BUSINESS ECONOMICS

N. Gregory Mankiw, Mark P. Taylor and Andrew Ashwin

CENGAGE

Australia • United States

CENGAGE Learning

Business Economics, 2nd Edition
N. Gregory Mankiw, Mark P. Taylor and Andrew Ashwin

Publisher: Annabel Ainscow

Commissioning Editor: Jenny Grene

Content Project Manager: Sue Povey

Manufacturing Manager: Eyvett Davis

Marketing Manager: Vicky Fielding

Typesetter: MPS Limited

Cover design: Adam Renvoize Creative

Text design: Design Deluxe Ltd

While the publisher has taken all reasonable care in the preparation of this book, the publisher makes no representation, express or implied, with regard to the accuracy of the information contained in this book and cannot accept any legal responsibility or liability for any errors or omissions from the book or the consequences thereof.

Products and services that are referred to in this book may be either trademarks and/or registered trademarks of their respective owners. The publishers and author/s make no claim to these trademarks. The publisher does not endorse, and accepts no responsibility or liability for, incorrect or defamatory content contained in hyperlinked material.

All the URLs in this book are correct at the time of going to press; however the Publisher accepts no responsibility for the content and continued availability of third party websites.

For product information and technology assistance,
contact **emea.info@cengage.com**.

For permission to use material from this text or product,
and for permission queries,
email **emea.permissions@cengage.com**.

British Library Cataloguing-in-Publication Data
A catalogue record for this book is available from the British Library.

ISBN: 978-1-4737-2244-6

Cengage Learning EMEA
Cheriton House, North Way, Andover, Hampshire, SP10 5BE
United Kingdom

Cengage Learning products are represented in Canada by Nelson Education Ltd.

For your lifelong learning solutions, visit **www.cengage.co.uk**

Purchase your next print book, e-book or e-chapter at
www.cengagebrain.com

Printed in China by RR Donnelley
Print Number: 02   Print Year: 2016

BRIEF CONTENTS

About the Authors   viii
Preface   ix
Acknowledgements   xiv

PART 1 The Economic and Business Environment – Setting the Scene   1

1   What Is Business Economics?   3
2   Economics and Business Decision Making   21
3   The Business Environment   33

PART 2 Microeconomics – The Market System   51

4   Supply and Demand: How Markets Work   53
5   Elasticity and Its Applications   86

PART 3 Microeconomics – The Limitations of Markets   119

6   Market Failure   121
7   The Consumer and Consumer Behaviour   149

PART 4 Microeconomics – The Economics of Firms in Markets   177

8   Business Goals and Behaviour   179
9   Firm Behaviour and the Organization of Industry   206
10   The Firm's Production Decisions   235

11   Market Structures   254
12   Other Types of Imperfect Competition   284
13   Corporate Strategy and Pricing Policy   312

PART 5 Microeconomics – Factor Markets   329

14   Labour Markets   331
15   Financial Markets   359

PART 6 Introduction to Macroeconomics   385

16   The Macroeconomic Environment   387
17   Aggregate Demand and Aggregate Supply   425
18   Macroeconomics – Employment and Unemployment   453
19   Macroeconomics – Inflation and Price Stability   469
20   Macroeconomics – Fiscal, Monetary and Supply-Side Policy   496

PART 7 Global Business and Economics   525

21   The Global Economy   527

Glossary   557
Index   565
Formulas   573

CONTENTS

About the Authors   viii
Preface   ix
Acknowledgements   xiv

Summary   49
Questions for review   49
Problems and applications   50

THE ECONOMIC AND BUSINESS ENVIRONMENT – SETTING THE SCENE   1

1 What Is Business Economics?   3

What is business economics?   4
Thinking as an economist   7
How people interact   11
How the economy as a whole works   14
Summary   19
Questions for review   19
Problems and applications   19

2 Economics and Business Decision Making   21

Economics: The science (or art) of decision making   22
Business decision making   25
Conclusion   30
Summary   31
Questions for review   32
Problems and applications   32

3 The Business Environment   33

The transformation process   34
The PESTLE framework   39
Shareholder value and stakeholders   46
Conclusion   47

MICROECONOMICS – THE MARKET SYSTEM   51

4 Supply and Demand: How Markets Work   53

The market forces of supply and demand   54
Markets and competition   56
Supply   58
Shifts versus movements along the supply curve   60
Demand   64
Shifts versus movements along the demand curve   65
Demand and supply together   70
How prices allocate resources   83
Summary   84
Questions for review   84
Problems and applications   85

5 Elasticity and Its Applications   86

Elasticity and its application   87
Price elasticity of supply   87
The price elasticity of demand   94
Other demand elasticities   103
Applications of supply and demand elasticity   110
Summary   115
Questions for review   115
Problems and applications   116

MICROECONOMICS – THE LIMITATIONS OF MARKETS   119

6 Market Failure   121

Introduction   122
Externalities   125
Using the demand curve to measure
   consumer surplus   127
Producer surplus   128
Government, business and externalities   134
Conclusion   145
Summary   146
Questions for review   147
Problems and applications   147

7 The Consumer and Consumer Behaviour   149

Introduction   150
Behavioural economics   161
Advertising and branding   164
Brand names   167
Asymmetric information   168
Conclusion   171
Summary   173
Questions for review   174
Problems and applications   174

MICROECONOMICS–THE ECONOMICS OF FIRMS IN MARKETS   177

8 Business Goals and Behaviour   179

The goals of firms   180
Financial objectives   185
Break-even analysis   190
Non-financial objectives   199
Summary   204
Questions for review   204
Problems and applications   205

9 Firm Behaviour and the Organization of Industry   206

The costs of production   207
What are costs?   207
Production and costs   210
The various measures of cost   213
Costs in the short run and in the long run   220
Isoquants and isocosts   224
Summary   230
Conclusion   231
Summary   232
Questions for review   232
Problems and applications   232

10 The Firm's Production Decisions   235

Introduction   236
The supply curve in a competitive market   244
Conclusion: Behind the supply curve   250
Summary   252
Questions for review   252
Problems and applications   252

11 Market Structures   254

Introduction   255
Imperfect competition   256

Monopoly   257
How monopolies make production
   and pricing decisions   260
The welfare cost of monopoly   266
Price discrimination   270
Public policy towards monopolies   275
Conclusion: The prevalence of monopoly   278
Summary   280
Questions for review   281
Problems and applications   281

12   Other Types of Imperfect Competition   284

Introduction   285
Oligopoly   291
Interdependence, game theory and the economics
   of competition   298
Public policies toward oligopolies   304
Conclusion   307
Summary   309
Questions for review   309
Problems and applications   309

13   Corporate Strategy and Pricing Policy   312

Introduction   313
Business strategy   313
Pricing strategies   320
Summary   327
Questions for review   327
Problems and applications   328

PART 5

MICROECONOMICS – FACTOR MARKETS   329

14   Labour Markets   331

The markets for the factors of production   332
The demand for labour   332

The supply of labour   339
The other factors of production: Land and capital   344
Earnings and discrimination   347
The economics of discrimination   352
Conclusion   355
Summary   356
Questions for review   357
Problems and applications   358

15   Financial Markets   359

Introduction   360
Financial institutions in the economy   360
Measuring the time value of money   365
Managing risk   366
Asset valuation   369
Savings and investments in the national
   income accounts   371
An overview of islamic finance   377
Conclusion   379
Summary   381
Questions for review   382
Problems and applications   382

PART 6

INTRODUCTION TO MACROECONOMICS   385

16   The Macroeconomic Environment   387

Introduction   388
The economy's income and expenditure   388
The components of GDP   392
Real versus nominal GDP   394
Measuring the cost of living   396
Production and growth   402
Economic growth, business and public policy   403
Unemployment   406
Specialization and trade   409
Open-economy macroeconomics:
   Basic concepts   411

The prices for international transactions:
    Real and nominal exchange rates   414
A model of exchange rate determination:
    Purchasing power parity   417
Conclusion   420
Summary   422
Questions for review   423
Problems and applications   423

17 Aggregate Demand and Aggregate Supply   425

Introduction   426
Three key facts about economic fluctuations   426
Explaining short-run economic fluctuations   427
The aggregate demand curve   430
The aggregate supply curve   436
Two causes of economic fluctuations   444
Conclusion   450
Summary   451
Questions for review   451
Problems and applications   452

18 Macroeconomics – Employment and Unemployment   453

Introduction   454
Identifying unemployment   454
Job search   457
Structural unemployment   460
Conclusion   465
Summary   467
Questions for review   467
Problems and applications   467

19 Macroeconomics – Inflation and Price Stability   469

Money growth and inflation   470
The classical theory of inflation   470
The costs of inflation   474
Inflation and unemployment   479
The Phillips curve   480
The role of expectations   483
The role of supply shocks   488
The cost of reducing inflation   490
Conclusion   492
Summary   494
Questions for review   494
Problems and applications   495

20 Macroeconomics – Fiscal, Monetary and Supply-Side Policy   496

Monetary policy, fiscal policy and supply-side
    policy   497
Monetary policy   497
Fiscal policy   502
Supply-side policies   510
How monetary policy influences aggregate
    demand   514
How fiscal policy influences aggregate demand   519
Conclusion   521
Summary   523
Questions for review   523
Problems and applications   524

PART 7

GLOBAL BUSINESS AND ECONOMICS   525

21 The Global Economy   527

The single European market and the euro   528
Common currency areas and European monetary
    union   530
Fiscal policy and common currency areas   535
Global business, culture and ethics   539
The costs and benefits of globalization   542
Business in emerging markets   545
Outsourcing   549
Foreign direct investment   551
Conclusion   552
Summary   554
Questions for review   555
Problems and applications   555

Glossary   557
Index   565
Formulas   573

N. GREGORY MANKIW is Robert M. Beren Professor of Economics and Chair of the Department of Economics at Harvard University. As a student, he studied economics at Princeton University and the Massachusetts Institute of Technology. As a teacher he has taught macroeconomics, microeconomics, statistics and principles of economics. Professor Mankiw is a prolific writer and a regular participant in academic and policy debates. His work has been published in scholarly journals such as the *American Economic Review, Journal of Political Economy* and *Quarterly Journal of Economics*. In addition to his teaching, research and writing, Professor Mankiw has been a research associate of the National Bureau of Economic Research, an advisor to the Federal Reserve Banks of Boston and New York, and the Congressional Budget Office. From 2003 to 2005, he served as chairman of the US President's Council of Economic Advisors.

MARK P. TAYLOR is Dean of Warwick Business School at the University of Warwick and Professor of International Finance. He obtained his first degree in philosophy, politics and economics from Oxford University and his master's degree in economics from London University, from where he also holds a doctorate in economics and international finance. Professor Taylor has taught economics and finance at various universities (including Oxford, Warwick and New York) and at various levels (including principles courses, advanced undergraduate and advanced postgraduate courses). He has also worked as a senior economist at the International Monetary Fund and at the Bank of England and, before becoming Dean of Warwick Business School, was a managing director at Black Rock, the world's largest financial asset manager, where he worked on international asset allocation based on macroeconomic analysis. His research has been extensively published in scholarly journals and he is today one of the most highly cited economists in the world. He was most recently a member of the Academic Advisory Group of the Bank of England Fair and Effective Markets Review.

ANDREW ASHWIN has over 20 years' experience as a teacher of economics. He has an MBA from the University of Hull and a PhD from the University of Leicester. Andrew is an experienced author writing a number of texts on Economics and Business for students at different levels and publications related to his PhD research. Andrew was Chair of Examiners for a major awarding body in England and Wales for Business and Economics and is a former Editor of the *Economics, Business and Enterprise Association* (EBEA) journal. Andrew is also a consultant to the qualifications regulator in England and Wales and is a Chartered Educational Assessor and a Fellow of the Chartered Institute of Educational Assessors.

PREFACE

How much of business is economics and how much of economics is business? This is a difficult question to answer but perhaps what is at the heart of both is decision making. This book is about decision making. Alfred Marshall, the great 19th-century British economist, in his textbook, *Principles of Economics* published in 1890 wrote: 'Economics is a study of mankind in the ordinary business of life.' For many people the ordinary business of life is interwoven with relationships with business. Every single day, billions of people around the world make decisions. When we make decisions we are being economists. A great proportion of these decisions are made by people in the context of their work which in turn is part of business. So Business and Economics are very closely linked.

A study of economics in a business context will help you understand the world in which you live. There are many questions about businesses and the economy that might spark your curiosity. Why do airlines charge less for a return ticket if the traveller stays over a Saturday night? Why are movie businesses prepared to pay some actors extremely large sums to star in films while others struggle to even get a bit part? Why are living standards so meagre in many African countries? Why do some countries have high rates of inflation while others have stable prices? Why do businesses produce many products that are so similar – surely they succeed only in cannibalizing their market? Why is it so important to have a better understanding of how consumers behave? Why have some European countries adopted a common currency? These are just a few of the questions that a course in Business Economics will help you answer.

The second reason to study Business Economics is that it will make you a more astute participant in the economy and in business. As you go about your life, you make many economic decisions. While you are a student, you decide how many years to stay in full-time education. When you have completed your degree you will have to decide on a career path and find a job (which may be difficult despite being highly qualified). Once you take a job, you decide how much of your income to spend, how much to save and how to invest your savings. In your daily work you will have to make many decisions and respond to an ever-changing environment. One day you may find yourself running your own small business or a large firm, and you will decide what prices to charge for your products and what products to offer for sale. The insights developed in the coming chapters will give you a new perspective on how best to make these decisions.

A study of Business Economics will give you a better understanding of the potential and limits of economic policy and how such policy can influence business behaviour. In your business career you may find yourself asking various questions about economics. What are the burdens associated with alternative forms of taxation? What are the effects of free trade with other countries? To what extent do businesses have a responsibility to protect the environment? How does the government budget deficit affect the economy and thus your business?

A study of Business Economics will go some way towards helping you make more sense of the world, your place in it and how business is affected and behaves as a consequence.

FOR WHOM IS THIS BOOK WRITTEN?

The book has been written with the non-specialist economist in mind but who has to embark on a course of study in economics as part of a degree in Business. Your degree might be Business Economics, it might be Business Management or it might be Sports Coaching and Management. An increasing number of degree courses will include some coverage of economic principles and this book is designed for just such courses. We have tried to put ourselves in the position of someone seeing economics for the first time and not necessarily looking forward to the prospect. Our goal has been to emphasize the material that *students* should and do find interesting about the study of the economy and business.

One result is that this book is briefer than many books used to introduce students to economics. Throughout this book we have tried to return to applications and policy questions as often as possible. All the chapters include case studies illustrating how the principles of economics are applied. In addition, 'In the News' boxes offer highlights from news events showing how economic ideas shed light on current issues facing business and society, along with questions to help you apply your knowledge to new contexts – a vitally important part of learning.

Readers should note that part of this book is adapted from Greg Mankiw's best-selling US undergraduate *Principles of Economics* text.

The adaptation to Professor Mankiw's text takes into account the needs of students and lecturers in the EMEA region and as such, may reflect different views to those in the original US text. Responsibility for the adaptation lies with Cengage Learning EMEA.

HOW IS THIS BOOK ORGANIZED?

In deciding what topics to include in the book we started with the typical course structures at universities offering some sort of Business Economics module as part of a degree programme. Some lecturers will choose to study topics in a slightly different order but our thinking was to try and present what we felt was a logical way of presenting an introduction to economics as it applies to a business context.

Introductory Material

Chapter 1, 'What is Business Economics?', sets the scene by introducing students to the economists' view of the world through the Ten Principles of Economics and business decision making. It previews some of the big ideas that recur throughout economics, such as opportunity cost, marginal decision making, the role of incentives, the gains from trade, and the efficiency of market allocations. Throughout the book, we refer regularly to the Ten Principles of Economics introduced in Chapter 1 to remind students that these ideas are the foundation for all economics. Chapter 2, 'Economics and Business Decision Making', explores decision making in more detail and includes a discussion about a crucial part of any business – recruiting and retaining customers. Chapter 3, 'The Business Environment', presents an overview of what we mean by business activity, how businesses transform inputs into outputs, the meaning of adding value and the internal and external environment within which businesses have to operate. We have looked at this environment through what is called the PESTLE framework – political, economic, social, technological and environmental.

Microeconomics – The Market System

The next two chapters introduce the market system through looking at the basic tools of supply and demand. Chapter 4, 'Supply and Demand: How Markets Work', develops the supply curve, the demand curve and the notion of market equilibrium. Chapter 5, 'Elasticity and Its Applications', introduces the concept of elasticity and uses it to analyse events in three different markets.

Microeconomics – The Limitations of the Market System

While many economies work based on market systems, they do, like most things, have their limitations. The next two chapters use the tools developed to look at Market Failure and the Consumer and Consumer Behaviour. You will learn that the costs and benefits of market activity are not always taken into account by decision makers and as a result the allocation of resources is less than efficient. In Chapter 7 you will learn that consumers (both businesses and individuals) do not always behave rationally and this can also lead to a less than efficient resource allocation. An understanding of consumer behaviour is an important aspect of business – after all, if we do not understand how the individuals and businesses we want to sell products to behave, then businesses will suffer and be more likely to fail.

Microeconomics – The Economics of Firms in Markets

Part 4 includes six chapters devoted to understanding and analysing the actions and behaviour of firms. Chapter 8 looks at business goals and behaviour to get an understanding of why businesses exist, what they aim to do and how changes to business goals can lead to different behaviour. Chapter 9 builds on some of the concepts introduced in Chapter 8 and covers firms' costs and revenues in the short and long run. Chapter 10 presents a model of the firm in equilibrium and how production decisions are made in competitive conditions. Chapter 11 follows up on this by looking at pricing decisions and an introduction to business strategy before Chapter 12 covers the effect on business behaviour of operating in different market structures such as when a firm has monopoly power. This enables you to understand how degrees of market power influence the way firms behave. Chapter 13 follows on by looking at other forms of market structure including monopolistic competition (not to be confused with monopoly) and oligopoly – competition amongst the few.

Microeconomics – Factor Markets

We complete our look at microeconomics with Part 5 which looks at the markets for labour and capital, two key components of factor inputs for a business. Chapter 14 emphasizes the link between factor prices and marginal productivity and discusses the determinants of equilibrium wages. Chapter 15 introduces important concepts in the theory and practice of financial markets including the time value of money, how asset prices are determined and the supply and demand for loanable funds.

Macroeconomics

The next five chapters cover the macroeconomic environment in which firms have to operate. Our overall approach to teaching macroeconomics is to examine the economy in the long run (when prices are flexible) before examining the economy in the short run (when prices are sticky). We believe that this organization simplifies learning macroeconomics for several reasons. First, the classical assumption of price flexibility is more closely linked to the basic lessons of supply and demand, to which you have already been introduced. Second, the classical dichotomy allows the study of the long run to be broken up into several, easily digested pieces. Third, because the business cycle represents a transitory deviation from the economy's long-run growth path, studying the transitory deviations is more natural after the long-run equilibrium is understood. Fourth, the macroeconomic theory of the short run is more controversial among economists than the macroeconomic theory of the long run. For these reasons, many upper-level courses in macroeconomics now follow this long-run-before-short-run approach; our goal is to offer introductory students the same advantage. There would be nothing to stop lecturers who prefer to approach the short run first from so doing – the book is flexible enough to allow this approach to be adopted.

Chapter 16 introduces some basic macroeconomic concepts including a discussion of the meaning of gross domestic product and related statistics from the national income accounts, the measurement and use of the consumer prices index, real and nominal interest rates, trade and exchange rates. These concepts are developed in the next four chapters which look in more detail at aggregate demand and supply, employment and unemployment, inflation and price stability and macroeconomic policy.

Global Business and Economics

We complete our journey through Business Economics by looking at the impact of doing business globally. Increasingly firms are involved in global trade and having some understanding of emerging markets, different business cultures and the European Union and the single market provides a foundation for what is likely to be further study as you progress through your degree.

LEARNING TOOLS

The purpose of this book is to help students learn the fundamental lessons of economics and to apply these lessons to a business context. Towards that end, we have used various learning tools that recur throughout the book.

- *Case Studies.* Economic theory is useful and interesting only if it can be applied to understanding actual events and policies. This book, therefore, contains numerous case studies that apply the theory that has just been developed in a business context.
- *'In the News' boxes.* One benefit that students gain from studying economics is a new perspective and greater understanding about news from around the world. To highlight this benefit, we have incorporated discussions of news events including excerpts from newspaper articles from around Europe, the Middle East, Africa and India. These articles, together with our brief introductions, show how basic economic theory can be applied and raise important questions

for discussion in business. To help further develop application skills we have included some questions at the end which can either be used as practice for self-study or as the basis for seminar or tutorial discussion.

- *'FYI' boxes.* These boxes provide additional material 'for your information'. Some of them offer a glimpse into the history of economic thought. Others clarify technical issues. Still others discuss supplementary topics that instructors might choose either to discuss or skip in their lectures but which students should find useful in supplementing their knowledge and understanding.

- *Definitions of key concepts.* When key concepts are introduced in the chapter, they are presented in **bold** typeface. In addition, their definitions are placed in the margins. This treatment should aid students in learning and reviewing the material.

- *Pitfall Preventions boxes.* The authors have used their collective teaching wisdom to outline areas where students make frequent mistakes and which can be a cause of confusion. The Pitfall Prevention boxes alert students to the potential for these mistakes.

- *Jeopardy Problems boxes.* These are problems designed to help you think as an economist. You will be given end-points or solutions and you have to think through the different ways in which the solutions or end-point given might have been arrived at using your knowledge of economics and business.

- *What if …? boxes.* Questions designed to get you thinking about different scenarios in business and economics.

- *Quick Quizzes.* After most major sections, you are offered a 'quick quiz' to check your comprehension of what you have just learned. If you cannot readily answer these quizzes, you should stop and reread material before continuing.

- *Chapter summaries.* Each chapter ends with a brief summary that reminds you of the most important lessons that you have just learned. Later in your study it offers an efficient way to revise for exams.

- *Questions for review.* At the end of each chapter are questions for review that cover the chapter's primary lessons. You can use these questions to check your comprehension and to prepare for exams.

- *Problems and applications.* Each chapter also contains a variety of problems and applications that ask you to apply the material you have learned. Some instructors may use these questions for private study assignments. Others may use them as a starting point for classroom discussions.

ACKNOWLEDGEMENTS

The authors would like to thank the following reviewers for their comments:

Andrew Abbott – University of Hull, UK
Dr Turner Anna – CEU Business School, Hungary
Emanuele Bracco – Lancaster University, UK
Dr Yu-Fu Chen – Dundee University, UK
Matthew T. Col – University College Dublin, Ireland
Gary Cook – University of Liverpool, UK
Dr John Duignan – University of the West of Scotland, UK
Aat van Eeden – Zuyd University of Applied Science, Netherlands
Robert Elliott – University of Birmingham, UK
John Forde – University of Salford, UK
Richard Godfrey – Cardiff School of Management, UK
Marco Gundermann – Cardiff Metropolitan University, UK
Dr Hala Helmi El Hadidi – British University, Egypt
Juan Garcia Lara – Universidad Carlos III Madrid, Spain
Qamarullah Bin Tariq Islam – Rajshahi University, Bangladesh; University
     of Glasgow, UK
Paul L. Latreille – Swansea University, UK
Dr Bobby Mackie – University of the West of Scotland, UK
Tim Maxfield – University of Worcester, UK
Pedro Martins – Queen Mary, University of London, UK
Fearghal J. McHugh – Galway Mayo Institute of Technology, Ireland
Natalie Moore – University of Nottingham, UK
Yoko Nagase – Oxford Brookes University, UK
Adel Nemeth – Jacobs University, Bremen
Dr Matthew Olczak – Aston University, UK
Quentin Outram – Leeds University Business School, UK
Bruce Philp – Nottingham Business School, UK
Julia Planko – Hogeschool Utrecht, Netherlands
Neil Reaich – Economics, Business and Enterprise Association
Jose R. Sanchez-Fung – Kingston University London, UK
Ulrich Schüle – School of Business FH Mainz-University of Applied Sciences,
     Germany
Cemil Selcuk – Cardiff University, UK
Vasilios Sogiakas – University of Glasgow, UK
Nicholas Spearman – University of the Witwatersrand, South Africa
Dr F Steffen – University of Liverpool Management School, UK
Michael Wood – London South Bank University, UK
Dr Michael Wynn-Williams – University of Greenwich, UK
Gaston Yalonetzky – Leeds University Business School, UK

CENGAGE
Learning®

MindTap

Turn the light on with MindTap

MindTap represents a new approach to online learning. A fully online learning solution, MindTap combines all of your learning tools, readings, multimedia, activities and assessments, into a singular Learning Path that guides you through your course.

Lecturers can easily personalize the experience by customizing the presentation of these learning tools and content to their students so that they have access to course content exactly when they need it.

MindTap can be fully integrated into most Learning Management Systems giving you a seamless experience. You will also have a dedicated team of Digital Course Support professionals to make your use of MindTap a success.

To find out more students can go to **login.cengagebrain.com** and instructors can go to **login.cengage.com** or speak to their local Cengage Learning EMEA representative.

MindTap is available with some of our bestselling titles across multiple disciplines including Accounting, Economics, Management, Psychology, Engineering and Chemistry

PART 1

THE ECONOMIC AND BUSINESS ENVIRONMENT – SETTING THE SCENE

1 WHAT IS BUSINESS ECONOMICS?

LEARNING OUTCOMES

After reading this chapter you should be able to:

- Explain what businesses do and what economics studies.
- Provide a definition and example of business activity in the public and private sector.
- Define scarcity.
- Explain the idea of a trade-off and provide at least one example.
- Give a definition of opportunity cost and provide at least three examples relating to individual and business decision making.

- Explain the difference between capitalist and communist economic systems in how they answer the fundamental questions of society.
- Outline how prices direct resources to different economic activities.
- Explain why specialization and trade can improve people's choices.
- Give an example of an externality.
- Explain the source of large and persistent inflation.

WHAT IS BUSINESS ECONOMICS?

Business studies and economics are invariably taught as separate subjects in many schools prior to university. Business studies focuses on issues and problems related to business organizations of different types and includes business objectives, marketing, business organization, human resources management, accounting and finance, operations management and the influence of external factors including management of change. Economics focuses on the workings of markets, firm behaviour, market structures, factor markets (such as the market for labour and capital), international trade and the workings of the economy as a whole including growth, unemployment, inflation and exchange rates.

There is one thing, however, which connects the two discipline areas and that is decision making. People in businesses have to make decisions every day and the way in which they make these decisions and the outcome of those decisions can be informed by using the models, methods and tools of economics. In addition, an understanding of the key concepts of economics is essential. The purpose of this book is to help you begin to think as an economist and to apply that thinking to business contexts to set you on the way to being a better decision maker. Businesses need people who understand the basic principles of business, who are flexible, can think in different ways and who are problem solvers who can cope with and confront change in a positive way. Having an understanding of the basic principles of economics will help in developing these skills.

What Is Business?

Business is an activity. It involves using inputs, which are broadly described as land, labour and capital, and turning them into some output which is then sold to customers. These outputs could be goods such as TVs, food, books, clothes, furniture, bricks, cars, glass and so on or services such as banking, insurance, accounting, tourism, repairs, medical care, entertainment, transportation, hotels, restaurants, etc. The customers who buy these outputs could be private individuals, other businesses or government bodies both from the domestic economy and from overseas. In the process of exchange of outputs, buyers pay a price to acquire the outputs and the money received by the seller represents the income of the business.

Business activity is carried out for different reasons. In some cases, the primary aim of a business is to ensure that the money received from selling outputs is greater than the cost of producing these outputs. In other words, the business is focused on making a profit and **profit** is the reward for the risk taken in carrying out business activity. Some business activity will be carried out with the primary intention of fulfilling a need, and whilst in most cases it is expected that the costs of providing the output must at the very least be covered by the income generated, any surplus that is generated is put back into the business or used for a good cause.

Because business activity has different aims, the organizations that provide outputs are different. The **private sector** is made up of different types of businesses. Some are very small, one-person organizations and some are giants with operations in many different countries employing many thousands of people. The main aim of these businesses is to generate profit but they will also have many other aims which might also include a recognition of their moral and ethical responsibilities to society as a whole. Other businesses in the private sector are set up with

profit the reward for taking risk in carrying out business activity

private sector business activity which is owned, financed and organized by private individuals

the primary aim of providing outputs or a service which meet a particular need. These businesses will include charitable organizations, voluntary work, fundraising and activities which have wider social and community benefits. This is referred to as the **third sector** or not-for-profit business.

In many countries a large amount of business activity is carried out by the government on behalf of the population as a whole. This is referred to as the **public sector**. The finance for public sector activity comes from tax payers and from the income that can be generated from the activity itself. Public sector activity is focused on providing goods and services to the public as a whole and in doing so maximizing the opportunities for access. Balancing the cost of providing education, health, legal, welfare, emergency services, roads and transport, and so on with the demand for these services is a considerable challenge to any government but, fundamentally, it might be expected that the cost of provision is at least met by the funds available.

One of the main decisions facing businesses is what the aims of the business should be. If the primary aim is to make profit, decisions made may be different but related to those which are made if the primary aim of the business is to provide a perceived social benefit. Public sector organizations have to make difficult decisions about the provision of services because funds may be limited. In most business activity, decisions might include how many people to employ, what each of those people will do to contribute to the business, how much employees get in return for their labour, who should receive a bonus scheme and who should not, how to increase output per worker, how best to manage costs, when to invest, how much to invest and where best to get the funds to invest from, what products to produce, what products not to produce, when to stop producing products, when to expand, when to contract, how best to manage the sales process and customer relations, whether to be environmentally friendly or whether to give the impression of being so, how to deal with competitors and whether to charge a high price or a low price (or one in-between). It is important to note at the outset that there are rarely simple and identifiable 'right' and 'wrong' answers in business. However meticulous the analysis carried out and data collected, ultimately judgements have to be made. When the judgements lead to positive outcomes, the decision makers are praised and may be lauded as having some special skill or insight but when the judgement leads to negative outcomes decision makers are criticized and may find themselves out of a job. Decision makers will seek to use many different techniques and methods to help them make better decisions, decisions that lead to the positive outcomes desired. A knowledge of the methods, tools and models of economics may be one way in which decision makers can understand the problems and issues they face and be in a better position to make decisions as a result. It is important to emphasize, however, that having a good understanding of economics is not going to automatically lead to business success, however that success is defined.

Businesses operate as part of society. Typically, business activity forms part of a society that is based on capitalist principles where resources are owned by private individuals, and trade and exchange is carried out largely for the purposes of making a profit. In some societies, resources are owned by the state and business activity is carried out for social, economic and political reasons, which may include a fundamental belief that society ought to be organized along more egalitarian lines than those which exist in capitalist societies. These are referred to as **communist economies**. Inequality is an outcome of **capitalist economies** and the gaps between the rich and poor and those who have and have not form fundamental areas of disagreement in decision making.

third sector business activity owned, financed and organized by private individuals but with the primary aim of providing needs and not making profit

public sector business activity owned, financed and organized by the state on behalf of the population as a whole

communist economies systems where resource inputs are largely owned by the state and exchange and trade is based on social, political and economic motives which may be primarily based on a belief of greater equality

capitalist economies systems where resource inputs are largely owned by private individuals and where the motive for exchange takes place primarily for profit

CASE STUDY

Measuring Businesses in Wales

Businesses can be classified in many different ways. One method commonly used by governments is based on business size. Data collected in Wales for 2014 are grouped according to the numbers employed in each business as shown in the following table.

According to numbers of employees	Number				Percentage of total		
	Enterprise count	Employment	Turnover (£m)	Number	Enterprise count	Employment	Turnover (£m)
All bands	231 110	1 058 500	116 643	1 406 253	100.0	100.0	100.0
Micro (0–9)	218 745	359 900	16 505	595 150	94.6	34.0	14.2
Small (10–49)	8 740	164 300	11 689	184 729	3.8	15.5	10.0
Medium (50–249)	2 030	130 000	13 597	145 627	0.9	12.3	11.7
Large (250+)	1 595	404 300	74 851	480 746	0.7	38.2	64.2

The data show that around 95 per cent of all businesses in Wales are small with each having less than ten employees. These account for 34 per cent of all employees, but just 14 per cent of turnover. Whereas the largest businesses, each with over 250 employees, make up just 0.7 per cent of the enterprises operating in Wales, but account for 38 per cent of the employment and over 64 per cent of the turnover.

The data provide useful information for governments to monitor trends, but it does not show how the businesses might be interconnected. For example, many small and medium sized businesses will be suppliers for larger businesses. Since they are interconnected, the decision of a large business can affect decisions of other smaller concerns. For example, in 2014 Pinewood Studios decided to set up a production centre near Cardiff in Wales. This decision will benefit many large and small suppliers who may in turn take on more employees and invest in new technology. Some suppliers may even move into the area to take advantage of being close to the studios.

One of the larger suppliers to the film studios is the builders' merchant, Jewson, which services the studios, but the investment will generate business opportunities for many smaller enterprises if the 241 independent media-related companies based at Pinewood's existing studios in England is anything to go by.

Source: StatsWales at **https://statswales.wales.gov.uk/Catalogue/Business-Economy-and-Labour-Market/Businesses/Business -Structure/Headline-Data/LatestBusinessStructureInWales-by-Sizeband-Measure**

The Fundamental Questions of Society

Regardless of the economic system in place, any country has some fundamental questions to answer. These questions are:

- What products will be produced?
- How will products be produced?
- Who will get the products that are produced?

These are profound questions and have equally profound implications. In any society, human beings have wants and needs; at the most basic level these wants and needs are food, clothing and shelter. To provide for these needs, resources, which we have classified as land, labour and capital, have to be organized to generate the products that society needs to answer the first question; there are many different ways in which products can be produced. The way in which products are produced might determine who gets access and this is determined by the economic system that is adopted. In a capitalist system, those who own resources may get access to a far greater proportion of the products produced than those who do not, whereas in a non-capitalist system resources are owned by the state and the state may determine a far greater degree of equality of access. Decisions made in capitalist economies will be based on different beliefs and priorities to those made in communist economies.

What Is Economics?

At its simplest, **economics** is the study of how society manages its resources. The management of society's resources is important because resources are scarce. **Scarcity** means that society has limited resources and therefore cannot produce all the products people desire. Just as a household cannot give every member everything he or she wants, a society cannot give every individual the highest standard of living to which he or she might aspire.

In capitalist societies, the fundamental questions of what is to be produced, how products are to be produced and who gets access to the products produced are answered through the combined actions of millions of households and firms. Economists therefore study how people make decisions: how much they work, what they buy, how much they save and how they invest their savings. Economists also study how people and people in businesses interact with one another. Economists analyse forces and trends that affect the economy as a whole, including the growth in average income, the fraction of the population that cannot find work and the rate at which prices change.

In communist societies, the fundamental questions are answered by the state making judgements about resource use and these judgements will be based on different belief systems from those in capitalist societies. Economists study how decisions are made in these societies and the implications of these decisions. In many countries, private individuals and the state operate together in answering the fundamental questions. These are referred to as **mixed economies**. The proportion of economic activity that is carried out by the private sector and public sector varies, but there are few instances of countries where the private and public sector do not coexist in addressing the fundamental questions.

In a sense, economics can be described as the science of decision making. In thinking as an economist in the context of business, there are particular concepts, models and methods that have developed within the discipline of economics. These can be applied and help in the analysis of business problems and issues.

economics the study of how society makes decisions in managing scarce resources

scarcity the limited nature of society's resources in relation to wants and needs

mixed economies economic systems that include elements of both private and public ownership of resources to answer the fundamental questions

THINKING AS AN ECONOMIST

We use the term 'the economy' on a regular basis but have you ever stopped to think about what the term really means? Whether we are talking about the economy of a group of countries, such as the European Union (EU) or the Middle East, or the economy of one particular country, such as South Africa (SA) or the United Kingdom (UK), or of the whole world, an economy is just a group of people interacting with one another as they go about their lives. This interaction is invariably through a process of exchange. Whether it be an individual buying a morning newspaper, a business buying several hundred tonnes of steel for a construction project or a government funding a higher education institution, the interaction

the economy the collective interaction between individuals in the process of production and exchange in a defined area

consists of millions of individuals all making decisions and together we describe these interactions as **the economy**. Because the behaviour of an economy reflects the behaviour of the individuals, both acting on their own and as part of businesses who make up the economy, we consider starting to think as an economist with four principles of individual decision making.

Principle 1: Decision Making Involves Trade-Offs

When we make decisions, we have to make a judgement between two or more courses of action. Each course of action will have certain benefits. If we choose one course of action we get the benefits of that action but usually have to give up the benefits of the other courses of action. Making decisions requires trading off the benefits of one action against the benefits of another.

Consider a business manager who must decide how to allocate her most valuable resource – her time. She can spend all of her time reflecting on strategy in her office which, if implemented successfully, could bring benefits to the business. Equally, she could spend all of her time walking around the premises talking to staff, gaining a better understanding of the business and motivating workers, which may bring benefits of improved productivity and efficiency; or she can divide her time between the two fields. For every hour she spends reflecting and strategizing, she gives up the benefits that could be gained for an hour she could have used talking to staff. Consider employees of this business deciding how to spend the income they receive from working at the business. They can buy food, clothing or a family holiday, each of which bring certain benefits. Or they can save some of the family income for retirement, which brings benefits in the future. If the family decide to save an extra €100 a month for retirement then they have to trade-off the benefits this brings in the future for the benefits incurred by spending that €100 on products today.

When people are grouped into societies, they face different kinds of trade-offs. Resources devoted to consumer goods such as clothing, food, cars, washing machines and so on could also be used for producing capital goods – equipment and machinery that is used for the production of other goods. The more society spends on consumer goods that bring benefits to people, the less we can spend on capital goods that bring the benefits of raising standards of living at some point in the future.

Also important in modern society is the trade-off between a clean environment and a high level of income. Laws that require firms to reduce pollution might raise the cost of production but bring the benefit to society as a whole (and possibly to the firm in the form of good publicity). Because of the higher costs, these firms may end up earning smaller profits, paying lower wages, charging higher prices or some combination of these three. Thus, while pollution regulations give us the benefit of a cleaner environment and the improved levels of health that come with it, they reduce the benefits that higher incomes would bring to firms' owners, workers and customers.

Recognizing that people and businesses face trade-offs does not by itself tell us what decisions they will or should make. A chief executive officer (CEO) should not abandon time set aside for reflection and thinking just because doing so would increase the time available to talk to workers. Society should not stop protecting the environment just because environmental regulations reduce our material standard of living. Nevertheless, acknowledging trade-offs is important because people and businesses are likely to make good decisions only if they understand the options that they have available and can quantify them in some way to make informed decisions.

Principle 2: The Cost of Something is What You Give Up to Get It

Because people and businesses face trade-offs, making decisions requires comparing not only the benefits but also the costs of alternative courses of action. In many cases, however, these costs and benefits are not as obvious as might first appear.

Consider the decision by a business to cease production of a product that is not selling very well. The benefit is that resources can be made available to invest in other parts of the business that are more successful. But what is the cost? To answer this question, you might be tempted to add up the money the business has to pay in redundancy to workers who may no longer be needed, to close down plant and get rid of defunct machinery and equipment. Yet this total does not truly represent what the business gives up when it ceases production of a product. First, it ignores many wider issues that the business might face as a result of its decision. How do competitors view the decision? Will they seek to use it as an example of the decline of the business? What about customers – will they be disappointed that the product has disappeared? A number of businesses have found themselves under pressure to bring back much loved products that may not have been financially viable and have incurred disappointment from customers and possible loss of loyalty as a result. Then there is the attitude among workers – is this closure the first of others, does it send negative signals to the rest of the workforce resulting in a decline in motivation and increases in staff turnover as workers seek to get out before they are pushed out? Second, it does not include the lost revenue from sales of the product. It may be that sales were low and not that it was not viable to continue with production. Assuming that sales were not zero, there will have been some revenue being generated and this will now be lost. This has to be taken into consideration.

The decision, therefore, has costs far greater than pure money costs. The cost of loss of goodwill, worker and customer loyalty and bad publicity also has to be taken into consideration in assessing the costs of the decision and these may not be immediately obvious and sometimes not easy to work out.

The **opportunity cost** of an action is what you give up to pursue that course of action. When making any decision, such as whether to close down production of a product, decision makers should be aware of the opportunity costs that accompany each possible action.

opportunity cost the cost expressed in terms of the benefits sacrificed of the next best alternative

> **Quick Quiz** You may have heard the adage 'there is no such thing as a free lunch'. What do you think this means in the context of trade-offs and opportunity cost?

Principle 3: Rational People and Businesses Think at the Margin

There are many aspects of economics which are based on assumptions. One such assumption is that people behave rationally. The extent to which this is indeed the case is debatable but, in some cases, businesses and individuals do make decisions based on a rational assessment (as far as is possible) of different options. The decision by a company worker of whether to put in the extra hour at the end of the working day might be based on the perceived costs and benefits of completing a task before going home. A publisher may have to make a decision about whether

marginal changes small
incremental adjustments to a plan
of action

to print an extra 1000 copies of a textbook when it is not certain that all these extra books will sell. Economists use the term **marginal changes** to describe small incremental adjustments to an existing plan of action. Keep in mind that 'margin' means 'edge', so marginal changes are adjustments around the edges of what you are doing. In many situations, people can make sensible decisions by thinking at the margin.

Consider an airline company deciding how much to charge passengers. Suppose that flying a 200-seat aeroplane from London to Warsaw costs the airline €50 000. In this case, the average cost of each seat is €50 000/200, which is €250. One might be tempted to conclude that the airline should never sell a ticket for less than €250. If the airline thinks at the margin it could raise its profits. Imagine that 24 hours before the plane is due to depart, there are still ten empty seats. Last-minute passengers accessing the booking area on the airline's website might be willing to pay €200 for a seat. Should the airline sell it to them? If the plane has empty seats, the cost of adding one more passenger is minuscule. Although the *average* cost of flying a passenger is €250, the *marginal* cost is merely the cost of the airline meal that the extra passenger will consume (which may have gone to waste in any case) and possibly a slight increase in the amount of aircraft fuel used. As long as the late booking passengers pay more than the marginal cost, selling them a ticket can be profitable. We assume that a rational decision maker takes an action if and only if the marginal benefit of the action exceeds the marginal cost.

Principle 4: People and Businesses Respond to Incentives

If people and businesses make decisions by comparing costs and benefits, their behaviour may change when the costs or benefits change. That is, people respond to incentives. When the price of an apple rises, for instance, people decide to eat more pears and fewer apples because the price paid to buy an apple is higher. At the same time, apple orchards decide to hire more workers and harvest more apples, because the benefit of selling an apple is also higher. The effect of price on the behaviour of buyers and sellers in a market is crucial for understanding how the economy works.

Public policy makers should never forget about incentives, because many policies change the costs or benefits that people face and, therefore, alter behaviour. A tax on petrol, for instance, encourages people to drive smaller, more fuel-efficient cars. For vehicle manufacturers this change in demand has to be accommodated and shifts resources into the production of smaller, more fuel-efficient cars and away from larger, more fuel expensive cars. It also encourages people to use public transport rather than drive and to live closer to where they work. This in turn has an effect on decisions about provision of public transport, and what type of transport, and housing provision. If the tax were large enough, people might explore electric cars, which requires investment by vehicle manufacturers in this technology and a host of other businesses that may be involved in setting up the infrastructure to facilitate the use of electric cars.

unintended consequences
the outcomes of decision making or
policy changes which are not anticipated and are unforeseen

When policy makers fail to consider how their policies affect incentives, they often end up with results they did not intend – these are referred to as **unintended consequences**. For example, if a government decided to make the wearing of safety helmets for cyclists a legal requirement, the primary focus of the law might be to help reduce the incidents of serious head injuries for cyclists. The unintended consequences might be that people decide not to cycle in the numbers they used to because wearing a cycle helmet is unfashionable. The number of people suffering head injuries might fall because fewer people are now cycling but, in addition, society loses the positive health benefits that cycling can bring, and businesses manufacturing and servicing bicycles might see demand fall. Public transport and roads may become busier because people switch to using buses and cars rather than cycling to work.

This is an example of the general principle that people respond to incentives. When analysing any policy or business decision, we must consider not only the direct effects but also the indirect effects that work through incentives. If the decision changes incentives, it will cause people to alter their behaviour.

CASE STUDY

Industry Quotas in Nigeria

In 2014 the Nigerian government introduced a new fish quota restricting imports of frozen fish by 25 per cent. The fish imports came from Asia, Europe and Russia. The introduction of the quota was intended to encourage the domestic mainly 'farmed' fishing industry. However, the ban resulted in a rise in the smuggling of fish and an increase in food inflation. Indeed, in December 2014 the Nigerian government decided to increase quotas to deserving importers, which has helped to reduce prices to consumers.

References: The Fish Site, **http://www.thefishsite.com/fishnews/23029/nigeria-begins -import-quota-policy-for-fish** and **http://www.thefishsite.com/fishnews/24777/new -import-quotas-crash-nigerian-fish-prices**

Quick Quiz The emphasis on road safety throughout Europe has increased over the last 25 years. Not only are cars packed with safety technology and devices, but roads are also designed to be safer with the use of safety barriers and better road surfaces, for example. Is there a case for believing that if people feel they are safer in their cars there is an incentive to drive faster because the marginal cost is now outweighed by the marginal benefit?

HOW PEOPLE INTERACT

As we go about our lives, many decisions affect not only ourselves but businesses and other people as well. The next three principles concern how people and businesses interact with one another.

Principle 5: Trade Can Make Everyone Better Off

The Americans, South Africans and the Japanese are often mentioned in the news as being competitors to Europeans in the world economy. In some ways this is true, because American, South African and Japanese firms do produce many of the same goods as European firms. Airbus and Boeing compete for the same customers in the market for aircraft. Toyota and Citroën compete for the same customers in the market for cars. South African and American fruit growers compete in the same market as European fruit growers, and South African and American wine producers compete in the same market as French, Spanish and Italian wine makers.

Yet it is easy to be misled when thinking about competition among countries. Trade between Europe and South Africa or the USA, or between Europe and Japan, is not like a sports contest where one side wins and the other side loses (a zero-sum game). In fact, the opposite is true: trade between two economies can make each economy better off.

Assuming business activity in the private sector in a capitalist system, when a business produces a product it competes against other businesses that are producing similar products. Despite this competition, a business would not be better off isolating itself from all other businesses. If it did, the business would have to supply all its own raw materials and components, find its own staff, arrange its own insurance, do its own banking, arrange its own security and so on. Businesses can benefit from their ability to trade with others. Trade allows each business to specialize in the activities it does best, whether it is farming, making clothes or home building. By trading with others, businesses can buy a greater variety of goods and services at lower cost and therefore (potentially) increase efficiency.

Countries as well as businesses benefit from the ability to trade with one another. Trade allows countries to specialize in what they do best and to enjoy a greater variety of goods and services. The Japanese and Americans, as well as the Egyptians and Brazilians, are as much our partners in the world economy as they are our competitors. While trade can bring benefits it must be borne in mind that with any trade there can be winners and losers.

Principle 6: Markets Can Be a Good Way to Organize Economic Activity

Communist economic systems have central planners in the government who guide economic activity. These planners decide what goods and services are produced, how much is produced, and who produces and consumes these goods and services. The theory behind central planning is that only the government can organize economic activity in a way that promotes economic well-being for the country as a whole.

In a capitalist system, the private ownership of resources means that individuals making millions of decisions every day determine economic activity. The interaction of buyers and sellers in markets allocates resources to different uses and addresses the fundamental economic questions. In a **market economy**, firms decide who to hire and what to make; individuals supplying labour decide which firms to work for and what to buy with their incomes. These individuals (collectively referred to as households) and firms interact in the marketplace, where prices and self-interest guide their decisions. The process of exchange in market economies is facilitated by prices that provide signals to consumers and producers, and lead to resources moving to different uses all of which are based on the self-interests of firms and households. Prices reflect both the value of a good to society and the cost to society of making the good.

market economy an economy that allocates resources through the decentralized decisions of many firms and households as they interact in markets for goods and services

In a pure market economy (one with no state involvement), no one is considering the economic well-being of society as a whole. Yet, despite self-interested decision makers, market economies have proven remarkably successful in organizing economic activity, and the vast majority of countries around the world base their economies on a market system to a greater and lesser extent. Proponents of market economies argue that they are the most effective way yet devised in allocating resources and improving standards of living. However, note the caveat in this principle. Markets *can be* a good way to organize economic activity. We emphasize *can be* because markets are not devoid of problems as we will outline in the next principle. The European debt crisis between 2007 and 2009 and its aftermath, which is still having an effect on millions of people, has cast doubt over a number of the models and assumptions that economists made about market systems. We will look at the reasons why markets may not work properly in later chapters.

FYI

Adam Smith and the Invisible Hand

Adam Smith's *The Wealth of Nations* is a landmark in economics. It reflected a point of view that was typical of so-called 'enlightenment' writers at the end of the 18th century – that individuals are usually best left to their own devices, without government guiding their actions. This political philosophy provides the intellectual basis for the market economy.

Why do decentralized market economies work? Here is Adam Smith's description of how people interact in a market economy:

> Man has almost constant occasion for the help of his brethren, and it is vain for him to expect it from their benevolence only. He will be more likely to prevail if he can interest their self-love in his favour, and show them that it is for their own advantage to do for him what he requires of them.…It is not from the benevolence of the butcher, the brewer, or the baker that we expect our dinner, but from their regard to their own interest.… Every individual…neither intends to promote the public interest, nor knows how much he is promoting it.…He intends only his own gain, and he is in this, as in many other cases, led by an invisible hand to promote an end which was no part of his intention. Nor is it always the worse for the society that it was no part of it. By pursuing his own interest he frequently promotes that of the society more effectually than when he really intends to promote it.
>
> *Wealth of Nations 1776*

Adam Smith, 1723–1790

Smith is arguing that participants in the economy are motivated by self-interest and that the 'invisible hand' of the marketplace guides this self-interest into promoting general economic well-being. Our analysis in the coming chapters will allow us to express Smith's conclusions more precisely and to analyse fully the strengths and weaknesses of the market's invisible hand.

Principle 7: Governments Can Sometimes Improve Market Outcomes

Markets only work if certain assumptions are upheld. One of these assumptions is that an effective system of property rights exists. **Property rights** are linked to the idea of ownership of resources, which forms the basis of the capitalist system. If an individual owns property, then there has to be some system in place to ensure that the rights associated with owning that property can be enforced. These rights might include the exclusive right to use and exploit the good to generate

property rights the exclusive right of an individual, group or organization to determine how a resource is used

income and the right to transfer ownership to another individual or organization. A farmer won't grow food if they expect their crop to be stolen, and a restaurant won't serve meals unless it is assured that customers will pay before they leave. A market-based system has to rely on the legal system and police to enforce rights over the things we produce and these are provided by the state.

A pure market system can lead to outcomes that may not be deemed desirable. Specifically, market outcomes may be seen as being inefficient or inequitable. Governments step in to promote efficiency and equity by seeking to either enlarge the economic cake or change the way in which the cake is divided.

market failure a situation in which a market left on its own fails to allocate resources efficiently

When market outcomes fail to lead to an efficient allocation of resources, economists call this **market failure**. One possible cause of market failure is an **externality**, which is the uncompensated impact of one person's actions on the well-being of a bystander or third party. For instance, the classic example of an external cost is pollution. Another possible cause of market failure is **market power**, which refers to the ability of a single person (or small group) to unduly influence market prices. For example, if everyone in a remote village in the Scottish Highlands needs water but there is only one well, the owner of the well may act in self-interest and in doing so make decisions that have wide social and economic implications. In the presence of externalities or market power, well designed public policy can enhance economic efficiency and social outcomes.

externality the uncompensated impact of one person's actions on the well-being of a bystander or third party

market power the ability of a single economic agent (or small group of agents) to have a substantial influence on market prices

? **what if** … the intervention by government actually leads to a worse outcome than if it had not done anything in the first place? Does this mean governments should never interfere in the market?

Market systems may also fail to ensure that economic prosperity is distributed equitably. A market economy rewards people according to their ability to produce things for which other people are willing to pay. The world's best footballer earns more than the world's best chess player simply because people are willing to pay more to watch football than chess. The invisible hand does not ensure that everyone has sufficient food, decent clothing and adequate health care. Many public policies, such as income tax and the social security system, aim to achieve a more equitable distribution of economic well-being.

To say that the government *can* improve on market outcomes at times does not mean that it always *will*. Public policy is made by a political process that is far from perfect. Sometimes policies are designed simply to reward the politically powerful. Sometimes they are made by well-intentioned leaders who are not fully informed or who are unduly swayed by lobbying from businesses with a great deal of influence and power. Well-intentioned policies can have unintended consequences. Thinking as an economist helps you to judge when a government policy is justifiable to promote efficiency or equity, and when it is not.

HOW THE ECONOMY AS A WHOLE WORKS

economic growth the increase in the amount of goods and services in an economy over a period of time

We started by discussing how individuals make decisions and then looked at how people interact with one another. All these decisions and interactions together make up 'the economy'. The last three principles concern the workings of the economy as a whole. A key concept in this section is **economic growth** – the percentage increase in the number of goods and services produced in an economy over a period of time, usually expressed over a quarter and annually.

Principle 8: An Economy's Standard of Living Depends on Its Ability to Produce Goods and Services

Table 1.1 shows **gross domestic product (GDP) per head** of the population in a number of selected countries. In 2013 the average annual income per head of population in the Netherlands was about $46 000, while it was lower in the UK and Germany at around $38 000 and $44 000, respectively, somewhat higher in Norway

gross domestic product (GDP) per head the market value of all final goods and services produced within a country in a given period of time divided by the population of a country to give a per capita figure

TABLE 1.1

Gross Domestic Product (GDP) Per Capita, Purchasing Power Parity, Current International $, 2013

Country	2013
Australia	43 202
Bahrain	43 850
Belgium	41 574
Brazil	15 037
Burkina Faso	1 684
Canada	42 752
Central African Republic	603
Denmark	43 782
Egypt	11 089
Finland	39 740
France	37 532
Germany	43 883
Greece	25 666
India	5 417
Italy	35 280
Japan	36 223
Kenya	2 795
Lebanon	17 173
Luxembourg	91 047
Malta	29 126
Mozambique	1 105
Netherlands	46 162
Norway	64 405
Oman	45 333
Saudi Arabia*	53 644
Singapore	78 763
South Africa	12 866
Spain	33 094
United Arab Emirates*	59 845
United Kingdom	38 259
Republic of Yemen	3959
Zimbabwe	1832

Note: the figures here represent GDP converted to international dollars using purchasing power parity rates.

*Figures for 2012

Source: World Bank, June 2015. **http://data.worldbank.org/indicator/NY.GDP.PCAP.PP.CD**

at around $64 000 and an enviable $91 000 in Luxembourg. By contrast, we can see differences in income and living standards around the world that are quite staggering. For example, in the same year, 2013, average income in South Africa, at around $13 000, was about a third of the level in Bahrain, while in Egypt it was around $11 000, in India around $5400, in Yemen about $4000 and in Burkina Faso it was only about $1700. The average income of the Central African Republic at $603 is around 0.66 per cent of the annual income per person in Luxembourg! Not surprisingly, this large variation in average income is reflected in various other measures of the quality of life and **standard of living**. Citizens of high-income countries have better nutrition, better health care and longer life expectancy than citizens of low-income countries, as well as more TV sets, more washing machines and more cars.

standard of living a measure of welfare based on the amount of goods and services a person's income can buy

Changes in the standard of living over time are also large. Over the last 50 years, average incomes in Western Europe and North America have grown at about 2 per cent per year (after adjusting for changes in the cost of living). At this rate, average income doubles every 35 years, and over the last half-century average income in many of these prosperous economies has risen approximately three-fold. Yet, average income in Ethiopia rose by only a third over this period – an average annual growth rate of around only 0.5 per cent.

What explains these large differences in living standards among countries and over time? Almost all variation in living standards is attributable to differences in countries' **productivity** – that is, the amount of goods and services produced from each hour of a worker's time. In nations where workers can produce a large quantity of goods and services per unit of time, most people enjoy a high standard of living; in nations where workers are less productive, most people must endure a more meagre existence. Similarly, the growth rate of a nation's productivity determines the growth rate of its average income. Productivity is not only important to a country's well-being but is also vital to that of businesses.

productivity the quantity of goods and services produced from each hour of a worker's time

The relationship between productivity and living standards also has profound implications for public policy. When thinking about how any policy will affect living standards, the key question is how it will affect our ability to produce goods and services. To boost living standards, policy makers need to raise productivity by ensuring that workers are well educated, have the tools needed to produce goods and services, and have access to the best available technology. These policies are important in providing the resource infrastructure that businesses need to be able to thrive. Without well-educated workers with high levels of employability skills, business costs would be higher because they would have to pay to train workers in these skills themselves. Without an adequate transport and communications network, business activity is hampered and again costs are higher and productivity lower.

Differences in standards of living not only occur between countries but also within countries.

Principle 9: Prices Rise When the Government Prints Too Much Money

In Germany in January 1921, a daily newspaper was priced at 0.30 marks. Less than 2 years later, in November 1922, the same newspaper was priced at 70 000 000 marks. All other prices in the economy rose by similar amounts. This episode is one of history's most spectacular examples of **inflation**, an increase in the overall level of prices in the economy.

inflation an increase in the overall level of prices in the economy

While inflation in Western Europe and North America has been much lower over the last 50 years than that experienced in Germany in the 1920s, inflation has at times been an economic problem. During the 1970s, for instance, the overall level of prices in the UK more than tripled. By contrast, UK inflation from 2000 to 2008 was about 3 per cent per year; at this rate it would take more than 20 years for prices to double.

In more recent times, Zimbabwe experienced German-like hyperinflation. In March 2007 inflation in the African state was reported to be running at 2200 per cent. This means that a good priced at the equivalent of €2.99 in March 2006 would be priced at €65.78 just a year later. Because high inflation imposes various costs on businesses and society, keeping inflation at a low level is a goal of economic policy makers around the world. It is difficult for businesses to plan ahead for investment, forecasting sales and revenues if the price level is not relatively stable.

What causes inflation? In almost all cases of high or persistent inflation, the culprit turns out to be the same – growth in the quantity of money. When a government creates large quantities of the nation's money, the value of the money falls. In Germany in the early 1920s, when prices were on average tripling every month, the quantity of money was also tripling every month. Although less dramatic, the economic history of other European and North American countries points to a similar conclusion: the high inflation of the 1970s was associated with rapid growth in the quantity of money and the low inflation of the 2000s was associated with slow growth in the quantity of money.

Principle 10: Society Faces a Short-Run Trade-Off between Inflation and Unemployment

When the government increases the amount of money in the economy, one result is inflation. Another result, at least in the short run, is a lower level of unemployment. The curve that illustrates this short-run trade-off between inflation and unemployment is called the **Phillips curve**, after the economist, A.W.H. Phillips, who first examined this relationship while working at the London School of Economics.

Phillips curve a curve that shows the short-run trade-off between inflation and unemployment

The Phillips curve remains a controversial topic among economists, but many economist today accepts the idea that society faces a short-run trade-off between inflation and unemployment. This simply means that, over a period of a year or two, many economic policies push inflation and unemployment in opposite directions. Policy makers face this trade-off regardless of whether inflation and unemployment both start out at high levels (as they were in the early 1980s), at low levels (as they were in the late 1990s) or somewhere in-between.

The trade-off between inflation and unemployment is only temporary, but it can last for several years. The Phillips curve is, therefore, crucial for understanding many developments in the economy. In particular, it is important for understanding the **business cycle** – the irregular and largely unpredictable fluctuations in economic activity, as measured by the number of people employed or the production of goods and services.

business cycle fluctuations in economic activity, such as employment and production

JEOPARDY PROBLEM

A government announces that unemployment has gone up by 75 000 over the last month but employment has risen by 40 000. How can this outcome arise?

Policy makers can exploit the short-run trade-off between inflation and unemployment using various policy instruments. By changing the amount that the government spends, the amount it taxes and the amount of money it prints, policy makers can influence the combination of inflation and unemployment that the economy experiences. Because these instruments of monetary and fiscal policy are potentially so powerful, how policy makers should use these instruments to control the economy, if at all, is a subject of continuing debate.

IN THE NEWS

University or Work?

Eighteen-year-olds who have achieved the entry requirements to UK universities must make the decision of whether to go to university or earn money. It is a big decision. A rational 18-year-old would consider the opportunity cost of a degree. This is the amount of money that person would have made, if he or she had instead chosen work, added onto the cost of the degree at around £9000 a year in fees. In 2014, despite a drop in the number of 18-year-olds in Britain, there was a 3 per cent rise in those opting to study at university. More than 500 000 young people secured places at UK universities. It seems that more young people are thinking that the gain from a university education is worth it. So what is the gain?

In terms of money, it will be the extra earnings the graduate will receive over a career also known as the lifecycle of wages. A study, commissioned by the UK government, compared the earnings (and employment) of those individuals who have a first degree (and 2+ A-levels) with those with 2+ A-levels and no higher education degree. The study simulated the predicted earnings (and employment status) of individuals and then averaged these to show that the private benefit of a degree, in terms of lifetime earnings net of tax and loan repayments, is large. For men it is in the order of £168 000 or 28 per cent more earnings and for women

it is even higher at £242 000 or 53 per cent of earnings on average.

If students were aware of the differences then it might help explain why for every 13 women going to university there are only ten men.

In non-monetary terms, those considering going to university would also consider the kudos of earning a degree along with the extra academic knowledge gained and the social life that goes alongside their studies. Maybe the non-monetary side is more important to young people as it is more immediate.

The study mentioned earlier also showed that the social benefit to the government is substantial at £264 000 from men and £318 000 for women graduates, which outweighed likely exchequer costs. This may explain why the government has removed limits to places. The government supports those who wish to attend by providing student loans for fees and to help cover some living expenses, but loan repayments depend on future earnings, so there is no guarantee that all the money loaned will be paid back.

Despite the increase in demand for places, there is growing competition between universities to supply those places, and universities have invested heavily in providing more places. Students, as consumers of education, are being fussier in their choice of university now they are paying higher rates for tuition fees.

Questions

1. What is meant by the opportunity cost of going to university?
2. Calculate the opportunity cost of a 3-year degree if the alternative is work paid at £20 000 per year.
3. Why might more students be choosing to go to university in 2014 than in previous years?
4. Average earnings for women are less than those for men, so why do more women than men go to university?
5. What are the costs and benefits of governments investing in higher education?

References:
1. BBC News, 19 December 2014, **http://www.bbc.co.uk/news /education-30537561**
2. Department for Business Innovation and Skills August 2014 BIS Research Paper No. 112 The Impact of University Degrees on the Lifecycle of Earnings: Some Further Analysis, **https://www .gov.uk/government/uploads/system /uploads/attachment_data/file/229498 /bis-13-899-the-impact-of-university -degrees-on-the-lifecycle-of-earnings -further-analysis.pdf**

SUMMARY

- The fundamental lessons about individual decision making are that people and businesses face trade-offs among alternative goals, that the cost of any action is measured in terms of foregone opportunities, that rational people and businesses make decisions by comparing marginal costs and marginal benefits, and that people and businesses change their behaviour in response to the incentives they face.

- The fundamental lessons about interactions among people and businesses are that trade can be mutually

beneficial, that markets are usually a good way of coordinating trade among people and businesses, and that the government can potentially improve market outcomes if there is some market failure or if the market outcome is inequitable.

- The fundamental lessons about the economy as a whole are that productivity is the ultimate source of living standards, that money growth is the ultimate source of inflation, and that society faces a short-run trade-off between inflation and unemployment.

QUESTIONS FOR REVIEW

1. Give three examples of trade-offs that a business manufacturing washing machines might have to face.

2. What is the opportunity cost to a business of purchasing a new IT system to manage its accounting at a cost of €55 000?

3. A business in the construction industry is considering investing in building ten new houses on the edge of a small town. How might it use thinking at the margin to make a decision whether to go ahead with the investment?

4. Why should policy makers think about incentives?

5. Why might trade among countries have some winners but also some losers?

6. What is it claimed the 'invisible hand' of the marketplace does?

7. Explain the two main causes of market failure and give an example of each.

8. Why is productivity important to businesses and to society as a whole?

9. What is inflation, and what causes it?

10. How are inflation and unemployment related in the short run?

PROBLEMS AND APPLICATIONS

1. Describe some of the trade-offs faced by each of the following:
   a. A decision by an entrepreneur starting a small business to borrow some start-up capital from a bank or raise the funds through borrowing from friends and relations.
   b. A member of the government deciding how much to spend on some new military hardware for the defence industry.
   c. A chief executive officer deciding whether to invest in a new more efficient heating system for the company's headquarters.
   d. A worker in a hotel deciding whether to accept the offer by her manager of extra shifts in the restaurant.

2. You work in a bank and were planning to spend Saturday going to watch your local football team with your

son and daughter. However, your boss has asked you if you would help prepare some important financial data for some new regulations that are being introduced by the government. It is not compulsory to come in over the weekend but it is made clear it would be looked upon favourably.
   a. If you decide to go to the football match, what is the true cost to you of that decision?
   b. If you decide to go into work for the weekend to help out your boss, what is the true cost of that decision?

3. A business operated by a sole trader generates €20 000 in profits and has the option of retaining the amount to reinvest into the business or putting the sum into a bank which would generate 2 per cent interest a year. What would your decision be and why, and what is the opportunity cost of your decision?

4. A smartphone manufacturer invests €20 million in developing a new phone design and 3D interface, but the development is not quite finished. At a recent meeting, your sales people report that a rival has just released a new phone which is estimated to reduce the expected sales of your new product to €12 million. If it would cost €4 million to finish development and make the product, should you go ahead and do so? What is the most that you should pay to complete development? Explain your answer.

5. Three members of the operations management team at a plant manufacturing steel tubing for construction projects are discussing a possible increase in production. Each suggests a way to make this decision.
   a. Team member 1: We should base the decision on whether labour productivity would rise if we increased output.
   b. Team member 2: We need to focus more on cutting our average cost per tube – this will help us to be more competitive against our rivals.
   c. Team member 3: We should only increase output if the extra revenue from selling the additional tubes would be greater than the extra costs.
   Who do you think is right? Why?

6. The financial crisis of 2007–2009 has had a significant impact on people in many countries. Does the crisis suggest that markets need to be more closely monitored and regulated to prevent such crises from occurring again?

7. Suppose the European Union adopted central planning for its economy, and you became the Chief Planner. Among the millions of decisions that you need to make for next year are how much food to produce, what land to use and who should receive the food produced and in what quantities.

a. To make these decisions intelligently, what information would you need about the food industry?
b. What information would you need about each of the people in the countries making up the European Union?
c. How would your decisions about food affect some of your other decisions, such as how much farm equipment to produce, how much labour to employ on farms and how much fertilizer to use? How might some of your other decisions about the economy change your views about food?

8. Explain whether each of the following government activities is motivated by a concern about equity or a concern about efficiency. In the case of efficiency, discuss the type of market failure involved.
   a. Regulating gas prices.
   b. Regulating advertising.
   c. Providing students with vouchers that can be used to buy university education.

9. Discuss each of the following statements from the standpoints of equity and efficiency.
   a. 'All students should have free access to higher education.'
   b. 'Businesses making workers redundant should be made to provide at least six months' pay as a redundancy payment to enable those affected time to find a new job.'
   c. 'Businesses should be made to pay more into workers' pension schemes to ensure that people have a decent standard of living when they retire.'

10. Imagine that you are a policy maker trying to decide whether to reduce the rate of inflation in your country. To make an intelligent decision, what would you need to know about inflation, unemployment and the trade-off between them?

2 ECONOMICS AND BUSINESS DECISION MAKING

LEARNING OUTCOMES

After reading this chapter you should be able to:

- Give examples of unconscious and conscious decisions by consumers and businesses.
- Explain the basic economic problem of scarce resources and unlimited wants.
- Give examples about how informed decision making can be based on assumptions about weighing up the value of costs and benefits.
- State at least two examples of the difficulties businesses face in accurately valuing costs and benefits.

- Explain the importance to businesses of decisions on investment, growth and expansion, using appropriate examples.
- Show why acquiring and keeping customers are important decisions for a business.
- Give an example to show how making decisions on keeping customers' needs to be assessed carefully.

ECONOMICS: THE SCIENCE (OR ART) OF DECISION MAKING

In every walk of life humans have to make decisions. In business, this is no different. Every day millions of people working in businesses at many different levels make decisions. Decisions arise because there is a choice of different actions. A business might have to make a decision about whether and how far to change price, whether to invest in new technology, hire or release workers, spend money on an advertising campaign and so on. In each case, it will have to weigh up the costs and benefits of making the decision and in doing so consider other possible options as part of the decision making process. Deciding between alternatives arises because resources are usually scarce relative to the demand. This is the heart of the economic problem.

The Economic Problem – Scarce Resources and Unlimited Wants and Needs

The central economic problem is one of scarce resources and unlimited wants and needs. The Earth is blessed with resources of all kinds: some we know about and some we still do not know exist. Oil, metals, land, minerals, plants, animals and so on all provide humans with the means to satisfy our needs; the essentials of life such as food, water, clothing and shelter, without which it would be difficult to survive, and our wants, all the things we would like to have which we believe make our lives more comfortable and happy.

However, these resources are scarce. By scarce resources we mean that they are insufficient in quantity relative to the demand for them. Few businesses have so much money that they can afford to satisfy all their wants and needs. As a result businesses have to make decisions about how they allocate income and scarce resources to different uses.

> **?** **what if …** you are living inside the Arctic Circle and are having some guests round to your house for a party. You go to a store which is selling packaged ice cubes in its freezer. Would you buy them? If so why and if not, why not?

When consumers choose between buying one product or another they undertake both conscious and subconscious processing. Understanding how consumers behave is important for businesses. Economists attempt to model decision-making behaviour and in building these models have to make assumptions. One such assumption is that humans weigh up the value of the costs and benefits of a decision. If the value of the benefits of a decision is greater than the value of the costs then this can be a reasonable basis on which to make a purchasing decision.

This assumption of rational behaviour may be relevant in many cases; it could be argued that businesses in particular have developed sophisticated ways of making rational decisions by identifying and quantifying costs and benefits to help them make decisions. Management accounting techniques, in particular, have been developed with the primary intention of assisting in decision making. Over the last 30 years, advances in technology and research in the field of neuroscience and psychology has opened up new information to how and why humans make decisions. This information is being used by businesses to help understand consumer behaviour and this can help in the design and development of new products as well as in the way in which existing products are marketed.

The Effect of Human Decision Making on Businesses

When consumers go to the supermarket, many will fill up the shopping trolley with similar products to those purchased on the last visit, almost on autopilot. Some might be tempted by the end-of-aisle or point-of-sale offers that seek to persuade consumers to give up hard earned cash in order to acquire the good in question, but this involves a little bit more mental computation than the buying on autopilot. Does the consumer really need (or want) the item concerned and does the amount of money being asked for the product (the price) represent value for money; in other words, will buying the product bring adequate benefits? Every time an individual makes a decision about the purchase of a product it has an effect on a business.

Consider the following example.

A new student walks into a university bookshop and looks at the copy of Mankiw, Taylor and Ashwin, which has been recommended by her lecturer. The student looks at the book, thinks it looks impressive but when she looks at the price she thinks it is a little high. Giving up €50 at that moment in time makes her think twice. She thinks about the freshers' welcome party for new members of the netball team which she is planning on going to, not to mention the freshers' ball at the end of the week. She puts the book back on the shelf and decides she will try her luck in the library instead.

The effect of this decision is that the bookshop will not receive €50 from the sale of the book. This is just another in a long line of decisions being made by students which has seen sales at the bookshop declining. At the end of the month the bookshop returns the unsold stock back to the publisher, Cengage Learning. The publisher has to adjust its inventories (stocks) and now has more stock of the book than it had anticipated. The bookshop may find that if it cannot encourage more students to use its facilities rather than spending their money on other things or even buying their books second hand or online, then it may not be able to cover the costs of stock, staffing, lighting and heating, administrative costs and rent for the premises. It may have to close down as a result.

For the publisher, the increase in stock means that it will not have to reprint the book at the time it planned to do so. The printing company in China finds that the reprint order it was expecting does not arrive and as a result they cut back on the amount of paper and ink they order from their suppliers. For paper manufacturers the fall in the order for paper means that they now do not need to hire as many workers and so some workers are made redundant.

These workers find their incomes are now much lower and so have to cut back on the family spending. They used to eat out at least once every two weeks but now decide they have to cut that out altogether. The restaurant where they used to eat notices a drop in the number of people walking through the door to eat and so does not need to order as many supplies of ingredients as previously …

And so on.

The simple decision by the student on its own may not seem to be that important but the combined effect of millions of decisions made every day by millions of people around the world do have significant effects on businesses. These decisions are important in other ways too.

Value for Money

A decision to buy this book is a message to the publisher and the authors that the book has some value – it helps with study, it makes the subject easier to understand, the support resources are helpful in getting through assessments, and ultimately the students can get the grade they are looking for. In other words, a decision to buy this book implies the buyer feels it will give value for money. We can define **value for money** as a situation where the satisfaction gained from using the book (however we choose to measure that satisfaction) is greater than the amount of money the individual had to hand over to acquire it (the price).

> **value for money** a situation (mostly subjective) where the satisfaction gained from purchasing and consuming a product is greater than the amount of money the individual had to hand over to acquire it (the price)

If enough students make such a decision this book will be very successful. The authors will be pleased because they will get royalties from the sale of each book and the publisher will be pleased because each sale represents revenue and if enough books are sold to more than cover the total costs of producing and selling the book, it will make a profit.

However, the decision to buy this book has an effect on other books which could have been bought for a Business Economics course. When you are in a book shop or looking at the choices on a website, choosing one book is an endorsement for the producer of that book, but what about the one you decide not to buy? If enough people make the choice to buy this book and not another, then the rival publisher may decide that its book does not have a market and declares the book out of print. The author is likely to get very few, if any, royalties and those people that worked hard to help produce the book may find their jobs in jeopardy if something similar happens to other books they are involved with.

This is why economists spend a great deal of time looking at the working of markets. A market is made up of two parties, buyers (consumers) and sellers (producers), coming together to agree on exchange. Businesses make products available and consumers make decisions about whether to buy these products. Every individual consumer decision is important in its own right but in order to get an understanding of the market as a whole we look at the effects of the aggregation of those decisions.

Why consumers make the decisions they do is the subject of continued debate and academic research. The developments in imaging technologies have revealed, in part (there is still much we do not know), how the brain functions when we make decisions. It is opening up fascinating new lines of enquiry and understanding. Neuroscience and developments in psychology are playing their part in helping economists to better understand human behaviour in a variety of contexts, including how they make purchasing decisions. Behavioural economics is becoming an increasingly important branch of the discipline and is being utilized not only by academic economists but also by businesses in a bid to better understand decision making and human behaviour.

CASE STUDY

Apple Is Gaining Market Share

In the last three months of 2014, Apple sold more than 74 million iPhones. Its market share grew by 46 per cent year-on-year to grab nearly 20 per cent of the market share for smartphones. While the average price of smartphones has fallen, due to price sensitivity, Apple's latest iPhone is more expensive than previous models. Clearly buyers feel they are getting

value for money and are prepared to pay a premium price to be a proud owner of the new iPhone.

In the smartphone market, Apple has managed to convince its customer base that its iPhone is great value for money despite the product being able to command a premium price over competitors. Data from web search analysis indicate that nine out of ten iPhone users will stay with the Apple brand when they buy a new phone. This brand loyalty compares favourably with Samsung, for whom less than eight out of ten customers say they will stay with the brand. It had been much worse for Samsung, which has managed to significantly improve brand loyalty from 37 per cent in 2011 to 77 per cent in 2014, but some of this has been through price reductions, something Apple currently does not need to do.

Apple is far from complacent and still has to work hard to convince customers to buy its products. Apple releases a new mobile operating system every year which unsurprisingly works best on the newest hardware released at a similar time. Prior to the launch, app developers update their apps for the new operating system. Apple's marketing is also slick and this helps add value to its products.

Reference: ZDNet (2015) **http://www.zdnet.com/article/idc-apple-samsung-smartphones-q4-2014/**

BUSINESS DECISION MAKING

Businesses are also interested in how they, themselves, make decisions about a whole host of things such as who to hire, when to hire, what to invest in, what not to invest in, how to improve productivity, whether to pursue an acquisition or not, whether to conduct an advertising campaign and if so how much to spend on it and when, among others. There are stakeholder decisions that affect the business and need to be understood, for example why some employees may be less committed to their work or to the principles and values of the business. How do governments make decisions and what impact will it have on businesses? What decision-making processes take place at suppliers? Are the decisions managers and owners make compatible, and if so how will these decisions affect local communities and the environment?

Quick Quiz Think about a recent purchase decision you made. What were the other options you could have chosen instead? Articulate the reasons why you eventually made the decision to purchase the product you did.

There are three important areas for business where decision making has to be considered carefully.

Investment

investment making money available to develop a project which will generate future returns including increasing future productive capacity

One of the key decisions that has to be made relates to investment. **Investment**, in this context, is about a business making money available to develop a project that will generate future returns including increasing future productive capacity. Examples of business investment might include:

- A chemical engineering firm deciding to hire a specialist chemist to work on the development of a particular process for a client.
- A tool-making firm investing in a new piece of machinery which helps make the firm more productive.
- A food manufacturing plant buying a new oven which helps improve temperature regulation of the cooking process or helps to increase the volume of ingredients being processed at any one time.
- A farmer considering whether to install a new milking parlour to replace an existing facility. The new parlour might provide the farmer with more information about the volume and quality of the milk being given by the herd, as well as automating some procedures which mean that more cows can be milked in a shorter amount of time. This might then free up the farmer to do other important jobs around the farm.
- A Chinese restaurant owner having to make a decision about which insurance company to use to renew its insurance policies to cover it for fire, theft, loss of profits, public liability (in case any customer or member of the public is injured or suffers in some way as a result of the business' actions), injury to employees (employers' liability), damage or loss to machinery and equipment and many other possible risks. Does it stick with its existing insurer who has provided good service but is quite expensive, or go with a new insurer with an unknown reputation but which is much cheaper?
- A road haulage company considering investing in a computerized monitoring system for all its fleet of vehicles which travel around Europe to help it improve its logistical planning, adherence to health and safety regulations and help improve tracking in the event of theft.

Cook pans in a food manufacturing plant – the decision to purchase these pieces of equipment will have been taken after carefully weighting up the costs and benefits and what contribution they will make to overall production and productivity.

There are some key characteristics which are common to this sort of investment decision. Any decision will bring with it some costs, both financial and otherwise, and will also bring with it benefits – these benefits could be to the business itself and to those who have an interest in the business (**stakeholders**) and the wider society. These costs and benefits have to be weighed up and we assume that a decision is worth taking if the value of the accrued benefits to the business outweighs the value of the total costs of the decision.

stakeholders groups or individuals with an interest in a business, such as workers, managers, suppliers, the local community, customers and owners.

? **what if ...** a business values two options equally? How might it make a decision which to invest in if it can only afford one of them?

Economists would argue that in order to make any informed decision we have to have some idea of the value of the relative costs and benefits. Calculating the financial cost of building and operating a new assembly plant for a manufacturing firm and estimating the financial benefits from the resulting expansion in production might be straightforward. What is not so easy is calculating the cost of the new plant on the ecosystem or the damage to the visual amenity of the area around which the plant will be built. The more accurately these sorts of costs can be calculated the more informed the decision. Economists try to find effective ways of calculating costs and benefits more accurately but ultimately there is always going to be some error term and a lack of information which will make the calculations and estimates less than perfect.

JEOPARDY PROBLEM

In the UK, there is a fierce on-going debate about the validity of investing millions of pounds into a new high-speed rail network linking the south with parts of the north-west and north-east of the country. What sort of factors might businesses argue need to be considered in arriving at a decision whether to go ahead with the investment? How and why might other stakeholders view the decision to go ahead differently?

Growth and Expansion

At some point in time, a business will have to make a decision about growth and expansion. It could be argued that a new business start-up is as much a part of growth and expansion as a decision by a large multinational business to acquire a new business by merger or takeover.

These decisions involve considerable risk to a business. **Risk** is the extent to which a decision leading to a course of action will result in some loss, damage, adverse effect or otherwise undesirable outcome to the decision maker. One of the first questions many businesses may ask themselves when making a decision is 'what could go wrong' and decisions relating to growth and expansion are no different.

risk the extent to which a decision leading to a course of action will result in some loss, damage, adverse effect or otherwise undesirable outcome to the decision maker

A business might grow through internal or external means. Internal growth comes from the business generating sufficient profits to be able to reinvest back into the business. This reinvestment might be in buying new premises, new plant and equipment, taking on more staff, more efficient computer systems or hiring a consultant to help identify new systems and processes of working which allow the business to sell more.

External growth by contrast is generally much quicker in that a firm can grow by either taking over or merging with another business. Merger and acquisition activity (M&A) tends to fluctuate with the swings in economic activity; when the economy is growing, M&A activity tends to be higher and vice versa. There are often grand claims made by business leaders about the benefits to the business of any such external growth. The word 'synergies' is used to describe how anticipated benefits will accrue to the business. **Synergy** refers to a situation where the combination of two or more businesses or business operations brings total benefits which are greater than those that would arise from the separate business entities. The idea of $2 + 2 = 5$ is often used to exemplify the principle.

synergy a situation where the combination of two or more businesses or business operations brings total benefits which are greater than those which would arise from the separate business entities

The reality tends to be less spectacular. There have been a number of very high-profile mergers and takeovers which have promised huge benefits to shareholders and customers alike which have proved to be illusory. Some estimates put the success rate of mergers and acquisitions at between 20 and 45 per cent. If we take the lower end of these estimates then only one in five mergers and acquisitions are successful. This, of course, depends on what we mean by 'success'. If the M&A did not bring the benefits promised at the outset then the process could be classed as not being successful although the business might still be in a better position than it was prior to the M&A.

Pitfall Prevention Terms such as 'success' or 'failure' are relative. This means that we have to be careful how we make judgements in relation to these terms. If a business tells its shareholders that a merger will yield a 40 per cent increase in efficiency within 5 years but in the event efficiency only increases by 20 per cent, should this be classed as a failure? Always make sure that you are clear in your definition of what is meant by 'success' or 'failure' when discussing business activity.

Acquiring and Keeping Customers

For any business to survive it must have customers, whether these customers are other businesses or final consumers. Acquiring customers involves some cost – marketing, advertising, promotion, putting in place appropriate services, having the right product in the right place at the right time and ensuring that the product meets the expectations of customers in terms of quality. It will also involve making decisions about how much money should be devoted to acquiring new customers? How much budget should a new advertising or promotion campaign be given? What is the best and most efficient way in which customers can be reached and persuaded to try the business' products?

Once a business has acquired customers, there are also decisions to be made about how these customers can be retained and at what cost. What emphasis should the business put on keeping customers in relation to acquiring new ones – should it be 80:20, 70:30, 60:40, 50:50 or some other proportion?

At what point is it appropriate to lose a customer? In principle, the answer can be given by reference to thinking at the margin. It might be worth losing a customer if the cost of retaining that customer becomes higher than the benefits that the customer brings – in other words, the revenue being generated by the customer is less than the cost of retaining that customer.

The balance between the cost of acquiring and keeping customers changes, depending in part on the wider economic environment. It is often said that it is much cheaper to keep existing customers than find new ones. The Chartered Institute of Marketing notes that the cost of acquiring a new customer depends on the industry or market sector, but that in general it is between four and ten times the cost of keeping an existing one. There are a number of factors that can affect the cost of both these things including the rate at which new competitors enter the industry, the extent to which existing competitors bring out new products and how close a substitute they are, pricing tactics being adopted, and levels of customer service. The latter can be important in retaining customers and includes such things as the expectations of customers not being met, the quality of the product in terms of how easy it is to use and how resilient it is, errors in billing customers and general customer service issues like the length of time customers have to wait to speak to someone, how knowledgeable customer service operatives are, the ease of accessing technical help, and how easy a website is to navigate.

All these factors are affected to a greater and lesser extent by the decisions a firm makes. Someone in the organization, for example, makes a decision about what telephone system to use, how many people there are to staff the system, where it is located and what its perceived role is. On the basis of this decision, the company could win and lose customers. Giving customers a frustrating time at the end of a phone but at low unit cost could be false economy.

Quick Quiz   What factors might a business have to consider in making a decision to outsource customer service operations to a low labour-cost economy?

CASE STUDY

The Importance of Customer Retention

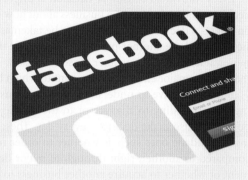

When you visit a restaurant there is on average a 70 per cent chance that you will never make the return visit. This statistic implies that restaurants need to focus on acquiring customers and not worry too much about keeping them. One strategy would be to just pay someone with great persuasive skills to stand outside the restaurant and attract the customers in, and spend less on a good chef. Zach Goldstein, CEO and founder of Thanx notes: 'Modern customers are promiscuous. With countless competing options, they don't mind spreading the love. Most brands write them off by focusing on customer acquisition, but customer retention is seven times more cost effective – they're already familiar with you.'

Taipei-based start-up Jessyfrup has developed a clever iPad application designed to get more returning customers into restaurants. Founder of Jessyfrup, Chu Hsuan Ting, found out that many restaurants in Taiwan use Yahoo ads, Google AdWords or Facebook ads to get customers from the Internet into their restaurants. These restaurants pay around US$300 every month for online advertising, mainly aimed at attracting customers who will only visit the restaurant once. It means the restaurants keep spending US$300 every month in order to get more customers. Jessyfrup's app is different in that it allows customers to input their mobile number into the restaurant's iPad app in person and then receive promotions/offers via SMS to encourage them to return. Not everyone wants to receive SMS promotions all the time so Jessyfrup uses its own data to work out the most appropriate time to send the SMS to each individual customer in an attempt to maximize customer retention.

Ting claims a restaurant using his system can reduce a US$300 monthly online advertising spend to around half of that simply because the restaurant will gain more repeat customers. If he is correct, then after paying a charge of around $70 a month a restaurant using the software could gain a net saving of around $80 a month. Of course some of this would need to be spent on getting a better chef, at least in some restaurants.

References: **http://www.virtualpressoffice.com/publicsiteContentFileAccess?fileContent Id=1882730&fromOtherPageToDisableHistory=Y&menuName=News&sId=&sInfo=**

http://e27.co/taipeis-jessyfrup-boosting-customer-retention-rates-local -businesses-20150105/

CONCLUSION

Economics can be seen as being a science of decision making. Because we are all affected in some way by scarce resources and unlimited wants and needs, we have to allocate resources to different uses and thus make choices. In making these choices we have to make decisions. There are increasingly more sophisticated ways of looking at how individuals and businesses make decisions but in order to analyse how economies work we make basic assumptions about behaviour. In making these assumptions we can then observe deviations and seek to develop more sophisticated models to understand why, which lead to better theories to help make predictions.

Every individual consumer decision is important in its own right because that decision sends messages to a business about how the consumer values the products on offer – a decision to purchase can be taken as a positive message whilst a decision to purchase another product is a message that somehow the rival product is more valuable to the consumer for some reason. This collective individual decision making has major effects on the extent to which businesses are successful or not.

Businesses have to understand these reasons in order to improve their offering. In responding to changes or to the messages they receive from consumers, businesses also make decisions every day. These decisions can range from seemingly mundane ones such as whether to order reams of paper from one supplier compared to another, right through to major decisions on new plant and equipment or whether to acquire another business to help meet consumer needs more effectively. Each is important in its own right.

We can look at business decision making in three main areas: decisions on investment in new productive capacity, on growth and expansion, and on acquiring and keeping customers. Collectively these decisions are related and will have knock-on effects on other decisions businesses have to make. For example, if a decision is taken to introduce an enterprise resource planning (ERP) system (a system that brings together management information from inside and outside the business to the whole organization which helps improve flows of information within the business) this might then lead to decisions having to be taken on hiring new staff, maybe reducing staffing in some areas, decisions on training needs and how to manage some of the disruption that will occur during transition.

We work on the basic assumption that businesses will weigh up the costs and benefits of a decision, attempting to quantify as far as possible these costs and benefits, and then making a decision based on the assessment of the value of the benefits in relation to the value of the costs. One of the problems businesses face in making decisions based on this principle is accurately valuing all the costs and benefits.

IN THE NEWS

Attracting Foreign Investment in South Africa

Attracting foreign investment is crucial to the future prosperity and economic growth of nations. However, it is not always easy to do business in some countries. A government can play an important role in ensuring its country is open and able to attract foreign investment from companies.

Saldanha Bay Iron Ore Terminal

The Organization for Economic Cooperation and Development (OECD) Restrictiveness Index ranks South Africa as an open economy for foreign direct investment (FDI). This openness is reflected in the overall trend of growing FDI into South Africa over the past two decades. So much so, that FDI in South Africa accounts for just over 40 per cent of GDP. In the last 5 years South Africa has received about one-quarter of all new investment projects in Africa. Companies from the USA, the European Union and increasingly from China, India and other Asian countries see South Africa as a good place to invest.

The 2014 *AT Kearney Foreign Direct Confidence Index* ranks South Africa in 13th position among the 25 leading economies. It has moved up two places from 2013. Over 130 foreign firms either entered South Africa or expanded their investments during 2013.

However, the South African government cannot afford to be complacent especially when viewing other data. The *2015 Ease of Doing Business* report ranks 189 countries and is compiled by the World Bank. It shows that South Africa's overall performance in the *Ease of Doing Business Index* declined, with the country dropping from 41st to 43rd. One explanation given is South Africa's poor or limited access to electricity. For example, it can take over 200 days to get connected to the grid. This is something that South Africa needs to sort out if it wishes to remain competitive to foreign investment and attract more inward flows of investment.

It also has some work to do on improving the transparency of credit information. The country also needs to ensure its regulations are appropriate and enforced.

While its ease of doing business ranking has fallen, South Africa has improved its world ranking in a range of other indicators such as:

- Starting a business – 64 to 61
- Registering property – 99 to 97
- Trading across borders – 106 to 100
- Enforcing contracts – 80 to 46

The improvement in the trading across borders indicator is important for a country like South Africa because it implies it is more attractive to foreign investment in manufactured and mineral products which are exported from South Africa to international markets. To support trade across borders, in 2015 South Africa announced a R9.65-billion investment in infrastructure projects at the port of Saldanha on its west coast. The project is designed to clear the bottlenecks affecting exports that has been constraining economic growth. This capital spending should have a positive impact in the future.

Questions

1. What is the link between foreign direct investment and GDP in a country like South Africa?
2. What is the value of indexes such as *Ease of Doing Business* to multinationals and countries like South Africa? Why might people also look at the trends in rank order of the index over a period of years?
3. Why are businesses as far afield as the USA, Europe and Asia keen to invest in developing countries like South Africa?
4. Why is infrastructure important for economic growth?
5. How might the South African government make its country more attractive to potential investors?

Reference: http://www.biznews.com/davos-2015/2015/01/19/minister-rob-davies-south-africa-open-business/Bottom of Form

SUMMARY

- Decision making is at the heart of economics.
- Millions of decisions are made every day by businesses and consumers and these decisions affect businesses in different ways.
- Businesses have to make decisions focused on three main areas:
  - investment
  - growth and expansion
  - acquiring and keeping customers.
- Assessing the value of the costs and benefits is a basis for making decisions.

- If the value of the benefits is greater than the value of the costs then the decision can be justified.
- It is not always easy to quantify the value of all the costs and benefits in making a decision.

- Neuroscience and psychology is revealing new ways in which people and businesses make decisions which may not always reflect a rational decision based on the value of costs and benefits.

QUESTIONS FOR REVIEW

1. Explain the difference between a conscious and a sub-conscious purchasing decision. Which do you think is more reliable and why?

2. Oil is a commodity and there are billions of barrels still waiting to be exploited. Why, then, do we refer to oil as a scarce resource?

3. Using some specific examples, explain the difference between wants and needs.

4. Explain what economists mean by 'making an informed, rational decision'.

5. Explain how a decision by a student to take a bus to a guest lecture by a famous economist at a nearby town hall, rather than a taxi, affects both transport businesses.

6. You buy a new t-shirt from Holister and have to pay €25 for it. How would you measure the value for money of this t-shirt?

7. Why is it difficult to accurately assess the costs and benefits of a decision such as whether to grant permission to a leisure business to open a new theme park on the outskirts of a town?

8. What is risk in the context of decision making by a business?

9. Why do you think the cost to businesses of acquiring customers is generally much higher than retaining them?

10. Using an appropriate example, outline three factors which could lead to an increase in the cost of keeping customers.

PROBLEMS AND APPLICATIONS

1. When you go into a shop to buy a product, how often do you make decisions based on conscious and sub-conscious factors?

2. You have to arrange a flight from Amsterdam to Rome and look at a travel website for the choices available to you. List the range of factors you will want to consider in making your choice about which airline to choose to make the flight. To what extent is the decision you arrive at 'rational'?

3. Food is essential for human life. Does this mean that all food items should be classed as 'needs' and not 'wants'?

4. A customer of a mobile phone network contacts the provider to explain that they are changing to another provider. To what extent should the provider be concerned about this decision by the customer? Explain your answer.

5. Two student friends attend a gig showcasing a new band which has had rave reviews from music journalists. At the end of the evening they talk about their experience; one says they thought the band lived up to expectations and the €20 was 'more than worth it'. The other thinks

the evening was a 'waste of money'. Give some possible explanations about why each student had a different perception of value for money in this instance.

6. Some business leaders put faith in 'gut instinct' in making decisions. To what extent would you advise basing decisions on gut instincts rather than 'rational' analysis?

7. Explain how investment in new productive capacity can help a business grow internally.

8. Evaluate the case for a builders' merchant spending more money on retaining its existing customers rather than acquiring new ones.

9. A business calculates that the cost of acquiring a new customer is €250 and the average yearly revenue received from each customer is €260. Should the business go ahead with its customer acquisition spending on this basis?

10. 'There is a science to decision making and a business should take notice of this science in helping to make its own decisions.' To what extent do you agree with this statement?

3 THE BUSINESS ENVIRONMENT

LEARNING OUTCOMES

After reading this chapter you should be able to:

- Give a definition of the meaning of business and business activity.

- List and give examples of the four factors of production.

- List the key characteristics and skills of entrepreneurs.

- Describe the transformation process and apply this to a series of everyday examples.

- Give a definition of the term 'value added'.

- Explain the main internal and external factors which affect business activity through using the PESTLE framework.

- Give a definition of the term 'shareholder value'.

- Describe how shareholder value can be affected by both increasing revenues and reputation.

THE TRANSFORMATION PROCESS

Decision making is a recurring theme of this book. Successful business is all about making decisions that help meet aims and objectives, and, as we have seen, economics can be seen as being a 'science' of decision making. We have seen how business activity involves taking a series of inputs and producing an output. The business might provide the output (goods and services) to someone who actually consumes the good or service (the final consumer). This is referred to as **B2C business**. **B2B business** is the term used when businesses sell goods or services to another business, who may either act as an intermediary in getting goods and services to the final consumer, or who will do something to those goods and services before selling them on to a final consumer.

In recent years there are also other forms of activity that could be classed as business activity where consumers interact with other consumers via social networking sites or specialist websites such as eBay, Amazon Marketplace, eBid, Quicksales, uBid and Overstock, which facilitate this type of trade. This is referred to as **C2C business**.

> **Pitfall Prevention**   The term 'business' in a question is generic – when considering answers to questions be sure to specify what type of business you are referring to so that you contextualize your answers and show some awareness that different businesses may be affected in different ways.

Factors of Production

A common feature that characterizes business activity is the **transformation process**. Any business has to utilize inputs, referred to as **factors of production**, and does something with them to produce an output – a semi-finished product or commodity (raw materials such as rubber, cocoa, coffee, wheat, tin, ores, etc.), which is then sold on to another business for producing a finished product which is sold to a consumer.

Economists classify these factors of production in four main ways, although there are some that argue for only three factors of production. The four are land, labour, capital and enterprise. Some class enterprise as a specialist form of labour but we will assume it is a separate factor of production.

Land   Land is a term that includes all the natural resources of the Earth and so might not only include pieces of land on which factories or offices are built, or which is farmed, but also things such as fish in the sea, minerals and ores from the ground, and so on.

Labour   Labour is all the physical and mental effort provided by humans in production. This includes human activity ranging from the work of a chief executive officer (CEO) at the head of a large public company right through to the person who has to clean the toilets.

Capital   In everyday language we use the term **capital** to refer to money. Economists use the term capital in a different way, although the two are linked.

B2C business business activity where the business sells goods and services to a final consumer

B2B business business activity where the business sells goods and services to another business

C2C business business activity where consumers exchange goods and services often facilitated by a third party such as an online auction site

transformation process the process in which businesses take factor inputs and process them to produce outputs which are then sold

factors of production a classification of inputs used in business activity which includes land, labour, capital and enterprise

land all the natural resources of the Earth which can be used in production

labour all the human effort, mental and physical, which is used in production

capital any item used in production which is not used for its own sake but for what it contributes to production

Capital refers to anything that is not used for its own sake but which makes a contribution to production. This might include equipment and machinery, buildings, offices, shops, computers, mainframes, desks, chairs, etc. Of course, in order to get capital, businesses need money but economists view money as a medium of exchange and so it is often more informative to look at the opportunity cost which can tell us a great deal about the relative values that businesses put on decision making.

> **Quick Quiz** Choose one product and write down some specific examples of the three factors of production covered so far which are used in the production of the product chosen.

Factors of production like land, labour and capital need organizing before they combine to produce outputs. Iron ore in the ground is useless until someone organizes the labour and capital to extract it and process it ready for another business to use in many different ways. A chemical company will not discover new processes unless humans combine with land and capital to work out what these processes might be and design them so that they are cost effective and viable. As individuals we would have problems cutting and styling our own hair unless someone with the necessary skill brings together the factors of production to enable us to sit and watch as our hair is transformed. This requires land for the salon building, equipment such as sinks, taps, chairs, scissors, dryers, colourings, chemicals, etc., not to mention someone or a group of people taking the risk of setting up the business in the first place.

This is the factor of **enterprise**. Entrepreneurs take the risk of organizing factors of production to generate business activity and in return hope to get a number of rewards which might include profit but might also be less obvious things such as self-satisfaction, personal challenge and the desire to take more control over one's life.

enterprise the act of taking risks in the organization of factors of production to generate business activity

We might often think of entrepreneurs as being exceptional individuals who have seemingly become incredibly successful and very wealthy. The names usually quoted in the same breath as the term 'entrepreneur' include Sergey Brin and Larry Page, Richard Branson, Mark Zuckerberg, Debbie Fields, Azim Premji and Lakshmi Mittal, among others, but these tend to be extreme examples. The reality is that the world is full of millions of people being entrepreneurial. They might include an individual who has set herself up in business as a painter and decorator, an electrician, builder, plumber, florist, carpet fitter, a child in a poverty stricken area of India making some money out of recycling rubbish in some way, a farmer running a dairy herd, a financial advisor, tyre fitter and many other examples.

The skills necessary to be an entrepreneur are well documented, but the extent individuals possess and utilize these skills varies in each case. The reasons why some entrepreneurs go on to make millions while others struggle to barely make a living is not simply to do with the degree of determination, initiative, planning, access to finance, asking the right questions, acting on hunches, taking risks, being willing to work hard and make things happen, thinking ahead and thinking creatively, it is also to do with being in the right place at the right time and having a large degree of luck.

Can this be classed as an entrepreneurial activity?

Entrepreneurs take risks and many of them fail: the rate of business failure in the 3 to 5 years after start-up is estimated to be around 30 per cent, although getting precise data is difficult because we have to be careful how we define 'business failure'. It is fairly clear that a business fails if it has to file for insolvency or, in the case of a sole trader, bankruptcy, but if the owner sells on the business after a few years because they do not feel they are getting enough of a return is that also an example of failure?

? **what if . . .** the number of business failures rises above 50 per cent, would this mean that it is not worth taking the risks to start up a new business?

It is clear that setting up a new business is challenging. Potentially high failure rates do not put off millions of people around the world from starting businesses and many will try again after (sometimes many) failures in the hope that lessons have been learned and the next time will see things work. The skills and qualities of entrepreneurs are many, but perhaps the most important is the willingness to take risks. This is one reason why some economists prefer to class enterprise as a factor of production in its own right rather than seeing it as just another form of labour.

Business activity is about bringing factors of production together to generate a product which is then sold. It is essentially a transformation process, therefore, with some types of business activity being very much more complex and risky than others. This is one reason why prices might be higher for some products compared to others and why some types of labour generate more income than do others.

Adding Value

How these factors are brought together, in what proportions and how they work together in the transformation process, could be very different, even in the same type of business operating in the same industry. Rarely are two firms producing cars or chemicals the same, although they may have many similarities. One of the key elements of the transformation process is adding value and this could be at any stage in this process.

added value the difference between the cost of factor inputs into production and the amount consumers are prepared to pay (the value placed on the product by consumers)

Added value is what a business does to inputs to convert them to outputs which customers (businesses or final consumers) are prepared to pay for. Adding value could be in the form of a piece of technology that makes a consumer's life much easier in some way, or does the job the product is designed for more effectively or more stylishly than other rival products on the market. It might even be that a business creates a product or service that no one has thought of before and which people are prepared to pay enough money for, and over a long enough period (often repeatedly), to enable the business to cover the costs of producing that product and to provide a sufficient return to those who own the business to persuade them to keep producing. There is a great deal of complexity that arises out of this relatively simple statement but it is at the heart of what business activity is about and how a business can survive. If it cannot add value then the business will ultimately fail.

CASE STUDY

Added Value Through the Use of Technology

Added value takes many forms. It is determined by the price a customer pays less the cost of the factor inputs. Many firms add value to their products or services through branding, developing a positive reputation and providing good customer experience since all these help raise the price customers are prepared to pay.

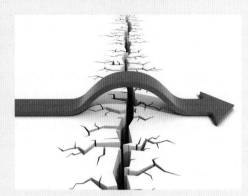

Elimination of obstacles is a priority for Amazon.

According to a CEI survey, 86 per cent of buyers are prepared to pay more for a better customer experience. It implies that a business spending money on this could see a rise in its revenue and profit.

Amazon is one such company paying close attention to improving its customer care, but making improvements won't happen without incurring costs. By using better software systems Amazon is trying to improve customer experience and provide a quicker return on the investment made.

For Amazon, advances in technology are critical in helping it to improve its website – essential for any internet retailer. There are four key elements that Amazon identified to improve the customer experience in finding and purchasing products.

First, Amazon is targeting the elimination of obstacles at the point of purchase for its B2C business. It wants the customer to have a quick and smooth buying experience without any hitches. Customers will be reluctant to buy from an online merchant where the process between a decision to buy and the payment process fails.

Second, Amazon provides interactive product displays so the e-commerce experience attempts to mirror an in-store experience. Customers can roll over images to zoom in and select colours and sizes, to see what is in stock and at what price.

Third, Amazon uses technology to allow it to personalize the site appearance so that it is different for each specific user. Once you have logged in, just look at your Amazon home page compared to a friend's home page. Check out the personalized recommendations.

Fourth, Amazon utilizes different platforms and apps from which customers can make their purchases.

References: **http://www.forbes.com/sites/steveolenski/2013/11/25/how-retail-brands-are-using-technology-to-provide-added-value-to-consumers/**

http://www.richrelevance.com/

Some products will fail because they do not meet market needs – there are not enough people willing to pay the price being asked which is sufficient to cover the costs of production and provide the return. The entrepreneur may have thought there was a market and whilst there invariably are some people who will buy the product, the key is whether there are *enough* people or businesses willing to pay for the product over time.

In other cases, a perfectly good product which has a market will fail because some other business comes along and offers a product which does something more and better. In other cases the product may fail because times have changed and there is simply no need for that product any more. Business activity is dynamic.

The transition in mobile phone technology is an excellent example of this dynamic process. The very idea of having a phone that can be used anywhere is relatively new, perhaps only 30 years old, but the changes over that period of time in what these products look like, their size and what they can do, have been significant. Initially, merely being able to contact and speak to another person away from the house was a major step forwards.

Then being able to send short messages was seen as a revolutionary step forwards. After that, combining a mobile phone with a device that could access the Internet was a goal of businesses in this industry but very quickly it became not only accessing the Internet but being able to send emails, record and transmit videos, watch TV, play music, record voices, download and read books, act as a calculator, a personal messaging system, diary, satellite navigation system and so on, which have all become part of our mobile phone to the extent that in many cases making phone calls represents only a fraction of their overall use. It is difficult to imagine the many hours of development and technological change that have led us to the situation we are currently at with mobile phones, and it is probably even harder for us to imagine what these devices might be like in 10 years' time. However, the point is that somebody has sat and thought about these things; they have asked what else could the technology allow us to do, what new technologies do we need to enable us to provide some even more wonderful things in the future? What sort of things do people want from these devices and perhaps equally important, what do they not want?

There were probably many different cases of products, phones, technologies that never actually made it past design or market research stage. Many ideas probably never worked but businesses in the industry took risks, marshalled the factors of production and made the transformations necessary to create a dynamic process. Competition has led to new products and new technologies which we are prepared to pay for and that we presumably think improve our lives (although there are always going to be disadvantages). If the advantages or costs outweigh the disadvantages then we tend to buy them and businesses will produce products as a result.

CASE STUDY

A Complex Transformation Process

It is entirely possible that you might be reading this case study on a computer device of some kind, perhaps a laptop, a smartphone, tablet, etc. One of the key elements of these technologies is the silicon chip. Intel is one of the largest chip makers in the world and the following case gives some indication as to the complexity of the transformation process.

One of the key inputs is sand, which includes large amounts of silicon. The silicon is purified by being melted and then cooled into an ingot – a cylindrical shape around 300 mm in diameter weighing 100 kg. This process is undertaken in Japan by companies such as Toshiba Ceramics. Other companies then take these ingots and slice them into thin wafers around 1 mm thick. Each wafer is then polished and Intel buys them in this state ready for manufacturing at its plants in Arizona and Oregon in the USA.

At these plants (called 'fabs') – which, incidentally, are identical in design and building orientation – the wafers are etched with integrated circuits which build layers and are the result of hundreds of individual processes. Once these processes are complete the wafers are then shipped to Intel's assembly and test plants in Malaysia. Here the wafers are tested and then sliced into pieces called dies and tested again to ensure they work. Those that do not pass this test are discarded and the ones that do are packaged and sent back to warehouses in Arizona. At this stage the packaging is anonymous so that it is not clear that they are from Intel, to help reduce the risk of theft in transportation. From the warehouses in Arizona the chips are then shipped to computer manufacturing plants across the world and to different manufacturers. The plants can be in Brazil, Taiwan, China, Malaysia, Ireland and other parts of the US such as Texas and Tennessee, depending on the manufacturer. Once the chips are put into the device this may then be shipped either to a retail outlet or direct to the customer. The humble chip in your device is likely to have travelled thousands of miles during its production process as it is transformed from sand into an extremely sophisticated electronic component capable of helping process millions of operations in a short amount of time.

THE PESTLE FRAMEWORK

Change will be happening all the time in any business and how it adapts to this change will be an important part of the extent to which the business is a success. In responding to change, there are some factors which the business will have some control over and others which it will not. The business can have some control over the inputs it buys and how it combines those inputs to produce its outputs. However, there are a number of external factors over which it has very little control but which it has to respond and react to.

In order to help understand and analyse these external factors, a framework is used which summarizes a number of broad, sometimes highly related and interacting areas, which business has to work within. This framework is referred to as the PESTLE framework with the acronym standing for:

- political
- economic
- social
- technological
- legal
- environmental.

We will take a brief look at each one in turn.

CASE STUDY

What Price for Cheap Milk?

In the UK, the four biggest supermarkets have been involved in a milk price war during 2014, which has seen the price of a four-pint plastic bottle of milk dropping from around £1.39 to £1 in Tesco, Sainsbury's and Morrisons. Asda is the cheapest of the big four supermarkets, selling four pints of milk for just 89p.

This provides challenges for marginal dairy farmers who supply the supermarkets with milk. The body that represents farmers, the National Farmers' Union (NFU), says around 60 dairy farmers gave up milk production in December 2014 alone. The NFU warned that fewer than 5000 dairy farmers could be left in the UK by 2025 if current rates of decline continue. At the end of 2014, the number of dairy farmers had dipped below 10 000 for the first time, a 50 per cent fall in numbers since 2002.

The NFU strongly feels that most dairy farmers in this country have lowered costs to a point now that they can't lower them any more. Very few farmers are making a profit as they receive less per litre then their average costs per litre.

Are the supermarkets to blame for the decline of dairy farming by mistreating their suppliers? Tesco sources its milk from a group of 600 farmers and said prices were always above the cost of production: 'Whatever price we charge our customers, it doesn't impact on how we pay our farmers,' a spokesperson said. Currently, Tesco pays farmers 32p per litre and the NFU states that the average costs for farmers is 28p per litre, but this masks the fact that costs vary between farms. Therefore, some marginal dairy farmers will have high costs while others are more efficient. It is the more marginal farmers who are struggling to survive.

If supermarkets are not to blame then the problem lies elsewhere. A deeper analysis of the market for milk shows that two-thirds of the milk sold goes to food processing companies. These operations are forcing prices down by setting prices around 25p per litre. They send some supplies as milk on to the supermarkets and make dairy products, like cheese and yoghurt, from the rest.

It is really a matter of supply and demand. World demand for dairy products has fallen as Russia has an import ban and China's consumption is less than expected. The more efficient farms have also increased yields and although some may make a loss on milk they do receive subsidies for the amount of land they have which can keep them in business. However, as all dairy farms are different, some are clearly struggling to make ends meet with high costs, including rents, and low prices, so we can expect more dairy farms to cease production in the UK in the coming years.

Suggested activity: Find out what has happened to the number of dairy farms and to milk prices since this article was written.

References: **http://www.theguardian.com/business/2015/jan/12/dairy-farmers-go-unpaid -milk-becomes-cheaper-than-water**

http://www.bbc.co.uk/news/blogs-magazine-monitor-31058356

Political

Politics refers to power – who has power, who makes decisions and how it affects individuals and business. Power can be wielded by local governments, national governments and supranational governments, where decision making or laws are made by groups or states outside national boundaries, such as the EU. In some countries power lies in the hands of a relatively small number of people, possibly linked to a royal family, tribal or religious group. In others the military may be an important element in the way in which political authority is framed.

In most countries in the EU, government is democratic with political parties submitting themselves for election periodically. Different systems determine who forms governments but one particular party or group of parties in coalition may have been given the power by the people to make decisions, policies and laws that affect individuals and businesses in various ways. In other countries it is a ruling elite or the military who make decisions and establish laws and the people in the country may have a very limited, or no say, in the political process. In still other countries, the rule of law may barely exist and in this case business activity may be very difficult to carry out.

Changes to laws, directions in policy or regulations can all affect businesses in different ways. Laws on employment, employee rights and responsibilities, health and safety, taxation, planning, trade, advertising and business govern- ance among many other things, all affect business and invariably raise the cost of doing business by involving the business in additional time, form filling or procedures. In some cases laws or regulations may be passed with the aim of helping a business by giving grants or special dispensation to operate. In this case there may also be a cost in terms of certain conditions to which the busi- ness has to adhere to get the benefit. For example, there may be a relaxation of planning regulations which mean a business can establish new premises more quickly but the *quid pro quo* (something given in return for something) is that the business has to remain at the premises for a certain period of time or employ a certain number of people.

Economic

Businesses have to operate within an economic environment. This relates to the extent of economic activity in different 'economies', which could include a very local economy, a regional economy, a national or supranational or global economy. There are also bodies which have supernational powers – the authority to act across different nations – such as the International Monetary Fund (IMF).

Economic activity, as we have seen, refers to the amount of buying and selling that takes place. This activity can be looked at within a local area, a region, nation and on a global scale. The rate at which buying and selling (or the number of trans- actions) takes place varies at different time periods for different reasons as we will see in more detail in later chapters.

Businesses are affected by these fluctuations in economic activity. For example, a restaurant will be affected by decisions of people to go out for a meal which may, in turn, be affected by how confident these people feel that they will continue to have a job in the future, or whether they have recently lost their job. If a restaurant finds that the number of people they serve in a week is falling then they will have to adjust the supplies that they purchase and this will then have an effect on other businesses. Those supplying wine, soft drinks, fresh fruit and vegetables and other ingredients will then be affected by falling sales.

Such an example might be characteristic of a decline in the local economy and can often happen when an area is highly dependent on a single employer who may either scale-back operations or even close down. A similar case will occur over regions and whole countries. The south of Italy, for example, suffers from a lower level of economic activity than the north, with standards of living, opportunities for employment and growth lower as a consequence. There are similar situations which occur in parts of the former East Germany and the Middle East. In the Palestinian territories, for example, economic activity is significantly affected by the ongoing political situation and this means that this region has a lower level of economic activity.

The financial crisis of 2007–2009 is still having a major impact on businesses and individuals across Europe. Governments have had to impose policies to cut public spending and increase taxes in order to reduce deficits and the reliance on borrowing. Small firms complain that they find it difficult to get access to capital that is priced reasonably and many larger firms have delayed investment programmes, citing the uncertain economic climate as a key reason. What we can see from the above is that businesses are affected by the swings in economic activity both locally, nationally and globally. In many cases these swings might be triggered by crises in the banking system, by political instability such as that witnessed in the Ukraine or by changes in interest rates, but the effects are magnified by the changes in confidence levels in individuals, businesses and governments.

It is possible to classify these effects as microeconomic or macroeconomic. The **microeconomic environment** refers to factors and issues that affect an individual firm operating in a particular market or industry. Changes in economic activity can affect some firms in a positive way and others in a negative way. For example, regardless of the level of economic activity, funeral directors may experience relatively stable levels of trade although in times of economic slowdown families may choose to spend smaller amounts on funerals or choose cheaper options than they may do when the economy is performing more strongly.

In times of weak economic growth retail businesses such as supermarkets may also find that whilst there may be changes to the type of products people buy, the volume of trade does not decline that much, meaning they are relatively insulated from declines in economic activity. Retail businesses which sell high end products such as electronic goods or fashion items, however, may find that they are very badly hit by economic slowdown and sales may fall dramatically whilst other businesses, such as second-hand shops, pawn shops or low-price discount stores, may actually find their business increases. These are all examples of specific businesses in particular markets.

The **macroeconomic environment** refers to the national or global economy within which the business operates. The things which can affect businesses from macroeconomic changes include variations in exchange rates, interest rates (which may be linked), policies on taxation, planning, competition and so on. Changes in these macroeconomic factors can affect the level of economic activity in the economy as a whole and as a result impact on businesses. As exchange rates change, businesses will be affected in different ways depending on the extent to which they buy and sell products from abroad and in what proportions. Costs could rise or fall (or a combination of the two) and demand could also rise or fall and the effects can be highly complex in businesses which trade extensively across different regions of the world.

microeconomic environment
factors and issues that affect an individual firm operating in a particular market or industry

macroeconomic environment
the national or global economy within which the business operates

Social

Businesses are affected by various trends, fashions, moods and changes in society. The move to improving the equality between men and women and diversity and inclusion in the workplace, for example, has led to businesses having to adapt their processes and their attitudes to employment, the way their businesses operate and how they monitor the attitudes and behaviour of workers.

Social changes affect our attitudes to things like recycling and the publicity which has been given to the problem of climate change and/or global warming has meant that many businesses now report the extent to which they have taken steps to monitor energy use, recycling, the use of natural resources and where they source raw materials. Building and office construction is changing to try and find ways to improve efficiency and make them 'greener'.

There are broad social changes that are also having an impact, such as the changing structure of the population. Many European and Middle Eastern economies, for example, are experiencing an ageing population with an increasing proportion of the population over the age of 65. This creates both opportunities and threats to businesses. Retirement ages may well rise in countries as governments struggle to afford state pensions and this changes employment dynamics. Businesses that offer pension support have already found that they have to adjust the type of pension they offer. Final salary schemes, where the pension the employees receive is based on a proportion of their salary at retirement, have been phased out and replaced by contributory pension schemes simply because some businesses were finding that they could not afford to sustain final salary schemes as people were living longer.

For some businesses the ageing population provides opportunities to develop products and services which are targeted at the needs of the growing number of people who are over 65, who tend to be more affluent and who are still relatively healthy and active. The pattern of housing demand changes, with smaller homes required to take account not only of single pensioners, but also the rising number of single families, which has followed rising divorce rates in many countries. Manufacturers are looking to develop vehicles which cater for the needs of older drivers through the provision of more intuitive technologies such as automatic parallel parking, sensors which mean the car can effectively 'see round corners', have active safety systems which warn the driver of potential hazards or danger ahead, voice operated functions and wi-fi capability in the car.

Other social changes such as the growth in the use of social networking sites, viral messaging and the Internet have opened up opportunities but also present threats. Facebook and Twitter provide the chance for businesses to showcase themselves and have their brand and message spread to large numbers of people very quickly and at low cost. The flipside of this is that the degree of control a business has over messaging and the reporting of the business is limited.

Employees can, sometimes innocently, compromise the business and damage the brand or reputation simply through an injudicious use of 140 characters or an ill-judged piece of behaviour, which is subsequently broadcast to millions on YouTube or Facebook. It is fair to say that most businesses are still trying to understand social networking and how best to utilize it. The problem is that social networking tends to change more quickly than the ability of a business to understand it and work out how to use it most effectively.

Technological

technology the application or use of knowledge in some way which enables individuals or businesses to have greater control over their environment

It is tempting to think of technology as some electronic gadget but the definition of technology is much wider. **Technology** is the use of knowledge in some way that enables individuals or businesses to have greater control over their environment. Businesses constantly think of ways in which they can employ knowledge in this way because it can help to reduce costs and improve efficiency. Technology can also help give a firm competitive advantage which is both distinctive and defensible.

The last 50 years have seen an explosion in technological developments that have provided both opportunities and threats for businesses. How businesses respond to these is crucial. Technological developments can also help to provide some answers to the most pressing problems that humans face, including the effect on the environment of business activity, how to feed the human population, how to provide access to the essentials of life such as water, how to treat killer diseases, save animals and plants from extinction and tackle global poverty.

> **Quick Quiz** Outline two examples where you think technology has improved our lives and two examples where you think technology has not led to an improvement in human welfare.

Legal

Laws and regulation can be national or supranational. The legal framework covers all aspects of society, and businesses have to abide by these laws. A strong legal system that is respected is fundamental to the principle of good governance, and helps provide confidence in the way in which a business operates and promotes trade. As we have seen in Chapter 1, trade can be beneficial but businesses will be reluctant to trade and customers put off buying if they lack confidence. For example, customers want to know that if they buy a litre of fuel from a petrol station they do actually get a litre of fuel dispensed from the pump; investors need to know that the information on which they base decisions is as accurate and truthful as possible, if a business comes up with a new idea, process or invention that they can protect the investment in the time, money and intellectual capital that they have made. Confidence between businesses, between businesses and customers and the legal and regulatory framework, is adhered to by most and which builds in adequate incentives to be adhered to, is important in facilitating business activity.

Laws and regulation govern the way in which financial accounts are reported, how labour markets work, what health and safety measures businesses need to put in place, how they can describe and advertise products, what information consumers must be given, what minimum standards must be met, how much pollution a business can create and many more. While a strong and respected legal and regulatory framework provides confidence, it also comes at a cost; businesses have to pay to implement legal and regulatory requirements and this not only means higher costs for them and possibly an effect on margins, but might also mean higher prices or more inconvenience for consumers. For example, data protection laws mean that husbands and wives often get frustrated at the fact that a business will not discuss issues relating to a spouse or partner separately.

> **?** ▪ **what if** ... a business sees an opportunity to sell its goods into a new market in an emerging economy but a report tells them that governance and the rule of law is weak. Should the business enter that market?

Environment

It is now rare for any business to fail to recognize the impact of its operations on the environment. This awareness may be as a result of a conscious policy decision to manage its operations to take account of that impact, or through being forced by law or regulation to do so. Economic growth across many countries around the world has meant that resource use is expanding and, as we saw in Chapter 1, resources are scarce in relation to demand. There is also concern about how we use resources in terms of efficiency, and how we manage the results of resource use in terms of the waste products generated and the impact on ecosystems and land use.

One of the major themes of the last 30 years has been a growing concern that the consequences of human activity could be having a negative effect on the wider ecosystem. There are plenty of studies to suggest that carbon emissions, largely produced by human activity, have been a direct cause of a gradual rise in average global temperatures which in turn could lead to greater volatility in global weather patterns, and also bring about a thawing of polar ice caps, rising sea levels and subsequent effects on those living in low-lying areas of the world. Major efforts have been made to gain global agreement on reducing carbon emissions and finding more environmentally friendly ways of producing goods, services and energy. This has not been easy to achieve. One of the reasons is that the richer countries, which have been accused of being responsible for these carbon emissions, are now asking for everyone to take the pain and cost of adjustment, and poorer countries are suggesting that such a move would jeopardize their efforts to grow and better provide for their people. They argue that the rich nations are the ones who caused the problems so the rich nations should be the ones who take most of the pain. To counter this, the rich nations say that there is little point in them taking action to reduce emissions if the emerging nations are going to more than replace any reductions they might make several times over in the coming years as they grow rapidly. It seems that whilst there is some consensus that the planet does face a problem, who is responsible and how it should be tackled is less in agreement.

One aspect of thinking like an economist is the necessity of thinking critically, of not accepting everything you hear or read without questioning its validity and reliability. In many countries in Europe, recycling is an obvious and significant feature of everyday life. Almost every business has recycling policies and facilities, universities vie with one another to be the 'greenest' institution, households, local government and businesses are required to recycle and to meet targets set by national and supranational government.

As business economists, we need to be thinking about the costs and benefits of recycling and as a result whether it makes economic sense. Not all recycling is

The potential for business activity to impact on the environment always exists. The argument centres on the extent to which governments, laws and regulations can help reduce the risk.

'good'; if the amount of resources necessary to recycle metal cans into other products was greater than the cost of producing the cans from scratch, would it be a sensible business decision to do it?

Equally, we need to remember to critically examine claims from 'scientists' about carbon emissions and climate change. If businesses are going to be required to make what are quite possibly very expensive and significant decisions on resource use and allocation, are the reasons for making those decisions based on sound information? How reliable are the studies carried out into the causes and effects of rising carbon emissions? Does the idea of 'global average temperature' actually mean anything? Simply, businesses have to ask the right questions to get the right information in order to make more informed decisions.

Pitfall Prevention While we classify external factors using the PESTLE framework, in analysing real business situations it is often not easy to simply classify factors affecting a business in a simple way – the factors tend to be interrelated and cause and effect are not readily identifiable.

SHAREHOLDER VALUE AND STAKEHOLDERS

We have seen how business activity is a transformation process but we have to ask ourselves why businesses carry out this activity and for whom? We can use two concepts to provide at least part of the answer: shareholder value and stakeholders.

Let us assume that shareholders is a term used to represent business owners as a whole rather than simply those people who have purchased shares in a business and become part owners in that business, because the principle is the same. Whoever runs the business on a day-to-day basis, be it managers or in smaller enterprises the owners themselves, the imperative is to seek growth in a variety of things which may include earnings and, in larger businesses, dividends and share price. Businesses have to take decisions which help to increase earnings while keeping costs under control. These decisions may include what to invest in (and what not) and when to invest, as well as how much and what the perceived returns might be. If investment decisions help to generate returns over a period then **shareholder value** will increase. Shareholder value is not simply profit, however, it is also the potential for the business to continue making profits over a period of time and to grow the profits.

shareholder value the overall value delivered to the owners of business in the form of cash generated and the reputation and potential of the business to continue growing over time

Investment decisions can be made that will secure short-term profit growth quickly but which might damage the future capacity of the business to compete and survive in the longer term. Poor decision making can lead to damage in lots of ways, for example signing up a celebrity to endorse products might help boost sales and earnings in the short term but could lead to longer-term damage if the celebrity happens to get involved in something that affects the reputation of the business. A business could dispose of waste at very low cost and secure short-term profit gains but if that method of waste disposal damages the environment then the longer-term earnings generation potential of the business could be affected in a negative way. In the two examples given, shareholder value could potentially decline in the future.

In addition to considering shareholder value, businesses increasingly have to take into account the fact that their operations affect a much wider group of people or individuals than simply owners. Employees, customers, managers, suppliers, the local community, government and the environment all have an interest in a business from different perspectives.

Most businesses will have to recognize the effect of its operations on these different stakeholders and have to take, often conflicting, perspectives into account when making decisions and running the business. For example, it might be tempting for a business to source new supplies from cheaper operators in emerging economies but in so doing it must consider how this might affect its wider stakeholders. Consumers might be supportive of such moves if it meant that prices are lower but quality is maintained. Suppliers in the domestic economy who lose contracts will be unlikely to support such a decision; some employees might be concerned about losing their jobs as a result and the local community might have a view about the ethical and moral basis for such a decision. Managers may feel the decision is justified if it enhances their reputation for managing complex change projects but owners/ shareholders may want to be convinced that the decision really will lead to long-term as well as short-term benefits. Reconciling the often conflicting interests of stakeholders is one of the most challenging aspects of any business, and economics can help in not only identifying the potential costs and benefits but also quantifying these costs and benefits to enable more informed decision making.

CONCLUSION

In this chapter we have provided an outline of what business is and how it has to operate in an environment. We have looked at how it takes in resources and transforms them into outputs which are then sold, either to other businesses or final consumers. As part of this transformation process, businesses operate in both an internal and an external environment. The internal environment includes factors over which the business has some control. The business can, for example, take action to change its prices, get a better understanding about its customers and markets, seek cheaper raw materials, outsource parts of its operations to countries with cheaper costs, negotiate with its bankers for cheaper finance and so on.

However, the business has little control over its external environment. We classify this external environment into a number of different areas represented by the acronym PESTLE. Understanding the political, economic, social, technological, legal and environmental influences enables decision makers to be able to analyse the position of the business and devise tactics and strategies to combat them or to put them in a better position to compete and win customers.

While we break down these factors to facilitate ease of analysis, in reality businesses have to deal with all of these factors at the same time and it is often difficult to distinguish which factor is the most significant or which to give greater emphasis to.

For example, a train operating company knows that it has to invest in high quality engines and rolling stock to provide a service to its customers that is perceived as representing value for money. It may know that there is a trend for more people to use trains but is this a social trend, an economic one or a political one? Are customers deliberately making decisions to use rail transport because they believe it is more environmentally friendly or are they doing it because the roads are too congested, or is it because work patterns are changing or because people have more disposable income and can afford to travel for business and for leisure? Have governments made decisions to increase the price of petrol to try and encourage reductions in the use of fossil fuels to help reduce the impact on the environment, or have they done so to raise money in the form of higher taxes? Has this political decision driven consumers to switch to rail use?

Rail companies will also have to consider the legal and regulatory framework. Safety on the rail networks is a key element of how train operators make decisions. They know that when accidents occur the loss of life and injury can be significant. Should they aim to meet minimum legal and regulatory standards or should they aim to go well beyond them? How much are customers prepared to pay to feel safe when they travel?

They also know that when accidents happen governments tend to tighten regulations and laws to meet increased public concerns. Any increase in legislation on safety will have microeconomic effects on the business – costs will be higher and so fares might have to increase. Technology may be employed to improve train and network safety but businesses will be looking at the balance between the costs of improving safety and the benefits and relative value of both.

If a train operating company invests in new, more efficient rolling stock and engines, should it buy the equipment from a local or national provider or from the supplier who offers the cheapest price for the quality it requires? How far will these sorts of decisions be influenced by political groups? Does the business have a responsibility to its domestic workers or to its supranational workers or to its shareholders? If the cheaper option also happens to be the most environmentally friendly one, should this override national employment considerations?

We can see that any decision is not going to be purely driven or influenced by one factor alone but by a mixture of them all. If decision making was easy then we would all be able to make the right decisions all the time. The fact that businesses ultimately have to make decisions and judgements based on what might possibly be imperfect information will inevitably lead to mistakes being made and less than efficient outcomes as a result.

IN THE NEWS

Tesco's Changing Attitude to Its Stakeholders

This article explores the trade-off between stakeholder objectives and how this is affected by a company's profitability.

Why do companies, like Tesco, the UK-based grocery chain store, exist? Is it to supply us with products and services, enhance shareholder value, employ local people, to give trade to its suppliers such as dairy farmers, pay taxes and support the community or something else? If Tesco or any business

could achieve all of these then they would indeed be friends to everyone. However, making all stakeholders happy is perhaps a challenge too far as there are trade-offs between stakeholder objectives and so businesses must prioritize especially when the external environment is uncertain.

In 2007, Tesco was a major growth company, generating big profits with a UK market share of 31.8 per cent. Subsequently, the

global economic crisis made for a challenging trading environment. In 2012 Tesco employed over 290 000 people on a full-time or part-time basis with one quarter of these under 25. In that year Tesco announced plans to expand. It claimed it was committed to creating 20 000 jobs in 2 years as net job creation.

By March 2014, however, Tesco's market share had dropped to 28.7 per cent and profits had been falling for several years. Keener competition from competitors like the upmarket grocer, Waitrose, and the discounters, Aldi and Lidl, has squeezed Tesco's customer base. Reports of inaccurate accounting practices also tarnished the Tesco brand.

Tesco publishes a detailed Tesco and Society Report annually. In 2014 the CEO at the time said that 'the last three years at Tesco have been all about one thing: making Tesco better for everyone in society, our customers, our colleagues, shareholders, suppliers and the communities we serve.' He later explained, 'If we are to succeed in the future, we need to become a sustainable retailer in every sense of the word. We need to make what matters better for society as a whole. Quite simply – better is better.'

In January 2015 the company confirmed that around 2000 staff would lose their jobs as a result of closing 43 stores across the UK and announced that senior staff at its head office might lose their jobs as a result of changes to its head office which employs around 8000 people. The new CEO said at the time: 'We have some very difficult changes to make. I am very conscious that the consequences of these changes are significant for all stakeholders in our business but we are facing the reality of the situation.'

Questions

1. Who are the stakeholders of Tesco and which stakeholders do you think it prioritizes and why?
2. In what way is the government a stakeholder in Tesco's success or its challenges?
3. **Why is there a conflict between different stakeholder objectives?**
4. **Why is it harder to meet stakeholder objectives when demand falls?**
5. **Use the PESTLE framework to show how Tesco is responding to change. Which factors does it have little control over and which can it influence?**

References: BBC News **http://www.bbc.co.uk/news/business-17252738**

International Business Times **http://www.ibtimes.co.uk/tesco-cut-thousands-jobs-head-office-following-store-closures-1485712**

Tesco plc **http://www.tescoplc.com/files/pdf/responsibility/2014/tesco_and_society_review_2014.pdf**

SUMMARY

- Business activity involves using factors of production and transforming them into products which are bought either by other businesses or final consumers.

- Business activity has to take place within an environment which is both internal and external.

- Businesses have some control over the internal environment but sometimes limited control over the external environment.

- The external environment can be looked at through the PESTLE framework – political, economic, social, technological, legal and environmental.

- Changes in the external environment can provide both opportunities and threats.

- Businesses have a responsibility to a wide range of stakeholders who have some direct or indirect interest in the business.

QUESTIONS FOR REVIEW

1. Using an example of a product of your choice, explain the principle of business activity.
2. Think about a business producing bottled spa water. Identify some examples of the four factors of production which are necessary to produce the output of that business.
3. Why do some economists argue for enterprise to be a separate factor of production rather than a specialist form of labour?
4. Think of a good and a service with which you are familiar and sketch a diagram, accompanied by a brief

description, of the transformation process which takes place to produce each.

5. Describe the value added at each stage of production of a loaf of bread up to the point it is purchased by the consumer.

6. In a country with a democratic political system, why might a business be concerned about a change in government?

7. Explain the possible differences between the microeconomic and macroeconomic environment effects on a business producing costume jewellery.

8. Explain how a concern over the effect on the environment of business activity can lead to not only environmental change but also technological, social and legal changes which could affect a business.

9. Explain how an investment decision might affect shareholder value in a positive way both in the short and long run.

10. Describe how a plan by a business to increase the price of its goods might cause a conflict between the interests of managers, shareholders, employees and customers.

PROBLEMS AND APPLICATIONS

1. Is there such a thing as a 'science of decision making'? Explain your answer in relation to business decision making.

2. To what extent is it the case that value added is always higher in a B2C business than a B2B business because businesses are more aware of value for money than are consumers?

3. Industries that use large amounts of capital in relation to other factors of production are said to be capital intensive. Is it necessarily the case that capital intensive businesses are more efficient than labour intensive ones? Explain your answer using relevant examples.

4. What do you think are the most important factors which separate those entrepreneurs that are deemed massively successful because they are worth millions, and those who just about manage to survive running their own business?

5. What do you think is the main reason for the relatively high rate of business failures 5 years after start-up? Justify your answer.

6. The price of a high-quality diamond ring used for weddings is €250. The price of a tonne of steel is €25. Does this mean that the transformation process in making a diamond ring is ten times more complex and costly than in making a tonne of steel? Explain your answer using the concept of added value.

7. A business making high-quality ball-point pens faces a number of challenges in the next year. It is concerned that a slow-down in the European economy along with a shift to the use of laptops and tablet devices by young people will begin to damage its long-term viability. What advice would you give the owners of this business to respond to these two external challenges? Explain your reasoning.

8. Should businesses be allowed to regulate their own activities or should governments legislate to force them to meet their social and environmental responsibilities? Explain your reasoning and use appropriate examples to illustrate your answer.

9. A pharmaceutical business reads a research report published by a leading university that suggests consumers are 20 per cent less likely to use over-the-counter medicines if these have not been advertised on TV over the last 12 months. What questions might the business want to ask of the research conducted before making any decision on whether to advertise?

10. Do you think that it is ever possible for a business to satisfy the conflicting demands of all stakeholders? Justify your reasoning.

PART 2

MICROECONOMICS – THE MARKET SYSTEM

4 SUPPLY AND DEMAND: HOW MARKETS WORK

LEARNING OUTCOMES

After reading this chapter you should be able to:

- List at least two characteristics of a competitive market.
- List the factors that affect the amount that producers wish to sell in a market.
- List the factors that affect the amount that consumers wish to buy in a market.
- Draw a graph of supply and demand in a market and find the equilibrium price and quantity.

- Shift supply and demand curves in response to an economic event and find the new equilibrium price and quantity.
- Describe the process by which a new equilibrium is reached.
- Explain how price acts as a signal to both producers and consumers.

THE MARKET FORCES OF SUPPLY AND DEMAND

Poor weather conditions in parts of Europe can have an effect on the yield of wheat crops and as a result businesses using wheat in the production of food products face higher costs. Slowing levels of economic growth in China cause the demand for steel to fall and this reduces prices for businesses across the rest of the world, meaning the price of both semi-finished and finished products where steel is a component part in production falls.

If a report is published linking food products with health risks, firms producing these foods face falling prices and a possible collapse in their markets. A change in exchange rates for currencies can have different effects on different businesses depending on the extent to which they trade with other businesses and customers abroad. Airlines know that they can charge higher prices at certain times of the year to certain destinations, than at other times where they may have to cut fares to fill aircraft. What do these events have in common? They are all related to markets containing buyers and sellers. In this chapter we are going to look at a fundamental aspect of business economics, the operation of markets and the interaction between the 'forces' of supply and demand.

Supply and demand are referred to as forces because they act in different ways and put pressure on prices to change. This chapter introduces the theory of supply and demand using a model of markets which has some predictive power. It considers how sellers and buyers behave and how they interact with one another. Price signals influencing both buyers and sellers change behaviour and go some way to allocating the economy's scarce resources.

At this point it is important to note an important distinction. We use the terms 'price' and 'cost' regularly in everyday life – often interchangeably. In this book we will refer to the two terms in a distinct way. **Price** is the amount of money a buyer (a business or a consumer) has to give up in order to acquire something. **Cost** refers to the payment to factor inputs in production. When we discuss suppliers we will be referring to cost in this sense.

price the amount of money a buyer (a business or a consumer) has to give up in order to acquire something

cost the payment to factor inputs in production

Assumptions of the Model of Supply and Demand

Economists use models to represent reality. No model is perfect and no model describes every situation. The model of supply and demand is built on a number of assumptions and is referred to as the *competitive market* model. It is important to keep these assumptions in mind at all times when using the model to analyse markets.

Assumption 1: Many Buyers and Sellers In a competitive market there are many buyers and sellers each of whom are responsible for buying or selling only a very small proportion of the total market. Buyers and sellers are assumed to be price takers – they have to accept the existing market price and neither can do anything to influence or set price; a seller cannot withhold supply in the hope of forcing price upwards and a buyer cannot influence price by varying the amount they choose to buy.

Assumption 2: Homogenous Goods Goods in the market are assumed to be identical and not subject to differentiation and as such buyers have no preference for the products of one supplier over another. This also implies that sellers will each charge the same price as there is no incentive for any seller to charge a price higher or lower than any other.

CASE STUDY

How Homogenous Can Tobacco Products Be?

In 2015 the UK parliament voted to ban the branding of cigarette packs. The measures will take effect in England from 2016, when manufacturers will have to use plain packets. This comes on top of a point of display ban introduced to supermarkets in 2012 and extended to all retailers in April 2015.

Tobacco companies might consider suing the UK government over the forced removal of branding cigarette packaging. 'We have a fundamental right to differentiate our brands from those of competitors,' said Imperial Tobacco. It feels the legislation is an infringement on intellectual property rights covering its brands and as a result it fears a drop in profits. It also claims the ban will increase counterfeit cigarette sales as these will be harder to detect.

Those in favour of the ban say the measures will improve public health and cut the number of child smokers.

The legislation follows that in other countries such as the Republic of Ireland and Australia. According to the Society for Research on Nicotine and Tobacco, the number of people able to name cigarette brands dropped from 65 per cent to 59 per cent in Australia just a year after the ban.

Reference: **http://www.ft.com/cms/s/0/82886136-a243-11e4-bbb8-00144feab7de.html#ax zz3Qb2qVneH**

Assumption 3: Perfect Information   Buyers and sellers are assumed to have perfect information in that they know all prices that exist, they know and understand the attributes of a product and sellers know and understand the production processes and capabilities in the market. Sellers are also assumed to be able to access the resources they need to produce a good.

Assumption 4: Freedom of Entry and Exit   There are no barriers to entry or exit in any industry meaning that firms are free to switch resources to alternative production at any time.

Assumption 5: Buyers and Sellers Are Clearly Defined   The actions of buyers and sellers are completely independent of each other. Sellers cannot influence demand and buyers cannot influence supply. The factors that influence buyers and sellers are thus distinct and independent.

Assumption 6: Clearly Defined Property Rights   The rights of ownership of resources and property are clear to all and enforced. This means that the decisions taken by buyers and sellers take into account all the associated costs and benefits and that the amount buyers are willing to pay and suppliers willing to supply takes account of all these costs and benefits.

Assumption 7: Zero Transaction Costs
In facilitating an exchange it is assumed that the buyer and the seller have no transaction costs. Transaction costs include the time taken to find appropriate goods, legal fees associated with transactions, transport costs associated with a purchase or fees charged by financial institutions such as interest rates on loans.

Assumption 8: Rational Behaviour
Buyers and sellers are assumed to act rationally. Buyers are seeking to maximize the utility or satisfaction from their purchases and sellers are seeking to maximize profits.

You might be thinking that these assumptions are absurd and are so unrealistic as to make the model redundant before you have even looked at it. Indeed, there are many who cast doubt on the validity of using a model which relies on so many unrealistic assumptions and suggest that its predictive powers are so limited as to be useless. In using the model of supply and demand, we have to be mindful of these assumptions and we can then look at different contexts and gain insight and understanding to behaviour and outcomes that might be different to that predicted by the model. Whilst these assumptions are unrealistic, the model of supply and demand does allow us to make some predictions and provides an approximation to many everyday experiences and a means of assessing how markets might behave differently when these assumptions are relaxed.

MARKETS AND COMPETITION

market a group of buyers and sellers of a particular good or service who come together to agree a price for exchange

The terms *supply* and *demand* refer to the behaviour of businesses and people as they interact with one another in markets. A **market** is a group of sellers and buyers of a particular good or service. The sellers as a group determine the supply of the product and the buyers as a group determine the demand for the product. Before discussing how sellers and buyers behave, let's first consider more fully what we mean by a 'market' and the various types of markets we observe in the economy.

Types of Markets

Markets take many forms. Sometimes markets are highly organized and some of the assumptions outlined above do hold. Markets for many agricultural commodities and for metals are two examples. In these markets, buyers and sellers meet at a specific time and place, where an auctioneer helps set prices and arrange sales. Many businesses rely on these highly organized markets and are affected by them because they have little control over the prices they have to pay for these products, which can affect their costs and margins considerably, both in a positive and a negative way. In agricultural markets there can be a large number of small farmers who are price takers and have to accept the reigning market price for their output.

More often, markets are less organized. For example, consider the market for perfume. Here many of the assumptions outlined are redundant. Businesses manufacturing and selling perfume are often very large and there are a relatively small amount of sellers in the industry. Each seller seeks to offer differentiated products for sale which they hope will be distinctive and popular. The buyers of perfume do not all meet together at any one time. These buyers are individuals, all of whom have different tastes, One person's ideal fragrance is another person's obnoxious smell and they do not all gather together in a room to shout out the prices they are willing to pay. There is no auctioneer calling out the price of perfume. Each seller of perfume posts a price for a bottle of perfume (which may be uncannily similar), and each buyer makes purchasing decisions based on a number of different factors many of which will not be rational. In addition, buyers and sellers in these markets are not necessarily independent. Sellers may have successfully (often over many years) attempted to influence buyer behaviour. In the perfectly competitive model this is not the case.

Even though it is not organized, the group of perfume sellers and buyers forms a market. Each seller is aware that their product is similar but different to that offered by other sellers. Each buyer knows that there are several sellers from which to choose. The price of perfume and the quantity of perfume sold are not determined by any single buyer or seller. Ultimately, the seller knows that if the price it is charging does not represent value for money in the eyes of the consumer, then the product will not generate the returns expected and the product may have to be modified or withdrawn from sale. Market forces still have an impact.

Competition exists when two or more firms are rivals for customers. The market for perfume, like most markets in the economy, is, given this definition, 'competitive'. Each firm strives to gain the attention and custom of buyers in the market. Economists, however, use the term *competitive market* in a different way to mean something very specific and is based on the assumptions outlined above.

> **competition** a market situation when two or more firms are rivals for customers

Competition: Perfect and Otherwise

The assumptions of the model of supply and demand refer to *perfectly competitive* markets. There are some markets in which the assumption of perfect competition apply to a degree. In the wheat market, for example, there are tens of thousands of farmers who sell wheat, and millions of consumers who use wheat and wheat products. Because no single buyer or seller can influence the price of wheat, each takes the price as given. The reason for making this assumption is so that we can look at how markets operate under these 'ideal' conditions and what the expected outcomes are. If we then observe in reality that these outcomes do not occur as we expect, then we can analyse what imperfections exist which help to explain this behaviour.

It is clear that not all goods and services are sold in perfectly competitive markets. Some markets have only one seller, and this seller sets the price. Such a seller is called a *monopoly*. Your local water company, for instance, may be a monopoly. Residents in your area probably have only one water company from which to buy this service. Some markets fall between the extremes of perfect competition and monopoly. One such market, called an *oligopoly*, has a few sellers that do not always compete aggressively. Airline routes are an example. If a route between two cities is serviced by only two or three carriers, the carriers may avoid rigorous competition so they can keep prices high. Another type of market is *monopolistic* or *imperfectly competitive*; it contains many sellers but each offers a slightly different product. Because the products are not exactly the same, each seller has some ability to set the price for its own product. An example is the market for magazines. Magazines compete with one another for readers and anyone can enter the market by starting a new one, but each magazine offers different articles and can set its own price.

Despite the diversity of market types we find in the world, we begin by studying perfect competition. Perfectly competitive markets are the easiest to analyse. Moreover, because some degree of competition is present in most markets, many of the lessons that we learn by studying supply and demand under perfect competition apply in more complicated markets as well.

CASE STUDY

The End of the Diamond Monopoly

Historically, the diamond industry was virtually under the control of one company, De Beers, making it a classic monopoly. The company, based in South Africa, had a market share of nearly 90 per cent in the late 1980s which gave it extensive monopoly power and consequently the diamond market was uncompetitive.

De Beers controlled prices by stockpiling diamonds when the market was weak. This raised prices to buyers called Sightholders. In times of heavy demand it would release diamonds onto the market and controlled prices at a desired level.

However, since the 1980s diamond discoveries in Russia, Australia and Canada helped to erode de Beers market share, so that by 2013 it had fallen to below 40 per cent. Now the forces of market supply and demand are more important in driving the diamond price and not the actions of one company.

A key date was 2004 when De Beers significant stock of diamonds was liquidated. Since then diamond prices have fluctuated as the market became more competitive. In 2007 diamond prices started to rise as stock markets approached their pre-crash peak, since there was an increase in global discretionary income leading to a greater consumer demand for polished diamonds. This didn't last and diamond prices tumbled as a result of the economic crisis and subsequent drop in demand. A post-recession recovery saw the market price rise, fuelled by the confidence of US consumers, who comprise 40 per cent of the market for polished diamonds.

Reference: Paul Zimnisky – Kitco Commentry, **http://www.kitco.com/ind/Zimnisky/2013 -06-06-A-Diamond-Market-No-Longer-Controlled-By-De-Beers.html**

SUPPLY

We are going to begin our look at markets by considering producers – businesses – and examine the behaviour of sellers. To focus our thinking and provide a context for our analysis, let's consider producers of rape seed which is used to make cooking oil. Rape seed, characterized by acres of bright yellow flowers, is grown widely across many parts of the world including Canada, China, India, France, Germany, Australia, the UK, Poland, Ukraine, the US, the Czech Republic, Russia, Belarus, Lithuania and Denmark. Some of the assumptions of the market model apply to the market for rape seed, including the fact that there are many sellers each of whom supply a relatively small proportion of the total market and the product is largely homogenous.

The distinctive yellow flowers of rape plants make an attractive sight in many countries at certain times of the year. The seed from the plants provides a valuable source of cooking oil.

The Supply Curve: The Relationship Between Price and Quantity Supplied

The quantity supplied of any good or service is the amount that sellers are willing and able to sell. There are many determinants of quantity supplied, but price plays a special role in our analysis. When the price of rape seed is high, selling rape seed is profitable, and so sellers are willing to supply more. Sellers of rape seed work longer hours, devote more planting to rape, invest in research and development on improvements to rape seed growing and hire extra workers in order to ensure supplies to the market rise. By contrast, when the price of rape seed is low, the business is less profitable, and so growers are less willing to plant rape. At a low price, some growers may even choose to shut down, and their **quantity supplied** falls to zero. Because the quantity supplied rises as the price rises, and falls as the price falls, we say that the quantity supplied is *positively related* to the price of the good. This relationship between price and quantity supplied is called the **law of supply**: other things being equal, when the price of a good rises, the quantity producers are willing to supply also rises, and when the price falls, the quantity supplied falls as well.

quantity supplied the amount of a good that sellers are willing and able to sell

law of supply the claim that, other things being equal, the quantity supplied of a good rises when its price rises

The table in Figure 4.1 shows the quantity Tramontana, a rape seed grower, is willing to supply, at various prices of rape seed. By convention, price is on the vertical axis and the quantity supplied on the horizontal axis. At a price below €50 per tonne, Tramontana does not supply any rape seed at all. As the price rises, it is willing to supply a greater and greater quantity. This is the **supply schedule**, a table that shows the relationship between the price of a good and the quantity supplied, holding constant everything else that influences how much producers of the good want to sell.

supply schedule a table that shows the relationship between the price of a good and the quantity supplied

The graph in Figure 4.1 uses the numbers from the table to illustrate the law of supply. The curve relating price and quantity supplied is called the supply curve. The **supply curve** slopes upwards because, other things being equal, a higher price means a greater quantity supplied.

supply curve a graph of the relationship between the price of a good and the quantity supplied

FIGURE 4.1

Tramontana's Supply Schedule and Supply Curve

The supply schedule shows the quantity supplied at each price. This supply curve, which graphs the supply schedule, shows how the quantity supplied of the good changes as its price varies. Because a higher price increases the quantity supplied, the supply curve slopes upward.

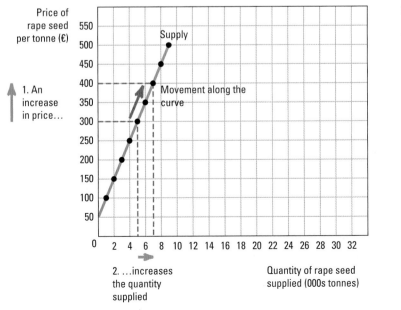

Price of rape seed (€)	Quantity of rape seed supplied (000s tonnes)
50	0
100	1
150	2
200	3
250	4
300	5
350	6
400	7
450	8
500	9

Market Supply versus Individual Supply

Market supply is the sum of the supplies of all sellers. The table in Figure 4.2 shows the supply schedules for two rape seed producers – Tramontana and Sedona. At any price, Tramontana's supply schedule tells us the quantity of rape seed Tramontana is willing to supply, and Sedona's supply schedule tells us the quantity of rape seed Sedona is willing to supply. The market supply is the sum of the two individual supplies.

The graph in Figure 4.2 shows the supply curves that correspond to the supply schedules. We sum the individual supply curves *horizontally* to obtain the market supply curve. That is, to find the total quantity supplied at any price, we add the individual quantities found on the horizontal axis of the individual supply curves. The market supply curve shows how the total quantity supplied varies as the price of the good varies. In reality, the market supply will be the amount all producers in the market are willing to offer for sale at each price.

> **Pitfall Prevention**   Be careful to ensure that you distinguish between individual and market supply in your analysis – the behaviour of one individual business may be different from the whole industry.

SHIFTS VERSUS MOVEMENTS ALONG THE SUPPLY CURVE

A distinction is made between a shift in the supply curve and a movement along the supply curve. A shift in the supply curve is caused by a factor affecting supply other than a change in its price. The factors affecting supply are outlined below. If any of these factors change, then the amount sellers are willing to offer for sale changes, whatever the price. The shift in the supply curve is referred to as an *increase or decrease in supply*. A movement along the supply curve occurs when there is a change in price assuming other factors affecting supply are held constant (*ceteris paribus*). This may occur because of a change in demand conditions. A change in price leads to a movement along the supply curve and is referred to as a *change in quantity supplied*.

Shifts in the Supply Curve

The supply curve for rape seed shows how much rape seed producers are willing to offer for sale at any given price, holding constant all the other factors beyond price that influence producers' decisions about how much to sell. This relationship can change over time and is represented by a shift in the supply curve. For example, suppose the price of fertilizer falls. Because fertilizer is an input into producing rape seed, the fall in its price means producing rape seed is now cheaper – the same quantity of rape seed can be harvested at lower cost which makes selling rape seed more profitable. This increases the supply of rape seed: at any given price,

FIGURE 4.2

Market Supply as the Sum of Individual Supplies

The quantity supplied in a market is the sum of the quantities supplied by all the sellers at each price. Thus, the market supply curve is found by adding horizontally the individual supply curves. At a price of €250, Tramontana is willing to supply 4000 tonnes of rape seed and Sedona is willing to supply 10 000 tonnes. The quantity supplied in the market at this price is 14 000 tonnes of rape seed.

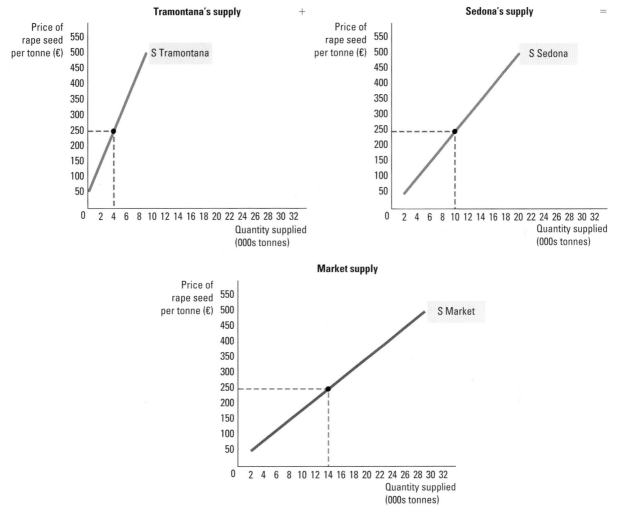

Price of rape seed (per tonne)	Tramontana (000s)		Sedona (000s)		Market (000s)
€0.00	0	+	0	=	0
50	0		2		2
100	1		4		5
150	2		6		8
200	3		8		11
250	4		10		14
300	5		12		17
350	6		14		20
400	7		16		23
450	8		18		26
500	9		20		29

FIGURE 4.3

Shifts in the Supply Curve

Any change that raises the quantity that sellers are willing to produce and offer for sale at a given price shifts the supply curve to the right. Any change that lowers the quantity that sellers are willing to produce and offer for sale at a given price shifts the supply curve to the left.

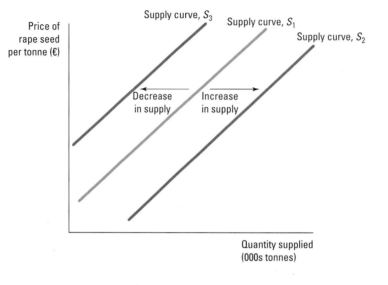

sellers are now willing to offer for sale a larger quantity. This is represented as a shift in the supply curve for rape seed to the right.

Figure 4.3 illustrates shifts in supply. Any change that raises quantity supplied at every price, such as a fall in the price of fertilizer, shifts the supply curve to the right and is called an *increase in supply*. Similarly, any change that reduces the quantity supplied at every price shifts the supply curve to the left and is called a *decrease in supply*.

There are many variables that can shift the supply curve. Here are some of the most important.

Input Prices   To produce their output of rape seed, sellers use various inputs: fertilizer, fuel for tractors, weed killer and harvesting machines. Growers will also have to pay for computers, machinery, farm buildings and the labour of workers used throughout the planting, growing, harvesting and distribution process. When the price of one or more of these inputs rises, producing rape seed is less profitable and firms supply fewer tonnes of rape seed. If input prices fall for some reason, then production may be more profitable and there is an incentive to supply more at each price. Thus, the supply of a good is negatively related to the price of the inputs used to make the good.

Technology   The technology for turning the inputs into rape seed is yet another determinant of supply. This technology might be related to the quality and viability of seed, improvements in plant breeding to create more uniform and productive plants, or in the use of fertilizers to improve soil quality and growth. Advances in technology increase productivity allowing more to be produced using fewer factor inputs. As a result costs, both total and unit, may fall and supply increases. The invention of harvesting machines, for example, reduces the amount of labour necessary to gather and process rape seed. By reducing firms' costs, the advance in technology raises the supply of rape seed.

Expectations   The amount of rape seed firms supply today may depend on their expectations of the future. For example, if growers expect the price of rape seed to rise in the future, they may put some of their current stock into storage and supply less to the market today. If government reports from health departments suggest that using cooking oil made from rape seed reduces the chance of heart disease then producers might reasonably expect an increase in sales and so plant more fields to rape in anticipation.

The Number of Sellers   Market supply will be affected by the number of firms in the industry. In the EU around 24 million tonnes of rape seed are harvested a year and at a price (as of August 2015) of approximately €677 per tonne this means a market value around €16.2 billion. If there were more farmers switching to rape production, then the amount of rape seed produced would be likely to rise. Equally, if some of the growers that currently plant rape closed down their operations the amount of rape seed produced would be likely to fall each year.

Natural/Social Factors   There are often many natural or social factors that affect supply. These include such things as the weather affecting crops, natural disasters, pestilence and disease, changing attitudes and social expectations (for example, over the production of organic food, the disposal of waste, reducing carbon emissions, ethical supply sourcing and so on) which can all have an influence on production decisions. Some or all of these may have an influence on the cost of inputs into production.

Summary

The supply curve shows what happens to the quantity supplied of a good when its price varies, holding constant all the other variables that influence sellers. When one of these other variables changes, the supply curve shifts. Table 4.1 lists all the variables that influence how much producers choose to sell of a good.

TABLE 4.1

Variables That Influence Sellers

This table lists the variables that affect how much producers choose to sell of any good. Notice the special role that the price of the good plays: a change in the good's price represents a movement along the supply curve, whereas a change in one of the other variables shifts the supply curve.

Variable	A change in this variable...
Price	Is represented as a movement along the supply curve
Input prices	Shifts the supply curve
Technology	Shifts the supply curve
Expectations	Shifts the supply curve
Number of sellers	Shifts the supply curve

> **Quick Quiz** Make up an example of a supply schedule for apples, and graph the implied supply curve. Give an example of something that would shift this supply curve. • Would a change in the price of apples shift this supply curve? Explain.

DEMAND

We now turn to the other side of the market and examine the behaviour of buyers. Once again, to focus our thinking, let's consider the market for rape seed.

The Demand Curve: The Relationship Between Price and Quantity Demanded

quantity demanded the amount of a good buyers are willing and able to purchase at different prices

The **quantity demanded** of any good is the amount of the good that buyers are willing and able to purchase. As we shall see, many things determine the quantity demanded of any good, but when analysing how markets work, one determinant plays a central role – the price of the good. If the price of rape seed rose, people would buy fewer tonnes of rape seed. Food manufacturers and retailers might switch to another form of cooking oil, such as sunflower oil. If the price of rape seed fell to €100 per tonne, people would buy more. Because the quantity demanded falls as the price rises and rises as the price falls, we say that the quantity demanded is *negatively related* to the price. This relationship between price and quantity demanded is true for most goods in the economy and, in fact, is so pervasive that economists call it the **law of demand**.

law of demand the claim that, other things being equal, the quantity demanded of a good falls when the price of the good rises

The table in Figure 4.4 shows how many tonnes of rape seed Hanse, a food processor, is willing and able to buy each year at different prices of rape seed. If rape seed were free, Hanse would be willing to take 10 000 tonnes of rape seed. At €200 per tonne, Hanse would be willing to buy 6000 tonnes of rape seed. As the price rises further, he is willing to buy fewer and fewer tonnes of rape seed. When the price reaches €500 per tonne, Hanse would not be prepared to buy any rape seed at all. This table is a **demand schedule**, a table that shows the relationship between the price of a good and the quantity demanded, holding constant everything else that influences how much consumers of the good want to buy.

demand schedule a table that shows the relationship between the price of a good and the quantity demanded

demand curve a graph of the relationship between the price of a good and the quantity demanded

The graph in Figure 4.4 uses the numbers from the table to illustrate the law of demand. The price of rape seed is on the vertical axis, and the quantity of rape seed demanded is on the horizontal axis. The downward sloping line relating price and quantity demanded is called the **demand curve**.

Market Demand versus Individual Demand

The demand curve in Figure 4.4 shows an individual's demand for a product. To analyse how markets work, we need to determine the *market demand*, which is the sum of all the individual demands for a particular good or service.

Hanse's Demand Schedule and Demand Curve

The demand schedule shows the quantity demanded at each price. The demand curve, which graphs the demand schedule, shows how the quantity demanded of the good changes as its price varies. Because a lower price increases the quantity demanded, the demand curve slopes downwards.

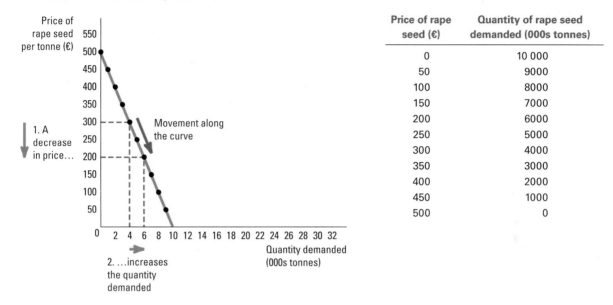

Price of rape seed (€)	Quantity of rape seed demanded (000s tonnes)
0	10 000
50	9000
100	8000
150	7000
200	6000
250	5000
300	4000
350	3000
400	2000
450	1000
500	0

The table in Figure 4.5 shows the demand schedules for rape seed of two food processers – Hanse and Michelle. At any price, Hanse's demand schedule tells us how many tonnes of rape seed he would be willing and able to buy at different prices, and Michelle's demand schedule tells us how many tonnes of rape seed she is willing and able to buy. The market demand at each price is the sum of the two individual demands.

The graph in Figure 4.5 shows the demand curves that correspond to these demand schedules. As we did with the market supply, we sum the individual demand curves *horizontally* to obtain the market demand curve.

Because we are interested in analysing how markets work, we shall work most often with the market demand curve. The market demand curve shows how the total quantity demanded of a good changes as the price of the good varies, while all the other factors that affect how much consumers want to buy, such as incomes and taste, amongst other things, are held constant.

SHIFTS VERSUS MOVEMENTS ALONG THE DEMAND CURVE

A shift in the demand curve is caused by a factor affecting demand other than a change in price. The factors affecting demand are outlined below. If any of these factors change, then the amount consumers wish to purchase changes, whatever the price. The shift in the demand curve is referred to as an *increase* or *decrease in demand*. A movement along the demand curve occurs when there is a change in price. This may

FIGURE 4.5

Market Demand as the Sum of Individual Demands

The quantity demanded in a market is the sum of the quantities demanded by all the buyers at each price. Thus, the market demand curve is found by adding horizontally the individual demand curves. At a price of €200, Hanse would like to buy 6000 tonnes of rape seed and Michelle would be prepared to buy 12 000 tonnes of rape seed. The quantity demanded in the market at this price, therefore, is 18 000 tonnes of rape seed.

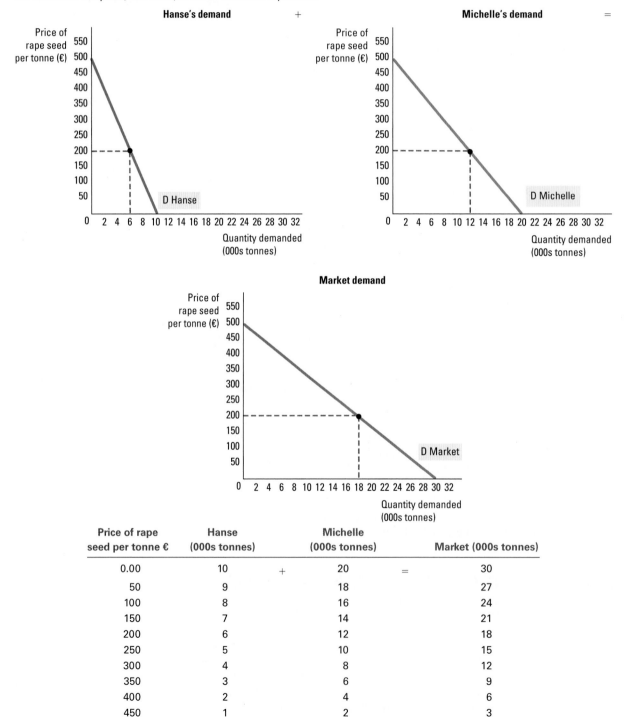

Price of rape seed per tonne €	Hanse (000s tonnes)		Michelle (000s tonnes)		Market (000s tonnes)
0.00	10	+	20	=	30
50	9		18		27
100	8		16		24
150	7		14		21
200	6		12		18
250	5		10		15
300	4		8		12
350	3		6		9
400	2		4		6
450	1		2		3
500	0		0		0

occur because of a change in supply conditions and the factors affecting demand are assumed to be held constant. A change in price leads to a movement along the demand curve and is referred to as a *change in quantity demanded*.

Movement Along the Demand Curve

We are going to briefly look at the economics behind a movement along the demand curve. Let us assume that the price of a particular variety of rape seed (Excalibur) falls, while all other rape seed varieties' (Vision, Dimension, Vistive and Fashion) prices remain constant. We know that the fall in price will lead to an increase in quantity demanded. There are two reasons for this increase:

1. **The income effect.** If we assume that incomes remain constant then a fall in the price of Excalibur means that growers who buy this variety can now afford to buy more with their income. In other words, their *real income*, what a given amount of money can buy at any point in time, has increased and part of the increase in quantity demanded can be put down to this effect.
2. **The substitution effect.** Now that Excalibur is lower in price compared to other rape seed varieties, some growers will choose to substitute the more expensive varieties with the now cheaper Excalibur. This switch accounts for the remaining part of the increase in quantity demanded.

Shifts in the Demand Curve

The demand curve for rape seed shows how many tonnes of rape seed buyers are willing to buy at any given price, holding constant the many other factors beyond price that influence consumers' buying decisions. As a result, this demand curve need not be stable over time. If something happens to alter the demand at any given price, the demand curve shifts. For example, suppose European health authorities discovered that people who regularly use rape seed oil live longer, healthier lives. The discovery would be likely to raise the demand for rape seed. At any given price, buyers would now want to purchase a larger quantity of rape seed at all prices and the demand curve for rape seed would shift.

Figure 4.6 illustrates shifts in demand. Any change that increases the quantity demanded at every price, such as our imaginary discovery by the European health authorities, shifts the demand curve to the right and is called an *increase in demand*. Any change that reduces the demand at every price shifts the demand curve to the left and is called a *decrease in demand*.

There are many variables that can shift the demand curve. Here are the most important.

Income   What would happen to the demand for rape seed if unemployment increases? Most likely, it would fall (how much it would fall is another question and will be dealt with in the next chapter) because of lower incomes. Lower incomes mean that people have less to spend in total, so they are likely to spend less on some – and probably most – goods. If the demand for a good falls when income falls, the good is called a **normal good**.

Not all goods are normal goods. If the demand for a good rises when income falls, the good is called an **inferior good**. An example of an inferior good might be bus rides. As income falls, people are less likely to buy a car or take a taxi and more likely to take the bus. As income falls, therefore, demand for bus rides tends to increase.

normal good a good for which, other things being equal, an increase in income leads to an increase in demand (and vice versa)

inferior good a good for which, other things being equal, an increase in income leads to a decrease in demand (and vice versa)

FIGURE 4.6

Shifts in the Demand Curve

Any change that raises the quantity that buyers wish to purchase at a given price shifts the demand curve to the right. Any change that lowers the quantity that buyers wish to purchase at a given price shifts the demand curve to the left.

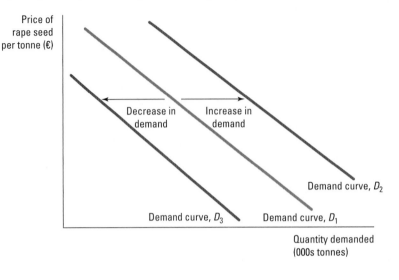

Prices of Related Goods   Suppose that the price of sunflower seed oil falls. The law of demand says that people will buy more sunflower seed oil. At the same time, people will probably buy less rape seed oil. Because sunflower seed oil and rape seed oil can both be used for cooking, they satisfy similar desires. When a fall in the price of one good reduces the demand for another good, the two goods are called **substitutes**. Substitutes are often pairs of goods that are used in place of each other, such as beef steak and Wiener schnitzel, pullovers and sweatshirts, and cinema tickets and movie downloads. The more closely related substitute products are, the more effect we might see on demand if the price of one of the substitutes changes.

substitutes two goods for which an increase in the price of one leads to an increase in the demand for the other (and vice versa)

Suppose that the price of woks falls. According to the law of demand, people will buy more woks. Yet, in this case, people will probably buy more rape seed oil as well, because rape seed oil and woks tend to be used together. When a fall in the price of one good raises the demand for another good, the two goods are called **complements**. Complements are often pairs of goods that are used together, such as petrol and cars, computers and software, bread and cheese, strawberries and cream, and bacon and eggs. As with substitutes not only do we need to identify what goods can be classed as complementary, we also need to be aware of the strength of the relationship between the two goods.

complements two goods for which an increase in the price of one leads to a decrease in the demand for the other (and vice versa)

Tastes   The most obvious determinant of demand are tastes and fashions. If people like rape seed oil, they buy more of it. Economists are increasingly interested in understanding and explaining people's tastes. The developments in neuroscience mean that we now have an increasing understanding of why people make decisions and this has come into the realm of economics. This helps economists examine what happens, and why, when tastes change. This knowledge is also very important to businesses seeking to get a better understanding of their market, how consumer's behave and why they behave in the ways they do.

Expectations   Buyers' expectations about the future may affect their demand for a good or service today. For example, if food processors and manufacturers who use rape seed oil in their production expect to earn higher revenues next month, they may be more willing to spend some of their current cash reserves buying rape seed oil. As another example, if buyers expect the price of rape seed to fall tomorrow, they may be less willing to buy rape seed at today's price.

The Size and Structure of the Population   A larger population, other things being equal, will mean a higher demand for all goods and services. Changes in the way the population is structured also influences demand. Many European countries have an ageing population and goods and services required by the elderly see an increase in demand. The demand for retirement homes, insurance policies suitable for elderly drivers and smaller cars, for example, may increase.

Pitfall Prevention   Many students confuse movements along and shifts in demand and supply curves. Using the correct phrasing (*change in supply/demand* refers to a shift in the curve, *change in quantity supplied/ demanded* refers to a movement along the curve) is one way to help prevent this confusion.

Summary   The demand curve shows what happens to the *quantity demanded* of a good when its price varies, holding constant all the other variables that influence buyers. When one or more of these other variables changes, the demand curve shifts leading to an *increase* or *decrease in demand*. Table 4.2 lists all the variables that influence how much consumers choose to buy of a good.

TABLE 4.2

Variables That Influence Buyers

This table lists the variables that affect how much consumers choose to buy of any good. Notice the special role that the price of the good plays: a change in the good's price represents a movement along the demand curve, whereas a change in one of the other variables shifts the demand curve.

Variable	A change in this variable...
Price	Is represented as a movement along the demand curve
Income	Shifts the demand curve
Prices of related goods	Shifts the demand curve
Tastes	Shifts the demand curve
Expectations	Shifts the demand curve
Number of buyers	Shifts the demand curve

Quick Quiz   Make up an example of a demand schedule for pizza, and graph the implied demand curve Give an example of something that would shift this demand curve. Would a change in the price of pizza shift this demand curve?

DEMAND AND SUPPLY TOGETHER

Having analysed supply and demand separately, we now combine them to see how they determine the quantity of a good bought and sold in a competitive market and its price.

Equilibrium

market equilibrium a situation in which the price has reached the level where quantity supplied equals quantity demanded

equilibrium or clearing price the price that balances quantity supplied and quantity demanded

equilibrium quantity the quantity supplied and the quantity demanded at the equilibrium price

Figure 4.7 shows the market supply curve and market demand curve together. Equilibrium is defined as a state of rest, a point where there is no force acting for change. Economists refer to supply and demand as being *market forces*. In any market the relationship between supply and demand exerts force on price. If supply is greater than demand or vice versa, then there is pressure on price to change. Notice, however, that there is one point at which the supply and demand curves intersect. This point is called the **market equilibrium**. The price at this intersection is called the **equilibrium or clearing price**, and the quantity is called the **equilibrium quantity**. Here the equilibrium price is €200 per tonne, and the equilibrium quantity is 7000 tonnes bought and sold.

At the equilibrium price, the quantity of the good that buyers are willing and able to buy exactly balances the quantity that sellers are willing and able to sell. The equilibrium price is sometimes called the *market-clearing price* because, at this price, everyone in the market has been satisfied: buyers have bought all they want to buy, and sellers have sold all they want to sell – there is neither a shortage nor a surplus.

The actions of buyers and sellers in a competitive market naturally move towards the equilibrium of supply and demand. To see why, consider what happens when the market price is not equal to the equilibrium price.

FIGURE 4.7

The Equilibrium of Supply and Demand

The equilibrium is found where the supply and demand curves intersect. At the equilibrium price, the quantity supplied equals the quantity demanded. Here the equilibrium price is €200: at this price, 7000 tonnes of rape seed are supplied and 7000 tonnes are demanded.

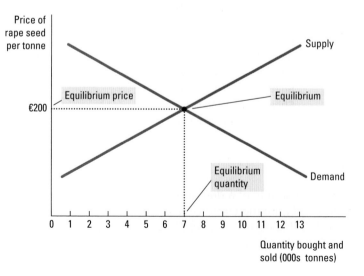

FIGURE 4.8

Markets Not in Equilibrium

In panel (a), there is a surplus. Because the market price of €250 is above the equilibrium price, the quantity supplied (10 000 tonnes) exceeds the quantity demanded (4000 tonnes). Suppliers try to increase sales by cutting the price of rape seed, and this moves the price toward its equilibrium level. In panel (b), there is a shortage. Because the market price of €150 is below the equilibrium price, the quantity demanded (10 000 tonnes) exceeds the quantity supplied (4000 tonnes). With too many buyers chasing too few goods, suppliers can take advantage of the shortage by raising the price. Hence, in both cases, the price adjustment moves the market towards the equilibrium of supply and demand.

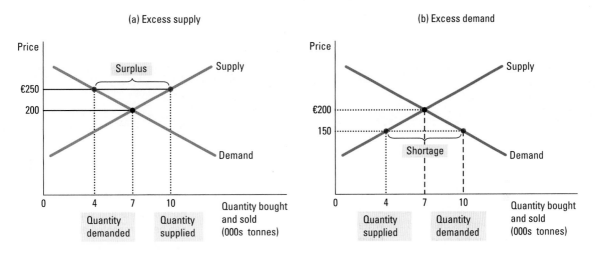

Suppose first that the market price is above the equilibrium price, as in panel (a) of Figure 4.8. At a price of €250 per tonne, the quantity suppliers would like to sell at this price (10 000 tonnes) exceeds the quantity which buyers are willing to purchase (4000 tonnes). There is a **surplus** of the good: suppliers are unable to sell all they want at the going price. A surplus is sometimes called a situation of *excess supply*. When there is a surplus in the rape seed market, sellers of rape seed find they cannot sell all the supplies they have and so the market responds to the surplus by cutting prices. Falling prices, in turn, increase the quantity demanded and decrease the quantity supplied. Prices continue to fall until the market reaches the equilibrium.

surplus a situation in which quantity supplied is greater than quantity demanded

Suppose now that the market price is below the equilibrium price, as in panel (b) of Figure 4.8. In this case, the price is €150 per tonne, and the quantity of the good demanded exceeds the quantity supplied. There is a **shortage** of the good: buyers who are unable to buy all they want at the going price. A shortage is sometimes called a situation of *excess demand*. When a shortage occurs in the rape seed market, buyers may find they cannot acquire all the supplies they need. With too many buyers chasing too few goods, the suppliers respond to the shortage by raising prices without losing sales. As the price rises, quantity demanded falls, quantity supplied rises and the market once again moves toward the equilibrium.

shortage a situation in which quantity demanded is greater than quantity supplied

The activities of the many buyers and sellers automatically push the market price towards the equilibrium price. Once the market reaches its equilibrium, all buyers and sellers are satisfied, and there is no upward or downward pressure on the price. How quickly equilibrium is reached varies from market to market, depending on how quickly prices adjust. In most free markets (which includes all the assumptions outlined earlier) surpluses and shortages are only temporary because prices eventually move towards their equilibrium levels. Indeed, this

law of supply and demand the claim that the price of any good adjusts to bring the quantity supplied and the quantity demanded for that good into balance

phenomenon is so pervasive that it is called the **law of supply and demand**: the price of any good adjusts to bring the quantity supplied and quantity demanded for that good into balance.

JEOPARDY PROBLEM

The market for bicycles has seen falling prices but not a change in the amount of bicycles bought and sold. Explain how this situation might have come about. Use diagrams to illustrate.

FYI

This FYI will be helpful if you have to use maths in your course. If you do not have to use maths then you can safely move on to the next section without affecting your overall understanding of this chapter.

Functions

In economics a lot of use is made of functions. Demand and supply equations are two examples of functions. Typically, functions are expressed as:

$$Y = f(x)$$

or simply $f(x)$

This means that the value of Y is dependent on the value of the terms in the bracket – in our example above there is only one value, x, so the value of Y is dependent on the value of x.

We know from this chapter that there are a number of factors affecting demand and supply. The general form of the function in such a case would look like:

$$Y = f(x_1 \ldots \ldots \ldots x_n)$$

where $x_1 \ldots \ldots x_n$ represents a range of variables.

Given the determinants of demand and supply we could write the demand and supply functions as:

$$D = f(P_n, P_n \ldots P_{n-1}, Y, T, P, A, E)$$

Where:

- P_n = Price
- $P_n \ldots P_{n-1}$ = Prices of other goods (substitutes and complements)
- Y = Incomes (the level and distribution of income)
- T = Tastes and fashions
- P = The level and structure of the population
- A = Advertising
- E = Expectations of consumers

and:

$$S = f(P_n, P_n \ldots P_{n-1}, H, N, F_1 \ldots F_m, E, S_f)$$

Where:

- P_n = Price
- $P_n \ldots P_{n-1}$ = Profitability of other goods in production and prices of goods in joint supply
- H = Technology
- N = Natural shocks
- $F_1 \ldots F_m$ = Costs of production
- E = Expectations of producers
- S_f = Social factors

Linear Equations

Both demand and supply functions can be represented as linear equations and be drawn as straight line graphs.

A linear equation normally looks like:

$$y = a + bx$$

In this equation, y is the value plotted on the vertical axis (the dependent variable), x is the value on the horizontal axis (the independent variable), a is a constant and b is the slope of the line or its gradient. Remember that demand looks at the relationship between price and the quantity demanded and supply is the relationship between price and the quantity supplied. In both cases, the quantity demanded and supplied are dependent on the price. So, price is the independent variable and the quantity the dependent variable.

Students of pure maths will notice that in economics, supply and demand graphs are the wrong way around – normally, the vertical Y axis represents the dependent variable and the X axis the independent variable. In supply and demand graphs, price, the independent variable, is drawn on the Y axis and quantity demanded and supplied, the dependent variable, on the X axis. The switch is attributed to Alfred Marshall (1842–1924) who developed supply and demand analysis in the latter part of the 19th century. It is important, therefore, to remember which is the dependent variable and which the independent variable as we progress through the analysis.

Applying the relationship between price and quantity demanded and supplied, we get typical equations such as:

$$Q_d = 2100 - 2.5p$$
$$Q_s = -10 + 6p$$

In the case of the demand curve the minus sign in front of the price variable tells us that there is a negative relationship between price and quantity demanded, whereas the plus sign in front of the price in the supply equation tells us that there is a positive relationship between price and quantity supplied.

You may also see demand and supply equations which look like:

$$P = 840 - 0.4Q_d \text{ or:}$$
$$P = -120 + 0.8Q_s$$

The equation $P = 840 - 0.4Q_d$ is just the inverse of the demand equation $Q_d = 2100 - 2.5p$. We found this by adopting the following method:

$$Q_d = 2100 - 2.5p$$
$$Q_d + 2.5p = 2100$$
$$2.5p = 2100 - Q_d$$
$$\frac{2.5p}{2.5} = \frac{2100 - Q_d}{2.5}$$
$$P = 840 - 0.4 Q_d$$

Remember, however, that because of the switching of supply and demand curves as noted above, you can get some odd looking equations which do not fit with the graphical analysis.

The important thing to remember when manipulating linear equations of this sort is that whatever you do to one side of the equation (multiply, add, divide or subtract a number or element) you must do the same thing to the other side.

Finding Price and Quantity

If we take the original two equations:

$$Q_d = 2100 - 2.5p$$
$$Q_s = -10 + 6p$$

We can dissect them in a bit more detail in relation to the standard $y = a + bx$ linear equation we first introduced. In our equations, the quantity demanded and supplied are one of the variables in the equation. In this case they are the dependent variable. Their value depends upon the price – the independent variable. In the case of the demand curve, the quantity demanded will be 2100 minus 2.5 times whatever the price is. If price is €6 then quantity demanded will be $2100 - 2.5(6) = 2085$. If price is €16 then quantity demanded will be $2100 - 2.5(16) = 2060$.

Looking at supply, if the price were €8 then the quantity supplied would be $-10 + 6(8) = 38$ and if price were €16 then quantity supplied would be $-10 + 6(16) = 86$.

If we used the other two equations we looked at:

$$P = 840 - 0.4Q_d$$

Or:

$$P = -120 + 0.8Q_s$$

Then we can arrive at values for P or Q assuming we have at least one of these two variables.

For demand, if $P = $ €6 then the quantity demanded would be:

$$P = 840 - 0.4Q_d$$
$$0.4Q_d = 840 - 6$$
$$\frac{0.4Q_d}{0.4} = \frac{834}{0.4}$$
$$Q_d = 2085$$

In the case of supply, if price = €8:

$$P = -120 + 0.8Q_s$$
$$8 = -120 + 0.8Q_s$$
$$\frac{8}{0.8} = \frac{-120 + 0.8Q_s}{0.8}$$
$$10 = -150 + Q_s$$
$$10 + 150 = Q_s$$
$$Q_s = 160$$

Finding Market Equilibrium: *The substitution method*

We know that in equilibrium, demand equals supply (D = S). To find the market equilibrium, therefore, we set the demand and supply equations equal to each other and solve for P and Q.

Take the following demand and supply equations:

$$Q_d = 32 - 3P$$
$$Q_s = 20 + 4P$$

We know that in equilibrium: $Q_d = Q_s$, so, equilibrium in this market will be where:

$$32 - 3P = 20 + 4P$$

This now allows us to solve for P and so find the equilibrium price. Subtract 20 from both sides and add 3p to both sides to get:

$$32 - 20 = 4P + 3P$$
$$12 = 7P$$

$P = $ €1.71 (rounded to the nearest whole cent).

We can now substitute the equilibrium price into our two equations to find the equilibrium quantity, rounded to the nearest whole number:

$$Q_d = 32 - 3P$$
$$Q_d = 32 - 3(1.71)$$
$$Q_d = 32 - 5.13$$
$$Q_d = 26.87$$
$$Q_d = 27$$
$$Q_s = 20 + 4P$$
$$Q_s = 20 + 4(1.71)$$
$$Q_s = 20 + 6.84$$
$$Q_s = 26.84$$
$$Q_s = 27$$

Note the figures for Q_d and Q_s before rounding, differ slightly because we had to round the price. Now look at this example:

$$P = 3 + 0.25Q_s$$
$$P = 15 - 0.75Q_d$$

In this case the equations are defined in terms of price but the principle of working out equilibrium is the same as we have used above. First, set the two equations equal to each other:

$$3 + 0.25Q_s = 15 - 0.75Q_d$$

Then solve for Q:

Add $0.75Q_d$ to both sides and then subtract 3 from both sides to get:

$$0.75Q_d + 0.25Q_s = 15 - 3$$
$$Q = 12$$

Substitute $Q = 12$ into one of the equations to find P.

$$P = 3 + 0.25Q_s$$
$$P = 3 + 0.25(12)$$
$$P = 6$$

To check, also substitute into the demand equation:

$$P = 15 - 0.75Q_d$$
$$P = 15 - 0.75(12)$$
$$P = 15 - 9$$
$$P = 6.$$

There is another way to find both the quantity and the price and that is through adopting the approach of solving simultaneous equations. Simultaneous equations require us to find two unknowns – price and quantity.

The elimination method

Look at the following two equations:

$$Q_d = 20 - 2P$$
$$Q_s = 2 + 2P$$

In this case, the terms are all neatly aligned above each other so it is a relatively simple task to add the two together. Note that we are trying to find equilibrium where $Q_d = Q_s$ so the value of Q is the same. Adding the two together we get:

$$Q_d = 20 - 2P$$
$$Q_s = 2 + 2P$$
$$2Q = 22$$
$$Q = 11$$

Notice that in the above equations we have a very convenient fact that the coefficient of p in each case is the same but with opposite signs. This makes this example very easy to eliminate P to isolate the Q value. This is not always the case, however, but it is important to remember that having two equal values with opposite signs allows us to get rid of them! We will come back to this later. We can now use the fact that we know Q, to find the equilibrium price by substituting Q into one of the equations thus:

$$Q_d = 20 - 2P$$
$$11 = 20 - 2P$$
$$2P = 20 - 11$$
$$2P = 9$$
$$P = 4.5$$

It is always worth checking your answer to make sure you have made no mistakes along the way so

in this case we will substitute our known value of Q into the second equation to check we get the same answer ($P = 4.5$):

$$Q_s = 2 + 2P$$
$$11 = 2 + 2P$$
$$11 - 2 = 2P$$
$$9 = 2P$$
$$P = 4.5$$

Sometimes we may have equations where the P and Q values are both on the same side of the equation. In this case we have to use a different technique – the elimination method.

Take the following two equations:

$$-3P + 4Q = 5 \quad (1)$$
$$2P - 5Q = -15 \quad (2)$$

We have labelled these two equations (1) and (2) to allow us to keep track of what we are doing and reduce the risk of making an error. Remember above when we noted the fact that having a nice convenient equation where the coefficient was equal but the signs opposite, enabled us to be able to eliminate one of the values to help solve the equation for the other unknown. That is what we need to do with these two equations. We have to manipulate the two equations to make either the 'P' terms or the 'Q' terms have the same coefficient but opposite signs. A knowledge of factors and lowest common denominators is useful here!

In this example we are going to manipulate the equations to get rid of the 'P' terms. This allows us to isolate the 'Q' terms and thus solve for Q and then find P.

$$-3P + 4Q = 5 \quad (1)$$
$$2P - 5Q = -15 \quad (2)$$

To eliminate P, multiply (1) by 2 and (2) by 3:

$$3 - 6P + 8Q = 10 \quad (3)$$
$$6P - 15Q = -45 \quad (4)$$

Add together (3) and (4):

$$-6P + 8Q = 10 \quad (3)$$
$$6P - 15Q = -45 \quad (4)$$
$$-7Q = -35$$

Divide both sides by -7

$$Q = 5$$

We can now substitute Q into equations (1) and (2) to find (and check) P. If $Q = 5$ then:

$$-3P + 4(5) = 5$$
$$-3P + 20 = 5$$
$$20 - 5 = 3P$$
$$15 = 3P$$
$$P = 5$$

$$2P - 5(5) = -15$$
$$2P - 25 = -15$$
$$2P = -15 + 25$$
$$2P = 10$$
$$P = 5$$

In this case the equilibrium price is €5 and the equilibrium quantity is 5.

Three Steps to Analysing Changes in Equilibrium

So far we have seen how supply and demand together determine a market's equilibrium, which in turn determines the price of the good and the amount of the good that buyers purchase and sellers produce. Markets are dynamic – demand and supply change all the time and in some markets these changes may be almost every second of every day – in foreign exchange markets, for example. The equilibrium price and quantity depend on the position of the supply and demand curves. When some event shifts one (or both) of these curves, the equilibrium in the market changes. The analysis of such a change is called *comparative statics* because it involves comparing two unchanging situations – an initial and a new equilibrium.

When analysing how some event affects a market, we proceed in three steps. First, we decide whether the event shifts the supply curve, the demand curve or, in some cases, both curves. Second, we decide whether the curve shifts to the right or to the left. Third, we use the supply and demand diagram to compare the initial and the new equilibrium, which shows how the shift affects the equilibrium price and quantity. It is important in the analysis that the process by which equilibrium changes is understood and that the changes involved are not instantaneous (although some schools of thought do refer to instantaneous changes in markets) – some markets will take longer to adjust to changes than others. Table 4.3 summarizes the three steps. To see how this recipe is used, let's consider various events that might affect the market for rape seed.

TABLE 4.3

A Three-Step Programme for Analysing Changes in Equilibrium

1. Decide whether the event shifts the supply or demand curve (or perhaps both).
2. Decide in which direction the curve shifts.
3. Use the supply and demand diagram to see how the shift changes the equilibrium price and quantity.

Example: A Change in Demand Suppose that a government-sponsored research project finds that using rape seed oil helps reduce the risk of heart disease and strokes. How does this event affect the market for rape seed? To answer this question, let's follow our three steps.

1. The news has a direct effect on the demand curve by changing people's taste for rape seed oil. That is, the report changes the amount of rape seed oil that consumers want to buy at any given price.
2. Because the report incentivizes people to use more rape seed oil, the demand curve SHIFTS to the right. Figure 4.9 shows this increase in demand as the shift in the demand curve from D_1 to D_2. This shift indicates that the quantity of rape seed oil demanded is higher at every price. The shift in demand has led to a shortage of rape seed oil in the market. At a price of €200 buyers now want to buy 26 000 tonnes of rape seed but sellers are only offering 12 000 tonnes for sale at this price. There is a shortage of 14 000 tonnes.
3. As Figure 4.9 shows, the shortage starts to force up prices and encourages growers to offer more rape for sale which is represented as a MOVEMENT ALONG the supply curve. The additional production incurs extra costs and so a higher price is required to compensate sellers. This raises the equilibrium price from €200 to €300 and the equilibrium quantity from 12 000 to 20 000 tonnes. In other words, the report increases the price of rape seed and the quantity of rape seed bought and sold.

FIGURE 4.9

How an Increase in Demand Affects the Equilibrium

An event that raises quantity demanded at any given price shifts the demand curve to the right. The equilibrium price and the equilibrium quantity both rise. Here, the report linking using rape seed oil to reductions in risk of ill health causes buyers to demand more rape seed. The demand curve shifts from D_1 to D_2, which causes the equilibrium price to rise from €200 to €300 and the equilibrium quantity to rise from 12 000 to 20 000 tonnes.

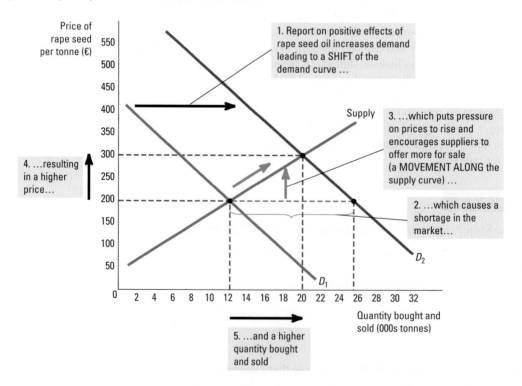

Shifts in Curves Versus Movements Along Curves – A Reminder When the report drives up the price of rape seed, the quantity of rape seed that growers supply rises, but the supply curve remains in the same position. Economists say there has been an increase in 'quantity supplied' but no *change* in 'supply'.

'Supply' refers to the position of the supply curve, whereas the 'quantity supplied' refers to the amount suppliers wish to sell at different prices. In this example, we assumed supply does not change. Instead, the report alters consumers' desire to buy at any given price and thereby shifts the demand curve. The increase in demand creates a shortage. The shortage means there are more buyers looking to purchase rape seed than there are sellers willing to sell. As a result, price starts to creep up as buyers are prepared to pay higher prices to get products. When the price rises growers are willing to offer more rape seed for sale and so the quantity supplied rises. This increase in quantity supplied is represented by the movement along the supply curve. The shortage will continue to be competed away by price rising until supply and demand are once again brought into equilibrium. The final result will be a rise in equilibrium price and in the amount bought and sold.

Example: A Change in Supply Suppose that, during another summer, bad weather destroys part of the seed crop for rape and drives up the world price of rape seed for planting. How does this event affect the market for rape seed?

1. The change in the price of seed, an input needed to grow rape, affects the supply curve. By raising the costs of production, it reduces the amount of rape seed that firms produce and sell at any given price. The demand curve does not change because the higher cost of inputs does not directly affect the amount of rape seed buyers wish to buy.
2. The supply curve shifts to the left because, at every price, the total amount that firms are willing and able to sell is reduced. Figure 4.10 illustrates this decrease in supply as a shift in the supply curve from S_1 to S_2. At a price of €200 sellers are now only able to offer 4000 tonnes of rape seed for sale but demand is still 12 000 tonnes of rape seed. The shift in supply to the left has created a shortage in the market. The shortage will create pressure on price to rise as buyers look to purchase rape seed.
3. As Figure 4.10 shows, the shortage raises the equilibrium price from €200 to €250 and lowers the equilibrium quantity from 12 000 to 9000 tonnes. As a result of the increase in seed for growing, the price of rape seed rises, and the quantity of rape seed bought and sold falls.

Example: A Change in Both Supply and Demand (i) Now suppose that the report and the bad weather occur during the same summer.

1. We determine that both curves must shift. The report affects the demand curve because it alters the amount of rape seed that buyers want to buy at any given price. At the same time, when the bad weather drives up the price of seed for growing rape, it alters the supply curve for rape seed because it changes the amount of rape seed that firms want to sell at any given price.
2. The curves shift in the same directions as they did in our previous analysis: the demand curve shifts to the right, and the supply curve shifts to the left. Figure 4.11 illustrates these shifts.

FIGURE 4.10

How a Decrease in Supply Affects the Equilibrium

An event that reduces supply at any given price shifts the supply curve to the left. The equilibrium price rises, and the equilibrium quantity falls. Here, an increase in the price of seed for growing rape plants (an input) causes sellers to supply less rape seed. The supply curve shifts from S_1 to S_2, which causes the equilibrium price of rape seed to rise from €200 to €250 and the equilibrium quantity to fall from 12 000 to 9000 tonnes.

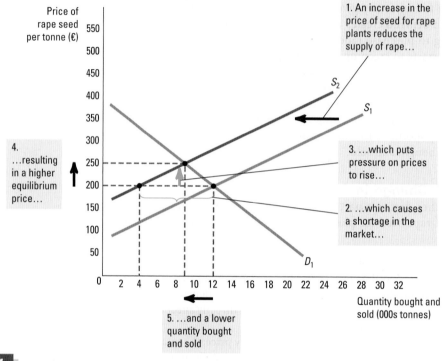

1. An increase in the price of seed for rape plants reduces the supply of rape...

4. ...resulting in a higher equilibrium price...

3. ...which puts pressure on prices to rise...

2. ...which causes a shortage in the market...

5. ...and a lower quantity bought and sold

FIGURE 4.11

A Shift in Both Supply and Demand (i)

Here we observe a simultaneous increase in demand and decrease in supply. Two outcomes are possible. In panel (a), the equilibrium price rises from P_1 to P_2, and the equilibrium quantity rises from Q_1 to Q_2. In panel (b), the equilibrium price again rises from P_1 to P_2, but the equilibrium quantity falls from Q_1 to Q_2.

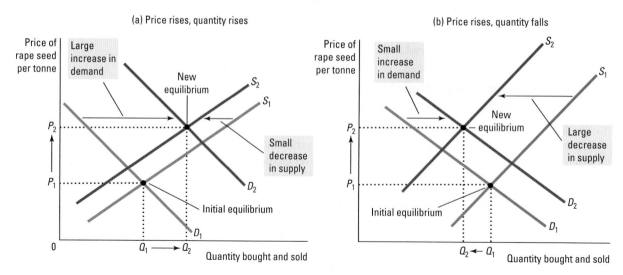

(a) Price rises, quantity rises

(b) Price rises, quantity falls

3. As Figure 4.11 shows, there are two possible outcomes that might result, depending on the relative size of the demand and supply shifts. In both cases, the equilibrium price rises. In panel (a), where demand increases substantially while supply falls just a little, the equilibrium quantity also rises. By contrast, in panel (b), where supply falls substantially while demand rises just a little, the equilibrium quantity falls. Thus, these events raise the price of rape seed, but their impact on the amount of rape seed bought and sold is ambiguous (that is, it could go either way).

Example: A Change in Both Supply and Demand (ii)

We are now going to look at a slightly different scenario but still with both supply and demand changing together. Assume that the details of the report have been leaked prior to official publication and the findings publicized on TV news stations. We know that the report is likely to increase demand for rape seed and so the demand curve will shift to the right. However, sellers' expectations that sales of rape seed will increase as a result of the forecasts mean that they take steps to expand production of rape seed. This would lead to a shift of the supply curve to the right – more rape seed is now offered for sale at every price.

1. We determine that both curves must shift. The report affects the demand curve because it alters the amount of rape seed that buyers want to buy at any given price. At the same time, the expectations of producers alter the supply curve for rape seed because they change the amount of rape seed that firms want to sell at any given price.
2. Both demand and supply curves shift to the right: Figure 4.12 illustrates these shifts.
3. As Figure 4.12 shows, there are three possible outcomes that might result, depending on the relative size of the demand and supply shifts. In panel (a), where demand increases substantially while supply rises just a little, the equilibrium price and quantity rises. By contrast, in panel (b), where supply rises substantially while demand rises just a little, the equilibrium price falls but the equilibrium quantity rises. In panel (c) the increase in demand and supply are identical and so equilibrium price does not change. Equilibrium quantity will increase, however. Thus, these events have different effects on the price of rape seed although the amount of rape seed bought and sold in each case is higher. In this instance the effect on price is ambiguous.

? **what if…** Malmo FF, a Swedish football team, is taken over by a rich Middle East backer? The team is strengthened and produces a series of excellent results which propel them to the top of the Swedish Allsvenskan. Demand for tickets to the 24 000 capacity stadium increases dramatically. Draw a supply and demand diagram to illustrate this market situation. Would the club increase ticket prices? If so, what might fans' reaction be? If the club does not increase prices why might it make this decision? What do you think would be the practical effect on fans and the prices they have to pay for tickets if prices were held at the original level? Assuming the improvement in the club's fortunes continues for several seasons, what might the long-term market situation look like?

FIGURE 4.12

A Shift in Both Supply and Demand (ii)

Here, again, we observe a simultaneous increase in demand and supply. Three outcomes are possible. In panel (a) the equilibrium price rises from P_1 to P_2 and the equilibrium quantity rises from Q_1 to Q_2. In panel (b), the equilibrium price falls from P_1 to P_2 but the equilibrium quantity rises from Q_1 to Q_2. In panel (c), there is no change to the equilibrium price but the equilibrium quantity rises from Q_1 to Q_2.

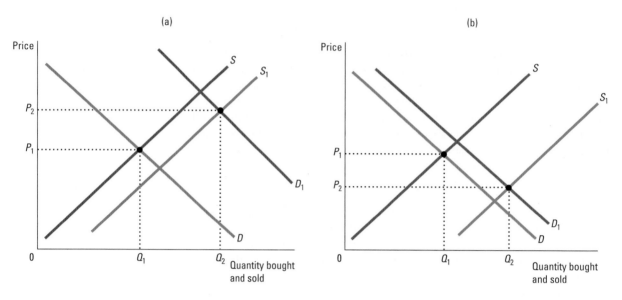

(a)

(b)

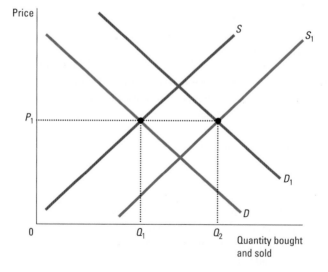

(c)

IN THE NEWS

The Strange Case of Changing Oil Prices

Oil prices reached a peak in 2012 but in 2014 prices fell sharply. The interaction of supply and demand of oil and interdependent markets for energy makes this a volatile market.

In February 2010 Brent crude was priced around $75 a barrel and rose to a peak of $125 a barrel just a year later. The price was relatively stable until the spring of 2014. In February 2014 the price was trading around $108 and a few months later, prices began to plummet. By February 2015 the price had fallen to below $50.

A global surplus has been the main cause of the fall in oil prices. Demand for oil is lower than expected, but supply has increased partly due to the increase in the supply of unconventional oil in the USA from fracking. At the same time Saudi Arabia has refused to cut production of crude oil. Some other oil-producing countries, such as Iran and Venezuela, argue that supply should be restricted in order to raise prices, but the influence and power of the Organization of Petroleum Exporting Countries (OPEC) acting as a cartel has declined.

Markets are interdependent; what happens in one market can have effects on others. For example, the additional supply of biofuels has affected the demand for

oil from carbon-based sources and car manufacturers have increased engine efficiency, further reducing the demand for oil, partly in response to sharp oil price rises in the past. The energy market is further complicated by concerns over global warming meaning many governments encourage the development of sustainable energy sources.

If prices continue to fall or remain low for any length of time this can mean that some forms of oil supply will no longer be economically viable and production will be cut as a reaction to price changes. This would particularly affect US shale oil suppliers and North Sea oil fields where production costs are higher. The key to keeping production going in these circumstances will be how easy it is to drive down costs. In January 2015, BP announced that it planned to cut 300 North Sea oil jobs to save costs in response to the falling price of crude oil.

If crude oil prices remain low, then the feasibility of new projects for energy supplies, both sustainable or otherwise, will be put into doubt. For existing projects, much of the costs are sunk costs which are committed and cannot be recovered. In the short-term,

therefore, firms involved with these projects may continue production.

Questions

1. Identify and explain three possible factors influencing the investment decisions of oil producers.
2. Explain how the market for crude oil and biofuel is interdependent.
3. Use supply and demand diagrams to show the effects of a) the overall growth in supply of oil; b) a decline in demand for oil products.
4. What evidence in the article supports shifts in the supply curve and what evidence supports a movement along the supply curve for oil.
5. What has happened to oil prices since 2015? Explain what factors have caused the change in the price of oil since 2015.

References: http://www.theweek.co.uk /business/oil-price/60838/oil-price -drops-again-amid-large-scale-strike -in-us

http://www.biofuelsdigest.com /bdigest/2015/02/01/the-oil-price-crash -of-14-what-lessons-have-we-learned/

https://uk.news.yahoo.com/bp-due-cut -north-sea-jobs-oil-costs-080428116 --finance.html#TRQgl0i

FYI

Prices as Signals

Our analysis so far has only brushed the surface of the way markets operate. Economists have conducted extensive research into the nature and determinants of both demand and supply. It is beyond the scope of this book to go into too much detail on these issues but it is useful to have a little bit of background knowledge on this to help understand markets more effectively.

At the heart of research into demand and supply is why buyers and sellers behave as they do. The development of magnetic resonance imaging (MRI) techniques has allowed researchers to investigate how the brain responds to different stimuli when making purchasing decisions (referred to as *neuroeconomics*). As time goes by our understanding of buyer and seller behaviour will improve and theories will have to be adapted to accommodate this new understanding.

However, much of the theory behind how markets work relies on the assumption of rational behaviour, defined in terms of humans preferring more to less and taking into account information prior to making a decision. The main function of price in a free market is to act as a signal to both buyers and sellers to help in decision making.

For buyers, price tells them something about what they have to give up to acquire the benefits that having the good will confer on them. These benefits are referred to as the *utility* (satisfaction) derived from consumption. If you are willing to pay €10 to go and watch a movie then economists will assume that the value of the benefits you gain from watching the movie is greater than the next best alternative – what else you could have spent your €10 on. We have noted in Chapter 1 that people face trade-offs and that the cost of something is what you have to give up to acquire it. This is fundamental to the law of demand. At higher prices, the sacrifice being made in terms of the value of the benefits gained from alternatives is greater and so we may be less willing to do so as a result. If the price of a ticket for the movie was €20 (other things being equal) then it might have to be a very good movie to persuade us that giving up what else €20 could buy is worth it.

For sellers price acts as a signal in relation to the profitability of production. For most sellers, increasing the amount of a good produced will incur some additional input costs. A higher price is required in order to compensate for the additional cost and to also enable the producer to gain some reward from the risk they are taking in production. That reward is termed profit.

If prices are rising in a free market then this acts as a different but related signal to buyers and sellers. Rising prices to a seller means that there is a shortage and thus there is an incentive to expand production because the seller knows that they will be able to sell what they produce. For buyers, a rising price changes the nature of the trade-off they have to face. They will now have to give up more in order to acquire the good and they will have to decide whether the value of the benefits they will gain from acquiring the good is worth the extra price they have to pay.

What we do know is that for both buyers and sellers, there are many complex processes that occur in decision making. While we do not fully understand all these processes yet, economists are constantly searching for new insights that might help them understand the workings of markets more fully. All of us go through these complex processes every time we make a purchasing decision – although we may not realize it! Having some appreciation of these processes is fundamental to thinking like an economist.

Summary

We have just seen four examples of how to use supply and demand curves to analyse a change in equilibrium. Whenever an event shifts the supply curve, the demand curve, or perhaps both curves, you can use these tools to predict how the event will alter the amount bought and sold in equilibrium and the price at which the good is bought and sold. Table 4.4 shows the predicted outcome for any combination of shifts in the two curves. To make sure you understand how to use the tools of supply and demand, pick a few entries in this table and make sure you can explain to yourself why the table contains the prediction it does.

TABLE 4.4

What Happens to Price and Quantity When Supply or Demand Shifts?

As a quick quiz, make sure you can explain each of the entries in this table using a supply and demand diagram.

	No change in supply	An increase in supply	A decrease in supply
No change in demand	P same	P down	P up
	Q same	Q up	Q down
An increase in demand	P up	P ambiguous	P up
	Q up	Q up	Q ambiguous
A decrease in demand	P down	P down	P ambiguous
	Q down	Q ambiguous	Q down

HOW PRICES ALLOCATE RESOURCES

This chapter has analysed supply and demand in a single market. Although our discussion has centred on the market for rape seed, the lessons learned here apply in many other markets as well. Whenever you go to a shop to buy something, you are contributing to the demand for that item. Whenever you look for a job, you are contributing to the supply of labour services. Because supply and demand are such pervasive economic phenomena, the model of supply and demand is a powerful tool for analysis. We shall be using this model repeatedly in the chapters which follow.

In this chapter we have begun to see how markets work. In any economic system, scarce resources have to be allocated among competing uses. Market economies harness the forces of supply and demand to serve that end. Supply and demand together determine the prices of the economy's many different goods and services; prices in turn are the signals that guide the allocation of resources. Consider the allocation of property on the seafront in a seaside resort. Because the amount of this property is limited, not everyone can enjoy the luxury of living by the beach. Who gets this resource? The answer is: whoever is willing and able to pay the price. The price of seafront property adjusts until the quantity of property demanded exactly balances the quantity supplied. Thus, in market economies, prices are the mechanism for rationing scarce resources.

Similarly, prices determine who produces each good and how much is produced. For instance, consider farming. Because we need food to survive, it is crucial that some people work on farms. What determines who is a farmer and who is not? The allocation of workers to farms is based on the job decisions of millions of workers. This system works because decisions depend on prices. The prices of food and the wages of farm workers (the price of their labour) adjust to ensure that enough people choose to be farmers.

SUMMARY

- Economists use the model of supply and demand to analyse competitive markets. In a competitive market, there are many buyers and sellers, each of whom has little or no influence on the market price.

- The supply curve shows how the quantity of a good supplied depends on the price. According to the law of supply, as the price of a good rises, the quantity supplied rises. Therefore, the supply curve slopes upward.

- In addition to price, other determinants of how much producers want to sell include input prices, technology, expectations, the number of sellers, and natural and social factors. If one of these factors changes, the supply curve shifts.

- The demand curve shows how the quantity of a good demanded depends on the price. According to the law of demand, as the price of a good falls, the quantity demanded rises. Therefore, the demand curve slopes downward.

- In addition to price, other determinants of how much consumers want to buy include income, the prices of substitutes and complements, tastes, expectations and the number of buyers. If one of these factors changes, the demand curve shifts.

- The intersection of the supply and demand curves determines the market equilibrium. At the equilibrium price, the quantity supplied equals the quantity demanded.

- The behaviour of sellers and buyers naturally drives markets toward their equilibrium. When the market price is above the equilibrium price, there is a surplus of the good, which causes the market price to fall. When the market price is below the equilibrium price, there is a shortage, which causes the market price to rise.

- To analyse how any event influences a market, we use supply and demand diagrams to examine how the event affects the equilibrium price and quantity. To do this we follow three steps. First, we decide whether the event shifts the supply curve or the demand curve (or both). Second, we decide which direction the curve shifts. Third, we compare the new equilibrium with the initial equilibrium.

- In market economies, prices are the signals that guide economic decisions and thereby allocate scarce resources. For every good in the economy, the price ensures that supply and demand are in balance. The equilibrium price then determines how much of the good buyers choose to purchase and how much sellers choose to produce.

QUESTIONS FOR REVIEW

1. What determines the quantity of a good that sellers supply?

2. What are the supply schedule and the supply curve, and how are they related? Why does the supply curve slope upwards?

3. Does a change in producers' technology lead to a movement along the supply curve or a shift in the supply curve? Does a change in price lead to a movement along the supply curve or a shift in the supply curve?

4. What determines the quantity of a good that buyers demand?

5. What are the demand schedule and the demand curve, and how are they related? Why does the demand curve slope downwards?

6. Does a change in consumers' tastes lead to a movement along the demand curve or a shift in the demand

curve? Does a change in price lead to a movement along the demand curve or a shift in the demand curve?

7. Carlos prefers asparagus to spinach. His income declines and as a result he buys more spinach. Is spinach an inferior or a normal good to Carlos? Explain your answer.

8. Define the equilibrium of a market. Describe the forces that move a market toward its equilibrium.

9. Cheese and wine are complements because they are often enjoyed together. When the price of wine rises, use the tools of supply and demand to predict what happens to the supply, demand, quantity supplied, quantity demanded and the price in the market for cheese.

10. Describe the role of prices in market economies.

PROBLEMS AND APPLICATIONS

1. Explain each of the following statements using supply and demand diagrams.
   a. When there is a drought in southern Europe, the price of olive oil rises in supermarkets throughout Europe.
   b. A slowdown in economic activity in China causes a fall in the price of steel on world markets.
   c. The price of skiing holidays rises dramatically during the two weeks in which schools have breaks in February.

2. 'An increase in the demand for mozzarella cheese raises the quantity of mozzarella demanded, but not the quantity supplied.' Is this statement true or false? Explain.

3. Consider the market for large family saloon cars. For each of the events listed here, identify which of the determinants of supply or demand is affected. Also indicate whether supply or demand is increased or decreased. Then show the effect on the price and quantity of large family saloon cars.
   a. People decide to have more children.
   b. A strike by steel workers raises steel prices.
   c. Engineers develop new automated machinery for the production of cars.
   d. The price of estate cars rises.
   e. A stock market crash lowers people's wealth.

4. During the 1990s, technological advances reduced the cost of computer chips. How do you think this affected the market for computers? For computer software? For typewriters?

5. Using supply and demand diagrams, show the effect of the following events on the market for sweatshirts.
   a. A drought in Egypt damages the cotton crop.
   b. The price of leather jackets falls.
   c. All universities require students to attend morning exercise classes in appropriate attire.
   d. New knitting machines are invented.

6. Suppose that in the year 2016 the number of births is temporarily high. How might this baby boom affect the price of baby-sitting services in 2021 and 2031? (Hint: 5-year-olds need babysitters, whereas 15-year-olds can be babysitters.)

7. The market for pizza has the following demand and supply schedules:

Price	Quantity demanded	Quantity supplied
€4	135	26
5	104	53
6	81	81
7	68	98
8	53	110
9	39	121

Graph the demand and supply curves. What is the equilibrium price and quantity in this market? If the actual price in this market were above the equilibrium price, what would drive the market towards the equilibrium? If the actual price in this market were below the equilibrium price, what would drive the market towards the equilibrium?

8. Suppose that the price of tickets to see your local football team play at home is determined by market forces. Currently, the demand and supply schedules are as follows:

Price	Quantity demanded	Quantity supplied
€10	50 000	30 000
20	40 000	30 000
30	30 000	30 000
40	20 000	30 000
50	10 000	30 000

a. Draw the demand and supply curves. What is unusual about this supply curve? Why might this be true?
b. What are the equilibrium price and quantity of tickets?
c. Your team plans to increase total capacity in its stadium by 10 000 seats next season. What admission price should it charge?

9. Market research has revealed the following information about the market for chocolate bars: the demand schedule can be represented by the equation $Q_d = 1600 - 300P$, where Q_d is the quantity demanded and P is the price. The supply schedule can be represented by the equation $Q_s = 1400 + 700P$, where Q_s is the quantity supplied. Calculate the equilibrium price and quantity in the market for chocolate bars.

10. What do we mean by a perfectly competitive market? Do you think that the example of rape seed used in this chapter fits this description? Is there another type of market that better characterizes the market for rape seed?

5 ELASTICITY AND ITS APPLICATIONS

LEARNING OUTCOMES

After reading this chapter you should be able to:

- Calculate elasticity using the midpoint method.
- Calculate the price elasticity of supply and demand.
- Distinguish between an inelastic and elastic supply and demand curve.
- Distinguish between the price elasticity of demand for necessities and luxuries.

- Calculate different elasticities – price, income and cross.
- Demonstrate the impact of the price elasticity of demand on total expenditure and total revenue under conditions of different demand elasticities.

ELASTICITY AND ITS APPLICATION

For businesses, the price they charge for the products they produce is a vital part of their product positioning – what the product offering is in relation to competitors. We have seen in Chapter 4 how markets are dynamic and that price acts as a signal to both sellers and buyers; when prices change, the signal is altered and producer and consumer behaviour changes.

Imagine a business producing silicon chips for use in personal computers, laptops and a variety of other electronic devices. Because the business earns all its income from selling silicon chips, it devotes much effort to making the factory as productive as it can be. It monitors how production is organized, staff recruitment and motivation levels, checks suppliers for cost effectiveness and quality, and studies the latest advances in technology. The business knows that the more chips it manufactures, the more will be available to sell, and the higher will be its income (assuming it can sell them).

One day a local university announces a major discovery. Scientists have devised a new material to produce chips which would help to increase computing power by 50 per cent. How should the business react to this news? Should it use the new material? Does this discovery make the business better off or worse off than before? In this chapter we will see that these questions can have surprising answers. The surprise will come from applying the most basic tools of economics – supply and demand – to the market for computer chips.

To apply the basic analysis of supply and demand covered in Chapter 4 to understand the impact of the scientists' discovery, we must first develop one more tool: the concept of *elasticity* also referred to as *price sensitivity*. We know from Chapter 4 that when price rises, demand falls and supply rises. What we did not discuss in the chapter was *how far* demand and supply change in response to changes in price – in other words, how sensitive supply and demand are to a change in prices. When studying how some event or policy affects a market, we can discuss not only the direction of the effects but their magnitude as well. **Elasticity**, a measure of how much buyers and sellers respond to changes in market conditions, allows us to turn statements about quantity supplied and demanded from the qualitative to the quantitative with the result that the analysis will have greater precision.

> **elasticity** a measure of the responsiveness of quantity supplied or quantity demanded to one of its determinants

PRICE ELASTICITY OF SUPPLY

The Price Elasticity of Supply and Its Determinants

The law of supply states that higher prices raise the quantity supplied. The **price elasticity of supply** measures how much the quantity supplied responds to changes in the price. Supply of a good is said to be *elastic* (or price sensitive) if the quantity supplied responds substantially to changes in the price. Supply is said to be *inelastic* (or price insensitive) if the quantity supplied responds only slightly to changes in the price.

> **Price elasticity of supply** a measure of how much the quantity supplied of a good responds to a change in the price of that good, computed as the percentage change in quantity supplied divided by the percentage change in price

The price elasticity of supply depends on the flexibility of sellers to change the amount of the good they produce. For example, seafront property has an inelastic supply because it is almost impossible to produce more of it quickly – supply is not very sensitive to changes in price. By contrast, manufactured goods, such as books, cars and television sets, have relatively elastic supplies because the firms that produce them can run their factories longer in response to a higher price – supply is more sensitive to changes in price.

Elasticity can take any value greater than or equal to zero. The closer to zero the more inelastic, and the closer to infinity the more elastic.

The Determinants of Price Elasticity of Supply

The Time Period   In most markets, a key determinant of the price elasticity of supply is the time period being considered. Supply is usually more elastic in the long run than in the short run. We can further distinguish between the short run and the very short run. Over very short periods of time, firms may find it virtually impossible to respond to a change in price by changing output. In the short run firms cannot easily change productive capacity to make more or less of a good but may have some flexibility. For example, it might take a month to employ new labour but after that time some increase in output can be accommodated. Overall, in the short run, the quantity supplied is not very responsive to the price. By contrast, over longer periods, firms can build new factories or close old ones, hire new staff and buy in more capital and equipment. In addition, new firms can enter a market and old firms can shut down. Thus, in the long run, the quantity supplied can respond substantially to price changes.

Productive Capacity   Most businesses, in the short run, will have a finite capacity – an upper limit to the amount that they can produce at any one time determined by the quantity of factor inputs they possess. How far they are using this capacity depends, in turn, on the state of the economy. In periods of strong economic growth, firms may be operating at or near full capacity. If demand and prices are rising for the product they produce, it may be difficult for the firm to expand output and so supply may be inelastic.

When the economy is growing slowly or is contracting, some firms may find they have to cut back output and may only be operating at 60 per cent of full capacity. In this situation, if demand later increased and prices started to rise, it may be much easier for the firm to expand output relatively quickly and so supply would be more elastic.

The Size of the Firm/Industry   It is possible that, as a general rule, supply may be more elastic in smaller firms or industries than in larger ones. For example, consider a small independent furniture manufacturer. Demand for its products may rise and in response the firm may be able to buy in raw materials (wood, for example), to meet this increase in demand. While the firm will incur a cost in buying in this timber, it is unlikely that the unit cost for the material will increase. Compare this to a situation where a steel manufacturer increases its purchase of raw materials (iron ore, for example). Buying large quantities of iron ore on global commodity markets can drive up unit price and, by association, unit costs.

The response of supply to changes in price in large firms/industries, therefore, may be less elastic than in smaller firms/industries. This is also related to the number of firms in the industry – the more firms there are in the industry the easier it is to increase supply, other things being equal.

The Mobility of Factors of Production   Consider a farmer whose land is currently devoted to producing wheat. A sharp rise in the price of rape seed might encourage the farmer to switch use of land from wheat to rape seed relatively easily. The mobility of the factor of production land, in this case, is relatively high and so supply of rape seed may be relatively elastic.

A number of multinational firms that have plants in different parts of the world now build each plant to be identical. What this means is that if there is disruption to one plant the firm can more easily transfer operations to another plant elsewhere and continue production 'seamlessly'. Car manufacturers utilize such an interchangeability of parts and operations. The chassis, for example, may be identical across a range of branded car models. This is the case with some Audi, Volkswagen, Seat and Skoda models. This means that the supply may be more elastic as a result.

Compare this to the supply of highly skilled oncology consultants. An increase in the wages of oncology consultants (suggesting a shortage exists) will not mean that a renal consultant or other doctors can suddenly switch to take advantage of the higher wages and increase the supply of oncology consultants. In this example, the mobility of labour to switch between different uses is limited and so the supply of these specialist consultants is likely to be relatively inelastic.

Ease of Storing Stock/Inventory In some firms, stocks can be built up to enable the firm to respond more flexibly to changes in prices. In industries where inventory build-up is relatively easy and cheap, the price elasticity of supply is more elastic than in industries where it is much harder to do this. Consider the fresh fruit industry, for example. Storing fresh fruit is not easy because it is perishable and so the price elasticity of supply in this industry may be more inelastic.

Computing the Price Elasticity of Supply

Economists compute the price elasticity of supply as the percentage change in the quantity supplied divided by the percentage change in the price. That is:

$$\text{Price elasticity of supply} = \frac{\text{Percentage change in quantity supplied}}{\text{Percentage change in price}}$$

For example, suppose that an increase in the price of milk from €0.20 to €0.25 a litre raises the amount that dairy farmers produce from 90 000 to 106 875 litres per month. We calculate the percentage change in price as:

$$\text{Percentage change in price} = (0.25 - 0.20)/0.20 \times 100 = 25\%$$

Similarly, we calculate the percentage change in quantity supplied as the change in supply (16 875 litres) divided by the original amount (90 000 litres) multiplied by 100:

$$\text{Percentage change in quantity supplied} = 16\,875/90\,000 \times 100 = 18.75\%$$

In this case, the price elasticity of supply is:

$$\text{Price elasticity of supply} = 18.75\%/25\% = 0.75$$

In this example, the elasticity of 0.75 reflects the fact that the quantity supplied changes proportionately three-quarters as much as the price. If price rose by 15 per cent, for example, supply would rise by $0.75 \times 15 = 11.25\%$.

The Midpoint Method of Calculating Percentage Changes and Elasticities

If you try calculating the price elasticity of supply between two points on a supply curve, you will quickly notice an annoying problem: the elasticity for a movement from point A to point B seems different from the elasticity for a movement from point B to point A. For example, consider these numbers:

Point A: Price = €4 Quantity Supplied = 80
Point B: Price = €6 Quantity Supplied = 125

Going from point A to point B, the price rises by 50 per cent – the change in price divided by the original price × 100 (2/4 × 100), and the quantity rises by 56.25 per cent (the change in quantity supplied divided by the original supply × 100: 45/80 × 100), indicating that the price elasticity of supply is 56.25/50 or 1.125.

By contrast, going from point B to point A, the price falls by 33 per cent (2/6 × 100), and the quantity falls by 36 per cent (45/125 × 100), indicating that the price elasticity of supply is 36/33 or 1.09.

Note, in the working above we have rounded the fall in price to the nearest whole number (33 per cent).

One way to avoid this problem is to use the *midpoint method* for calculating elasticities. In the example above we used a standard way to compute a percentage change – divide the change by the initial level and multiply by 100. By contrast, the midpoint method computes a percentage change by dividing the change by the midpoint (or average) of the initial and final levels. In our example, the midpoint between point A and point B is:

Midpoint: Price = €5 Quantity = 102.5

€5 is the midpoint of €4 and €6. Therefore, according to the midpoint method, a change from €4 to €6 is considered a 40 per cent rise, because $((6 - 4)/5) \times 100 = 40$. Similarly, a change from €6 to €4 is considered a 40 per cent fall $((4 - 6)/5) \times 100 = -40$. Looking at the quantity, moving from Point A to Point B gives $(125 - 80)/102.5 \times 100 = 43.9\%$ and for a price fall $(80 - 125)/102.5 \times 100 = -43.9\%$.

Because the midpoint method gives the same answer regardless of the direction of change (as indicated by the negative sign), it is often used when calculating price elasticities between two points.

According to the midpoint method, when going from point A to point B, the price rises by 40 per cent, and the quantity rises by 43.9 per cent. Similarly, when going from point B to point A, the price falls by 40 per cent, and the quantity falls by 43.9 per cent. In both directions, the price elasticity of supply equals 1.0975 (1.1 to 1 decimal place).

We can express the midpoint method with the following formula for the price elasticity of supply between two points, denoted (Q_1, P_1) and (Q_2, P_2):

$$\text{Price elasticity of supply} = \frac{(Q_2 - Q_1)/([Q_2 + Q_1]/2)}{(P_2 - P_1)/([P_2 + P_1]/2)}$$

The numerator is the percentage change in quantity computed using the midpoint method, and the denominator is the percentage change in price computed using the midpoint method.

The Variety of Supply Curves

Because the price elasticity of supply measures the responsiveness of quantity supplied to the change in price, it is reflected in the appearance of the supply curve (assuming we are using similar scales on the axes of diagrams being used). Figure 5.1 shows five cases. In the extreme case of a zero elasticity, as shown in panel (a), supply is *perfectly inelastic* and the supply curve is vertical. In this case, the quantity

FIGURE 5.1

The Price Elasticity of Supply

The price elasticity of supply determines whether the supply curve is steep or flat (assuming that the scale used for the axes is the same). Note that all percentage changes are calculated using the midpoint method.

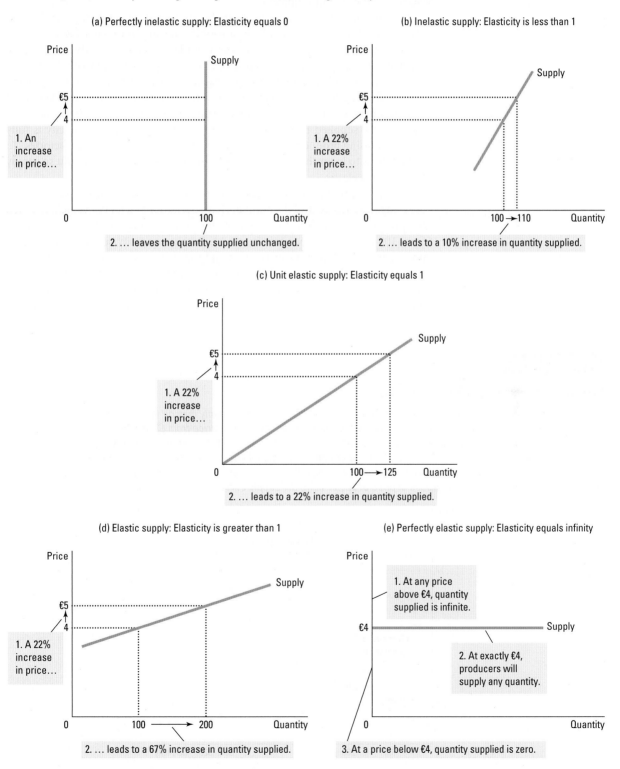

supplied is the same regardless of the price. As the elasticity rises, the supply curve gets flatter, which shows that the quantity supplied responds more to changes in the price. At the opposite extreme, shown in panel (e), supply is *perfectly elastic*. This occurs as the price elasticity of supply approaches infinity and the supply curve becomes horizontal, meaning that very small changes in the price lead to very large changes in the quantity supplied.

In some markets, the elasticity of supply is not constant but varies over the supply curve. Figure 5.2 shows a typical case for an industry in which firms have factories with a limited capacity for production. For low levels of quantity supplied, the elasticity of supply is high, indicating that firms respond substantially to changes in the price. In this region, firms have capacity for production that is not being used, such as buildings and machinery sitting idle for all or part of the day. Small increases in price make it profitable for firms to begin using this idle capacity. As the quantity supplied rises, firms begin to reach capacity. Once capacity is fully used, increasing production further requires the construction of new factories. To induce firms to incur this extra expense, the price must rise substantially, so supply becomes less elastic.

Figure 5.2 presents a numerical example of this phenomenon. Each case uses the midpoint method and the numbers have been rounded for convenience. When the price rises from €3 to €4 (a 29 per cent increase), the quantity supplied rises from 100 to 200 (a 67 per cent increase). Because quantity supplied moves proportionately more than the price, the supply curve has elasticity greater than 1. By contrast, when the price rises from €12 to €15 (a 22 per cent increase), the quantity supplied rises from 500 to 525 (a 5 per cent increase). In this case, quantity supplied moves proportionately less than the price, so the elasticity is less than 1.

FIGURE 5.2

How the Price Elasticity of Supply Can Vary

Because firms often have a maximum capacity for production, the elasticity of supply may be very high at low levels of quantity supplied and very low at high levels of quantity supplied. Here, an increase in price from €3 to €4 increases the quantity supplied from 100 to 200. Because the increase in quantity supplied of 67 per cent (computed using the midpoint method) is larger than the increase in price of 29 per cent, the supply curve is elastic in this range. By contrast, when the price rises from €12 to €15, the quantity supplied rises only from 500 to 525. Because the increase in quantity supplied of 5 per cent (rounded up) is smaller than the increase in price of 22 per cent, the supply curve is inelastic in this range.

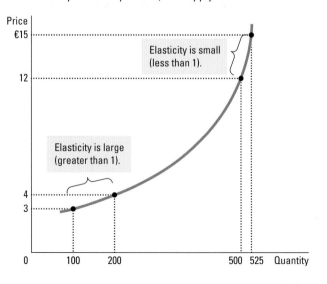

Total Revenue and the Price Elasticity of Supply

When studying changes in supply in a market we are often interested in the result-ing changes in the **total revenue** received by producers. In any market, total rev-enue received by sellers is the price of the good times the quantity of the good sold ($P \times Q$). This is highlighted in Figure 5.3 which shows an upward sloping supply curve with an assumed price of €5 and a supply of 100 units. The height of the box under the supply curve is P and the width is Q. The area of this box, $P \times Q$, equals the total revenue received in this market. In Figure 5.3, where P = €5 and Q = 100, total revenue is €5 × 100, or €500.

total revenue the amount received by sellers of a good, com-puted as the price of the good times the quantity sold

FIGURE 5.3

The Supply Curve and Total Revenue

The total amount received by sellers equals the area of the box under the supply curve, P × Q. Here, at a price of €5, the quantity supplied is 100 and the total revenue is €500.

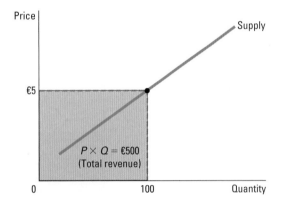

The change in total revenue as a result of a price change will depend on the price elasticity of supply. If supply is inelastic, as in Figure 5.4, then an increase in

FIGURE 5.4

How Total Revenue Changes When Price Changes: Inelastic Supply

With an inelastic supply curve, an increase in the price leads to an increase in quantity supplied that is proportionately smaller. Therefore, total revenue (the product of price and quantity) increases. Here, an increase in the price from €4 to €5 causes the quantity supplied to rise from 80 to 100, and total revenue rises from €320 to €500.

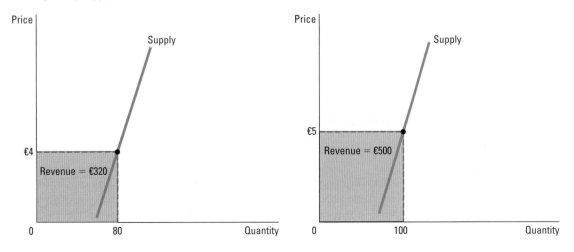

the price which is proportionately larger causes an increase in total revenue. Here an increase in price from €4 to €5 causes the quantity supplied to rise only from 80 to 100, and so total revenue rises from €320 to €500.

If supply is elastic then a similar increase in price brings about a much larger than proportionate increase in supply. In Figure 5.5, we assume a price of €4 and a supply of 80 with total revenue of €320. Now a price increase from €4 to €5 leads to a much greater than proportionate increase in supply from 80 to 150 with total revenue rising to €750.

FIGURE 5.5

How Total Revenue Changes When Price Changes: Elastic Supply

With an elastic supply curve, an increase in price leads to an increase in quantity supplied that is proportionately larger. Therefore, total revenue (the product of price and quantity) increases. Here, an increase in the price from €4 to €5 causes the quantity supplied to rise from 80 to 150, and total revenue rises from €320 to €750.

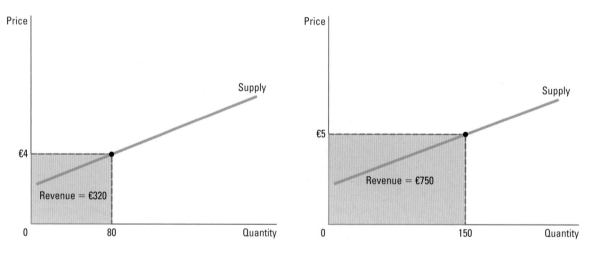

THE PRICE ELASTICITY OF DEMAND

Businesses cannot directly control demand. They can seek to influence demand (and do) by utilizing a variety of strategies and tactics but ultimately the consumer decides whether to buy a product or not. One important way in which consumer behaviour can be influenced is through a firm changing the prices of its goods (many firms do have some control over the price they can charge although as we have seen, in perfectly competitive markets this is not the case as the firm is a price taker). An understanding of the price elasticity of demand is important in anticipating the likely effects of changes in price on demand.

CASE STUDY

Travel and Fuel Prices

The UK pump price of petrol or diesel fell by around 20 per cent in 2014, but what effect has this had on demand? Perhaps not as much as you might expect, since our journey into work or collecting and dropping off our children to their school and friends will broadly remain the same. Overall the link between changes in demand and fuel price changes is not that strong.

According to the Energy Information Administration (EIA), in the USA petrol and diesel prices would have to decrease by between 25 per cent to 50 per cent for car travel to increase 1 per cent.

This calculation suggests that car fuel is price inelastic, but it is difficult to state an accurate level of elasticity. This is because demand is also influenced by other factors than price. For example, older people drive less miles than younger people and the UK has an ageing population. The level of car ownership, where people live and changes in the quality and price of public transport are also contributory factors. In fact, 1.8 per cent more cars were registered for use in the UK during 2014. In the three months to the end of September 2014, there was a 2.2 per cent increase in the total distance travelled in the UK compared to the same time a year earlier.

The implication is that lower fuel prices will individually not lead to us to drive a lot further, but it will lead to an increase in our disposable income. If we are spending less on fuel for our cars than before the price drop, then we can use the surplus money for other things such as air travel to go on holiday.

If a fall in the price of aviation fuel was to persist and led to a fall in air fares of say 10 per cent, it would likely lead to an increase in passenger numbers of over 10 per cent. Our demand for leisure air travel is price elastic.

The price drop of fuel should have been good news for airline companies and passengers. The low-fare carrier easyJet saw passenger numbers rise 6.5 per cent and its seats occupied rise to nearly 91 per cent. Its competitor, Ryanair, had a similar increase of 6 per cent. However, it is surprisingly complicated to attribute the components of added value (of which fuel is one) for an airline ticket, not least because different prices are charged to different consumers for the same journey in similar seats. As well as this price discrimination, the ticket price includes a charge to cover airport duties and overheads, so in effect fuel is only part of an airline's costs and accounts for less than half of the price of a ticket. Airline companies understand the impact of airfare changes on demand, and plan prices to keep their airplanes as close to full capacity as possible. Operating close to capacity means they may not have to pass on the fuel savings to their customers.

References: **EIA http://www.eia.gov/todayinenergy/detail.cfm?id=19191**

**Telegraph http://www.telegraph.co.uk/finance/personalfinance/insurance/11341256
/How-falling-petrol-prices-pushed-up-car-insurance-costs.html**

The Price Elasticity of Demand and Its Determinants

price elasticity of demand
a measure of how much the quantity demanded of a good responds to a change in the price of that good, computed as the percentage change in quantity demanded divided by the percentage change in price

The law of demand states that a fall in the price of a good raises the quantity demanded. The **price elasticity of demand** measures how much the quantity demanded responds to a change in price. Demand for a good is said to be *elastic* or price sensitive if the quantity demanded responds substantially to changes in the price. Demand is said to be *inelastic* or *price insensitive* if the quantity demanded responds only slightly to changes in the price.

The price elasticity of demand for any good measures how willing consumers are to move to or away from a good as its price changes. Thus, the elasticity reflects the many economic, social and psychological forces that influence consumer tastes. Based on experience, however, we can state some general rules about what determines the price elasticity of demand.

Availability of Close Substitutes Goods with close substitutes tend to have a more elastic demand because it is easier for consumers to switch from that good to others. For example, butter and spread are easily substitutable. A small increase in the price of butter, assuming the price of spread is held fixed, causes the quantity of butter sold to fall by a relatively large amount. As a general rule, the closer the substitute the more elastic the good is because it is easier for consumers to switch from one to the other. By contrast, because eggs are a food without a close substitute, the demand for eggs is likely to be less elastic than the demand for butter.

Necessities versus Luxuries Necessities tend to have relatively inelastic demands, whereas luxuries have relatively elastic demands. People use gas and electricity to heat their homes and cook their food. If the price of gas and electricity rose together, people would not demand dramatically less of them. They might try and be more energy-efficient and reduce their demand a little, but they would still need hot food and warm homes. By contrast, when the price of sailing dinghies rises, the quantity of sailing dinghies demanded falls substantially. The reason is that most people view hot food and warm homes as necessities and a sailing dinghy as a luxury. Of course, whether a good is a necessity or a luxury depends not on the intrinsic properties of the good but on the preferences of the buyer. For an avid sailor with little concern over their health, sailing dinghies might be a necessity with inelastic demand and hot food and a warm place to sleep a luxury with elastic demand.

Definition of the Market The elasticity of demand in any market depends on how we draw the boundaries of the market. Narrowly defined markets tend to have more elastic demand than broadly defined markets, because it is easier to find close substitutes for narrowly defined goods. For example, food, a broad category, has a fairly inelastic demand because there are no good substitutes for food. Ice cream, a narrower category, has a more elastic demand because it is easy to substitute other desserts for ice cream. Vanilla ice cream, a very narrow category, has a very elastic demand because other flavours of ice cream are good substitutes for vanilla.

Proportion of Income Devoted to the Product Some products have a relatively high price and take a larger proportion of income than others. Buying a new suite of furniture for a lounge, for example, tends to take up a large amount of income, whereas buying an ice cream might account for only a tiny proportion of income. If the price of a three-piece suite rises by 10 per cent, therefore, this is likely to have a greater effect on demand for this furniture than a similar 10 per cent increase in the price of an ice cream. The higher the proportion of income devoted to the product the greater the elasticity is likely to be.

Time Horizon   Goods tend to have more elastic demand over longer time horizons. When the price of petrol rises, the quantity of petrol demanded falls only slightly in the first few months. Over time, however, people buy more fuel-efficient cars, switch to public transport and move closer to where they work. Within several years, the quantity of petrol demanded falls more substantially. Similarly, if the price of a unit of electricity rises much above an equivalent energy unit of gas, demand may fall only slightly in the short run because many people already have electric cookers or electric heating appliances installed in their homes and cannot easily switch. If the price difference persists over several years, however, people may find it worth their while to replace their old electric heating and cooking appliances with new gas appliances and the demand for electricity will fall.

Computing the Price Elasticity of Demand

The principles for computing price elasticity of demand are similar to those discussed when we looked at price elasticity of supply. The price elasticity of demand is computed as the percentage change in the quantity demanded divided by the percentage change in the price. That is:

$$\text{Price elasticity of demand} = \frac{\text{Percentage change in quantity demanded}}{\text{Percentage change in price}}$$

Suppose that a 10 per cent increase in the price of a packet of breakfast cereal causes the amount you buy to fall by 20 per cent. Because the quantity demanded of a good is negatively related to its price, the percentage change in quantity will always have the opposite sign to the percentage change in price. In this example, the percentage change in price is a *positive* 10 per cent (reflecting an increase), and the percentage change in quantity demanded is a *negative* 20 per cent (reflecting a decrease). For this reason, price elasticities of demand are sometimes reported as negative numbers. In this book we follow the common practice of dropping the minus sign and reporting all price elasticities as positive numbers. (Mathematicians call this the *absolute value*.) With this convention, a larger price elasticity implies a greater responsiveness of quantity demanded to price.

Using this convention we calculate the elasticity of demand as:

$$\text{Price elasticity of demand} = \frac{20\%}{10\%} = 2$$

In this example, the elasticity is 2, reflecting that the change in the quantity demanded is proportionately twice as large as the change in the price.

Pitfall Prevention We have used the term 'relatively' elastic or inelastic at times throughout the analysis so far. It is important to remember that elasticity can be any value greater than or equal to 0. We can look at two goods, both of which are classed as 'inelastic' but where one is more inelastic than the other. If we are comparing good X, which has an elasticity of 0.2 and good Y, which has an elasticity of 0.5, then both are inelastic but good Y is *relatively* elastic by comparison. As with so much of economics, careful use of terminology is important in conveying a clear understanding.

Using the Midpoint Method

As with the price elasticity of supply, we use the midpoint method to calculate price elasticity of demand. We can express the midpoint method with the following formula for the price elasticity of demand between two points, denoted (Q_1, P_1) and (Q_2, P_2):

$$\text{Price elasticity of demand} = \frac{(Q_2 - Q_1)/([Q_2 + Q_1]/2)}{(P_2 - P_1)/([P_2 + P_1]/2)}$$

The numerator is the proportionate change in quantity, and the denominator is the proportionate change in price, both computed using the midpoint method.

The Variety of Demand Curves

Economists classify demand curves according to their elasticity. Demand is *elastic* when the elasticity is greater than 1, so that quantity changes proportionately more than the price. Demand is *inelastic* when the elasticity is less than 1, so that quantity moves proportionately less than the price. If the elasticity is exactly 1, so that quantity moves the same amount proportionately as price, demand is said to have *unit elasticity*.

Because the price elasticity of demand measures how much quantity demanded responds to changes in the price, it is closely related to the slope of the demand curve. The following heuristic (rule of thumb), again assuming we are using comparable scales on the axes, is a useful guide: the flatter the demand curve that passes through a given point, the greater the price elasticity of demand. The steeper the demand curve that passes through a given point, the smaller the price elasticity of demand.

Figure 5.6 shows five cases, each of which uses the same scale on each axis. This is an important thing to remember because simply looking at a graph and the shape of the curve without recognizing the scale can result in incorrect conclusions about elasticity. In the extreme case of a zero elasticity shown in panel (a), demand is *perfectly inelastic*, and the demand curve is vertical. In this case, regardless of the price, the quantity demanded stays the same. As the elasticity rises, the demand curve gets flatter and flatter, as shown in panels (b), (c) and (d). At the opposite extreme shown in panel (e), demand is *perfectly elastic*. This occurs as the price elasticity of demand approaches infinity and the demand curve becomes horizontal, reflecting the fact that very small changes in the price lead to huge changes in the quantity demanded.

Total Expenditure, Total Revenue and the Price Elasticity of Demand

When studying changes in demand in a market, we are interested in the amount paid by buyers of the good which will in turn represent the total revenue that sellers receive. **Total expenditure** is given by the total amount bought multiplied by the price paid. We can show total expenditure graphically, as in Figure 5.7. The height of the box under the demand curve is P, and the width is Q. The area of this box, $P \times Q$, equals the total expenditure in this market. In Figure 5.7, where $P = €4$ and $Q = 100$, total expenditure is $€4 \times 100 = €400$.

total expenditure the amount paid by buyers, computed as the price of the good times the quantity purchased

FIGURE 5.6

The Price Elasticity of Demand

The steepness of the demand curve indicates the price elasticity of demand (assuming the scale used on the axes are the same). Note that all percentage changes are calculated using the midpoint method.

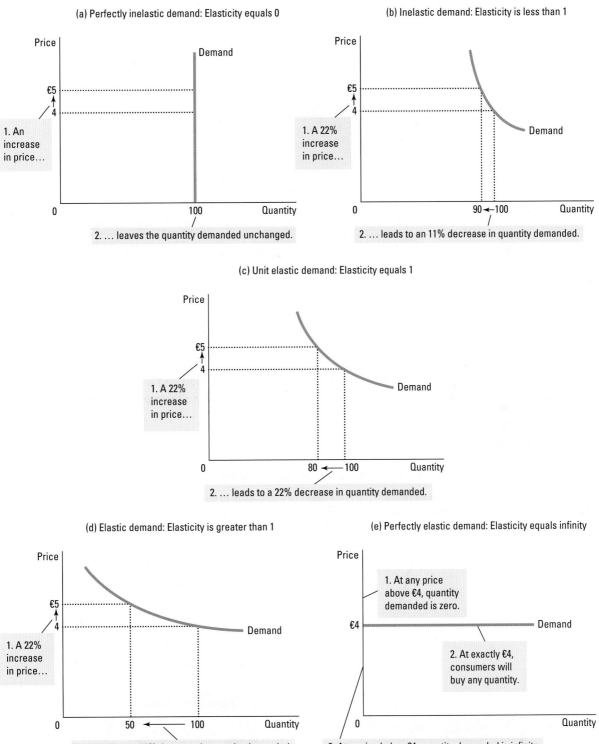

FIGURE 5.7

Total Expenditure

The total amount paid by buyers, and received as revenue by sellers, equals the area of the box under the demand curve, $P \times Q$. Here, at a price of €4, the quantity demanded is 100, and total expenditure is €400.

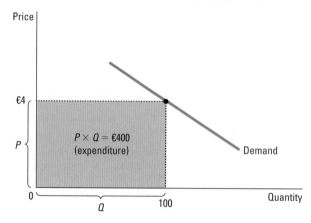

For businesses, having some understanding of the price elasticity of demand is important in decision making. If a firm is thinking of changing price how will the demand for its product react? The firm knows that there is an inverse relationship between price and demand but the effect on its revenue will be dependent on the price elasticity of demand. It is entirely possible that a firm could reduce its price and increase total revenue. Equally, a firm could raise price and find its total revenue falling. At first glance this might sound counter-intuitive but it all depends on the price elasticity of demand for the product.

If demand is price inelastic, as in Figure 5.8, then an increase in the price causes an increase in total expenditure. Here an increase in price from €1 to €3 causes the quantity demanded to fall only from 100 to 80, and so total expenditure rises from €100 to €240. An increase in price raises $P \times Q$ because the fall in Q is proportionately smaller than the rise in P.

FIGURE 5.8

How Total Expenditure Changes When Price Changes: Inelastic Demand

With an inelastic demand curve, an increase in the price leads to a decrease in quantity demanded that is proportionately smaller. Therefore, total expenditure (the product of price and quantity) increases. Here, an increase in the price from €1 to €3 causes the quantity demanded to fall from 100 to 80, and total expenditure rises from €100 to €240.

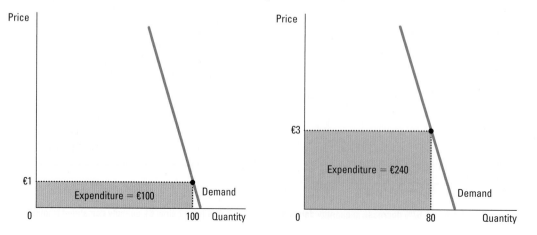

We obtain the opposite result if demand is elastic: an increase in the price causes a decrease in total expenditure. In Figure 5.9, for instance, when the price rises from €4 to €5, the quantity demanded falls from 50 to 20, and so total expenditure falls from €200 to €100. Because demand is elastic, the reduction in the quantity demanded is so great that it more than offsets the increase in the price. That is, an increase in price reduces $P \times Q$ because the fall in Q is proportionately greater than the rise in P.

FIGURE 5.9

How Total Expenditure Changes When Price Changes: Elastic Demand

With an elastic demand curve, an increase in the price leads to a decrease in quantity demanded that is proportionately larger. Therefore, total expenditure (the product of price and quantity) decreases. Here, an increase in the price from €4 to €5 causes the quantity demanded to fall from 50 to 20, so total expenditure falls from €200 to €100.

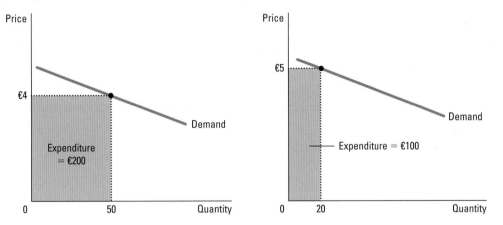

Although the examples in these two figures are extreme, they illustrate a general rule:

- When demand is price inelastic (a price elasticity less than 1), price and total expenditure move in the same direction.
- When demand is price elastic (a price elasticity greater than 1), price and total expenditure move in opposite directions.
- If demand is unit price elastic (a price elasticity exactly equal to 1), total expenditure remains constant when price changes.

? **what if...** a high street clothes retailer is planning its summer sales campaign and wants to cut prices to help it get rid of stock, increase footfall (the number of customers entering its premises) and revenue. It knows of the concept of price elasticity of demand but how does it set about estimating the price elasticity of demand for its products so that it can more accurately set price cuts which will achieve its aims?

Elasticity and Total Expenditure Along a Linear Demand Curve

Look at the straight line demand curve shown in Figure 5.10. A linear demand curve has a constant slope. The slope is defined as the ratio of the change in price ('rise') to the change in quantity ('run'). This particular demand curve's slope is constant because each €1 increase in price causes the same 2-unit decrease in the quantity demanded.

FIGURE 5.10

Elasticity of a Linear Demand Curve

The slope of a linear demand curve is constant, but its elasticity is not. The demand schedule in the table was used to calculate the price elasticity of demand by the midpoint method. At points with a low price and high quantity, the demand curve is price inelastic. At points with a high price and low quantity, the demand curve is price elastic.

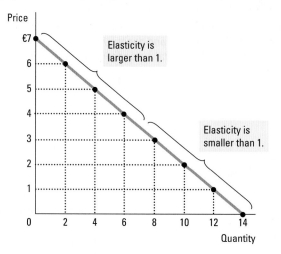

Price	Quantity	Total revenue (Price × Quantity)	Per cent change in price	Per cent change in quantity	Price elasticity	Quantity description
€7	0	€0	15	200	13.0	Elastic
6	2	12	18	67	3.7	Elastic
5	4	20	22	40	1.8	Elastic
4	6	24	29	29	1.0	Unit elastic
3	8	24	40	22	0.6	Inelastic
2	10	20	67	18	0.3	Inelastic
1	12	12	200	15	0.1	Inelastic
0	14	0				

Even though the slope of a linear demand curve is constant, the elasticity is not. The reason is that the slope is the ratio of *changes* in the two variables, whereas the elasticity is the ratio of *percentage changes* in the two variables. You can see this by looking at the table in Figure 5.10, which shows the demand schedule for the linear demand curve in the graph. The table uses the midpoint method to calculate the price elasticity of demand. At points with a low price and high quantity, the demand curve is price inelastic. At points with a high price and low quantity, the demand curve is price elastic.

The table also presents total expenditure at each point on the demand curve. These numbers illustrate the relationship between total expenditure and price elasticity. When the price is €1, for instance, demand is price inelastic and a price increase to €2 raises total expenditure. When the price is €5, demand is price elastic, and a price increase to €6 reduces total expenditure. Between €3 and €4, demand is exactly unit price elastic and total expenditure is the same at these two prices.

In analysing markets, we will use both demand and supply curves on the same diagram. We will refer to changes in total revenue when looking at the effects of changes in equilibrium conditions but remember that revenue for sellers represents the same identity as expenditure for buyers.

OTHER DEMAND ELASTICITIES

In addition to the price elasticity of demand, economists also use other elasticities to describe the behaviour of buyers in a market.

The Income Elasticity of Demand

The **income elasticity of demand** measures how the quantity demanded changes as consumer income changes. It is calculated as the percentage change in quantity demanded divided by the percentage change in income.

$$\text{Income elasticity of demand} = \frac{\text{Percentage change in quantity demanded}}{\text{Percentage change in income}}$$

> **income elasticity of demand** a measure of how much the quantity demanded of a good responds to a change in consumers' income, computed as the percentage change in quantity demanded divided by the percentage change in income

Most goods are *normal goods*: higher income increases quantity demanded. Because quantity demanded and income change in the same direction, normal goods have positive income elasticities. A few goods, such as bus rides, are *inferior goods*: higher income lowers the quantity demanded. Because quantity demanded and income move in opposite directions, inferior goods have negative income elasticities.

Even among normal goods, income elasticities vary substantially in size. Necessities, such as food and clothing, tend to have small income elasticities because consumers, regardless of how low their incomes, choose to buy some of these goods. Luxuries, such as caviar and diamonds, tend to have high income elasticities because consumers feel that they can do without these goods altogether if their income is too low.

The Cross-Price Elasticity of Demand

The **cross-price elasticity of demand** measures how the quantity demanded of one good changes as the price of another good changes. It is calculated as the percentage change in quantity demanded of good 1 divided by the percentage change in the price of good 2.

$$\text{Cross-price elasticity of demand} = \frac{\text{Percentage change in quantity demanded of good 1}}{\text{Percentage change in the price of good 2}}$$

> **cross-price elasticity of demand** a measure of how much the quantity demanded of one good responds to a change in the price of another good, computed as the percentage change in quantity demanded of the first good divided by the percentage change in the price of the second good

Whether the cross-price elasticity is a positive or negative number depends on whether the two goods are substitutes or complements. Substitutes are goods that are typically used in place of one another, such as broccoli and cabbage. An increase in the price of broccoli induces people to eat cabbage instead. Because the price of broccoli and the quantity of cabbage demanded move in the same direction, the cross-price elasticity is positive. Conversely, complements are goods that are typically used together, such as computers and software. In this case, the cross-price elasticity is negative, indicating that an increase in the price of computers reduces the quantity of software demanded. As with price elasticity of demand, cross-price elasticity may increase over time: a change in the price of electricity will have little effect on demand for gas in the short run but much stronger effects over several years.

Pitfall Prevention When referring to elasticity it is easy to forget which *type* of elasticity you are referring to. It is sensible to ensure that you use the correct terminology to make sure you are thinking clearly about the analysis and being accurate in your referencing to elasticity. If you are analysing the effect of changes in income on demand then you must specify *income elasticity*, whereas if you are analysing changes in prices on supply then you must specify *price elasticity of supply* and so on.

FYI

The Mathematics of Elasticity

We present this section for those who require some introduction to the maths behind elasticity. For those who do not need such a technical explanation, this section can be safely skipped without affecting your overall understanding of the concept of elasticity.

Point Elasticity of Demand

Figure 5.10 showed that the value for elasticity can vary at every point along a straight line demand curve. Point elasticity of demand allows us to be able to be more specific about the elasticity at different points. In the formula repeated below, the numerator (the top half of the fraction) describes the change in quantity in relation to the base quantity and the denominator the change in price in relation to the base price.

$$ped = \frac{\left(\dfrac{Q_2 - Q_1}{((Q_2 + Q_1)/2)}\right) \times 100}{\left(\dfrac{P_2 - P_1}{((P_2 + P_1)/2)}\right) \times 100}$$

If we cancel out the 100s in the above equation and rewrite it a little more elegantly (using the Greek letter delta (Δ) to mean 'change in') we get:

$$ped = \frac{\dfrac{\Delta Q}{Q}}{\dfrac{\Delta P}{P}}$$

Where the $\Delta Q = Q_2 - Q_1$ and $\Delta P = P_2 - P_1$

Rearranging the above we get:

$$ped = \frac{\Delta Q}{Q} \times \frac{P}{\Delta P}$$

There is no set order required to this equation so it can be re-written as:

$$ped = \frac{\Delta Q}{\Delta P} \times \frac{P}{Q}$$

The eagle eyed among you will notice that the expression $\Delta Q/\Delta P$ is the slope of a linear demand curve. Look at the example in Figure 5.11. Here we have two demand curves, D_1 and D_2, given by the equations:

$$P = 20 - 5Q$$
and
$$Q = 5 - 0.25P$$

For demand curve D_1, the vertical intercept is 20 and the horizontal intercept is 4 and so the slope of the line D_1 is −5.

FIGURE 5.11

Point Elasticity of Demand

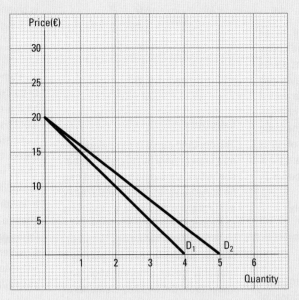

For demand curve D_2, the vertical intercept is 20 and the horizontal intercept is 5, the slope of the line D_2 is −4. To verify this let us take demand curve D_1; if price were 10 then the quantity would be $20 - 5Q$. Rearranging

gives $5Q = 20 - 10$, $5Q = 10$, so $Q = 2$. Looking at demand curve D_2 if price were 10, then the quantity would be $5 - (0.25 \times 10) = 2.5$.

Now let us assume that price falls from 10 to 5 in each case. The

quantity demanded for D_1 would now be $5 = 20 - 5Q$, $5Q = 15$, $Q = 3$ and for D_2, $5 - (0.25 \times 5) = 3.75$.

Representing this graphically for demand curve D_1, we get the result shown in Figure 5.12.

FIGURE 5.12

Price Elasticity of Demand

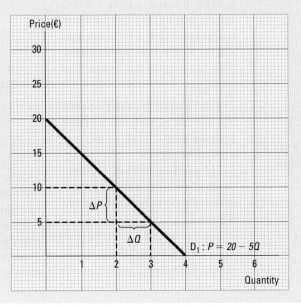

The slope of the line as drawn is:

$$\frac{\Delta P}{\Delta Q} = \frac{-5}{1} = -5$$

The slope is the same at all points along a linear demand curve. The ratio of P/Q at different points on the demand curve, however, will differ because of the price which we start with prior to a change. Using demand curve D_1, the ratio of P/Q at the initial price of 10 is $10/2 = 5$. At a price of 5, the ratio of P/Q given by the demand curve D_1 would be $5/3 = 1.67$.

Going back to our formula:

$$ped = \frac{\Delta Q}{\Delta P} \times \frac{P}{Q}$$

The first part of the equation $(\Delta Q/\Delta P)$ is the (inverse) slope of the demand curve and the second part of the equation P/Q gives us a specific point on the demand curve relating to a particular price and quantity combination. Multiplying these two terms gives us the price elasticity of demand at a particular point and so is referred to as *point elasticity of demand*. The price elasticity of demand when price changes from 10 to 5 in demand curve D_1 above, would be:

$$ped = \frac{\Delta Q}{\Delta P} \times \frac{P}{Q}$$

$$ped = \frac{1}{5} \times \frac{10}{2}$$

$$ped = 1$$

If we were looking at a fall in price from 15 to 10 we would get:

$$ped = \frac{\Delta Q}{\Delta P} \times \frac{P}{Q}$$

$$ped = \frac{1}{5} \times \frac{15}{1}$$

$$ped = 3$$

And if looking at a price fall from 5 to 2.5 then we would get:

$$ped = \frac{\Delta Q}{\Delta P} \times \frac{P}{Q}$$

$$ped = \frac{0.5}{2.5} \times \frac{5}{3}$$

$$ped = 0.33$$

Calculus

The demand curve is often depicted as a linear curve but there is no reason why it should be linear and can be curvilinear. To measure elasticity accurately in this case economists use calculus.

If you are following a quantitative methods course you will probably cover differentiation and integration, the two key elements of calculus. Differentiation is used to calculate rates of change through finding a derivative. A derivative tells you the slope of a curve at a particular point. The slope of a curve is given by $\frac{\Delta y}{\Delta x}$ or $\frac{rise}{run}$. The derivative is rise over run per run or the rate of change in one variable (say quantity) as a result of a very small or infinitesimal change in another variable (say price). Given a basic function $y = ax + b$ the derivative is found using the linear function rule $\frac{dy}{dx} = a$. If the function is of the form $y = x^n$ the derivative, $\frac{dy}{dx}$ is found using the power rule: $\frac{dy}{dx} = nx^{n-1}$.

The rules of calculus applied to a demand curve give a far more accurate measurement of *ped* at a particular point.

For a linear demand function, the approximation to the point elasticity at the initial price and quantity is given by:

$$\frac{(Q_2 - Q_1)}{(P_2 - P_1)} \cdot \frac{P_1}{Q_1}$$

which gives exactly the same result as the point elasticity which is defined in terms of calculus and is given by :

$$\frac{dQ}{dP} \cdot \frac{P}{Q}$$

Point elasticity defined in terms of calculus gives a precise answer; all the other formulae are approximations of some sort. The formula looks similar but it must be remembered that what we are talking about in this instance is an infinitesimally small change in quantity following an infinitesimally small change in price expressed by the formula:

where $\frac{dQ}{dP}$ is the derivative of a linear function. Given our basic linear equation of the form:

$Q = a - bP$, the linear function rule gives $\frac{dQ}{dP}$ as the coefficient of $P - (-b)$

Take the following demand equation:

$$Q = 60 - 3P$$

To find the price elasticity of demand when price $= 15$. First of all we need to find Q.

$$Q = 60 - 3P$$
$$Q = 60 - 3(15)$$
$$Q = 15$$

We calculate $\frac{dQ}{dP}$ as -3. Substitute this into the formula to get:

$$ped = -3\left(\frac{15}{15}\right)$$

$$ped = -3$$

It is useful to remember that given an elasticity figure we can calculate the expected change in demand as a result of a change in price. For example, if the *ped* is given as 0.6 then an increase in price of 5 per cent will result in a fall in quantity demanded of 3 per cent.

By using the inverse of the elasticity equation, for any given value of *ped* we can calculate how much of a price change is required to bring about a desired change in quantity demanded. Suppose that a government wanted to reduce the demand for motor vehicles as part of a policy to reduce congestion and pollution. What sort of price change might be required to bring about a 10 per cent fall in demand?

Assume that the *ped* for motor vehicles is 0.8. The inverse of the basic elasticity formula is:

$$\frac{1}{ped} - \frac{\%\Delta P}{\%\Delta Q}$$

Substituting our known values into the formula we get:

$$\frac{1}{0.8} = \frac{\%\Delta P}{10}$$

$$1.25 = \frac{\%\Delta P}{10}$$

$$\%\Delta P - 12.5$$

To bring about a reduction in demand of 10 per cent, the price of motor vehicles would have to rise by 12.5 per cent.

Other Elasticities

Income and cross-elasticity of demand are all treated in exactly the same way as the analysis of price elasticity of demand above.

Income elasticity of demand (yed) would be:

$$yed = \frac{\Delta Q}{\Delta Y} \cdot \frac{Y}{Q}$$

Using calculus:

$$yed = \frac{dQ}{dY} \cdot \frac{Y}{Q}$$

For cross-elasticity the formulas would be:

$$xed = \frac{\Delta Q_a}{\Delta P_b} \times \frac{P_b}{Q_a}$$

$$xed = \frac{dQ_a}{dP_b} \times \frac{P_b}{Q_a}$$

Where Q_a is the quantity demanded of one good, *a*, and P_b is the price of a related good, *b* (either a substitute or a complement).

In Chapter 4 we saw that demand can be expressed as a multivariate function where demand is dependent on a range of variables which include price, incomes, tastes and so on. It is possible to calculate the elasticities of all these other factors using the same principles as those outlined above. In each case it is usual to calculate the elasticity with respect to a change in one of the variables whilst holding the others constant.

For example, take the demand equation $Q = 1400 - 4P + 0.04Y$. This equation tells us that demand is dependent on the price and also the level of income. From this equation we can calculate the *ped* and *yed*. In this example we will use calculus to find both elasticities assuming $P = 50$ and $Y = 8000$. Given these values:

$$Q = 1400 - 4(50) + 0.04(8000)$$

$$Q = 1400 - 200 + 320$$

$$Q = 1520$$

With:

$$\frac{dQ}{dP} = -4$$

$$ped = -4\left(\frac{50}{1520}\right)$$

$$ped = -0.132$$

Given:

$$\frac{dQ}{dY} = 0.04$$

$$yed = 0.04\left(\frac{8000}{1520}\right)$$

$$yed = 0.21$$

Now look at this demand equation:

$$Q_a = 100 - 8P_a - 6P_b + 4P_c + 0.015Y$$

This equation gives the relationship between demand and the prices of other goods labelled *a*, *b* and *c* respectively. We can use this to find the respective cross-elasticities. Assume that the price of good *a* is 20, the price of good *b*, 40, the price of good *c*, 80 and $Y = 20\,000$. Substituting these into our formula gives:

$$Q_a = 100 - 8(20) - 6(40)$$
$$+ 4(80) + 0.015(20\,000)$$

$$Q_a = 100 - 160 - 240 + 320 + 300$$

$$Q_a = 320$$

The change in demand of good *a* with respect to changes in the price of good *b* is given by:

$$\frac{dQ_a}{dP_b} = -6$$

$$xed = -6\left(\frac{40}{320}\right)$$

$$xed = -6(0.125)$$

$$xed = -0.75$$

The relationship between good *a* and *b* is that they are complements – a rise in the price of good *b* will lead to a fall in the quantity demanded of good *a*.

The change in the price of good *a* with respect to changes in the price of good *c* is given by:

$$\frac{dQ_a}{dP_c} = 4$$

$$xed = 4\left(\frac{80}{320}\right)$$

$$xed = 4(0.25)$$

$$xed = 1$$

In this case the relationship between the two goods is that they are substitutes – a rise in the price of good c would lead to a rise in the quantity demanded of good a.

Price Elasticity of Supply

Many of the principles outlined above apply also to the price elasticity of supply. The formula for the price elasticity of supply (*pes*) using the point method is:

$$pes = \frac{\Delta Q_s}{\Delta P} \times \frac{P}{Q_s}$$

Using calculus:

$$pes = \frac{dQ_s}{dP} \times \frac{P}{Q_s}$$

However, we need to note a particular issue with *pes* which relates to the graphical representation of supply curves.

This is summarized in the following:

- A straight line supply curve intersecting the y-axis at a positive value has a *pes* > 1.

- A straight line supply curve passing through the origin has a *pes* = 1.
- A straight line supply curve intersecting the x-axis at a positive value has a *pes* < 1.

To see why any straight line supply curve passing through the origin has a *pes* of 1 we can use some basic knowledge of geometry and similar triangles. Figure 5.13 shows a straight line supply curve S_1 passing through the origin. The slope of the supply curve is given by $\frac{\Delta P}{\Delta Q_s}$. We have highlighted a triangle shaded blue with the ratio $\frac{\Delta P}{\Delta Q_s}$ relating to a change in price of 7.5 and a change in quantity supplied of 1. The larger triangle formed by taking a price of 22.5 and a quantity supplied of 3 shows the ratio of the price and quantity at this point $\left(\frac{P}{Q}\right)$. The two triangles formed by these are both classed as similar triangles – they have different lengths to their three sides but the internal angles are all the

same. The ratio of the sides must therefore be equal as shown by equation 1 below:

$$\frac{\Delta P}{\Delta Q_s} = \frac{P}{Q_s} \qquad (1)$$

Given our definition of point elasticity of supply, if we substitute equation 1 into the formula and rearrange we get:

$$pes = \frac{\Delta Q_s}{\Delta P} = \frac{P}{Q_s}$$

Therefore:

$$pes = 1$$

Elasticity and Total Expenditure/Revenue

We have used the term 'total expenditure' in relation to the demand curve to accurately reflect the fact that demand is related to buyers and when buyers pay for products this represents expenditure. Many books use the term expenditure and revenue interchangeably and in this short section

FIGURE 5.13

Point Elasticity of Supply

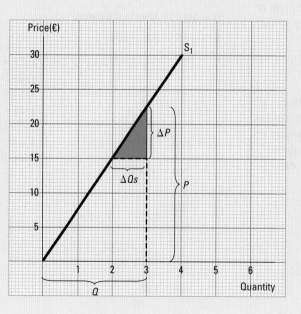

we are going to refer to revenue. Total revenue is found by multiplying the quantity purchased by the average price paid. This is shown by the formula:

$$TR = P \times Q$$

Total revenue can change if either price or quantity, or both, change. This can be seen in Figure 5.14 where a rise in the price of a good from P_0 to P_1 has resulted in a fall in quantity demanded from Q_0 to Q_1.

We can represent the change in price as ΔP. The new price is $(P + \Delta P)$. The change in quantity is ΔQ and the new quantity will be $(Q + \Delta Q)$. TR can be represented thus:

$$TR = (P + \Delta P)(Q + \Delta Q)$$

If we multiply out this expression as shown then we get:

$$TR = PQ + P\Delta Q + \Delta PQ + \Delta P\Delta Q$$

In Figure 5.14, this can be seen graphically.

As a result of the change in price there is an additional amount of revenue shown by purple rectangle (ΔPQ). However, this is offset by the reduction in revenue caused by the fall in quantity caused by the increase in price shown by the blue rectangle ($P\Delta Q$). There is also an area indicated by the yellow rectangle which is equal to $\Delta P\Delta Q$. This leaves us with a formula for the change in TR as:

$$\Delta TR = \Delta PQ + P\Delta Q + \Delta P\Delta Q$$

Let us substitute some figures into our formula to see how this works in practice. Assume the original price of a product is 15 and the quantity demanded at this price is 750. When price rises to 20 the quantity demanded falls to 500.

Using the equation:

$$TR = PQ + P\Delta Q + \Delta PQ + \Delta P\Delta Q$$

TR is now:

$$TR = 15(750) + 15(-250)$$
$$+ 5(750) + 5(-250)$$
$$TR = 10\,000$$

The change in TR is:

$$\Delta TR = \Delta PQ + P\Delta Q + \Delta P\Delta Q$$
$$\Delta TR = 5(750) + 15(-250) + 5(-250)$$
$$\Delta TR = 3750 - 3750 - 1250$$
$$\Delta TR = -1250$$

In this example the effect of the change in price has been negative on TR. We know from our analysis of price elasticity of demand that this means the percentage change in quantity demand was greater than the percentage change in price – in other words, *ped* must be price elastic at this point (>1). For the change in TR to be positive, therefore, the *ped* must be <1.

We can express the relationship between the change in TR and *ped* as an inequality as follows:

$$ped = \frac{\Delta Q}{\Delta P} \times \frac{P}{Q} > 1$$

When price increases, revenue decreases if *ped* meets this inequality. Equally, for a price increase to result in a rise in revenue *ped* must meet the inequality:

$$ped = \frac{\Delta Q}{\Delta P} \times \frac{P}{Q} < 1$$

FIGURE 5.14

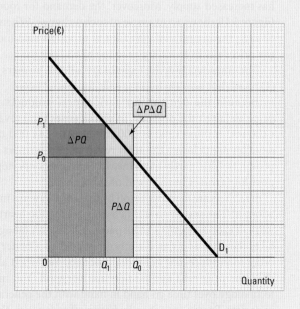

JEOPARDY PROBLEM

A business selling plumbing equipment to the trade (i.e. professional plumbers only) increases the price of copper piping by 4 per cent and reduces the price of radiators by 5 per cent. A year later the company analyses its sales figures and finds that revenue for copper piping rose in the first three months after the price rise but then fell dramatically thereafter, while the revenue for sales of radiators also fell throughout the period.

Explain what might have happened to bring about this situation. Illustrate your answer with diagrams where appropriate.

APPLICATIONS OF SUPPLY AND DEMAND ELASTICITY

Here we apply the versatile tools of supply, demand and elasticity to answer two questions.

Why Are Improvements in Agricultural Technologies Not Always Good News for Farmers?

Over the last 50 years, the technology used in agriculture has increased dramatically. It might seem at first sight that this would be good news for farmers. We can analyse the effect to see if it is good news for farmers by using the three steps we introduced in Chapter 4. Improvements in technology have led to increases in productivity and increases in supply of agricultural products. This shifts the supply curve for agricultural products to the right and lowers the market price of food.

The demand curve remains the same because consumers' desire to buy agricultural products at any given price is not affected by the fact that technology has increased supply. Moreover, the demand for food is relatively price inelastic. Figure 5.15 shows an example of such a change. When the supply curve shifts from S_1 to S_2, the quantity of agricultural products sold increases from 500 to 550, and the price falls from €200 per tonne to €80 per tonne.

The improvement in technology allows farmers to produce more products (Q rises), but now each tonne sells for less (P falls).

Because the demand for agricultural products is assumed to be relatively price inelastic, the decrease in price causes total revenue for farmers to fall from €100 000 million (200 × 500 million) to €44 000 million. Thus, technological developments lower the total revenue that farmers receive for the sale of their products. This partly explains why governments step in to provide income support for farmers in the form of subsidies.

If farmers are made worse off by the developments in new technology, why do they adopt it? The answer to this question goes to the heart of how competitive markets work. If each farmer is a small part of the market for agricultural products, he or she takes the price as given. For any given price, it is better to use the new technology in order to produce and sell more products. Yet, when all farmers do this, the supply rises, the price falls and farmers are worse off. You might expect that increases in technology over time go hand in hand with the general increase in living standards in society. People are generally better off today than they were 50 years ago. Would demand for agricultural products not increase as incomes increase? Research has shown that the income elasticity of demand for food is income inelastic meaning that as incomes increase demand for food increases by a proportionately smaller amount. Even if the demand curve for agricultural products shifts to the right as a result of this rise in incomes, it does not shift far enough to the right to compensate for the price reduction caused by the increase in supply and so farmers still see a fall in revenue.

FIGURE 5.15

An Increase in Supply of Agricultural Products

When an advance in agricultural technology increases the supply of agricultural products from S₁ to S₂, the price falls. Because the demand for agricultural products is price inelastic, the increase in the quantity sold from 500 million to 550 million is proportionately smaller than the decrease in the price from €200 to €80 per tonne. As a result, farmers' total revenue falls from €100 000 million (€200 × 500 million) to €44 000 million (€80 × 550 million).

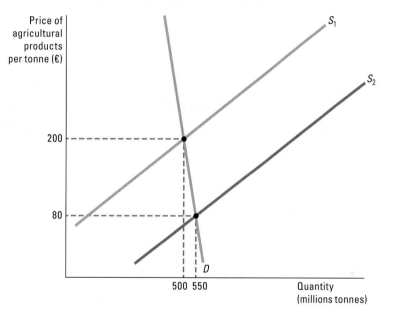

When analysing the effects of technology, it is important to keep in mind that what is bad for farmers is not necessarily bad for society as a whole. Improvements in technology can be bad for some famers who find it difficult to survive, but it represents good news for consumers of agricultural products who see the price of food falling.

Why Do Prices of Ski Holidays Differ So Much at Different Times of the Season?

For many people, winter provides the opportunity to take a snow sports holiday. There are considerable variations in the prices that they have to pay for their holiday which is highly dependent on when they are able to travel. For example, a quick check of a ski company website for the 2014–2015 season revealed the prices shown in Table 5.1 for seven-night ski trips per person to Austria, leaving from London.

There is a considerable variation in the prices that holidaymakers have to pay – £616 being the greatest difference. Prices are particularly high leaving on 27 December and 14 February – why? The reason is that at this time of the season the demand for ski holidays increases substantially because they coincide with annual holiday periods: 27 December is part of the Christmas/New Year holiday and when schoolchildren are also on holiday; 14 February is also the start of a week's school holiday for many UK children.

TABLE 5.1

Prices for 7-night Ski Holidays in Austria, From London

Departure date	Price per person (£)
27 December 2014	1000
3 January 2015	436
10 January 2015	450
17 January 2015	384
24 January 2015	439
31 January 2015	449
7 February 2015	479
14 February 2015	895
21 February 2015	415

The supply of ski holidays does have a limit – there will be a finite number of accommodation places and passes for ski-lifts and so the elasticity of supply is relatively inelastic (Figure 5.16). It is difficult for tour operators to increase supply of accommodation or ski-passes easily in the short run in the face of rising demand at these times. The result is that the increase in demand for ski holidays at these peak times results in prices rising significantly to choke off the excess demand as highlighted in Figure 5.16. If holidaymakers are able to be flexible about when they take their holidays then they will be able to benefit from lower prices for the same holiday. Away from these peak periods the demand for ski holidays is lower and so tour operators have spare capacity – the supply curve out of peak times is more elastic in the very short run. If there was a sudden increase in demand in mid-January, for example, then tour operators would have the capacity to accommodate that demand so prices would not rise as much as when that capacity is strictly limited.

FIGURE 5.16

The Supply of Ski Holidays in Europe

The supply curve for ski holidays is relatively inelastic in the short run. An increase in demand from D_1 to D_2 at peak times leads to a relatively large increase in price per person.

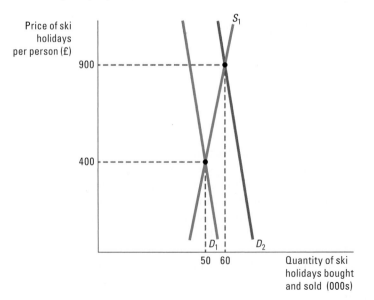

Cases for which supply is very inelastic in the short run but more elastic in the long run may see different prices exist in the market. Air and rail travel and the use of electricity may all be examples where prices differ markedly at peak times compared with off-peak times because of supply constraints and the ability of firms to be able to discriminate between customers at these times.

Quick Quiz How might a drought that destroys half of all farm crops be good for farmers? If such a drought is good for farmers, why don't farmers destroy their own crops in the absence of a drought?

IN THE NEWS

Governments and international health organizations around the world are concerned at the effects on people from smoking tobacco. One way to reduce smoking is through taxation, but how effective is it?

According to the World Health Organization, tobacco is addictive and harmful to users and others. Every year around 100 000 people die from smoking-related illnesses in the UK alone. Tobacco use has a knock-on effect to governments in terms of the extra costs to public health provision.

Typically, demand for tobacco is influenced by three factors: changes in price, real incomes and in tastes and preferences. Legislation on marketing seeks to change people's preferences. The UK government has passed legislation limiting the marketing of tobacco ever since 1965 and this has had some success. In 2016 this will be reinforced with the introduction of standardized packaging. This makes packets less appealing and helps reinforce health messages.

Increasing tobacco taxation leads to higher prices and can also reduce real incomes, both will have an impact on consumption, but tobacco is seen to be price inelastic

so it requires big price increases to significantly reduce demand.

Both strategies have had some success. Although some 10 million people smoked in the UK in 2013, smoking rates have more than halved since 1974. Today, 22 per cent of men and 19 per cent of women smoke which compares favourably to the levels in 1974 when 51 per cent of men and 41 per cent of women smoked.

Many people believe that taxation is an effective way of reducing smoking, especially since smoking rates are much higher among poorer people. In 2013, 14 per cent of adults employed in managerial and professional jobs smoked, compared to 29 per cent in routine and manual occupations.

Any increase in tobacco tax is usually passed onto the consumer since the tobacco industry is an oligopoly. Therefore to be effective tax increases have to increase prices of tobacco above inflation. Such an increase will encourage some

Tobacco crop growing

smokers to quit, make others reduce their consumption and help prevent new users from taking up the habit.

There is evidence that the numbers smoking shows an inverse relationship to increases in real excise tax on tobacco from 2004 to 2007. Also, the quantity each smoker consumes goes down with any increase in excise duty. Overall it is believed that a 10 per cent increase in the price of tobacco will lead to a 4.1 to 4.8 per cent fall in demand for buying tobacco products in the UK. The reason the drop in demand is not higher is down to the addictive nature of smoking. Within this figure responsiveness rates are higher for lower income earners since the share of income spent on tobacco generally falls as people's incomes rise.

Questions

1. What advantages does an increase in tobacco excise duty tax have for the government that imposes it?

2. What justification is there for governments to levy extra taxes on tobacco?

3. What are the main determinants of the price elasticity of demand for tobacco products and why are poor smokers more price sensitive than the rich?

4. Calculate the price elasticity of demand on lower income consumers consuming 100 000 packs if there is a tax increase of £1.50

bringing the price of a packet of cigarettes up to £7.50 resulting in a fall in demand to 87 000.

5. What long-term strategy might a global tobacco company adopt if the UK government announces it has plans for year on year real increases in excise duty on tobacco products?

Reference: Adapted from http://www.who.int/tobacco/economics/meetings/dublin_demand_for_tob_feb2012.pdf

---

FYI

Estimates of Elasticities

We have discussed the concept of elasticity in general terms but there is empirical evidence on elasticity of products in the real world. We present some examples of estimates of price elasticity of supply and demand for a range of products in Table 5.2. It must be remembered that the following are estimates and you may find other data where the elasticities differ from those given here.

TABLE 5.2

Estimates of Price Elasticity of Supply

Good	PES estimate
Public transport in Sweden	0.44 to 0.64
Labour in South Africa	0.35 to 1.75
Beef	
• Zimbabwe	2.0
• Brazil	0.11 to 0.56
• Argentina	0.67 to 0.96
Corn (short run in US)	0.96
Housing, long run in selected US cities	Dallas: 38.6
	San Francisco: 2.4
	New Orleans: 0.9
	St. Louis: 8.1
Uranium	2.3 to 3.3
Recycled aluminium	0.5
Oysters	1.64 to 2.00
Retail store space	3.2
Natural gas (short run)	0.5

Source: http://signsofchaos.blogspot.co.uk/2005_11_01_archive.html

Estimates of Price Elasticity of Demand

Good	PED estimate
Tobacco	0.4
Milk	0.3
Wine	0.6
Shoes	0.7
Cars	1.9
Particular brand of car	4.0
Movies	0.9
Entertainment	1.4
Furniture	3.04
Fuel	0.4
Bread	0.25

SUMMARY

- The price elasticity of supply measures how much the quantity supplied responds to changes in the price. This elasticity often depends on the time horizon under consideration. In most markets, supply is more elastic in the long run than in the short run.

- The price elasticity of supply is calculated as the percentage change in quantity supplied divided by the percentage change in price. If the elasticity is less than 1, so that quantity supplied moves proportionately less than the price, supply is said to be price inelastic. If the elasticity is greater than 1, so that quantity supplied moves proportionately more than the price, supply is said to be price elastic.

- The price elasticity of demand measures how much the quantity demanded responds to changes in the price. Demand tends to be more price elastic if close substitutes are available, if the good is a luxury rather than a necessity, if the market is narrowly defined or if buyers have substantial time to react to a price change.

- The price elasticity of demand is calculated as the percentage change in quantity demanded divided by the

percentage change in price. If the elasticity is less than 1, so that quantity demanded moves proportionately less than the price, demand is said to be price inelastic. If the elasticity is greater than 1, so that quantity demanded moves proportionately more than the price, demand is said to be price elastic.

- Total revenue, the total amount received by sellers for a good, equals the price of the good times the quantity sold. For price inelastic demand curves, total revenue rises as price rises. For price elastic demand curves, total revenue falls as price rises.

- The income elasticity of demand measures how much the quantity demanded responds to changes in consumers' income. The cross-price elasticity of demand measures how much the quantity demanded of one good responds to changes in the price of another good.

- The tools of supply and demand can be applied in many different kinds of markets. This chapter uses them to analyse the market for agricultural products and for ski holidays.

QUESTIONS FOR REVIEW

1. How is the price elasticity of supply calculated? Explain what the calculation measures.

2. Is the price elasticity of supply usually larger in the short run or in the long run? Why?

3. What are the main factors that affect the price elasticity of supply? Think of some examples to use to illustrate the factors you cover.

4. Define the price elasticity of demand and the income elasticity of demand.

5. List and explain some of the determinants of the price elasticity of demand. Think of some examples to use to illustrate the factors you cover.

6. If the price elasticity of demand is greater than 1, is demand price elastic or price inelastic? If the price elasticity equals 0, is demand perfectly price elastic or perfectly price inelastic?

7. Draw a supply and demand diagram with the demand curve more inelastic than the supply curve. Show the equilibrium price, equilibrium quantity and the total revenue received by producers. Use your diagram to show under what circumstances producers see a rise in total revenue.

8. If demand is price elastic, how will an increase in price change total revenue? Explain.

9. What do we call a good whose income elasticity is less than 0?

10. Outline some of the factors that will affect the elasticity of supply and demand for houses for private purchase in the short run and the long run.

PROBLEMS AND APPLICATIONS

1. Seafront properties along the promenade at Brighton on the south coast of England have a price inelastic supply, and cars have a price elastic supply. Suppose that a rise in population doubles the demand for both products (that is, the quantity demanded at each price is twice what it was).
   a. What happens to the equilibrium price and quantity in each market?
   b. Which product experiences a larger change in price?
   c. Which product experiences a larger change in quantity?
   d. What happens to total consumer spending on each product?

2. Because better weather makes farmland more productive, farmland in regions with good weather conditions is more expensive than farmland in regions with bad weather conditions. Over time, however, as advances in technology have made all farmland more productive, the price of farmland (adjusted for overall inflation) has fallen. Use the concept of price elasticity to explain why productivity and farmland prices are positively related across space but negatively related over time.

3. For each of the following pairs of goods, which good would you expect to have a more price elastic demand and why?
   a. Required textbooks or mystery novels.
   b. Beethoven recordings or classical music recordings in general.
   c. Heating oil during the next six months or heating oil during the next five years.
   d. Lemonade or water.

4. Suppose that business travellers and holidaymakers have the following demand for airline tickets from Birmingham to Naples:

Price (€)	Quantity demanded (business travellers)	Quantity demanded (holidaymakers)
150	2100	1000
200	2000	800
250	1900	600
300	1800	400

   a. As the price of tickets rises from €200 to €250, what is the price elasticity of demand for (i) business travellers and (ii) holidaymakers? (Use the midpoint method in your calculations.)
   b. Why might holidaymakers have a different price elasticity from business travellers?

5. Suppose that your demand schedule for streamed movies is as follows:

Price (€)	Quantity demanded (income = €10 000)	Quantity demanded (income = €12 000)
8	40	50
10	32	45
12	24	30
14	16	20
16	8	12

   a. Use the midpoint method to calculate your price elasticity of demand as the price of streamed movies increases from €8 to €10 per movie if (i) your income is €10 000, and (ii) your income is €12 000.
   b. Calculate your income elasticity of demand as your income increases from €10 000 to €12 000 if (i) the price is €12, and (ii) the price is €16 per streamed movie.

6. Two drivers – Jan and Lou – each drive up to a petrol station. Before looking at the price, each places an order. Jan says, 'I'd like 30 litres of petrol.' Lou says, 'I'd like €30-worth of petrol.' What is each driver's price elasticity of demand?

7. Consider public policy aimed at smoking.
   a. Studies indicate that the price elasticity of demand for cigarettes is about 0.4. If a packet of 20 cigarettes in the UK is currently priced at £9.00 and the government wants to reduce smoking by 20 per cent, by how much should it increase the price?
   b. If the government permanently increases the price of cigarettes, will the policy have a larger effect on smoking one year from now or five years from now? Explain.
   c. Studies also find that teenagers have a higher price elasticity of demand for cigarettes than do adults. Why might this be true?

8. Pharmaceutical drugs have a price inelastic demand, and computers have a price elastic demand. Suppose that technological advance doubles the supply of both products (that is, the quantity supplied at each price is twice what it was).
   a. What happens to the equilibrium price and quantity in each market?
   b. Which product experiences a larger change in price?
   c. Which product experiences a larger change in quantity?
   d. What happens to total consumer spending on each product?

9. Suppose that there is severe flooding in a region in which there is a high concentration of wheat farmers.
   a. Farmers whose crops were destroyed by the floods were much worse off, but farmers whose crops were not destroyed benefited from the floods. Why?
   b. What information would you need about the market for wheat to assess whether farmers as a group were hurt or helped by the floods?

10. Explain why the following might be true: a drought around the world raises the total revenue that farmers receive from the sale of grain, but a drought only in France reduces the total revenue that French farmers receive.

PART 3

MICROECONOMICS – THE LIMITATIONS OF MARKETS

6 MARKET FAILURE

LEARNING OUTCOMES

After reading this chapter you should be able to:

- See how decision making and transactions can often ignore social costs and benefits leading to externalities.

- Define market failure and give examples of how it arises.

- Explain the difference between private and social costs.

- Draw diagrams to show consumer and producer surplus and be able to identify changes in both as a result of changes in price.

- Use diagrams to explain how both negative and positive externalities arise and show the welfare costs of inefficient resource allocation.

- Discuss different government-led solutions to market failure including regulation, taxes and subsidies.

- Analyse the use of tradable permits.

- Use diagrams to show how taxes and subsidies affect businesses, price and output and how the incidence of tax is shared between consumers and producers.

- Evaluate the arguments surrounding the economic analysis of pollution.

- Consider some of the issues relating to social and ethical responsibility of firms.

- Analyse the use of property rights as a means of correcting externalities.

INTRODUCTION

We have looked at markets and how firms operate in those markets. Efficiency has been a recurring feature of the discussion of markets and firms but we have to be careful how we define efficiency. Efficiency can be looked at in three different ways. Efficiency is about getting the most we can from scarce resources. More specifically we can define efficiency in relation to business in four ways:

- Technical efficiency – a business can improve its technical efficiency if it could find a way of using its existing resources to produce more. It may be that it could use machinery instead of people that do the same job but do it much faster without having to take a break!
- Productive efficiency – a business can improve productive efficiency by producing output at the lowest cost possible. If it can find a way of sourcing cheaper raw materials, for example, which allows it to reduce costs, then it can improve its productive efficiency.
- Allocative efficiency – this looks at efficiency from the perspective of consumers. Are the products being produced by businesses actually wanted and valued by consumers (both individual consumers and business consumers)? Efficiency occurs where the goods and services being produced match the demand by consumers. Allocative efficiency occurs where the cost of resources used to produce the products is equal to the value placed on the product by consumers represented by the price they are willing to pay.
- Social efficiency – when businesses produce products they incur costs – raw materials, wages, rents, interest payments, insurance, plant and equipment and so on – the private costs. However, there are also costs which businesses may not take into account such as the pollution they generate in production. These are costs borne by society as a whole. Social efficiency occurs where the private and social cost of production is equal to the private and social benefits derived from their consumption.

In recent years there has been a greater awareness of the effects that a firm's operations have on its wider stakeholders and takes into account the perspective of social efficiency. We know, for example, that cigarette and alcohol manufacturers produce products which can result in serious health issues for users and problems for society as a whole – a case of over production and consumption. We know that there is a way to reduce the instances of sexually transmitted diseases, including the very serious problem of HIV AIDS, through wider use of condoms, but this is a product which is under-used.

Market theory in its purest sense is based on an assumption that markets work efficiently and when they do, resources are allocated efficiently. The reality is much more complex than this, partly because of the definition of efficiency that is used. Market failure occurs where the market does not allocate resources efficiently.

Sources of Market Failure

There are a number of sources of market failure which can be summarized as follows:

- In many cases there is imperfect knowledge of and between buyers and sellers. This might arise because consumers do not have adequate technical knowledge or where advertising can mislead or misinform. Producers are likely to be unaware of all the opportunities open to them and cannot always accurately measure productivity. For both consumers and producers, decisions are often based not on rational assessment of the costs and benefits but a wide range of rules of thumb (called heuristics).

- Goods are not homogenous – they are differentiated through branding, technology, labelling and product information, amongst other methods.
- Resource immobility – firms cannot substitute or move factors of production from one use to another easily. Labour can be both geographically and occupationally immobile, some capital items have limited uses (for example, what else could the Channel Tunnel be used for?) and land cannot be moved to where it might be needed nor exploited if it is not suitable.
- Market power. In some markets there are not large numbers of sellers but the market may be dominated by a relatively small number of very large firms which have some element of monopoly power. Firms with monopoly power might indulge in collusion, price fixing, rigging of markets and the erection of barriers to entry.
- There are some products which cannot be provided in sufficient quantity by the market, for example, merit goods and public goods.
- Inequality exists in factor or income endowment, for example through unequal wealth distribution, the location of resources (for example, oil and mineral reserves), where poverty exists and through discrimination.
- Decisions may be made which do not take into account all costs and benefits. In particular, decision makers may consider just the private costs and benefits but not the social costs and benefits and so resources are not allocated efficiently.

The market failures examined in this chapter fall under a general category called *externalities*. An externality arises when an individual or business engages in an activity that influences the well-being of a bystander (a third party) who neither pays nor receives any compensation for that effect. If the impact on the bystander is adverse, it is called a *negative externality*; if it is beneficial, it is called a *positive externality*.

Private and Social Costs

When making decisions, businesses and individuals are likely to consider the private costs and private benefits. In deciding to publish a textbook, for example, a publishing business incurs various private costs such as the cost of paper, printing, marketing, editorial work, paying author royalties and various overheads such as administration. The publisher will take into account a number of private benefits which include the share of profits to owners or shareholders, and the employment of individuals within the business. However, in making the decision to publish the book the business may not take into consideration the cost (or benefit) to society that is imposed as a result of that decision. Distribution of textbooks contributes to congestion, road wear and tear; there are the emissions that the vehicles give off, the noise pollution and the increased risk of accident which may cause injury or even death to a third party. Firms that make and sell paper, which is used in the production of books, also create, as a by-product of the manufacturing process, a chemical called dioxin. Scientists believe that once dioxin enters the environment it raises the population's risk of cancer, birth defects and other health problems. There may also be some social benefits of the decision; knowledge development is improved as a result of the book being available, employees of the firm will spend the money they earn on goods and services in the local area and workers at paper mills will have jobs.

These social costs and benefits are not necessarily taken into consideration by the business when making the decision to publish the book. The internal costs and benefits may be far more important in the firm's decision making. The social costs and benefits are borne by a third party. The cost of repairing damaged roads, the cost of dealing with accident and injury, delays caused as a result of congestion, the effects and costs of dealing with pollution and so on, all have to be borne by others – often the taxpayer. Equally, any social benefits arising from the decision are gained by those not party to the initial decision without them having to pay for the benefit derived.

In the presence of externalities, society's interest in a market outcome extends beyond the well-being of buyers and sellers who participate in the market; it also includes the well-being of bystanders who are affected indirectly. For a business this might be its wider stakeholders. Because buyers and sellers neglect the external effects of their actions when deciding how much to demand or supply, the market equilibrium is not efficient when there are externalities. That is, the equilibrium fails to maximize the total benefit to society as a whole. The release of dioxin into the environment, for instance, is a negative externality. Self-interested paper firms will not consider the full cost of the pollution they create and, therefore, will emit too much pollution unless the government prevents or discourages them from doing so.

Externalities come in many varieties, as do the policy responses that try to deal with the market failure. Here are some examples:

- The exhaust from cars is a negative externality because it creates smog that other people have to breathe. Drivers do not take into consideration this externality and so tend to drive too much thus increasing pollution. The government attempts to solve this problem by setting emissions standards for cars. It also taxes petrol in order to reduce the amount that people drive. These policy remedies have effects on business costs and behaviour which might ultimately have to be passed onto the consumer in the form of higher prices. The benefits might be that more research and development (R&D) into efficient cars is carried out by firms looking to gain some competitive advantage in the market – something that might benefit both firms and consumers.
- Airports create negative externalities because people who live near the airport or on the flight path are disturbed by noise. Airports and airlines do not bear the full cost of the noise and, therefore, may be less inclined to spend money on noise reduction technologies. The government may address this problem by regulating the times that airlines can take-off and land at an airport, or by providing subsidies to help local homeowners invest in triple glazing and other sound proofing measures for homes on the flight path.
- Research into new technologies provides a positive externality because it creates knowledge that other people can use. Because inventors and business R&D units cannot capture the full benefits of their inventions, they tend to devote too few resources to research. The government addresses this problem partially through the patent and intellectual property system, which gives inventors and businesses an exclusive use over their inventions or right to exploit intellectual property for a period of time, and through the provision of subsidies to encourage firms to invest in R&D.
- The provision of public transport brings benefits to many people not only because it helps them get around more easily but it also helps relieve congestion thus benefiting other road users. Governments are often prepared to subsidize public transport because there are positive benefits to society as a whole.
- Immunization programmes against communicable diseases and infections are often provided free of charge by a country's health service. The benefits not

only accrue to the individuals who receive the inoculations but in far wider circles. Those who are inoculated are less likely to pass on infection to others, in particular the more vulnerable members of society, days lost through work are reduced which in turn helps businesses operate more effectively. Recent studies in the UK suggest that around 180 million working days are lost each year due to illness, with an estimated cost to the economy amounting to £2.5 billion (€3.44 billion). The indirect costs due to the fall in consumer service levels as a result of employee absence were estimated at £17 billion (€23.44 billion). If an immunization system contributes to a reduction in the instances of employee absence this can have significant effects on businesses.

In each of these cases, some decision maker fails to take account of the external effects of his or her behaviour. The government responds by trying to influence this behaviour to protect the interests of bystanders.

EXTERNALITIES

Welfare Economics: An Overview

Firms rely on consumers. Consumers buy products from firms but their behaviour will depend on a variety of factors, not least their willingness to pay for a product. Whenever you go into a shop or choose a product online, you are making complex neural calculations – there will be a price which you are prepared to pay to acquire a product and there will be a slightly higher price which for some reason you are not prepared to pay. The maximum price is the **willingness to pay** and it measures how much a buyer values a product. Buyers are invariably happy to buy products at prices less than their willingness to pay but would refuse to buy at a price more than their willingness to pay. We can also assume that the buyer would be indifferent about buying a good at a price exactly equal to their willingness to pay.

> **willingness to pay** a measure of how much a buyer values a good by the amount they are prepared to pay to acquire the good

When buying a good a consumer can expect to derive some benefit. The willingness to pay is a reflection of the value of the benefit that the buyer expects to receive. This is why firms spend large sums of money trying to understand how consumers value products and what affects their behaviour. If a consumer buys a product for €10 but would have been prepared to pay €20 we say that the buyer receives *consumer surplus* of €10. **Consumer surplus** is the amount a buyer is willing to pay for a good minus the amount the buyer actually pays for it. We refer to 'getting a bargain' regularly in everyday language. In economics, a bargain means paying much less for something than we expected or anticipated and as a result we get a greater degree of consumer surplus than we expected. Consumer surplus measures the benefit to buyers of participating in a market.

> **consumer surplus** the amount a buyer is willing to pay for a good minus the amount the buyer actually pays for it

CASE STUDY

Auctions, Online Shopping and Consumer Surplus

We all want a bargain and by this we mean that we can buy something for less than the price we were really prepared to pay for it. Achieving this gives us the consumer a surplus which we can choose to spend on other things. On the other side, sellers will try to maximize the price they get from selling each product.

Take the souqs in North Africa where there can be hundreds of stalls, thousands of people, and numerous items for sale, but not a single visible price. Here the buyer and seller face each other and haggle over the price. The result is that each customer can end up paying a different price for the same product sold by one trader. In the souq the advantage is with the seller especially if the buyer is an unsuspecting tourist, but that is not the case with online auctions.

On eBay the advantage is loaded onto the buyer. In most auctions on eBay there will be one item for sale, but many potential purchasers. The seller must seek out the person who is prepared to pay the highest price by having a time related online auction. Bidders drop out when the price bid for the item for sale rises above the maximum price they are willing to pay. It tells us what all the bidders who drop out were prepared to pay, but gives us no idea on the price the winner was willing to pay. Therefore the winner is likely to derive a consumer surplus. The bidding process can reveal some information about those involved. When initial bids are made, these might be at low prices and if no-one else bids, the winner may only pay a low price and get considerable consumer surplus. However, as soon as other bidders join in and the price is raised, it becomes clearer which bidders are serious and perhaps may be prepared to pay relatively high prices and which are not. Without these other bidders it is difficult to know how much any one individual is prepared to pay.

Some early research by Jank and Shmueli analysing over 4500 US and UK auctions found that buyers were likely to have paid around 30 per cent of the higher value of the merchandise they successfully bid for. This suggests that sellers could set higher prices and still be successful in selling their goods.

Like sellers in the souqs, the Internet allows small-scale sellers to operate (as well as large ones), but here the prices are more transparent. Buyers can find out about the quality of the products through reading user reviews and can relatively quickly search many sellers. Through good online research, customers can end up paying much less than they would have been prepared to pay. The consumer surplus gained from internet shopping will vary across countries. The average consumer surplus across 13 of the G20 countries represents about 4.4 per cent of GDP, according to a 2012 report by the Boston Consulting Group.

References: Adapted from **http://www.reuters.com/article/2008/01/28/us-ebay-consumers-idUSN2742167120080128**

http://theinconsequentialdiary.com/2012/04/22/bargaining-in-the-arab-market-morocco/

http://www.bcg.com/documents/file100409.pdf

USING THE DEMAND CURVE TO MEASURE CONSUMER SURPLUS

Consumer surplus is closely related to the demand curve for a product. The market demand curve represents the willingness and ability to pay of all consumers in the market. Because buyers always want to pay less for the goods they buy, lower prices makes buyers of a good better off. But how much does buyers' well-being rise in response to a lower price? We can use the concept of consumer surplus to answer this question precisely.

Figure 6.1 shows a demand schedule for a market – let's assume that it is the market for tickets for a music festival. If the festival organizers set the price at P_1, Q_1 consumers will want to buy a ticket. The marginal buyer represented by the point Q_1 has a willingness to pay of just P_1; at any price above P_1, this festival goer is not willing to pay. However, all the buyers represented by the amount $0 - Q_1$ were willing to pay a price higher than P_1 to get tickets. All these buyers gained some degree of consumer surplus shown by the area above the price and below the demand curve. In panel (a) of Figure 6.1, consumer surplus at a price of P_1 is the area of triangle ABC. Now suppose that the price set by the festival organizers was set at P_2 rather than P_1, as shown in panel (b). The consumer surplus now equals area ADF. The increase in consumer surplus attributable to the lower price is the area BCFD.

This increase in consumer surplus is composed of two parts. First, those buyers who would have bought Q_1 of the good at the higher price P_1 are better off because they now pay less. The increase in consumer surplus of existing buyers is the reduction in the amount they are now being asked to pay; it equals the area of the rectangle BCED. Second, some new buyers enter the market because they are now willing and able to buy tickets at the lower price. As a result, the quantity

FIGURE 6.1

How the Price Affects Consumer Surplus

In panel (a) the price is P_1, the quantity of festival tickets demanded is Q_1 and consumer surplus equals the area of the triangle ABC. If the ticket price is set at P_2 rather than P_1, as in panel (b), the quantity demanded would be Q_2 rather than Q_1, and the consumer surplus rises to the area of the triangle ADF. The increase in consumer surplus (area BCFD) occurs in part because existing consumers now pay less (area BCED) and in part because new consumers enter the market at the lower price (area CEF).

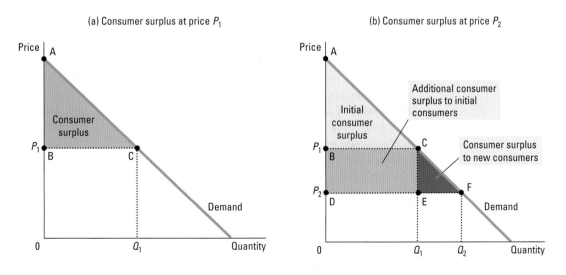

demanded for festival tickets would be Q_2 rather than Q_1. The consumer surplus these newcomers receive is the area of the triangle CEF.

The lesson from this example holds for all demand curves: the area below the demand curve and above the price measures the consumer surplus in a market. The reason is that the height of the demand curve measures the value buyers place on the good, as measured by their willingness to pay for it. The difference between this willingness to pay and the market price is each buyer's consumer surplus. Thus, the total area below the demand curve and above the price is the sum of the consumer surplus of all buyers in the market for a good or service.

What Does Consumer Surplus Measure?

Our goal in developing the concept of consumer surplus is to make normative judgements about the desirability of market outcomes. Firms can also use the concept of consumer surplus in designing branding, advertising and promotion campaigns and deciding on pricing strategies.

Because consumer surplus measures the benefit that buyers receive from a good *as the buyers themselves perceive it*, it is a good measure of economic well-being if businesses want to respect and possibly exploit the preferences of buyers. A key assumption of consumer surplus is that consumers are the best judges of how much benefit they receive from the goods they buy. This may not always be the case.

> **Quick Quiz** Draw a demand curve for MP3 downloads. In your diagram, show a price of MP3 downloads per tune and the consumer surplus that results from that price. Explain in words what this consumer surplus measures.

PRODUCER SURPLUS

We now turn to the other side of the market and consider the benefits sellers receive from participating in a market. The analysis of sellers' welfare is similar to our analysis of buyers' welfare.

Cost and the Willingness to Sell

As with our analysis of the buyer side, sellers are willing to offer goods for sale if the price they receive exceeds the cost. Here the term cost should be interpreted as the producer's opportunity cost. Cost is a measure of a firm's willingness to sell their product. Each producer in a market would be eager to sell their products at a price greater than their cost, would refuse to sell their products at a price less than their cost, and would be indifferent about selling their products at a price exactly equal to cost.

If a producer is able to sell a product at a price that is higher than the lowest amount they would be willing to sell that product for, then they will receive some benefit. We say that the producer receives *producer surplus*. **Producer surplus** is the amount a seller is paid minus the cost of production. Producer surplus measures the benefit to sellers of participating in a market. The total producer surplus in a market is the value of the sum of all the individual producer surplus.

producer surplus the amount a seller is paid minus the cost of production

Using the Supply Curve to Measure Producer Surplus

Just as consumer surplus is closely related to the demand curve, producer surplus is closely related to the supply curve. It is not surprising that sellers always want to receive a higher price for the goods they sell. How far sellers' well-being will rise in response to a higher price can be calculated precisely by using the concept of producer surplus. Figure 6.2 shows a typical upward sloping supply curve. Let us assume that this is the supply curve for firms providing online rental access to movies per time period. At a price of P_1, firms can expect to sell Q_1 rentals over the time period. The producer surplus is the area below the price and above the supply curve. In panel (a) of Figure 6.2, at the price of P_1 the producer surplus is the area of triangle ABC.

Panel (b) shows what happens if the price of online movie rentals rises from P_1 to P_2. Producer surplus now equals area ADF. This increase in producer surplus has two parts. First, those sellers who were already selling Q_1 of the good at the lower price P_1 are better off because they now get more for what they sell. The increase in producer surplus for existing sellers equals the area of the rectangle BCED. Second, some new sellers enter the market because they are now willing to produce the good at the higher price, resulting in an increase in the quantity supplied from Q_1 to Q_2. The producer surplus of these newcomers is the area of the triangle CEF.

FIGURE 6.2

How the Price Affects Producer Surplus

In panel (a) the price is P_1, the quantity demanded is Q_1 and producer surplus equals the area of the triangle ABC. When the price rises from P_1 to P_2, as in panel (b), the quantity supplied rises from Q_1 to Q_2 and the producer surplus rises to the area of the triangle ADF. The increase in producer surplus (area BCFD) occurs in part because existing producers now receive more (area BCED) and in part because new producers enter the market at the higher price (area CEF).

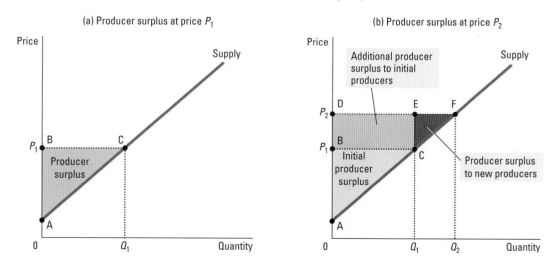

As this analysis shows, we use producer surplus to measure the well-being of sellers in much the same way as we use consumer surplus to measure the well-being of buyers. Because these two measures of economic welfare are so similar, it is natural to use them together to analyse market inefficiencies.

These inefficiencies and changes in welfare can be estimated by referring to the **deadweight loss**. The deadweight loss is the fall in total surplus that results when a tax (or some other policy) distorts a market outcome. This can be considered by

deadweight loss the fall in total surplus that results from a market distortion, such as a tax

calculating the changes in both producer and consumer surplus as a result of the tax or policy change minus the benefits (which may be the tax revenue accruing to the government, for example). Figure 6.3 summarizes the effects of a tax by comparing welfare before and after the tax is imposed. The third column in the table in Figure 6.3 shows the changes. The tax causes consumer surplus to fall by the area B + C and producer surplus to fall by the area D + E. Tax revenue rises by the area B + D. Not surprisingly, the tax makes buyers and sellers worse off and the government better off.

The change in total welfare includes the change in consumer surplus (which is negative), the change in producer surplus (which is also negative), and the change in tax revenue (which is positive). When we add these three pieces together, we find that total surplus in the market falls by the area C + E. Thus, the losses to buyers and sellers from a tax exceed the revenue raised by the government. The area C + E measures the size of the deadweight loss as the fall in total surplus.

FIGURE 6.3

How a Tax Affects Welfare

A tax on a good reduces consumer surplus (by the area B + C) and producer surplus (by the area D + E). Because the fall in producer and consumer surplus exceeds tax revenue (area B + D), the tax is said to impose a deadweight loss (area C + E).

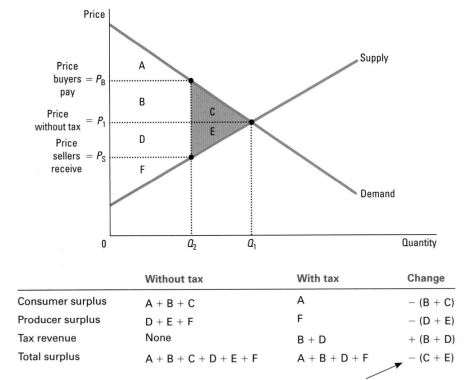

	Without tax	With tax	Change
Consumer surplus	A + B + C	A	– (B + C)
Producer surplus	D + E + F	F	– (D + E)
Tax revenue	None	B + D	+ (B + D)
Total surplus	A + B + C + D + E + F	A + B + D + F	– (C + E)

The area C + E shows the fall in total surplus and is the deadweight loss of the tax.

Quick Quiz Draw a supply curve for MP3 downloads. In your diagram show a price of MP3 downloads and the producer surplus that results from that price. Explain in words what this producer surplus measures.

Market Inefficiencies

To make our analysis concrete, we will consider a specific market – the market for aluminium. Figure 6.4 shows the supply and demand curves in the market for aluminium.

Remember that supply and demand curves contain important information about costs and benefits. The demand curve for aluminium reflects the value of aluminium to consumers, as measured by the prices they are willing to pay. At any given quantity, the height of the demand curve shows the willingness to pay of the marginal buyer. In other words, it shows the value to the consumer of the last unit of aluminium bought. Similarly, the supply curve reflects the costs of producing aluminium. At any given quantity, the height of the supply curve shows the cost of the marginal seller. In other words, it shows the cost to the producer of the last unit of aluminium sold.

In the absence of government intervention, the price adjusts to balance the supply and demand for aluminium. The quantity produced and consumed in the market equilibrium, shown as Q_{MARKET} in Figure 6.4, is efficient in the sense that it maximizes the sum of producer and consumer surplus. That is, the market allocates resources in a way that maximizes the total value to the consumers who buy and use aluminium minus the total costs to the producers who make and sell aluminium.

FIGURE 6.4

The Market for Aluminium

The demand curve reflects the value to buyers, and the supply curve reflects the costs of sellers. The equilibrium quantity, Q_{MARKET}, maximizes the total value to buyers minus the total costs of sellers. In the absence of externalities, therefore, the market equilibrium is efficient.

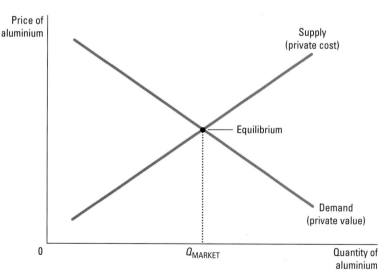

Negative Externalities

Now let's suppose that aluminium factories emit pollution: for each unit of aluminium produced, a certain amount of a pollutant enters the atmosphere. This pollutant may pose a health risk for those who breathe the air; it is a negative externality. There is a cost involved in dealing with the effects of the pollutant which may be the health care that those affected have to receive. This cost may not be taken into consideration by producers of aluminium who may only consider the private costs of production. How does this externality affect the efficiency of the market outcome?

Because of the externality, the cost to *society* of producing aluminium is larger than the cost to the aluminium producers. For each unit of aluminium produced, the *social* (or *external*) *cost* includes the private costs of the aluminium producers plus the costs to those bystanders affected adversely by the pollution. Figure 6.5 shows the social cost of producing aluminium. The social cost curve is above the supply curve because it takes into account the external costs imposed on society by aluminium producers. At every price the social cost is higher than the private cost so we can say that the social cost curve is the sum of the private costs and the social or external cost. The difference between these two curves reflects the social or external cost of the pollution emitted.

What quantity of aluminium should be produced? To answer this question, we can refer to our analysis of consumer and producer surplus. The ideal would be to maximize the total surplus derived from the market – the value to consumers of aluminium minus the cost of producing aluminium with the proviso that the cost of producing aluminium includes the external costs of the pollution.

This ideal would be the level of aluminium production at which the demand curve crosses the social cost curve. This intersection determines the optimal amount of aluminium from the standpoint of society as a whole. As a general principle the socially efficient output occurs where the marginal social cost equals the marginal social benefit at a particular output. Below this level of production, the value of the aluminium to consumers (as measured by the height of the demand curve) exceeds the social cost of producing it (as measured by the height of the social cost curve). Producing any more than this level means the social cost of producing additional aluminium exceeds the value to consumers.

FIGURE 6.5

Pollution and the Social Optimum

In the presence of a negative externality, such as pollution, the social cost of the good exceeds the private cost. The optimal quantity, Q_{OPTIMUM}, is therefore lower than the equilibrium quantity, Q_{MARKET}.

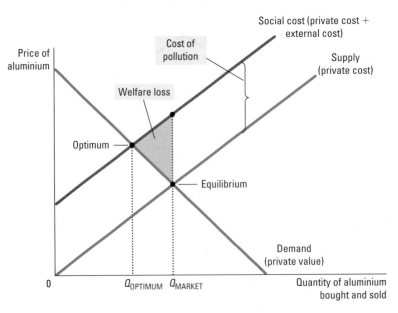

Note that the equilibrium quantity of aluminium, Q_{MARKET}, is larger than the socially optimal quantity, $Q_{OPTIMUM}$. The reason for this inefficiency is that the market equilibrium reflects only the private costs of production. In the market equilibrium, the marginal consumer values aluminium at less than the social cost of producing it. That is, at Q_{MARKET} the demand curve lies below the social cost curve. Thus, reducing aluminium production and consumption below the market equilibrium level raises total economic well-being. We can measure changes in well-being by the welfare loss associated with different market outcomes. We measure the difference in the value placed on each marginal unit of production of aluminium between $Q_{OPTIMUM}$ and Q_{MARKET} by consumers as shown by the shaded triangle in Figure 6.5.

How can society hope to achieve the optimal outcome? The answer is to somehow force the decision maker to take into consideration some or all of the social costs of the decision. In our example, one way to do this would be to tax aluminium producers for each tonne of aluminium sold. The tax would shift the supply curve for aluminium upward by the size of the tax. If the tax accurately reflected the social cost of the pollution released into the atmosphere, the new supply curve would coincide with the social cost curve. In the new market equilibrium, aluminium producers would produce the socially optimal quantity of aluminium.

The use of such a tax is called **internalizing an externality** because it gives buyers and sellers in the market an incentive to take account of the external effects of their actions. Aluminium producers would, in essence, take the costs of pollution into account when deciding how much aluminium to supply because the tax would make them pay for these external costs.

internalizing an externality
altering incentives so that people take account of the external effects of their actions

Positive Externalities

Although some activities impose costs on third parties, others yield benefits. Education, for example, yields positive externalities because a more educated population means firms can employ more flexible and productive employees which helps improve productive and technical efficiency and increases the potential for economic growth, which benefits everyone. Notice that the productivity benefit of education is not necessarily an externality: the consumer of education (the student) reaps most of the benefit in the form of higher wages. But if some of the productivity benefits of education spill over and benefit other people, as is the case if economic growth is stimulated, then this effect would count as a positive externality as well.

The analysis of positive externalities is similar to the analysis of negative externalities. As Figure 6.6 shows, the demand curve does not reflect the value to society of the good. The value placed on an activity such as education is valued less by consumers than the total value to society. Because the social value (or external benefit) is greater than the private value, the social value curve lies above the demand curve. The social value curve is the private value plus the external benefit to society at each price. At every price the benefit to society is greater than the private benefit, hence the social value curve lies to the right of the private benefit curve. The optimal quantity is found where the social value curve and the supply curve (which represents costs) intersect. Hence, the socially optimal quantity is greater than the quantity determined by the private market.

Once again, the government can correct the market failure by inducing market participants to internalize the externality. The appropriate response in the case of positive externalities is exactly the opposite to the case of negative externalities. To move the market equilibrium closer to the social optimum, a positive externality requires a subsidy. In fact, that is exactly the policy many governments follow by heavily subsidizing education.

FIGURE 6.6

Education and the Social Optimum

In the presence of a positive externality, the social value of the good exceeds the private value. The optimal quantity, $Q_{OPTIMUM}$, is therefore higher than the equilibrium quantity, Q_{MARKET}.

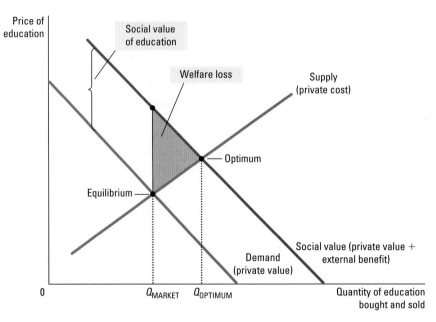

To summarize: negative externalities lead markets to produce a larger quantity than is socially desirable. Positive externalities lead markets to produce a smaller quantity than is socially desirable. To remedy the problem, the government can internalize the externality by taxing goods that have negative externalities and subsidizing goods that have positive externalities.

JEOPARDY PROBLEM

From a social efficiency perspective, consider the situation where an orbital motorway around a busy major city is highly congested during the day but is largely deserted between the hours of 11.00 pm and 5.30 am. What steps might be taken to improve the efficiency of such a road system?

GOVERNMENT, BUSINESS AND EXTERNALITIES

It is widely acknowledged by firms that their activities result in both positive and negative externalities and that market failure means that resources are not allocated as efficiently as they might be. In virtually every country, governments step in to try and influence business behaviour in an attempt to counter market failure and provide the incentives to change behaviour to generate an outcome which is seen as benefiting society as a whole.

There are two main ways in which governments intervene in business: *command-and-control policies* regulate behaviour directly. *Market-based policies* provide incentives for private decision makers to behave differently and resolve the perceived problem.

Regulation

The government can remedy an externality by making certain behaviours either required or forbidden. For example, it is a crime in any European country for firms to dump poisonous chemicals into the water supply. In this case, the external costs to society far exceed the benefits to the polluter. The government therefore institutes a command-and-control policy that prohibits this act altogether.

In most cases of pollution, however, the situation is not this simple. Despite the stated goals of some environmentalists, it would be impossible to prohibit all polluting activity. For example, virtually all forms of transport – even the horse – produce some undesirable polluting by-products. But it would not be sensible for the government to ban all transport. Thus, instead of trying to eradicate pollution altogether, society has to weigh the costs and benefits to decide the kinds and quantities of pollution it will allow.

Environmental regulations can take many forms. Sometimes the government may dictate a maximum level of pollution that a factory may emit, or set permitted noise levels for an airline. At other times the government requires that firms adopt a particular technology to reduce emissions or will only grant a licence to operate if certain criteria are met. In all cases, to design good rules, government regulators need to know the details about specific industries and about the alternative technologies that could be adopted. This information is often difficult for government regulators to obtain.

Market-Based Policies – Pigovian Taxes and Subsidies

Instead of regulating behaviour in response to an externality, the government can use market-based policies to align private incentives with social efficiency. For instance, as we saw earlier, the government can internalize the externality by taxing activities that have negative externalities and subsidizing activities that have positive externalities. Taxes enacted to correct the effects of negative externalities are called **Pigovian taxes**, after the English economist Arthur Pigou (1877–1959), an early advocate of their use.

Pigovian tax a tax enacted to correct the effects of a negative externality

Pigovian taxes as a way to deal with pollution can have benefits over regulations because such taxes can reduce pollution at a lower cost to society. To see why, let us consider an example.

Suppose that two factories – a paper mill and a steel mill – are each dumping 500 tonnes of effluent into a river each year. The government decides that it wants to reduce the amount of pollution. It considers two solutions:

- Regulation. The government could tell each factory to reduce its pollution to 300 tonnes of effluent per year.
- Pigovian tax. The government could levy a tax on each factory of €50 000 for each tonne of effluent it emits.

The regulation would dictate a level of pollution, whereas the tax would give factory owners an economic incentive to reduce pollution.

Proponents of a tax would first point out that a tax is just as effective as regulation in reducing the overall level of pollution. The government can achieve whatever level of pollution it wants by setting the tax at the appropriate level. The higher the tax, the larger the reduction in pollution. Indeed, if the tax is high enough, the factories will close down altogether, reducing pollution to zero.

Regulation on the other hand, requires each factory to reduce pollution by the same amount, but an equal reduction is not necessarily the least expensive way to clean up the water. It is possible that the paper mill can reduce pollution at lower cost than the steel mill. If so, the paper mill would respond to the tax by reducing pollution substantially to avoid the tax, whereas the steel mill would respond by reducing pollution less and paying the tax.

In essence, the Pigovian tax places a price on the right to pollute. Just as markets allocate goods to those buyers who value them most highly, a Pigovian tax allocates pollution to those factories that face the highest cost of reducing it. Whatever the level of pollution the government chooses, it can achieve this goal at the lowest total cost using a tax.

Pigovian taxes can also be better for the environment. Under the command-and-control policy of regulation, the factories have no reason to reduce emissions further once they have reached the target of 300 tonnes of effluent. By contrast, the tax gives the factories an incentive to develop cleaner technologies, because a cleaner technology would reduce the amount of tax the factory has to pay.

Pigovian taxes are unlike most other taxes. Many taxes distort incentives and move the allocation of resources away from the social optimum. The reduction in economic well-being – that is, in consumer and producer surplus – exceeds the amount of revenue the government raises, resulting in a deadweight loss. By contrast, when externalities are present, society also cares about the well-being of the bystanders who are affected. Pigovian taxes correct incentives for the presence of externalities and thereby move the allocation of resources closer to the social optimum. Thus, while Pigovian taxes raise revenue for the government, they also enhance economic efficiency.

Tradable Pollution Permits

Returning to our example of the paper mill and the steel mill, let us suppose that the government adopts regulation and requires each factory to reduce its pollution to 300 tonnes of effluent per year. Then one day, after the regulation is in place and both mills have complied, the two firms go to the government with a proposal. The steel mill wants to increase its emission of effluent by 100 tonnes. The paper mill has agreed to reduce its emission by the same amount if the steel mill pays it €5 million. Should the government allow the two factories to make this deal?

From the standpoint of economic efficiency, allowing the deal is good policy. The deal must make the owners of the two factories better off, because they are voluntarily agreeing to it. Moreover, the deal does not have any external effects because the total amount of pollution remains the same. Thus, social welfare is enhanced by allowing the paper mill to sell its right to pollute to the steel mill.

The same logic applies to any voluntary transfer of the right to pollute from one firm to another. If the government allows firms to make these deals, it will, in essence, have created a new scarce resource: pollution permits. A market to trade these permits governed by the forces of supply and demand will help allocate the right to pollute. The firms that can reduce pollution only at high cost will be willing to pay the most for the pollution permits. The firms that can reduce pollution at low cost will prefer to sell whatever permits they have.

One advantage of allowing a market for pollution permits, sometimes referred to as a 'cap and trade' system as outlined in the illustration below, is that the initial allocation of pollution permits among firms does not matter from the standpoint of economic efficiency. Those firms that can reduce pollution most easily would be willing to sell whatever permits they get, and those firms that can reduce pollution only at high cost would be willing to buy whatever permits they need. As long as there is a free market for the pollution rights (an important assumption), the final allocation will be efficient whatever the initial allocation.

Although reducing pollution using permits may seem quite different from using Pigovian taxes, in fact the two policies have much in common. In both cases, firms pay for their pollution. With Pigovian taxes, polluting firms must pay a tax to the government. With pollution permits, polluting firms must pay to buy the permit. (Even firms that already own permits must pay to pollute: the opportunity cost of polluting is what they could have received by selling their permits on the open market.) Both Pigovian taxes and pollution permits internalize the externality of pollution by making it costly for firms to pollute.

The similarity of the two policies can be seen by considering the market for pollution. Both panels in Figure 6.7 show the demand curve for the right to pollute.

FIGURE 6.7

The Equivalence of Pigovian Taxes and Pollution Permits

In panel (a) the government sets a price on pollution by levying a Pigovian tax, and the demand curve determines the quantity of pollution. In panel (b) the government limits the quantity of pollution by limiting the number of pollution permits, and the demand curve determines the price of pollution. The price and quantity of pollution are the same in the two cases.

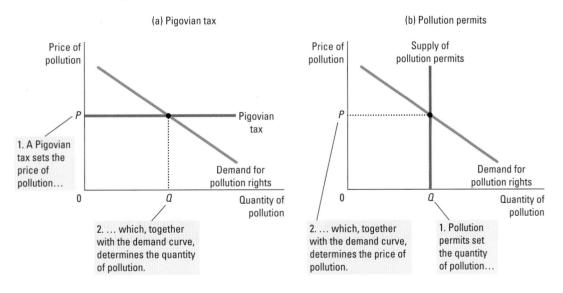

This curve shows that the lower the price of polluting, the more firms will choose to pollute. In panel (a) the government uses a Pigovian tax to set a price for pollution. In this case, the supply curve for pollution rights is perfectly elastic (because firms can pollute as much as they want by paying the tax), and the position of the demand curve determines the quantity of pollution. In panel (b) the government sets a quantity of pollution by issuing pollution permits. In this case, the supply curve for pollution rights is perfectly inelastic (because the quantity of pollution is fixed by the number of permits), and the position of the demand curve determines the price of pollution. Hence, for any given demand curve for pollution, the government can achieve any point on the demand curve either by setting a price with a Pigovian tax or by setting a quantity with pollution permits.

In some circumstances, however, selling pollution permits may be better than levying a Pigovian tax. Suppose the government wants no more than 600 tonnes of effluent to be dumped into the river. The government may not know the demand curve for pollution and so is not sure what size tax would achieve its goal. In this case, it can simply auction off 600 pollution permits. The auction price would yield the appropriate size of the Pigovian tax.

A number of governments around the world have used such a system as a way to control pollution. In 2002, European Union environment ministers unanimously agreed to set up a market to trade pollution permits for carbon dioxide (CO_2), the main so-called greenhouse gas of concern. Pollution permits, like Pigovian taxes, are increasingly being viewed as a cost-effective way to keep the environment clean.

A Formal Analysis of Taxes and Subsidies

Many governments, whether national or local, use taxes to raise revenue for public projects, such as roads, schools and national defence. Businesses in most countries face considerable tax burdens whether it is administering income tax payments to national revenue services, paying value added or sales taxes, paying taxes on profits, excise duties and other taxes such as religious taxes (in countries like Saudi Arabia and Germany, for example) or taxes related to employment referred to as payroll taxes. In some cases, firms can pass on some of the burden of these taxes to consumers.

tax incidence the manner in which the burden of a tax is shared among participants in a market

Economists use the term **tax incidence** to refer to the distribution of a tax burden. We can analyse the incidence of tax by using the tools of supply and demand.

How Taxes on Sellers Affect Market Outcomes

Consider a tax levied on sellers of a good. Suppose the government imposes a tax on sellers of nail varnish remover of €0.50 per bottle. What are the effects of this tax? We can analyse the effect using three steps.

Step One   The immediate impact of the tax is on the sellers of nail varnish remover. The quantity of nail varnish remover demanded at any given price is the same; thus, the demand curve does not change. By contrast, the tax on sellers makes the nail varnish remover business less profitable at any given price, so it shifts the supply curve.

Step Two   Because the tax on sellers raises the cost of producing and selling nail varnish remover, it reduces the quantity supplied at every price. The supply curve shifts to the left (or, equivalently, upward).

We can be precise about the magnitude of the shift. For any market price of nail varnish remover, the effective price to sellers – the amount they get to keep after paying the tax – is €0.50 lower. For example, if the market price of a bottle is €3.00, the effective price received by sellers would be €2.50. To induce sellers to supply any given quantity, the market price must now be €0.50 higher to compensate for the effect of the tax. Thus, as shown in Figure 6.8, the supply curve shifts *upward* from S_1 to S_2 by exactly the size of the tax (€0.50).

FIGURE 6.8

A Tax on Sellers

When a tax of €0.50 is levied on sellers, the supply curve shifts up by €0.50 from S₁ to S₂. The equilibrium quantity falls from 100 to 90 bottles. The price that buyers pay rises from €3.00 to €3.30. The price that sellers receive (after paying the tax) falls from €3.00 to €2.80. Even though the tax is levied on sellers, buyers and sellers share the burden of the tax.

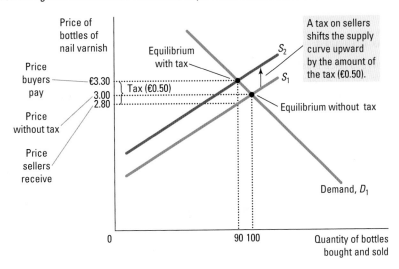

Step Three   Having determined how the supply curve shifts, we can now compare the initial and the new equilibrium. The figure shows that the equilibrium price of nail varnish remover rises from €3.00 to €3.30, and the equilibrium quantity falls from 100 to 90 bottles. The tax reduces the size of the nail varnish remover market and buyers and sellers share the burden of the tax. Because the market price rises, buyers pay €0.30 more for each bottle of nail varnish remover than they did before the tax was enacted. Sellers receive a higher price than they did without the tax, but the effective price (after paying the tax) falls from €3.00 to €2.80.

Implications   A tax on sellers places a wedge between the price that buyers pay and the price that sellers receive. The wedge between the buyers' price and the sellers' price is the same, and would be the same regardless of whether the tax is levied on buyers or sellers. In reality most governments levy taxes on sellers rather than on buyers, however. The wedge shifts the relative position of the supply and demand curves. In the new equilibrium, buyers and sellers share the burden of the tax.

Elasticity and Tax Incidence

When a good is taxed, buyers and sellers of the good share the burden of the tax. But how exactly is the tax burden divided? Only rarely will it be shared equally. To see how the burden is divided, consider the impact of taxation in the two markets in Figure 6.9. In both cases, the figure shows the initial demand curve, the initial supply curve, and a tax that drives a wedge between the amount paid by buyers and the amount received by sellers. The difference in the two panels is the relative elasticity of supply and demand. Panel (a) of Figure 6.9 shows a tax in a market with very elastic supply and relatively inelastic demand. That is, sellers are very responsive to changes in the price of the good (so the supply curve is relatively flat), whereas buyers are not very responsive (so the demand curve is relatively steep). When a tax is imposed on a market with these elasticities, the price received by sellers does not fall much, so sellers bear only a small burden. By contrast, the price paid by buyers rises substantially, indicating that buyers bear most of the burden of the tax. If the price elasticity of demand is low (represented in panel (a) by a steep curve) then demand will fall proportionately less in response to a rise in price – buyers are not very price sensitive. The seller can shift the burden of the tax onto the buyer, safe in the knowledge that demand will only fall by a relatively small amount.

FIGURE 6.9

How the Burden of a Tax is Divided

In panel (a), the supply curve is price elastic and the demand curve is price inelastic. In this case, the price received by sellers falls only slightly, while the price paid by buyers rises substantially. Thus, buyers bear most of the burden of the tax. In panel (b), the supply curve is price inelastic and the demand curve is price elastic. In this case, the price received by sellers falls substantially, while the price paid by buyers rises only slightly. Thus, sellers bear most of the burden of the tax.

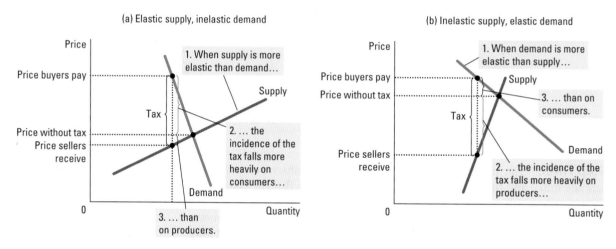

Panel (b) of Figure 6.9 shows a tax in a market with relatively price inelastic supply and very price elastic demand (represented by a flatter curve). In this case, sellers are not very responsive to changes in the price (so the supply curve is steeper), while buyers are very responsive. The figure shows that when a tax is imposed, the price paid by buyers does not rise much, while the price received by sellers falls substantially. Thus, sellers bear most of the burden of the tax. In this case, sellers know that if they try to pass on the tax to buyers that demand will fall by a relatively large amount.

The two panels of Figure 6.9 show a general lesson about how the burden of a tax is divided: a tax burden falls more heavily on the side of the market that is less price elastic. Why is this true? In essence, the price elasticity measures the willingness of buyers or sellers to leave the market when conditions become unfavourable. If demand is price inelastic, it means that buyers do not have good alternatives to consuming this particular good. If supply is price inelastic, it means that sellers do not have good alternatives to producing this particular good. When the good is taxed, the side of the market with fewer good alternatives cannot easily leave the market and must, therefore, bear more of the burden of the tax.

> **Quick Quiz** In a supply and demand diagram, show how a tax on car sellers of €1000 per car affects the quantity of cars sold and the price of cars. In your diagram, show the change in the price paid by car buyers and the change in price received by car sellers.

How Subsidies Affect Market Outcomes

A **subsidy** is the opposite of a tax. Subsidies are levied when governments want to encourage the consumption of a good which they deem is currently under-produced. Subsidies are generally given to sellers and have the effect of reducing the cost of production, as opposed to a tax which increases the cost of production. Subsidies exist in a variety of different areas including education, transport, agriculture, regional development, housing and employment.

> **subsidy** a payment to buyers and sellers to supplement income or lower costs and which thus encourages consumption or provides an advantage to the recipient

Subsidies in education help to make the cost of attending higher education lower than it would otherwise be. Most European countries provide subsidies for transport systems and the common agricultural policy oversees subsidies to farmers. In Switzerland some €2.5 billion is spent on subsidies for rail transport, in Germany the figure is nearer to €9 billion, whilst in the UK subsidies account for around €3 billion and in France €6.8 billion.

Figure 6.10 shows how a subsidy works using the rail system as an example. In the absence of a subsidy the equilibrium number of journeys bought and sold is Q_e and the equilibrium train ticket for each journey is price P_e. We again use a three-step approach to analyse the effect.

Step One   If the government gives a subsidy of €20 per journey to train operators, it is the supply curve for journeys which is affected; the demand curve is not affected because the number of train journeys demanded at each price stays the same. The subsidy to train operators reduces the cost of providing a train journey and so the supply curve will shift downwards to the right.

FIGURE 6.10

A Subsidy on Rail Transport

When a subsidy of €20 per journey is given to sellers, the supply curve shifts to the right by €20 from S_1 to S_2. The equilibrium quantity rises from Q_e to Q_1 journeys per year. The price that buyers pay for a journey falls from €75 to €60. The subsidy results in lower prices for passengers and an increased number of journeys available. Even though the subsidy is given to sellers, buyers and sellers share the benefits of the subsidy.

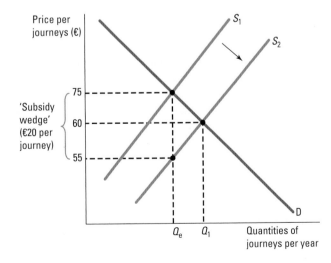

Step Two   Because the subsidy reduces the cost to the train operators, the supply curve shifts to the right by the amount of the subsidy. If the cost of providing a train journey was an average of €75 and the subsidy was €20, the supply curve would shift so that train operators would now supply train journeys at an effective cost €20 lower. They would now be willing to supply more train journeys at every price.

Step Three   Comparing the initial and the new equilibrium we can see that the equilibrium price of each train journey is now lower at €60 and the equilibrium number of journeys travelled increases to Q_1. Passengers and train operators both benefit from the subsidy as passengers can obtain train tickets at a lower price than before the subsidy and have more journeys available, and sellers receive more revenue than they did before the subsidy allowing them the potential to invest in the service they provide. The precise division of the benefits between buyers and sellers will depend on the relative price elasticities of demand and supply.

Implications   There is considerable debate surrounding the value of subsidies. We have seen from the example how price and quantity can be affected following the imposition of a subsidy. In the case of transport, it may have the effect of altering the incentives for people to travel on the train rather than on the roads, and so have the benefit of reducing congestion on the roads and the pollution that is associated with road use. There are also costs associated with subsidies; the subsidy has to be financed and this generally falls on the taxpayer. Subsidies may also encourage firms to overproduce, which has a wider effect on the market. Subsidies on commodities such as cotton, bananas and sugar distort the workings of the market and change global comparative advantage. Overproduction leads to excess supply on world markets and drives down prices, as well as diverting trade to rich countries who can support producers through subsidies at the expense of poor countries, whose producers cannot compete because prices are lower than the free market price.

> **?** **what if…** A government imposed a subsidy on a product with a highly price inelastic demand curve but a very price elastic supply curve. What do you think would be the effects in both the short term and the long term for consumers and businesses in this market?

Property Rights

In some cases, private solutions to externalities can occur but need some form of legal back-up to be able to work. One such example is the establishment of property rights. In order for any economy to work efficiently, a system of property rights has to be established and understood. The principle behind property rights is this: if an individual decided to throw a brick through the window of someone else's house, the house owner would have the rights to expect legal redress. Assuming the individual who caused the damage can be identified and the proof that it was they who caused the damage, the property owner can expect compensation, under the law, to put right the damage. This may include replacing the window pane and for any emotional trauma experienced by the house owner.

With things such as rivers, streams, land and air it is less easy to establish who the legal owners are. If some system could be devised whereby the ownership of property could be established, then those who cause damage to that property can be brought to book. Extending property rights, therefore, might be one area where externalities can be internalized. For example, if property rights over the air that we breathe can be extended, then any firm polluting that air (in whatever way, noise, smell, smoke, etc.) could face prosecution for doing so. The threat of prosecution is sufficient to act as an incentive to change behaviour.

Extension of property rights also means that the owner of the property (which can be intellectual as well as physical) can also exercise the right to sell or share that property if they so wish at some mutually agreeable price. Extending property rights allows individuals, groups and organizations to be able to arrive at efficient solutions. If, for example, an individual was assigned property rights for the air 1 km above their property, then if a nearby factory wanted to pollute that air they would have to enter into negotiations with the house owner to do so at some mutually agreeable price. The resulting right to pollute could also be sold to another party. A more developed system of property rights can, therefore, improve well-being. It has also been identified as playing a crucial role in good governance, particularly relevant for developing countries to be able to attract the sort of inward investment that will help their economies to grow.

There are problems with extending property rights, however. How do we apportion rights to such things as air, the seas, rivers and land? The cost of establishing property rights and getting international agreement on what they entail is considerable, and may counteract the social benefits provided. If property rights were extended to the volume of air 1 km above a person's property, imagine the complexity of the negotiations that would have to be carried out with any business nearby, or airlines and the military for the right to share that air. Property owners may also have insufficient knowledge about their rights and exactly what they mean; it is also not a costless exercise to prove that property rights have been violated.

In the music and movie industry the complexities of property rights have been the subject of debate and countless lawsuits in recent years. It not only relates to the issues of file sharing, pirating, copying CDs and DVDs for personal use and downloading, but also to the artists/actors themselves and the rights to the music that they have written and performed on stage and screen. Similar issues are also being experienced in the publishing industry as digital technologies mean the traditional printed book is under some pressure and pirating becomes a growing problem.

Intellectual property law is an incredibly complex area and different countries interpret property rights in different ways, making any international agreement even more difficult. Despite the complexities, there have been efforts to extend property rights to help bring social benefits. In many parts of Europe, property rights over public spaces such as national parks, rivers and seas have meant that environmental laws can be established and enforced and this has led to an improvement in well-being for millions who are able to use these spaces, enjoy cleaner rivers and exploit the resources of the sea.

Objections to the Economic Analysis of Pollution

Some environmentalists argue that it is in some sense morally wrong to allow anyone to pollute the environment in return for paying a fee. Clean air and clean water, they argue, are fundamental human rights that should not be debased by considering them in economic terms. How can you put a price on clean air and clean water? The environment is so important, they claim, that we should protect it as much as possible, regardless of the cost.

Critics of this view note that people face trade-offs. Certainly, clean air and clean water have value. But their value must be compared to their opportunity cost – that is, to what one must give up to obtain them. Eliminating all pollution is impossible. Trying to eliminate all pollution would reverse many of the technological advances that allow us to enjoy a high standard of living. Few people would be willing to accept poor nutrition, inadequate medical care or shoddy housing to make the environment as clean as possible.

A clean environment is a normal good–it has a positive income elasticity: rich countries can afford a cleaner environment than poor ones and, therefore, usually have more rigorous environmental protection. In addition, like most other goods, clean air and water obey the law of demand: the lower the price of environmental protection, the more the public will want. The economic approach of using pollution permits and Pigovian taxes reduces the cost of environmental protection and should, therefore, increase the public's demand for a clean environment.

> **Quick Quiz** A glue factory and a steel mill emit smoke containing a chemical that is harmful if inhaled in large amounts. Describe three ways the town government might respond to this externality. What are the pros and cons of each solution?

Social and Ethical Responsibility

Many firms complain about government interference in business and about the taxes they have to pay. Some will also argue that the subsidy system is fundamentally flawed because it is unfair (not unsurprisingly, the ones who are most vociferous in this condemnation of subsidies are the ones who do not receive any). There is an argument that government could reduce its involvement in markets if firms behaved more responsibly. Unfortunately, firms do not always behave responsibly (even if we were able to accurately define what the term 'responsible' meant in this context).

social responsibility the responsibility a firm has for the impact of their product and activities on society

ethical responsibility the moral basis for business activity and whether what the business does 'is right' and is underpinned by some moral purpose – doing what is 'right'

Social responsibility refers to the responsibility a firm has for the impact of their product and activities on society. **Ethical responsibilities** refer to the moral basis for business activity and whether what the business does is 'right' and is underpinned by some moral purpose – doing what is 'right'.

The problem arises when asking 'doing what is right for whom?' A private sector firm is primarily responsible to its shareholders – the owners of the business – who in turn will wish to see the firm grow, expanding sales and profits. In so doing there may be a conflict with the responsibility a firm has to the health and welfare of its customers. Drug companies have a responsibility to develop new products, market them and generate profits for their shareholders. In so doing, to what extent should they compromise the health and safety of those who consume their products?

Many businesses will claim to have a socially responsible code of practice that they adhere to, as well as an ethical stance to their activities, but such claims are sometimes refuted and criticized by opponents. It is all very well claiming to have no artificial colouring and preservative in food products, for example, but this might be disingenuous at the very least if the product is high in salt and sugars which can contribute to obesity, heart disease and high blood pressure if consumed in too high a quantity.

Part of the policy response by governments could be passing legislation that forces businesses to give clearer information on packaging to help consumers make more informed choices about what they buy. Such legislation would impose additional costs on businesses and ultimately would put up the price of the product to the consumer and thus reduce consumer surplus. Are consumers willing to pay such a price for the extra information? If firms do engage in activities that increase levels of responsibility and ethical standards, this comes at a cost. Many European consumers enjoy low prices for clothing whilst some firms in the Middle East who manufacture these products receive very low prices for their efforts. Would consumers in Europe be willing to pay higher prices for their clothes in order that

Middle East manufacturers get higher prices and so can improve wages and conditions for employees? It is not at all clear that such a philanthropic approach would be embraced by consumers.

The issues therefore are complex and open to subjective interpretation. The solution may be to try to arrive at some form of balance between the rights of people to choose their own lifestyle, be informed about the consequences of that lifestyle and to be protected from the unknown by the government. Where that balance lies though is not at all clear.

CONCLUSION

The invisible hand is powerful but not omnipotent. A market's equilibrium maximizes the sum of producer and consumer surplus. When buyers and sellers in the market are the only interested parties, this outcome is efficient from the standpoint of society as a whole. But when there are external effects, such as pollution, evaluating a market outcome requires taking into account the well-being of third parties as well. In this case, the invisible hand of the marketplace may fail to allocate resources efficiently.

Because of the problem of externalities, the government often steps in to try to rectify market failure. When government does intervene in the market, firms are affected either because they have to pay taxes, receive subsidies or through the regulations that are imposed. These interventions invariably impose costs on businesses and in many countries there are complaints from business representatives of the burden of taxes and regulation.

Society as a whole has to make a judgement about the extent to which such government interference confers benefits on society as a whole which are greater than the costs of that intervention. It can be argued that firms should take more responsibility for their actions but getting agreement on what that responsibility should be and whether consumers are prepared to pay for increased social and ethical responsibility in the form of higher prices will always be difficult.

Yet, even now, society should not abandon market forces entirely. Rather, the government can address the problem by requiring decision makers to bear the full costs of their actions. Pigovian taxes on emissions and pollution permits, for instance, are designed to internalize the externality of pollution. Increasingly, they are being seen as effective policies for those interested in protecting the environment. Market forces, properly redirected, can be an effective remedy for market failure.

IN THE NEWS

Pricing Pollution

China accounts for nearly 30 per cent of greenhouse gas emissions. This article looks at how it intends to control these emissions.

In 2014 average global temperature was some 0.69°C above the 20th-century average. Many scientists argue that this long-term trend has been caused by the increase in greenhouse gases into the atmosphere, largely as a result of the burning of fossil fuels.

The effects of the rise in global temperatures varies across the world, but the external costs of the increase in carbon dioxide emissions might be more cases of extreme weather events. Some areas are experiencing more flooding whilst others face drought. In January 2013, Beijing, China's capital, monitored air pollution some 40 times that considered safe by the World Health Organization. The cause was said to be atmospheric conditions trapping pollution from 5 million cars and 200 coal-fired power stations.

According to the World Bank, China had an annual average economic growth rate of 7.7 per cent between 2010 and 2014. China is already the world's biggest carbon-emitting nation accounting for nearly 30 per cent of global greenhouse emissions and high continued growth rates could exacerbate the problem.

In 2014 China announced its intention to introduce a national carbon permit trading market in 2016, making it the world's biggest emissions trading scheme,

overshadowing the European trading scheme by a factor of two. It is likely to regulate between 3 and 4 billion tonnes of carbon dioxide by 2020 in a permit trading market worth 400 billion yuan or around 43 billion pounds sterling. This prices pollution at €10 a tonne, above current prices for permits in Europe which are around €6 per tonne.

To gain experience of carbon trading China has already launched several regional schemes.

The system works by placing a cap on carbon dioxide emissions from manufacturers and power generation companies. Industries emitting levels above their cap will have to buy permits in the open market. As the permit price rises, then alternative greener sources become more viable and it pays polluters to invest in systems to control and reduce emissions.

One issue is compliance by industry. The regional pilot schemes launched in 2013 show that compliance from polluters is good, but that might be down to the issuing of too many permits. If that is the case then industry has less of an incentive to cut emissions.

Chongqing, one of the regional pilot schemes, handed out 125 million permits in 2013 for 242 local companies targeted with reducing their carbon emissions, many of which burn coal. In 2014 the number of permits was reduced to

116 million, representing a decline of 7.2 per cent. It suggests the Chinese government is responding to pressures to focus attention on the negative externalities associated with industrial growth.

Questions

1. Outline some of the external costs associated with pollution.
2. Use supply and demand analysis to explain how a market for carbon permits aims to reduce the overall level of carbon emissions in nations who operate such a system. As part of your answer, explain the role the price of permits play as a signal to businesses in controlling their pollution.
3. Outline the key factors in a cap and trade scheme which are necessary to bring about desired reductions in carbon emissions.
4. Why might green products be 'dependent' on a successful trade in carbon permits?
5. Evaluate the importance of overall emissions control targets to the successful creation of a carbon trading market in China.

References: **http://reneweconomy.com.au/2014/china-plans-65bn-carbon-market-at-around-18tonne-48911**

http://uk.reuters.com/article/2015/03/10/china-carbon-chongqing-idUKL4N0WC3OU20150310?feedType=RSS&feedName=rbssFinancialServicesAndRealEstateNews

SUMMARY

- Market failure occurs when resources are not allocated efficiently.
- Typically, market failure occurs because of a lack of perfect information between firms and buyers or because firms have some element of market power.

- When a transaction between a buyer and seller directly affects a third party, the effect is called an externality. Negative externalities, such as pollution, cause the socially optimal quantity in a market to be less than the equilibrium quantity. Positive externalities, such as technology spillovers, cause the socially optimal quantity to be greater than the equilibrium quantity.

- Those affected by externalities can sometimes solve the problem privately. For instance, when one business confers an externality on another business, the two businesses can internalize the externality by merging.
- When private parties cannot adequately deal with external effects, such as pollution, the government often steps in. Sometimes the government prevents socially inefficient activity by regulating behaviour. At other times it internalizes an externality using Pigovian taxes. Another public policy is to issue permits. For instance, the government could protect the environment by issuing a limited number of pollution permits. The end result of this policy is largely the same as imposing Pigovian taxes on polluters.

QUESTIONS FOR REVIEW

1. Identify, using examples, three sources of market failure.

2. Using an appropriate example, explain the difference between a private cost and a social cost and a private benefit and a social benefit.

3. Give an example of a negative externality and an example of a positive externality.

4. Use a supply-and-demand diagram to explain the effect of a negative externality in production.

5. In a supply-and-demand diagram, show producer and consumer surplus in the market equilibrium.

6. In what way does the patent system help society solve an externality problem?

7. List some of the ways that the problems caused by externalities can be solved without government intervention.

8. How does a tax imposed on a good with a high price elasticity of demand affect the market equilibrium? Who bears most of the burden of the tax in this instance?

9. How does a subsidy on a good affect the price paid by buyers, the price received by sellers and the quantity bought and sold?

10. What are Pigovian taxes? Why do economists prefer them over regulations as a way to protect the environment from pollution?

PROBLEMS AND APPLICATIONS

1. Do you agree with the following statements? Why or why not?
   a. 'The benefits of Pigovian taxes as a way to reduce pollution have to be weighed against the deadweight losses that these taxes cause.'
   b. 'When deciding whether to levy a Pigovian tax on consumers or producers, the government should be careful to levy the tax on the side of the market generating the externality.'

2. Consider the market for fire extinguishers.
   a. Why might fire extinguishers exhibit positive externalities?
   b. Draw a graph of the market for fire extinguishers, labelling the demand curve, the social value curve, the supply curve and the social cost curve.
   c. Indicate the market equilibrium level of output and the efficient level of output. Give an intuitive explanation for why these quantities differ.
   d. If the external benefit is €10 per extinguisher, describe a government policy that would result in the efficient outcome.

3. The cost of producing Blu-ray DVD players has fallen over the past few years. Let's consider some implications of this fact.
   a. Use a supply-and-demand diagram to show the effect of falling production costs on the price and quantity of Blu-ray DVD players sold.
   b. In your diagram, show what happens to consumer surplus and producer surplus.
   c. Suppose the supply of Blu-ray DVD players is very price elastic. Who benefits most from falling production costs – consumers or producers of Blu-ray DVD players?

4. The government decides to reduce air pollution by reducing the use of petrol. It imposes €0.50 tax for each litre of petrol sold.
   a. Should it impose this tax on petrol companies or motorists? Explain, using a supply-and-demand diagram.
   b. If the demand for petrol were more price elastic, would this tax be more effective or less effective in

reducing the quantity of petrol consumed? Explain with both words and a diagram.

c. Are consumers of petrol helped or hurt by this tax? Why?

d. Are workers in the oil industry helped or hurt by this tax? Why?

5. Assume that it is rumoured that the French government subsidizes cattle farming, and that the subsidy is larger in areas with more tourist attractions. Can you think of a reason why this policy might be efficient?

6. Many observers believe that the levels of pollution in our economy are too high.

a. If society wishes to reduce overall pollution by a certain amount, why is it efficient to have different amounts of reduction at different firms?

b. Command-and-control approaches often rely on uniform reductions among firms. Why are these approaches generally unable to target the firms that should undertake bigger reductions?

c. Economists argue that appropriate Pigovian taxes or tradable pollution rights will result in efficient pollution reduction. How do these approaches target the firms that should undertake bigger reductions?

7. The Pristine River has two polluting firms on its banks. European Industrial and Creative Chemicals each dump 100 tonnes of effluent into the river each year. The cost of reducing effluent emissions per tonne equals €10 for European Industrial and €100 for Creative. The government wants to reduce overall pollution from 200 tonnes to 50 tonnes per year.

a. If the government knew the cost of reduction for each firm, what reductions would it impose to reach its overall goal? What would be the cost to each firm and the total cost to the firms together?

b. In a more typical situation, the government would not know the cost of pollution reduction at each

firm. If the government decided to reach its overall goal by imposing uniform reductions on the firms, calculate the reduction made by each firm, the cost to each firm and the total cost to the firms together.

c. Compare the total cost of pollution reduction in parts (a) and (b). If the government does not know the cost of reduction for each firm, is there still some way for it to reduce pollution to 50 tonnes at the total cost you calculated in part (a)? Explain.

8. 'A fine is a tax for doing something wrong. A tax is a fine for doing something right.' Discuss.

9. Some people object to market-based policies to reduce pollution, claiming that they place a monetary value on cleaning our air and water. Critics reply that society implicitly places a monetary value on environmental cleanup even under command-and-control policies. Discuss why this is true.

10. There are three industrial firms in Eurovia.

Firm	Initial pollution level	Cost of reducing pollution by 1 unit
A	70 units	€20
B	80	25
C	50	10

The government wants to reduce pollution to 120 units, it gives each firm 40 tradable pollution permits.

a. Who sells permits and how many do they sell? Who buys permits and how many do they buy? Briefly explain why the sellers and buyers are each willing to do so. What is the total cost of pollution reduction in this situation?

b. How much higher would the costs of pollution reduction be if the permits could not be traded?

7 THE CONSUMER AND CONSUMER BEHAVIOUR

LEARNING OUTCOMES

After reading this chapter you should be able to:

- Analyse how a consumer's optimal choices are determined.
- Describe how firms use advertising and branding to influence consumer behaviour and the arguments for and against advertising.
- Examine the problems caused by asymmetric information.
- State the assumptions of the standard economic model.
- Calculate total and marginal utility as consumption increases.

- Draw a budget constraint on a graph if you are given the value of income and the prices of the goods.
- Explain the relationship between relative prices and the marginal rate of substitution between two goods at the consumer's optimum.
- Describe different heuristics and be able to give examples of each.
- Present an argument for and against advertising.
- Explain how signalling and screening help to reduce asymmetric information.

INTRODUCTION

Business activity requires a producer and a consumer – businesses cannot survive without some individual, group or other business buying their output. It makes sense, therefore, for businesses to have an understanding of how consumers think and behave. How do consumers make decisions about purchases? What makes a consumer choose one product repeatedly over the many others that are available? How are they influenced by advertising (if at all) and how important are brands in influencing consumer behaviour? We are going to look at all of these issues in this chapter.

First of we all are going to present a classical theory of consumer behaviour based on an assumption of rational behaviour which is referred to as the *standard economic model*. The model presented can explain some consumer behaviour in some situations but as with all models it has its limitations. Over the last 30 years more research has been done into how consumers make purchasing decisions and the existence of technology such as functional magnetic resonance imaging (fMRI) and positive emission tomography (PET) have allowed researchers to analyse how the brain responds to different stimuli and what parts of the brain become active when purchasing decisions are made or when individuals are exposed to stimuli such as advertising.

This research along with that of psychologists and anthropologists among other disciplines has led to the development of different, sometimes competing, sometimes complementary, theories of consumer behaviour. We are going to look at some of these theories.

We are then going to look at advertising and branding and how businesses can use these to influence consumer behaviour and the extent to which they are successful in doing so. In looking at these areas we need to recognize that consumers are not homogenous. Consumers come in many forms – some are individuals, some are large organizations such as other businesses, government or its agents, and some are small businesses. These are not all going to behave the same and so an understanding of those upon whom you rely is going to be of some importance in a successful business.

The Standard Economic Model

When you walk into a shop, you are invariably confronted with a wide range of goods. Most people have limited financial resources and cannot buy everything they want. How are purchasing choices made, therefore?

One assumption might be that you consider the constraint that is your income, the prices of the various goods being offered for sale and the value they represent (more of this shortly) and choose to buy a bundle of goods that, given your resources, best suits your needs and desires and maximizes value. This is a constrained optimization problem that forms the basis of many classical economic theories.

We can summarize some key assumptions of the standard economic model as:

- Buyers (or economic agents as they are sometimes referred to) are rational.
- More is preferred to less.
- Buyers seek to maximize their utility.
- Consumers act in self-interest and do not consider the utility of others.

Value

value the worth to an individual of owning an item represented by the satisfaction derived from its consumption

A key concept in consumer behaviour is value. Value is a subjective term – what one person or business thinks represents value is often different to that of some other individual or business. **Value** can be seen as the worth to an individual of owning an item represented by the satisfaction derived from its consumption. Classical economists used the term **utility** to refer to the satisfaction derived from consumption. Utility is an ordinal concept; we can use some measure of utility to represent consumer choices in some order but that order tells us nothing about the differences in the values we use. For example, if a group of five people were asked to rank different brands of cola in order of preference using a 10-point scale (with each point referred to as a *util*) we might be able to conclude that brand X was the most popular, followed by brand Y and brand Z. If person 1 ranked brand X at 10 utils while person 2 ranked the same brand as 5 utils we cannot say that person 1 values brand X twice as much as person 2, only that they place it higher in their preferences.

One way in which we can measure value is the amount consumers are prepared to pay. It is highly likely that at some point in your life you will have said something like, 'I wouldn't have that if you paid me', or similar. How much of our limited income we are prepared to pay is a reflection of the value we put on acquiring a good. It might not tell us much about the satisfaction from actually consuming the good (the buyer might not be the final consumer) but it does give some idea of value. For example, two friends, Alexa and Monique are in a store looking at shoes. Alexa picks up a pair priced at €100. Monique looks at her friend and asks why on earth she is thinking of buying them? No way would Monique pay that sort of money for those shoes. A discussion ensues about the shoes; clearly there is a difference of opinion on them and thus how much they are 'worth'. If Alexa buys the shoes, then the value to her must be at least €100 because that is what she has to give up in money terms in order to acquire it. It may be that Alexa would have been prepared to pay much more than €100 for the shoes, in which case she is getting consumer surplus. Monique leaves the store baffled at her friend's purchasing decision. Monique clearly feels that giving up €100 to buy those shoes was a 'waste of money'.

The amount buyers are prepared to pay for a good, therefore, tells us something about the value they place on it. It is not just the amount of money we hand over that reflects value but what that amount of money could have bought; the opportunity cost. We could make a reasonable assumption that Monique believed there was a way in which she could allocate €100 to get more value – in other words, the alternative that €100 could buy (whatever that might be) represented greater value than acquiring the particular pair of shoes Alexa chose.

Total and Marginal Utility

Given that utility can be used as a word to represent satisfaction derived from consumption we can look at what happens to utility as consumption increases. Given our assumption that consumers prefer more to less, intuition might tell us that total utility increases as consumption increases. This may be true up to a point. To understand this let us use an example.

You have spent two hours in the gym working very hard. You are hot, sweaty and very thirsty. After your shower you go to the nearest café and order a glass of orange juice. If you were asked to rate the satisfaction derived from consuming the orange juice out of 10 (utils) at that time, you might rate it at 10. You order a second glass as you are still thirsty; the second glass still brings some satisfaction but if asked to rate it you might give it 8. Total utility is now 18 utils – the second glass has increased total utility. However, you did not rate the second glass quite as high as the first because some of your thirst has been quenched. **Marginal utility** measures the addition to total utility as a result of the consumption of an extra unit. The marginal utility of the first glass was 10 but for the second glass the marginal utility was 8.

utility the satisfaction derived from consumption

marginal utility the addition to total utility as a result of one extra unit of consumption

If you now ordered a third glass you might rate this at 5. Total utility is now 23 but the marginal utility of the third glass is 5. By the time you get to the fifth or sixth glass the marginal utility is likely to be very low and at some point could even be negative. For example, if you have already had 8 glasses of orange juice your stomach might be telling you that it really does not need another one – having the ninth glass might actually make you physically sick and so the marginal utility of the ninth glass would be negative. It follows that total utility will actually start to decline at this point.

This example illustrates a general principle called the law of **diminishing marginal utility**. This simply states that the more a consumer has of a given commodity the smaller the satisfaction gained from consuming each extra unit. As consumption of a good rises, total utility will rise at first but at a slower rate until some point at which the consumer becomes satiated (has had enough) after which point total utility will fall and marginal utility will be negative.

This principle is important in considering the relationship between price and the demand curve. Diminishing marginal utility implies that we value successive units of consumption less than the previous and so it makes sense that consumers are not prepared to pay as much for successive units of consumption. To encourage consumers to buy more, sellers have to reduce prices, which partly explains why the demand curve slopes downwards from left to right.

Many firms will be acutely aware that they have rivals competing for consumers and that consumers have a choice. Switching between one good and another is a feature of business. The marginal rate of substitution (MRS) measures how much of one good a consumer requires in order to be compensated for a one-unit reduction in consumption of another good. The marginal rate of substitution between two goods depends on their marginal utilities. For example, if the marginal utility of good X is twice the marginal utility of good Y, then a person would need 2 units of good Y to compensate for losing 1 unit of good X, and the marginal rate of substitution equals 2. More generally, the marginal rate of substitution equals the marginal utility of one good divided by the marginal utility of the other good.

diminishing marginal utility a 'law' that states that marginal utility will fall as consumption increases

What Consumers Can Afford

Most people would like to increase the quantity or quality of the goods they consume – to take longer holidays, drive fancier cars or eat at better restaurants. People consume less than they desire because their spending is *constrained*, or limited, by their income. To keep things simple, we use a model which examines the decisions facing a consumer who buys only two goods: cola and pizza. Of course, real people buy thousands of different kinds of goods. Yet using this model greatly simplifies the problem without altering the basic insights about consumer choice.

Suppose that the consumer has an income of €1000 per month and that they spend their entire income each month on cola and pizza. The price of a litre of cola is €2 and the price of a pizza is €10. The table in Figure 7.1 shows some of the many combinations of cola and pizza that the consumer can buy. The first line in the table shows that if the consumer spends all their income on pizza, they can eat 100 pizzas during the month, but they would not be able to buy any cola at all. The second line shows another possible consumption bundle: 90 pizzas and 50 litres of cola. And so on. Each consumption bundle in the table costs exactly €1000.

The graph in Figure 7.1 illustrates these consumption bundles that the consumer can choose. The vertical axis measures the number of litres of cola, and the horizontal axis measures the number of pizzas. Three points are marked on this figure. At point A, the consumer buys no cola and consumes 100 pizzas. At point B, the consumer buys no pizza and consumes 500 litres of cola. At point C, the consumer buys 50 pizzas and 250 litres of cola. Point C, which is exactly at the middle of the line from A to B, is the point at which the consumer spends an equal amount (€500) on cola and pizza. Of course, these are only three of the different combinations of cola and pizza that the consumer can choose shown by the line from A to B. This line, called the **budget constraint**, shows the consumption bundles that the consumer can afford. In this case, it shows the trade-off between cola and pizza that the consumer faces.

> **budget constraint** the limit on the consumption bundles that a consumer can afford

FIGURE 7.1

The Consumer's Budget Constraint

The budget constraint shows the various bundles of goods that the consumer can afford for a given income. Here the consumer buys bundles of cola and pizza. The table and graph show what the consumer can afford if their income is €1000, the price of cola is €2 and the price of pizza is €10.

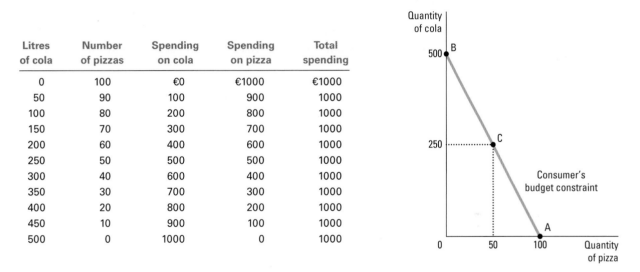

Litres of cola	Number of pizzas	Spending on cola	Spending on pizza	Total spending
0	100	€0	€1000	€1000
50	90	100	900	1000
100	80	200	800	1000
150	70	300	700	1000
200	60	400	600	1000
250	50	500	500	1000
300	40	600	400	1000
350	30	700	300	1000
400	20	800	200	1000
450	10	900	100	1000
500	0	1000	0	1000

The slope of the budget constraint measures the rate at which the consumer can trade one good for the other. The slope between two points is calculated as the change in the vertical distance divided by the change in the horizontal distance ('rise over run'). From point A to point B, the vertical distance is 500 litres, and the horizontal distance is 100 pizzas. Because the budget constraint slopes downward, the slope is a negative number – this reflects the fact that to get one extra pizza, the consumer has to *reduce* their consumption of cola by five litres. In fact, the slope of the budget constraint (ignoring the minus sign) equals the *relative price* of the two goods – the price of one good compared to the price of the other. A pizza costs five times as much as a litre of cola, so the opportunity cost of a pizza is 5 litres of cola. The budget constraint's slope of 5 reflects the trade-off the market is offering the consumer: 1 pizza for 5 litres of cola.

> **Quick Quiz** Draw the budget constraint for a person with income of €1000 if the price of cola is €5 per litre and the price of pizza is €10. What is the slope of this budget constraint?

Preferences – What the Consumer Wants

The consumer's preferences allow them to choose among different bundles of cola and pizza. If you offer the consumer two different bundles, they chooses the bundle that best suits their tastes. If the two bundles suit their tastes equally well, we say that the consumer is *indifferent* between the two bundles.

Just as we have represented the consumer's budget constraint graphically, we can also represent their preferences graphically. We do this with indifference curves. An **indifference curve** shows the bundles of consumption that make the consumer equally happy. In this case, the indifference curves show the combinations of cola and pizza with which the consumer is equally satisfied.

Figure 7.2 shows two of the consumer's many indifference curves. The consumer is indifferent among combinations A, B and C, because they are all on the same curve. Not surprisingly, if the consumer's consumption of pizza is reduced, say from point A to point B, consumption of cola must increase to keep them equally happy. If consumption of pizza is reduced again, from point B to point C, the amount of cola consumed must increase yet again.

The slope at any point on an indifference curve equals the rate at which the consumer is willing to substitute one good for the other. This is the MRS. In this case, the MRS measures how much cola the consumer requires in order to be compensated for a one-unit reduction in pizza consumption. Notice that because the indifference curves are not straight lines, the MRS is not the same at all points on a given indifference curve. The rate at which a consumer is willing to trade one good for the other depends on the amounts of the goods they are already consuming. That is, the rate at which a consumer is willing to trade pizza for cola depends on whether they are hungrier or thirstier, which in turn depends on how much pizza and cola they have at the outset.

> **indifference curve** a curve that shows consumption bundles that give the consumer the same level of satisfaction

---

FIGURE 7.2

The Consumer's Preferences

The consumer's preferences are represented with indifference curves, which show the combinations of cola and pizza that make the consumer equally satisfied. Because the consumer prefers more of a good, points on a higher indifference curve (I_2) are preferred to points on a lower indifference curve (I_1). The marginal rate of substitution (MRS) shows the rate at which the consumer is willing to trade cola for pizza.

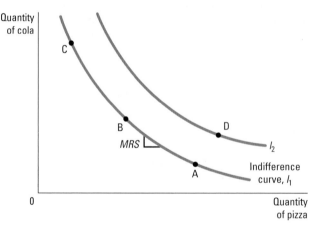

The consumer is equally happy at all points on any given indifference curve, but they prefer some indifference curves to others. We assume that consumers would rather have more of a good than less of it. Because they prefer more consumption to less, higher indifference curves are preferred to lower ones. The idea that buyers can rank preferences from best to worst (or vice versa) is captured by **expected utility theory**. In Figure 7.2, any point on curve I_2 is preferred to any point on curve I_1.

A consumer's set of indifference curves gives a complete ranking of the consumer's preferences. That is, we can use indifference curves to rank any two bundles of goods. For example, the indifference curves in Figure 7.2 tell us that point D is preferred to point A because point D is on a higher indifference curve than point A. This may be obvious because point D offers the consumer both more pizza and more cola. However, point D is also preferred to point C because point D is on a higher indifference curve. Point D has less cola than point C, but it has more than enough extra pizza to make the consumer prefer it. By seeing which point is on the higher indifference curve, we can use the set of indifference curves to rank any combinations of cola and pizza.

expected utility theory the idea that buyers can rank preferences from best to worst (or vice versa)

> **Pitfall Prevention** Remember that an indifference curve shows bundles of goods which give equal utility so that consumers have no preference between them – they are equally preferred. However, it is assumed that consumers always prefer more to less so would prefer to be on the highest indifference curve possible.

Optimization – What the Consumer Chooses

We have the two pieces necessary to consider the consumer's decision about what to buy. Remembering the assumptions we set out earlier in the chapter, we can state that the consumer would like to end up with the best possible combination of cola and pizza – that is, the combination on the highest possible indifference curve. But the consumer can only make choices under the constraint of their budget, which measures the total resources available to them.

Figure 7.3 shows the consumer's budget constraint and three of their many indifference curves. The highest indifference curve that the consumer can reach (I_2 in the figure) is the one that just barely touches the budget constraint. The point at which this indifference curve and the budget constraint touch is called the *optimum*. The consumer would prefer point A, but cannot afford that point because it lies above their budget constraint. The consumer can afford point B, but that point is on a lower indifference curve and, therefore, provides the consumer less satisfaction. The optimum represents the best combination of consumption of cola and pizza available to the consumer given their budget constraint.

Notice that, at the optimum, the slope of the indifference curve equals the slope of the budget constraint. We say that the indifference curve is *tangential* to the budget constraint. The slope of the indifference curve is the marginal rate of substitution between cola and pizza, and the slope of the budget constraint is the relative price of cola and pizza. Thus, the consumer chooses consumption of the two goods so that the marginal rate of substitution equals the relative price. That is:

$$MRS = \frac{P_x}{P_y}$$

Because the marginal rate of substitution equals the ratio of marginal utilities, we can write this condition for optimization as:

$$\frac{MU_x}{MU_y} = \frac{P_x}{P_y}$$

The Consumer's Optimum

The consumer chooses the point on their budget constraint that lies on the highest indifference curve. At this point, called the optimum, the MRS equals the relative price of the two goods. Here the highest indifference curve the consumer can reach is I₂. The consumer prefers point A, which lies on indifference curve I₃, but the consumer cannot afford this bundle of cola and pizza. In contrast, point B is affordable, but because it lies on a lower indifference curve, the consumer does not prefer it.

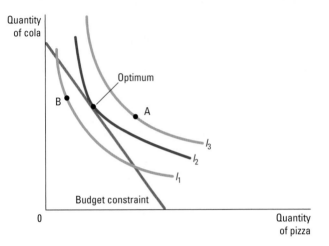

Now rearrange this expression to become:

$$\frac{MU_x}{P_x} = \frac{MU_y}{P_y}$$

This equation has a simple interpretation: at the optimum, the marginal utility per euro spent on good X equals the marginal utility per euro spent on good Y. Why? If this equality did not hold, the consumer could increase utility by changing behaviour, switching spending from the good that provided lower marginal utility per euro and more on the good that provided higher marginal utility per euro. This would be the rational thing to do.

This analysis of consumer choice shows how market prices reflect the marginal value that consumers place on goods. In making consumption choices, the consumer takes as given the relative price of the two goods and then chooses an optimum at which their MRS equals this relative price. The relative price is the rate at which the *market* is willing to trade one good for the other, whereas the MRS is the rate at which the *consumer* is willing to trade one good for the other. At the consumer's optimum, the consumer's valuation of the two goods (as measured by the MRS) equals the market's valuation (as measured by the relative price). As a result of this consumer optimization, market prices of different goods reflect the value that consumers place on those goods.

How Changes in Income Affect the Consumer's Choices

Now that we have seen how the consumer makes the consumption decision, let's examine how consumption responds to changes in income. To be specific, suppose that income increases. With higher income, the consumer can afford more of both goods. The increase in income, therefore, shifts the budget constraint outward, as in Figure 7.4. Because the relative price of the two goods has not changed, the slope of the new budget constraint is the same as the slope of the initial budget constraint. That is, an increase in income leads to a parallel shift in the budget constraint.

FIGURE 7.4

An Increase in Income

When the consumer's income rises, the budget constraint shifts out. If both goods are normal goods, the consumer responds to the increase in income by buying more of both of them. Here the consumer buys more pizza and more cola.

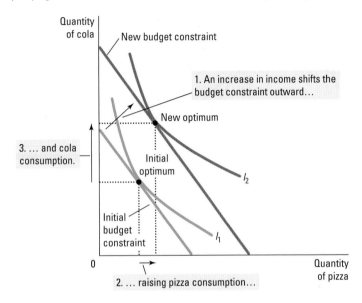

The expanded budget constraint allows the consumer to choose a better combination of cola and pizza. In other words, the consumer can now reach a higher indifference curve. Given the shift in the budget constraint and the consumer's preferences as represented by their indifference curves, the consumer's optimum moves from the point labelled 'initial optimum' to the point labelled 'new optimum'.

Notice that in Figure 7.4 the consumer chooses to consume more cola and more pizza. Although the logic of the model does not require increased consumption of both goods in response to increased income, this situation is the most common one. Remember that if a consumer wants more of a good when their income rises, economists call it a normal good. The indifference curves in Figure 7.4 are drawn under the assumption that both cola and pizza are normal goods.

Figure 7.5 shows an example in which an increase in income induces the consumer to buy more pizza but less cola. If a consumer buys less of a good when their income rises, economists call it an inferior good. Figure 7.5 is drawn under the assumption that pizza is a normal good and cola is an inferior good.

How Changes in Prices Affect the Consumer's Choices

Let's now use this model of consumer choice to consider how a change in the price of one of the goods alters the consumer's choices. Suppose, in particular, that the price of cola falls from €2 to €1 a litre. It is no surprise that the lower price expands

An Inferior Good

A good is an inferior good if the consumer buys less of it when their income rises. Here cola is an inferior good: when the consumer's income increases and the budget constraint shifts outward, the consumer buys more pizza but less cola.

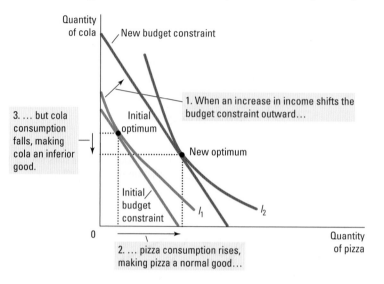

the consumer's set of buying opportunities. In other words, a fall in the price of any good causes the budget constraint to pivot. With their available income of €1000 the consumer can now buy twice as many litres of cola than before but the same amount of pizza. Figure 7.6 shows that point A in the figure stays the same (100 pizzas). Yet if the consumer spends their entire income of €1000 on cola, they can now buy 1000 rather than only 500 litres. Thus, the end point of the budget constraint pivots outwards from point B to point C.

A Change in Price

When the price of cola falls, the consumer's budget constraint pivots outward and changes slope. The consumer moves from the initial optimum to the new optimum, which changes their purchases of both cola and pizza. In this case, the quantity of cola consumed rises and the quantity of pizza consumed falls.

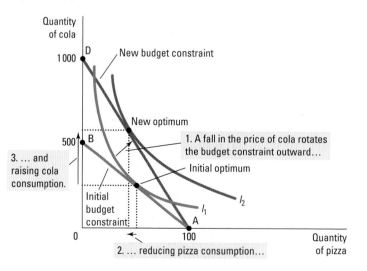

Notice that in this case the pivoting of the budget constraint changes its slope. (This differs from what happened previously when prices stayed the same but the consumer's income changed.) As we have discussed, the slope of the budget constraint reflects the relative price of cola and pizza. Because the price of cola has fallen to €1 from €2, while the price of pizza has remained at €10, the consumer can now trade a pizza for 10 rather than 5 litres of cola. As a result, the new budget constraint is more steeply sloped.

How such a change in the budget constraint alters the consumption of both goods depends on the consumer's preferences. For the indifference curves drawn in this figure, the consumer buys more cola and less pizza.

Income and Substitution Effects

The impact of a change in the price of a good on consumption can be decomposed into two effects which we briefly introduced in Chapter 4: an **income effect** and a **substitution effect**. To see what these two effects are, consider how our consumer might respond when they learn that the price of cola has fallen. They might reason in the following ways:

> *Great news! Now that cola is cheaper, my income has greater purchasing power – my income now buys me more. I am, in effect, richer than I was. Because I am richer, I can buy both more cola and more pizza.*

(This is the income effect.)

> *Now that the price of cola has fallen, I get more litres of cola for every pizza that I give up. Because pizza is now relatively more expensive, I should buy less pizza and more cola.*

(This is the substitution effect.)

income effect the change in consumption that results when a price change moves the consumer to a higher or lower indifference curve

substitution effect the change in consumption that results when a price change moves the consumer along a given indifference curve to a point with a new marginal rate of substitution

The decrease in the price of cola makes the consumer better off. If cola and pizza are both normal goods, the consumer will want to spread this improvement in their purchasing power over both goods. This income effect tends to make the consumer buy more pizza and more cola. Yet, at the same time, consumption of cola has become less expensive relative to consumption of pizza. This substitution effect tends to make the consumer choose more cola and less pizza.

Now consider the end result of these two effects. The consumer certainly buys more cola, because the income and substitution effects both act to raise purchases of cola. But it is ambiguous whether the consumer buys more pizza, because the income and substitution effects work in opposite directions. This conclusion is summarized in Table 7.1.

We can interpret the income and substitution effects using indifference curves. The income effect is the change in consumption that results from the movement to a higher indifference curve. The substitution effect is the change in consumption that results from being at a point on an indifference curve with a different marginal rate of substitution.

Figure 7.7 shows graphically how to decompose the change in the consumer's decision into the income effect and the substitution effect. When the price of cola falls, the consumer moves from the initial optimum, point A, to the new optimum, point C. We can view this change as occurring in two steps. First, the consumer moves *along* the initial indifference curve I_1 from point A to point B. The consumer is equally happy at these two points, but at point B the marginal rate of substitution reflects the new relative price. (The dashed line through point B reflects the new relative price by being parallel to the new budget constraint). Next, the consumer *shifts* to the higher indifference curve I_2 by moving from point B to point C. Even though points B and C are on different indifference curves, they have the same marginal rate of substitution. That is, the slope of the indifference curve I_1 at point B equals the slope of the indifference curve I_2 at point C.

Although the consumer never actually chooses point B, this hypothetical point is useful to clarify the two effects that determine the consumer's decision. Notice that the change from point A to point B represents a pure change in the marginal rate of substitution without any change in the consumer's welfare. Similarly, the change from point B to point C represents a pure change in welfare without any change in the marginal rate of substitution. Thus, the movement from A to B shows the substitution effect, and the movement from B to C shows the income effect.

FIGURE 7.7

Income and Substitution Effects

The effect of a change in price can be broken down into an income effect and a substitution effect. The substitution effect – the movement along an indifference curve to a point with a different marginal rate of substitution – is shown here as the change from point A to point B along indifference curve I₁. The income effect – the shift to a higher indifference curve – is shown here as the change from point B on indifference curve I₁ to point C on indifference curve I₂.

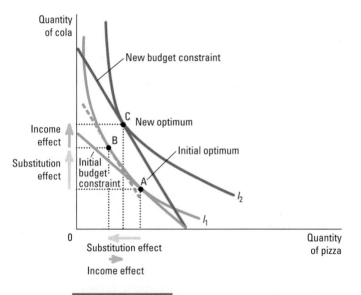

TABLE 7.1

Income and Substitution Effects When the Price of Cola Falls

Good	Income effect	Substitution effect	Total effect
Cola	Consumers are richer, so they buy more cola.	Cola is relatively cheap, so consumers buy more cola.	Income and substitution effects act in same direction, so consumers buy more cola.
Pizza	Consumers are richer, so they buy more pizza.	Pizza is relatively more expensive, so consumers buy less pizza.	Income and substitution effects act in opposite directions, so the total effect on pizza consumption is ambiguous.

> **?** **what if…** a rise in prices takes place at the same time as a fall in incomes? How would this affect consumer optimum?

BEHAVIOURAL ECONOMICS

The standard economic model described above has some merits but the key assumption that consumers behave rationally in making purchasing decisions does have some limitations. Why, for example, do consumers complain about a €0.10 increase in a litre of fuel but are happy to spend €5 on a lottery ticket where the chances of winning are considerably less than being struck by lightning? Why do people make pledges to get fitter, eat more healthily or quit habits like smoking, but fail in their efforts very quickly? Why do employees get angry if they find out that a colleague is getting a higher pay rise than them? Why do people give up a considerable amount of time to queue (often in very inclement weather) to grab a 'bargain' at the sales when they could have used the time queuing to earn more than they 'save' getting the bargain? Why do people queue for hours to get their hands on the latest technology device from Apple, or the latest version of a video game or to watch a new release of a cult movie?

Many of the things we do in life and the decisions we make cannot be explained as those of rational beings. (Rational beings are sometimes referred to by economists as *homoeconomicus*.) Although in some ways humans reflect the rational, calculating people assumed in economic theory, in reality they are far more complex. They can be forgetful, impulsive, confused, emotional and short-sighted. Economists have suggested that humans are only 'near rational' or that they exhibit 'bounded rationality'. **Bounded rationality** is the idea that humans make decisions under the constraints of limited, and sometimes unreliable, information, that they face limits to the amount of information they can process and that they face time constraints in making decisions.

> **bounded rationality** the idea that humans make decisions under the constraints of limited, and sometimes unreliable, information that they are unable to fully process

Studies of human decision making, primarily in the field of psychology but now widely adopted by economics, have tried to detect systematic mistakes that people make. We outline some of the key findings below.

People Are Overconfident   Imagine that you were asked some numerical questions, such as the number of African countries in the United Nations, the height of the tallest mountain in Europe and so on. Instead of being asked for a single estimate, however, you were asked to give a 90 per cent confidence interval – a range such that you were 90 per cent confident the true number falls within it. When psychologists run experiments like this, they find that most people give ranges that are too small: the true number falls within their intervals far less than 90 per cent of the time. That is, most people are too sure of their own abilities.

People Give Too Much Weight to a Small Number of Vivid Observations   Imagine that you are thinking about buying a new smartphone by company X. To learn about its reliability, you read *Consumer Reports*, which has surveyed 1000 owners of the particular smartphone that you are looking at. Then you run into a friend who owns such a phone and she tells you that she is really unhappy with the phone. How do you treat your friend's observation? If you think rationally, you will realize that she has only increased your sample size from 1000 to 1001, which does not provide much new information. Placing a reliance on your friend's opinion should be of little importance but in reality people do place a disproportionate degree of importance on such information.

In addition, a process called the *reticular activation system* (RAS) works to bring your attention to instances of this smartphone – you will suddenly start to notice more of them. The RAS is an automatic mechanism in the brain that brings relevant information to our attention. This effect may also exert an influence on decision making which has little to do with rationality – simply noticing more of the smartphones does not change their reliability.

People Are Reluctant to Change Their Mind

People tend to interpret evidence to confirm beliefs they already hold. In one study, subjects were asked to read and evaluate a research report on whether capital punishment deters crime. After reading the report, those who initially favoured the death penalty said they were more sure in their view, and those who initially opposed the death penalty also said they were more sure in their view. The two groups interpreted the same evidence in exactly opposite ways.

People Have a Natural Tendency to Look for Examples Which Confirm Their Existing View or Hypothesis

Nassim Nicholas Taleb, the author of the book *The Black Swan*, calls this 'naïve empiricism'. People identify, select or observe limited examples of past instances and quote them as evidence for a viewpoint or hypothesis. For example, extreme weather events can be selected as evidence of climate change or a rise in the price of petrol of 10 per cent is quoted as being symptomatic of a broader increase in prices of all goods.

People Use Rules of Thumb – Heuristics

The standard economic model implies that to act rationally buyers will consider all available information in making purchasing decisions and weigh up this information to maximize utility subject to a budget constraint. In reality it is likely that many consumers will (a) not have access to sufficient information to be able to make a fully rational choice and (b) even if they did they would not be able to process this information fully, partly due to a lack of mental facility (not everyone can do arithmetic quickly in their head nor make statistical calculations on which to base their choices). Instead, when making decisions many people will use shortcuts that help simplify the decision-making process. These shortcuts are referred to as **heuristics** or *rules of thumb*. Some of these heuristics can be deep-seated and firms can take advantage of them to influence consumer behaviour.

There are a number of different types of heuristics:

Anchoring refers to the tendency for people to start with something they are familiar with or know and make decisions or adjustments based on this anchor. For example, a consumer may base the price they expect to pay for a restaurant meal on the last two prices they paid when eating out. If the price at the next restaurant is higher than this anchor price it may be that the consumer thinks the restaurant is 'expensive' or 'not good value for money' and may choose not to go again, whereas if the price they pay is lower than the anchor price they might see the restaurant as being good value for money and choose to return again. Often these anchors are biased and so the adjustment or decision is flawed in some way.

Availability refers to cases where decisions are made based on an assessment of the risks of the likelihood of something happening. If examples readily come to mind as a result of excessive media coverage, for example, decisions may be taken with a skewed assessment of the risks. If a consumer brings to mind the idea that the last couple of winters have been particularly bad then they might be more likely to buy equipment to help them combat adverse weather for the next winter. Consumers

heuristics rules of thumb or shortcuts used in decision making

who use commuter trains are more likely to give negative feedback about the service they have received if their recent experience has been of some delays or cancellations even if the overall level of punctuality of the train operator has been very high.

Representativeness People tend to make judgements by comparing how representative something is to an image or stereotype that they hold. For example, people may be more prepared to pay money to buy a lottery ticket if a close friend has just won a reasonable amount of money on the lottery or make an association that if Bose headphones are good quality (for example) then its home theatre systems are also going to be good quality.

Persuasion heuristics are linked to various attributes that a consumer attaches to a product or a brand. For example, it has been shown that size does matter to consumers and so marketers can exploit this by making more exaggerated claims in adverts or using facts and figures to make the product more compelling in the mind of the consumer. The more that the marketers can highlight the positive attributes of their product (and the negative ones of their rivals) the more likely consumers are to make choices in favour of their product. In addition consumers are also persuaded by people they like and respect. This may be utilized by firms through the people they use in adverts and celebrity endorsements but may also be important in terms of the people a firm employs to represent them in a sales or marketing capacity. It may also be relevant in cases where friends or colleagues discuss products and is one of the reasons why firms are keen to build a better understanding of how social media, like Facebook and Twitter, can be exploited. Finally, persuasion heuristics can manifest themselves in the 'bandwagon' effect – if a large number of people go and see a movie and rave about it then there is even more incentive for others to go and see it as well. Firms may look to try and create a bandwagon effect to utilize this persuasion heuristic in their marketing.

Simulation heuristics occur where people use mental processes to establish the likely outcome of something. The easier it is to simulate or visualize that outcome the more likely the individual is to make a decision based on it. For example, if it is easy to imagine a product which makes you look good, then you are more likely to buy it. Pharmaceutical firms know that consumers are more likely to buy and take medicines that deal with known and experienced symptoms (things like headaches, strained muscles, sore throats and runny noses) which are easy to visualize and imagine, than taking regular medicines for something like high cholesterol because it is hard to build a mental process for the effects of high cholesterol.

Expected Utility Theory and Framing Effects

In our discussion of the standard economic model we referred to expected utility theory – the idea that preferences can and will be ranked by buyers. Expected utility theory is important in that every day we have to make decisions based on ranking preferences. Imagine you are faced with buying your first car. You have limited income and so have to go to second-hand dealers. You are wary of the potential problems inherent in buying a second-hand car – you know that if the car develops a mechanical fault it often costs more to repair than to replace so you go to the dealers with this in mind. You find two cars that you like – one is priced at €500 and its age suggests that it has a 50 per cent chance of breaking down in the first year. The second car is €900 but has a 20 per cent chance of breaking down in the first year. Which do you choose? Expected utility theory says that consumers can rank the preference between these two options. We assumed that if the car breaks down it is more expensive to repair than to replace so our calculations are based on replacing the car rather than repairing it (we are talking rational human beings after all here).

Behavioural economics has lots of applications. Here a simple mat insert into a public urinal focuses the male attention and helps reduce the costs of cleaning. It's all about understanding behaviour to help change behaviour.

The expected replacement cost of the first car would be the price we paid (€500) multiplied by the probability of it breaking down (50 per cent) which works out as €500 × 0.50 = €250. The expected replacement cost of the second car is 0.2 × 900 = €180. The rational choice, therefore, would be to purchase the more expensive car. The problem is that the way in which such choices are presented can affect our judgements and the rational decision is violated.

Research into this area is extensive and persuasive. Essentially, choices can be affected by the way in which they are framed. In our example above, if you were faced with the choice of buying a car which has an 80 per cent chance of losing €720 in a year's time, or another car which has a 50 per cent chance of losing €250 after a year, which would you now choose? In this second case the two options are presented differently but are essentially the same as the first set of choices. The risks now appear different.

Firms are careful to frame the way they present products and information to consumers to influence purchasing decisions and exploit these differences in perception. For example, firms selling insurance know that people make judgements about the extent to which they are exposed to risk in deciding whether to take out insurance and how much cover they need. Adverts and marketing, therefore, may be framed to give the impression to consumers that they face increased risk.

ADVERTISING AND BRANDING

Knowledge of these different heuristics is important to firms in advertising. It is nearly impossible to go through a typical day in a modern economy without being bombarded with advertising. Whether you are reading a newspaper, watching television or driving down the motorway, some firm will try to convince you to buy its product. Such behaviour is typical in non-competitive markets where firms sell differentiated products.

The amount of advertising varies substantially across products. Firms that sell highly differentiated consumer goods, such as over-the-counter drugs, perfumes, soft drinks, razor blades, breakfast cereals or dog food, typically spend between 10 and 20 per cent of revenue on advertising. Firms that sell industrial products, such as drill presses and communications satellites, typically spend very little on advertising. And firms that sell homogeneous products, such as wheat, peanuts or crude oil, spend nothing at all.

The Debate Over Advertising

There are billions spent on advertising around the world. Is society wasting the resources it devotes to advertising? Or does advertising serve a valuable purpose? Assessing the social value of advertising is difficult and often generates heated argument among economists. Let's consider both sides of the debate.

CASE STUDY

Can Anyone Escape Advertising?

Advertising is far more prevalent than we often appreciate. Imagine taking a trip to watch your local football team. You pick up the junk mail at the front door putting it to one side to look at later and set off to catch the bus.

Two delivery vehicles pass by, each promoting their business on the side and back of the vehicles. At the bus stop a man is carrying two bags in supermarket colours, slogan and logos. He is with his son who is wearing clothes clearly identifying several well-known clothing companies. There are other football fans waiting for the bus with their club shirts and scarves. One has just finished his Costa coffee takeaway.

On the bus, there are plenty of 'sites' used to advertise goods sold by the bus company. As you carry on the journey, you notice several food takeaways and you decide to buy some fish and chips to eat before the game. The paper they are wrapped in has a half page advert for carpets and another giving me 0 per cent interest should I choose to buy a certain model of car.

The match programme tells you that a betting company has sponsored the game. All around the stadium are advertising hoardings. The ones opposite the TV cameras are electronic and change every minute or so. As you look up into the sky, a plane trailing a banner promoting a furniture store sale passes by.

An interesting thought experiment might be estimating how much you would have spent if you had bought a product from each advert you have witnessed on your relatively short journey! The chances are, though, that you will not respond to every advert you see, so what is the purpose of advertising?

We might filter information received from adverts but some advertising does raise awareness and might lead to individuals making more informed choices.

It has long been recognized that psychology has a lot to do with advertising. Sutherland and Sylvester (2000) argue that advertising influences the order in which we evoke or notice the alternatives we consider, rather than persuade us to buy. The primary aim of advertising, they argue, is to generate a series of small effects, which ultimately influence our behaviour and may cause us to view differently the products or the brands that we choose, especially in a crowded marketplace with a large amount of competition.

Exactly how adverts work, therefore, is not easy to quantify. Sutherland and Sylvester suggest that many involved in the advertising industry do not really understand why some adverts seem to work and others don't work anything like as well.

Reference: Sutherland, M. and Sylvester, A.K. (2000) *Advertising and the Mind of the Consumer: What Works, What Doesn't and Why*, 2nd ed. London, Kogan Page.

The Critique of Advertising Critics of advertising argue that firms advertise in order to manipulate people's tastes. Much advertising is psychological rather than informational. Consider, for example, the typical television advert for some brand of soft drink. The advert most likely does not tell the viewer about the product's price or quality. Instead, it might show a group of happy people at a party on a beach on a beautiful sunny day. In their hands are cans of the soft drink. The goal of the advert is to convey a subconscious (if not subtle) message: 'You too can have many friends and be happy and beautiful, if only you drink our product.' Critics of advertising argue that such an advert creates a desire that otherwise might not exist.

Critics also argue that advertising impedes competition. Advertising often tries to convince consumers that products are more different than they truly are. By increasing the perception of product differentiation and fostering brand loyalty, advertising makes buyers less concerned with price differences among similar goods. With a less elastic demand curve, each firm charges a larger mark-up over marginal cost.

The Defence of Advertising   Defenders of advertising argue that firms use advertising to provide information to customers. Advertising conveys the prices of the goods being offered for sale, the existence of new products and the locations of retail outlets. This information allows customers to make better choices about what to buy and thus enhances the ability of markets to allocate resources efficiently.

Defenders also argue that advertising fosters competition. Because advertising allows customers to be more fully informed about all the firms in the market, customers can more easily take advantage of price differences. Thus, each firm has less market power. In addition, advertising allows new firms to enter more easily, because it gives entrants a means to attract customers from existing firms.

Advertising as a Signal of Quality

Many types of advertising contain little apparent information about the product being advertised. Consider a firm introducing a new breakfast cereal. A typical advertisement might have some highly paid actor eating the cereal and exclaiming how wonderful it tastes. How much information does the advertisement really provide?

The answer is: more than you might think. Defenders of advertising argue that even advertising that appears to contain little hard information may in fact tell consumers something about product quality. The willingness of the firm to spend a large amount of money on advertising can itself be a *signal* to consumers about the quality of the product being offered.

Consider a hypothetical problem facing two firms – Nestlé and Kellogg. Each company has just come up with a recipe for a new breakfast cereal, which it plans to sell for €3 a box. To keep things simple, let's assume that the €3 is all profit. Each company knows that if it spends €10 million on advertising, it will get 1 million consumers to try its new cereal. And each company knows that if consumers like the cereal, they will buy it not once but many times.

Let's consider Nestlé's decision. Based on market research, Nestlé knows that its cereal is only mediocre. Although advertising would sell one box to each of 1 million consumers, the consumers would quickly learn that the cereal is not very good and stop buying it. Nestlé decides it is not worth paying €10 million in advertising to get only €3 million in sales. So it does not bother to advertise. It sends its cooks back to the drawing board to find another recipe.

Kellogg, on the other hand, knows that its cereal is great. Each person who tries it will buy a box a month for the next year. Thus, the €10 million in advertising will bring in €36 million in sales. Advertising is profitable here because Kellogg has a good product that consumers will buy repeatedly. Thus, Kellogg chooses to advertise.

Now that we have considered the behaviour of the two firms, let's consider the behaviour of consumers. We began by asserting that consumers are inclined to try a new cereal that they see advertised. But is this behaviour rational? Should a consumer try a new cereal just because the seller has chosen to advertise it?

In fact, it may be completely rational for consumers to try new products that they see advertised. In our story, consumers decide to try Kellogg's new cereal because Kellogg advertises. Kellogg chooses to advertise because it knows that its cereal is quite good, while Nestlé chooses not to advertise because it knows that its cereal is only mediocre. By its willingness to spend money on advertising, Kellogg signals to consumers the quality of its cereal. Each consumer thinks, quite sensibly, 'Wow, if the Kellogg Company is willing to spend so much money advertising this new cereal, it must be really good.'

What is most surprising about this theory of advertising is that the content of the advertisement is irrelevant. Kellogg signals the quality of its product by its willingness to spend money on advertising. (This example is used for illustrative purposes only and is not meant to infer that Nestlé deliberately produces inferior products!) What the advertisements say is not as important as the fact that consumers know ads are expensive. By contrast, cheap advertising cannot be effective at signalling quality to consumers. In our example, if an advertising campaign cost less than €3 million, both Nestlé and Kellogg would use it to market their new cereals. Because both good and mediocre cereals would be advertised, consumers could not infer the quality of a new cereal from the fact that it is advertised. Over time, consumers would learn to ignore such cheap advertising.

This theory can explain why firms pay celebrities large amounts of money to make advertisements that, on the surface, appear to convey no information at all. The information is not in the advertisement's content, but simply in its existence and expense.

BRAND NAMES

Advertising is closely related to the existence of **branding**. In many markets, there are two types of firms. Some firms sell products with widely recognized brand names, while other firms sell generic substitutes. For example, in a typical supermarket, you can find Pepsi next to less familiar colas, or Kellogg's cornflakes next to the supermarket's own brand of cornflakes, made for it by an unknown firm. Most often, the firm with the famous brand name spends more on advertising and charges a higher price for its product.

> **branding** the means by which a business creates an identity for itself and highlights the way in which it differs from its rivals

Just as there is disagreement about the economics of advertising, there is disagreement about the economics of brand names and branding. Let's consider both sides of the debate.

Critics of brand names argue that branding causes consumers to perceive differences that do not really exist. In many cases, the generic good is almost indistinguishable from the brand-name good. Consumers' willingness to pay more for the brand-name good, these critics assert, is a form of irrationality fostered by advertising. Economist Edward Chamberlin, one of the early developers of the theory of monopolistic competition, concluded from this argument that brand names were bad for the economy. He proposed that the government discourage their use by refusing to enforce the exclusive trademarks that companies use to identify their products.

More recently, economists have defended brand names as a useful way for consumers to ensure that the goods they buy are of high quality. There are two related arguments. First, brand names provide consumers with *information* which cannot be easily judged in advance of purchase. Second, brand names give firms an *incentive* to meet the needs of consumers, because firms have a financial stake in maintaining the reputation of their brand names. Note that branding does not always equate to high quality. Some firms will happily admit their goods are 'cheap and cheerful' but point out that they provide consumers with value for money. A number of discount stores, for example, have expanded in recent years, partly because of the difficult economic times that many countries have experienced. Firms such as Lidl, Netto, Poundstretcher and Poundland are interested in developing their brand names as much as Armani and Ralph Lauren. Consumers are able to associate the brand name with value for money – important when times are difficult.

To see how these arguments work in practice, consider a famous brand name: Ibis hotels. Imagine that you are driving through an unfamiliar town and you need somewhere to stay for the night. You see a Hotel Ibis and a local hotel next door to it. Which do you choose? The local hotel may in fact offer better accommodation at lower prices, but you have no way of knowing that. In contrast, Hotel Ibis offers a consistent product across many European cities. Its brand name is useful to you as a way of judging the quality of what you are about to buy.

The Ibis brand name also ensures that the company has an incentive to maintain quality. For example, if some customers were to become very ill from bad food served at breakfast at a Hotel Ibis, the news would be disastrous for the company. Ibis would lose much of the valuable reputation that it has built up over the years and, as a result, it would lose sales and profit, not just in the hotel that served the bad food, but in its many hotels across Europe. By contrast, if some customers were to become ill from bad food served at breakfast in a local hotel, that restaurant might have to close down, but the lost profits would be much smaller. Hence, Ibis has a greater incentive to ensure that its breakfast food is safe.

The debate over brand names centres on the question of whether consumers are rational in preferring brand names over generic substitutes. Critics of brand names argue that brand names are the result of an irrational consumer response to advertising. Defenders of brand names argue that consumers have good reason to use brand-name products because they can be more confident in the quality and consistency of message of these products.

Quick Quiz How might advertising make markets less competitive? How might it make markets more competitive? • Give the arguments for and against brand names.

JEOPARDY PROBLEM

A firm manufacturing batteries in a market with a number of competitors spends a large amount of money over a 3-year period both advertising its product and building its brand image. It finds, in the following years, that if it increases its price its revenue increases. Its internal research suggests this is contrary to what would have happened prior to the advertising campaign. What has changed in the intervening years to lead to this outcome?

ASYMMETRIC INFORMATION

'I know something you don't know.' This statement is a common taunt among children, but it also conveys a deep truth about how people sometimes interact with one another. Many times in life, one person knows more about what is going on than another. A difference in access to relevant knowledge is called an *information asymmetry*.

Examples abound. A worker knows more than their employer about how much effort they put into their job. A seller of a used car knows more than the buyer about the car's condition. The first is an example of a *hidden action*, whereas the second is an example of a *hidden characteristic*. In each case, the party in the dark (the employer, the car buyer) would like to know the relevant information, but the informed party (the worker, the car seller) may have an incentive to conceal it.

Because asymmetric information is so prevalent, economists have devoted much effort in recent decades to studying its effects. And, indeed, the 2001 Nobel Prize in economics was awarded to three economists (George Akerlof, Michael Spence and Joseph Stiglitz) for their pioneering work on this topic. Let's discuss some of the insights that this research has revealed.

Hidden Actions: Principals, Agents and Moral Hazard

Moral hazard is a problem that arises when one person, called the **agent**, is performing some task on behalf of another person, called the **principal**. If the principal cannot perfectly monitor the agent's behaviour, the agent tends to undertake less effort than the principal considers desirable and is not fully responsible for the consequences of their actions. The phrase *moral hazard* refers to the risk, or 'hazard', of inappropriate or otherwise 'immoral' behaviour by the agent.

Moral hazard can lead to **adverse selection**. This means that the market process may end up with 'bad' outcomes because of asymmetric information. Adverse selection is a feature of banking, finance and insurance industries. A bank, for example, sets rules and regulations for its accounts which may lead to some customers, who are not very profitable to the bank, adversely selecting the bank – customers the bank would rather not have. In insurance, the person seeking insurance cover has more information about his or her situation than the insurer. A person who knows they are high risk will look to buy insurance but not necessarily divulge the extent of the risk they pose to the insurance company. How does the insurance company distinguish between its high-risk and low-risk customers? The insurance company would rather take on the low-risk customers than the high-risk ones but high-risk customers adversely select the insurance company. In finance, some investment banks have been accused of putting very risky assets into financial products and clients buying these products do not know the full extent of the risk they are buying – clients are dealing with suppliers who they would have been better off not dealing with. In such a situation, the principal tries various ways to encourage the agent to act more responsibly (such as pricing insurance for high-risk customers higher than for low-risk ones).

moral hazard the tendency of a person who is imperfectly monitored to engage in dishonest or otherwise undesirable behaviour

agent a person who is performing an act for another person, called the principal

principal a person for whom another person, called the agent, is performing some act

adverse selection the tendency for the mix of unobserved attributes to become undesirable from the standpoint of an uninformed party

? **what if…** governments believed that the market is the best regulator of banks and sought to increase competition in the banking industry. Would this reduce moral hazard?

The employment relationship is the classic example. The employer (business) is the principal, and the worker is the agent. The moral hazard problem is the temptation of imperfectly monitored workers to shirk their responsibilities. How do firms respond to this problem?

- Better monitoring. Human resources departments in larger firms develop processes to improve the monitoring of workers and to also put in place performance management systems to help provide incentives for employees to meet their employment responsibilities.

- High wages. According to *efficiency wages theories*, some employers may choose to pay their workers a wage above the level that equilibrates supply and demand in the labour market. A worker who earns an above-equilibrium wage is less likely to shirk, because if they are caught and fired, they might not be able to find another high-paying job.
- Delayed payment. Firms can delay part of a worker's compensation, so if the worker is caught shirking and is fired, they suffer a larger penalty. One example of delayed compensation is the year-end bonus. Similarly, a firm may choose to pay its workers more later in their lives. Thus, the wage rises that workers receive as they age may reflect not just the benefits of experience but also a response to moral hazard.

These various mechanisms to reduce the problem of moral hazard need not be used alone. Employers can use a combination of them.

Beyond the workplace, there are many other examples of moral hazard that affect businesses. Individuals with insurance cover, be it fire, motor vehicle or medical insurance, may behave differently as a result of having that cover. A motorist, for example, might drive more recklessly in the knowledge that in the event of an accident the cost will be met primarily by the insurance company. Similarly, families choosing to live near a river may benefit from the scenic views but the increased risk of flooding imposes a cost to the insurance company and the government in the event of a serious flood. The financial crisis raised the issue of bankers' bonuses. One argument put forward was that banks were acting recklessly in giving large bonuses to workers which encouraged inappropriate and risky investment. Such behaviour was encouraged because bankers 'knew' that governments would step in to prevent banks from failing.

Many regulations are aimed at addressing the problem: an insurance company may require homeowners to buy smoke detectors or pay higher premiums if there is a history of reckless driving (or even refuse to provide insurance cover to the individual), the government may prohibit building homes on land with high risk of flooding and new regulations may be introduced to curb the behaviour of banks. But the insurance company does not have perfect information about how cautious homeowners are, the government does not have perfect information about the risk that families undertake when choosing where to live and regulators do not know fully the risks that bankers take in investment decisions. As a result, the problem of moral hazard persists.

Signalling to Convey Private Information

signalling an action taken by an informed party to reveal private information to an uninformed party

Markets respond to problems of asymmetric information in many ways. One of them is **signalling**, which refers to actions taken by an informed party for the sole purpose of credibly revealing his private information.

We have seen examples of signalling earlier in this chapter; firms may spend money on advertising to signal to potential customers that they have high-quality products. The intention is that the informed party is using a signal to convince the uninformed party that the informed party is offering something of high quality.

What does it take for an action to be an effective signal? Obviously, it must be costly. If a signal were free, everyone would use it, and it would convey no information. For the same reason, there is another requirement: the signal must be less costly, or more beneficial, to the person with the higher-quality product. Otherwise, everyone would have the same incentive to use the signal and it would reveal nothing.

Screening to Induce Information Revelation

When an informed party takes actions to reveal their private information, the phenomenon is called signalling. When an uninformed party takes actions to induce the informed party to reveal private information, the phenomenon is called **screening**.

Some screening is common sense. A person buying a used car may ask that it be checked by a car mechanic or a trade association before the sale. A seller who refuses this request reveals their private information that the car is not of high quality. The buyer may decide to offer a lower price or to look for another car.

Other examples of screening are more subtle. For example, consider a firm that sells car insurance. The firm would like to charge a low premium to safe drivers and a high premium to risky drivers. But how can it tell them apart? Drivers know whether they are safe or risky, but the risky ones won't admit to it. A driver's history is one piece of information (which insurance companies in fact use), but because of the intrinsic randomness of car accidents, history is an imperfect indicator of future risks.

The insurance company might be able to sort out the two kinds of drivers by offering different insurance policies that would induce them to separate themselves. One policy would have a high premium and cover the full cost of any accidents that occur. Another policy would have low premiums but would have, say, a €1000 excess. (That is, the driver would be responsible for the first €1000 of damage, and the insurance company would cover the remaining risk). Notice that the excess is more of a burden for risky drivers because they are more likely to have an accident. Thus, a low-premium policy with a relatively large excess would attract the safe drivers, while the high-premium policy with a low excess would attract the risky drivers. Faced with these two policies, the two kinds of drivers would reveal their private information by choosing different insurance policies.

screening an action taken by an uninformed party to induce an informed party to reveal information

Quick Quiz A person who buys a life insurance policy pays a certain amount per year and receives for their family a much larger payment in the event of their death. Would you expect buyers of life insurance to have higher or lower death rates than the average person? How might this be an example of moral hazard? Of adverse selection? How might a life insurance company deal with these problems?

CONCLUSION

This chapter has examined different but complementary models of consumer behaviour. The standard economic model relies on a set of assumptions with rational human beings at its heart. Economists are always looking to refine their models and the developments in technology and the influence of other disciplines has led to theories of consumer behaviour which go some way to helping understand the imperfections in the standard economic model. Firms are increasingly using these insights to help develop marketing strategies to influence consumer behaviour and increase sales. Advertising and branding are two of these areas which are used by firms to influence consumer behaviour and are features of imperfect competition. Finally we looked at issues which arise from asymmetric information. The very fact that most businesses know more about their product than do consumers gives rise to potential problems, and we looked in particular at moral hazard and adverse selection and how it affects the financial industry.

If there is a unifying theme to these topics, it is that life is messy. Information is imperfect, government is imperfect and people are imperfect. Of course, you knew this long before you started studying economics, but economists need to understand these imperfections as precisely as they can if they are to explain, and perhaps even improve, the world around them.

IN THE NEWS

What Information Should You Give Your Life Insurer?

The arrangement of any life insurance is between the policyholder and the life insurance company. One has to disclose information for the other to establish the risk of the policy. This article looks at the challenges and consequences of using genetic testing as a means of reducing asymmetric information when arranging a life insurance policy.

Some individuals who have a family history of certain types of illness later in life may want to know the risk that they might face so that they can make life-changing decisions. One cheap and fast way of finding out is through genetic predictive screening. This involves a person giving either a blood or saliva sample and then having the sample tested for known gene defects. It helps doctors to make predictions about the risk or chance of someone getting future illnesses such as dementia or cancer. Having this information can be very important

for the individual and the health practitioners, but the informed party may not wish to divulge this to other organizations such as their current or potential future employer or life insurance companies. As a consequence, the person could go to a private clinic where the results would not even be passed on to his or her own doctor. An individual who has failed the gene test could then take out a large life cover knowing full well that he or she is more likely to claim on it than the average person. It would simply not be in their interests to make a full disclosure to the life insurance company.

However, many life insurance companies argue that they need this information as part of their screening process. If they had access to genetic testing, they could adjust their insurance premiums to reflect this. To the insurance companies,

restricting this information means in the end they have to cover more payouts. They will want to protect themselves from the obvious risk of a potential high payout.

If some insurance companies could get hold of this information by insisting on these tests then they could gain a competitive advantage since they could refuse to provide the insurance cover where the results of tests suggest the risk is much higher and then offer cheaper premiums to those where test results show much lower risk factors.

If genetic testing became a compulsory requirement for people buying life insurance, then those at high risk might be unable to buy life cover or get a mortgage. What currently happens in the UK is that insurance companies rely on the honesty of the customer by asking if the person has undergone a gene test and if so what the result was. But will this change?

In the US, insurance companies cover general health costs which for most people are free in the UK within the National Health Service. In Kentucky, the death rate from lung cancer is 50 per cent higher than the US average. Today, most insurance companies serving the state are paying for screening that could detect lung cancer in high-risk patients with a long history of smoking. Early detection leads to more successful long-term outcomes for patients and consequently saves insurance companies money. This is an example of diagnostic testing. It goes further. Worried by obesity and its impact on health, some US insurance companies will reimburse their clients who join fitness classes and attend nutritional counselling.

The debate will continue around who should have access to people's personal health information.

At present there are laws preventing discrimination based on the results of genetic tests. In the UK these laws restrict what employers can ask about pre-employment medical checks. Also customers seeking life insurance will not be asked, nor be put under pressure, to take a predictive test in order to obtain insurance cover for sums less than £500 000 of life insurance. Nor do they need to disclose the results of a predictive test taken after the insurance cover has started. Of course it may be in a customer's favour to disclose predictive genetic test information.

Questions

1. **What is the moral hazard that can face a customer taking out life insurance?**
2. **Why is it in the interests of the life insurer to gain the maximum**
health information they can about the potential client?
3. **Research any life insurance company and explain how it attempts to gain disclosure information from its customers.**
4. **In what situations will reducing the asymmetric information benefit both parties?**
5. **Why do consumers need protection and why might many businesses agree that this protection by law is necessary?**

References: http://www.globalchange.com/genescreen.htm

http://www.permianbasin360.com/news-article/d/story/lung-cancer-screenings-now-covered-by-most-insuran/39334/ix6stN8dxUOUUENQF3MsoA

https://www.abi.org.uk/~/media/Files/Documents/Publications/Public/2014/Genetics/Concordat%20and%20Moratorium%20on%20Genetics%20and%20Insurance.pdf

SUMMARY

- The standard economic model assumes humans behave rationally and seek to maximize utility subject to the constraint of limited income.

- Increased consumption raises total utility up to a point but marginal utility falls as consumption increases and is called the law of diminishing marginal utility.

- A consumer's budget constraint shows the possible combinations of different goods they can buy given their income and the prices of the goods. The slope of the budget constraint equals the relative price of the goods.

- The consumer's indifference curves represent their preferences. An indifference curve shows the various bundles of goods that make the consumer equally happy. Points on higher indifference curves are preferred to points on lower indifference curves. The slope of an indifference curve at any point is the consumer's marginal rate of substitution – the rate at which the consumer is willing to trade one good for the other.

- The consumer optimizes by choosing the point on their budget constraint that lies on the highest indifference curve. At this point, the slope of the indifference curve (the marginal rate of substitution between the goods) equals the slope of the budget constraint (the relative price of the goods).

- When the price of a good falls, the impact on the consumer's choices can be broken down into an income effect and a substitution effect. The income effect is the change in consumption that arises because a lower price makes the consumer better off. The substitution effect is the change in consumption that arises because a price change encourages greater consumption of the good that has become relatively cheaper. The income effect is reflected in the movement from a lower to a higher indifference curve, whereas the substitution effect is reflected by a movement along an indifference curve to a point with a different slope.

- The study of psychology and economics reveals that human decision making is more complex than is assumed in conventional economic theory. People are not always rational, they use rules of thumb (heuristics) and are influenced by the way in which information is presented (framing effects) which may alter outcomes.

- The product differentiation inherent in imperfectly competitive markets leads to the use of advertising and brand names. Critics of advertising and brand names argue that firms use them to take advantage of consumer irrationality and to reduce competition.

Defenders of advertising and brand names argue that firms use them to inform consumers and to compete more vigorously on price and product quality.

- In many economic transactions, information is asymmetric. When there are hidden actions, principals may be concerned that agents suffer from the problem of moral hazard. When there are hidden characteristics, buyers may be concerned about the problem of adverse selection among the sellers. Private markets sometimes deal with asymmetric information with signalling and screening.

QUESTIONS FOR REVIEW

1. A consumer goes into a coffee shop and has four cups of coffee. Explain what we might observe about the total utility and marginal utility of the individual. How does your explanation illustrate the law of diminishing returns?

2. A consumer has income of €3000. Bread is priced at €3 a loaf and cheese is priced at €6 a kilo.
   a. Draw the consumer's budget constraint. What is the slope of this budget constraint?
   b. Draw a consumer's indifference curves for bread and cheese. Pick a point on an indifference curve for bread and cheese and show the marginal rate of substitution. What does the marginal rate of substitution tell us?

3. Show a consumer's budget constraint and indifference curves for bread and cheese. Show the optimal consumption choice. If the price of bread is €3 a loaf and the price of cheese is €6 a kilo, what is the marginal rate of substitution at this optimum?

4. The price of cheese rises from €6 to €10 a kilo, while the price of bread remains at €3 a loaf. For a consumer

with a constant income of €3000, show what happens to consumption of bread and cheese. Decompose the change into income and substitution effects.

5. Explain and give an example of the following heuristics:
   a. Representative heuristics
   b. Availability heuristics
   c. Simulation heuristics
   d. Adjustment heuristics

6. How might advertising with no apparent informational content in fact convey information to consumers?

7. Explain two benefits that might arise from the existence of brand names.

8. What is moral hazard? List three things an employer might do to reduce the severity of this problem.

9. What is adverse selection? Give an example of a market in which adverse selection might be a problem.

10. Define *signalling* and *screening*, and give an example of each.

PROBLEMS AND APPLICATIONS

1. Jacqueline divides her income between coffee and croissants (both of which are normal goods). An early frost in Brazil causes a large increase in the price of coffee.
   a. Show how this early frost might affect Jacqueline's budget constraint.
   b. Show how this early frost might affect Jacqueline's optimal consumption bundle assuming that the substitution effect outweighs the income effect for croissants.
   c. Show how this early frost might affect Jacqueline's optimal consumption bundle assuming that the income effect outweighs the substitution effect for croissants.

2. Surette buys only orange juice and yoghurt.
   a. In 2016, Surette earns €50 000, orange juice is priced at €2 a carton and yoghurt is priced at €4 a tub. Draw Surette's budget constraint.
   b. Now suppose that all prices increase by 10 per cent in 2017 and that Surette's salary increases by 10 per cent as well. Draw Surette's new budget constraint. How would Surette's optimal combination of orange juice and yoghurt in 2017 compare to her optimal combination in 2016?

3. Economist George Stigler once wrote that, according to consumer theory, 'if consumers do not buy less of a commodity when their incomes rise, they will surely

buy less when the price of the commodity rises.' Explain this statement using the concepts of income and substitution effects.

4. Choose three products you purchased recently. Think about the reasons that you made the particular purchase decision in each case in relation to the various heuristics.

5. Look at the following two statements:
   a. Which would you prefer – a 50 per cent chance of winning €150 or a 50 per cent chance of winning €100?
   b. Would you prefer a decision that guarantees a €100 loss or would you rather take a gamble where the chance of winning €50 was rated at 50 per cent but the chance of losing €200 was also rated at 50 per cent?
   c. What would your choice be in a.?
   d. What would your choice be in b.?
   e. What is the difference between these two sets of statements and how do they illustrate the concept of framing?

6. Each of the following situations involves moral hazard. In each case, identify the principal and the agent, and explain why there is asymmetric information. How does the action described reduce the problem of moral hazard?
   a. Landlords require tenants to pay security deposits.
   b. Firms compensate top executives with options to buy company shares at a given price in the future.
   c. Car insurance companies offer discounts to customers who install anti-theft devices in their cars.

7. Some AIDS activists believe that health insurance companies should not be allowed to ask applicants if they are infected with the HIV virus that causes AIDS. Would this rule help or hurt those who are HIV-positive? Would it help or hurt those who are not HIV-positive? Would it exacerbate or mitigate the problem of adverse selection in the market for health insurance? Do you think it would increase or decrease the number of people without health insurance? In your opinion, would this be a good policy?

8. For each of the following pairs of firms, explain which firm would be more likely to engage in advertising:
   a. A family-owned farm or a family-owned restaurant.
   b. A manufacturer of forklift trucks or a manufacturer of cars.
   c. A company that invented a very reliable watch or a company that invented a less reliable watch that costs the same amount to make.

9. The government is considering two ways to help the needy: giving them cash, or giving them free meals at soup kitchens. Give an argument for giving cash. Give an argument, based on asymmetric information, for why the soup kitchen may be better than the cash handout.

10. Describe three adverts that you have seen on TV. In what ways, if any, were each of these adverts socially useful? In what ways were they socially wasteful? Did the adverts affect the likelihood of you buying the product? Why or why not?

PART 4

MICROECONOMICS—
THE ECONOMICS OF FIRMS
IN MARKETS

8 BUSINESS GOALS AND BEHAVIOUR

LEARNING OUTCOMES

After reading this chapter you should be able to:

- Explain the point of profit maximization where marginal cost equals marginal revenue and draw a diagram to illustrate.

- Show the related point of profit maximization using total revenue and total cost curves and thus the point of revenue maximization.

- Explain the relationship between price elasticity of demand, marginal revenue and revenue maximization.

- Explain how costs can be minimized at the point where the average cost curve is at its lowest.

- Outline some basic tactics and strategies for maximizing market share.

- Provide alternative definitions of the concept of shareholder value.

- Give explanations of non-financial objectives such as environmental and ethical objectives and consider the impact on stakeholders and stakeholder conflicts.

- Outline the principles of social enterprise.

THE GOALS OF FIRMS

It might seem obvious that businesses exist to make profits and indeed, for many that is a key requirement. However, it is too simplistic to analyse business just based on that assumption. Changes in the last 30 years have led to businesses in the private sector having to balance a wider range of objectives along with making profit. As noted in Chapter 1, for some businesses, other aims take priority and in the public sector, simply covering cost may be an aim as part of the overall priority of providing products which benefit society as a whole. We have also seen that a market mechanism can allocate products efficiently but when imperfections exist, the market may not work as effectively in allocating scarce resources. In some cases, the government steps in to regulate or influence market outcomes. There are some products which have characteristics which make it very difficult for the market to work at all and in those cases, the government may have to provide for the needs of its citizens. We can identify different types of products by looking at two characteristics:

excludable the property of a good whereby a person can be prevented from using it or gaining benefit when they do not pay for it

- Is the good **excludable**? Can people who do not pay for the use of a good be prevented from using the good or gaining benefit from it?
- Is the good **rival**? Does one person's use of the good diminish another person's ability to use it?

Using these two characteristics, we can further categorize goods in four ways:

rival the property of a good whereby one person's use diminishes other people's use

1. **Private goods** are both excludable and rival. Consider a chocolate bar, for example. A chocolate bar is excludable because it is possible to prevent someone else from eating it – you just don't give it to them. A chocolate bar is rival because if one person eats it, another person cannot eat the same bar.

private goods goods that are both excludable and rival

2. **Public goods** are neither excludable nor rival. That is, people cannot be prevented from using a public good, and one person's use of a public good does not reduce another person's ability to use it. For example, a country's national defence system protects all of the country's citizens equally and the fact that one person is being defended does not affect whether or not another citizen is defended.

public goods goods that are neither excludable nor rival

3. **Common resources** are rival but not excludable. For example, fish in the ocean are a rival good: when one person catches fish, there are fewer fish for the next person to catch. Yet these fish are not an excludable good because, given the vast size of an ocean, it is difficult to stop fishermen from taking fish out of it when, for example, they have not paid for a licence to do so.

common resources goods that are rival but not excludable

4. When a good is excludable but not rival, it is an example of a *natural monopoly*. For instance, consider fire protection in a small town. It is easy to exclude people from using this good: the fire service can just let their house burn down. Yet fire protection is not rival. Firefighters spend much of their time waiting for a fire, so protecting an extra house is unlikely to reduce the protection available to others. In other words, once a town has paid for the fire service, the additional cost of protecting one more house is small.

In this chapter we are going to look at the wide range of factors that might drive business activity primarily through the provision of private goods.

aims the long-term goals of a business

Aims and Objectives

objectives the means by which a business will be able to achieve its aims

As a general rule, **aims** are the long-term goals of the business. These aims are often captured in the business mission and vision statement. **Objectives** are the means by which a business will seek to achieve its aims. They are invariably measurable targets which are set to help the business identify the extent to which it is on target to meet its aims.

Many firms will summarize their overall goals through a mission or vision statement.

If you look at the mission statements of large businesses, it is likely that you will not find many instances where profit is specifically referred to. Instead it is likely that there will be references, in one form or another, to customers, environmental and social responsibility, quality, shareholder value, stakeholder well-being and to employees.

This highlights the complex web of stakeholder responsibilities which now guide many firms' long term goals. Many of these goals are interlinked – references to 'economic success' or 'profitability', for example, are linked to shareholder value; quality may not only be associated with customer satisfaction but, depending on the definition, with social and environmental responsibility.

Strategies and Tactics

A **strategy** is generally regarded as being to do with the long term – where the business wants to be at some point in the future. A **tactic**, on the other hand, is seen more as a short-term framework for decision making. Tactics are the 'how' to the question posed by strategy, which is the 'where'. To get to where you want to be in the future (the strategy) requires certain steps to be put in place to enable the business to progress towards that place (the tactics).

> **strategy** a series of actions, decisions and obligations that lead to the firm gaining a competitive advantage and exploiting the firm's core competencies

> **tactic** short-term framework for decision making

How long the time period which defines 'the future' is more difficult to identify and there is much debate about the use of the term. For example, one often hears sports managers talking of the 'strategy they devised for the game'. In this case is the 'future' the time period when the game has finished? If the 'strategy' is to win a particularly difficult game against fierce rivals then in the context of decision making this could be seen as being 'long term'. The team manager will then employ tactics to use in the game to achieve the desired goal of winning the match. These tactics will be the 'how' in terms of what formation is put out, which players will play where, who marks who, whether to focus on defence or attack, which particular opposition players to target to limit their influence on the game and the sort of 'plays', set piece moves etc. that will be used at certain times in the game.

Others would argue that winning the game is not an example of strategy because it is not the long term. The long term would be where the team wants to be at the end of the season, what financial position it wants to be in or where it wants to be in 5 years' time.

Because there is so much debate on these points we cannot come to any definitive conclusion and this should be borne in mind as you read this book and others; you are likely to see many different interpretations. For the purposes of this book we will use the definitions of strategy and tactics as given above. We will also refer more generally to a firm having 'goals' which is a more generic term which can be understood by all and which does not embroil us in the debate over semantics. This is not meant to detract from the seriousness of the debate, however. Having a clear understanding of what is being done in a business, what decisions are being made, when and why, are all vitally important for business success.

Despite the varying goals that exist, private sector firms must make a profit if they are to survive in the long run – rarely will any business activity be able to continue if costs are consistently greater than revenues. Some private sector businesses whose primary aim is to provide some sort of social benefit will still have to at least cover their costs in the long run. These businesses may not refer to 'profit' but to 'surpluses' and seek to ensure that any surplus is re-invested back in to the business to help better achieve the social aim rather than be distributed amongst owners of the business.

There is, however, a theoretical point at which a firm can maximize its profit and this may be something that influences a wide range of business decision making, including how much to produce, what price to charge and how to monitor and control costs. In balancing out the other objectives a firm has, there will be an inevitable impact on profits. For example, if a firm expresses a goal to reduce its environmental impact then this is likely to have an impact on its costs and this may mean that profit will be less than the maximum that could be made if this focus was not part of its decision making.

The Public Sector and the Private Sector

In Chapter 1 we introduced the distinction between the public sector and the private sector. Public sector provision of products might be through some sort of public corporation which is ultimately responsible to a national parliament but which operates as an independent entity in a similar way to many private sector businesses. Day-to-day decisions are made by managers but the overall finance for the business comes from a mixture of government funding and charges for products. The goals of such organizations may be to provide high-quality services to customers at reasonable prices such that the operation is able to at least cover its costs. Any profit (or surplus) is used for reinvesting to improve the quality of the customer provision. These products are sometimes provided free at the point of use and in other cases consumers have to pay a price, although the price might be much lower than would be the case if the product was provided by a private sector firm. Business activity in the public sector may take place because it is difficult to charge people for the products concerned because they are not excludable or rival, or people may not be able to afford to pay for them and so access to these products may be lower than is deemed desirable. Table 8.1 shows some typical examples of business activity which is carried out in the public sector across the Europe, Middle East and Africa (EMEA) territories. It is clear from this table that some of the goods provided are obviously public goods while there are other examples where

TABLE 8.1

Business Activity in the Private and Public Sector

Type of good	Public good or both public and private
Health care	Both
Dental care	Both
Pension provision	Both
Street lighting	Public
Roads	Both
Public parks	Public
Beaches	Both
Justice	Public
Police	Public
Refuse collection	Both
Education	Both

the goods are private goods but the public sector may choose to also provide them. This may be because some goods can be classed as merit goods. A **merit good** is one which could be provided by the private sector but which may also be offered by the public sector because it is believed that a less than optimal amount would be available to the public if resource allocation was left entirely to the private sector. This may be because people either would not be able to afford them or because they do not see such purchases as a priority. For example, some people may choose not to take out private health insurance because they think that they will not get ill or would rather spend their money on something that gives more immediate gratification. It is not until they get ill or have an accident and face health cost bills that they realize they may have made an unwise decision.

The examples given in Table 8.1 highlight how some goods can be both public and private goods or obviously public goods. For example, street lighting is a public good because it is almost impossible for a private business to be able to provide this good and charge individuals for the privilege. Beaches, on the other hand, can be both a private good and a public good. Users can be charged for use if a business has bought a stretch of beach and is able to allow only certain people to use it following payment. Many beaches are provided by the state for the benefit of all. Both private and public beaches have a cost of provision as they have to be kept clean and have lifeguards and other safety features. In the case of public provision, the taxpayer will ultimately fund the cost, whilst if the beach was owned by a private firm the cost would be covered by the payments members make to access the beach.

In many countries, the public sector accounts for a significant proportion of business activity as highlighted in Table 8.2 which shows government expenditures as a percentage of GDP in 2014 for a selection of countries.

> **merit good**   a good which could be provided by the private sector but which may also be offered by the public sector because it is believed that a less than optimal amount would be available to the public if resource allocation was left entirely to the private sector

TABLE 8.2

Government Expenditures as a Percentage of GDP (Selected Countries), 2014

Country	Government expenditure as a percentage of GDP
Austria	50.5
Denmark	57.6
Germany	45.4
Greece	51.9
Iceland	47.3
Ireland	48.1
Italy	49.8
Kuwait	38.5
Netherlands	49.8
Norway	43.9
Poland	43.5
South Africa	32.1
Turkey	34.9
United Kingdom	48.5
United States	41.6

Source: **http://www.heritage.org/index/explore?view=by-variables**

Private sector businesses can be small firms owned by just one person, or large multinational businesses that operate around the world (globally). In the case of large businesses, there might be many thousands of owners involved. Few firms in the private sector can afford to take their eye off financial performance even if profit is not the major goal. We are going to split business goals into two sections – financial and non-financial objectives – but it is important to remember there may be very close links between the two.

CASE STUDY

Who Calls the Shots?

In the UK, local authorities play a pivotal role in providing community sports and recreation facilities, since they are charged with some responsibility for the health outcomes of the population they serve. Despite this there is no legal requirement for the local authorities to provide facilities themselves.

Wiltshire Local Authority serves a largely rural population of around 470 000 people and currently operates 23 sports and recreational facilities in towns all across the county. Some of its facilities are run by a partner organization called People and Places. One such centre is located in the town of Royal Wootton Basset. People and Places is a big organization, employing over 6000 staff and running well over 100 sports and recreation centres across the UK for many different local authorities. What makes People and Places interesting is that it is a social enterprise, meaning it is a not-for-profit organization and has no shareholders. Any surplus made can be entirely reinvested into providing better and more sustainable facilities, working with its local authority partners. People and Places prides itself on its investment in staff and it supports young people in work by offering a range of apprenticeships. It earned the title of leisure operator of the year both in 2013 and 2014. The aims of the organization are to increase active participation in sport and recreation for the communities it serves on behalf of its local authority partners, and further to support and develop local sports and community clubs.

Not too far away from Royal Wootton Bassett is Swindon, and, if you live there and have enough money, you could become a member of a David Lloyd Leisure and Fitness Club. The gym group, David Lloyd Leisure, has some similarities with People and Places since it also employs 6000 people and it too values staff and provides effective training. It also prides itself in the service it gives its customers. David Lloyd Leisure operates in some 88 centres in the UK, a slightly smaller number than People and Places. It too has a target to become more sustainable. Now come the differences. First, it aims for a different market segment: those with plenty of disposable income. Second, it also trades overseas. Third and significantly, it aims to make a profit in order to pay back its owners who set aside money for future investment. In 2013 the private limited company made a profit of nearly £15 million on a turnover of around £205 million. It was purchased in 2013 by TDR for £750 million. TDR is a private equity firm that believes it can improve the efficiency and return from David Lloyd Leisure. TDR has earmarked a further £50 million for expansion, believing that David Lloyd Leisure had been underinvested in over recent years. However, TDR is a much bigger business and has a varied portfolio. This includes owning a debt purchasing company, a chain of pubs, a business that looks after vacant properties, and UK restaurant chains Pizza Express and Ask.

TDR even owns a fishing tackle operation, so fitness is only a small part of its overall operation.

References: **http://www.davidlloyd.co.uk**

**http://www.independent.co.uk/news/business/news/david-lloyd-leisure-fitness
-clubs-sold-for-healthy-750m-8801039.html**

**http://www.sportandrecreation.org.uk/lobbying-and-campaigning/policyareas
/access-facilities/local-authorities**

http://www.placesforpeopleleisure.org/find-a-leisure-centre

FINANCIAL OBJECTIVES

As we look at some financial objectives of business, it is important to bear in mind some of the models being presented here are simply that – models. They will help to conceptualize what we mean by certain principles and to enable us to understand why businesses make some decisions. We are not suggesting that firms sit down and chart their marginal revenue and marginal costs to find the exact point where they are equal and then announce they are maximizing profits. The point is that these models help explain a principle and so help us understand why, for example, a rail company might charge a different price for the same journey at different times of the day or why an airline or holiday company will slash prices of seats or package holidays at the last minute or why sometimes it is better to think about reducing output rather than constantly looking to increase it.

Profit Maximization

A basic assumption of classical economics is that a firm in a competitive market tries to maximize profit. We are going to explore this principle in more detail using the example of a competitive firm which we shall call Waterlane Farm Dairy.

Waterlane Farm produces a quantity of milk Q and sells each unit at the market price P. The farm's total revenue is $P \times Q$. For example, if a litre of milk sells for €0.35 and the farm sells 10 000 litres per day, its total revenue is €3500 per day.

Because Waterlane Farm is small compared with the world market for milk, it takes the price as given by market conditions. This means, in particular, that the price of milk does not depend on the quantity of output that Waterlane Farm produces and sells. If Waterlane doubles the amount of milk it produces, the price of milk remains the same, and its total revenue doubles. As a result, total revenue is proportional to the amount of output.

TABLE 8.3

Total, Average and Marginal Revenue for Waterlane Farm Dairy, a Competitive Firm

Quantity (Q) 000s	Price (P) €	Total revenue (TR = P × Q) €	Average revenue (AR = TR/Q) €	Marginal revenue (MR = ΔTR/ΔQ) €
1 litres	0.35	350	0.35	
2	0.35	700	0.35	350
3	0.35	1050	0.35	350
4	0.35	1400	0.35	350
5	0.35	1750	0.35	350
6	0.35	2100	0.35	350
7	0.35	2450	0.35	350
8	0.35	2800	0.35	350

Table 8.3 shows the revenue for Waterlane Farm Dairy. The first two columns show the amount of output the farm produces and the price at which it sells its output. The third column is the farm's total revenue. The table assumes that the price of milk is €0.35 a litre, so total revenue is simply €0.35 times the number of litres. This allows us to ask two questions:

1. How much revenue does the farm receive for the typical litre of milk?
2. How much additional revenue does the farm receive if it increases production of milk by one litre?

average revenue total revenue divided by the quantity sold

The fourth column in the table shows **average revenue**, which is total revenue (from the third column) divided by the amount of output (from the first column). Average revenue tells us how much revenue a firm receives for the typical unit sold. In Table 8.3, you can see that average revenue equals €0.35, the price of a litre of milk. This illustrates a general lesson that applies not only to competitive firms but to other firms as well. Total revenue is the price times the quantity ($P \times Q$), and average revenue is total revenue ($P \times Q$) divided by the quantity (Q). Therefore, in a perfectly competitive market, a firm's average revenue equals the price of the good.

marginal revenue the change in total revenue from an additional unit sold

The fifth column shows **marginal revenue**, which is the change in total revenue as a result of an increase in output. Increasing output from 1000 to 2000 litres changes total revenue from €350 to €700, so the marginal revenue provided by the additional sale of 1000 litres of milk is €350. We can calculate the marginal revenue from the sale of one litre of milk by dividing €350 by the increase in output (1000 litres). Doing this tells us that the farm adds €0.35 to total revenue, therefore the marginal revenue of one litre of milk is €0.35. This result illustrates a lesson that applies only to competitive firms. Total revenue is $P \times Q$, and P is fixed for a competitive firm. Therefore, when Q rises by one unit, total revenue rises by P euros. For competitive firms, marginal revenue equals the price of the good.

Quick Quiz When a competeitive firm doubles the amount it sells, what happens to the price of its output and its total revenue?

Let us put together our knowledge of the firm's costs and its revenues to examine how the firm maximizes profit.

Thought Experiment   Before we do this, consider the following thought experiment to help conceptualize what we are about to analyse.

You have €100 in your pocket. You have a collection of souvenir flags for sale. Each flag costs an extra €5 to produce. If you could sell one extra flag to a customer for €10, would you make the transaction? Hopefully your answer is 'yes'. By doing so you will incur an additional cost of €5 to produce the flag but will gain €10 for selling it; with the result you have a surplus of €5 which you put into your pocket meaning you have added to the €100 and now have €105.

If you found it difficult to sell the next flag at €10 but a customer offered you €8, would you be prepared to sell it? Again, your answer ought to be 'yes'. This transaction yields a surplus of €3, not as much as the previous transaction but it still yields a surplus which adds to the amount in your pocket to make the sum €108. Would you prefer to have €108 in your pocket rather than €105? Presumably, the rational person would say 'yes'.

Now consider a situation where you could only persuade a customer to buy the next flag if you charged €4. Would you now make the transaction? In this case you sell the flag for less than the cost of producing the extra flag so you would pay out €5 in costs but only receive €4 in revenue from the sale of the flag. The sale would be made at a loss of €1 and so the money in your pocket would now be €107. Assuming we are behaving rationally, there would be no incentive for you to enter into this particular transaction since it would leave you worse off.

What if you could make a sale of a flag at a price of €5? In this situation you would make neither any surplus nor any loss. Given that you are not any worse off, there is no reason why the transaction should not be carried out.

Identifying the Point of Profit Maximization

Now let's apply this thought experiment to an example using Waterlane Farm. Consider Table 8.4. In the first column of the table is the number of litres of milk Waterlane Farm Dairy produces. The second column shows the farm's total revenue assuming the market price is €0.35. The third column shows the farm's total cost of producing the different quantities of milk.

TABLE 8.4

Profit Maximization: A Numerical Example

Quantity (Q) 000s	Total revenue (TR) €	Total cost (TC) €	Profit (TR − TC) €	Marginal revenue (MR = $\Delta TR/\Delta Q$) €	Marginal cost (MC = $\Delta TC/\Delta Q$) €	Change in profit (MR − MC) €
0 litres	0	200	−200			
1	350	250	100	350	50	300
2	700	400	300	350	150	200
3	1050	700	350	350	300	50
4	1400	1050	350	350	350	0
5	1750	1430	320	350	380	−30
6	2100	1830	270	350	400	−50
7	2450	2250	200	350	420	−70
8	2800	2700	100	350	450	−100

The fourth column shows the farm's profit, which is computed by subtracting total cost from total revenue. If the farm produces nothing, it has a loss of €200. This is because the farm will incur some costs regardless of whether it produces any milk. These costs are called *fixed costs*. If it produces 1000 litres, it generates a profit of €100. If it produces 2000 litres, it has a profit of €300, and so on.

What is the profit maximizing output? This can be found by comparing the marginal revenue and marginal cost from additional output (remember the thought experiment above when analysing this). The fifth and sixth columns in Table 8.4 compute marginal revenue and marginal cost from the changes in total revenue and total cost, and the last column shows the change in profit for each additional litre produced. Expanding output from 0 to 1000 litres of milk generates additional revenue of €350 at an additional cost of €50; hence, producing this additional 1000 litres adds €300 to profit. The next 1000 litres produced has a marginal revenue of €350 and a marginal cost of €150, so the extra 1000 litres adds €200 to total profit. As long as marginal revenue exceeds marginal cost, increasing the quantity produced adds to profit and it is worth Waterlane Farm producing this extra milk. Once Waterlane Farm has reached 3000 litres of milk, however, the situation changes. The next thousand litres would add €350 to total revenue but at an additional cost of €380, so producing this next thousand litres would reduce profit by €30 (from €350 to €320). It does not make sense for Waterlane Farm to produce the extra thousand litres and so as a result, the farm would not produce beyond 3000 litres. We can apply this same principle if looking at the marginal revenue and marginal cost of an additional unit of output. In the example of Waterlane Farm, the decision might be about whether to produce an extra litre of milk.

Waterlane Farm can apply the principle of thinking at the margin to help them make decisions. If marginal revenue is greater than marginal cost it is worth increasing the production of milk. If Waterlane Farm was able to identify the marginal revenue (MR) and marginal cost (MC) of producing one extra litre of milk and could vary its output decisions around these marginal decisions then it could identify the profit maximizing output as being where $MC = MR$.

Figure 8.1 is a diagrammatic representation of the profit maximizing output. The vertical axis shows the costs and revenue and the horizontal axis, output. The marginal cost curve is given by MC, shown rising as output rises. The firm's demand curve is shown as $P = AR = MR$. Remember that a competitive firm is a price taker. If the market price is given by P_1 then the average revenue and marginal revenue per unit is the same as the price. Imagine that the firm is producing at Q_1. At this level of output, marginal revenue (P_1) is greater than marginal cost (MC_1). That is, in producing the Q_1th unit, the additional revenue (P_1) would exceed the additional costs (MC_1), profit would increase. Hence, if marginal revenue is greater than marginal cost, as it is at Q_1, it is worth the firm increasing output because profit will rise.

A similar argument applies when output is at Q_2. In this case, marginal cost is greater than marginal revenue. The firm makes a loss on this Q_2nd unit of $MC_2 - P_1$ which has a negative effect on profit. If the firm reduced production to Q_3, the MC would still be greater than the MR but the negative effect on profit would now be less ($MC_3 - P_1$). If marginal revenue is less than marginal cost, the firm can increase profit by reducing production. Where do these marginal adjustments to the level of production end? Regardless of whether the firm begins with production at a low level (such as Q_1) or at a high level (such as Q_2), the firm can increase profit by adjusting production until the quantity produced reaches Q_{MAX}. This analysis confirms the general rule for profit maximization: at the profit-maximizing level of output, marginal revenue and marginal cost are exactly equal.

FIGURE 8.1

Profit Maximization for a Competitive Firm

This figure shows the marginal cost curve (MC) and demand curve facing a competitive firm. The market price (P₁), equals marginal revenue (MR) and average revenue (AR). At the quantity Q₁, marginal revenue P₁ exceeds marginal cost MC₁, so increasing output to this level would increase profit. At the quantity Q₂ marginal cost MC₂ is above marginal revenue P₁, so it would be worth the firm reducing production to increase profit. The profit maximizing quantity Q_MAX is found where marginal cost exceeds marginal revenue.

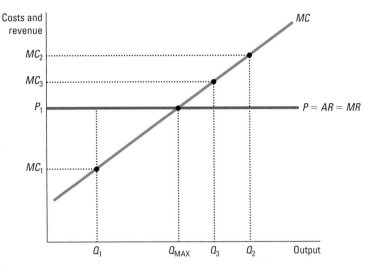

FYI

The Mathematics of Profit Maximization

Assume that the equations for an inverse demand curve and total cost facing a firm are given as:

$$P = 230 - Q$$

and:

$$TC = 40 + Q^2$$

To find the marginal revenue and marginal cost we differentiate both equations using the power function rule:

$$\frac{dy}{dx} = nx^{n-1}$$

So, $MC = \dfrac{d(TC)}{dQ} = -2Q$

$$TR = P \times Q$$
$$TR = (230 - Q)Q$$
$$TR = 230Q - Q^2$$
$$MR = \frac{d(TR)}{dQ} = 230 - 2Q$$

Setting the profit maximizing output at $MC = MR$ gives us:

$$-Q = 230 - 2Q$$
$$Q = 230$$

Profit would be maximized at an output level of 230. It should be noted that the outcome figures are not always neat round numbers. The point, as has been made earlier, is that this is a model to help firms make decisions and as a result this firm might aim for an output level between two values and know that it is maximizing profit.

JEOPARDY PROBLEM

> A firm finds itself in a position of seeing an increase in sales growth of 15 per cent over the previous year and productivity is up by 5 per cent. The firm's directors, however, have reported losses of €25 million compared to a profit of €15 million in the previous year. How could this have happened?

BREAK-EVEN ANALYSIS

When a new business starts up, or if an existing business decides to develop a new product, one initial goal may be to achieve break-even. Break-even refers to the output level at which the total costs of production are equal to the total revenue generated from selling that output. Many firms will look at break-even analysis as part of their planning tools. They can look at the variables involved and how different figures plugged into these variables can affect decision making.

Figure 8.2 shows how we can represent break-even graphically. The vertical axis shows both costs and revenues and the horizontal axis shows output and sales. A firm faces fixed costs which must be paid regardless of whether it produces any output. The fixed cost curve, FC, is represented as a horizontal line at a cost of C. Variable costs (VC) are zero when the firm produces no output but rise as output rises. The VC curve shows these costs rising in direct proportion to output. Total cost is the sum of variable costs and fixed cost ($TC = VC + FC$) and so the TC curve has a vertical intercept equal to the level of fixed costs

---

FIGURE 8.2

Break-Even Analysis

A break-even chart shows a firm's total cost, made up of fixed and variable costs and its total revenue. The output level where TR = TC is the break-even point shown by output Q_{BE}. Any output level below Q_{BE} would mean that the firm was producing at a loss because TC would be greater than TR but any output above Q_{BE} would mean the firm was operating at a profit. At output level Q_1, the amount of profit is indicated by the shaded triangle B. The distance between Q_{BE} and Q_1 is called the margin of safety and denotes how far sales could fall before the firm starts to make losses.

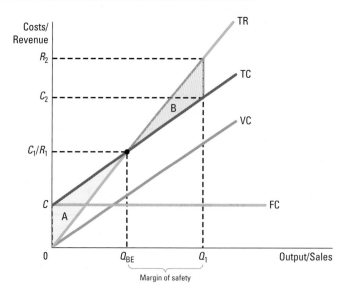

(C) and then rises as output rises. The vertical distance between the TC and VC curve is constant because of the proportional relationship between output and VC assumed above.

The total revenue curve is dependent on the price that the firm chooses to charge for its product. The higher the price charged the steeper the TR curve. The break-even level of output in Figure 8.2 is the amount where $TC = TR$ which is depicted as Q_{BE}. At this output level the TC are C_1 and the TR the same at R_1 shown by C_1/R_1 in Figure 8.2. At any output level below Q_{BE} the firm will find that its TC is greater than TR and so it will make a loss on that output. The range of output in which a loss is made is represented by the area shown by the shaded triangle A.

At output levels above Q_{BE}, for example Q_1, the firm's TR, shown by R_2, is greater than its TC, shown by C_2 and as a result it makes profits on this output equal to the value represented by the distance $R_2 - C_2$. The total amount of profit made at output Q_1 is represented by the shaded triangle B. If the firm did operate at Q_1 then it could experience a fall in sales and still be generating a profit provided sales did not fall below the break-even output Q_{BE}. The distance between the break-even output and current production where TR is greater than TC is called the **margin of safety**.

We can also look at the break-even point in a more mathematical way. A firm needs to aim at selling its output at a price greater than the variable cost of production.

Imagine a firm producing chocolate bars. The ingredient costs are €0.30 per bar and the labour costs are estimated at €0.10 per bar. Total variable costs are €0.40 per bar. If the selling price of the chocolate bar is €0.60 then every bar sold covers the variable costs of production and leaves €0.20 which can be used to help pay off the fixed costs which also have to be paid. This sum is called the **contribution**. The contribution is the difference between the selling price and the variable cost per unit. Knowing the contribution per unit, the break-even output can be given by:

$$\text{Break-even} = \frac{\text{Fixed costs}}{\text{Contribution per unit}}$$

The break-even point can be affected by the costs of production. Any change in fixed costs, for example, will shift the FC line up or down and thus the TC curve. Equally, changes in raw materials costs can affect the variable costs and as a result the TC curve.

The firm can use break-even analysis to assess the impact of the changes in costs and make decisions as a result. These planning decisions can be extended to analyse the possible effects of changes in prices and hence revenue. We know that $TR = P \times Q$. If a firm changes its price the shape of the TR curve will alter. If a firm chooses to increase its price then the TR curve will pivot and become steeper as shown in Figure 8.3. With the TR curve now indicated as TR_1, the firm will not have to sell as many products to cover its costs and so the break-even output will be lower at Q_{BE2}. A firm might choose to reduce its price, in which case the TR curve will become flatter. In this case TR curve will now be represented as TR_2 and the firm will now have to sell more products in order to cover its costs and so the break-even output would rise to Q_{BE3}.

Limitations of Break-Even Analysis

As mentioned above, break-even is best seen as a planning tool and the outline given here is a simplistic one. There are a number of limitations with break-even analysis. First, there is an assumption that all output is sold. This is not the case for many firms where

margin of safety the distance between the break-even output and current production where total revenue is greater than total cost

contribution the difference between the selling price and the variable cost per unit

FIGURE 8.3

The Effect on Break-Even Output of Changes in Price

Total revenue is found by multiplying price times the quantity sold. If the price is increased the TR curve will become steeper as shown by the curve TR₁. As a result, the firm would now only need to produce output Q_{BE2} in order to break-even. If price was reduced the TR curve becomes flatter indicated by curve TR₂ and the firm would have to sell a higher output level, Q_{BE3} in order to break even.

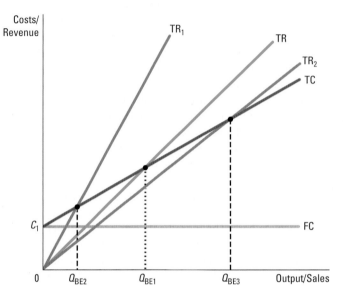

production takes place but products are not immediately sold and as such firms have stock (inventory).

Second, the shape of the *TR* and *TC* curves is unlikely to be smooth as not every additional product a firm sells can be sold at the same price. Equally, given the dynamic nature of markets, any estimation of costs or revenues is not likely to be relevant for very long.

Third, we know that if a firm changes price, demand will be affected. Break-even analysis says nothing about what the effect of a price change on actual sales will be, nor how long it will take a firm to sell the output level to break-even. The effect on sales of a change in price will be dependent on the price elasticity of demand.

Revenue Maximization

In recent years there has been criticism of some executives in businesses because their reward packages seem to have grown disproportionately in comparison to the performance of the business. One of the problems with this is understanding the definition of 'performance'. Executives might be persuaded to focus on goals which may give an impression of the business doing well, such as targeting sales. Other things being equal, a rise in sales is a 'good' thing although of course this might not say anything about the cost involved in achieving any such increase in sales.

We know that total revenue is price multiplied by quantity sold. The goal of revenue maximization may also be referred to as *sales revenue maximization*.

The principle is straightforward. There are three ways to increase sales: do something with price, something to influence how much is sold, or a combination of the two. We have seen how both reducing and increasing price can increase total revenue depending on the price elasticity of demand for the product. There are a number of pricing strategies that can be employed and we will look at these in more detail in Chapter 11. Equally, firms will use a number of tactics to try and increase sales which will include other elements of the marketing mix apart from price:

- the product itself;
- how consumers are able to access the product (place);
- how consumers are made aware of the product (promotion);
- the processes involved which includes things like customer service commitments and the information customers can access;
- a focus on the people who are involved in the business (the employees and physical evidence);
- how the firm is viewed in the eyes of its customers, and the extent to which the view conforms with prior assumptions. For example, going into a car showroom and seeing new cars which are dirty and poorly presented in a shabby environment would not be an image most car dealers would want to present.

Graphical Representation of Sales Revenue Maximization   We know from our look at the theory of demand that in order to increase demand, a firm needs to reduce its price. We also know that along a straight line demand curve the elasticity ranges from elastic through to inelastic.

The price elasticity of demand (*ped*) varies at every point along a straight line demand curve. The higher up the demand curve (towards the vertical axis) where price is relatively high but quantity demanded relatively low, *ped* will be elastic, whereas at the lower end of the demand curve (towards the horizontal axis) the price is relatively low but quantity demanded relatively high and as a result *ped* will be inelastic. There will also be a point midway between these two ranges where the *ped* is of unit elasticity.

This knowledge is important when looking at market structure and imperfect competition such as oligopoly and monopoly where the firm does not face a horizontal demand curve where $P = AR = MR$. In markets where firms are not operating under the assumptions of perfect competition, they will face a downward sloping demand curve. Given that the demand curve slopes down from left to right, in order to sell an additional unit the producer must offer it at a lower price than previous units and so the *MR* will always be lower than the average revenue. Graphically, the marginal revenue (*MR*) curve lies below the demand curve (the *AR* curve) as shown in Figure 8.4. *MR* is the addition to total revenue as a result of selling one more (or one fewer) units of production. When the addition to total revenue does not change as a result of the sale of one extra unit of production, the *MR* is zero. The definition of unit elasticity is that the percentage change in quantity demanded is equal to the percentage change in price and so there will be no change in total revenue. It follows that the *MR* curve cuts the horizontal axis where the *ped* = 1. This is summarized in Figure 8.4.

What this tells us is that the total revenue curve will be positive when the price elasticity of the demand curve is elastic, at its maximum when price elasticity is equal to 1 and begins to decline when the price elasticity of the demand curve is inelastic.

The total revenue curve can be graphed as in Figure 8.5 showing the relationship between sales revenue on the vertical axis in euros, and the volume of sales on

FIGURE 8.4

Changing Price Elasticity of Demand Along a Demand Curve and Marginal Revenue

If the firm faces a downward sloping demand curve, then the slope of the curve is constant but the price elasticity of demand is not. In order to sell additional quantities, the firm must reduce price and so the addition to total revenue – the marginal revenue – will be less than the price (average revenue). The MR curve will lie below the demand curve. At the point where ped = unity (1), the addition to TR will be zero and so this represents the horizontal intercept of the MR curve. At points where the ped is less than unity (ped = inelastic), the MR is negative as the addition to R is falling.

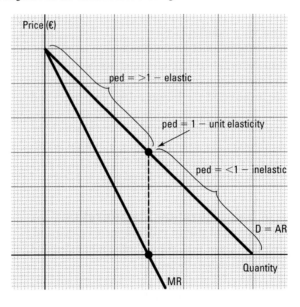

FIGURE 8.5

The Total Revenue Curve

Panel (a) shows the TR curve for a firm in a competitive market. If the firm is a price taker then P = AR = MR and the demand curve it faces will be horizontal. The TR curve will be a positive curve rising in direct proportion to sales. Panel (b) shows the TR curve for a firm facing a downward sloping demand curve. As sales increase TR starts to rise but the rate of growth in TR will gradually begin to slow, reaching a maximum and then beginning to decline.

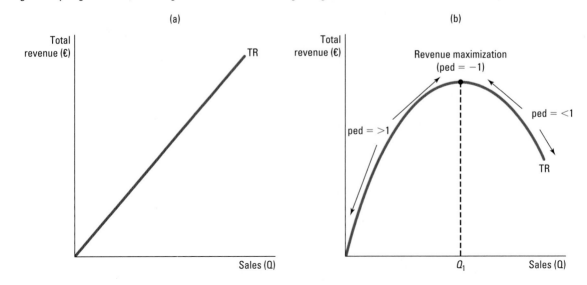

the horizontal axis. Panel (a) shows the *TR* for a price taking firm in competitive conditions where $P = AR = MR$. In this situation the *TR* curve will be a positive curve rising in direct proportion to sales. Panel (b) shows the situation for a firm facing a downward sloping demand curve. The *TR* curve begins as a positive function of sales rising as more sales are achieved, reaching a maximum at a volume of sales of Q_1 and then declining thereafter. This is because the firm has to reduce prices in order to sell more output and is linked to the explanation given of the shape of the *MR* and demand curve in Figure 8.4.

We have seen how a firm can achieve profit maximization at the point where $MR = MC$. At this point the gap between the total revenue curve and the total cost curve is at a maximum. We can transpose the *TC* curve onto the *TR* curve shown in panel (b) of Figure 8.5 to get the situation depicted in Figure 8.6. From this we can see that the point of profit maximization occurs when sales volumes are at Q_{PM}. At this point the distance between the *TR* and *TC* curves is at its maximum. However, the point of sales revenue maximization occurs where sales volume is Q_{SM} to the right of the profit maximizing sales level. This implies that if sales revenue maximization is pursued as a goal by a firm, it may be that it achieves this goal at lower profits, and this is likely to be because the cost of generating additional sales rises faster than the increase in revenue generated. This could be due to very expensive marketing campaigns, for example, or aggressive pricing tactics which drive out rivals but at very reduced margins.

Figure 8.6 also shows a sales volume of Q_L. At this level of sales, *TC* is greater than *TR* and the firm is making a loss. Despite generating much higher sales, this is being achieved at greater and greater cost and if continued the firm would continue to make increasing losses.

FIGURE 8.6

Profit Maximization and Revenue Maximization

This figure transposes a TC *curve onto the* TR *curve for a firm facing a downward sloping demand curve. The point of profit maximization occurs where the distance between the* TR *and* TC *curves is at a maximum at a sales level of* Q_{PM}. *This is not the sales revenue maximizing position, however; this is achieved where sales are* Q_{SM} *and the* TR *curve is at a maximum. If the firm continued to try to push sales growth the* TR *would start to decline. At a sales level of* Q_L, *the firm makes a loss as* TC *is greater than* TR *at that sales level.*

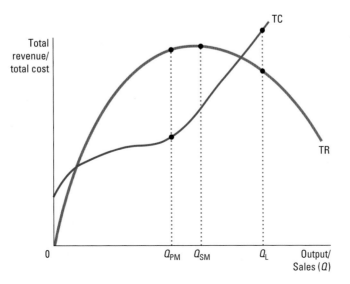

> **Pitfall Prevention** In the discussion of the difference between profit maximization and sales revenue maximization, it is easy to get confused over the difference between total and marginal values. Ensure that you keep the distinction clear and understand the relationship between the two.

Cost Minimization

product life cycle a diagram representing the life cycle of a product from launch through to growth, maturity and decline

Most products go through a process, referred to as the product life cycle, starting with development, launch, growth, maturity and then decline. The **product life cycle** is a simplistic model to describe these typical processes. A typical product life cycle looks like that shown in Figure 8.7 which has sales on the vertical axis and time on the horizontal axis.

Sales are clearly zero during the development stage and so at the point of launch the vertical and horizontal intercept will be 0. As the product gains traction in the market, sales will start to rise often picking up speed as a firm's marketing campaigns take effect. At some point sales will start to slow and at this point the market is either saturated as a result of new firms entering to take advantage of profits that exist and which have been highlighted by the product concerned, or where tastes change and the market begins to mature and stagnate. After a certain point, the market will start to decline and sales will gradually taper off. This is the decline stage of the product life cycle.

FIGURE 8.7

The Product Life Cycle

The product life cycle can be represented by a graph which shows sales on the vertical axis and time on the horizontal axis. At the introduction stage sales begin to rise slowly and then may pick up speed. Sales will continue to grow until the market matures after which time sales will start to decline.

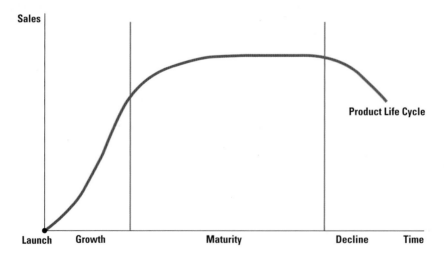

The reason why we have introduced the product life cycle is that there are links between the position of a product and the goal of minimizing cost. It can be assumed that every firm might want to keep costs to a minimum, but as a specific strategy this might be particularly relevant in a mature market, where the product faces little prospect of significant sales growth from year to year although the firm wishes to stay in the market. By sales growth we mean year-on-year increases in sales. For example, assume that unit sales in year X_1 are 1 million. If, in year X_2 sales rise to 1.2 million then sales growth will have been 20 per cent. If in year X sales are 1.25 million then sales growth will have been 4.16 per cent. However, if in year X sales remain at 1.25 million then sales growth will be zero but the firm might still wish to stay in the market because sales are deemed healthy at this level. The firm may see relatively stable revenues from such sales levels being generated for the foreseeable future although the prospect of growing sales in the future is just not feasible.

In such a market how does the firm increase profit? It knows it can do little to increase revenue given the maturity of the market and so the other option is to focus on costs. This could mean looking at making its human resource management more efficient by not only looking at whether it has the optimal number of staff to carry out its operations effectively, but whether those staff are in the right positions, whether talent is being exploited and whether the business can be reorganized to bring about a more optimal structure which allows it to continue meeting customer expectations but at the same time cut costs – both total and unit.

Productivity   Increasing productivity can be a way in which firms control or cut costs. Productivity is a measure of output per factor of production per unit of time. It can be summarized in the following formula:

$$\text{Productivity} = \frac{\text{Total output}}{\text{Units of the factor}}$$

If, for example, a cutlery manufacturer produced 20 000 sets of cutlery per month and employed 200 workers, then output per worker (productivity) would be 100 sets per month. Increasing productivity is an important goal for firms because of the contribution it makes to reducing unit costs.

To see how productivity can help a focus on controlling costs, assume that our cutlery manufacturer sells each set for a price of €75 and that the current unit cost of production is €50 so the margin on unit sales is €25. If the firm sells all 20 000 units a month it generates revenues of €1.5 million and costs will be €1 million.

Now assume that the firm makes some organizational changes which include reducing the tiers of management and streamlining the sales function. In addition, new machinery in its factory helps workers to operate more efficiently and as a result of these changes productivity per worker rises to 120 units per month. Clearly there will have been some costs involved in making these changes but if the proportionate increase in costs is less than the proportionate increase in productivity then the firm's unit costs can fall thus improving its margins.

If workers are paid an average of €2500 per month with a productivity level of 100 units per month then we can work out that the unit labour costs to produce the cutlery sets is €25. If wages stay the same but the new changes increase productivity to 120 units per month, the unit labour costs are now only €20.83 per set. Other things being equal, the firm can now increase its margin from €25 to €29.17. Assuming it continues to sell all 20 000 units per month its profit increases by €83 400 per month.

It is also possible that the firm, in recognition of the changes the workforce are having to adjust to, could even pay the workers a higher wage and still see an increase in profit provided the increase in wages was more than offset by the rise in productivity.

supply chain the various processes, activities, organizations and resources used in moving a product from business to business or business to consumer

The Supply Chain   For many firms the supply chain can be long and complex. The **supply chain** is the various processes, activities, organizations and resources used in moving a product from business to business or business to consumer. Because of the complexities of the supply chain there are lots of opportunities for firms to focus on these activities and processes to find ways of increasing efficiency and reducing both total and unit costs.

One advocate of such a focus is Michael Porter whose theory of competitive advantage has been a foundation of strategic analysis of firms for many years. In his book *Competitive Advantage*[1] Porter states: 'If a firm can achieve and sustain overall cost leadership, then it will be an above-average performer in its industry provided it can command prices at or near the industry average.' A focus on any aspect of the supply chain may help to give the firm a competitive advantage if that advantage is both distinctive and defensible, that is, if it is unique to the business and not easy to copy in the short to medium term by the firm's rivals. Such advantages may be developed through employing specialists to analyse all aspects of the firm's supply chain operations. Investment in new equipment and machinery, designing new processes, putting in place new systems, finding ways to rationalize back-office functions (such activities as administration, payments and accounts offices, IT and human resources management, which help keep a business running smoothly but may not have direct contact with customers), streamlining distribution networks and finding cheaper suppliers or outsourcing various aspects of the supply chain.

If these are put in place the firm may well be able to experience benefits which help them to move closer to the minimum point on the short-run average cost curve or, if a change in scale is achieved, a new short-run average cost curve at a lower point on the long-run average cost curve.

Shareholder Value

Shareholder value refers to the way in which shareholders receive reward for the risk they have taken in investing in the business. This risk is rewarded through either (or both) an increase in the share price of the business or in the value of the dividends paid to shareholders.

Shareholders are the part owners of a business. Owning a share in a business represents a claim to the future earnings of that business. Those earnings will be dependent, in part, on the way in which the business is led and managed. The decisions of the executives and managers in a firm will affect the ability of the firm to generate revenues and to control costs and therefore make profits over time. The profits will be partly distributed to shareholders in the form of dividends. Investors may also buy shares in the hope that the price will rise and as a result the shares can be sold at a personal profit to the investor.

Fundamental to shareholder value is the idea that if a CEO focuses attention on improving the performance of the company through various measures, then the stock price will invariably follow if it is assumed that stock prices accurately reflect fundamental values (something that has been called into question in the years following the financial crisis).

The definition of performance, however, is where there is lots of debate. Should performance include just measures of profit? Do increases in the rate of growth

---

[1]Porter E.M. (2004) *Competitive Advantage: Creating and sustaining superior performance*, p.13. New York, Free Press.

of sales revenue over time signify good performance? Some would suggest firms focus on what is termed **free cash flow**. Free cash flow is the cash generated from the firm's operations minus that spent on capital assets. What this figure represents is the ability of the business to generate cash over and above that necessary to carry out its operations, service its assets and expand those assets. Cash generation is necessary to enable any firm to be able to expand over time and to develop new products and thus maintain its competitiveness.

free cash flow the cash generated from the firm's operations minus that spent on capital assets

NON-FINANCIAL OBJECTIVES

The following represents a summary of what can be called non-financial objectives. Of course, in reality, financial and non-financial objectives are often hard to disentangle, partly because as mentioned above, decisions that affect one part of a business are also likely to affect another part. A decision to expand market share, for example, can lead to increases in revenue and profit and as a result improve shareholder value.

Satisficing

The theory of satisficing was developed by Carnegie Tech Nobel-laureate, Herbert Simon in 1956. Simon argued that human beings do not act as rational automatons and are unable to compute optimized outcomes with mathematical precision. For example, CEOs may not have either the time nor brain capacity to sit and calculate the profit maximizing output. Instead they tend to behave using a mix of satisfying and sufficing, termed satisficing. CEOs, for example, have to satisfy shareholder demands and make healthy profits but not necessarily by maximizing profit. The profit level must be sufficient to satisfy shareholder demands.

As a result, the assumption of profit maximizing or any other sort of maximizing or minimizing might not hold in the real world where uncertainty, the complexity of organizations and the vagaries of human behaviour mean that decisions are regularly made which are sub-optimal.

Linked to this is so-called **agency theory**, whereby managers in a firm are viewed as being agents of shareholders and may pursue their own self-interest rather than the interests of the shareholders. If the interests of shareholders and managers diverge then there can be an agency problem and measures may need to be put into place to more closely align the interests of owners and managers.

agency theory where managers act as the agents of shareholders and as a result there may be a divorce between ownership and control such that managers pursue their own self-interests rather than the interests of shareholders

Market Power

Market power might include a number of different characteristics. It can involve firms seeking growth through acquisition (merger or takeover) both within their core market and outside it. The latter is referred to as conglomerate acquisitions and leads to firms having interests across a range of diverse and often totally unrelated markets. The Indian Tata Group, for example, owns businesses involved with information technology and communications, engineering, automotive, chemicals, energy and consumer products such as beverages and ceramics.

Expanding power can give a firm considerable influence over its market and enable it to have some influence over price or on output. We will look in more

market share the proportion of total sales accounted for by a product/business in a market

detail at the effects on firm behaviour in markets where the assumptions of highly competitive firms is dropped, in later chapters. Part of the drive to expand market power might also involve a desire to increase market share. **Market share** refers to the proportion of total sales in a market accounted for by an individual firm. In the global personal computer (PC) market in January 2015, for example, Lenovo accounted for around 20 per cent of shipments of PCs in the fourth quarter of the year. In the same period, Hewlett Packard (HP) accounted for around 19.7 per cent, Dell for around 13.5 per cent, Acer for 7.7 per cent and Apple for 7.1 per cent (source of data, IDC Worldwide Quarterly PC Tracker, quoted by ZDNet).

Many CEOs will want to monitor market share, partly because it gives some indication of the market power of the firm, but also because there may be personal gratification in expanding market share ahead of rivals; the CEO network can often be very close and highly competitive.

Market share can be expanded through sub-optimal tactics such as cutting prices. The aim is to encourage consumers to switch and once they have been won over, to then retain them. We saw in Chapter 2 how recruiting and retaining customers have different costs. The tactic of cutting prices to win over customers can be an expensive one in terms of the effect on margins and profits; prices might be cut to the point where the firm is selling products at below cost in an attempt to win market share. In the longer term such a tactic is not sustainable but in the short term it may well be sufficient to win a significant number of new or returning customers.

Social, Ethical and Environmental Objectives

Few large firms will neglect the concern amongst their wider stakeholders of the social, ethical and environmental impact of a firm's operations. The vast majority have incorporated some sort of social and environmental responsibility reporting into their operations in addition to the annual report of financial accounts. Critics have argued that some firms use social and environmental issues as a cynical marketing tool and this may be true in some cases, but regardless of the reasons for introducing such policies, many firms have changed the way they run their operations to improve levels of social and environmental responsibility.

Examples of the sort of things that have been introduced include a greater awareness of the effects of pollution in all its forms, and measures to reduce it through increasing efficiency in the use of resources; developing operations to utilize cleaner technologies to reduce the environmental impact; sourcing raw materials from renewable sources; looking at options to recycle including making products that are almost fully recyclable; and reducing energy and water use.

Such measures are not only beneficial to the environment as a whole but also to businesses. Initial investment costs in cleaner energy systems, for example, can be high but the longer-term effects can be significant in terms of reduced unit costs. The social and environmental movement has forced businesses to take a long hard look at themselves and their operations and to make changes to the way they operate and this can be no bad thing for any business looking to find ways of improving – however the definition of 'improving' is framed.

In addition to environmental objectives firms have increasingly developed social and ethical responsibilities in recognition of the wider stakeholders they interact with. These include local sponsorship programmes; being involved in charity work; monitoring closely the way workers are treated, especially if the firm outsources part of its operations; basing decision making not simply on profitability but on what is perceived to be 'right and proper'; doing work with the local community including getting employees to work with local projects; developing closer relationships with suppliers; and promoting diversity.

Ethical decision making involves conducting operations which conform to accepted moral codes – doing things the 'right' way. Such decision making includes the way in which a business manages and reports its financial affairs to help reduce the instances of fraud, bribery and corruption. Other aspects of ethical decision making include giving workers freedom of speech (a particularly relevant point given the increasing use of social media such as Facebook and Twitter as a means of communicating), paying taxes fairly, producing products which are safe (but which may be more costly to produce), and making decisions about who to trade with, who to recruit as suppliers and why those decisions have been made. For example, a firm may choose not to engage in trade with the government of a country which it sees as being repressive, even if such trade could be lucrative.

> **?** ■   **what if ...** a firm has been making significant losses for 5 years which is pushing it to the brink of insolvency. It is offered the prospect of entering into a lucrative trade deal with a very corrupt government which would enable it to not only reverse the losses but also safeguard the jobs of its workers. What should the business do?

Putting into place social, ethical and environmental policies can be expensive and invariably requires considerable changes in a corporate culture and the way the business operates. Many businesses will look at such changes as being long term in their ultimate effects and benefits, and part of the process involves convincing shareholders that these benefits will outweigh the initial costs. If carefully considered and developed, some of these policies can be seen as being sources of competitive advantage which can be distinctive and defensible and therefore make very good business sense, let alone the impact on the firm's reputation and credibility.

It must be remembered, however, that moves to improve social, ethical and environmental responsibility and the incorporation of policies as part of the goals of a firm do not happen everywhere. The vast majority of businesses are small and medium sized and it may be impractical for many small businesses to have such goals. In addition, the geographical spread of business means that efforts to promote such policies as business goals may be confined to parts of developed Western economies. Problems in securing deals on reducing carbon emissions, for example, highlight the tensions that exist between emerging economies and mature economies.

Brand Recognition

A brand is a means of creating awareness and identity in a product or range of products such that consumers come to recognize and associate the product when making purchasing decisions. A brand does not have to be associated with high value, high price or quality. A brand has to clearly reflect to the consumer what the association and personality is – what it means. Brands such as Dolce and Gabbana, for example, have associations with high quality fashion, whereas a brand such as Netto or Poundland have an association with low prices and value for money. If a shopper goes to Netto, they do not expect (nor want) expensively laid out and equipped stores; they expect to be able to buy a range of goods at competitive prices.

Building a brand and subsequent brand recognition may be a goal of business activity. Many firms spend significant sums of money on building brand recognition over time and it should come as no surprise that guarding that hard-earned recognition is something firms are keen to protect. Laws in many countries recognize such efforts and attempts by other firms to imitate a brand can be challenged in the courts.

Ultimately, the goal of brand recognition is designed to influence consumer behaviour. When an individual goes into a fuel station, for example, the array of chocolate bars by the pay station is designed to encourage impulse buying. Brand recognition may be an important factor and is why consumers, almost without thinking, go for a chocolate bar they are aware of and recognize as satisfying their needs. Creating a situation when consumers default to the purchase of one brand ahead of rivals would be the ultimate goal of many businesses in this area, and the developments in neuroscience are beginning to reveal more about how brand association and recognition works and influences purchasing decisions.

Reputation and Image

Linked with social, ethical and environmental responsibility and branding is a goal to develop reputation and image. This might be a reputation for high levels of customer service, quality, reliability, value for money, technically sophisticated products, social awareness, design, style – anything that the firm thinks will help it to gain a competitive edge and which it can exploit.

Social Enterprise

Social enterprises are a combination of charity and business activity. The concept developed in Italy in the 1980s and is a growing feature of business activity throughout Europe. Social enterprises generate surpluses in order to survive in the long term, but these surpluses are invested into some social or community-based project rather than being shared between the owners through dividends. These sorts of businesses are referred to as being part of the *not-for-profit* or *third sector* activity.

The goals of the business in such cases might be to generate surpluses to help communities access water supplies in less developed countries, promote recycling or fair trade, provide affordable homes, help young people to take a more active role in society and so on.

Quick Quiz Are the different business goals outlined above mutually exclusive – i.e. is it possible to be a socially and environmentally responsible business whilst at the same time minimizing cost and maximizing profit?

IN THE NEWS

Print or Electronic News?

The newspaper print industry faces considerable challenges which include rising newsprint costs, declining advertising revenue and lower circulation figures. Competition from electronic media is also a factor; this form of media competition has much lower overheads since there is no need to pay for printing presses or delivery fleets. Access to the news is immediate and the sites can be changed all the time, so it is capable of being more up to date than print newspapers.

The National Readership Survey suggests that newsprint readership and circulation fell by an average of 13 per cent between 2013 and 2014, but with the figure varying across different publications. Circulation figures from the Audit Bureau point to a more moderate decline of 6 per cent but, either way, the figures point to the challenges the industry faces. Regional newspapers are facing similar difficulties. Many have sales below their break-even output. Some have closed and others are only published weekly or online. *Trinity Mirror*, which owns the *Daily Mirror* and a number of other regional newspapers, announced the closure of seven regional papers in November 2014.

However, in the past newspapers have successfully weathered the decline in circulation, for example, the drop in the market as a direct result of competition from TV news, so can they survive now? One option is to join the market for online readership, but it is not that simple.

The *Guardian* and *Daily Mail* have both gone for a mass reach model by making their online content free. According to Media Briefing the *Mail*'s monthly circulation for June 2014 was 10.8 million for the printed paper and 9.5 million for the website, whilst the *Guardian* boasts a monthly circulation of 3.8 million print to 9.6 million using the Web. Maintaining or increasing circulation makes the titles more attractive for advertisers to buy space, but having free access results in a loss of potential revenue from subscription fees.

Another approach is to only offer access to the websites through subscription, an option chosen by *The Times*. *The Times* had a monthly print in June 2014 of 4.4 million compared to an online circulation of only 302 000. If *The Times* average online subscription was £2 a week then every new subscriber kept for a year would bring in just over £100, so if the paper could increase online subscriptions in a year by say 10 000 it would increase revenue by £1 million. You don't need vast numbers because overheads are low, but erecting a paywall means you lose social reach.

So do paywalls work or do you have to give away your online content for free? Sales of *The Times* now account for just over half of its revenue whilst 44 per cent comes from advertising. *The Times* originally lost around 90 per cent of its online users when it went over to a subscription, but user numbers have increased year on year by 8 per cent and there are now just over 150 000 digital-only subscribers (others get the printed copy as well). This data can also be a bit misleading since any glance at *The Times* website will show that there are a number of discounted offers not to mention packages that are non-paying through bulk fees arranged with a number of employers. This is evidence of *The Times* having to work much harder than non-paying sites in order to reach new audiences.

Questions

1. **What is meant by the term break-even and what is its significance to the newspaper business?**
2. **What stage in the product life cycle is the printed newspaper industry in? Justify your answer.**
3. **Explain which of the following goals you think are most relevant to the newspaper industry today: increased market share, maximizing social reach, maximizing profits, expanding sales, surviving, diversifying.**

4. If it cost £30 million to run an online pay-by-subscription newspaper and the subscription averaged £50 a year, what level of readership is required to start making a profit? What advice would you give the online publication if it made a loss of £5 million in the first year and £2 million in the second year?

5. What strategies are open to the newspaper industry attempting to arrest the decline in printed circulation?

References: http://www.themediabriefing.com/article/newspaper-publishers

-nrs-abc-circulation-readership-digital-june-2014

http://uk.businessinsider.com/the-times-swings-back-into-profit-and-posts-digital-subscriber-uplift-2014-12?r=US

SUMMARY

- We have looked at a range of business goals. Some of these can be classified as aims and others, objectives.

- The 'traditional' (classical) assumption of profit maximization is one example of a financial objective or goal but increasingly other goals are becoming just as important.

- Brand recognition or a well-developed set of policies to minimize the environmental impact of a business' operations, for example, could be seen as being routes to generate increased sales and thus contribute to higher profits. The aim could still be profit maximization, the objective to help achieve this through promoting brand recognition or environmental responsibility.

- Others might argue that brand recognition or social and environmental awareness is a long-term aim in itself.

- Rather than be overly concerned with such distinctions, it is important to recognize that business goals are varied and dependent in part on the type of business and the type of business organization.

- All these goals are interrelated and can be seen as being parts of a jigsaw. Ultimately, businesses in the private sector need to generate profits – they will have to close down if the business' activities are unsustainable.

- Of concern to the business economist, therefore, are the ways in which the stakeholder demands on business can be reconciled.

- It is safe to say that it is unlikely that all stakeholder demands can be met so business owners have to balance these competing demands and find a way of carrying out business which maximizes overall benefits at minimum cost.

- It is important to recognize that there will always be some cost involved in carrying out business and so regardless of the environmental, social and ethical claims of a firm, there will be some areas of operation where criticism can be levelled at the business' activities. How these criticisms are managed is often a crucial part of the role of CEOs and managers.

QUESTIONS FOR REVIEW

1. Using an example, explain the difference between aims and objectives.

2. Explain why a business maximizes profit where $MC = MR$.

3. Explain why, at the point of maximum TR, the price elasticity of demand for a good is -1.

4. What is meant by the terms 'break-even point' and 'margin of safety'?

5. What is the meaning of the term 'productivity'?

6. How can increases in factor productivity help a firm to achieve cost minimization?

7. Why might a firm have a goal of increasing market share?

8. Using examples, explain the difference between social and environmental objectives.

9. Explain how an objective to base decisions on strong ethical principles can lead to stakeholder conflict.

10. What is a social enterprise?

PROBLEMS AND APPLICATIONS

1. Why can it be difficult to distinguish between aims and objectives and strategies and tactics?

2. A firm faces the following cost and demand equations:

$$P = 100 - Q$$
$$TC = 10 - 5Q^2$$

   Find the profit maximizing output.

3. A firm faces the following cost and revenue schedules:

Output (Q)	TR	TC
0	0	3
1	6	5
2	12	8
3	18	12
4	24	17
5	30	23
6	36	30
7	42	38
8	48	47

   Calculate the profit, marginal revenue and marginal cost, and state what the profit maximizing output will be for the firm under the assumption that it seeks to maximize profit.

4. A firm has the following information available to its managers:
   Fixed costs are €1500, price is €8 and the variable costs are €0.50 per unit. What is the break-even output for this firm?

5. The firm in Question 4 above is operating at its break-even output. A discussion is being held about making a decision to change price with the aim of increasing profit. It is operating at 98 per cent capacity. The sales director wants to reduce price but the operations manager wants to increase price. Which of these two options would you recommend the firm take and why?

6. If a firm faces a downward sloping demand curve, why doesn't total revenue continue rising as a firm sells more of its output?

7. Workers in a firm have petitioned the management for a 5 per cent pay increase. How might the firm's management approach negotiations on the pay claim. (Hint: the management may be interested in raising the issue of productivity.)

8. Which of the following do you think is the most important element of shareholder value: the dividend to shareholders, the firm's share price or free cash flow? Explain your answer.

9. How might an energy firm such as BP or Shell claim that they can maximize shareholder value but at the same time emphasize their environmental and social credentials?

10. A firm is operating in a market in which the good it sells is in the maturity stage of its life cycle. How does knowledge of this shape its decisions about what its goals for that product might be? How might these decisions be influenced if the firm had a new product in development which it believed could take significant market share in the future?

9 FIRM BEHAVIOUR AND THE ORGANIZATION OF INDUSTRY

LEARNING OUTCOMES

After reading this chapter you should be able to:

- Explain why the marginal cost curve must intersect the average total cost curve at the minimum point of the average total cost curve.

- Explain why a production function might exhibit increasing marginal product at low levels of output and decreasing marginal product at high levels of output.

- Explain why, as a firm expands its scale of operation, it tends to first exhibit economies of scale, then constant returns to scale, then diseconomies of scale.

- Show, by using isoquant curves and isocost lines, how firms can arrive at the least-cost input combination.

THE COSTS OF PRODUCTION

The economy is made up of thousands of firms that produce the goods and services we enjoy every day: Mercedes Benz produces cars, Miele produces kitchen appliances and Nestlé produces food and drink. Some firms, such as these three, are large; they employ thousands of workers and have thousands of shareholders who share in the firms' profits. Other firms, such as the local hairdresser's salon or pizzeria, are small; they employ only a few workers and may be owned by a single person or family.

As we examine firm behaviour in more detail you will gain a better understanding of what decisions lie behind the supply curve in a market which we introduced in Chapter 4. In addition, it will introduce you to a part of economics called *industrial organization* – the study of how firms' decisions regarding prices and quantities depend on the market conditions they face. The town in which you live, for instance, may have several restaurants but only one water supply company. How does this difference in the number of firms affect the prices in these markets and the efficiency of the market outcomes? The field of industrial organization addresses exactly this question.

Before we turn to these issues, however, we need to discuss the costs of production. All firms, regardless of size, incur costs as they make the goods and services that they sell. A firm's costs are a key determinant of its production and pricing decisions. In this chapter, we define some of the variables that economists use to measure a firm's costs, and we consider the relationships among them. We will also introduce a model to look at how a firm might maximize production given certain constraints such as its budgets and the factors of production it has available.

WHAT ARE COSTS?

We begin our discussion of costs at Flavio's Pizza Factory. By examining some of the issues that Flavio faces in his business, we can learn some lessons about costs that apply to all firms in the economy.

Total Revenue, Total Cost and Profit

The amount of pizzas Flavio sells multiplied by the price he sells the pizzas at is the total revenue the firm receives. If Flavio sells 500 000 pizzas a year and the average price of each pizza sold is €5 his total revenue will be €5 × 500 000 = €2.5 million.

To produce those 500 000 pizzas, Flavio will have had to employ labour, buy machinery and equipment, run and maintain that equipment, buy the raw materials to make the pizzas (flour, cheese, tomatoes and so on), pay rent or a mortgage on the factory, pay off loans he may have secured (both the sum borrowed and any interest charged), pay for market research, marketing costs such as advertising and promotion, administration costs (such as managing the firm's payroll, monitoring the finances, processing sales and purchase invoices), and many other everyday payments down to the cost of using the telephone, energy, postage, maintaining the buildings and so on. These represent Flavio's **total cost**.

total cost the market value of the inputs a firm uses in production

If Flavio subtracts all the costs over the year from the revenues received in the same year he will either have a surplus (i.e. his revenue will be greater than his costs) or possibly have spent more on costs than received in revenues.

Profit is the reward for the risk taken in carrying out production and is calculated as follows:

$$Profit = Total\ revenue - Total\ cost$$

We can express this in the formula:

$$\pi = TR - TC$$

where the Greek letter pi (π) represents profit.

Let us assume for the moment that Flavio's objective is to make his firm's profit as large as possible – in other words, he wants to maximize profit. Flavio needs to be able to measure his total revenue and his total costs. We know how to calculate total revenue, in many cases that is a relatively easy thing to do, but the measurement of a firm's total cost is more subtle and open to different interpretations.

> **Pitfall Prevention** It is important to understand the distinction between profit and cash flow – the latter is the money flowing into and out of a business over a period of time, whereas profit takes into consideration the total revenue and total cost. A firm could be profitable but have cash flow problems which could force it out of business.

Costs as Opportunity Costs

When measuring costs at Flavio's Pizza Factory, or any other firm, it is important to keep in mind that the cost of something is what you give up to get it. Recall that the *opportunity cost* of an item refers to the sacrifice of the benefits of the next best alternative. To calculate opportunity cost we divide the sacrifice (the numerator) by the gain (the denominator):

$$Opportunity\ cost = \frac{Sacrifice}{Gain}$$

When economists speak of a firm's cost of production, they include the opportunity costs of making its output of goods and services.

A firm's opportunity costs of production are sometimes obvious but sometimes less so. When Flavio pays €1000 for a stock of flour, he can no longer use that €1000 to buy something else; he has to sacrifice what else that €1000 could have purchased. Because these costs require the firm to pay out some money, they are called **explicit costs**. By contrast, some of a firm's opportunity costs, called **implicit costs**, do not require a cash outlay. Imagine that Flavio is skilled with computers and could earn €100 per hour working as a programmer. For every hour that Flavio works at his pizza factory, he gives up €100 in income, and this forgone income is also classed as part of his costs by an economist.

This distinction between explicit and implicit costs highlights an important difference between how economists and accountants analyse a business. Economists are interested in studying how firms make production and pricing decisions. Because these decisions are based on both explicit and implicit costs, economists include both when measuring a firm's costs. By contrast, accountants have the job of keeping track of the money that flows into and out of firms. As a result, they measure the explicit costs but often ignore the implicit costs.

The difference between economists and accountants is easy to see in the case of Flavio's Pizza Factory. When Flavio gives up the opportunity to earn money as a computer programmer, his accountant will not count this as a cost of his pizza

explicit costs input costs that require an outlay of money by the firm

implicit costs input costs that do not require an outlay of money by the firm

business. Because no money flows out of the business to pay for this cost, it never shows up on the accountant's financial statements. An economist, however, will count the foregone income as a cost because it will affect the decisions that Flavio makes in his pizza business. This is an important part of thinking like an economist. If the wage as a computer programmer rose from €100 to €500 per hour, the opportunity cost of running the business in terms of what Flavio is sacrificing in foregone income has risen. Flavio might decide he could earn more by closing the business and switching to computer programming.

The Cost of Capital as an Opportunity Cost An important implicit cost of almost every firm is the opportunity cost of the financial capital that has been invested in the business. Suppose, for instance, that Flavio used €300 000 of his savings to buy his pizza factory from the previous owner. If Flavio had instead left this money deposited in a savings account that pays an interest rate of 5 per cent, he would have earned €15 000 per year (assuming simple interest). To own his pizza factory, therefore, Flavio has given up €15 000 a year in interest income. This forgone €15 000 is an implicit opportunity cost of Flavio's business. An economist views the €15 000 in interest income that Flavio gives up every year as a cost of his business, even though it is an implicit cost. Flavio's accountant, however, will not show this €15 000 as a cost because no money flows out of the business to pay for it.

To explore further the difference between economists and accountants, let's change the example slightly. Suppose now that Flavio did not have the entire €300 000 to buy the factory but, instead, used €100 000 of his own savings and borrowed €200 000 from a bank at an interest rate of 5 per cent. Flavio's accountant, who only measures explicit costs, will now count the €10 000 interest paid on the bank loan every year as a cost because this amount of money now flows out of the firm. By contrast, according to an economist, the opportunity cost of owning the business is still €15 000. The opportunity cost equals the interest on the bank loan (an explicit cost of €10 000) plus the forgone interest on savings (an implicit cost of €5000).

Economic Profit versus Accounting Profit

Now let's return to the firm's objective – profit. Because economists and accountants measure costs differently, they also measure profit differently. An economist measures a firm's **economic profit** as the firm's total revenue minus all the opportunity costs (explicit and implicit) of producing the goods and services sold. An accountant measures the firm's **accounting profit** as the firm's total revenue minus only the firm's explicit costs.

Figure 9.1 summarizes this difference. Notice that because the accountant ignores the implicit costs, accounting profit is usually larger than economic profit. For a business to be profitable from an economist's standpoint, total revenue must cover all the opportunity costs, both explicit and implicit.

economic profit total revenue minus total cost, including both explicit and implicit costs

accounting profit total revenue minus total explicit cost

Quick Quiz Richard Collishaw is a dairy farmer who is also a skilled metal worker. He makes unique garden sculptures that could earn him €40 an hour. One day, he spends 10 hours working with his dairy herd. The cost of operating the machinery and plant used in the milking process is €200. What opportunity cost has he incurred? What cost would his accountant measure? If the milk produced will yield €400 in revenue, does Richard earn an accounting profit? Does he earn an economic profit? Would you advise Richard to continue as a farmer or switch to metal working?

FIGURE 9.1

Economists versus Accountants

Economists include all opportunity costs when analysing a firm, whereas accountants measure only explicit costs. Therefore, economic profit is smaller than accounting profit.

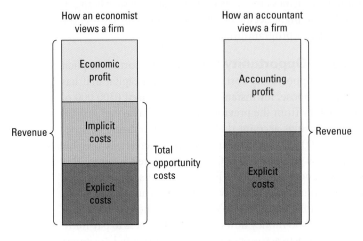

PRODUCTION AND COSTS

We have seen how the transformation process is characterized by firms buying inputs to carry out production. There is a relationship between the amount of inputs used, the cost of production and the amount produced. In this section we examine the link between a firm's production process and its total cost using Flavio's Pizza Factory as an example.

The Production Function

production function the relationship between the quantities of inputs used to make a good and the quantity of output of that good

The relationship between factor inputs can be expressed as a mathematical relationship called a production function. The **production function** shows the amount of output which can be produced given different combinations of factor inputs, land, labour and capital. This should be fairly intuitive – if Flavio increases the number of people working in his factory then the amount of pizzas produced would be likely to rise. However, it could also be possible that Flavio might decide to cut the number of workers he employs and buy a machine which can do their job and still increase the amount of pizzas produced.

In reality, firms face complex decisions over how to organize production and a whole discipline has grown up around this called operations management which in turn is closely linked to organizational behaviour and organizational design. Some firms rely on large amounts of labour compared to other factors for production and are referred to as *labour intensive*, whereas other firms have relatively small amounts of labour but very large amounts of capital and are referred to as *capital intensive*.

Let us assume there are two factor inputs, labour (L) and capital (K). The production function can be expressed as follows:

$$Q = f(L_1, K_1)$$

This states that the level of output (Q) is dependent upon the amount of labour and capital employed. More complex production functions are developed which include more specific dependent variables which can have different values. For example, we can specify a particular amount of labour, a particular amount of capital, as well as a certain quantity of land. Using this as a model, we can then vary some factor inputs whilst holding the others constant and analyse the effect on the level of output.

Obviously, this is a very simple introduction to the production function and as we will see later, changing the amount of factor inputs can have different consequences.

> **?** **what if ...** Flavio's factory had a total floor area of 2000 square metres, three-quarters of which was taken up with machinery. Flavio employs 50 workers. If he employs a further ten workers, will output of pizzas increase? If he employs another ten will output continue to increase? What do you think would happen to output if Flavio continued to increase the number of workers he employs?

The Short Run and the Long Run

In business, the distinction between the short run and the long run is of considerable importance. The **short run** is defined as the period of time in which some factors of production cannot be altered. The **long run** is that period of time when all factors of production can be altered. The distinction is really conceptual rather than specific. Many businesses will not be able to calculate the short run or the long run but they will know that the distinction will be an important consideration in their decision making. The long run for a market trader in a local street market may be weeks or months but for an energy supply company could be 20 years.

In the short run, let us assume that the size of Flavio's factory is fixed (a not unreasonable assumption) but that Flavio can vary the quantity of pizzas produced by changing the number of workers.

Table 9.1 shows how the quantity of pizzas Flavio's factory produces per hour depends on the number of workers. As you see in the first two columns, if there are no workers in the factory Flavio produces no pizzas. When there is 1 worker he produces 50 pizzas. When there are 2 workers he produces 90 pizzas, and so on.

short run the period of time in which some factors of production cannot be changed

long run the period of time in which all factors of production can be altered

TABLE 9.1

A Production Function and Total Cost: Flavio's Pizza Factory

Number of workers	Output (quantity of pizzas produced per hour)	Marginal product of labour (per hour)	Cost of factory	Cost of workers	Total cost of inputs (cost of factory + cost of workers)
0	0		€30	€0	€30
		50			
1	50		30	10	40
		40			
2	90		30	20	50
		30			
3	120		30	30	60
		20			
4	140		30	40	70
		10			
5	150		30	50	80

FIGURE 9.2

Flavio's Production Function

The production function in panel (a) shows the relationship between the number of workers hired and the quantity of output produced. Here the number of workers hired (on the horizontal axis) is from the first column in Table 9.1, and the quantity of output produced (on the vertical axis) is from the second column. The production function gets flatter as the number of workers increases, which reflects diminishing marginal product. The total cost curve in panel (b) shows the relationship between the quantity of output produced and total cost of production. Here the quantity of output produced (on the horizontal axis) is from the second column in Table 9.1, and the total cost (on the vertical axis) is from the sixth column. The total cost curve gets steeper as the quantity of output increases because of diminishing marginal product.

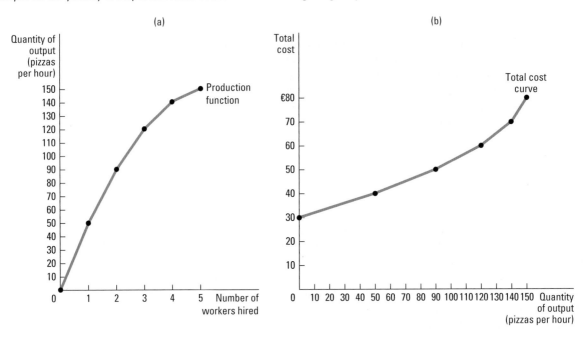

Figure 9.2 (panel (a)) presents a graph of these two columns of numbers. The number of workers is on the horizontal axis, and the number of pizzas produced is on the vertical axis. This is a graph of the production function.

If Flavio is able to estimate his production function, how would such information help him in his decision making? This is what we are trying to model. Remember that a model is a representation of reality. No-one is suggesting that every firm or business person sits down, works out production functions and graphs them (although there are plenty of examples of very sophisticated analysis of this sort which does take place) but the important thing from our perspective is the conceptualization of the decision-making process.

Decision making may involve Flavio thinking at the margin. If you were Flavio you might want to have some understanding of the effect on the amount of pizzas produced of employing an extra worker. You might also want to compare this outcome with how much you had to pay the extra worker. To help make these decisions, the third column in the table gives the marginal product of a worker. The **marginal product** of any input in the production process is the increase in the quantity of output obtained from one additional unit of that input. Employing the first worker adds 50 pizzas per hour to total production. Hiring the second worker increases pizza production from 50 to 90, so the marginal product of this second worker is 40 pizzas. Notice that as the number of workers increases, the marginal product of each successive worker declines. The second worker has a marginal

marginal product the increase in output that arises from an additional unit of input product of 40 pizzas, the third, 30 pizzas and the fourth, 20 pizzas. This property of the production function is called **diminishing marginal product**. At first, when only a few workers are hired, they have easy access to Flavio's kitchen equipment. As the number of workers increases, additional workers have to share equipment and work in more crowded conditions. Hence, as more and more workers are hired, each additional worker contributes less to the production of pizzas.

diminishing marginal product the property whereby the marginal product of an input declines as the quantity of the input increases

Diminishing marginal product is also apparent in Figure 9.2 (panel (a)). The production function's slope ('rise over run') tells us the change in Flavio's output of pizzas ('rise') for each additional input of labour ('run'). That is, the slope of the production function measures the marginal product of a worker. As the number of workers increases, the marginal product declines, and the production function becomes flatter.

From the Production Function to the Total Cost Curve

The last three columns of Table 9.1 are reproduced as a graph in Figure 9.2 (panel (b)) to show Flavio's cost of producing pizzas. In this example, the cost of operating the factory is €30 per hour and the cost of a worker is €10 per hour. If Flavio hires 1 worker, his total cost is €40. If he hires 2 workers, his total cost is €50, and so on. With this information, the table now shows how the number of workers Flavio hires is related to the quantity of pizzas he produces and to his total cost of production.

We are interested in studying firms' production and pricing decisions. For this purpose, the most important relationship in Table 9.1 is between quantity produced (in the second column) and total costs (in the sixth column). Panel (b) of Figure 9.2 graphs these two columns of data with the quantity produced on the horizontal axis and total cost on the vertical axis. This graph is called the *total cost curve.*

Now compare the total cost curve in panel (b) of Figure 9.2 with the production function in panel (a). These two curves are opposite sides of the same coin. The total cost curve gets steeper as the amount produced rises, whereas the production function gets flatter as production rises. These changes in slope occur for the same reason. High production of pizzas means that Flavio's kitchen is crowded with many workers. Because the kitchen is crowded, each additional worker adds less to production, reflecting diminishing marginal product. Therefore, the production function is relatively flat. But now turn this logic around: when the kitchen is crowded, producing an additional pizza requires a lot of additional labour and is thus very costly. Therefore, when the quantity produced is large, the total cost curve is relatively steep.

Quick Quiz If Farmer Schmidt plants no seeds on his farm, he gets no harvest. If he plants 1 bag of seeds he gets 3 tonnes of wheat. If he plants 2 bags he gets 5 tonnes. If he plants 3 bags he gets 6 tonnes. A bag of seeds is priced at €100, and seeds are his only cost. Use these data to graph the farmer's production function and total cost curve. Explain their shapes.

THE VARIOUS MEASURES OF COST

Our analysis of Flavio's Pizza Factory demonstrated how a firm's total cost reflects its production function. From data on a firm's total cost we can derive several related measures of cost. To see how these related measures are derived, we consider the example in Table 9.2. Workers at Flavio's factory regularly use Lia's Coffee Bar.

TABLE 9.2

The Various Measures of Cost: Lia's Coffee Bar

Quantity of coffee (cups per hour)	Total cost	Fixed cost	Variable cost	Average fixed cost	Average variable cost	Average total cost	Marginal cost
0	€3.00	€3.00	€0.00	–	–	–	
							€0.30
1	3.30	3.00	0.30	€3.00	€0.30	€3.30	
							0.50
2	3.80	3.00	0.80	1.50	0.40	1.90	
							0.70
3	4.50	3.00	1.50	1.00	0.50	1.50	
							0.90
4	5.40	3.00	2.40	0.75	0.60	1.35	
							1.10
5	6.50	3.00	3.50	0.60	0.70	1.30	
							1.30
6	7.80	3.00	4.80	0.50	0.80	1.30	
							1.50
7	9.30	3.00	6.30	0.43	0.90	1.33	
							1.70
8	11.00	3.00	8.00	0.38	1.00	1.38	
							1.90
9	12.90	3.00	9.90	0.33	1.10	1.43	
							2.10
10	15.00	3.00	12.00	0.30	1.20	1.50	

The first column of the table shows the number of cups of coffee that Lia might produce, ranging from 0 to 10 cups per hour. The second column shows Lia's total cost of producing coffee. Figure 9.3 plots Lia's total cost curve. The quantity of coffee (from the first column) is on the horizontal axis, and total cost (from the second column) is on the vertical axis. Lia's total cost curve has a shape similar to Flavio's. In particular, it becomes steeper as the quantity produced rises, which (as we have discussed) reflects diminishing marginal product.

FIGURE 9.3

Lia's Total Cost Curve

Here the quantity of output produced (on the horizontal axis) is from the first column in Table 9.2, and the total cost (on the vertical axis) is from the second column. As in Figure 9.2, the total cost curve gets steeper as the quantity of output increases because of diminishing marginal product.

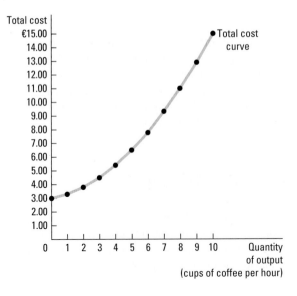

Fixed and Variable Costs

Lia's total cost can be divided into two types. Some costs, called **fixed costs**, are not determined by the amount of output produced; they can change but not as a result of changes in the amount produced. They are incurred even if the firm produces nothing at all. Lia's fixed costs include any rent she pays because this cost is the same regardless of how much coffee Lia produces. Similarly, if Lia needs to hire staff to serve the drinks, regardless of the quantity of coffee sold, the worker's salary is a fixed cost. The third column in Table 9.2 shows Lia's fixed cost, which in this example is €3.00.

Some of the firm's costs, called **variable costs**, change as the firm alters the quantity of output produced. Lia's variable costs include the cost of coffee beans, water, milk, sugar and paper cups: the more coffee Lia makes, the more of these items she needs to buy. Similarly, if Lia pays her workers overtime to make more coffee, the wages of these workers are variable costs. The fourth column of the table shows Lia's variable cost. The variable cost is 0 if she produces nothing, €0.30 if she produces 1 cup of coffee, €0.80 if she produces 2 cups and so on.

A firm's total cost is the sum of fixed and variable costs. In Table 9.2 total cost in the second column equals fixed cost in the third column plus variable cost in the fourth column.

> **fixed costs** costs that are not determined by the quantity of output produced

> **variable costs** costs that are dependent on the quantity of output produced

Average and Marginal Cost

As the owner of her firm, Lia has to decide how much to produce. A key part of this decision is how her costs will vary as she changes the level of production. In making this decision, Lia might ask two questions about the cost of producing coffee:

- How much does it cost to make the typical cup of coffee?
- How much does it cost to increase production of coffee by 1 cup?

Although at first these two questions might seem to have the same answer; they do not. Both answers will turn out to be important for understanding how firms make production decisions.

To find the cost of the typical unit produced, we would divide the firm's total costs by the quantity of output it produces. For example, if the firm produces 2 cups per hour, its total cost is €3.80, and the cost of the typical cup is €3.80/2, or €1.90. Total cost divided by the quantity of output is called **average total cost**. Because total cost is just the sum of fixed and variable costs, average total cost can be expressed as the sum of average fixed cost and average variable cost. **Average fixed cost** is the fixed cost divided by the quantity of output, and **average variable cost** is the variable cost divided by the quantity of output.

Although average total cost tells us the cost of the typical unit, it does not tell us how much total cost will change as the firm alters its level of production. The last column in Table 9.2 shows the amount that total cost rises when the firm increases production by 1 unit of output. This number is called **marginal cost**. For example, if Lia increases production from 2 to 3 cups, total cost rises from €3.80 to €4.50, so the marginal cost of the third cup of coffee is €4.50 minus €3.80, or €0.70.

It may be helpful to express these definitions mathematically:

> **average total cost** total cost divided by the quantity of output

> **average fixed cost** fixed costs divided by the quantity of output

> **average variable cost** total variable cost divided by the quantity of output

> **marginal cost** the increase in total cost that arises from an extra unit of production

$$\text{Average total cost} = \text{Total cost/Quantity}$$

$$ATC = \frac{TC}{Q}$$

and

$$\text{Marginal cost} = \text{Change in total cost/Change in quantity}$$

$$MC = \Delta TC/\Delta Q$$

Here the Greek letter delta, Δ, represents the change in a variable. These equations show how average total cost and marginal cost are derived from total cost. Average total cost tells us the cost of a typical unit of output if total cost is divided evenly over all the units produced. Marginal cost tells us the increase in total cost that arises from producing an additional unit of output.

> **Pitfall Prevention** Confusion over the relationship between average and marginal concepts is a source of problems in understanding. It is often useful to think of the relationship using something concrete from your own life such as the relationship between the average number of goals/points you score in a hockey, rugby, netball or football match (or whatever sport you take part in) and what happens to your average and marginal points/goal tally as you play additional games.

FYI

The Mathematics of Margins

The concept of the margin refers to small changes in variables such as revenue and costs. We know that total revenue is a function of (is dependent upon) the price and the number of units sold. Total cost is a function of the factor inputs used in production given by the sum of the fixed and variable costs. Given that both total revenue and total cost are functions we can use calculus to derive the respective marginal revenue and marginal costs.

Consider the following demand function:

$$P = 200 - 4Q$$

We know that $TR = P \times Q$

Substituting the demand function into the TR formula we get:

$$TR = (200 - 4Q)\, Q$$
$$TR = 200Q - 4Q^2$$

Using the power function rule outlined in Chapter 4, we can derive marginal revenue (MR) by:

$$MR = \frac{d(TR)}{dQ}$$

MR in the example above is:

$$\frac{d(TR)}{dQ} = 200 - 8Q$$

If demand was 10 pizzas, marginal revenue would be $200 - 8(10) = 120$. If demand rose by 1 unit to 11 then total revenue would rise by $200 - 8(11) = 112$.

We can apply a similar approach to deriving the marginal cost. Take the TC function:

$$TC = Q^2 + 14Q + 20$$

We can look at the expression $Q^2 + 14Q$ and conclude that this part of the function is where the value of Q is dependent on some factor and will vary. As a result this is the variable cost component. The last term in the function, denoted by the value 20, is not dependent on Q and so is the fixed cost element. We know that when differentiating this term the result is zero. We would expect this to be the case because, by definition, fixed costs are not affected by changes in output. Marginal cost, therefore, relates to changes in the variable costs of production.

To derive the marginal cost, we use:

$$MC = \frac{d(TC)}{dQ}$$

Differentiating our TC function gives:

$$MC = \frac{d(TC)}{dQ} = 2Q + 14$$

If output is 15, then $MC = 2(15) + 14 = 44$

If output rises to 16 then $MC = 2(16) + 14 = 46$

FIGURE 9.4

Lia's Average Cost and Marginal Cost Curves

This figure shows the average total cost (ATC), average fixed cost (AFC), average variable cost (AVC) and marginal cost (MC) for Lia's Coffee Bar. All of these curves are obtained by graphing the data in Table 9.2. These cost curves show three features that are typical of many firms: (1) Marginal cost rises with the quantity of output. (2) The average total cost curve is U-shaped. (3) The marginal cost curve crosses the average total cost curve at the minimum of average total cost.

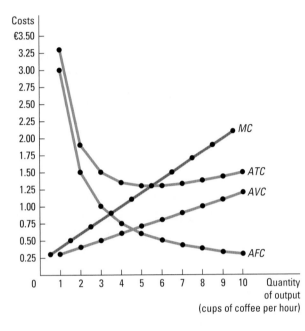

Cost Curves and Their Shapes

Just as in previous chapters we found graphs of supply and demand useful when analysing the behaviour of markets, we will find graphs of average and marginal cost useful when analysing the behaviour of firms. Figure 9.4 graphs Lia's costs using the data from Table 9.2. The horizontal axis measures the quantity the firm produces, and the vertical axis measures marginal and average costs. The graph shows four curves: average total cost (*ATC*), average fixed cost (*AFC*), average variable cost (*AVC*), and marginal cost (*MC*).

The cost curves shown here for Lia's Coffee Bar have some features that are common to the cost curves of many firms in the economy. Let's examine three features in particular: the shape of marginal cost, the shape of average total cost, and the relationship between marginal and average total cost.

Rising Marginal Cost Lia's marginal cost rises with the quantity of output produced. This reflects the property of diminishing marginal product. When Lia is producing a small quantity of coffee she has few workers and much of her equipment is not being used. Because she can easily put these idle resources to use, the marginal product of an extra worker is large, and the marginal cost of an extra cup of coffee is small. By contrast, when Lia is producing a large quantity of coffee her bar is crowded with workers and most of her equipment is fully utilized. Lia can produce more coffee by adding workers, but these new workers have to work in crowded conditions and may have to wait to use the equipment. Therefore, when the quantity of coffee being produced is already high, the marginal product of an extra worker is low, and the marginal cost of an extra cup of coffee is large.

U-Shaped Average Total Cost   Lia's average total cost curve takes on a U-shape. To understand why this is so, remember that average total cost is the sum of average fixed cost and average variable cost. Average fixed cost always declines as output rises because the fixed cost does not change as output rises and so gets spread over a larger number of units. Average variable cost typically rises as output increases because of diminishing marginal product. Average total cost reflects the shapes of both average fixed cost and average variable cost. As shown in Figure 9.4 at very low levels of output, such as 1 or 2 cups per hour, average total cost is high because the fixed cost is spread over only a few units. Average total cost then declines as output increases until the firm's output reaches 5 cups of coffee per hour, when average total cost falls to €1.30 per cup. When the firm produces more than 6 cups, average total cost starts rising again because average variable cost rises substantially. If further units of output were produced the average total cost curve would continue to slope upwards giving the typical U-shape referred to.

The bottom of the U-shape occurs at the quantity that minimizes average total cost. This quantity is sometimes called the **efficient scale** of the firm. For Lia, the efficient scale is 5 or 6 cups of coffee. If she produces more or less than this amount, her average total cost rises above the minimum of €1.30.

efficient scale the quantity of output that minimizes average total cost

The Relationship Between Marginal Cost and Average Total Cost

If you look at Figure 9.4 (or back at Table 9.2) you will see that whenever marginal cost is less than average total cost, average total cost is falling. Whenever marginal cost is greater than average total cost, average total cost is rising. This feature of Lia's cost curves is not a coincidence from the particular numbers used in the example: it is true for all firms and is a basic mathematical relationship.

To see why, refer to your understanding of averages and consider what happens to average cost as output goes up by one unit. If the cost of the extra unit is above the average cost of units produced up to that point, then it will tend to pull up the new average cost of a unit. If the new unit actually costs less than the average cost of a unit up to that point, it will tend to drag the new average down. But the price of an extra unit is what economists call marginal cost, so what we have just asserted is tantamount to saying that if marginal cost is less than average cost, average cost will be falling; and if marginal cost is above average cost, average cost will be rising.

This relationship between average total cost and marginal cost has an important corollary: the marginal cost curve crosses the average total cost curve at its minimum. Why? At low levels of output, marginal cost is below average total cost, so average total cost is falling. But after the two curves cross, marginal cost rises above average total cost. For the reason we have just outlined, average total cost must start to rise at this level of output. Hence, at this point of intersection the cost of an additional unit is the same as the average and so the average does not change and the point is the minimum of average total cost.

Typical Cost Curves

In the examples we have studied so far, the firms' exhibit diminishing marginal product and, therefore, rising marginal cost at all levels of output. Yet actual firms are often a bit more complicated than this. The principle of diminishing marginal product in the short run does hold but when it occurs varies depending on the type of firm and the nature of the production process. In many firms, diminishing marginal product does not start to occur until possibly significant numbers of workers are hired. The particular features of the production process might mean that marginal product rises as additional workers are hired because a team of workers can divide tasks and work more productively than individual workers. Firms do analyse their cost structures and make decisions on changes based on how factor inputs can be better organized to increase productivity and the principle of diminishing marginal product, whilst explained simply in our example, still holds and informs decision making even in complex business operations.

The table in Figure 9.5 shows the cost data for a firm, called Berit's Bagel Bin. These data are used in the graphs. Panel (a) shows how total cost (*TC*) depends on the quantity produced, and panel (b) shows average total cost (*ATC*), average fixed cost (*AFC*), average variable cost (*AVC*) and marginal cost (*MC*).

FIGURE 9.5

Berit's Cost Curves

Many firms, like Berit's Bagel Bin, experience increasing marginal product before diminishing marginal product and, therefore, have cost curves shaped like those in this figure. Panel (a) shows how total cost (TC) depends on the quantity produced. Panel (b) shows how average total cost (ATC), average fixed cost (AFC), average variable cost (AVC) and marginal cost (MC) depend on the quantity produced. These curves are derived by graphing the data from the table. Notice that marginal cost and average variable cost fall for a while before starting to rise.

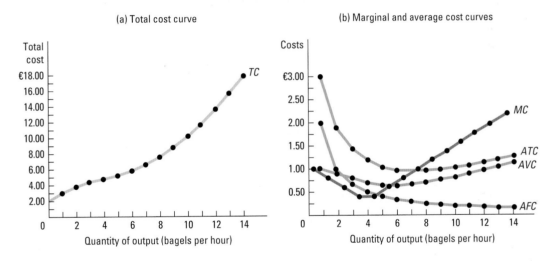

Quantity of bagels (per hour)	Total cost (€)	Fixed cost (€)	Variable cost (€)	Average fixed cost (€)	Average variable cost (€)	Average total cost (€)	Marginal cost (€)
Q	TC = FC + VC	FC	VC	AFC = FC/Q	AVC = VC/Q	ATC = TC/Q	MC = ΔTC/ΔQ
1	3.00	2.00	1.00	2.00	1.00	3.00	
2	3.80	2.00	1.80	1.00	0.90	1.90	0.80
3	4.40	2.00	2.40	0.67	0.80	1.47	0.60
4	4.80	2.00	2.80	0.50	0.70	1.20	0.40
5	5.20	2.00	3.20	0.40	0.64	1.04	0.40
6	5.80	2.00	3.80	0.33	0.63	0.96	0.60
7	6.60	2.00	4.60	0.29	0.66	0.95	0.80
8	7.60	2.00	5.60	0.25	0.70	0.95	1.00
9	8.80	2.00	6.80	0.22	0.76	0.98	1.20
10	10.20	2.00	8.20	0.20	0.82	1.02	1.40
11	11.80	2.00	9.80	0.18	0.89	1.07	1.60
12	13.60	2.00	11.60	0.17	0.97	1.14	1.80
13	15.60	2.00	13.60	0.15	1.05	1.20	2.00
14	17.80	2.00	15.80	0.14	1.13	1.27	2.20

In the range of output from 0 to 4 bagels per hour, the firm experiences increasing marginal product, and the marginal cost curve falls. After 5 bagels per hour, the firm starts to experience diminishing marginal product, and the marginal cost curve starts to rise. This combination of increasing then diminishing marginal product also makes the average variable cost curve U-shaped.

Despite these differences from our previous example, Berit's cost curves share the three properties that are most important to remember:

- Marginal cost eventually rises with the quantity of output.
- The average total cost curve is U-shaped.
- The marginal cost curve crosses the average total cost curve at the minimum of average total cost.

Quick Quiz Suppose BMW's total cost of producing 4 cars is €60 000 and its total cost of producing 5 cars is €85 000. What is the average total cost of producing 5 cars? What is the marginal cost of the fifth car? • Draw the marginal cost curve and the average total cost curve for a typical firm, and explain why these curves cross where they do.

COSTS IN THE SHORT RUN AND IN THE LONG RUN

So far we have discussed the behaviour of costs in the short run. We are now going to look in more detail at the relationship between the short and long run.

The Relationship Between Short-Run and Long-Run Average Total Cost

For many firms, the division of total costs between fixed and variable costs depends on the time horizon. Consider, for instance, a car manufacturer, such as Renault. Over a period of only a few months, Renault cannot adjust the number or sizes of its car factories. To increase output it could try to make use of its existing plant and maybe hire more workers at the factories it already has. The cost of these factories is, therefore, a fixed cost in the short run. By contrast, over a period of several years, Renault can expand the size of its factories, build new factories or close old ones. Thus, the cost of its factories is a variable cost in the long run.

Because many decisions are fixed in the short run but variable in the long run, a firm's long-run cost curves differ from its short-run cost curves. Figure 9.6 shows an example. The figure presents three short-run average total cost curves representing the cost structures for a small, medium and large factory. It also presents the long-run average total cost curve. As the firm adjusts the size of the factory to the quantity of production, it moves along the long-run curve, and it is adjusting the size of the factory to the quantity of production.

This graph shows how short-run and long-run costs are related. The long-run average total cost curve is a much flatter U-shape than the short-run average total cost curve. In addition, all the short-run curves lie on or above the long-run curve. These properties arise because firms have greater flexibility in the long run.

FIGURE 9.6

Average Total Cost in the Short and Long Runs

Because fixed costs are variable in the long run, the average total cost curve in the short run differs from the average total cost curve in the long run.

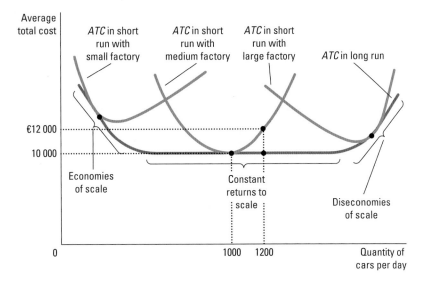

In essence, in the long run, the firm chooses which short-run curve it wants to use. But in the short run, it has to use whatever short-run curve it chose in the past.

The figure shows an example of how a change in production alters costs over different time horizons. When Renault wants to increase production from 1000 to 1200 cars per day, it has little choice in the short run but to hire more workers at its existing medium-sized factory. Because of diminishing marginal product, average total cost rises from €10 000 to €12 000 per car. In the long run, however, Renault can expand both the size of the factory and its workforce, and average total cost returns to €10 000.

CASE STUDY

In It for the Long Run

The aviation industry is very competitive. One good example is the budget carriers in India. Between January and October 2014 the market leader was IndiGo with 30 per cent of the domestic flights. The next major player was Jet Airways with around 22 per cent of the market share, followed by SpiceJet and the state-owned Air India. Next comes the much smaller GoAir with only 9 per cent of the market but it is still able to compete successfully and make a profit even at a much smaller scale of operation

(unlike Air India with losses covered by the government). GoAir, founded in 2004, has just 19 aircraft and is unlikely to increase the number of new planes it buys dramatically. It has seen off competition from Kingfisher, Air Decca, Air Sahara and Paramount Airways, and it intends to survive and prosper. It is confident of its future despite expansion plans by IndiGo, the market leader, to buy a further 250 aircraft and other new firms seeking to enter the market.

One reason for IndiGo wanting to expand is because the potential demand for air travel is likely to grow in the long run. Another is to reap the benefits of economies of scale. If successful, then such a growth strategy will see it benefit at the expense of competitors.

So how is a profitable carrier, like GoAir going to react? It sees its best chance of survival is to avoid a rapid expansion and instead concentrate on improving efficiency. Current regulations forbid outsourcing of maintenance, baggage and security, so there will be few savings to be made in these areas of operation. Jeh Wadia, the founder of GoAir, thinks he can lower his firm's average cost curves in the short run by filling each plane with more passengers and reducing the number of empty seats per flight. He is also targeting punctuality and having a quicker and more efficient turnaround. On the measure of punctuality IndiGo has the best record of 92.8 per cent in 2014, with GoAir coming second on 87.5 per cent. Air India's punctuality is poor at only 63.3 per cent, suggesting it has much to do if it is to become competitive.

Another tack for the carriers is to play off airports and the authorities. India's states are keen to attract budget airlines. In this way carriers can keep their landing costs down and already some of India's 29 states have reduced aviation fuel tax in a bid to attract the airlines to fly into their state. Perhaps it will be the expanding airlines that will have more bargaining power.

Adapted from: **http://www.economist.com/news/business/21635004-prospering-indias -aviation-market-requires-patience-and-discipline-short-haul-long**

Economies and Diseconomies of Scale

economies of scale the property whereby long-run average total cost falls as the quantity of output increases

diseconomies of scale the property whereby long-run average total cost rises as the quantity of output increases

constant returns to scale the property whereby long-run average total cost stays the same as the quantity of output changes

The shape of the long-run average total cost curve conveys important information about the technology for producing a good. When long-run average total cost declines as output increases, there are said to be **economies of scale**. When long-run average total cost rises as output increases, there are said to be **diseconomies of scale**. When long-run average total cost does not vary with the level of output, there are said to be **constant returns to scale**. In this example, Renault has economies of scale at low levels of output, constant returns to scale at intermediate levels of output and diseconomies of scale at high levels of output.

What might cause economies or diseconomies of scale? Economies of scale often arise because higher production levels allow *specialization* among workers and increase the possibility that technology can be used, which permits each worker to become better at his or her assigned tasks. For instance, modern assembly line production may require fewer workers in relation to the technology used but still produce more cars. If Renault were producing only a small quantity of cars, it could not take advantage of this approach and would have higher average total cost. Diseconomies of scale can arise because of *coordination problems* that are inherent in any large organization. The more cars Renault produces, the more stretched the management team becomes, and the less effective the managers become at keeping costs down.

This analysis shows why long-run average total cost curves are often U-shaped. At low levels of production, the firm benefits from increased size because it can take advantage of greater specialization. Coordination problems, meanwhile, are not yet acute. By contrast, at high levels of production, the benefits of specialization have already been realized, and coordination problems become more severe as the firm grows larger. Thus, long-run average total cost is falling at low levels of production because of increasing specialization and rising at high levels of production because of increasing coordination problems.

The Implications of Economies of Scale

Economies of scale are the advantages of large-scale production that result in lower average or unit costs. Imagine a firm which makes bricks. The firm's existing plant has a maximum capacity of 100 000 bricks per week and the total costs are €30 000 per week. The average cost for each brick, assuming the plant operates at full capacity, is €0.30. The firm sets a price of €0.40 per brick giving it a profit margin of €0.10 per brick. If it sells all 100 000 bricks it produces each week, the total revenue per week will be €40 000.

Now imagine that in the long run the firm expands. It doubles the size of its plant. The total costs, obviously, increase – they are now using more land and putting up more buildings, as well as hiring extra labour and buying more equipment and raw materials. All of this expansion will increase the total cost. However, it is not always the case that a doubling of capacity will also lead to a doubling of the cost.

Following this expansion, assume TC is now €50 000 per week. The expansion of the plant means that the firm can double its output so its capacity is now 200 000 bricks per week. The percentage increase in the total costs is less than the percentage increase in output. Total costs have risen by €20 000 or 66 per cent and total output by 100 per cent, which means that the average cost per brick is now €0.25.

The firm now faces two scenarios. In scenario 1, the firm could maintain its price at €0.40 and increase its profit margin on each brick sold from €0.10 to €0.15. Assuming it sells all the bricks it produces its revenue would increase to €80 000 per week.

In scenario 2, the firm might choose to reduce its price to improve its competitiveness against its rivals. It could maintain its former profit margin of €0.10 and reduce the price to €0.35 improving the chances of increasing its competitiveness. In this case, if it sells all it produces its revenue would be €70 000 per week.

What the firm chooses to do would be dependent on its competitive position. If it played a dominant role in the market it might be able to increase its price and still sell all it produces. If it was in a more competitive market it might not have sold all its capacity in the first place so being able to reduce its price might mean that it can now increase sales against its rivals and increase its total revenue as a result.

Economies of scale, therefore, occur where the proportionate rise in output as a result of the expansion or growth of the firm, as defined by a rise in all the factor inputs, is greater that the proportionate rise in costs as a result of the expansion.

Quick Quiz If Airbus produces 9 jets per month, its long-run total cost is €9.0 million per month. If it produces 10 jets per month, its long-run total cost is €9.5 million per month. Does Airbus exhibit economies or diseconomies of scale?

ISOQUANTS AND ISOCOSTS

One of the issues facing businesses in considering production economics is to attempt to maximize output but with a constraint of factor inputs. We have seen that different firms have different ratios of factor inputs in the production process. This can vary not only between industries but also within industries. For example, some farms are far more land intensive than others which may be far more capital or labour intensive. Output levels for all three types of farm may be similar. What businesses are interested in is how they can utilize their factors of production in different ways to maximize output at minimum cost.

The use of isocost and isoquant lines provides a model to help conceptualize the process.

Production Isoquants

production isoquant a function which represents all the possible combinations of factor inputs that can be used to produce a given level of output

A **production isoquant** is a function which represents all the possible combinations of factor inputs that can be used to produce a given level of output. For the sake of simplicity we are going to assume just two factor inputs, labour and capital. To further focus our thinking, let us assume that the capital in question is a machine that coats pizzas with a tomato base, then adds the filling and then bakes the pizzas. The electricity needed to power this machine varies with the amount of pizzas produced. The labour will be the workers who mix and produce the dough for the pizza base and who feed the machine and then package the finished pizzas.

Figure 9.7 shows a graphical representation of the production isoquants that relate to the combinations of labour and capital that can be used to produce pizzas. An output level of $Q = 600$ could be produced using 5 units of labour and 1 unit of power for the machine (point A), or 2 units of labour and 2 units of power (point B). The isoquant line $Q = 600$ connects all the possible combinations of capital and labour which could produce an output of 600 pizzas. Given the level of capital and labour inputs for Flavio's factory, a series of isoquants can be drawn for different levels of output. Figure 9.7 shows the isoquants for output levels of $Q = 600$, $Q = 750$, $Q = 900$ and $Q = 1050$. In theory, the whole of the graphical space could be covered with isoquants all relating to the different levels of possible output.

As mentioned previously, few businesses will sit down and draw out isoquants in the way we have done here but the reality is that firms do regularly make decisions about factor combinations in deciding output. Firms will often look at the option of substituting capital for labour by making staff redundant and investing instead in new equipment. Firms may also look at replacing existing machinery with new ones or look for outsourcing opportunities, both of which would have an effect on the shape and position of the isoquants.

Substituting one factor for another will have costs and may not be easy; machinery may be highly specialized and workers may have skills that machines simply cannot replicate (the ability to make clients feel confident and at ease, for example).

marginal rate of technical substitution the rate at which one factor input can be substituted for another at a given level of output

The slope of the isoquant represents the **marginal rate of technical substitution** (MRTS). This is the rate at which one factor input can be substituted for another at a given level of output. Referring to Figure 9.7, take the output level $Q = 1050$ and a combination of labour and capital at 5 and 6 units respectively. If Flavio considered cutting 2 units of labour he would have to increase the amount of power used on the machine employed by 3 to 9 in order to maintain output at 1050. The MRTS would be given by the ratio of the change in capital to the change in labour, $\Delta K/\Delta L$. The change in capital is from 6 to 9 units and the change in labour is from

5 to 3. The MRTS = 3/–2 or –1.5. (Note, these changes are in opposite directions and so the MRTS would be a negative number.) This tells us that Flavio has to increase the amount of power used by 1.5 for every 1 unit of labour released to maintain production at $Q = 1050$.

FIGURE 9.7

Production Isoquants for Flavio's Pizza Factory

Given the possibility of employing different amounts of capital and labour, the isoquant map connects together combinations of capital and labour which could be employed to produce different levels of output of pizzas. For an output level Q = 600, 4 units of power for the machine and 1 unit of labour could produce 600 pizzas but so could the combination 2 units of power for the machine and 2 units of labour. 5 units of power and 5 units of labour could produce an output level Q = 900; a combination of 2 units of power and 10 units of labour could also produce 900 pizzas.

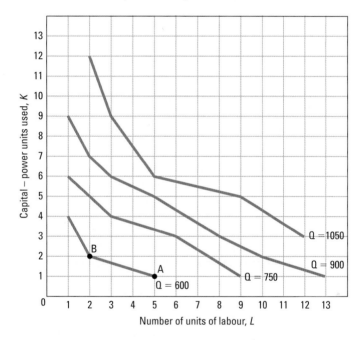

The way we have drawn the isoquants in Figure 9.7 would suggest different MRTS because the slope of each isoquant is different.

It is common to see isoquants drawn as smooth curves as shown in Figure 9.8. Clearly, in such a situation the use of calculus to calculate the MRTS would be advantageous because it would provide a much more accurate value at every point on each curve. Using calculus, the derivative of capital with respect to labour dK/dL, would give us this precise value.

Isocost Lines

Our analysis so far has looked at different combinations of factor inputs to produce given outputs. A business has to take into consideration the obvious fact that factor inputs cost money. Labour has to be paid, wages and salaries and energy to power the machines have to be purchased. Firms have budgets which have to be adhered to. Isocost lines take the cost of factor inputs into consideration. An **isocost line** shows the different combination of factor inputs which can be purchased with a given budget.

isocost line the different combination of factor inputs which can be purchased with a given budget

FIGURE 9.8

Production Isoquants

It is common to represent production isoquants as a series of smooth curves representing the different combinations of capital and labour which would be used to produce different levels of output represented in this Figure as Q = X, Q = X₁, 2 = X₂, etc.

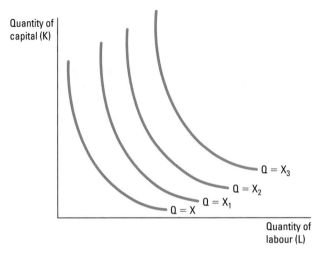

Assume that the price of power to operate the pizza machine Flavio has to buy is given by the general form $P_K K$, and the price of labour is given the general form $P_L L$. Given a cost constraint represented by TC_{KL} we can express the relationship as:

$$P_K K + P_L L = TC_{KL}$$

Now assume that the price of capital per unit to make pizzas is €1000 per month and the price of labour, €500 per month. Our formula would look like this:

$$1000K + 500L = TC_{KL}$$

Using 3 capital units and 9 units of labour would cost 1000(3) + 500(9) = €7500. Are there other combinations of capital and labour that would produce pizzas at a cost of €7500? We can find this out by rearranging the equation to give:

$$€7500 = 1000K + 500L$$

We can now find values for K and L which satisfy this equation. For example, dividing both sides by 1000 and solving for K we get:

$$K = \frac{7500}{1000} - \frac{500L}{1000}$$
$$K = 7.5 - 0.5L$$

Table 9.3 shows combinations of whole units of capital and labour that satisfy this equation. For example, if 5 units of labour were used then:

$$K = 7.5 - 0.5(5)$$
$$K = 7.5 - 2.5$$
$$K = 4.0$$

The information can be graphed as in Figure 9.9 with units of capital on the vertical axis and units of labour on the horizontal axis. The isocost line $TC_{KL} = 7500$

connects all the combinations of labour and capital to make pizzas which cost €7500. At point A, 5 units of capital and 4.5 units of labour will have a total cost of €7500 but so will the combination of 1.5 units of capital and 12 units of labour at point B.

TABLE 9.3

Factor combinations to satisfy the equation $K = 7.5 - 0.5L$

K	L
7.0	1
6.0	3
5.0	5
4.0	7
3.0	9
2.0	11
1.0	13
0.0	15

FIGURE 9.9

Isocost Lines

Isocost lines connect combinations of capital and labour that a business can afford to buy given a budget constraint. The isocost line shown relates to a budget constraint of €7500. With this budget constraint Flavio could spend all the money on 7 units of capital but would not be able to afford any workers, giving the vertical intercept. If the business chose to spend the budget entirely on labour then it would be able to purchase 15 units of labour but no machines. Any point on the isocost line between these two extremes connects together combinations of capital and labour that could be purchased with the available budget. At point A, Flavio could afford to buy 5 units of capital and 4.5 units of labour; at point B, he could afford to buy 1.5 units of labour and 12 units of labour.

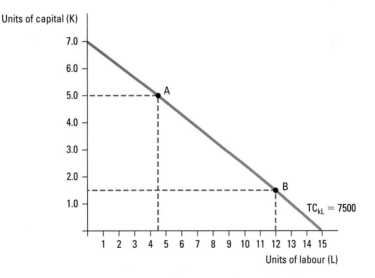

Other isocost lines could be drawn connecting combinations of capital and labour at different levels of total cost. For each of these isocost lines, the vertical intercept shows how many units of capital Flavio could buy with his budget constraint if he employed zero units of labour. The horizontal intercept shows how many units of labour Flavio could buy if zero units of capital were purchased. The isocost line shows the combinations of capital and labour that Flavio could purchase given his budget constraint.

The slope of the isocost line is the ratio of the price of labour to capital P_L/P_K. As the isocost line is a straight line the slope is constant throughout. In this example, the slope is $500/1000 = 0.5$. This tells us that for every one additional unit of labour employed he has to reduce the amount of capital by 0.5 and for every one additional unit of capital employed he must reduce labour by 2 units.

The Least-Cost Input Combination

We now know the combination of factor inputs needed to produce given quantities of output (pizzas in our case) given by the isoquant curves and the cost of using different factor combinations given by the isocost lines. We can put these together to find the least cost input combination.

Figure 9.10 shows different isoquants relating to three different output levels $Q = X$, $Q = X_1$ and $Q = X_2$ and three isocost lines relating to three different budget constraints TC_{KL1}, TC_{KL2} and TC_{KL3}.

Any point where the isocost line cuts the isoquant line is a possible combination of factors that could be used. The more resources a firm has at its disposal the higher the output it can produce. The question we want to ask is: what is the best or optimum combination? Let us assume that Flavio has a budget constraint of TC_{KL2}. He could produce output $Q = X$ and employ the combination of factors of production at point A. Similarly, he could employ fewer units of capital and more units of labour and afford to produce the same output at point B. However, we could reasonably assume that if there was a way in which a business could use its existing budget and resources to produce more output then it would do so. It may make such a decision if it thought that it could sell more output.

FIGURE 9.10

The Least-Cost Input Combination

The figure shows different isoquants relating to three different output levels $Q = X$, $Q = X_1$ and $Q = X_2$ and three isocost lines relating to three different budget constraints TC_{KL1}, TC_{KL2} and TC_{KL3}. Given isocost line TC_{KL3} any of the outputs represented by A–E are possible but the optimum is at point E where the isoquant $Q = X_2$ is tangential to the isocost line TC_{KL3}.

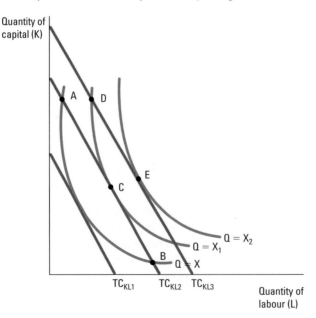

Starting at point A, therefore, Flavio could reduce the amount of capital used and increase the amount of labour to produce a higher output level $Q = X_1$ at point C.

Flavio might like to produce an output $Q = X_1$ using the combination of factors given by point D, however, that combination falls on a different isocost line, TC_{KL3}.

Flavio does not have the funds to be able to afford this combination. However, he can afford to employ capital and labour where the combination of factors given at point C is exactly the same as the cost of employing those factors. At point C the isoquant curve is tangential to the isocost line. This is the least-cost input combination. Given Flavio's budget constraint there is no incentive for him to change the combination of factors of production employed at this point because to do so would mean that those resources would not be producing at maximum efficiency at minimum cost. Flavio might like to produce an output level given by $Q = X_2$ at point E but given his budget constraint he cannot afford to produce that level of output. The optimum point, therefore, given existing productivity levels of factor inputs and the price of factor inputs, is C.

At this point of tangent, the point of least-cost input occurs where the marginal rate of technical substitution is equal to the ratio of the prices of factors. This is represented by the equation:

$$\frac{MP_L}{MP_K} = \frac{P_L}{P_K}$$

This is also sometimes given as:

$$\frac{MP_L}{P_L} = \frac{MP_K}{P_K}$$

JEOPARDY PROBLEM

Flavio has been able to increase the amount of pizzas he is producing without increasing the budget he has available. How might this outcome be possible?

IN THE NEWS

From Gran's Kitchen to Large-Scale Production for the Jam Boy

In this chapter we have noted how businesses are dynamic and constantly looking to exploit new opportunities in the way they operate production. This article shows how one business starting out at a very small and local scale has expanded to become an international concern.

Some people just have that entrepreneurial spirit and can take

the hard knocks on the road to success. Fraser Doherty is one such young entrepreneur. His start was modest, but he had strong ambitions to expand in a market where national jam sales have gone down in recent years. When he was 14 and still at school he made 12 jars of jam using his gran's recipe and sold these to neighbours. Soon he was making 20 jars to satisfy

demand and then 40, and so on. He found new outlets in local markets around his home city of Edinburgh and was cooking in the evenings and at weekends to satisfy demand. Production had risen to 1000 jars a week, but this was the maximum capacity he could achieve from his kitchen facilities. He wanted to grow, but could he take his idea further? He left school as a 16-year-old,

confident that he could succeed in the jam business, but he knew he needed a unique selling point. As a result he developed a new product called SuperJam, made from 100 per cent fruit and no added sugar, but his production remained 1000 jars a week, limited by his kitchen facilities.

The next stage for his business to develop was to find more retail outlets. As a 16-year-old with limited business experience, Fraser turned up at a 'meet the buyer' day organized by Waitrose, an up-market UK supermarket. Waitrose liked his idea but asked him to find a factory in order to meet new production levels of at least 20 000 jars a week. Doing this would see a significant reduction in his unit costs, enabling him to sell to Waitrose at a competitive price.

Given his age and limited finances, he could not open up a factory of his own and instead sought out an existing jam manufacturer. Trying to find one who shared in the dream of a boy was no easy task. It took him 2 years, but he persevered and found a jam manufacturer willing to take the risk. Now he started to produce his kitchen recipe on a much grander scale. At this point he could afford to lower the price he could sell jam to Waitrose for. The launch of SuperJam went well with one Waitrose store in his hometown, selling 1500 jars on the opening day, more jam than the branch normally sold in a month.

He now produces over 50 000 jars in a day supplying some 2000 supermarkets around the world including in the UK, Austria, Russia, Denmark, the USA, Finland and Ireland.

Questions

1. For SuperJam, what is the difference between the short run and long run?
2. Explain why increasing output has led to lower unit costs for SuperJam?
3. Explain the types of economies of scale experienced by SuperJam.
4. Why might SuperJam have succeeded in growing quickly in a market that is in overall decline?
5. What were the advantages and disadvantages to Fraser of using an existing factory to make his jam, rather than building a new factory?

Reference: **http://shop.superjam.co.uk /pages/about-us**

SUMMARY

Let us just summarize this section by thinking through this logically. If you were Flavio faced with a budget constraint, it might be reasonable to assume that you would want to ensure that you use your money in the best way possible to produce the maximum amount possible. Taking a factor input combination such as that at A, if there was a way in which you could reorganize those factor inputs so that they did not cost you anymore, but you could produce more pizzas, it would make sense to do so.

Cutting back on the use of capital and increasing labour means the additional output produced is greater but does not cost any more. Provided the benefit of doing this is greater than the cost incurred, it makes sense to make such a decision. If there is still a way to continue cutting capital use and increasing labour which would bring about increased production of pizzas, then it is clearly sensible to continue doing so until you reach a point where there is no benefit in shifting resources any further.

The least-cost input combination can change if the cost of labour or capital changes (in which case the slope of the isocost line would change) or if both prices changed equally then the isocost line would shift either inwards or outwards depending on the direction of the price change. The shape of the isoquant curve might also change if the marginal productivity of either capital or labour changed.

Remember early in this analysis how we mentioned that this approach was a way of conceptualizing how businesses behave. The assumption is that firms want to maximize output at minimum cost. Firms will have some idea of the productivity of factor inputs and also of the cost of buying in factors. They will continually be looking to find ways to reorganize factors of production they employ to increase output but keep costs under control. The use of this model helps us to understand the logic behind business restructuring, outsourcing, seeking out cheaper suppliers, using different raw materials in different ways, spending money on training workers to be more effective in their jobs, and other ways of influencing productivity, and helps explain why businesses are dynamic and constantly changing and evolving organizations.

CONCLUSION

The purpose of this chapter has been to develop some tools that we can use to study how firms make production and pricing decisions. You should now understand what economists mean by the term *costs* and how costs vary with the quantity of output a firm produces. To refresh your memory, Table 9.4 summarizes some of the definitions we have encountered.

By themselves, of course, a firm's cost curves do not tell us what decisions the firm will make. But they are an important component of that decision.

TABLE 9.4

The Many Types of Cost: A Summary

Term	Definition	Mathematical description
Explicit costs	Costs that require an outlay of money by the firm	–
Implicit costs	Costs that do not require an outlay of money by the firm	–
Fixed costs	Costs that do not vary with the quantity of output produced	FC
Variable costs	Costs that do vary with the quantity of output produced	VC
Total cost	The market value of all the inputs that a firm uses in production	$TC = FC + VC$
Average fixed cost	Fixed costs divided by the quantity of output	$AFC = FC/Q$
Average variable cost	Variable costs divided by the quantity of output	$AVC = VC/Q$
Average total cost	Total cost divided by the quantity of output	$ATC = TC/Q$
Marginal cost	The increase in total cost that arises from an extra unit of production	$\dfrac{d(TC)}{dQ}$

SUMMARY

- Profit equals total revenue minus total cost.

- When analysing a firm's behaviour, it is important to include all the opportunity costs of production. Some of the opportunity costs, such as the wages a firm pays its workers, are explicit. Other opportunity costs, such as the wages the firm owner gives up by working in the firm rather than taking another job, are implicit.

- A firm's costs reflect its production process. A typical firm's production function gets flatter as the quantity of an input increases, displaying the property of diminishing marginal product. As a result, a firm's total cost curve gets steeper as the quantity produced rises.

- A firm's total costs can be divided between fixed costs and variable costs. Fixed costs are costs that are not determined by the quantity of output produced. Variable costs are costs that directly relate to the amount produced and so change when the firm alters the quantity of output produced.

- From a firm's total cost, two related measures of cost are derived. Average total cost is total cost divided by the quantity of output. Marginal cost is the amount by which total cost changes if output increases (or decreases) by 1 unit.

- When analysing firm behaviour, it is often useful to graph average total cost and marginal cost. For a typical firm, marginal cost rises with the quantity of output. Average total cost first falls as output increases and then rises as output increases further. The marginal cost curve always crosses the average total cost curve at the minimum of average total cost.

- A firm's costs often depend on the time horizon being considered. In particular, many costs are fixed in the short run but variable in the long run. As a result, when the firm changes its level of production, average total cost may rise more in the short run than in the long run.

- The use of isoquants and isocosts helps conceptualize the reasons why firms make decisions to change factor combinations used in production and how the prices of factor combinations can also influence those decisions.

QUESTIONS FOR REVIEW

1. What is the relationship between a firm's total revenue, total cost and profit?

2. Give an example of an opportunity cost that an accountant might not count as a cost. Why would the accountant ignore this cost?

3. What is marginal product, and what does it mean if it is diminishing?

4. Draw a production function that exhibits diminishing marginal product of labour. Draw the associated total cost curve. (In both cases, be sure to label the axes.) Explain the shapes of the two curves you have drawn.

5. Define total cost, average total cost and marginal cost. How are they related?

6. Draw the marginal cost and average total cost curves for a typical firm. Explain why the curves have the shapes that they do and why they cross where they do.

7. How and why does a firm's average total cost curve differ in the short run and in the long run?

8. Define economies of scale and explain why they might arise. Define diseconomies of scale and explain why they might arise.

9. Define an isoquant, an isocost line and the least-cost input combination.

10. Using the isocost, isoquant model, explain why firms might make a decision to cut the labour force and invest in capital equipment instead.

PROBLEMS AND APPLICATIONS

1. This chapter discusses many types of costs: opportunity cost, total cost, fixed cost, variable cost, average total cost and marginal cost. Fill in the type of cost that best completes each phrase below.
   a. The true cost of taking some action is its _____.
   b. _____ is falling when marginal cost is below it, and rising when marginal cost is above it.
   c. A cost that does not depend on the quantity produced is a _____.

d. In the breakfast cereal industry in the short run, _____ includes the cost of cereals such as wheat and corn and sugar, but not the cost of the factory.

e. Profits equal total revenue minus _____.

f. The cost of producing an extra unit of output is the _____.

2. Patrice is thinking about opening a café. He estimates that it would cost €500 000 per year to rent the premises, buy the equipment to make hot drinks and snacks and to buy in the ingredients. In addition, he would have to leave his €50 000 per year job as an accountant.

a. Define opportunity cost.

b. What is Patrice's opportunity cost of running the café for a year? If Patrice thought he could sell €510 000 worth of coffee and snacks in a year, should he open the café? Explain your answer.

3. A commercial fisherman notices the following relationship between hours spent fishing and the quantity of fish caught:

Hours	Quantity of fish (in kilograms)
0	0
1	10
2	18
3	24
4	28
5	30

a. What is the marginal product of each hour spent fishing?

b. Use these data to graph the fisherman's production function. Explain its shape.

c. The fisherman has a fixed cost of €10 (his fishing rod). The opportunity cost of his time is €5 per hour. Graph the fisherman's total cost curve. Explain its shape.

4. Clean Sweep is a company that makes brooms and then sells them door-to-door. Here is the relationship between the number of workers and Clean Sweep's output in a given day:

Workers	Output	Marginal product	Average total cost	Marginal cost
0	0			
1	20			
2	50			
3	90			
4	120			
5	140			
6	150			
7	155			

a. Fill in the column of marginal product. What pattern do you see? How might you explain it?

b. A worker costs €100 a day, and the firm has fixed costs of €200. Use this information to calculate total cost at each level of output.

c. Fill in the column for average total cost. (Recall that $ATC = TC/Q$.) What pattern do you see?

d. Now fill in the column for marginal cost. (Recall that $MC = \Delta TC/\Delta Q$.) What pattern do you see?

e. Compare the column for marginal product and the column for marginal cost. Explain the relationship.

f. Compare the column for average total cost and the column for marginal cost. Explain the relationship.

5. Suppose that you and your roommate have started a bagel delivery service on campus. List some of your fixed costs and describe why they are fixed. List some of your variable costs and describe why they are variable.

6. Consider the following cost information for a pizzeria:

Q (dozens)	Total cost	Variable cost
0	€300	€0
1	350	50
2	390	90
3	420	120
4	450	150
5	490	190
6	540	240

a. What is the pizzeria's fixed cost?

b. Construct a table in which you calculate the marginal cost per dozen pizzas using the information on total cost. Also calculate the marginal cost per dozen pizzas using the information on variable cost. What is the relationship between these sets of numbers? Comment.

7. You are thinking about setting up a lemonade bar. The bar itself costs €200 a week to rent. The ingredients for each glass of lemonade cost €0.50.

a. What is your fixed cost of doing business? What is your variable cost per glass?

b. Construct a table showing your total cost, average total cost and marginal cost for output levels varying from 0 to 100 litres. (Hint: there are 4 glasses in a litre.) Draw the three cost curves.

8. Healthy Harry's Juice Bar has the following cost schedules:

Q (vats)	Variable cost	Total cost
0	€0	€30
1	10	40
2	25	55
3	45	75
4	70	100
5	100	130
6	135	165

a. Calculate average variable cost, average total cost and marginal cost for each quantity.
b. Graph all three curves. What is the relationship between the marginal cost curve and the average total cost curve? Between the marginal cost curve and the average variable cost curve? Explain your answer.

9. Consider the following table of long-run total cost for three different firms:

Quantity	1	2	3	4	5	6	7
Firm A	€60	€70	€80	€90	€100	€110	€120
Firm B	11	24	39	56	75	96	119
Firm C	21	34	49	66	85	106	129

a. Does each of these firms experience economies of scale or diseconomies of scale?

10. Given the equation $K = 2000 - 250L$, calculate the combination of capital and labour between $L = 1$ and $L = 10$ which would produce an output with a total cost of €400.
a. Draw the resulting isocost curve with this data.
b. On your diagram draw a series of isoquants and explain how a business would either find the point where they minimized total cost given a constraint on output or maximize output given a budget constraint.

10 THE FIRM'S PRODUCTION DECISIONS

LEARNING OUTCOMES

After reading this chapter you should be able to:

- See how the supply curve for a competitive firm is derived in the short run and the long run.

- Cover the difference in the equilibrium position of a competitive firm in the short run and the long run.

- State the assumptions of the model of a highly competitive firm.

- Calculate and draw cost and revenue curves and show the profit-maximizing output.

- Show, using diagrams and basic maths, the conditions under which a firm will shut down temporarily and exit the market in the long run.

- Explain the difference between normal and abnormal profit.

- Explain why a firm will continue in production even if it makes zero profit.

- Use diagrams to explain the short- and long-run equilibrium position for a firm in a highly competitive market.

INTRODUCTION

Given a firm has an understanding about its costs and revenues and the various goals the business has, this allows decisions to be made about how much to supply and about when to cease production. Most products will have a life cycle which includes the phases from launch, through growth maturity and decline. Firms will have to make decisions about levels of production during these phases and ultimately whether to continue production.

 Firms are affected by the general state of the economy and changing tastes and fashions. In times of economic downturn, some firms will find that demand for their product falls to such an extent that it becomes impossible to continue production and so close down. VHS video recorders and cathode ray tube TVs are no longer produced by most of the major electrical manufacturers, for example. Such external effects mean that decisions will have to be taken on changes to production levels and indeed whether production should continue at all. We will look at the principles governing these decisions in this chapter.

Competition and Competitive Markets

Where more than one firm offers the same or a similar product in a market, there is competition. However, there are different degrees of competition ranging from highly competitive markets through to markets where supply may be from a small number of very large firms or in some cases, just one firm. The more competitive the market, the smaller each firm is in comparison to the size of the market. Where firms can influence the market price of the good they sell through being able to differentiate its product offering in some way, they will have some element of *market power*. Firms may differentiate their product and so reduce the perceived substitutability by making the product itself different in some way or through the way they build relationships with consumers, encourage purchasing habits, provide levels of customer service and after sales service, and so on.

We will examine the behaviour of firms with market power in a later chapter.

Our analysis of competitive firms in this chapter will be based on the assumption that each firm is small in relation to the overall size of the market and thus they are price takers. This will shed light on the decisions that lie behind the supply curve in a competitive market. Not surprisingly, we will find that a market supply curve is tightly linked to firms' costs of production. Among a firm's various costs – fixed, variable, average and marginal – which ones are most relevant for its decision about the quantity to supply at any given price? We will see that all these measures of cost play important and interrelated roles.

Few markets have all the characteristics of perfectly competitive markets. In previous chapters, we have used milk production as one example of a perfectly competitive market. There are many thousands of small firms who produce milk. Each has limited control over the price because many other sellers are offering an homogenous product; milk from one farm is essentially identical to that from other farms. It is assumed that because each seller is small they can sell all they want at the going price. There is little reason to charge less, and if a higher price is charged, buyers will go elsewhere.

Entry into the dairy industry is relatively easy – anyone can decide to start a dairy farm and for existing dairy farmers it is relatively easy to leave the industry. It should be noted that much of the analysis of competitive firms does not rely on the assumption of free entry and exit because this condition is not necessary for firms to be price takers. But as we will see later in this chapter, entry and exit are often powerful forces shaping the long-run outcome in competitive markets.

While on the sellers' side, the market exhibits many characteristics of perfect competition, it is not the case that there are many thousands of individual buyers. The vast majority of individuals buy and use milk but we do not buy it at source from farmers but from retailers who have processed and packaged the product. Farmers may have to sell their milk to large firms who manage this processing and distribution to retailers. These firms may seek to exploit market power. However, for the purposes of analysis, we are going to assume that no single buyer of milk can influence the price of milk because each buyer purchases a small amount relative to the size of the market.

The model for the analysis of firm behaviour in this chapter is based on the assumption of perfect competition. We can then begin to drop some of these assumptions and analyse how firm behaviour may differ as a result.

The Marginal Cost Curve and the Firm's Supply Decision

Recall that the point of profit maximization is the output level where marginal cost = marginal revenue ($MC = MR$). Consider the profit-maximizing position for a competitive firm as shown in Figure 10.1. The figure shows a horizontal line at the market price (P). The price line is horizontal because the firm is a price taker: the price of the firm's output is the same, regardless of the quantity

FIGURE 10.1

Profit Maximization for a Competitive Firm

This figure shows the marginal cost curve (MC), the average total cost curve (ATC) and the average variable cost curve (AVC). It also shows the market price (P), which equals marginal revenue (MR) and average revenue (AR). At the quantity Q_1, marginal revenue, MR_1 exceeds marginal cost MC_1, so raising production increases profit. At the quantity Q_2 marginal cost MC_2 is above marginal revenue MR_2, so reducing production increases profit. The profit-maximizing quantity Q_{MAX} is found where the horizontal price line intersects the marginal cost curve.

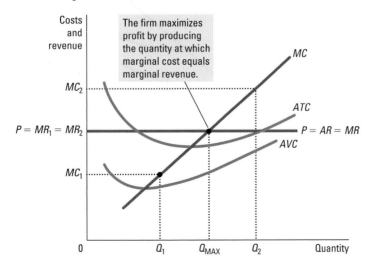

that the firm decides to produce. For a competitive firm, the firm's price equals both its average revenue (*AR*) and its marginal revenue (*MR*). The firm can sell all it wants at the reigning market price. If the firm is currently selling 100 units and the market price is €2 per unit then the average revenue (*AR* = *TR/Q*) will be 200/100 = €2. If it now sells an additional unit at €2 its average revenue will be 202/101 = €2 and the marginal revenue will also be €2. Therefore under these highly competitive conditions, *P* = *AR* = *MR*.

Figure 10.2 shows how a competitive firm responds to an increase in the price which may have been caused by a change in global market conditions. Remember that competitive firms are price takers and have to accept the market price for their product. Prices of commodities such as grain, sugar, cotton, coffee, pork bellies and so on are set by organized international markets, and so the individual firm has limited power to influence price. When the price is P_1, the firm produces quantity Q_1, the quantity that equates marginal cost to the price (which remember is the same as marginal revenue). Assume that an outbreak of tuberculosis results in the need to slaughter a large proportion of dairy cattle and as a result there is a shortage of milk on the market. When the price rises to P_2, the individual firm finds that marginal revenue is now higher than marginal cost at the previous level of output, so the firm will seek to increase production (assuming it is not one of the firms whose dairy herd has been wiped out). The new profit-maximizing quantity is Q_2, at which marginal cost equals the new higher price. In essence, because the firm's marginal cost curve determines the quantity of the good the firm is willing to supply at any price, it is the competitive firm's supply curve.

FIGURE 10.2

Marginal Cost as the Competitive Firm's Supply Curve (1)

An increase in the price from P_1 to P_2 leads to an increase in the firm's profit-maximizing quantity from Q_1 to Q_2. Because the marginal cost curve shows the quantity supplied by the firm at any given price, it is the competitive firm's supply curve.

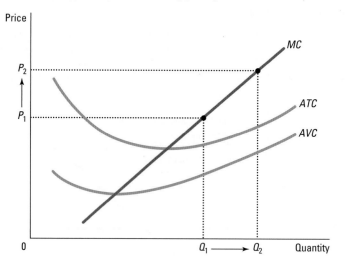

A similar, but reversed, situation would occur if the price fell for some reason as shown in Figure 10.3. In this situation, the firm would find that at the initial equilibrium output level, Q_1, marginal cost would be greater than marginal revenue with a new price of P_2 and so the firm would look to cut back production to the new profit-maximizing output level Q_2.

FIGURE 10.3

Marginal Cost as the Competitive Firm's Supply Curve (2)

A fall in the price from P$_1$ to P$_2$ leads to a decrease in the firm's profit-maximizing quantity from Q$_1$ to Q$_2$. The marginal cost curve shows the quantity supplied by the firm at any given price.

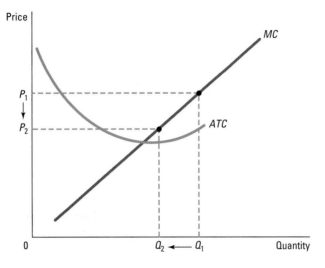

The Firm's Short-Run Decision to Shut Down

Clearly, in reality, the profit-maximizing output might be hard to identify because it relies on the firm being able to identify all its costs and revenues accurately over a period of time and to have the capacity to expand and contract quickly in response to changing market conditions. We also know that firms make losses – sometimes very big losses. If we assume that a firm exists to make a profit do we conclude that if it makes a loss it will shut down its operations? This is obviously not the case in some situations although at some point a decision to cease operating will be taken. How does the firm make that sort of decision?

We can distinguish between a temporary shutdown of a firm and the permanent exit of a firm from the market. A *shutdown* refers to a short-run decision not to produce anything during a specific period of time because of current market conditions. This is different to a complete cessation of operations referred to as exit. *Exit* is a long-run decision to leave the market. The short-run and long-run decisions differ because most firms cannot avoid their fixed costs in the short run but can do so in the long run. A firm that shuts down temporarily still has to pay its fixed costs, whereas a firm that exits the market saves both its fixed and its variable costs.

For example, consider the production decision that a milk producer faces. The cost of the land and the capital equipment, such as tractors, milking parlours and sheds, form part of the farmer's fixed costs. If the firm decides to suspend the supply of milk, the cost of the land and capital cannot be recovered. When making the short-run decision whether to shut down production for a period, the fixed cost of land and capital is said to be a *sunk cost*. By contrast, if the dairy farmer decides to leave the industry altogether, they can sell the land and some of the capital equipment. When making the long-run decision whether to exit the market, the cost of land and capital is not sunk. (We return to the issue of sunk costs shortly.)

Now let's consider what determines a firm's shutdown decision in the short run. If the firm shuts down, it loses all revenue from the sale of the products it is not now producing and which could be sold. At the same time, it does not have to pay

The decision to shut down a firm affects large numbers of people, not just employees who may lose their jobs, and can be a lengthy process and a costly decision to make.

the variable costs of making its product (but must still pay the fixed costs). Common sense would tell us that a firm shuts down if the revenue that it would get from producing is less than its variable costs of production; it is simply not worth producing a product which costs more to produce than the revenue generated by its sale. Doing so would reduce profit or make any existing losses even greater.

A little bit of mathematics can make this shutdown criterion more useful. If TR stands for total revenue and VC stands for variable costs, then the firm's decision can be written as:

$$\text{Shut down if } TR < VC$$

The firm shuts down if total revenue is less than variable cost. By dividing both sides of this inequality by the quantity Q, we can write it as:

$$\text{Shut down if } TR/Q < VC/Q$$

Notice that this can be further simplified. TR/Q is total revenue divided by quantity, which is average revenue (AR). For a competitive firm, average revenue is simply the good's price P. Similarly, VC/Q is average variable cost AVC. Therefore, the firm's shutdown criterion is:

$$\text{Shut down if } P < AVC$$

That is, a firm chooses to shut down if the price of the good is less than the average variable cost of production. This is our common sense interpretation: when choosing to produce, the firm compares the price it receives for the typical unit to the average variable cost that it must incur to produce the typical unit. If the price does not cover the average variable cost, the firm is better off stopping production altogether. The firm can reopen in the future if conditions change so that price exceeds average variable cost.

> **?**   **what if . . .** the price the firm received was equal to AVC in the long run – would the firm still be able to continue in production indefinitely?

We now have a full description of a competitive firm's profit-maximizing strategy. If the firm produces anything, it produces the quantity at which marginal cost equals the price of the product. Yet if the price is less than average variable cost at that quantity, the firm is better off shutting down and not producing anything. These results are illustrated in Figure 10.4. The competitive firm's short-run supply curve is the portion of its marginal cost curve that lies above average variable cost.

sunk cost a cost that has already been committed and cannot be recovered

Sunk Costs   Economists say that a cost is a **sunk cost** when it has already been committed and cannot be recovered. In a sense, a sunk cost is the opposite of an opportunity cost: an opportunity cost is what you have to give up if you choose to do one thing instead of another, whereas a sunk cost cannot be avoided, regardless of the choices you make. Because nothing can be done about sunk costs, you can ignore them when making decisions about various aspects of life, including business strategy.

Our analysis of the firm's shutdown decision is one example of the importance of recognizing sunk costs. We assume that the firm cannot recover its fixed costs by temporarily stopping production. As a result, the firm's fixed costs are sunk in the short run, and the firm can safely ignore these costs when deciding how much to produce. The firm's short-run supply curve is the part of the marginal cost curve that lies above average variable cost, and the size of the fixed cost does not matter for this supply decision.

FIGURE 10.4

The Competitive Firm's Short-Run Supply Curve

In the short run, the competitive firm's supply curve is its marginal cost curve (MC) above average variable cost (AVC). If the price falls below average variable cost, the firm is better off shutting down.

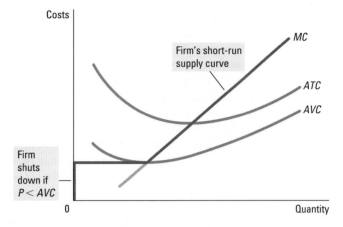

CASE STUDY

Big Production Decisions at Mount Gibson Iron Limited

Mount Gibson Iron has two key operations in Western Australia where iron ore deposits are of a very high quality and low in impurities. One of its operations is at Extension Hill and the other is at Koolan Island in Western Australia. Mount Gibson Iron has to make a big decision in 2015 about both these large-scale operations due to significant shocks. The first is external to the company and is down to a drop in world iron ore prices. In February 2014 the world price for iron ore per dry metric tonne was $120.65 and just a year later it had fallen to $62.69. Internally, Mount Gibson Iron still has good cash reserves, but it faces another significant problem in one of its two mines making matters much worse.

In October 2014 a sea wall gave way at the Koolan Island mine, flooding the pit. The company was forced to suspend all operations at Koolan Island, except care and maintenance. The flood has knocked out around 40 per cent of the company's total iron ore production from the two mines. It had already spent vast sums on site equipment and its port facilities on Koolan Island. These costs are not easily recoverable. The company has also had to make significant redundancy payments which it hopes will be covered by insurance it had taken out for both property damage and business disruption.

(Continued)

The short-term decision is to mothball facilities until a proper assessment of the future of the mine can be made. Koolan Island mine will now be treated as a new project, which means the costs of a 1-year rebuild of the wall will be assessed as sunk costs in any calculations. Since the company has obligations to shareholders, any decision about whether to start production up again or close the mine down completely will be based on the mines prospective future viability. This is subject to the mine's reserves, the trend in iron ore price, the exchange rates (since iron ore is priced in US dollars) as well as the costs of repair.

Mount Gibson's second mine at Extension Hill produces around 5 million tonnes a year. The mine had production costs of around $49 a tonne in December 2014 and the company feels this can be reduced to $45 a tonne by June 2015 by efficiency savings. Add to this royalties of 7.5 per cent and shipping costs of between $10 to $12, then it cannot afford for world iron ore prices to drop much further otherwise its margin will disappear.

The effects of lower iron ore prices and the sea wall disaster have resulted in significant impairment charges as it rebalances the value of its assets.

References: **http://www.indexmundi.com/commodities/?commodity=iron-ore&months=60**

http://www.Mountgibsoniron.com.au/wp-content/uploads/2014/12/5-12-14-Koolan -Island-Update.pdf

http://www.Mountgibsoniron.com.au/wp-content/uploads/2015/02/Investor-Call -Dec-Half-2014-.wav

http://www.smh.com.au/business/mining-and-resources/mount-gibson-iron -weighs-options-after-posting-870m-loss-20150217-13g6o9.html

The Firm's Long-Run Decision to Exit or Enter a Market

The firm's long-run decision to exit the market is similar to its short-run decision in some respects. If the firm exits, it again will lose all revenue from the sale of its product, but now it saves on both fixed and variable costs of production. Thus, the firm exits the market if the revenue it would get from producing is less than its total costs.

We can again make this criterion more useful by writing it mathematically. If *TR* stands for total revenue and *TC* stands for total cost, then the firm's criterion can be written as:

$$\text{Exit if } TR < TC$$

The firm exits if total revenue is less than total cost in the long run. By dividing both sides of this inequality by quantity *Q*, we can write it as:

$$\text{Exit if } TR/Q < TC/Q$$

We can simplify this further by noting that *TR/Q* is average revenue, which, of course for a competitive firm is the same as the price *P*, and that *TC/Q* is average total cost *ATC*. Therefore, the firm's exit criterion is:

$$\text{Exit if } P < ATC$$

That is, a firm chooses to exit if the price of the good is less than the average total cost of production.

One of the financial objectives for new firms starting up is to make profit. The entry criterion where some profit will be made is:

$$\text{Enter if } P > ATC$$

The criterion for entry is exactly the opposite of the criterion for exit.

We can now describe a competitive firm's long-run profit-maximizing strategy. If the firm is in the market, it aims to produce at the quantity at which marginal cost equals the price of the good. Yet if the price is less than average total cost at that quantity, the firm chooses to exit (or not enter) the market. These results are illustrated in Figure 10.5. The competitive firm's long-run supply curve is the portion of its marginal cost curve that lies above average total cost.

FIGURE 10.5

The Competitive Firm's Long-Run Supply Curve

In the long run, the competitive firm's supply curve is its marginal cost curve (MC) above average total cost (ATC). If the price falls below average total cost, the firm is better off exiting the market.

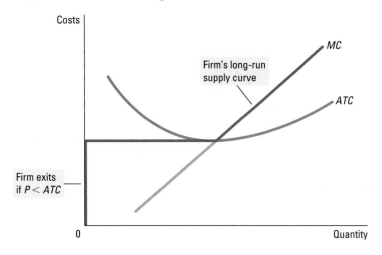

Measuring Profit in Our Graph for the Competitive Firm

As we analyse exit and entry, it is useful to be able to analyse the firm's profit in more detail. Recall that profit (π) equals total revenue (TR) minus total cost (TC):

$$\pi = TR - TC$$

We can rewrite this definition by multiplying and dividing the right-hand side by Q:

$$\pi = (TR/Q) - (TC/Q) \times Q$$

But note that TR/Q is average revenue, which is the price P, and TC/Q is average total cost ATC. Therefore:

$$\pi = (P - ATC) \times Q$$

This way of expressing the firm's profit allows us to measure profit in our graphs. Panel (a) of Figure 10.6 shows a firm earning positive profit. As we have already discussed, the firm maximizes profit by producing the quantity at which price equals marginal cost. Now look at the shaded rectangle. The height of the rectangle is $P - ATC$, the difference between price and average total cost. The width of the rectangle is Q, the quantity produced. Therefore, the area of the rectangle is $(P - ATC) \times Q$, which is the firm's profit.

Similarly, panel (b) of this figure shows a firm with losses (negative profit). In this case, maximizing profit means minimizing losses, a task accomplished once again by producing the quantity at which price equals marginal cost. Now consider the shaded rectangle. The height of the rectangle is $ATC - P$, and the width is Q. The area is $(ATC - P) \times Q$, which is the firm's loss. Because a firm in this situation is not making enough revenue to cover its average total cost, the firm would choose to exit the market.

FIGURE 10.6

Profit as the Area Between Price and Average Total Cost

The area of the shaded box between price and average total cost represents the firm's profit. The height of this box is price minus average total cost (P − ATC), and the width of the box is the quantity of output (Q). In panel (a), price is above average total cost, so the firm has positive profit. In panel (b), price is less than average total cost, so the firm has losses.

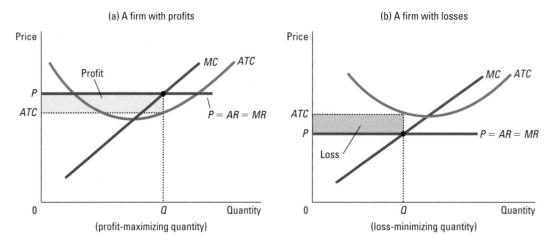

(a) A firm with profits

(b) A firm with losses

> **Quick Quiz** How does the price faced by a profit-maximizing competitive firm compare to its marginal cost? Explain. When does a profit-maximizing competitive firm decide to shut down? When does a profit-maximizing competitive firm decide to exit a market?

THE SUPPLY CURVE IN A COMPETITIVE MARKET

Now that we have examined the supply decision of a single firm, we can discuss the supply curve for a market. There are two cases to consider. First, we examine a market with a fixed number of firms. Second, we examine a market in which the number of firms can change as old firms exit the market and new firms enter. Both cases are important, for each applies over a specific time horizon. Over short periods of time it is often difficult for firms to enter and exit, so the assumption of a fixed number of firms is appropriate. But over long periods of time, the number of firms can adjust to changing market conditions.

The Short Run: Market Supply with a Fixed Number of Firms

Consider first a market with 1000 identical firms. For any given price, each firm supplies a quantity of output so that its marginal cost equals the price, as shown in panel (a) of Figure 10.7. That is, as long as price is above average variable cost, each firm's marginal cost curve is its supply curve. The quantity of output supplied to the market equals the sum of the quantities supplied by each of the 1000 individual firms. Thus, to derive the market supply curve, we add the quantity supplied by each firm in the market. As panel (b) of Figure 10.7 shows, because the firms are identical, the quantity supplied to the market is 1000 times the quantity supplied by each firm.

FIGURE 10.7

Market Supply with a Fixed Number of Firms

When the number of firms in the market is fixed, the market supply curve, shown in panel (b), reflects the individual firms' marginal cost curves, shown in panel (a). Here, in a market of 1000 firms, the quantity of output supplied to the market is 1000 times the quantity supplied by each firm.

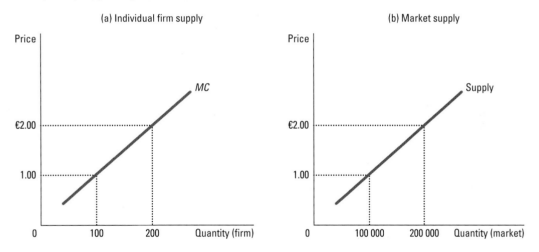

The Long Run: Market Supply with Entry and Exit

Now consider what happens if firms are able to enter or exit the market. Let's suppose that everyone has access to the same technology for producing the good and access to the same markets to buy the inputs into production. Therefore, all firms and all potential firms have the same cost curves.

Decisions about entry and exit in a market of this type depend on the incentives facing the owners of existing firms and the entrepreneurs who could start new firms. If firms already in the market are profitable, then new firms will have an incentive to enter the market. This entry will expand the number of firms, increase the quantity of the good supplied, and drive down prices and profits. Conversely, if firms in the market are making losses, then some existing firms will exit the market. Their exit will reduce the number of firms, decrease the quantity of the good supplied, and drive up prices and profits. At the end of this process of entry and exit, firms that remain in the market must be making zero economic profit.

Pitfall Prevention When talking about zero economic profit, it is important to remember the distinction between economic profit and accounting profit. When economists talk of zero profit they are referring to economic profit.

Recall that we can write a firm's profits as:

$$\pi = (P - ATC) \times Q$$

This equation shows that an operating firm has zero profit if, and only if, the price of the good equals the average total cost of producing that good. If price is above average total cost, profit is positive, which encourages new firms to enter. If price is less than average total cost, profit is negative, which encourages some firms to exit. The process of entry and exit ends only when price and average total cost are driven to equality.

This analysis has a surprising implication. We noted earlier in the chapter that competitive firms produce so that price equals marginal cost. We just noted that free entry and exit forces price to equal average total cost. But if price is to equal both marginal cost and average total cost, these two measures of cost must equal each other. Marginal cost and average total cost are equal, however, only when the firm is operating at the minimum of average total cost. Recall that the level of production with lowest average total cost is called the firm's efficient scale. Therefore, the long-run equilibrium of a competitive market with free entry and exit must have firms operating at their efficient scale.

Panel (a) of Figure 10.8 shows a firm in such a long-run equilibrium. In this figure, price P equals marginal cost MC, so the firm is profit-maximizing. Price also equals average total cost ATC, so profits are zero. New firms have no incentive to enter the market, and existing firms have no incentive to leave the market.

FIGURE 10.8

Market Supply with Entry and Exit

Firms will enter or exit the market until profit is driven to zero. Thus, in the long run, price equals the minimum of average total cost, as shown in panel (a). The number of firms adjusts to ensure that all demand is satisfied at this price. The long-run market supply curve is horizontal at this price, as shown in panel (b).

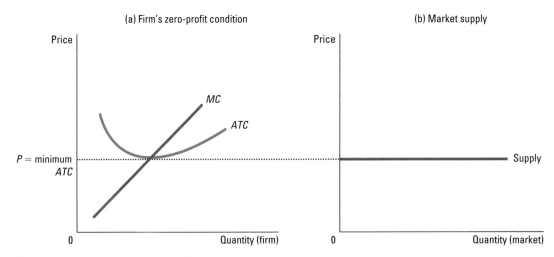

From this analysis of firm behaviour, we can determine the long-run supply curve for the market. In a market with free entry and exit, there is only one price consistent with zero profit – the minimum of average total cost. As a result, the long-run market supply curve must be horizontal at this price, as in panel (b) of Figure 10.8. Any price above this level would generate profit, leading to entry and an increase in the total quantity supplied. Any price below this level would generate losses, leading to exit and a decrease in the total quantity supplied. Eventually, the number of firms in the market adjusts so that price equals the minimum of average total cost, and there are enough firms to satisfy all the demand at this price.

Why do Competitive Firms Stay in Business if They Make Zero Profit?

At first, it might seem odd that competitive firms earn zero profit in the long run. After all, people start businesses to make a profit. If entry eventually drives profit to zero, there might seem to be little reason to stay in business.

To understand the zero-profit condition more fully, recall that profit equals total revenue minus total cost, and that total cost includes all the opportunity costs of the firm. In particular, total cost includes the opportunity cost of the time and money that the firm's owners devote to the business. In the zero-profit equilibrium, the firm's revenue must compensate the owners for the time and money that they expend to keep their business going.

Consider an example. Suppose that a farmer had to invest €1 million to open their farm, which otherwise could have been deposited in a bank to earn €50 000 a year in interest. In addition, the farmer had to give up another job that would have paid them €30 000 a year. Then the farmer's opportunity cost of farming includes both the interest they could have earned and the forgone wages – a total of €80 000. This sum must be calculated as part of the farmer's total costs. In some situations zero profit is referred to as **normal profit** – the minimum amount required to keep factor inputs in their current use. Even if profit is driven to zero, the revenue from farming compensates them for these opportunity costs.

> **normal profit** the minimum amount required to keep factors of production in their current use

Keep in mind that accountants and economists measure costs differently; accountants keep track of explicit costs but usually do not consider implicit costs. As a result, in the zero-profit equilibrium, economic profit is zero, but accounting profit is positive. Our farmer's accountant, for instance, would conclude that the farmer earned an accounting profit of €80 000, which is enough to keep the farmer in business. In the short run as we shall see, profit can be above zero or normal profit which is referred to as **abnormal profit**.

> **abnormal profit** the profit over and above normal profit

? **what if ...** a firm earned profit which was only 1 per cent less than zero profit. Would it still be worthwhile continuing in production?

A Shift in Demand in the Short Run and Long Run

Because firms can enter and exit a market in the long run but not in the short run, the response of a market to a change in demand depends on the time horizon. To see this, let's trace the effects of a shift in demand. This analysis will show how a market responds over time, and it will show how entry and exit drive a market to its long-run equilibrium.

Suppose the market for milk begins in long-run equilibrium. Firms are earning zero profit, so price equals the minimum of average total cost. Panel (a) of Figure 10.9 shows the situation. The long-run equilibrium is point A, the quantity sold in the market is Q_1, and the price is P_1.

FIGURE 10.9

An Increase in Demand in the Short Run and Long Run

The market starts in a long-run equilibrium, shown as point A in panel (a). In this equilibrium, each firm makes zero profit, and the price equals the minimum average total cost. Panel (b) shows what happens in the short run when demand rises from D_1 to D_2. The equilibrium goes from point A to point B, price rises from P_1 to P_2, and the quantity sold in the market rises from Q_1 to Q_2. Because price now exceeds average total cost, firms make profits, which over time encourage new firms to enter the market. This entry shifts the short-run supply curve to the right from S_1 to S_2 as shown in panel (c). In the new long-run equilibrium, point C, price has returned to P_1 but the quantity sold has increased to Q_3. Profits are again zero, price is back to the minimum of average total cost, but the market has more firms to satisfy the greater demand.

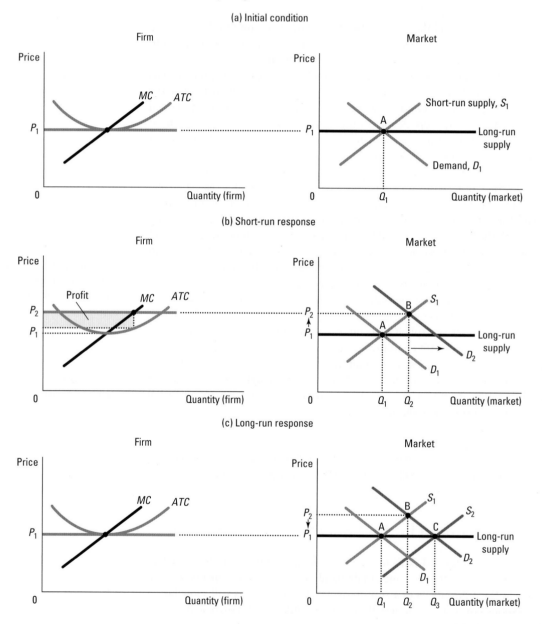

Now suppose scientists discover that milk has miraculous health benefits. As a result, the demand curve for milk shifts outward from D_1 to D_2, as in panel (b). The short-run equilibrium moves from point A to point B; as a result, the quantity rises from Q_1 to Q_2 and the price rises from P_1 to P_2. All of the existing firms respond to the higher price by raising the amount produced. Because each firm's supply curve reflects its marginal cost curve, how much they each increase production is determined by the marginal cost curve. In the new short-run equilibrium, the price of milk exceeds average total cost, so the firms are making positive or abnormal profit.

Over time, the profit in this market encourages new firms to enter. Some farmers may switch to milk production from other farm products, for example. As the number of firms grows, the short-run supply curve shifts to the right from S_1 to S_2, as in panel (c), and this shift causes the price of milk to fall. Eventually, the price is driven back down to the minimum of average total cost, profits are zero and firms stop entering. Thus, the market reaches a new long-run equilibrium, point C. The price of milk has returned to P_1, but the quantity produced has risen to Q_3. Each firm is again producing at its efficient scale, but because more firms are in the dairy business, the quantity of milk produced and sold is higher.

Why the Long-Run Supply Curve Might Slope Upwards

So far we have seen that entry and exit can cause the long-run market supply curve to be horizontal. The essence of our analysis is that there are a large number of potential entrants, each of which faces the same costs. As a result, the long-run market supply curve is horizontal at the minimum of average total cost. When the demand for the good increases, the long-run result is an increase in the number of firms and in the total quantity supplied, without any change in the price.

The reality is that the assumptions we have made in our model do not hold in all cases. There are, as a result, two reasons that the long-run market supply curve might slope upward. The first is that some resources used in production may be available only in limited quantities. For example, consider the market for farm products. Anyone can choose to buy land and start a farm, but the quantity and quality of land is limited. As more people become farmers, the price of farmland is bid up, which raises the costs of all farmers in the market. Thus, an increase in demand for farm products cannot induce an increase in quantity supplied without also inducing a rise in farmers' costs, which in turn means a rise in price. The result is a long-run market supply curve that is upwards sloping, even with free entry into farming.

A second reason for an upwards sloping supply curve is that firms may have different costs. For example, consider the market for painters. Anyone can enter the market for painting services, but not everyone has the same costs. Costs vary in part because some people work faster than others, use different materials and equipment and because some people have better alternative uses of their time than others. For any given price, those with lower costs are more likely to enter than those with higher costs. To increase the quantity of painting services supplied, additional entrants must be encouraged to enter the market. Because these new entrants have higher costs, the price must rise to make entry profitable for them. Thus, the market supply curve for painting services slopes upwards even with free entry into the market.

Notice that if firms have different costs, some firms earn profit even in the long run. In this case, the price in the market reflects the average total cost of the *marginal firm* – the firm that would exit the market if the price were any lower. This firm earns zero profit, but firms with lower costs earn positive profit. Entry does not eliminate this profit because would-be entrants have higher costs than firms already in the market. Higher-cost firms will enter only if the price rises, making the market profitable for them.

Thus, for these two reasons, the long-run supply curve in a market may be upwards sloping rather than horizontal, indicating that a higher price is necessary to induce a larger quantity supplied. Nevertheless, the basic lesson about entry and exit remains true. Because firms can enter and exit more easily in the long run than in the short run, the long-run supply curve is typically more elastic than the short-run supply curve.

> **Quick Quiz** In the long run with free entry and exit, is the price in a market equal to marginal cost, average total cost, both, or neither? Explain with a diagram.

CONCLUSION: BEHIND THE SUPPLY CURVE

We have been discussing the behaviour of competitive profit-maximizing firms. Marginal analysis has given us a theory of the supply curve in a competitive market and, as a result, a deeper understanding of market outcomes.

We have learned that when you buy a good from a firm in a competitive market, you can be assured that the price you pay is close to the cost of producing that good. In particular, if firms are competitive and profit-maximizing, the price of a good equals the marginal cost of making that good. In addition, if firms can freely enter and exit the market, the price also equals the lowest possible average total cost of production.

Although we have assumed throughout this chapter that firms are price takers, many of the tools developed here are also useful for studying firms in less competitive markets. In subsequent chapters we will examine the behaviour of firms with market power. Marginal analysis will again be useful in analysing these firms, but it will have quite different implications.

IN THE NEWS

The Growth in the Tablet Market

Businesses like Apple, Samsung and Microsoft are hardly the epitome of the perfectly competitive firm that we have been describing, but the market dynamics in which they operate can bear some comforting resemblances to the model outlined in this chapter.

There are few people in the world today who are not touched in some way by mobile devices. Ever since the mobile phone became a product accessible to very large numbers of people, firms have been looking to find ways of expanding the mobile technology market. The development of text messaging, emails, the Web, listening to music, playing games and watching video have all been included on mobile devices with varying degrees of success over the past decade.

Apple's introduction of the iPad developed a new concept in mobile devices – the tablet. The iPad was launched in January 2010. Since that time sales have risen quickly reaching over 32 million in 2011, over 58 million in 2012, 71 million in 2013, and 68 million in 2014. There have been six 9.7-inch iPad versions and three versions of the iPad mini. The success of the iPad made it clear that there was a demand for these types of devices with potential large profits to be made – Apple reported its fiscal first quarter 2015 profits of $18 billion on a turnover of $74.6 billion in April 2015 with a very healthy margin (this profit is attributed to all its products including the iPad). Apple was one of the first companies to launch a tablet PC but other electrical manufacturers were not far behind and saw the market potential.

When the iPad was first introduced, the price was relatively high at between €500 to €950 depending on the model. The abnormal profits that could be earned on these devices meant that there was an incentive for rivals to follow suit and launch their own tablet PC versions. Amazon had launched its Kindle in 2007 but this device did not have the functionality of an iPad and was more of an eBook service than a tablet PC. There had been other tablet PC devices prior to the

iPad but Apple did have the advantage of launching at a time when 3G and Wi-Fi access was more widely available and accessible.

Following the release of the iPad, the Galaxy Tab from Samsung, Research in Motion's BlackBerry Playbook, Vizio's Via, the Toshiba Thrive, LG's Optimus and the Motorola Xoom all appeared on the market. Amazon sought to get in on the act by updating its Kindle to the Kindle Fire which included far more functionality, mimicking a tablet PC.

How the market reacts to this influx of supply is dependent on the degree of substitutability between these different devices. This is not a perfect market with homogenous products and each device is different in terms of looks, functionality and usability. We are not talking about an industry supply curve, therefore, that is the summation of individual firm's supply curves.

However, for the consumer, the effect is that they have a far wider choice and with greater choice and competition between sellers, the pressure on prices to fall exists. Along with greater competition come the improvements in production techniques and knowledge, which individual manufacturers will be looking to exploit to lower production costs and increase productivity and efficiency, thus allowing them to have more flexibility on pricing in what is a growing and increasingly competitive market.

The result has been a gradual reduction in the real prices of tablet PCs as competition and production efficiencies rise. The latest iPad 2 sells for between €460 and €799

depending on the model, and the Samsung Tab comes in at a much lower price.

The actual stage of tablets in the product life cycle is hard to gauge. The first quarter sales figures in 2015 suggest a fall in Apple iPad sales compared with those a year earlier. This may be down to increased competition in the tablet market or a result of substitute products such as the phablet, a product straddling the smart phone and tablet or even the smartwatch.

Questions

1. Apple was one of the first businesses to enter the tablet PC market. What costs would it have had to take into account in deciding whether the market was worth entering?

2. Our model assumes freedom of entry and exit for a market that may not be present in markets which are not highly competitive. Outline some factors that might prevent entry into the tablet PC market.

3. Using diagrams, explain how short-run profits in the tablet PC industry might be competed away in the long term to lead to normal profits being made in this market.

4. What factors might affect the length of time which could constitute the long run in the tablet PC market?

5. Assess the factors which would allow a firm like Apple to continue making abnormal profits in the long run in this market.

SUMMARY

- Because a competitive firm is a price taker, its revenue is proportional to the amount of output it produces. The price of the good equals both the firm's average revenue and its marginal revenue.

- To maximize profit, a firm chooses a quantity of output such that marginal revenue equals marginal cost. Because marginal revenue for a competitive firm equals the market price, the firm chooses quantity so that price equals marginal cost. Thus, the firm's marginal cost curve is its supply curve.

- In the short run when a firm cannot recover its fixed costs, the firm will choose to shut down temporarily if the price of the good is less than average variable cost. In the long run when the firm can recover both fixed and

variable costs, it will choose to exit if the price is less than average total cost.

- In a market with free entry and exit, profits are driven to zero in the long run. In this long-run equilibrium, all firms produce at the efficient scale, price equals the minimum of average total cost, and the number of firms adjusts to satisfy the quantity demanded at this price.

- Changes in demand have different effects over different time horizons. In the short run, an increase in demand raises prices and leads to profits, and a decrease in demand lowers prices and leads to losses. But if firms can freely enter and exit the market, then in the long run the number of firms adjusts to drive the market back to the zero-profit equilibrium.

QUESTIONS FOR REVIEW

1. What is meant by a 'competitive firm'?

2. Draw the cost curves for a typical firm in a perfectly competitive market. For a given price, explain how the firm chooses the level of output that maximizes profit.

3. Under what conditions will a firm shut down temporarily? Explain.

4. Under what conditions will a firm exit a market? Explain.

5. Under what conditions will a firm enter a market? Explain.

6. Does a firm's price equal marginal cost in the short run, in the long run, or both? Explain.

7. Does a firm's price equal the minimum of average total cost in the short run, in the long run, or both? Explain.

8. Explain why a firm will continue in production even if it makes zero profit.

9. If a firm is making abnormal profit in the short run, what will happen to these profits in the long run assuming the conditions for a highly competitive market exist?

10. Are market supply curves typically more elastic in the short run or in the long run? Explain.

PROBLEMS AND APPLICATIONS

1. What are the characteristics of a competitive market? Which of the following drinks do you think is best described by these characteristics? Why aren't the others?
   a. tap water
   b. bottled water
   c. cola
   d. beer

2. Your flatmate's long hours in the chemistry lab finally paid off – she discovered a secret formula that lets people do an hour's worth of studying in 5 minutes. So

far, she's sold 200 doses, and faces the following average total cost schedule:

Q	Average total cost
199	€199
200	200
201	201

If a new customer offers to pay your flatmate €300 for one dose, should she make one more? Explain.

3. You go out to the best restaurant in town and order a lobster dinner for €40. After eating half of the lobster, you realize that you are quite full. Your date wants you to finish your dinner, because you can't take it home and because 'you've already paid for it'. What should you do? Relate your answer to the material in this chapter.

4. PC Camera GmbH faces costs of production as follows:

Quantity	Total fixed costs (€)	Total variable costs (€)
0	100	0
1	100	50
2	100	70
3	100	90
4	100	140
5	100	200
6	100	360

   a. Calculate the company's average fixed costs, average variable costs, average total costs and marginal costs at each level of production.
   b. The price of a PC camera is €50. Seeing that it can't make a profit the chief executive officer (CEO) decides to shut down operations. What are the firm's profits/losses? Was this a wise decision? Explain.
   c. Vaguely remembering her introductory business economics course, the chief financial officer (CFO) tells the CEO it is better to produce 1 PC camera because marginal revenue equals marginal cost at that quantity. What are the firm's profits/losses at that level of production? Was this the best decision? Explain.

5. 'High prices traditionally cause expansion in an industry, eventually bringing an end to high prices and manufacturers' prosperity.' Explain, using appropriate diagrams.

6. Suppose the book printing industry is competitive and begins in long-run equilibrium.
   a. Draw a diagram describing the typical firm in the industry.
   b. Hi-Tech Printing Company invents a new process that significantly reduces the cost of printing books. What happens to Hi-Tech's profits and the price of books in the short run when Hi-Tech's patent prevents other firms from using the new technology?
   c. What happens in the long run when the patent expires and other firms are free to use the technology?

7. Many small boats are made of fibreglass, which is derived from crude oil. Suppose that the price of oil rises.
   a. Using diagrams, show what happens to the cost curves of an individual boat-making firm and to the market supply curve.
   b. What happens to the profits of boat-makers in the short run? What happens to the number of boat-makers in the long run?

8. Suppose that the European Union textile industry is competitive, and there is no international trade in textiles. In long-run equilibrium, the price per unit of cloth is €30.
   a. Describe the equilibrium using graphs for the entire market and for an individual producer.

   Now suppose that textile producers in non-EU countries are willing to sell large quantities of cloth in the EU for only €25 per unit.
   b. Assuming that EU textile producers have large fixed costs, what is the short-run effect of these imports on the quantity produced by an individual producer? What is the short-run effect on profits? Illustrate your answer with a graph.
   c. What is the long-run effect on the number of EU firms in the industry?

9. Assume that the gold-mining industry is competitive.
   a. Illustrate a long-run equilibrium using diagrams for the gold market and for a representative gold mine.
   b. Suppose that an increase in jewellery demand induces a surge in the demand for gold. Using your diagrams from part (a), show what happens in the short run to the gold market and to each existing gold mine.
   c. If the demand for gold remains high, what would happen to the price over time? Specifically, would the new long-run equilibrium price be above, below or equal to the short-run equilibrium price in part (b)? Is it possible for the new long-run equilibrium price to be above the original long-run equilibrium price? Explain.

10. The liquorice industry is competitive. Each firm produces 2 million liquorice bootlaces per year. The bootlaces have an average total cost of €0.20 each and they sell for €0.30.
   a. What is the marginal cost of a liquorice bootlace?
   b. Is this industry in long-run equilibrium? Why or why not?

11 MARKET STRUCTURES

LEARNING OUTCOMES

After reading this chapter you should be able to:

- List three reasons why a monopoly can remain the sole seller of a product in a market.

- Use a monopolist's cost curves and the demand curve it faces to show the profit earned by a monopolist.

- Show the deadweight loss from a monopolist's production decision.

- Show why forcing a natural monopoly to set its selling price equal to its marginal cost of production creates losses for the monopolist.

- Demonstrate the surprising result that price discrimination by a monopolist can raise economic welfare above that generated by standard monopoly pricing.

INTRODUCTION

If you own a personal computer, it probably uses some version of Windows, the operating system sold by the US company, Microsoft Corporation. When Microsoft first designed Windows many years ago, it applied for and received a copyright, first from the US government and then from many of the governments of the world. The copyright gives Microsoft the exclusive right to make and sell copies of the Windows operating system. So if a person wants to buy a copy of Windows, he or she has little choice but to give Microsoft the price that the firm has decided to charge for its product. One version or another of Windows is the operating system used by around 90 per cent of the desktop PCs in the world. Microsoft is said to have a *monopoly* in the market for Windows.

If you use a PC or laptop, there is a very high chance that when you use a search engine it will be Google, which dominates the search engine market with a market share of around 68 per cent.

In most countries, the option for consumers to purchase utilities like gas, water and electricity is limited to a very small number of firms and in some cases there might only be one supplier.

Across many parts of Europe, consumers have choice in where they do their weekly grocery shopping but the market is likely to be dominated by a relatively small number of very large firms. Once in those large supermarkets, the choice may seem very wide indeed but it might be a surprise to learn that many of the choices on offer are actually produced by a small number of firms. In the breakfast cereal aisle, for example, there is a very wide range of choice available but most are produced by four very large firms, Nestlé, Kellogg, General Mills and Quaker. Equally, toothpaste, detergents, soaps, washing up liquid and so on, are likely to be made by Procter & Gamble, Colgate-Palmolive, Kimberley-Clarke and Unilever.

There is a choice in the purchase of mobile phones and mobile phone service providers but again the market is dominated by a small number of very large firms. Samsung, Apple, Nokia, LG, Huawei, HTC and Sony are the main suppliers of handsets, EE, O2, Vodafone, Verizon, T-Mobile, AT&T, Etisalat and Orascom being very large firms across Europe and the Middle East which dominate mobile phone service provision. Things change fast in this market too – at the time of writing, EE are subject to a takeover bid by British Telecom and O2 has been acquired by Hutchison Whampoa, owners of the Three network.

If you are a business and want to employ a firm of accountants to check your books and provide financial advice, it is very likely that you might turn to one of the so-called 'Big-Four' accounting firms, KPMG, Deloitte, PwC (PriceWaterhouseCoopers) and Ernst & Young.

You might think there is lots of choice if you want to buy some takeaway food or go to a restaurant or bar. How often, in reality, do you go back to the same place on a regular basis? If you analyse your behaviour it is likely that you will tend to have a degree of loyalty to particular brands for a variety of reasons.

What these examples highlight is that our everyday lives are influenced to a very large extent by interaction with a relatively small number of very large firms. Many markets are not characterized by a large number of relatively small firms who are price takers and have no influence of price selling, products that are very similar (homogenous). Even if we do have to buy a homogenous product like petrol or diesel, for example, we will tend to buy from a small number of very big suppliers such as BP, Shell, Texaco and Esso.

IMPERFECT COMPETITION

The business decisions of many of these firms we have used as examples are not well described by the model of a competitive market we have been assuming in the previous chapters. The reality is that firms can be *price makers* rather than having to be *price takers* and do not sell homogenous products. In some way or another, either because of some physical difference or because our psychology tells us, products are not homogenous and the degree to which one product is a substitute for another can be influenced by firms. If firms can influence price or control the amount they supply, or in some way present their product as being something very different, then they have some element of market power. A firm such as Microsoft has few close competitors and such a dominant market share that it can influence the market price of its product. When a firm has some element of market power its behaviour is different to that under the assumptions which characterized a highly competitive market.

Pitfall Prevention   Care is needed when using the word 'competitive' in economic analysis. In everyday usage, we use competitive to describe the degree of rivalry between groups or individuals. In economics, a firm in a competitive market is one which operates under the assumptions of a competitive market structure. Once we relax those assumptions we are interested in how a firm's behaviour changes. Competition between firms in market structures where there is considerable market power is certainly intense but the options available to firms and their behaviours are different to those firms operating under more perfectly competitive conditions.

In this chapter we examine the idea of imperfect competition and in particular the extreme form of imperfect competition, monopoly. In the next chapter we will look at other forms of imperfect competition.

An imperfectly competitive market is one where the assumptions of perfect competition do not hold and at the extreme of imperfect competition is monopoly.

A monopoly, in the extreme case, is a single supplier of a good with no competitors. Just as the extreme model of perfect competition does not exist in its purest form, there are few examples of a perfect monopoly. However, what we can identify are certain characteristics in particular markets where firms behave as if they are a monopoly supplier. A firm with an 90 per cent market share such as Microsoft in the Windows operating system market is not a pure monopoly – there are other operating systems such as Apple's Mac OS, and Linux, for example, but the market power that Microsoft can wield is considerable.

Where a firm has some element of market power it can alter the relationship between a firm's costs and the price at which it sells its product to the market. A competitive firm takes the price of its output as given by the market and then chooses the quantity it will supply so that price equals marginal cost. By contrast, the price charged by firms with market power exceeds marginal cost. This result is clearly true in the case of Microsoft's Windows. The marginal cost of Windows – the extra cost that Microsoft would incur by making one more copy of the program available – is only a few euros. The market price of Windows is many times marginal cost.

It is perhaps not surprising that firms with considerable market power can charge relatively high prices for their products. Customers of monopolies might seem to have little choice but to pay whatever the monopoly charges. But, if so, why is a copy of Windows priced at about €100 and not €1000? Or €10 000? The reason is that if Microsoft set the price that high, fewer people would buy the product.

People would buy fewer computers, switch to other operating systems or make illegal copies. Monopolies cannot achieve any level of profit they want because high prices reduce the amount that their customers buy. Although monopolies can control the prices of their goods, their profits are not unlimited. In other words, under conditions of imperfect competition firms do not face a horizontal demand curve which suggests they can sell any amount they offer at the going market price. Instead, firms face a downward sloping demand curve which means that if they want to sell more products they have to accept lower prices. If this is the case then price does not equal average revenue and marginal revenue is lower. This is partly what leads to changed behaviour.

We are going to start our analysis of behaviour of firms under imperfect competition by looking at monopolies. A **monopoly** is a firm which is the sole supplier of a product in a market. In reality we describe firms as monopolies even though there are other suppliers, as we have seen in the case of operating systems. Because there are concerns about the effect of market power on consumers and suppliers, most national competition policy defines monopolies in a much stricter way. A firm might be able to exercise some monopoly power if it has 25 per cent or more of the market. However, for the purposes of our analysis let us assume that there is only one supplier in the market. Remember that features of our analysis will apply fairly closely to situations where a firm dominates the market even though there are other suppliers. When we looked at firms under highly competitive conditions we saw that the profit maximizing output would occur where $MC = MR$. We also saw that if market conditions change, any abnormal or subnormal profit would disappear in the long run as new firms enter and leave the industry. In a competitive market firms are price takers and $P = AR = MR$. A firm operating as a monopoly does not face these same conditions and so production and pricing decisions are different.

> **monopoly** a firm that is the sole seller of a product without close substitutes

As we examine the production and pricing decisions of monopolies, we also consider the implications of monopoly for society as a whole. We base our analysis of monopoly firms, like competitive firms, on the assumption that they aim to maximize profit. But this goal has very different ramifications for competitive and monopoly firms. In a competitive market, firms are operating efficiently and consumers not only have choice but pay 'low' prices. Because monopoly firms face different market conditions, the outcome in a market with a monopoly is often different and not always in the best interest of society. It is these market imperfections that form the basis for so much government policy.

MONOPOLY

The fundamental cause of monopoly is *barriers to entry*: a monopoly remains the only seller in its market because other firms cannot enter the market and compete with it. Barriers to entry, in turn, have four main sources which we will briefly discuss.

Monopoly Resources

The simplest way for a monopoly to arise is for a single firm to own a key resource. For example, consider the market for water in a small town on a remote Scottish island not served by the water company from the mainland. If dozens of town residents on the island have working wells, the competitive model we have previously described is likely to hold. In such a situation the price of a litre of water is driven to equal the marginal cost of pumping an extra litre. But if there is only one well in town and it is impossible to get water from anywhere else, then the owner of the well has a monopoly on water. Not surprisingly, the monopolist has much greater market power than any single firm in a competitive market. In the case of a necessity like water, the monopolist could command quite a high price, even if the marginal cost is low.

Although exclusive ownership of a key resource is a potential cause of monopoly, in practice monopolies rarely arise for this reason. Actual economies are large, and resources are owned by many people. Indeed, because many goods are traded internationally, the natural scope of their markets is often worldwide. There are, therefore, few examples of firms that own a resource for which there are no close substitutes.

Government-Created Monopolies

In many cases, monopolies arise because the government has given one person or firm the exclusive right to sell some good or service. European kings, for example, once granted exclusive business licences to their friends and allies in order to raise money – a highly prized monopoly being the exclusive right to sell and distribute salt in a particular region of Europe. Even today, governments sometimes grant a monopoly (perhaps even to itself) because doing so is viewed to be in the public interest. In Sweden, the retailing of alcoholic beverages is carried out under a state-owned monopoly known as the Systembolaget, because the Swedish government deems it to be in the interests of public health to be able to directly control the sale of alcohol.

The patent and copyright laws are two important examples of how the government creates a monopoly to serve the public interest. When a pharmaceutical company discovers a new drug, it can apply to the government for a patent. If the government deems the drug to be truly original, it approves the patent, which gives the company the exclusive right to manufacture and sell the drug for a fixed number of years – often 20 years. Similarly, when a novelist finishes a book, they can copyright it. The copyright is a government guarantee that no one can print and sell the work without the author's permission. The copyright makes the novelist a monopolist in the sale of their novel.

The effects of patent and copyright laws are easy to see. Because these laws give one producer a monopoly, they lead to higher prices than would occur under competition. But by allowing these monopoly producers to charge higher prices and earn higher profits, the laws also encourage some desirable behaviour. Drug companies are allowed to be monopolists in the drugs they discover in order to encourage research. Authors are allowed to be monopolists in the sale of their books to encourage them to write more and better books.

Thus, the laws governing patents and copyrights have benefits and costs. The benefits of the patent and copyright laws are the increased incentive for creative activity. These benefits are offset, to some extent, by the costs of monopoly pricing, which we examine fully later in this chapter.

Natural Monopolies

natural monopoly a monopoly that arises because a single firm can supply a good or service to an entire market at a smaller cost than could two or more firms

An industry is a **natural monopoly** when a single firm can supply a good or service to an entire market at a lower cost than could two or more firms. A natural monopoly arises when there are economies of scale over the relevant range of output. Figure 11.1 shows the average total costs of a firm with economies of scale. In this case, a single firm can produce any amount of output at least cost. That is, for any given amount of output, a larger number of firms leads to less output per firm and higher average total cost.

FIGURE 11.1

Economies of Scale as a Cause of Monopoly

When a firm's average total cost curve continually declines, the firm has what is called a natural monopoly. In this case, when production is divided among more firms, each firm produces less, and average total cost rises. As a result, a single firm can produce any given amount at the smallest cost.

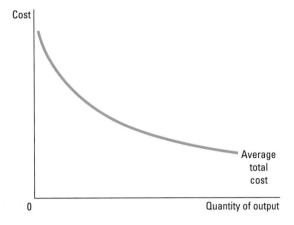

An example of a natural monopoly is the distribution of water. To provide water to residents of a town, a firm must build a network of pipes throughout the town. If two or more firms were to compete in the provision of this service, each firm would have to pay the fixed cost of building a network. Thus, the average total cost of water is lowest if a single firm serves the entire market.

When a firm is a natural monopoly, it is less concerned about new entrants eroding its monopoly power. Normally, a firm has trouble maintaining a monopoly position without ownership of a key resource or protection from the government. The monopolist's profit attracts entrants into the market, and these entrants make the market more competitive. By contrast, entering a market in which another firm has a natural monopoly is unattractive. Would-be entrants know that they cannot achieve the same low costs that the monopolist enjoys because, after entry, each firm would have a smaller piece of the market.

External Growth

Many of the largest firms in the world have grown partly through acquisition, merger or takeover of other firms. As they do so, the industry becomes more concentrated; there are fewer firms in the industry. Earlier we mentioned the Big Four accounting firms. This is an example where smaller accounting firms have merged or been taken over and has resulted in a number of large firms dominating the industry. One effect of this type of growth is that a firm might be able to develop monopoly power over its rivals and erect barriers to entry to make it harder for new firms to enter. It is for this reason that governments monitor such acquisitions to see if there are implications for competition.

Quick Quiz Identify three examples of firms with monopoly power, and explain the primary reason for the source of the monopoly power of each.

HOW MONOPOLIES MAKE PRODUCTION AND PRICING DECISIONS

Now that we know how monopolies arise, we can consider how a monopoly firm decides how much of its product to make and what price to charge for it. The analysis of monopoly behaviour in this section is the starting point for evaluating whether monopolies are desirable and what policies the government might pursue in monopoly markets.

Monopoly versus Competition

The key difference between a competitive firm and a monopoly is the monopoly's ability to influence the price of its output. A competitive firm is small relative to the market in which it operates and, therefore, takes the price of its output as given by market conditions and is assumed to be able to sell all its output. By contrast, because a monopoly is the sole producer in its market, it can alter the price of its good by adjusting the quantity it supplies to the market.

Because a monopoly is the sole producer in its market, its demand curve is the market demand curve. Thus, the monopolist's demand curve slopes downward for all the usual reasons, as in panel (b) of Figure 11.2. If the monopolist raises the price of its good, consumers buy less of it. Looked at another way, if the monopolist reduces the quantity of output it sells, the price of its output increases.

FIGURE 11.2

Demand Curves for Competitive and Monopoly Firms

Because competitive firms are price takers, they in effect face horizontal demand curves, as in panel (a). Because a monopoly firm is the sole producer in its market, it faces the downward sloping market demand curve, as in panel (b). As a result, the monopoly has to accept a lower price if it wants to sell more output.

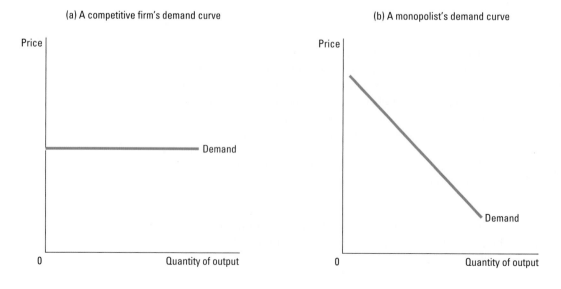

> **Pitfall Prevention** Because a monopolist faces a downwards sloping demand curve it can either set price and accept the level of demand to determine its sales or it can fix output at a certain level and allow the market to determine the price it can charge – it cannot do both, i.e., it cannot fix price *and* output together.

The market demand curve provides a constraint on a monopoly's ability to profit from its market power. A monopolist would prefer, if it were possible, to charge a high price and sell a large quantity at that high price. The market demand curve makes that outcome impossible. In particular, the market demand curve describes the combinations of price and quantity that are available to a monopoly firm. By adjusting the quantity produced (or, equivalently, the price charged), the monopolist can choose any point on the demand curve, but it cannot choose a point off the demand curve.

What point on the demand curve will the monopolist choose? As with competitive firms, we assume that the monopolist's goal is to maximize profit. Because the firm's profit is total revenue minus total costs, our next task in explaining monopoly behaviour is to examine a monopolist's revenue.

A Monopoly's Revenue

Consider a town with a single producer of water. Table 11.1 shows how the monopoly's revenue might depend on the amount of water produced.

The first two columns show the monopolist's demand schedule. If the monopolist produces just 1 litre of water, it can sell that litre for €1. If it produces 2 litres, it must lower the price to €0.90 in order to sell both litres. And if it produces 3 litres, it must lower the price to €0.80, and so on. If you graphed these two columns of numbers, you would get a typical downward sloping demand curve.

TABLE 11.1

A Monopoly's Total, Average and Marginal Revenue

Quantity of water	Price €	Total revenue €	Average revenue €	Marginal revenue €
(Q)	(P)	(TR = P × Q)	(AR = TR/Q)	(MR = ΔTR/ΔQ)
0 litres	1.1	0.0	–	
				1.0
1	1.0	1.0	1.0	
				0.8
2	0.9	1.8	0.9	
				0.6
3	0.8	2.4	0.8	
				0.4
4	0.7	2.8	0.7	
				0.2
5	0.6	3.0	0.6	
				0.0
6	0.5	3.0	0.5	
				−0.2
7	0.4	2.8	0.4	
				−0.4
8	0.3	2.4	0.3	

The third column of the table presents the monopolist's *total revenue*. It equals the quantity sold (from the first column) times the price (from the second column). The fourth column computes the firm's *average revenue*, the amount of revenue the firm receives per unit sold. We compute average revenue by taking the number for total revenue in the third column and dividing it by the quantity of output in the first column. As we discussed in the previous chapter, average revenue always equals the price of the good. This is true for monopolists as well as for competitive firms.

The last column of Table 11.1 computes the firm's *marginal revenue*, the amount of revenue that the firm receives for each additional unit of output. We compute marginal revenue by taking the change in total revenue when output increases by 1 unit. For example, when the firm is producing 3 litres of water it receives total revenue of €2.40. Raising production to 4 litres increases total revenue to €2.80. Thus, marginal revenue is €2.80 minus €2.40, or €0.40.

Table 11.1 shows a result that is important for understanding monopoly behaviour: a monopolist's marginal revenue is always less than the price of its good. For example, if the firm raises production of water from 3 to 4 litres, it will increase total revenue by only €0.40, even though it will be able to sell each litre for €0.70. For a monopoly, marginal revenue is lower than price because a monopoly faces a downward sloping demand curve. To increase the amount sold, a monopoly firm must lower the price of its good. Hence, to sell the fourth litre of water, the monopolist must get less revenue for each of the first three litres.

Marginal revenue for monopolies is very different from marginal revenue for competitive firms. When a monopoly increases the amount it sells, it has two effects on total revenue ($P \times Q$):

- *The output effect.* More output is sold, so Q is higher, which tends to increase total revenue.
- *The price effect.* The price falls, so P is lower, which tends to decrease total revenue.

Because a competitive firm can sell all it wants at the market price, there is no price effect. When it increases production by 1 unit, it receives the market price for that unit, and it does not receive any less for the units it was already selling. That is, because the competitive firm is a price taker, its marginal revenue equals the price of its good. By contrast, when a monopoly increases production by 1 unit, it must reduce the price it charges for every unit it sells, and this cut in price reduces revenue on the units it was already selling. As a result, a monopoly's marginal revenue is less than its price.

Figure 11.3 graphs the demand curve and the marginal revenue curve for a monopoly firm. (Because the firm's price equals its average revenue, the demand curve is also the average revenue curve.) These two curves always start at the same point on the vertical axis because the marginal revenue of the first unit sold equals the price of the good. But thereafter, for the reason we just discussed, the monopolist's marginal revenue is less than the price of the good. Thus, a monopoly's marginal revenue curve lies below its demand curve.

You can see in Figure 11.3 (as well as in Table 11.1) that marginal revenue can even become negative. Marginal revenue is negative when the price effect on revenue is greater than the output effect. In this case, when the firm produces an extra unit of output, the price falls by enough to cause the firm's total revenue to decline, even though the firm is selling more units.

Profit Maximization

Now that we have considered the revenue of a monopoly firm, we are ready to examine how such a firm maximizes profit. We apply the logic of marginal analysis to the monopolist's decision about how much to produce.

FIGURE 11.3

Demand and Marginal Revenue Curves for a Monopoly

The demand curve shows how the quantity affects the price of the good. The marginal revenue curve shows how the firm's revenue changes when the quantity increases by 1 unit. Because the price on all units sold must fall if the monopoly increases production, marginal revenue is always less than the price.

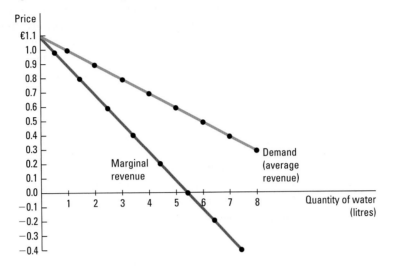

Figure 11.4 graphs the demand curve, the marginal revenue curve and the cost curves for a monopoly firm. All these curves should seem familiar: the demand and marginal revenue curves are like those in Figure 11.3, and the cost curves are like those we encountered in earlier chapters. These curves contain all the information we need to determine the level of output that a profit-maximizing monopolist will choose.

FIGURE 11.4

Profit Maximization for a Monopoly

A monopoly maximizes profit by choosing the quantity at which marginal revenue equals marginal cost (point A). It then uses the demand curve to find the price that will induce consumers to buy that quantity (point B).

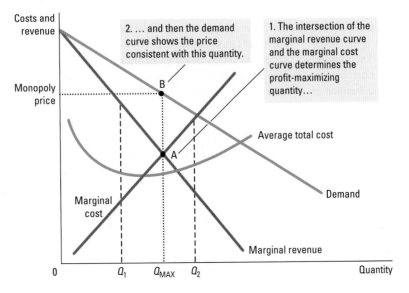

Suppose, first, that the firm is producing at a low level of output, such as Q_1. In this case, marginal cost is less than marginal revenue. If the firm increased production by 1 unit, the additional revenue would exceed the additional costs, and profit would rise. Thus, when marginal cost is less than marginal revenue, the firm can increase profit by producing more units.

A similar argument applies at high levels of output, such as Q_2. In this case, marginal cost is greater than marginal revenue. If the firm reduced production by 1 unit, the costs saved would exceed the revenue lost. Thus, if marginal cost is greater than marginal revenue, the firm can raise profit by reducing production.

In the end, the firm adjusts its level of production until the quantity reaches Q_{MAX}, at which marginal revenue equals marginal cost. Thus, the monopolist's profit-maximizing quantity of output is determined by the intersection of the marginal revenue curve and the marginal cost curve. In Figure 11.4, this intersection occurs at point A.

Remember that competitive firms choose to produce at the quantity of output at which marginal revenue equals marginal cost. In following this rule for profit maximization, competitive firms and monopolies are alike. But there is also an important difference between these types of firm: the marginal revenue of a competitive firm equals its price, whereas the marginal revenue of a monopoly is less than its price. That is:

$$\text{For a competitive firm: } P = (MR = MC)$$

$$\text{For a monopoly firm: } P > (MR = MC)$$

Assuming profit maximization, the decision to produce at a point where marginal revenue and marginal cost are equal is the same for both types of firm. What differs is the relationship of the price to marginal revenue and marginal cost.

FYI

Why a Monopoly Does Not Have a Supply Curve

You may have noticed that we have analysed the price in a monopoly market using the market demand curve and the firm's cost curves. We have not made any mention of the market supply curve. By contrast, when we analysed prices in competitive markets, the two most important words were always *supply* and *demand*.

What happened to the supply curve? Although monopoly firms make decisions about what quantity to supply, a monopoly does not have a supply curve. A supply curve tells us the quantity that firms choose to supply at any given price. This concept makes sense when we are analysing price-taking competitive firms. But a monopoly firm is a price maker, not a price taker. It is not meaningful to ask what such a firm would produce at any price because the firm sets the price at the same time it chooses the quantity to supply.

Indeed, the monopolist's decision about how much to supply is impossible to separate from the demand curve it faces. The shape of the demand curve determines the shape of the marginal revenue curve, which in turn determines the monopolist's profit-maximizing quantity. In a competitive market, supply decisions can be analysed without knowing the demand curve, but that is not true in a monopoly market. Therefore, we never talk about a monopoly's supply curve.

How does the monopoly find the profit-maximizing price for its product? The demand curve answers this question because the demand curve relates the amount that customers are willing to pay to the quantity sold. Thus, after the monopoly firm chooses the quantity of output that equates marginal revenue and marginal cost, it uses the demand curve to find the price consistent with that quantity. In Figure 11.4, the profit-maximizing price is found at point B.

We can now see a key difference between markets with competitive firms and markets with a monopoly firm: in competitive markets, price equals marginal cost. In monopolized markets, price exceeds marginal cost. As we will see in a moment, this finding is crucial to understanding the social cost of monopoly.

A Monopoly's Profit

How much profit does the monopoly make? To see the monopoly's profit, recall that the profit equation can be written:

$$\text{Profit} = (P - ATC) \times Q$$

This is the same as the profit equation for competitive firms and allows us to measure the monopolist's profit in our graph.

Consider the shaded box in Figure 11.5. The height of the box (the distance BC) is price minus average total cost, $P - ATC$, which is the profit on the typical unit sold.

The width of the box (the distance DC) is the quantity sold Q_{MAX}. Therefore, the area of this box is the monopoly firm's total profit.

FIGURE 11.5

The Monopolist's Profit

The area of the box BCDE equals the profit of the monopoly firm. The height of the box (BC) is price minus average total cost, which equals profit per unit sold. The width of the box (DC) is the number of units sold.

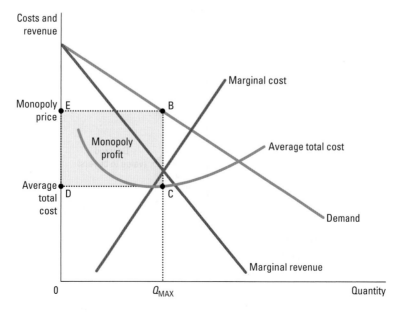

THE WELFARE COST OF MONOPOLY

Is monopoly a good way to organize a market? We have seen that a monopoly, in contrast to a competitive firm, charges a price above marginal cost. From the standpoint of consumers, this high price makes monopoly undesirable. At the same time, however, the monopoly is earning profit from charging this high price. From the standpoint of the owners of the firm, the high price makes monopoly very desirable. Is it possible that the benefits to the firm's owners exceed the costs imposed on consumers, making monopoly desirable from the standpoint of society as a whole?

We can answer this question using the concepts of consumer and producer surplus as our measure of economic well-being. Total surplus is the sum of consumer surplus and producer surplus. Consumer surplus is consumers' willingness to pay for a good minus the amount they actually pay for it. Producer surplus is the amount producers receive for a good minus their costs of producing it. In this case, there is a single producer – the monopolist.

The Deadweight Loss

We begin by considering what the monopoly firm would do if it were run not only for the profit earned by the firm's owners but also for the benefits received by the firm's consumers. The monopoly owners try to maximize total surplus, which equals producer surplus (profit) plus consumer surplus. Keep in mind that total surplus equals the value of the good to consumers minus the costs of making the good incurred by the monopoly producer.

Figure 11.6 analyses what level of output the monopoly owners would choose.

FIGURE 11.6

The Efficient Level of Output

A monopoly owner who wanted to maximize total surplus in the market would choose the level of output where the demand curve and marginal cost curve intersect. Below this level, the value of the good to the marginal buyer (as reflected in the demand curve) exceeds the marginal cost of making the good. Above this level, the value to the marginal buyer is less than marginal cost.

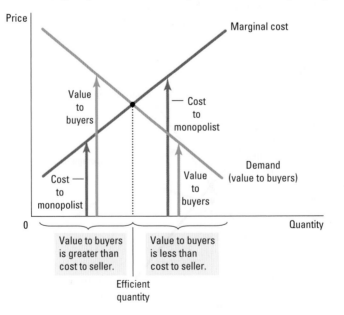

The demand curve reflects the value of the good to consumers, as measured by their willingness to pay for it. The marginal cost curve reflects the costs of the monopolist. Thus, the socially efficient quantity is found where the demand curve and the marginal cost curve intersect. Below this quantity, the value to consumers exceeds the marginal cost of providing the good, so increasing output would raise total surplus. Above this quantity, the marginal cost exceeds the value to consumers, so decreasing output would raise total surplus.

The monopoly owner could achieve this efficient outcome by charging the price found at the intersection of the demand and marginal cost curves. Thus, like a competitive firm and unlike a profit maximizing monopoly, a monopoly owner would charge a price equal to marginal cost. Because this price would give consumers an accurate signal about the cost of producing the good, consumers would buy the efficient quantity.

We can evaluate the welfare effects of monopoly by comparing the level of output that the monopolist chooses where the aim is to maximize profit to the level of output that a monopoly owner would choose if its aim was to maximize total surplus in the market. As we have seen, the profit maximizing monopolist chooses to produce and sell the quantity of output at which the marginal revenue and marginal cost curves intersect as opposed to the quantity at which the demand and marginal cost curves intersect which an owner would choose if maximizing total surplus. Figure 11.7 shows the comparison. The profit maximizing monopolist produces less than the socially efficient quantity of output.

FIGURE 11.7

The Inefficiency of Monopoly

Because a profit maximizing monopoly charges a price above marginal cost, not all consumers who value the good at more than its cost buy it. Thus, the quantity produced and sold by this monopoly producer is below the socially efficient level. The deadweight loss is represented by the area of the triangle between the demand curve (which reflects the value of the good to consumers) and the marginal cost curve (which reflects the costs of the monopoly producer).

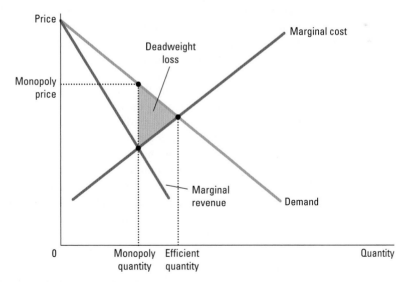

We can also view the inefficiency of monopoly in terms of the monopolist's price. Because the market demand curve describes a negative relationship between the price and quantity of the good, a quantity that is inefficiently low is equivalent to a price that is inefficiently high. When a monopolist charges a price above marginal cost, some potential consumers value the good at more than its marginal cost but less than the monopolist's price. These consumers do not end up buying the good. Because the value these consumers place on the good is greater than the cost of providing it to them, this result is inefficient. Thus, monopoly pricing prevents some mutually beneficial trades from taking place.

The inefficiency of monopoly can be measured in Figure 11.7 which shows the deadweight loss. Recall that the demand curve reflects the value to consumers and the marginal cost curve reflects the costs to the monopoly producer. Thus, the area of the deadweight loss triangle between the demand curve and the marginal cost curve equals the total surplus lost because of monopoly pricing.

The deadweight loss is caused because a monopoly exerts its market power by charging a price above marginal cost, creating a wedge. The wedge causes the quantity sold to fall short of the social optimum. In this situation a private firm gets the monopoly profit.

JEOPARDY PROBLEM

How might a situation arise through which a government granting monopoly rights to a TV company to provide national TV broadcasting of certain sporting events leads to an overall increase in welfare in society?

The Monopoly's Profit: A Social Cost?

It is tempting to decry monopolies for 'profiteering' at the expense of the public. And, indeed, a monopoly firm does earn a higher profit by virtue of its market power. According to the economic analysis of monopoly, however, the firm's profit is not in itself necessarily a problem for society.

Welfare in a monopolized market, like all markets, includes the welfare of both consumers and producers. Whenever a consumer pays an extra euro to a producer because of a monopoly price, the consumer is worse off by a euro, and the producer is better off by the same amount. This transfer from the consumers of the good to the owners of the monopoly does not affect the market's total surplus – the sum of consumer and producer surplus. In other words, the monopoly profit itself does not represent a shrinkage in the size of the economic pie; it merely represents a bigger slice for producers and a smaller slice for consumers. Unless consumers are for some reason more deserving than producers – a judgement that goes beyond the realm of economic efficiency – the monopoly profit is not a social problem.

The problem in a monopolized market arises because the firm produces and sells a quantity of output below the level that maximizes total surplus. The deadweight loss measures how much the economic pie shrinks as a result. This inefficiency is connected to the monopoly's high price: consumers buy fewer units when the firm raises its price above marginal cost. But keep in mind that the profit earned on the units that continue to be sold is not the problem. The problem stems from the inefficiently low quantity of output. Put differently, if the high monopoly price did not discourage some consumers from buying the good, it would raise producer surplus by exactly the amount it reduced consumer surplus, leaving total surplus the same as could be achieved by a monopoly owner aiming to maximize total surplus.

There is, however, a possible exception to this conclusion. Suppose that a monopoly firm has to incur additional costs to maintain its monopoly position. For example, a firm with a government-created monopoly might need to hire lobbyists to convince lawmakers to continue its monopoly. In this case, the monopoly may use up some of its monopoly profits paying for these additional costs. If so, the social loss from monopoly includes both these costs and the deadweight loss resulting from a price above marginal cost.

Quick Quiz How does a monopolist's quantity of output compare to the quantity of output that maximizes total surplus?

? **what if . . .** a monopolist did not have a primary goal of maximizing profit (i.e. where the aim was based on profit satisficing). What would determine the size of the welfare loss?

CASE STUDY

Short-Term Monopoly Drugs

Pharmaceutical companies are in direct competition with each other, but this competition is distorted by the use of patents. These patents encourage the pharmaceutical companies to invest heavily in researching and developing new treatments. Up to €3 billion can go into developing and trialling new drugs, and it is high risk because the treatment may never reach the market. The patent protects a pharmaceutical company from other companies copying its treatments for a number of years, typically 20 years. Without the patent, there would be much less incentive to innovate into new products because the companies would not be able to recoup the research and development costs.

- Patents help create a short-term monopoly for a particular drug. The company is able to set its own prices and earn a monopoly profit. It sets prices to maximize profits and not just to cover production and research costs. Clearly, a significant part of the profit is used to fund future drug research, but these companies are in business to make money for shareholders and there is an argument that the companies exploit the patent system fully to maximize shareholder returns.
- Evidence of large profits can be seen in the price drop once a drug loses its patent. The entry of generic drugs brings back competition and as a result the price falls since the companies producing the generic drugs do not bear the research and development cost and the market decides on the price levels, not the company.
- A pharmaceutical company nearing the end of a patent will not want to lose its monopoly position and will look for ways that it can keep prices

above the market level. It could invest in heavily branding the drug prior to the patent ending in order to differentiate it from generic forms. For example, Nurofen is branded ibuprofen and commands a price several times that of its generic form. Another strategy is to pay other pharmaceutical companies to delay producing a generic product. AstraZeneca made a deal with three big generic manufacturers that helped to protect Nexium from competition between 2008 and May 2014.

- Such pay-for-delay deals mean additional costs for consumers including the National Health Service in the UK. These types of deals seem to be beyond the initial purpose of having patents and can be the target of competition laws, especially since governments have had a hand in the creation of the monopoly in the first place.

- Pharmaceutical companies with protected products use variable pricing or price discrimination by selling products at discount to poorer countries. This allows the companies to capture consumer surplus and generate even more sales. It also satisfies critics who think such companies overcharge those who cannot afford to pay. To be successful, the companies need to be sure that drugs sold cheaply in poorer countries don't find a way back to the richer nations.

References: **http://www.economist.com/news/finance-and-economics/21604575-drug -companies-are-adept-extending-lifespan-patents-consumers**

http://www.forbes.com/sites/peterubel/2013/12/12/whats-fair-about-price-discrimination -in-pharmaceutical-markets/

http://www.theguardian.com/commentisfree/2013/feb/22/hiv-aids-deaths -pharmaceutical-industry

PRICE DISCRIMINATION

So far we have been assuming that the monopoly firm charges the same price to all customers. Yet in many cases firms try to sell the same good to different customers for different prices, even though the costs of producing for the two customers are the same. This practice is called **price discrimination**.

price discrimination the business practice of selling the same good at different prices to different customers

Before discussing the behaviour of a price-discriminating monopolist, we should note that price discrimination is not possible when a good is sold in a competitive market. In a competitive market, there are many firms selling the same good at the market price. No firm is willing to charge a lower price to any customer because the firm can sell all it wants at the market price. And if any firm tried to charge a higher price to a customer, that customer would buy from another firm. For a firm to price discriminate, it must have some market power.

A Parable About Pricing

To understand why a monopolist would want to price discriminate, let's consider a simple example. Imagine that you are the chief executive officer of Readalot Publishing Company. Readalot's best-selling author has just written her latest novel. To keep things simple, let's imagine that you pay the author a flat €2 million for the exclusive rights to publish the book. Let's also assume – for simplicity – that the cost of printing the book is zero. Readalot's profit, therefore, is the revenue it gets from selling the book minus the €2 million it has paid to the author. Given these assumptions, how would you, as Readalot's CEO, decide what price to charge for the book?

Your first step in setting the price is to estimate what the demand for the book is likely to be. Readalot's marketing department tells you that the book will attract two types of readers. The book will appeal to the author's 100 000 diehard fans. These fans will be willing to pay as much as €30 for the book. In addition, the book will appeal to about 400 000 less enthusiastic readers who will be willing to pay up to €5 for the book.

What price maximizes Readalot's profit? There are two natural prices to consider: €30 is the highest price Readalot can charge and still get the 100 000 diehard fans, and €5 is the highest price it can charge and still get the entire market of 500 000 potential readers. At a price of €30, Readalot can sell 100 000 copies, has revenue of €3 million, and makes profit of €1 million. At a price of €5, it sells 500 000 copies, has revenue of €2.5 million, and makes profit of €500 000. Thus, Readalot maximizes profit by charging €30 and forgoing the opportunity to sell to the 400 000 less enthusiastic readers.

Notice that Readalot's decision causes a deadweight loss. There are 400 000 readers willing to pay €5 for the book, and the marginal cost of providing it to them is zero. Thus, €2 million of total surplus is lost when Readalot charges the higher price. This deadweight loss is the usual inefficiency that arises whenever a monopolist charges a price above marginal cost.

Now suppose that Readalot's marketing department makes an important discovery: these two groups of readers are in separate markets. All the diehard fans live in Switzerland and all the other readers live in Turkey. Moreover, it is difficult for readers in one country to buy books in the other. How does this discovery affect Readalot's marketing strategy?

In this case, the company can make even more profit. To the 100 000 Swiss readers, it can charge €30 for the book. To the 400 000 Turkish readers, it can charge €5 for the book (or the Turkish lira equivalent). In this case, revenue is €3 million in Switzerland and €2 million in Turkey, for a total of €5 million. Profit is then €3 million, which is substantially greater than the €1 million the company could earn charging the same €30 price to all customers. Not surprisingly, Readalot chooses to follow this strategy of price discrimination.

Although the story of Readalot Publishing is hypothetical, it describes accurately the business practice of many publishing companies. New novels are often initially released as an expensive hardcover edition and later released in a cheaper paperback edition. The difference in price between these two editions far exceeds the difference in printing costs. The publisher's goal is just as in our example. By selling the hardcover to diehard fans (and libraries) who must have the book as soon as it is published and the paperback to less enthusiastic readers who don't mind waiting, the publisher price discriminates and raises its profit.

? **what if ...** the price elasticity of demand does not vary widely between different markets – would a monopolist still be able to practise price discrimination?

The Moral of the Story

The story of Readalot Publishing provides three lessons about price discrimination. The first is that price discrimination is a rational strategy for a profit-maximizing monopolist. In other words, by charging different prices to different customers, a monopolist can increase its profit. In essence, a price-discriminating monopolist charges each customer a price closer to his or her willingness to pay than is possible with a single price.

The second lesson is that price discrimination requires the ability to separate customers according to their willingness to pay. In our example, customers were separated geographically. But sometimes monopolists choose other differences, such as age or income, to distinguish among customers. Energy companies are able to discriminate through setting different prices at different times of the day with off-peak usage priced lower than peak time. Similarly, rail companies charge different prices to passengers at certain times of the day with peak travel attracting a much higher price than off-peak travel. Where there is a difference in the price elasticity of demand the monopolist can exploit this and practise price discrimination. Between the hours of 6.00AM and 9.30AM on weekday mornings, for example, the price elasticity of demand for rail travel is relatively low, whereas between 9.30AM and 4.00PM it tends to be relatively high. A higher price can be charged at the peak time but during the off-peak period, the firm may benefit from charging a lower price and encouraging more passengers to travel; the cost of running the train is largely fixed and the marginal cost of carrying an additional passenger is almost zero. Lowering the price, therefore, is a way of utilizing the capacity on the train and adding to profit.

A corollary to this second lesson is that certain market forces can prevent firms from price discriminating. In particular, one such force is *arbitrage*, the process of buying a good in one market at a low price and selling it in another market at a higher price in order to profit from the price difference. In our example, suppose that Swiss bookshops could buy the book in Turkey for €5 and resell it to Swiss readers at a price well below €30. This arbitrage would prevent Readalot from price discriminating because no Swiss resident would buy the book at the higher price. In fact, the increased use of the Internet for buying books and other goods through companies like Amazon and eBay is likely to affect the ability of companies to price discriminate internationally. Where firms can enforce the division of the market, as in the case of rail fares, they can practise price discrimination. A passenger buying a ticket at off-peak rates is not allowed to travel on a train running during peak periods, and hence arbitrage is circumvented.

The third lesson from our parable is that price discrimination can raise economic welfare. Recall that a deadweight loss arises when Readalot charges a single €30 price, because the 400 000 less enthusiastic readers do not end up with the book, even though they value it at more than its marginal cost of production. By contrast, when Readalot price discriminates, all readers end up with the book, and the outcome is efficient. Thus, price discrimination can eliminate the inefficiency inherent in monopoly pricing.

Note that the increase in welfare from price discrimination shows up as higher producer surplus rather than higher consumer surplus. In our example, consumers are no better off for having bought the book: the price they pay exactly equals the value they place on the book, so they receive no consumer surplus. The entire increase in total surplus from price discrimination accrues to Readalot Publishing in the form of higher profit.

The Analytics of Price Discrimination

Let us consider a little more formally how price discrimination affects economic welfare. We begin by assuming that the monopolist can price discriminate perfectly. *Perfect price discrimination* describes a situation in which the monopolist knows exactly the willingness to pay of each customer and can charge each customer a different price. In this case, the monopolist charges each customer exactly his willingness to pay, and the monopolist gets the entire surplus in every transaction.

Welfare With and Without Price Discrimination

Panel (a) shows a monopolist that charges the same price to all customers. Total surplus in this market equals the sum of profit (producer surplus) and consumer surplus. Panel (b) shows a monopolist that can perfectly price discriminate. Because consumer surplus equals zero, total surplus now equals the firm's profit. Comparing these two panels, you can see that perfect price discrimination raises profit, raises total surplus and lowers consumer surplus.

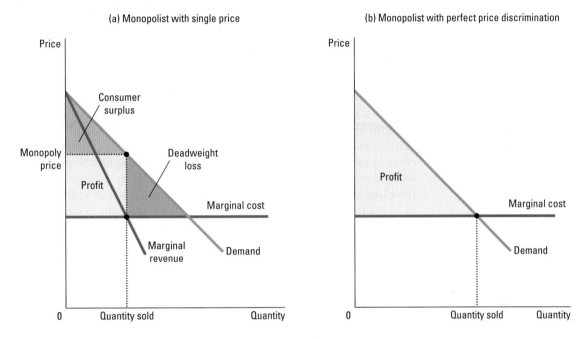

Figure 11.8 shows producer and consumer surplus with and without price discrimination. Without price discrimination, the firm charges a single price above marginal cost, as shown in panel (a). Because some potential customers who value the good at more than marginal cost do not buy it at this high price, the monopoly causes a deadweight loss. Yet when a firm can perfectly price discriminate, as shown in panel (b), each customer who values the good at more than marginal cost buys the good and is charged his willingness to pay. All mutually beneficial trades take place, there is no deadweight loss, and the entire surplus derived from the market goes to the monopoly producer in the form of profit.

In reality, of course, price discrimination is not perfect. Customers do not walk into shops with signs displaying their willingness to pay. Instead, firms price discriminate by dividing customers into groups: young versus old, weekday versus weekend shoppers, Germans versus British, and so on. Unlike those in our parable of Readalot Publishing, customers within each group differ in their willingness to pay for the product, making perfect price discrimination impossible.

How does this imperfect price discrimination affect welfare? The analysis of these pricing schemes is quite complicated, and it turns out that there is no general answer to this question. Compared to the monopoly outcome with a single price, imperfect price discrimination can raise, lower or leave unchanged total surplus in a market. The only certain conclusion is that price discrimination raises the monopoly's profit – otherwise the firm would choose to charge all customers the same price.

Examples of Price Discrimination

Firms use various business strategies aimed at charging different prices to different customers. Now that we understand the economics of price discrimination, let's consider some examples.

Cinema Tickets Many cinemas charge a lower price for children and senior citizens than for other patrons. This fact is hard to explain in a competitive market. In a competitive market, price equals marginal cost, and the marginal cost of providing a seat for a child or senior citizen is the same as the marginal cost of providing a seat for anyone else. Yet this fact is easily explained if cinemas have some local monopoly power and if children and senior citizens have a lower willingness to pay for a ticket. In this case, cinemas raise their profit by price discriminating.

Airline Prices Seats on aeroplanes are sold at many different prices. Most airlines charge a lower price for a round-trip ticket between two cities if the traveller stays over a Saturday night. At first this seems odd. Why should it matter to the airline whether a passenger stays over a Saturday night? The reason is that this rule provides a way to separate business travellers and personal travellers. A passenger on a business trip has a high willingness to pay and, most likely, does not want to stay over a Saturday night. By contrast, a passenger travelling for personal reasons has a lower willingness to pay and is more likely to be willing to stay over a Saturday night. Thus, the airlines can successfully price discriminate by charging a lower price for passengers who stay over a Saturday night.

Discount Coupons Many companies offer discount coupons to the public in newspapers and magazines. A buyer simply has to cut out the coupon in order to get €0.50 off their next purchase. Why do companies offer these coupons? Why don't they just cut the price of the product by €0.50?

The answer is that coupons allow companies to price discriminate. Companies know that not all customers are willing to spend the time to cut out coupons. Moreover, the willingness to clip coupons is related to the customer's willingness to pay for the good. A rich and busy executive is unlikely to spend her time cutting discount coupons out of a magazine, and they are probably willing to pay a higher price for many goods. A person who is unemployed is more likely to clip coupons and has a lower willingness to pay. Thus, by charging a lower price only to those customers who cut out coupons, firms can successfully price discriminate.

Quantity Discounts So far in our examples of price discrimination the monopolist charges different prices to different customers. Sometimes, however, monopolists price discriminate by charging different prices to the same customer for different units that the customer buys. Traditionally, English bakers would give you an extra cake for nothing if you bought 12. While the quaint custom of the 'baker's dozen' (i.e. 13 for the price of 12) is largely a thing of the past, many firms offer lower prices to customers who buy large quantities. This is a form of price discrimination because the customer effectively pays a higher price for the first unit bought than for the last. Quantity discounts are often a successful way of price discriminating because a customer's willingness to pay for an additional unit declines as the customer buys more units.

PUBLIC POLICY TOWARDS MONOPOLIES

We have seen that monopolies, in contrast to competitive markets, fail to allocate resources efficiently. Monopolies produce less than the socially desirable quantity of output and, as a result, charge prices above marginal cost. Policy makers in the government can respond to the problem of monopoly in one of four ways, by:

- trying to make monopolized industries more competitive
- regulating the behaviour of the monopolies
- turning some private monopolies into public enterprises
- doing nothing at all.

All industrialized countries have some sort of process for legally prohibiting mergers that are against the public interest.

The earliest moves towards using legal remedies to monopoly power were taken in the US in the late 19th and early 20th centuries, forming the basis of legislation that has become known in the USA as the anti-trust laws (in the UK and the rest of Europe, anti-trust law and anti-trust policy are more commonly referred to as competition law and competition policy, although usage of both terms is becoming widespread). These laws cover proposed mergers between two companies which already have substantial market share and are closely examined by the authorities, who might well decide that the merger would make the industry in question substantially less competitive and, as a result, would reduce the economic well-being of the country or region as a whole.

In Europe, each country has a competition authority. In the UK it is the Competition and Markets Authority (CMA); in Germany it is the Federal Cartel Office (*Bundeskartellamt*); in 2009 the French Competition Authority (*Autorité de la Concurrence*) began discharging its regulatory powers following reform of competition regulation; and in Italy the Anti-trust Authority (*Autorità Garante della Concorrenza e del Mercato*) oversees competition issues. National competition authorities such as these cooperate with each other and with the EU Competition Commission through the European Competition Network (ECN). The aim of the network is to coordinate activities and share information to help enforce EU competition law in member states where the opportunities for cross-border business have increased as the EU has developed and expanded.

While each national country can enforce its own competition legislation, these laws have to be in line with overall EU competition legislation. In the UK, for example, the Competition Act 1998 and the Enterprise Act 2002 both deal with competition issues within the UK but cross-border competition cases would be dealt with under EU law. There are well-defined criteria for deciding whether a proposed merger of companies belonging to more than one European Union country is subject to reference exclusively to the European Commission rather than to national authorities, such as the size of the worldwide or European turnover of the companies in question.

Competition legislation covers three main areas:

- Acting against cartels and cases where businesses engage in restrictive business practices which prevent free trade.
- Banning pricing strategies which are anti-competitive such as price fixing, predatory pricing, price gouging and so on, and through behaviour which might lead to a restriction in competition such as the sharing of information or carving up markets between different firms, rigging bids in tender processes or deliberately restricting production to reduce competition.
- Monitoring and supervising acquisitions and joint ventures.

The legislation allows competition authorities the right to fine firms who are found guilty of restricting competition, ordering firms to change behaviour and banning proposed acquisitions. The investigation will consider whether the acquisition, regardless of what size company it produces, is in the public interest. This is in recognition of the fact that companies sometimes merge not to reduce competition but to lower costs through more efficient joint production. These benefits from mergers are referred to as *synergies*.

Clearly, the government must be able to determine which mergers are desirable and which are not. That is, it must be able to measure and compare the social benefit from synergies to the social costs of reduced competition.

Regulation

Another way in which the government deals with the problem of monopoly is by regulating the behaviour of monopolists. This solution is common in the case of natural monopolies, for instance utility companies like water, gas and electricity companies. These companies are not allowed to charge any price they want. Instead, government agencies regulate their prices.

What price should the government set for a natural monopoly? This question is not as easy as it might at first appear. One might conclude that the price should equal the monopolist's marginal cost. If price equals marginal cost, customers will buy the quantity of the monopolist's output that maximizes total surplus, and the allocation of resources will be efficient.

FIGURE 11.9

Marginal Cost Pricing for a Natural Monopoly

Because a natural monopoly has declining average total cost, marginal cost is less than average total cost. Therefore, if regulators require a natural monopoly to charge a price equal to marginal cost, price will be below average total cost, and the monopoly will lose money.

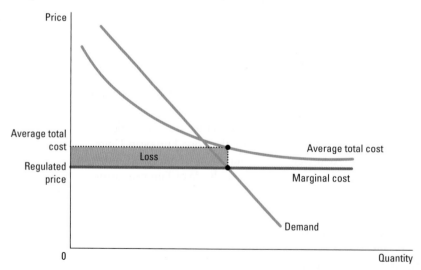

There are, however, two practical problems with marginal-cost pricing as a regulatory system. The first is illustrated in Figure 11.9. Natural monopolies, by definition, have declining average total cost. When average total cost is declining, marginal cost is less than average total cost. If regulators are to set price equal to marginal cost, that price will be less than the firm's average total cost, and the firm will lose money. Instead of charging such a low price, the monopoly firm would just exit the industry.

Regulators can respond to this problem in various ways, none of which is perfect. One way is to subsidize the monopolist. In essence, the government picks up the losses inherent in marginal-cost pricing. Yet to pay for the subsidy, the government needs to raise money through taxation, which involves its own deadweight losses. Alternatively, the regulators can allow the monopolist to charge a price higher than marginal cost. If the regulated price equals average total cost, the monopolist earns exactly zero economic profit. Yet average-cost pricing leads to deadweight losses, because the monopolist's price no longer reflects the marginal cost of producing the good. In essence, average-cost pricing is like a tax on the good the monopolist is selling.

The second problem with marginal-cost pricing as a regulatory system (and with average-cost pricing as well) is that it gives the monopolist no incentive to reduce costs. Each firm in a competitive market tries to reduce its costs because lower costs mean higher profits. But if a regulated monopolist knows that regulators will reduce prices whenever costs fall, the monopolist will not benefit from lower costs. In practice, regulators deal with this problem by allowing monopolists to keep some of the benefits from lower costs in the form of higher profit, a practice that requires some departure from marginal-cost pricing.

For example, in the UK, utility companies have often been subject to price caps whereby the regulator determines that the real price of the company's product – a kilowatt hour of electricity, for example – should fall by a given number of percentage points each year, reflecting productivity rises. Say, for example, this is 2 per cent. The company would then be allowed to raise its prices each year by the inflation rate *minus* 2 per cent. If the company increases its productivity by, say 4 per cent each year, however (in other words it can produce the same amount of output with 4 per cent fewer inputs), then in real terms its profits will go up each year. In this way, the system of price caps aims to give natural monopolies the motivation to improve efficiency and productivity that would be supplied by the invisible hand in a competitive market.

Public Ownership

The third policy used by the government to deal with monopoly is public ownership. That is, rather than regulating a natural monopoly that is run by a private firm, the government can run the monopoly itself. An industry owned by the government is called a nationalized industry. This solution is common in many European countries, where the government owns and operates utilities such as the telephone, water and electric companies.

Whether private or public ownership of natural monopolies is preferable will be dependent on how the ownership of the firm affects the costs of production. Private owners have an incentive to minimize costs as long as they reap part of the benefit in the form of higher profit. If the firm's managers are doing a bad job of keeping costs down, the firm's owners will fire them. By contrast, if the government bureaucrats who run a monopoly do a bad job, the losers are the customers and taxpayers, whose only recourse is the political system. The bureaucrats may become a special interest group and attempt to block cost reducing reforms. If you believe that the voting booth is a less reliable way of ensuring firms are well run when compared to the profit motive, then this may determine whether you prefer to see private or publicly owned natural monopolies.

Doing Nothing

Each of the foregoing policies aimed at reducing the problem of monopoly has drawbacks. As a result, some economists argue that it is often best for the government not to try to remedy the inefficiencies of monopoly pricing. Here is the assessment of economist George Stigler, who won the Nobel Prize for his work in industrial organization, writing in the *Fortune Encyclopedia of Economics*:

> *A famous theorem in economics states that a competitive enterprise economy will produce the largest possible income from a given stock of resources. No real economy meets the exact conditions of the theorem, and all real economies will fall short of the ideal economy – a difference called 'market failure'. In my view, however, the degree of 'market failure' for the American economy is much smaller than the 'political failure' arising from the imperfections of economic policies found in real political systems.*

As this quotation makes clear, determining the proper role of the government in the economy requires judgements about politics as well as economics.

Quick Quiz Describe the ways policy makers can respond to the inefficiencies caused by monopolies. List a potential problem with each of these policy responses.

CONCLUSION: THE PREVALENCE OF MONOPOLY

This chapter has discussed the behaviour of firms that have control over the prices they charge. We have seen that these firms behave very differently from the competitive firms studied in the previous chapter. Table 11.2 summarizes some of the key similarities and differences between competitive and monopoly markets.

TABLE 11.2

Competition Versus Monopoly: A Summary Comparison

	Competition	Monopoly
Similarities		
Goal of firms	Maximize profits	Maximize profits
Rule for maximizing	$MR = MC$	$MR = MC$
Can earn economic profits in the short run?	Yes	Yes
Differences		
Number of firms	Many	One
Marginal revenue	$MR = P$	$MR < P$
Price	$P = MC$	$P > MC$
Produces welfare-maximizing level of output?	Yes	No
Entry in long run?	Yes	No
Can earn economic profits in long run?	No	Yes
Price discrimination possible?	No	Yes

From the standpoint of public policy, a crucial result is that monopolists produce less than the socially efficient quantity and charge prices above marginal cost. As a result, they cause deadweight losses. In some cases, these inefficiencies can be mitigated through price discrimination by the monopolist, but at other times they call for policy makers to take an active role.

How prevalent are the problems of monopoly? There are two answers to this question.

In one sense, monopolies are common. Most firms have some control over the prices they charge. They are not forced to charge the market price for their goods, because their goods are not exactly the same as those offered by other firms. A Honda Accord is not the same as a Volkswagen Passat. Ben and Jerry's ice cream is not the same as Wall's. Each of these goods has a downward sloping demand curve, which gives each producer some degree of monopoly power.

Yet firms with substantial monopoly power are quite rare. Few goods are truly unique. Most have substitutes that, even if not exactly the same are very similar. Ben and Jerry's can raise the price of its ice cream a little without losing all its sales; but if it raises it very much, sales will fall substantially.

In the end, monopoly power is a matter of degree. It is true that many firms have some monopoly power. It is also true that their monopoly power is usually limited. In these cases, we will not go far wrong assuming that firms operate in competitive markets, even if that is not precisely the case.

IN THE NEWS

Should Google be More Regulated or Just Told it is Too Big?

The most dominant search engine in Europe is Google making it a real monopoly, but the threat of abuse of monopoly power doesn't come from pricing end users as the service is not paid for by the user. Its market power lies elsewhere.

Just log into the Internet on a personal computer and what is the most likely search engine to come up? Google. The company would argue that it is a great search engine and that is why people use it. It has 68 per cent of the market of Web searches in the USA and over 90 per cent in many European countries. Because it is such a popular service, it attracts more users and collects more data than other search engines, so it is better able to find the things searchers want. This makes it even more dominant giving it a monopoly status in the market.

But does it abuse its dominance? One worry about monopolies is that they create barriers to entry, preventing competition; so just how effective is Google at preventing competition? Google is a technology monopoly. Other technology monopolies have been dominant in the past but their dominance does not last forever because technology companies fail to quickly adapt with the times while other technology companies come up with something new and exciting. The market can change very quickly with the addition of new rivals and new technologies. One such threat for Google is the growth in the use of Smartphones, with users more dependent on apps than the Web.

Another way a monopoly can exert its power is through monopoly pricing, although the consumer does not have to pay a price to browse through Google, but Google has to generate income and profit and does so through advertisers. Advertisers pay for clicks onto their sites. They may feel there really isn't much alternative to Google as it is the dominant search engine. In this way Google has become a monopoly to those advertising on the net.

Like all other search engines, Google is a gatekeeper of information by directing users to websites. One concern expressed by critics of Google's monopoly power is over neutrality because Google has entwined its own products within search results. There is the potential for Google to prioritize its own sites rather than its rivals, so pushing other websites down the ranking. It means customers using Google may not visit the most appropriate websites from their searches. It also damages rivals

and non-rivals and their advertising revenue or sales. Some also claim that Google has the power to determine the terms in business areas that Google doesn't even compete in. For example, Google doesn't run dating sites, but sets rules through which they advertise against each other. The lack of neutrality distorts markets outside of the search industry. Another potential abuse is the misuse of personal information especially about privacy.

The European Union (EU) is worried about aspects of Google's dominance and in November 2014, its parliament voted in favour of breaking up Google's monopoly in Europe in an attempt to reduce its power and the concerns outlined above.

Questions

1. What is the source of monopoly power for Google?

2. **What types of barriers to entry are most relevant to potential competitors wishing to enter the search engine market?**

3. **Examine possible reasons why the EU parliament might want to break up Google.**

4. **What methods are open to governments and regulatory authorities to ensure there is less abuse of monopoly power?**

5. **How might technological developments lead to a reduction in Google's influence?**

References: http://money.cnn.com/2015/03/19/technology/google-monopoly-ftc/

http://www.economist.com/news/leaders/21635000-european-moves-against-google-are-about-protecting-companies-not-consumers-should-digital

http://uk.businessinsider.com/google-monopoly-and-antitrust-law-2014-11?r=US

http://www.nytimes.com/2009/12/28/opinion/28raff.html?_r=0

SUMMARY

- Imperfect competition is where the assumptions of perfect competition are dropped and firms have some degree of market power.

- Having market power means firms' behaviour may be different to that which operates under competitive conditions.

- At the extreme of imperfect competition is monopoly.

- A monopoly is a firm that is the sole seller in its market. A monopoly arises when a single firm owns a key resource, when the government gives a firm the exclusive right to produce a good, or when a single firm can supply the entire market at a smaller cost than many firms could.

- Because a monopoly is the sole producer in its market, it faces a downward sloping demand curve for its product. When a monopoly increases production by 1 unit,

it causes the price of its good to fall, which reduces the amount of revenue earned on all units produced. As a result, a monopoly's marginal revenue is always below the price of its good.

- Like a competitive firm, a monopoly firm maximizes profit by producing the quantity at which marginal revenue equals marginal cost. The monopoly then chooses the price at which that quantity is demanded. Unlike a competitive firm, a monopoly firm's price exceeds its marginal revenue, so its price exceeds marginal cost.

- A monopolist's profit-maximizing level of output is below the level that maximizes the sum of consumer and producer surplus. That is, when the monopoly charges a price above marginal cost, some consumers who value the good more than its cost of production do not buy it. As a result, monopoly causes deadweight losses.

- Policy makers can respond to the inefficiency of monopoly behaviour in four ways. They can use competition law to try to make the industry more competitive. They can regulate the prices that the monopoly charges. They can turn the monopolist into a government-run enterprise. Or, if the market failure is deemed small compared to the inevitable imperfections of policies, they can do nothing at all.

- Monopolists often can raise their profits by charging different prices for the same good based on a buyer's willingness to pay. This practice of price discrimination can raise economic welfare by getting the good to some consumers who otherwise would not buy it. In the extreme case of perfect price discrimination, the deadweight losses of monopoly are completely eliminated. More generally, when price discrimination is imperfect, it can either raise or lower welfare compared to the outcome with a single monopoly price.

QUESTIONS FOR REVIEW

1. Explain the difference between a perfectly competitive market and an imperfectly competitive market.

2. Do firms which operate in a market where there is a dominant firm not face competition? Explain.

3. Give an example of a government-created monopoly. Is creating this monopoly necessarily bad public policy? Explain.

4. Define natural monopoly. What does the size of a market have to do with whether an industry is a natural monopoly?

5. Why is a monopolist's marginal revenue less than the price of its good? Can marginal revenue ever be negative? Explain.

6. Draw the demand, marginal revenue and marginal cost curves for a monopolist. Show the profit-maximizing level of output. Show the profit-maximizing price.

7. In your diagram from the previous question, show the level of output that maximizes total surplus. Show the deadweight loss from the monopoly. Explain your answer.

8. What gives the government the power to regulate mergers between firms? From the standpoint of the welfare of society, give a good reason and a bad reason that two firms might want to merge.

9. Describe the two problems that arise when regulators tell a natural monopoly that it must set a price equal to marginal cost.

10. Give two examples of price discrimination. In each case, explain why the monopolist chooses to follow this business strategy.

PROBLEMS AND APPLICATIONS

1. A publisher faces the following demand schedule for the next novel of one of its popular authors:

Price (€)	Quantity demanded
100	0
90	100 000
80	200 000
70	300 000
60	400 000
50	500 000
40	600 000
30	700 000
20	800 000
10	900 000
0	1 000 000

The author is paid €2 million to write the book, and the marginal cost of publishing the book is a constant €10 per book.

a. Compute total revenue, total cost and profit at each quantity. What quantity would a profit-maximizing publisher choose? What price would it charge?

b. Compute marginal revenue. (Recall that $MR = \Delta TR/\Delta Q$.) How does marginal revenue compare to the price? Explain.

c. Graph the marginal revenue, marginal cost and demand curves. At what quantity do the marginal revenue and marginal cost curves cross? What does this signify?

d. In your graph, shade in the deadweight loss. Explain in words what this means.

e. If the author was paid €3 million instead of €2 million to write the book, how would this affect the publisher's decision regarding the price to charge? Explain.

f. Suppose the publisher was not profit-maximizing but was concerned with maximizing economic efficiency. What price would it charge for the book? How much profit would it make at this price?

2. Suppose that a natural monopolist was required by law to charge average total cost. On a diagram, label the price charged and the deadweight loss to society relative to marginal-cost pricing.

3. Consider the delivery of mail. In general, what is the shape of the average total cost curve? How might the shape differ between isolated rural areas and densely populated urban areas? How might the shape have changed over time? Explain.

4. Suppose the Eau de Jeunesse Water Company has a monopoly on bottled water sales in France. If the price of tap water increases, what is the change in Eau de Jeunesse's profit-maximizing levels of output, price and profit? Explain in words and with a graph.

5. The Wise Economists, a top rock band, have just finished recording their latest music album. Their record company's marketing department determines that the demand for downloads for the album is as follows:

Price (€)	Number of downloads
24	10 000
22	20 000
20	30 000
18	40 000
16	50 000
14	60 000

The company can produce the album with no fixed cost and a variable cost of €5 per download:

a. Find total revenue for quantity equal to 10 000, 20 000 and so on. What is the marginal revenue for each 10 000 increase in the quantity sold?

b. What quantity of downloads would maximize profit? What would the price be? What would the profit be?

c. If you were The Wise Economists agent, what recording fee would you advise them to demand from the record company? Why?

6. A company is considering building a bridge across a river. The bridge would cost €2 million to build and nothing to maintain. The following table shows the company's anticipated demand over the lifetime of the bridge:

Price per crossing (€)	Number of crossings (000s)
8	0
7	100
6	200
5	300
4	400
3	500
2	600
1	700
0	800

a. If the company were to build the bridge, what would be its profit-maximizing price? Would that be the efficient level of output? Why or why not?

b. If the company is interested in maximizing profit, should it build the bridge? What would be its profit or loss?

c. If the government were to build the bridge, what price should it charge for passengers and vehicles to use the bridge? Explain your answer.

d. Should the government build the bridge? Explain.

7. The Placebo Drug Company holds a patent on one of its discoveries.

a. Assuming that the production of the drug involves rising marginal cost, draw a diagram to illustrate Placebo's profit-maximizing price and quantity. Also show Placebo's profits.

b. Now suppose that the government imposes a tax on each bottle of the drug produced. On a new diagram, illustrate Placebo's new price and quantity. How does each compare to your answer in part (a)?

c. Although it is not easy to see in your diagrams, the tax reduces Placebo's profit. Explain why this must be true.

d. Instead of the tax per bottle, suppose that the government imposes a tax on Placebo of €110 000 regardless of how many bottles are produced. How does this tax affect Placebo's price, quantity and profits? Explain.

8. Pablo, Dirk and Franz run the only bar in town. Pablo wants to sell as many drinks as possible without losing money. Dirk wants the bar to bring in as much revenue as possible. Franz wants to make the largest possible profits. Using a single diagram of the bar's demand curve and its cost curves, show the price and quantity combinations favoured by each of the three partners. Explain.

9. The Best Computer Company just developed a new computer chip, on which it immediately acquires a patent.

a. Draw a diagram that shows the consumer surplus, producer surplus and total surplus in the market for this new chip.

b. What happens to these three measures of surplus if the firm can perfectly price discriminate? What is the change in deadweight loss? What transfers occur?

10. Many schemes for price discriminating involve some cost. For example, discount coupons take up time and resources from both the buyer and the seller. This question considers the implications of costly price discrimination. To keep things simple, let's assume that our monopolist's production costs are simply proportional to output, so that average total cost and marginal cost are constant and equal to each other.

a. Draw the cost, demand and marginal revenue curves for the monopolist. Show the price the monopolist would charge without price discrimination.

b. In your diagram, mark the area equal to the monopolist's profit and call it X. Mark the area equal to consumer surplus and call it Y. Mark the area equal to the deadweight loss and call it Z.

c. Now suppose that the monopolist can perfectly price discriminate. What is the monopolist's profit? (Give your answer in terms of X, Y and Z.)

d. What is the change in the monopolist's profit from price discrimination? What is the change in total surplus from price discrimination? Which change is larger? Explain. (Give your answer in terms of X, Y and Z.)

e. Now suppose that there is some cost of price discrimination. To model this cost, let's assume that the monopolist has to pay a fixed cost C in order to price discriminate. How would a monopolist make the decision whether to pay this fixed cost? (Give your answer in terms of X, Y, Z and C.)

f. How would a monopoly owner, who cares about total surplus, decide whether the monopolist should price discriminate? (Give your answer in terms of X, Y, Z and C.)

g. Compare your answers to parts (e) and (f). How does the monopolist's incentive to price discriminate differ from the monopoly owner interested in maximizing total surplus? Is it possible that the monopolist will price discriminate even though it is not socially desirable?

12 OTHER TYPES OF IMPERFECT COMPETITION

LEARNING OUTCOMES

After reading this chapter you should be able to:

- Show the long-run adjustment that takes place in a monopolistically competitive market when a firm generates economic profits.

- Show why monopolistically competitive firms produce at less-than-efficient scale in the long run.

- Discuss the inefficiencies of monopolistically competitive markets.

- Describe the characteristics of oligopoly and monopolistic competition.

- Describe the conditions under which an oligopolistic market generates the same outcome as a monopolistic market.

- Show why the outcome of the prisoners' dilemma may change if the game is repeated.

- Show why some business practices that appear to reduce competition may have a legitimate business purpose.

INTRODUCTION

In Chapter 11 we looked at an extreme form of imperfect competition – monopoly. We saw how a firm's behaviour might be different to that of a competitive market if it was the only supplier in the market.

In most markets we do not see the extremes described in perfect competition or monopoly, instead there are often many firms competing with each other but some are much larger than others. The competition between firms might be very localized, for example, between a number of restaurants in a typical city centre, be based on differences in price, on differences in the product, the quality of the service provided, or through exploiting human psychology to make it appear there is a difference between competing products or encouraging customer loyalty.

These things and more are all characteristic of imperfect competition. In conditions of imperfect competition, products are not homogenous. There might be many substitutes for a product in the market but in some way or another, the firm tries to make their product different to rivals so that the degree of substitutability is reduced. In differentiating products the firm is able to have some control over the price that they charge. The sellers in this market are price makers rather than price takers and price will be above marginal cost.

Monopolistic Competition

Because these markets have some features of competition and some features of monopoly it is called **monopolistic competition**. Monopolistic competition describes a market with the following attributes:

monopolistic competition
a market structure in which many firms sell products that are similar but not identical

- *Many sellers*. There are many firms competing for the same group of customers with each firm being small compared to the market as a whole.
- *Product differentiation*. Each firm produces a product that is at least slightly different from those of other firms. The firm is able to have some control over the extent to which it can differentiate its product from its rivals, thus reducing the degree of substitutability and garnering an element of customer or brand loyalty. Therefore, rather than being a price taker, each firm faces a downward sloping demand curve.
- *Free entry*. Firms can enter (or exit) the market without restriction. Thus, the number of firms in the market adjusts until economic profits are driven to zero.

Table 12.1 lists examples of the types of market with these attributes.

Competition with Differentiated Products

To understand monopolistically competitive markets, we first consider the decisions facing an individual firm. We then examine what happens in the long run as firms enter and exit the industry. Next, we compare the equilibrium under monopolistic competition to the equilibrium under perfect competition. Finally, we consider whether the outcome in a monopolistically competitive market is desirable from the standpoint of society as a whole.

The Monopolistically Competitive Firm in the Short Run

Each firm in a monopolistically competitive market is, in many ways, like a monopoly. Because its product is different from those offered by other firms, it

TABLE 12.1

Examples of Markets Which Have Characteristics of Monopolistic Competition

Architects	Vets
Restaurants	Hotel accommodation
Conference organizers	Air conditioning systems
Wedding planners	Pest control
Plumbing	Removal services
Coach hire	Beauty consultants
Funeral directors	Shop fitters
Fabric manufacturers	Waste disposal
Tailors	Dentists
Music teachers	Children's entertainers
Tyre fitters	Gas engineers
Garden centres	Steel fabricators
Landscape architects	Driving schools
Environmental consultants	Opticians
Furniture manufacturers	Chimney sweeps

faces a downward sloping demand curve. If we assume that a monopolistically competitive firm aims for profit maximization, it chooses the quantity at which marginal revenue equals marginal cost and then uses its demand curve to find the price consistent with that quantity.

Figure 12.1 shows the cost, demand and marginal revenue curves for two typical firms, each in a different monopolistically competitive industry.

FIGURE 12.1

Monopolistic Competitors in the Short Run

Monopolistic competitors maximize profit by producing the quantity at which marginal revenue equals marginal cost. The firm in panel (a) makes a profit because, at this quantity, price is above average total cost. The firm in panel (b) makes losses because, at this quantity, price is less than average total cost.

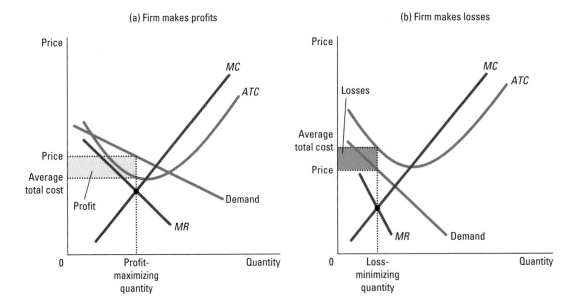

In both panels of this figure, the profit-maximizing quantity is found at the intersection of the marginal revenue and marginal cost curves. The two panels in this figure show different outcomes for the firm's profit. In panel (a), price exceeds average total cost, so the firm makes a profit. In panel (b), price is below average total cost. In this case, the firm is unable to make a positive profit, so the best the firm can do is to minimize its losses.

All this should seem familiar. A monopolistically competitive firm chooses its quantity and price just as a monopoly does. In the short run, these two types of market structure are similar.

The Long-Run Equilibrium

The situations depicted in Figure 12.1 prompt changes in behaviour which result in a different outcome in the long run. When firms are making profits, as in panel (a), new firms have an incentive to enter the market (remember that there is free entry and exit into the market). This entry means that more firms are now offering products for sale in the industry. The increase in supply causes the price received by all firms in the industry to fall. If an existing firm wishes to sell more, it must reduce its price. There are now more substitutes available in the market and the effect is that there is an increase in the number of products from which customers can now choose which reduces the demand faced by each firm already in the market. In other words, profit encourages entry, and entry shifts the demand curves faced by the incumbent firms to the left. As the demand for incumbent firms' products falls, these firms experience declining profit.

Conversely, when firms are making losses, as in panel (b), firms in the market have an incentive to exit. As firms exit, the supply will fall and price will rise. There are now fewer substitutes and so customers have fewer products from which to choose. This decrease in the number of firms effectively expands the demand faced by those firms that stay in the market. In other words, losses encourage exit, and exit has the effect of shifting the demand curves of the remaining firms to the right. As the demand for the remaining firms' products rises, these firms experience rising profit (that is, declining losses).

This process of entry and exit continues until the firms in the market are making exactly zero economic profit. Figure 12.2 depicts the long-run equilibrium. Once the market reaches this equilibrium, new firms have no incentive to enter, and existing firms have no incentive to exit.

> **?** **what if …** a firm operating in a very localized market making short-run abnormal profit could erect some sort of barrier to entry – would it still be able to make abnormal profits in the long run?

Notice that the demand curve in this figure just barely touches the average total cost curve. Mathematically, we say the two curves are *tangential* to each other. These two curves must be tangential once entry and exit have driven profit to zero. Because profit per unit sold is the difference between price (found on the demand curve) and average total cost, the maximum profit is zero only if these two curves touch each other without crossing.

To sum up, two characteristics describe the long-run equilibrium in a monopolistically competitive market:

- As in a monopoly market, price exceeds marginal cost. This conclusion arises because profit maximization requires marginal revenue to equal marginal cost

FIGURE 12.2

A Monopolistic Competition in the Long Run

In a monopolistically competitive market, if firms are making abnormal profit, new firms enter and the demand curves for the incumbent firms shift to the left. Similarly, if firms are making losses (subnormal profit), some of these firms exit and the demand curves of the remaining firms shift to the right. Because of these shifts in demand, a monopolistically competitive firm eventually finds itself in the long-run equilibrium shown here. In this long-run equilibrium, price equals average total cost, and the firm earns zero (normal) profit.

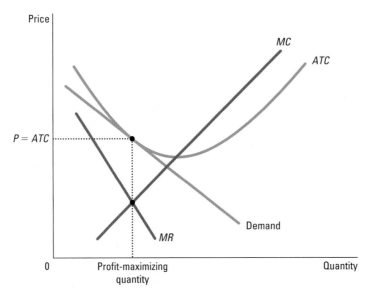

and because the downward sloping demand curve makes marginal revenue less than the price.

- As in a competitive market, price equals average total cost. This conclusion arises because free entry and exit drive economic profit to zero.

The second characteristic shows how monopolistic competition differs from monopoly. Because a monopoly is the sole seller of a product without close substitutes, it can earn abnormal profit, even in the long run. By contrast, because there is free entry into a monopolistically competitive market, the economic profit of a firm in this type of market is driven to zero.

Monopolistic Versus Perfect Competition

Figure 12.3 compares the long-run equilibrium under monopolistic competition to the long-run equilibrium under perfect competition. There are two noteworthy differences between monopolistic and perfect competition – excess capacity and the mark-up.

Excess Capacity As we have just seen, entry and exit drive each firm in a monopolistically competitive market to a point of tangency between its demand and average total cost curves. Panel (a) of Figure 12.3 shows that the quantity of output at this point is smaller than the quantity that minimizes average total cost. Thus, under monopolistic competition, firms produce on the downward sloping portion of their average total cost curves. In this way, monopolistic competition contrasts starkly with perfect competition. As panel (b) of Figure 12.3 shows, free entry in competitive markets drives firms to produce at the minimum of average total cost.

FIGURE 12.3

Monopolistic Versus Perfect Competition

Panel (a) shows the long-run equilibrium in a monopolistically competitive market, and panel (b) shows the long-run equilibrium in a perfectly competitive market. Two differences are notable. (1) The perfectly competitive firm produces at the efficient scale, where average total cost is minimized. By contrast, the monopolistically competitive firm produces at less than the efficient scale. (2) Price equals marginal cost under perfect competition, but price is above marginal cost under monopolistic competition.

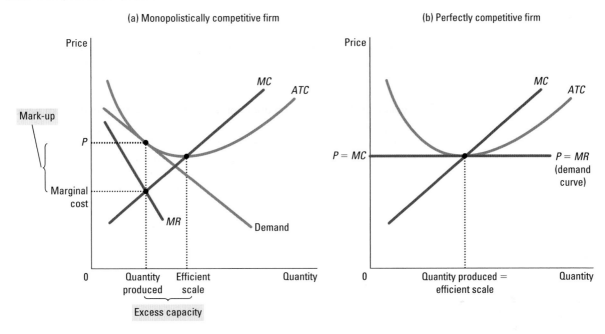

The quantity that minimizes average total cost is called the *efficient scale* of the firm. In the long run, perfectly competitive firms produce at the efficient scale, whereas monopolistically competitive firms produce below this level. Firms are said to have *excess capacity* under monopolistic competition. In other words, a monopolistically competitive firm, unlike a perfectly competitive firm, could increase the quantity it produces and lower the average total cost of production.

Mark-up Over Marginal Cost   A second difference between perfect competition and monopolistic competition is the relationship between price and marginal cost. For a competitive firm, such as that shown in panel (b) of Figure 12.3, price equals marginal cost. For a monopolistically competitive firm, such as that shown in panel (a), price exceeds marginal cost, because the firm always has some market power.

How is this mark-up over marginal cost consistent with free entry and zero profit? The zero-profit condition ensures only that price equals average total cost. It does *not* ensure that price equals marginal cost. Indeed, in the long-run equilibrium, monopolistically competitive firms operate on the declining portion of their average total cost curves, so marginal cost is below average total cost. Thus, for price to equal average total cost, price must be above marginal cost. Because of this a monopolistically competitive firm is always eager to get another customer. Because its price exceeds marginal cost, an extra unit sold at the posted price means more profit.

One characteristic of monopolistic competition is the use of advertising and establishment of brand names. Advertising and branding are important in understanding the behaviour of firms in imperfect competition.

Summary

- A monopolistically competitive market is characterized by three attributes: many firms, differentiated products and free entry.
- The equilibrium in a monopolistically competitive market differs from that in a perfectly competitive market in two related ways. First, each firm in a monopolistically competitive market has excess capacity. That is, it operates on the downward sloping portion of the average total cost curve. Second, each firm charges a price above marginal cost.
- Monopolistic competition does not have all the desirable properties of perfect competition. There is the standard deadweight loss of monopoly caused by the mark-up of price over marginal cost. In addition, the number of firms (and thus the variety of products) can be too large or too small. In practice, the ability of policy makers to correct these inefficiencies is limited.
- The product differentiation inherent in monopolistic competition leads to the use of advertising and brand names.

Table 12.2 summarizes the differences between monopolistic competition, perfect competition and monopoly.

TABLE 12.2

Monopolistic Competition: Between Perfect Competition and Monopoly Market Structure

	Market structure		
	Perfect competition	Monopolistic competition	Monopoly
Features that all three market structures share			
Assumed goal of firms	Maximize profits	Maximize profits	Maximize profits
Rule for maximizing	$MR = MC$	$MR = MC$	$MR = MC$
Can earn abnormal profits in the short run?	Yes	Yes	Yes
Features that monopoly and monopolistic competition share			
Price taker?	Yes	No	No
Price	$P = MC$	$P > MC$	$P > MC$
Produces welfare-maximizing level of output?	Yes	Yes	Yes
Features that perfect competition and monopolistic competition share			
Number of firms	Many	Many	One
Entry in long run?	Yes	Yes	No
Can earn abnormal profits in long run?	No	No	Yes

FYI

Contestable Markets

Most economics textbooks up to the late 1970s covered market structures ranging from perfect competition at one extreme to monopoly at the other. Changes in the way businesses actually operated in the real world meant that there were some gaps between the theory and the observed behaviour of firms. This led to the development of a new theory which was incorporated into the explanation of market structures. The theory of contestable markets was developed by William J. Baumol, John Panzar and Robert Willig in 1982.

The key characteristic of a perfectly contestable market is that firms are influenced by the threat of new entrants into a market. We have seen how, in monopolistically competitive markets, despite the fact that each firm has some monopoly control over its product, the ease of entry and exit means that in the long run profits can be competed away as new firms enter the market. The suggestion by Baumol and colleagues was that firms may deliberately limit profits made to discourage new entrants. The other characteristics of a perfectly contestable market are that there are no barriers to entry or exit and no sunk costs. Firms in the market will recognize that with no barriers to entry other firms can enter easily and this changes their behaviour.

Those firms in the market may have the advantage of knowledge and experience of the market and jealously guard this as a means of erecting barriers to entry. Firms may also attempt to erect other artificial barriers which might include operating at over-capacity, providing the opportunity to flood the market and drive down price in the event of a threat of entry. Firms will also carry out aggressive marketing and branding strategies to 'tighten' up the market or find ways of reducing costs and increasing efficiency to gain competitive advantage. Searching out sources of competitive advantage was a topic written on extensively by Michael Porter, who defined competitive advantage as being the advantages firms can gain over another which are both distinctive and defensible. These sources are not simply to be found in terms of new product development but through close investigation and analysis of the supply chain, where little changes might make a difference to the cost base of a firm which it can then exploit to its advantage.

The threat of entry means that firms behave as if the market were highly competitive but incumbents will not necessarily attempt to maximize profit. Profits might be limited by what was termed *entry limit pricing*. This refers to a situation where

a firm will keep prices lower than they could be in order to deter new entrants. Similarly, firms may also practise *predatory* or *destroyer pricing* whereby the price is held below average cost for a period to try and force out competitors or prevent new firms from entering the market. Incumbent firms may be in a position to do this because they may have been able to gain some advantages of economies of scale which new entrants may not be able to exploit.

Hit-and-run tactics might be evident in a contestable market where firms enter the industry, take the profit and get out quickly (which is possible because of the freedom of entry and exit). In other cases firms may indulge in what is termed *cream-skimming* – identifying parts of the market that are high in value added and exploiting those markets.

The theory of contestable markets has been widely adopted as a beneficial addition to the theory of the firm and there has been extensive research into its application. There are numerous examples of markets exhibiting contestability characteristics including financial services; airlines, especially flights on domestic routes; the IT industry and in particular internet service providers (ISPs), software and Web developers; energy supplies and the postal service.

OLIGOPOLY

The Europeans love chocolate. The average German eats about 180, 62-gram bars of chocolate a year. The Belgians are not far behind at 177 bars, the Swiss around 173 and the British eat around 164 bars per year. There are many firms producing chocolate in Europe including Anthon Berg in Denmark, Camille Bloch, Lindt and Favarger in Switzerland, Guylian and Godiva in Belgium, and Hachez in Germany. However, Europeans are likely to find that what they are eating has probably been made by one of three companies: Cadbury (owned by US firm, Kraft), Mars or Nestlé. These firms dominate the chocolate industry in the EU. Being so large and dominant they are able to influence the quantity of chocolate bars produced and, given the market demand curve, the price at which chocolate bars are sold.

oligopoly competition amongst the few – a market structure in which only a few sellers offer similar or identical products and dominate the market

The European market for chocolate bars fits a model of imperfect competition called **oligopoly** – literally, competition among the few. The essence of an oligopolistic market is that there are a few sellers which dominate the market and where the products they sell are identical or near identical. In this situation, competition between these large firms might be focused on strategic interactions among them. As a result, the actions of any one seller in the market can have a large impact on the profits of all the other sellers. That is, oligopolistic firms are interdependent in a way that competitive firms are not.

There is no magic number that defines 'few' from 'many' when counting the number of firms. Do the approximately dozen companies that now sell cars in Europe make this market an oligopoly or more competitive? The answer is open to debate. Similarly, there is no sure way to determine when products are differentiated and when they are identical. Are different brands of milk really the same? Again, the answer is debatable. When analysing actual markets, economists have to keep in mind the lessons learned from studying all types of market structure and then apply each lesson as it seems appropriate.

Our goal is to see how the interdependence that characterizes oligopolistic markets shapes the firms' behaviour and what problems it raises for public policy.

Markets With Only a Few Dominant Sellers

concentration ratio the proportion of total sales in an industry accounted for by a given number of firms

If a market is dominated by a relatively small number of sellers it is said to be *concentrated*. The **concentration ratio** refers to the proportion of the total market share accounted for by the top x number of firms in the industry. For example, a five-firm concentration ratio of 80 per cent means that five firms account for 80 per cent of market share; a three-firm concentration ratio of 72 per cent would indicate that three firms account for 72 per cent of total market sales and so on.

There are a number of examples of oligopolistic market structures including brewing, banking, mobile phone networks, the chemical and oil industries, the grocery/supermarket industry, detergents, and entertainment. Note that in each of these industries there might be many sellers in the industry (there are thousands of small independent breweries across Europe, for example) but sales are dominated by a relatively small number of firms. In brewing, the industry is dominated by A-BInBev, Heineken, Carlsberg and SABMiller.

A key feature of oligopoly is the tension that exists between firms of cooperation and self-interest. The group of oligopolists is best off cooperating and acting like a monopolist – producing a smaller quantity of output and charging a price above marginal cost. Yet because each oligopolist cares about only its own profit, there are powerful incentives at work that hinder a group of firms from maintaining the monopoly outcome.

A Duopoly Example

To understand the behaviour of oligopolies, let's consider an oligopoly with only two members, called a *duopoly*. Duopoly is the simplest type of oligopoly. Oligopolies with three or more members face the same problems as oligopolies with only two members, so we do not lose much by starting with the case of duopoly.

Imagine a town in which only two residents – Ishaq and Coralie – own wells that produce water safe for drinking. Each Saturday, Ishaq and Coralie decide how many litres of water to pump, bring the water to town, and sell it for whatever price the market will bear. To keep things simple, suppose that Ishaq and Coralie can pump as much water as they want without cost. That is, the marginal cost of water equals zero.

TABLE 12.3

The Demand Schedule for Water

Quantity (in litres)	Price per litre (€)	Total revenue (and total profit) €
0	1.20	0
10	1.10	11.00
20	1.00	20.00
30	0.90	27.00
40	0.80	32.00
50	0.70	35.00
60	0.60	36.00
70	0.50	35.00
80	0.40	32.00
90	0.30	27.00
100	0.20	20.00
110	0.10	11.00
120	0	0

Table 12.3 shows the town's demand schedule for water. The first column shows the total quantity demanded, and the second column shows the price. If the two well owners sell a total of 10 litres of water, water is priced at €1.10 a litre. If they sell a total of 20 litres, the price falls to €1.00 a litre. And so on. If you graphed these two columns of numbers, you would get a standard downward sloping demand curve.

The last column in Table 12.3 shows the total revenue from the sale of water. It equals the quantity sold times the price. Because there is no cost to pumping water, the total revenue of the two producers equals their total profit.

Let's now consider how the organization of the town's water industry affects the price of water and the quantity of water sold.

Competition, Monopolies and Cartels

Consider what would happen if the market for water were perfectly competitive. In a competitive market, the production decisions of each firm drive price equal to marginal cost. In the market for water, marginal cost is zero. Thus, under competition, the equilibrium price of water would be zero, and the equilibrium quantity would be 120 litres. The price of water would reflect the cost of producing it, and the efficient quantity of water would be produced and consumed.

Now consider how a monopoly would behave. Table 12.3 shows that total profit is maximized at a quantity of 60 litres and a price of €0.60 a litre. A profit-maximizing monopolist, therefore, would produce this quantity and charge this price. As is standard for monopolies, price would exceed marginal cost. The result would be inefficient, for the quantity of water produced and consumed would fall short of the socially efficient level of 120 litres.

What outcome should we expect from our duopolists? One possibility is that Ishaq and Coralie get together and agree on the quantity of water to produce and the price to charge for it. Such an agreement among firms over production and price is called **collusion**, and the group of firms acting in unison is called a **cartel**. Once a cartel is formed, the market is in effect served by a monopoly, and we can apply our analysis from Chapter 11. That is, if Ishaq and Coralie were to collude, they would agree on the monopoly outcome because that outcome maximizes the total profit that the producers can get from the market. Our two producers would produce a total of 60 litres, which would be sold at a price of €0.60 a litre. Once again, price exceeds marginal cost, and the outcome is socially inefficient.

A cartel must agree not only on the total level of production but also on the amount produced by each member. In our case, Ishaq and Coralie must agree how to split between themselves the monopoly production of 60 litres. Each member of the cartel will want a larger share of the market because a larger market share means larger profit. If Ishaq and Coralie agreed to split the market equally, each would produce 30 litres, the price would be €0.60 a litre and each would get a profit of €18.

collusion an agreement among firms in a market about quantities to produce or prices to charge

cartel a group of firms acting in unison

CASE STUDY

OPEC and the World Oil Market

Our story about the town's market for water is fictional, but if we change water to crude oil, and Ishaq and Coralie to Iran and Iraq, the story is closer to being accurate. A few countries, mostly in the Middle East, produce much of the world's oil. These countries together make up an oligopoly. Their decisions about how much oil to pump are much the same as Ishaq and Coralie's decisions about how much water to pump.

The countries that produce most of the world's oil formed a cartel, called the Organization of Petroleum Exporting Countries (OPEC). As originally formed in 1960, OPEC included Iran, Iraq, Kuwait, Saudi Arabia and Venezuela. By 1973, eight other nations had joined: Qatar, Indonesia, Libya, the United Arab Emirates, Algeria, Nigeria, Ecuador and Gabon. These countries then controlled about three-quarters of the world's oil reserves. Like any cartel, OPEC tries to raise the price of its product through a coordinated reduction in quantity produced. OPEC attempts to set production levels for each of the member countries.

The problem that OPEC faces is much the same as the problem that Ishaq and Coralie face in our story. The OPEC countries would like to maintain a high price for oil. But each member of the cartel is tempted to increase its production to get a larger share of the total profit. OPEC members frequently agree to reduce production but then cheat on their agreements.

OPEC was most successful at maintaining cooperation and high prices in the period from 1973 to 1985. The price of crude oil rose from $3 a barrel in 1972 to $11 in 1974 and then to $35 in 1981. But in the mid-1980s, member countries began arguing about production levels, and OPEC became ineffective at maintaining cooperation. By 1986 the price of crude oil had fallen back to $13 a barrel.

In recent years, the members of OPEC have continued to meet regularly, but the cartel has been less successful at reaching and enforcing agreements. Although the price of oil rose significantly in 2007 and 2008, the primary cause was increased demand in the world oil market, in part from a booming Chinese economy, rather than restricted supply. While this lack of cooperation among OPEC nations has reduced the profits of the oil-producing nations below what they might have been, it has benefited consumers around the world.

Things have become even harder for OPEC. The OPEC countries now produce around 35 per cent of global output of oil. However, the power of OPEC to control world oil prices by limiting supply is diminishing. It is largely down to the US energy revolution. Fracking is the process of using high-pressure water to extract oil and gas held in shale rock. It has resulted in a rapid rise in the supply of oil. US oil imports fell by over 40 per cent between 2008 and 2013. Other countries are now considering allowing the use of the new technologies despite some environmental concerns. Such government policy leads to further increases in supply and an outward shift of the supply curve. At the same time, Saudi Arabia refused OPECs request to cut production. This, coupled with lower than expected demand, helped to force prices down. In February 2011 Brent crude oil was priced at $125 a barrel and remained high until the spring of 2014 when in a few months prices fell sharply. In February 2015 the price had fallen to around $53 a barrel.

References: **http://nation.time.com/2014/02/07/fracking-energy-boom-natural-gas-geopolitics-iran/**

http://www.theweek.co.uk/business/oil-price/60838/oil-price-drops-again-amid-large-scale-strike-in-us

? ■ **what if** ... one of the firms entering into a cartel had much more market power than the other firms in the agreement – would this mean the cartel is more likely to succeed or not?

The Equilibrium for an Oligopoly

Although oligopolists would like to form cartels and earn monopoly profits, often that is not possible. Competition laws prohibit explicit agreements among oligopolists as a matter of public policy. In addition, squabbling among cartel members over how to divide the profit in the market sometimes makes agreement among them impossible. Let's therefore consider what happens if Ishaq and Coralie decide separately how much water to produce.

At first, one might expect Ishaq and Coralie to reach the monopoly outcome on their own, for this outcome maximizes their joint profit. In the absence of a binding agreement, however, the monopoly outcome is unlikely. To see why, imagine that Ishaq expects Coralie to produce only 30 litres (half of the monopoly quantity). Ishaq might reason as follows:

> *I could produce 30 litres as well. In this case, a total of 60 litres of water would be sold at a price of €0.60 a litre. My profit would be €18 (30 litres × €0.60 a litre). Alternatively, I could produce 40 litres. In this case, a total of 70 litres of water would be sold at a price of €0.50 a litre. My profit would be €20 (40 litres × €0.50 a litre). Even though total profit in the market would fall, my profit would be higher, because I would have a larger share of the market.*

Of course, Coralie might reason the same way. If so, Ishaq and Coralie would each bring 40 litres to town. Total sales would be 80 litres, and the price would fall to €0.40. Thus, if the duopolists individually pursue their own self-interest when deciding how much to produce, they produce a total quantity greater than the monopoly quantity, charge a price lower than the monopoly price and earn total profit less than the monopoly profit.

Although the logic of self-interest increases the duopoly's output above the monopoly level, it does not push the duopolists to reach the competitive allocation. Consider what happens when each duopolist is producing 40 litres. The price is €0.40, and each duopolist makes a profit of €16. In this case, Ishaq's self-interested logic leads to a different conclusion:

> *Right now my profit is €16. Suppose I increase my production to 50 litres. In this case, a total of 90 litres of water would be sold, and the price would be €0.30 a litre. Then my profit would be only €15. Rather than increasing production and driving down the price, I am better off keeping my production at 40 litres.*

Nash equilibrium a situation in which economic actors interacting with one another each choose their best strategy given the strategies that all the other actors have chosen

The outcome in which Ishaq and Coralie each produce 40 litres looks like some sort of equilibrium. In fact, this outcome is called a **Nash equilibrium** (named after economic theorist John Nash, whose life was portrayed in the book, *A Beautiful Mind*, and the film of the same name). A Nash equilibrium is a situation in which economic actors interacting with one another each choose their best strategy given the strategies the others have chosen. In this case, given that Coralie is producing 40 litres, the best strategy for Ishaq is to produce 40 litres. Similarly, given that Ishaq is producing 40 litres, the best strategy for Coralie is to produce 40 litres. Once they reach this Nash equilibrium, neither Ishaq nor Coralie has an incentive to make a different decision.

This example illustrates the tension between cooperation and self-interest. Oligopolists would be better off cooperating and reaching the monopoly outcome. Yet because they pursue their own self-interest, they do not end up reaching the monopoly outcome and maximizing their joint profit. Each oligopolist is tempted to raise production and capture a larger share of the market. As each of them tries to do this, total production rises, and the price falls.

At the same time, self-interest does not drive the market all the way to the competitive outcome. Like monopolists, oligopolists are aware that increases in the amount they produce reduce the price of their product. Therefore, they stop short of following the competitive firm's rule of producing up to the point where price equals marginal cost.

In summary, when firms in an oligopoly individually choose production to maximize profit, they produce a quantity of output greater than the level produced by monopoly and less than the level produced by competition. The oligopoly price is less than the monopoly price but greater than the competitive price (which equals marginal cost).

JEOPARDY PROBLEM

An oligopolistic market consists of a four-firm concentration ratio of 80 per cent. An economist does some research on this market and finds that prices have remained stable in the market for the last 5 years. What might the explanation be for this behaviour?

How the Size of an Oligopoly Affects the Market Outcome

We can use the insights from this analysis of duopoly to discuss how the size of an oligopoly is likely to affect the outcome in a market. Suppose, for instance, that Jean and Patrice suddenly discover water sources on their property and join Ishaq and Coralie in the water oligopoly. The demand schedule in Table 12.3 remains the same, but now more producers are available to satisfy this demand. How would an increase in the number of sellers from two to four affect the price and quantity of water in the town?

If the sellers of water could form a cartel, they would once again try to maximize total profit by producing the monopoly quantity and charging the monopoly price. Just as when there were only two sellers, the members of the cartel would need to agree on production levels for each member and find some way to enforce the agreement. As the cartel grows larger, however, this outcome is less likely. Reaching and enforcing an agreement becomes more difficult as the size of the group increases.

If the oligopolists do not form a cartel – perhaps because competition laws prohibit it – they must each decide on their own how much water to produce. To see how the increase in the number of sellers affects the outcome, consider the decision facing each seller. At any time, each well owner has the option to raise production by 1 litre. In making this decision, the well owner weighs two effects:

- *The output effect.* Because price is above marginal cost, selling 1 more litre of water at the going price will raise profit.
- *The price effect.* Raising production will increase the total amount sold, which will lower the price of water and lower the profit on all the other litres sold.

If the output effect is larger than the price effect, the well owner will increase production. If the price effect is larger than the output effect, the owner will not raise production. (In fact, in this case, it is profitable to reduce production). Each oligopolist continues to increase production until these two marginal effects exactly balance, taking the other firms' production as given.

Now consider how the number of firms in the industry affects the marginal analysis of each oligopolist. The larger the number of sellers, the less concerned each seller is about its own impact on the market price. That is, as the oligopoly grows in size, the magnitude of the price effect falls. When the oligopoly grows very large, the price effect disappears altogether, leaving only the output effect. In this extreme case, each firm in the oligopoly increases production as long as price is above marginal cost.

We can now see that a large oligopoly is essentially a group of competitive firms. A competitive firm considers only the output effect when deciding how much to produce: because a competitive firm is a price taker, the price effect is absent. Thus, as the number of sellers in an oligopoly grows larger, an oligopolistic market looks more and more like a competitive market. The price approaches marginal cost, and the quantity produced approaches the socially efficient level.

> **Pitfall Prevention** Remember that in an oligopolistic market structure there can be many hundreds and, in some cases, thousands of firms but the crucial thing to remember is that the market is dominated by a small number of very large firms.

This analysis of oligopoly offers a new perspective on the effects of international trade. Imagine that Toyota and Honda are the only car manufacturers in Japan, Volkswagen and BMW are the only car manufacturers in Germany, and Citroën and Peugeot are the only car manufacturers in France. If these nations prohibited international trade in cars, each would have a motorcar oligopoly with only two members, and the market outcome would likely depart substantially from the competitive ideal. With international trade, however, the car market is a world market, and the oligopoly in this example has six members. Allowing free trade increases the number of producers from whom each consumer can choose, and this increased competition keeps prices closer to marginal cost. Thus, the theory of oligopoly provides another reason why all countries can benefit from free trade.

> **Quick Quiz** If the members of an oligopoly could agree on a total quantity to produce, what quantity would they choose? If the oligopolists do not act together but instead make production decisions individually, do they produce a total quantity more or less than in your answer to the previous question? Why?

INTERDEPENDENCE, GAME THEORY AND THE ECONOMICS OF COMPETITION

As we have seen, oligopolies would like to reach the monopoly outcome, but doing so requires cooperation, which at times is difficult to maintain. In this section we look more closely at the problems people face when cooperation is desirable but difficult. To analyse the economics of cooperation, we need to learn a little about **game theory**.

game theory the study of how people behave in strategic situations

Game theory is the study of how people behave in strategic situations. By 'strategic' we mean a situation in which each person, when deciding what actions to take, must consider how others might respond to that action. One of the main features of oligopolistic markets is interdependence. Because the number of firms in an oligopolistic market is small, each firm must act strategically. Each firm knows that its decisions will be monitored and studied by its rivals and that its rivals will react to its decisions. If one firm is contemplating increasing price it must consider whether its rivals will also increase their price, keep their prices the same or possibly lower prices. If one firm is planning on introducing a new variation of its product, a new distribution system which gives it some supply chain cost advantages, or is planning a major marketing campaign to boost sales of its products, it has to consider what its rivals will do in response. Does the firm seek to introduce new products or systems to a market quickly and gain the benefits of what are referred to as 'first mover advantage'? If it introduces a new product or system, how quickly and closely will rivals seek to copy? Will rivals wait to see what mistakes the first mover in the market makes and learn from those mistakes before introducing competitive products/systems? Should a firm seek to enter into some agreement with its rivals and if it does so what risks does it undertake? The risks might include a lack of trust in the agreement and the potential for the rival to renege on any agreement and the possible legal ramifications of entering into a collusive agreement. Each firm knows that its profit depends not only on how much it produces but also on how much the other firms produce. The interdependence between firms in an oligopoly means that the study of how individuals and groups behave in strategic situations takes on an importance for understanding the behaviour of oligopolies.

A particularly important 'game' is called the **prisoners' dilemma**. This game provides insight into the difficulty of maintaining cooperation. Many times in life, people fail to cooperate with one another even when cooperation would make them all better off. An oligopoly is just one example. The story of the prisoners' dilemma contains a general lesson that applies to any group trying to maintain cooperation among its members.

prisoners' dilemma a particular 'game' between two captured prisoners that illustrates why cooperation is difficult to maintain even when it is mutually beneficial

The Prisoners' Dilemma

The prisoners' dilemma is a story about two criminals who have been captured by the police. Let's call them Mr Green and Mr Blue. The police have enough evidence to convict Mr Green and Mr Blue of a relatively minor crime, possessing stolen property, so that each would spend a year in prison. The police also suspect that the two criminals have committed an armed jewellery robbery together, but they lack hard evidence to convict them of this major crime. The police question Mr Green and Mr Blue in separate rooms, and they offer each of them the following deal:

Right now we can lock you up for 1 year. If you confess to the jewellery robbery and implicate your partner, however, we'll give you immunity and you can go free. Your partner will get 20 years in prison. But if you both confess to the crime, we won't need your testimony and we can avoid the cost of a trial, so you will each get an intermediate sentence of 8 years.

If Mr Green and Mr Blue, heartless criminals that they are, care only about their own sentences, what would you expect them to do? Would they confess or remain silent? Figure 12.4 shows their choices. Each prisoner has two strategies: confess or remain silent. The sentence each prisoner gets depends on the strategy he chooses and the strategy chosen by his partner in crime.

Consider first Mr Green's decision. He reasons as follows:

I don't know what Mr Blue is going to do. If he remains silent, my best strategy is to confess, since then I'll go free rather than spending a year in prison. If he confesses, my best strategy is still to confess, since then I'll spend 8 years in prison rather than 20. So, regardless of what Mr Blue does, I am better off confessing.

In the language of game theory, a strategy is called a **dominant strategy** if it is the best strategy for a player to follow regardless of the strategies pursued by other players. In this case, confessing is a dominant strategy for Mr Green. He spends less time in prison if he confesses, regardless of whether Mr Blue confesses or remains silent.

dominant strategy a strategy that is best for a player in a game regardless of the strategies chosen by the other players

FIGURE 12.4

The Prisoners' Dilemma

In this game between two criminals suspected of committing a crime, the sentence that each receives depends both on their decision whether to confess or remain silent and on the decision made by the other. Mr Blue and Mr Green each have the choice of confessing or remaining silent. If Mr Blue chooses to confess but Mr Green also confesses, each gets 8 years in prison as indicated by the top left quadrant. If Mr Blue chooses to remain silent but Mr Green confesses, Mr Blue will get 20 years in prison but Mr Green will go free as shown in the bottom left quadrant.

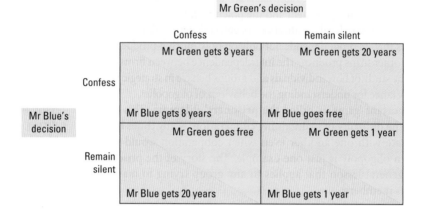

Now consider Mr Blue's decision. He faces exactly the same choices as Mr Green, and he reasons in much the same way. Regardless of what Mr Green does, Mr Blue can reduce his time in jail by confessing. In other words, confessing is also a dominant strategy for Mr Blue.

In the end, both Mr Green and Mr Blue confess, and both spend 8 years in prison. Yet, from their standpoint, this is a terrible outcome. If they had *both* remained silent, both of them would have been better off, spending only 1 year in prison on the possession charge. By each pursuing his own interests, the two prisoners together reach an outcome that is worse for each of them.

To see how difficult it is to maintain cooperation, imagine that, before the police captured Mr Green and Mr Blue, the two criminals had made a pact not to confess. Clearly, this agreement would make them both better off *if* they both live up to it, because they would each spend only 1 year in prison. But would the two criminals in fact remain silent, simply because they had agreed to? Once they are being questioned separately, the logic of self-interest takes over and leads them to confess. Cooperation between the two prisoners is difficult to maintain, because cooperation is individually irrational.

Oligopolies as a Prisoner's Dilemma

What does the prisoners' dilemma have to do with markets and imperfect competition? It turns out that the game oligopolists play in trying to reach the monopoly outcome is similar to the game that the two prisoners play in the prisoners' dilemma.

Consider an oligopoly with two firms, BP and Shell, in a hypothetical situation. Both firms refine crude oil. After prolonged negotiation, the two firms agree to keep refined oil production low in order to keep the world price of refined oil high. After they agree on production levels, each firm must decide whether to cooperate and live up to this agreement or to ignore it and produce at a higher level. Figure 12.5 shows how the profits of the two firms depend on the strategies they choose.

FIGURE 12.5

An Oligopoly Game

In this game between members of an oligopoly, the profit that each earns depends on both its production decision and the production decision of the other oligopolist.

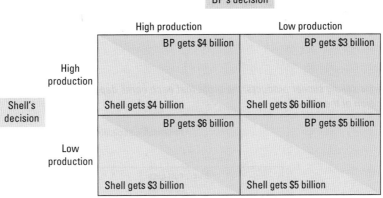

Suppose you are the CEO of BP. You might reason as follows:

If Shell keeps to its agreement and limits production, we both earn $5 billion in profit. If I can trust Shell to keep its side of the deal, I could raise production and sell more refined oil on world markets. In this scenario, my firm earns profit of $6 billion and so I am better off with high production. If I can't trust Shell to live up to the agreement and it produces at a high level but I stick to low production, then my firm earns $3 billion but Shell earns $6 billion. In this case I am better off also opting for high production and earning $4 billion. So, regardless of what Shell chooses to do, my firm is better off reneging on our agreement and producing at a high level.

Producing at a high level is a dominant strategy for BP. Of course, Shell reasons in exactly the same way, and so both firms produce at a high level. The result is the inferior outcome (from BP and Shell's standpoint) with lower profits for each firm compared to them both sticking to their original agreement of keeping production low.

This example illustrates why oligopolies have trouble maintaining monopoly profits. The monopoly outcome is jointly rational for the oligopoly, but each oligopolist has an incentive to cheat. Just as self-interest drives the prisoners in the prisoners' dilemma to confess, self-interest makes it difficult for the oligopoly to maintain the cooperative outcome with low production, high prices and monopoly profits.

Other Examples of the Prisoners' Dilemma

We have seen how the prisoners' dilemma can be used to understand the problem facing oligopolies. The same logic applies to many other situations as well. Here we consider two examples in which self-interest prevents cooperation and leads to an inferior outcome for the parties involved.

Advertising   When two firms advertise to attract the same customers, they face a problem similar to the prisoners' dilemma. For example, consider the hypothetical decisions facing two games console manufacturers, Sony and Microsoft, which is represented in Figure 12.6. If neither company advertises, the two companies split the market and earn €4 billion in profit each. If both advertise, they again split the market, but profits are lower at €3 billion each, since each company must bear the cost of advertising. Yet if one company advertises while the other does not, the one that advertises attracts customers from the other. If Sony advertise but Microsoft do not, Sony earns €5 billion in profit whilst Microsoft earns just €2 billion. Figure 12.6 shows that advertising is a dominant strategy for each firm. Thus, both firms choose to advertise, even though both firms would be better off if neither firm advertised.

FIGURE 12.6

An Advertising Game

In this game between firms selling similar products, the profit that each earns depends on both its own advertising decision and the advertising decision of the other firm.

Microsoft's decision

	Advertise	Don't advertise
Advertise	Microsoft gets €3 billion / Sony gets €3 billion	Microsoft gets €2 billion / Sony gets €5 billion
Don't advertise	Microsoft gets €5 billion / Sony gets €2 billion	Microsoft gets €4 billion / Sony gets €4 billion

Sony's decision

Common Resources Common resources tend to be subject to overuse because they are rival in consumption but not excludable, for example, fish in the sea. One can view this problem as an example of the prisoners' dilemma.

Imagine that two mining companies – Kazakhmys and Vedanta – own adjacent copper mines. The mines have a common pool of copper worth €12 million. The decision matrix for each company is shown in Figure 12.7. Drilling a shaft to mine the copper costs €1 million. If each company drills one shaft, each will get half of the copper and earn a €5 million profit as indicated by the bottom right quadrant (€6 million in revenue minus €1 million in costs).

Because the pool of copper is a common resource, the companies will not use it efficiently. Suppose that either company could drill a second shaft. If one company has two of the three shafts, that company gets two-thirds of the copper, which yields a profit of €6 million. If Vedanta drills two wells but Kazakhmys only drills one well, Vedanta faces costs of €2 million and gains profits of €6 million. Kazakhmys has €1 million in costs and takes profit of €3 million. This outcome is shown in the bottom left quadrant. Yet if each company drills a second shaft, the two companies again split the copper. In this case, each bears the cost of a second shaft, so profit is only €4 million for each company. Drilling two wells is a dominant strategy for each company. Once again, the self-interest of the two players leads them to an inferior outcome.

Why Firms Sometimes Cooperate

The prisoners' dilemma shows that cooperation is difficult. But is it impossible? Not all prisoners, when questioned by the police, decide to turn in their partners in crime. Cartels sometimes do manage to maintain collusive arrangements, despite the incentive for individual members to defect. Very often, the reason that players can solve the prisoners' dilemma is that they play the game not once but many times.

FIGURE 12.7

A Common Resources Game

In this game between firms mining copper from a common pool, the profit that each earns depends on both the number of shafts it drills and the number of shafts drilled by the other firm.

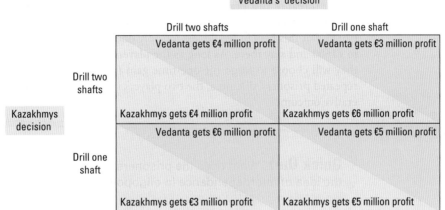

		Vedanta's decision	
		Drill two shafts	Drill one shaft
Kazakhmys decision	**Drill two shafts**	Vedanta gets €4 million profit Kazakhmys gets €4 million profit	Vedanta gets €3 million profit Kazakhmys gets €6 million profit
	Drill one shaft	Vedanta gets €6 million profit Kazakhmys gets €3 million profit	Vedanta gets €5 million profit Kazakhmys gets €5 million profit

To see why cooperation is easier to enforce in repeated games, let's return to our duopolists, Ishaq and Coralie. Recall that Ishaq and Coralie would like to maintain the monopoly outcome in which each produces 30 litres, but self-interest drives them to an equilibrium in which each produces 40 litres. Figure 12.8 shows the game they play. Producing 40 litres is a dominant strategy for each player in this game.

FIGURE 12.8

Ishaq and Coralie's Oligopoly Game

In this game between Ishaq and Coralie, the profit that each earns from selling water depends on both the quantity he or she chooses to sell and the quantity the other chooses to sell.

		Ishaq's decision	
		Sell 40 litres	Sell 30 litres
Coralie's decision	**Sell 40 litres**	Ishaq gets €1600 profit Coralie gets €1600 profit	Ishaq gets €1500 profit Coralie gets €2000 profit
	Sell 30 litres	Ishaq gets €2000 profit Coralie gets €1500 profit	Ishaq gets €1800 profit Coralie gets €1800 profit

Imagine that Ishaq and Coralie try to form a cartel. To maximize total profit they would agree to the cooperative outcome in which each produces and sells 30 litres. Yet, if Ishaq and Coralie are to play this game only once, neither has any incentive to live up to this agreement. Self-interest drives each of them to renege and produce and sell 40 litres.

Now suppose that Ishaq and Coralie know that they will play the same game every week. When they make their initial agreement to keep production low, they can also specify what happens if one party reneges. They might agree, for instance, that once one of them reneges and produces 40 litres, both of them will produce 40 litres forever after. This penalty is easy to enforce, for if one party is producing at a high level, the other has every reason to do the same.

The threat of this penalty may be all that is needed to maintain cooperation. Each person knows that defecting would raise his or her profit from €1800 to €2000. But this benefit would last for only one week. Thereafter, profit would fall to €1600 and stay there. As long as the players care enough about future profits, they will choose to forgo the one-time gain from defection. Thus, in a game of repeated prisoners' dilemma, the two players may well be able to reach the cooperative outcome.

Quick Quiz What does the prisoners' dilemma teach us about the idea of interdependence in oligopolistic markets?

PUBLIC POLICIES TOWARD OLIGOPOLIES

Cooperation among oligopolists is undesirable from the standpoint of society as a whole, because it leads to production that is too low and prices that are too high. To move the allocation of resources closer to the social optimum, policy makers try to induce firms in an oligopoly to compete rather than cooperate. Let's consider how policy makers do this and then examine the controversies that arise in this area of public policy.

Restraint of Trade and Competition Law

One way that policy discourages cooperation is through the common law. Normally, freedom of contract is an essential part of a market economy. Businesses and households use contracts to arrange mutually advantageous trades. In doing this, they rely on the court system to enforce contracts. Yet, for many centuries, courts in Europe and North America have deemed agreements among competitors to reduce quantities and raise prices to be contrary to the public interest. They have therefore refused to enforce such agreements.

Given the long experience of many European countries in tackling abuses of market power, it is perhaps not surprising that competition law is one of the few areas in which the European Union has been able to agree on a common policy. The European Commission can refer directly to the Treaty of Rome to prohibit price-fixing and other restrictive practices such as production limitation, and is especially likely to do so where a restrictive practice affects trade between EU member countries. The EU Competition Commission sets out its role as follows:

> *The antitrust area covers two prohibition rules set out in the Treaty on the Functioning of the European Union.*
>
> - *First, agreements between two or more firms which restrict competition are prohibited by Article 101 of the Treaty, subject to some limited exceptions. This provision covers a wide variety of behaviours. The most obvious example of illegal conduct infringing [the Article] is a cartel between competitors (which may involve price-fixing or market sharing).*
> - *Second, firms in a dominant position may not abuse that position (Article 102 of the Treaty). This is for example the case for predatory pricing aiming at eliminating competitors from the market.*
>
> *The Commission is empowered by the Treaty to apply these prohibition rules and enjoys a number of investigative powers to that end (e.g. inspection in business and non-business premises, written requests for information, etc.). It may also impose fines on undertakings which violate EU antitrust rules. Since 1 May 2004, all national competition authorities are also empowered to apply fully the provisions of the Treaty in order to ensure that competition is not distorted or restricted. National courts may also apply these prohibitions so as to protect the individual rights conferred to citizens by the Treaty.*
>
> ***http://ec.europa.eu/competition/antitrust/overview_en.html***

Controversies Over Competition Policy

Over time, much controversy has centred on the question of what kinds of behaviour competition law should prohibit. Most commentators agree that price-fixing agreements among competing firms should be illegal. Yet competition law has been used to condemn some business practices whose effects are not obvious. Here we consider three examples.

Resale Price Maintenance   One example of a controversial business practice is *resale price maintenance*, also called *fair trade*. Imagine that Superduper Electronics sells Blu-ray DVD players to retail stores for €100. If Superduper requires the retailers to charge customers €150, it is said to engage in resale price maintenance. Any retailer that charged less than €150 would have violated its contract with Superduper.

At first, resale price maintenance might seem anti-competitive and, therefore, detrimental to society. Like an agreement among members of a cartel, it prevents the retailers from competing on price. For this reason, the courts have often viewed resale price maintenance as a violation of competition law.

Yet some economists defend resale price maintenance on two grounds. First, they deny that it is aimed at reducing competition. To the extent that Superduper Electronics has any market power, it can exert that power through the wholesale price, rather than through resale price maintenance. Moreover, Superduper has no incentive to discourage competition among its retailers. Indeed, because a cartel of retailers sells less than a group of competitive retailers, Superduper would be worse off if its retailers were a cartel.

Second, economists believe that resale price maintenance has a legitimate goal. Superduper may want its retailers to provide customers with a pleasant showroom and a knowledgeable salesforce. Yet, without resale price maintenance, some customers would take advantage of one store's service to learn about the Blu-ray DVD player's special features and then buy the item at a discount retailer that does not provide this service. To some extent, good service is a public good among the retailers that sell Superduper products. We know that when one person provides a public good, others are able to enjoy it without paying for it. In this case, discount retailers would free ride on the service provided by other retailers, leading to less service than is desirable. Resale price maintenance is one way for Superduper to solve this free-rider problem.

The example of resale price maintenance illustrates an important principle: business practices that appear to reduce competition may in fact have legitimate purposes. This principle makes the application of competition law all the more difficult. The competition authorities in each EU nation under the European Competition Network are in charge of enforcing these laws and must determine what kinds of behaviour public policy should prohibit as impeding competition and reducing economic well-being. Often that job is not easy.

Predatory Pricing   Firms with market power normally raise prices above the competitive level. But should policy makers ever be concerned that firms with market power might charge prices that are too low? This question is at the heart of a second debate over competition policy.

Imagine that a large airline, call it National Airlines, has a monopoly on some route. Then Fly Express enters and takes 20 per cent of the market, leaving National with 80 per cent. In response to this competition, National starts slashing its fares. Some anti-trust analysts argue that National's move could be anti-competitive: the price cuts may be intended to drive Fly out of the market so National can recapture its monopoly and raise prices again. Such behaviour is called *predatory pricing*.

Although it is common for companies to complain to the relevant authorities that a competitor is pursuing predatory pricing, some economists are sceptical of this argument and believe that predatory pricing is rarely, and perhaps never, a profitable business strategy. Why? For a price war to drive out a rival, prices have to be driven below cost. Yet if National starts selling cheap tickets at a loss, it had better be ready to fly more planes, because low fares will attract more customers. Fly Express, meanwhile, can respond to National's predatory move by cutting back on flights. As a result, National ends up bearing more than 80 per cent of the losses, putting Fly Express in a good position to survive the price war. In such cases, the predator can suffer more than the prey.

Economists continue to debate whether predatory pricing should be a concern for competition policy makers. Various questions remain unresolved. Is predatory pricing ever a profitable business strategy? If so, when? Are the authorities capable of telling which price cuts are competitive and thus good for consumers and which are predatory? There are no simple answers.

Tying   A third example of a controversial business practice is *tying*. Suppose that Makemoney Movies produces two new films – *Spiderman* and *Hamlet*. If Makemoney offers cinemas the two films together at a single price, rather than separately, the studio is said to be tying its two products.

Some economists have argued that the practice of tying should be banned. Their reasoning is as follows: imagine that *Spiderman* is a blockbuster, whereas *Hamlet* is an unprofitable art film. Then the studio could use the high demand for *Spiderman* to force cinemas to buy *Hamlet*. It seems that the studio could use tying as a mechanism for expanding its market power.

Other economists are sceptical of this argument. Imagine that cinemas are willing to pay €20 000 for *Spiderman* and nothing for *Hamlet*. Then the most that a cinema would pay for the two films together is €20 000 – the same as it would pay for *Spiderman* by itself. Forcing the cinema to accept a worthless film as part of the deal does not increase the cinema's willingness to pay. Makemoney cannot increase its market power simply by bundling the two films together.

Why, then, does tying exist? One possibility is that it is a form of price discrimination. Suppose there are two cinemas. City Cinema is willing to pay €15 000 for *Spiderman* and €5000 for *Hamlet*. Country Cinema is just the opposite: it is willing to pay €5000 for *Spiderman* and €15 000 for *Hamlet*. If Makemoney charges separate prices for the two films, its best strategy is to charge €15 000 for each film, and each cinema chooses to show only one film. Yet if Makemoney offers the two films as a bundle, it can charge each cinema €20 000 for the films. Thus, if different cinemas value the films differently, tying may allow the studio to increase profit by charging a combined price closer to the buyers' total willingness to pay.

Tying remains a controversial business practice. Microsoft had been investigated for 'tying' its internet browser, Internet Explorer (IE), and other software like its Windows Media Player with its Windows operating system. Complaints have been made about the way in which Microsoft allegedly makes it more difficult for other browsers to be interoperable – that is, work within a range of other platforms. The European Commission imposed a fine of $1.4 billion in 2008 on Microsoft for breaching EU competition rules. As part of that investigation, the EU insisted that Microsoft made more of its code available to other software manufacturers to ensure greater interoperability. Microsoft had argued that such a move would compromise its security and that the code constituted sensitive commercial information. In March 2013, the Commission imposed a further €561 million on Microsoft for failing to promote a range of web browsers rather than just IE across the EU. Microsoft had introduced a pop-up browser selection window in 2010 but had not included this option in an update of Windows 7 in February 2011. Microsoft said that the non-inclusion was a 'technical error' for which it apologized.

The argument that tying allows a firm to extend its market power to other goods is not well founded, at least in its simplest form. Yet economists have proposed more elaborate theories for how tying can impede competition. Given our current economic knowledge, it is unclear whether tying has adverse effects for society as a whole.

All the analysis is based on an assumption that rivals may have sufficient information to be able to make a decision and that the decision will be a rational one based on this information. In reality firms do not have perfect information and do not behave rationally. Most firms in oligopolistic markets work very hard to protect sensitive information and only give out what they have to by law. Some information may be given to deliberately obfuscate the situation and hide what their true motives/strategies/tactics are. Economists have tried to include these imperfections into theories. Behavioural economics has offered some greater insights into the observed behaviour of the real world which often does not conform to the assumptions implied by the assumption of rationality.

CONCLUSION

Oligopolies would like to act like monopolies, but self-interest drives them closer to competition. Thus, oligopolies can end up looking either more like monopolies or more like competitive markets, depending on the number of firms in the oligopoly and how cooperative the firms are. The story of the prisoners' dilemma shows why oligopolies can fail to maintain cooperation, even when cooperation is in their best interest.

Policy makers regulate the behaviour of oligopolists through competition law. The proper scope of these laws is the subject of ongoing controversy. Although price fixing among competing firms clearly reduces economic welfare and should be illegal, some business practices that appear to reduce competition may have legitimate if subtle purposes. As a result, policy makers need to be careful when they use the substantial powers of competition law to place limits on firm behaviour.

IN THE NEWS

The Open Skies International Policy

The open skies international policy is designed to make air travel more competitive and has over 30 years opened up air travel by reducing the restrictions on international route rights and ending state subsidies to airlines. The increased competition has benefitted consumers. It has generally worked well, at least until recently. The three major US carriers, United, American Airlines and Delta, want to introduce some protection from the Gulf countries believing that their airlines receive government subsidies. The response has been a denial and that the American airlines should stop complaining and start competing.

One way to assess the nature of competition in a market is to look at what is happening to prices. In 2014 oil prices fell by over 50 per cent. This should be great news for airlines and their customers since oil is the biggest cost input for airlines. However, the reduction in airfares has been much slower and less significant that the fall in oil prices.

This might suggest a reason for regulatory and competition authorities to intervene. Some arguments that the airlines might put forward in their defence include that they hedge for fuel to negate the effects of future price rises, so they are locked into promising to buy fuel at prices higher than that in the current market. They also claim that demand for air travel is high and that airlines are operating close to capacity. Lastly they claim they need the profits to reinvest in new

aircraft, something the Gulf carriers are certainly doing.

Theory tells us that if costs fall then some providers will try to lower their prices for popular routes and shift capacity to these routes in order to capture market share, something that doesn't seem to have happened. It suggests that there is either too little competition because of landing rights or that so-called competitors are deliberately avoiding competition. Chuck Schumer, a US Senator, noted: 'ticket prices should not shoot up like a rocket and come down like a feather'.

Three American carriers, three European carriers and three Gulf carriers dominate long-haul travel, which might suggest the industry has an oligopoly structure. This might also be said of other markets; the big six energy firms in the UK control over 90 per cent of the market and the big four banks share 77 per cent of the market between them. Other markets with high concentration ratios include mobile phone operators where further mergers are predicted. There are significant barriers to entry in these markets, not least from the difficulty of customers switching companies. There are often penalties incurred by consumers for switching providers before lengthy contracts are finished.

Although we are familiar with the idea of competitive markets it is not always easy to determine which markets are competitive; government competition policy is mostly designed to scrutinize competition.

Questions

1. To what extent does the concentration ratio determine the competitiveness of a market?
2. To what extent have the authorities in countries around the world been successful in preventing anti-competitive practices in air travel? Justify your answer.
3. Why might it be tempting for airline companies to collude or cooperate and why would this practice be difficult to prove?
4. To what extent should self-interest of oligoplies benefit consumers?
5. What type of practices can be considered anti-competitive in the article and how may authorities deal with these?

References: http://www.nytimes.com /2015/03/24/business/dealbook /as-oil-prices-fall-air-fares-still-stay -high.html

http://www.thenational.ae/business /aviation/us-told-open-skies-policy -crucial-for-jobs-and-trade-ties

SUMMARY

- A monopolistically competitive market is characterized by three attributes: many firms, differentiated products and free entry.

- The equilibrium in a monopolistically competitive market differs from that in a perfectly competitive market in two related ways. First, each firm in a monopolistically competitive market has excess capacity. That is, it operates on the downward sloping portion of the average total cost curve. Second, each firm charges a price above marginal cost.

- Monopolistic competition does not have all the desirable properties of perfect competition. There is the standard deadweight loss of monopoly caused by the mark-up of price over marginal cost. In addition, the number of firms (and thus the variety of products) can be too large or too small. In practice, the ability of policy makers to correct these inefficiencies is limited.

- Oligopolists maximize their total profits by forming a cartel and acting like a monopolist. Yet, if oligopolists make decisions about production levels individually, the result is a greater quantity and a lower price than under the monopoly outcome. The larger the number of firms in the oligopoly, the closer the quantity and price will be to the levels that would prevail under competition.

- The prisoners' dilemma shows that self-interest can prevent people from maintaining cooperation, even when cooperation is in their mutual interest.

- Policy makers use competition law to prevent oligopolies from engaging in behaviour that reduces competition. The application of these laws can be controversial, because some behaviour that may seem to reduce competition may in fact have legitimate business purposes.

QUESTIONS FOR REVIEW

1. Describe the three attributes of monopolistic competition. How is monopolistic competition like monopoly? How is it like perfect competition?

2. Draw a diagram depicting a firm in a monopolistically competitive market that is making profits in the short run.
   a. Now show what happens to this firm as new firms enter the industry.
   b. Now draw the diagram of the long-run equilibrium in a monopolistically competitive market. How is price related to average total cost? How is price related to marginal cost?

3. Does a monopolistic competitor produce too much or too little output compared to the most efficient level? What practical considerations make it difficult for policy makers to solve this problem?

4. If a group of sellers could form a cartel, what quantity and price would they try to set?

5. How does the number of firms in an oligopoly affect the outcome in its market?

6. What is the prisoners' dilemma, and what does it have to do with oligopoly?

7. Give two examples other than oligopoly to show how the prisoners' dilemma helps to explain behaviour.

8. What kinds of behaviour do competition laws prohibit?

9. What is resale price maintenance, and why is it controversial?

10. Why might predatory pricing not be a useful tactic for an oligopolistic firm to pursue?

PROBLEMS AND APPLICATIONS

1. Classify the following markets as perfectly competitive, monopolistic or monopolistically competitive, and explain your answers.
   a. wooden HB pencils
   b. bottled water
   c. copper
   d. local telephone service
   e. strawberry jam
   f. lipstick

2. Sparkle is one firm of many in the market for toothpaste, which is in long-run equilibrium.
   a. Draw a diagram showing Sparkle's demand curve, marginal revenue curve, average total cost curve,

and marginal cost curve. Label Sparkle's profit-maximizing output and price.

b. What is Sparkle's profit? Explain.

c. On your diagram, show the consumer surplus derived from the purchase of Sparkle toothpaste. Also show the deadweight loss relative to the efficient level of output.

d. If the government forced Sparkle to produce the efficient level of output, what would happen to the firm? What would happen to Sparkle's customers?

3. If you were thinking of entering the ice cream business, would you try to make ice cream that is just like one of the existing (successful) brands? Explain your decision using the ideas of this chapter.

4. In 2014, oil prices fell by around 40 per cent and towards the end of the year touched $57 a barrel. The Organization of Petroleum Exporting Countries (OPEC), a cartel of leading oil producers, did not, as some anticipated, do anything to restrict output to force the price back up even though most OPEC members had been budgeting for oil prices to be nearer to $100 a barrel. One of the reasons for the falling price of oil has been the increase in supply of shale oil, particularly in the United States, indeed, the US became the world's biggest oil producer in 2014 because of the investment in shale oil production. But, shale oil is not cheap to extract, with many analysts suggesting that costs range from between $50 and $100 a barrel.

a. Why do you suppose OPEC might have decided not to cut oil supplies?

b. What might be the long-term outcome on the oil industry if prices continued to fall and remained below $50 per barrel for any length of time? Why might OPEC eventually benefit?

5. A large share of the world supply of diamonds comes from Russia and South Africa. Suppose that the marginal cost of mining diamonds is constant at €1000 per diamond, and the demand for diamonds is described by the following schedule:

Price (€)	Quantity
8000	5000
7000	6000
6000	7000
5000	8000
4000	9000
3000	10 000
2000	11 000
1000	12 000

a. If there were many suppliers of diamonds, what would be the price and quantity?

b. If there was only one supplier of diamonds, what would be the price and quantity?

c. If Russia and South Africa formed a cartel, what would be the price and quantity? If the countries split the market evenly, what would be South Africa's production and profit? What would happen to South Africa's profit if it increased its production by 1000 while Russia stuck to the cartel agreement?

d. Use your answer to part (c) to explain why cartel agreements are often not successful.

6. This chapter discusses companies that are oligopolists in the market for the goods they sell. Many of the same ideas apply to companies that are oligopolists in the market for the inputs they buy. If sellers who are oligopolists try to increase the price of goods they sell, what is the goal of buyers who are oligopolists?

7. A ban on cigarette advertising on television, which many countries imposed in the 1970s, actually led to increased profits of cigarette companies. Explain, using the ideas in this chapter, why this might have arisen. Could the ban still be good public policy? Explain your answer.

8. Assume that two airline companies decide to engage in collusive behaviour.

Let's analyse the game between two such companies. Suppose that each company can charge either a high price for tickets or a low price. If one company charges €100, it earns low profits if the other company charges €100 also, and high profits if the other company charges €200. On the other hand, if the company charges €200, it earns very low profits if the other company charges €100, and medium profits if the other company charges €200 also.

a. Draw the decision box for this game.

b. What is the Nash equilibrium in this game? Explain.

c. Is there an outcome that would be better than the Nash equilibrium for both airlines? How could it be achieved? Who would lose if it were achieved?

9. Farmer Collishaw and Farmer Scott graze their cattle on the same field. If there are 20 cows grazing in the field, each cow produces €4000 of milk over its lifetime. If there are more cows in the field, then each cow can eat less grass, and its milk production falls. With 30 cows on the field, each produces €3000 of milk; with 40 cows, each produces €2000 of milk. Cows are priced at €1000 apiece.

a. Assume that Farmer Collishaw and Farmer Scott can each purchase either 10 or 20 cows, but that neither knows how many the other is buying when he makes his purchase. Calculate the pay-offs of each outcome.

b. What is the likely outcome of this game? What would be the best outcome? Explain.

c. There used to be more common fields than there are today. Why?

10. Little Kona is a small coffee company that is considering entering a market dominated by Big Brew. Each company's profit depends on whether Little Kona enters and whether Big Brew sets a high price or a low price as highlighted in the decision box in Figure 12.9. Big Brew threatens Little Kona by saying, 'If you enter, we're going to set a low price, so you had better stay out'. Do you think Little Kona should believe the threat? Why or why not? What do you think Little Kona should do?

FIGURE 12.9

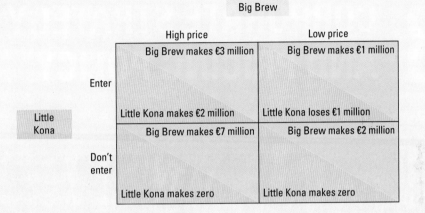

Big Brew

		High price	Low price
	Enter	Big Brew makes €3 million Little Kona makes €2 million	Big Brew makes €1 million Little Kona loses €1 million
Little Kona	**Don't enter**	Big Brew makes €7 million Little Kona makes zero	Big Brew makes €2 million Little Kona makes zero

13 CORPORATE STRATEGY AND PRICING POLICY

LEARNING OUTCOMES

After reading this chapter you should be able to:

- Give a clear definition of strategy.
- Outline at least two frameworks for strategic analysis.
- Outline some benefits and limitations of strategic planning.
- Outline the main features of the resource-based model.
- Explain the idea of emergent strategy.

- Outline the idea of logical incrementalism.
- Explain the main features of market-based strategies including value chain analysis, cost leadership, differentiation and niche marketing.
- Analyse the processes and challenges of implementing strategy.
- Explain the concept of the margin.
- Discuss the issues facing firms in making pricing decisions covering a range of pricing strategies.

INTRODUCTION

In this chapter we will be looking at aspects of corporate strategy and pricing policy. Strategy is a subject with many different points of view but we will present an outline of the key issues. We are going to start by looking at the idea of corporate strategy and then at some of the principal pricing strategies that firms in imperfectly competitive markets can adopt. Pricing strategies are not relevant in perfect competition because firms are price takers and have no control over the price they charge.

BUSINESS STRATEGY

There are many books written on strategy and there are intense debates between academics, between business leaders and between academics and business leaders about exactly what it means. What follows is an outline of the main schools of thought. Strategy can be individual to particular firms and industries and is highly complex, differing from organization to organization.

What is Strategy?

To take a broad definition, strategy can be seen as a series of actions, decisions and obligations which lead to the firm gaining a competitive advantage and exploiting the firm's core competencies. This definition implies the future and as such we can shorten this definition to note that strategy is about where the business wants to be at some point in the future and what steps it needs to take to get there. It is, therefore, about setting the overall direction of the business but in times of change much of this direction will be carried out in an environment of uncertainty.

The Strategic Hierarchy

Typically we might expect the strategic direction of the firm to be formulated at the highest levels of the business and this strategy then informs decisions and behaviour lower down the organization. This may be the case in many firms but we must also be aware that organizations now recognize that the senior team do not always have all the answers and increasingly, strategy is formulated at lower levels of the organization. Such strategic formulation and management is likely to be carried out in the context of the firm's overall strategy but that overall strategy may be formulated around a series of strategic intents rather than being anything specific. **Strategic intent** was picked up by Max Boisot in 1995 following the development of the idea by Gary Hamel and C.K. Prahalad in an article in the *Harvard Business Review* in 1989.

Strategic intent refers to establishing and sharing a vision of where a business wants to be at some point in the future and encouraging all those involved in the business to understand and work towards achieving this vision. Strategic intent can be thought of as a framework for decision making in an uncertain environment where detailed plans can be very quickly blown off course. Whenever key decisions need to be made, the decision maker/s need to refer back to the strategic intent and ask themselves the question: what decision would help to allow the firm to operate at a higher level in line with the vision?

strategic intent a framework for establishing and sharing a vision of where a business wants to be at some point in the future and encouraging all those involved in the business to understand and work towards achieving this vision

Strategic Planning

If a firm is able to articulate where it wants to be in the future then it needs to put something in place to help it achieve that goal and this might be a plan of some description. Strategic planning aims to put in place a system for decision making which is designed to help the business achieve its long-term goals. Such a plan may include four elements: establishing the purpose, objectives, strategies and tactics, commonly referred to by the acronym POST.

In order to develop the plan there needs to be a clear understanding of the organization and where it stands in relation to its external environment. Such an awareness-building exercise might start with an analysis of the firm and its market, its place within that market and to understand the market itself.

SWOT analysis an analysis of the firm's strengths, weaknesses, opportunities and threats

This might be carried out by various means such as a **SWOT analysis** (an analysis of the firm's strengths, weaknesses, opportunities and threats) or analysing its product portfolio using the Boston Consulting Group's matrix. This matrix classifies the firm's products in four ways: as cash cows, rising stars, problem children or dogs. Each of these classifications relates to the extent to which the product is part of a growing market and the proportion of market share the product has.

A cash cow will be a product that is in a mature market – the market is not growing but the product has a high market share and as such does not require significant expenditure to maintain sales. A problem child will be a product which has a low market share in a growing market. There might be something that is preventing the product from capturing more of the market and the firm may have to invest more money if the product is to make any progress or decide to withdraw it from the market – something which would be sensible if the cost of supporting it was much higher than the revenues it was projected to bring in. A rising star is a product which is part of a growing market and whose market share is also rising. This type of product may be a future cash cow. A dog is a product in a market which is declining and it may also have a low market share. This is a product which is a candidate for withdrawal from the market. These different categories can be represented in a matrix as shown in Figure 13.1.

FIGURE 13.1

The Boston Consulting Group Matrix

The Boston Consulting Group matrix classifies products in relation to market share (horizontal axis) and the extent to which it is a part of a growing market (vertical axis). The matrix then groups products into four classifications: Stars, Dogs, Cash Cows and Problem Children.

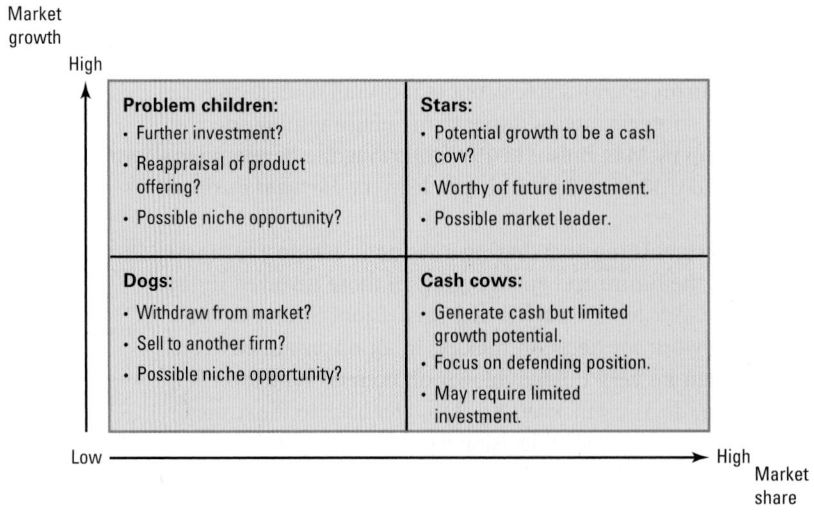

Market growth

High

Problem children:	Stars:
• Further investment?	• Potential growth to be a cash cow?
• Reappraisal of product offering?	• Worthy of future investment.
• Possible niche opportunity?	• Possible market leader.

Dogs:	Cash cows:
• Withdraw from market?	• Generate cash but limited growth potential.
• Sell to another firm?	• Focus on defending position.
• Possible niche opportunity?	• May require limited investment.

Low ──────────────────────────────► High

Market share

Many larger firms have large product portfolios so using the Boston Matrix may be one way in which they can analyse this portfolio. The firms can make decisions about supporting products, whether new product development needs to be carried out (which may be the case if they have a number of cash cows), and their overall market presence. It is a framework, therefore, for making decisions and reflects the firm's obligations and where it wants to be in the future.

Similarly, a firm might use a framework referred to as Porter's Five Forces. This was developed by Michael Porter in the 1980s and is cited extensively in literature relating to strategy. The Five Forces framework allows a firm to analyse its own competitive strength set in the context of external factors. This includes the existing competitive rivalry between suppliers in the market, the potential threat posed by new entrants, how much bargaining power buyers and suppliers in the market have and what threat is provided by substitute products.

The Five Forces model has been, and remains, extremely influential in business strategy. It is not, however, without its limitations. In particular, the movement of businesses to build collaboration through things such as joint ventures, supplier agreements, buyer agreements, research and development collaboration, and cost sharing all mean that buyer and supplier power might be moderated and not simply be seen as a threat. It is also important that a business recognizes the importance and role of its internal culture and the quality of its human resources in influencing its competitive strategy.

Regardless of the model used, the firm needs to have a clear understanding of its position in the market and that of its competitors to be able to formulate actions that will enable it to be where it wants to be in the future. Some element of planning, therefore, will be essential but the dynamic nature of business means that plans have to be flexible and subject to constant amendment if they are to be of any longer-term benefit. Few firms would create a plan and then stick rigidly to it. The strategic plan may be a way in which the firm outlines its strategy but how does it choose this strategy in the first place?

There are a number of different approaches which have been suggested. The following provides a brief outline of each.

Resource-Based Model

Every firm uses resources. It could be argued that each firm has a unique set of resources and it can use this uniqueness as the basis for choosing its strategy. Resources could be unique because the firm owns a particular set of assets which few other firms have, or employs a particularly brilliant team of production designers; it could be the location of the business that is unique or the way in which the firm has designed and organized its production operations. These resources can be analysed to find, identify and isolate **core competencies**. Core competencies are the things a business does which are the source of competitive advantage over its rivals. Firms can be in the same industry and have access to similar resources but for some reason one firm might better utilize these resources to achieve returns that are above others in the industry. The firm's strategy can be developed once these unique features have been identified and exploited and it is this which helps provide the competitive advantage.

core competencies the things a business does which are the source of competitive advantage over its rivals

Remember that competitive advantage refers to the advantages a firm has over its rivals which are both distinctive and defensible. What this tells us is if a firm is able to identify its core competencies it can exploit these in order to achieve greater returns and its rivals will not be able to quickly or cheaply find a way to emulate what the firm does in order to erode the advantage/s the firm has.

If a firm develops a strategy that starts to move away from its core competencies then there is a potential for failure unless it can also develop core competencies in this new area. For example, a firm like 3M has core competencies in substrates (the base material onto which something will be printed or laminated or protected), coatings and adhesives. It might use its expertise in these areas to formulate a strategy which seeks to exploit these competencies but if it decides that it will branch out to another area, for example, into cleaning products to complement its Scotch-guard protection brand, then it might find the expertise needed in that area is not something it possesses and as such may end up making below average returns.

There are plenty of examples of firms that have tried to branch out into new areas outside their expertise and have failed. Harley Davidson, for example, attempted to move into the perfume market, Bic, the ball point pen manufacturer, into ladies underwear and the women's magazine, *Cosmopolitan*, attempted to launch a range of yoghurts. In each case the moves were unsuccessful, partly because consumers failed to understand the association between what were established brands and a new departure, but also because the new ideas did not represent the core competencies of each firm.

Emergent Strategy

The dynamic and often chaotic nature of the business environment means that whatever plans a business has are likely to be outdated almost as soon as they are written, or overtaken by events which occur and which are outside the control of the business. The model of emergent strategy recognizes this reality.

A firm might start off with an intended (sometimes referred to as deliberate) strategy which is planned, deliberate and focused on achieving stated long-term goals. However, it is highly likely that some part of this intended strategy will not be realized and as situations and circumstances change the firm will have to make decisions. These decisions are made with the overall intended strategy in mind but adjusted to take account of the changed circumstances.

Over time this decision making forms a pattern which becomes emergent strategy. This implies that firms may adopt broad policies of intent rather than detailed plans so that they can respond to changed circumstances and also that they can learn as they go along.

Logical Incrementalism

The term logical incrementalism was used by James Brian Quinn, a professor of management at Amos Tuck School, Dartmouth, Colorado. Quinn suggests that managers might be seen to be making various incremental decisions in response to events which may not seem to have any coherent structure. However, these responses may have some rational basis whereby the firm has an overall strategy but local managers respond to local situations. The overall strategy can be realized but incrementally. Such incremental decisions may be affected by resource constraints at a local level which mean that trade-offs and compromises have to be made in order to adjust to these local conditions.

Market-Based Strategy

Market-based strategy turns the focus onto the business environment in which the firm operates and strategy is chosen based on an understanding of the competitive environment. Analysis of the competitive environment is focused on two key areas – the firm's cost structure and how it differentiates itself from its rivals.

It is often assumed that a firm can adopt pricing strategies regardless of other factors in an attempt to win market share or expand sales, but as will be noted later in this chapter, flexibility on the choice of pricing strategy is partly dependent on whether a firm can afford to adopt a pricing strategy. For example, it is only possible to adopt prices that are lower in comparison to rivals if the firm's cost base allows it to do so.

Value Chain Analysis   One of the first things a business has to do is to look at its value chain and examine every aspect to determine where inefficiencies may exist and where cost benefits can be gained. The term **value chain** refers to all the activities and operations which a firm carries out and how value is added at each of these stages. If the value created is greater than the cost of making the good or service available to the consumer then the firm will generate profit. It makes sense, therefore, to focus on these value stages and extract maximum value at minimum cost as the basis of creating sustainable competitive advantage.

> **value chain** the activities and operations which a firm carries out and how value is added at each of these stages

Crucially, value chain analysis can focus on aspects of the business which may have been seen as being unimportant but necessary. For example, publishers have warehouses where stock is processed prior to delivery to customers, whoever those customers may be – book shops, university campuses, online retailers and so on. Time spent looking at ways in which orders can be processed and shipped in the minimum time possible and at minimum cost could help create competitive advantage. If such efficient processes can be developed, it can not only help manage costs within the business and improve productivity, but the reputation of the firm can be enhanced and may result in additional sales in the market when competition is strong. Two Business Economics textbooks may be as good as each other but if one publisher can guarantee order-shipment-delivery times weeks ahead of the other, and with 99.99 per cent reliability, then this may be the reason why a customer chooses one book over another.

Porter outlined a number of key value chain activities:

- Inbound logistics includes goods inwards, warehousing and stock control.
- Operations relates to the processes that transform inputs into outputs.
- Outbound logistics focuses on fulfilling orders, shipping and distribution, marketing and sales, which deals with making consumers aware of the product and ensuring that products get to consumers at the right time, at the right place, at the right price and in sufficient quantities.
- Service, which is associated with the functions that help build product value and reputation and includes customer relations, customer service and maintenance and repair (or lack of it).

By exploiting value chain analysis a firm can identify ways of reducing its costs below that of its competitors and thus gain competitive advantage, which is distinctive and defensible. This is the essence of **cost leadership**. A firm might be able to identify particular efficiencies as described above or exploit possible economies of scale to gain the advantage over its rivals. As the firm progresses through these processes it can also benefit from the *learning curve* (sometimes also referred to as the *experience curve*). This states that as tasks and processes are repeated, the firm will become more efficient and effective at carrying out those tasks, and in a cumulative way, build in further improvements and efficiencies as time progresses.

> **cost leadership** a strategy to gain competitive advantage through reducing costs below competitors

Cost leadership may be beneficial in markets where price competition is fierce, where there is a limit to the degree of differentiation of the product possible, where the needs of consumers are similar and where consumers can relatively easily substitute one rival product for another – in other words, they incur low switching costs.

> **Quick Quiz** Why might a firm want to reduce maintenance and repair to a bare minimum as a means of increasing value?

A detailed analysis of every aspect of the firm's value chain can reveal small but possibly important activities where efficiencies can be improved to generate added value and reduce cost. Ensuring that the various functions and activities are coordinated can also help generate competitive advantage.

Travelling around many countries these days, you might notice extremely large distribution centres located near to major arterial roadways, airports, ports or railways. The development of these massive distribution centres has come through value chain analysis. A number of retail chain stores have such a system where the distribution centre acts as a hub receiving supplies and distributing them along 'spokes'. Such systems have helped give firms cost advantages as well as improving reputation for efficient delivery and order processing. Hub-and-spoke systems are also used by airlines to help simplify routes and keep costs under control as well as get passengers to their destinations as efficiently as possible.

If a firm is able to generate cost advantages through value chain analysis it can gain a position of being a cost leader and as such has greater flexibility in being able to set prices which help maximize revenues or profit.

Differentiation   The second focus of market-based strategies is on differentiation. **Differentiation** is the way in which a firm seeks to portray or present itself as being different or unique in some way. This can be physical in the form of the actual product itself, or mental and emotional through the way in which the business is able to develop its brands, advertise and promote itself and create emotional attachments to its products. Firms attempting to differentiate themselves do need to be aware of the importance of taking into account changing tastes and fashions. What differentiates a firm one year might become a burden the next and the perception of the business becomes difficult to change as time moves on.

Apple has been very successful at differentiating itself from its rivals both in terms of the functionality of its products but also in its design and the way in which it creates a loyal following of customers who are keen to snap up its products whenever they are released. Similarly, firms like Bose and Bang & Olufsen have created a reputation for high-quality sound systems and enviable design which sets them apart from their rivals. Food manufacturers like Heinz increasingly place an emphasis on quality, on the use of natural ingredients and low fat and sodium as a means of differentiating themselves. Hotel chains such as Holiday Inn place an emphasis on consistency so that wherever a guest stays, in whatever country it may be, there are certain features that are familiar and comforting so that guests do not experience any shocks.

Niche Strategies   A **market niche** is an (often) small segment of an existing market with specific wants and needs which are not currently being met by the market. Focusing on a niche might allow a business to identify some very specific customer requirements which it can meet profitably. Imagine a firm which develops flip-flops which have a built-in supportive arch. It is unlikely that 'everyone' will buy this product but for those people who suffer from foot problems, such as fallen arches or flat feet, the product might be extremely useful – so much so that they are prepared to pay a premium price for the comfort they bring.

differentiation the way in which a firm seeks to portray or present itself as being different or unique in some way

market niche a small segment of an existing market with specific wants and needs which are not currently being met by the market

The niche market in this case is a small section of the overall market for summer footwear who have podiatry problems (a podiatrist is a specialist in the treatment of foot problems).

Niche strategies are often beneficial to small firms which have developed specialized products but are certainly not unique to these types of business. Small businesses, in addition, may not have the resources to compete in terms of cost. If producing a mass market product they may have problems in differentiating themselves from their bigger rivals. In such cases, niche marketing may be an appropriate strategy to follow.

Larger firms may also target niche markets by creating trademarks, brands or securing patents. In such cases, firms may be able to not only target a wider market but also specific niches within it. In our flip-flop example, a large firm such as SSL International, the owner of the Dr Scholl footwear brand, might patent the design of foot support flip-flops and secure the niche market as a result.

> **Quick Quiz** What are the key features of a market niche? Give three examples of niche products with which you are familiar.

Strategic Implementation

Having analysed the firm and the market and then decided on some strategy, the next phase is to implement the strategy. This is invariably the most challenging part of strategic management. Implementation involves the way in which the plans and direction are actually put into practice and decisions that a firm takes to translate words into action.

Those who have created the strategy – often the senior leaders and managers in a business – have to communicate the vision and strategy to a range of stakeholders (not just the employees) and then make sure that the structures, design, people and operations are in place to deliver the strategy. In addition, the senior team will have to put in place systems to monitor progress of the strategy. This is not to suggest that the whole process is simply a top-down approach; as noted earlier, an increasing number of firms recognize that strategy has to be a focus at all levels of the business and that individuals and groups lower down the hierarchy have to have the flexibility and freedom to make choices and decisions. The caveat is seeking to ensure that these choices and decisions are made with the overall strategy in mind.

One framework which has been suggested for managing strategic implementation is the FAIR framework. This stands for Focus, Alignment, Integration and Review. In the focus phase, senior managers identify shorter-term objectives in conjunction with departmental or functional heads and in line with the overall strategic goals. These shorter-term objectives then have to be aligned throughout the functional and departmental areas of the organization, with resourcing and practical implications considered and worked through. These plans are then integrated into the day-to-day operational processes and workflows but management of these processes has to be reviewed periodically to see the extent to which the strategy is being implemented and what the results are.

Summary

This brief overview of a very complex topic has outlined some of the issues and thinking on strategy. There are many excellent books and articles on strategy

and strategic management, many of which go into much greater detail about the debates and differing perspectives that characterize the field of strategy. Ultimately, however, a firm has to have some understanding of itself and its market, identify and articulate a clear vision about where it wants to be in the future and find ways of implementing the strategic choices it has made.

PRICING STRATEGIES

One of the key decisions any firm operating in an imperfectly competitive market has to make is on the price to charge for its products. There are a number of pricing strategies (some argue they should properly be called tactics). The purpose of pricing strategies is to influence sales in some way or to reflect something about the product that the firm wishes to communicate to its customers and potential customers. At its simplest, there are only a few things a firm can do – either set price lower than its rivals, set price higher in order to reflect a standard or some suggestion of quality, or seek to set price at a similar level to that of its rivals.

Of course, the ability of the firm to use price as a means of influencing sales depends to a large extent on its costs. The difference between the cost of production and price can be looked at as a **margin** – the amount of profit a firm makes on each sale. Of course, this definition does depend on how 'cost of production' is calculated and what costs are included. However, for our purposes, looking at margins as the profit a firm makes from each sale is sufficient for our analysis. A firm operating at a higher cost base than its rivals will struggle in the long term to match the low prices its rivals may be able to charge because they have a lower average cost.

margin the amount of profit a firm makes on each sale

CASE STUDY

Why do We Pay the Same Price to See a Good Film as We do for a Flop?

The price of theatre tickets, football tickets and airline tickets varies according to the level of demand but this is generally not the case with cinema tickets. There is some variation in cinema ticket prices according to the time of day, day of the week and from price discrimination

according to age, however the price you pay does not depend on the quality and popularity of the film you decide to see. That price is fixed. Consequently some films play to empty seats. It may make sense to lower prices for relatively unpopular films in an effort to attract more cinema goers.

Todd Juenger, a media analyst, thinks that cinemas and the film industry have got it all wrong. He points out that cinemas are very inefficient since, on average, they operate at only 7 per cent of their capacity. Perhaps the pricing strategy is down to pride because if a film studio discounted a film in order to encourage more people to see it, then that studio would be owning up to producing a film of poor quality. The studios earn revenue from receiving a percentage of the price of each ticket sold. They also receive more income from DVD sales.

Having a fixed ticket price means there is a price ceiling on popular films which could command premium ticket prices. So why not have higher prices for blockbusters? Having fixed prices means lower demand for poor films and too high a demand for successful films, so what happens to alleviate the problem? The multiplexes provide an answer. The less popular films are shown in the smaller capacity auditoriums and the blockbusters use the higher capacity auditoriums. Popular films can also run for longer periods. This is decided by each multiplex and is an alternative to price adjustments.

Price adjustments in cinemas had been tried for a few years under the easyGroup brand easyCinema. It was based on the successful easyJet model with low headline ticket prices for early bookers and then increasing prices according to demand. The business model failed, partly because easyCinema wanted to negotiate a fixed price per film but the film studios refused this, preferring the model of receiving a percentage of each ticket sold. This has not deterred easyGroup from trying other ventures – there are some 24 easyGroup brands. As well as getting flights, you can book your easyHotel room, hire your easyCar and even order an easyPizza, but get in early to get the best prices.

Reference: **http://filmjunk.com/2012/04/16/theatre-owners-considering-variable-movie -ticket-prices-based-on-movie-quality/**

Cost-Plus Pricing

This is perhaps the simplest form of pricing. The firm calculates the cost of production per unit and then sets price above this cost. The price can therefore reflect the margin or mark-up that the firm desires. For this reason cost plus pricing is also referred to as *mark-up pricing* or *full-cost pricing*. Let us take an example. Assume that a hairdresser calculates the average cost of a styling to include the cost of the stylist's time, the chemicals used during the styling as well as working out how the fixed costs could be attributed to each customer (for example, the cost of heating and lighting, rent on the premises, rates, insurance, drinks and magazines given to customers, performing rights fees for music played in the salon and so on) at €30. If the salon owner desired a profit margin of 10 per cent then they should charge a price of €33 but if a mark-up of 50 per cent was required then the customer will be charged €45. The formula for calculating price given a desired mark-up percentage is:

Selling price = Total cost per unit × (1 + percentage mark-up, expressed as
a proportion)

If our salon owner calculated the total cost per customer of a simple wash, cut and blow-dry at €12 and the desired mark-up was 25 per cent then the price charged would be:

$$12 \times (1 + 0.25) = 12 \times 1.25 = €15$$

One of the benefits of cost-plus pricing is that the firm can see very easily what overall profit it is likely to make if it sells the desired number of units. It is also possible to set different prices with the same mark-up as shown in the examples above. The total cost per unit of doing a simple wash, cut and blow-dry is not the same as someone having a completely new style with highlights, but by using this formula the salon owner could be sure that the different prices charged generate the same percentage mark-up.

One of the problems is that basing price simply on a desired mark-up does not take into account market demand and the competition. In reality many firms will take these factors into consideration and adjust the size of the mark-up accordingly. Assume that our salon owner knows that there is another salon in town that charges €14 for a wash, cut and blow-dry and that the owner wants to undercut the rival. They set the price at €13. What is the mark-up now?

To calculate the mark-up in this case we use the formula:

$$Mark\text{-}up \ (per \ cent) = \left(\frac{Selling \ Price \ - \ Total \ Cost \ Per \ Unit}{Total \ Cost} \right) \times 100$$

The mark-up percentage, therefore, will be $\frac{13 \ - \ 12}{12} \times 100 = 8.3\%$.

The mark-up is not the same as the margin. In the example above the margin is the difference between the selling price and total cost per unit which is €1. This margin is then expressed as a percentage of the selling price and so would be $\frac{1}{13} \times 100 = 7.69\%$

It is possible that the salon owner might have a desired margin level (let's say it is 20 per cent) in which case this can be used to determine the selling price using the formula:

$$Selling \ Price = \frac{Total \ Cost \ Per \ Unit}{(1 \ - \ Margin)}$$

In our example the selling price will now be:

$$\frac{12}{(1 - 0.20)} = \frac{12}{0.8} = €15$$

Quick Quiz Using examples, explain the difference between mark-up and margin.

Contribution or Absorption Cost Pricing

This is related to cost-plus pricing and is based on the same principles but instead of attempting to calculate the total cost per unit, the firm will estimate the variable cost only and then add some mark-up to determine the selling price. The difference between the variable cost per unit and the selling price is called the contribution. This sum represents a contribution to the fixed costs which must also be paid. Recall the analysis of the break-even point in Chapter 8. As the firm sells more and more units the contribution eventually covers the fixed costs and, for all subsequent sales, the contribution will add to profit.

Contribution pricing may be useful if it is difficult for the firm to ascribe fixed costs to output easily, which may be the case in some service industries.

Psychological Pricing

The basis of psychological pricing is that humans respond to different prices in different ways and for some reason may, as a result, behave differently or have a different emotional response. The classic example of psychological pricing is that of a firm charging €5.99 for a product rather than €6.00. This is partly due to the way we view things – many people may look at the first figure in a price and pay little attention to the last two digits (called the *left-digit effect*). If the firm believes that customers would see the number '5' as being 'reasonable' but '6' as being too expensive then setting the price at €5.99 might encourage consumers to purchase believing they are getting some sort of discount.

Psychological pricing is based on a fundamental assumption that consumers do not behave rationally. If they did then why would they be willing to buy something at €15.49 but not at €15.50? It could also be argued that psychological pricing treats consumers as if they are not very bright and cannot see through the tactic. One can only conclude that the prevalence of use of this tactic would suggest that it does work.

Penetration Pricing

As the name suggests, penetration pricing is a tactic that is used to gain some penetration in a market. The firm sets its price at the lowest possible level in order to capture sales and market share. This is a tactic that may be used when a firm launches a new product onto the market and wants to capture market share. Once that market share has been captured and some element of brand loyalty built up, the firm may start to push up the price. If this is the longer-term aim then there could be a problem with consumers getting used to low prices and being put off when prices begin to rise. At this point, the price elasticity of demand is crucial to the longer-term success of the product. If consumers are sensitive about price then increases might lead to a switch to substitutes or the consumer leaving the market altogether.

Penetration pricing assumes that firms will operate at low margins while pursuing such a tactic, but if successful and sales volumes are high, then total profit could still be relatively high. Penetration pricing implies that a firm needs to have considerable control over its costs to enable it to operate at low margins.

Quick Quiz Why does penetration pricing tend to be a tactic that is associated with high-volume products?

Market Skimming

Market or price skimming is a tactic that can be used to exploit some advantage a firm has which allows it to sell its products at a high price. The term 'skimming' refers to the fact that the firm is trying to 'skim' profits while market conditions prevail by setting price as high as demand will allow.

Such a situation can arise when a firm launches a new product onto the market which has been anticipated for some time. Companies like Apple are very good at building such anticipation (some would call it hype) so that when the product does finally launch, the market price can be set relatively high. It may be that some months later the price of the product starts to fall, partly because of the need to persuade consumers who are marginal buyers, i.e. those that are not devoted to the product and would only consider buying at lower prices, or because the competition has reacted and launched substitutes.

The high initial prices imply that the firm is able to generate relatively high margins in the early stages of the product. These may be used to help offset the development costs, which in the case of technology products like smartphones, tablets and gaming consoles (where market skimming is not unusual as a pricing tactic), can be relatively high.

Destroyer or Predatory Pricing

This is a tactic designed to drive out competition. A firm uses its dominance in the market and its cost advantages to set price below a level its competitors are able to match. The intention is that some rivals will be forced from the market and so competition is reduced. Ultimately the firm which instigated the strategy is able to operate with greater monopoly power. This tactic is illegal in many countries and comes under anti-competitive laws; however it is often difficult to prove.

Loss-Leader

The use of loss-leaders is a tactic that is often seen in larger businesses and especially in supermarkets. A loss-leader is a product deliberately sold below cost and therefore at a loss in an attempt to encourage sales of other products. At holiday times, for example, many supermarkets will sell alcohol at prices below cost and advertise this in the hope and expectation that consumers will come into the store, buy the products which are on offer but also buy other things as well. The other items that are bought generate a profit and this profit offsets the losses made on the loss-leader.

The type of product chosen to be the loss-leader can be important. Often a firm will choose something that it thinks consumers will have a good understanding of in terms of value and original price. By doing this it hopes that the 'incredible' offer it is making will be noticed more obviously by the consumer and thus encourage the consumer to take advantage.

Products which are complements may also be the target of such a tactic. For example, selling a Blu-ray DVD player at a loss may encourage consumers to buy Blu-ray DVDs; or a firm sells wet shavers at low prices but consumers find that replacement blades tend to be sold at relatively high prices (and often packaged in large quantities so that not just one new blade can be purchased). Potential drawbacks could occur if the consumer is highly disciplined and only buys the goods on offer, but evidence suggests this is relatively unusual.

Quick Quiz How might a firm calculate whether a loss-leader has been a successful tactic?

Premium or Value Pricing

The type of market a firm operates in can be a determinant of the pricing strategy it adopts. On the one hand, fast selling consumer goods at a price which is competitive, might generate large volume sales for firms but yields low margins (such as chocolate bars, newspapers and ball point pens). At the other end of the scale, a firm might deliberately set its price high to reflect the quality or exclusivity of the product. It knows that sales volumes will be low but that the margins are high and as a result profits can still be high on low sales.

Premium pricing may be a feature of certain types of technology-based products, luxury yachts, some motor cars, jewellery, designer fashion items, hotels, perfumes and first class travel. In each of these cases the firm may deliberately set prices high or restrict output so that price rises relative to demand.

Competition Pricing

Competition pricing occurs where a firm will note the prices charged by its rivals and either set its own price at the same level or below, in order to capture sales. One of the problems with this is that firms have to have a very clear understanding of their competitors. For example, if a rival firm was charging a particular price for a product because it benefited from economies of scale and had lower average costs, then a new firm coming into the market and looking to compete on price might find that it cannot do so because it does not have the cost advantages. It could also be the case that a rival has set price based on established brand loyalty and simply setting a price at or below this in an attempt to capture sales may not work because the price difference is insufficient to break the loyalty that consumers have for the branded product.

In markets where competition is limited, 'going rate' pricing may be applicable and each firm charges similar prices to that of its rivals and in each case price may be well above marginal cost. Such a situation might be applicable to the banking sector, petrol and fuel, supermarkets and some electrical goods where prices tend to be very similar across different sellers.

Price Leadership

In some markets, a firm may be dominant and is able to act as a price leader. In such cases, rivals have difficulty in competing on price; if they charge too high a price they risk losing market share. Reducing prices could result in the price leader matching price and forcing smaller rivals out of the market. The other option, therefore, is to act as a follower and follow the pricing leads of rivals especially where those rivals have a clear dominance of market share.

? **what if . . .** a firm which is seen as a price leader, increases prices by 10 per cent but its rivals who are classed as followers decide not to raise price in this case?

Marginal-Cost Pricing

This typically occurs when a firm faces a situation where the marginal cost of producing an extra unit is very low and where the bulk of the costs are fixed costs. In such a situation the cost of selling an additional unit is either very low or non-existent and as a result the firm is able to be flexible about the prices it can charge.

An example occurs in the transport industry on airlines and trains. If an airline operates a scheduled flight with 300 seats available from Amsterdam to Riyadh, then the bulk of the costs will be incurred regardless of how many seats are sold. Let us assume that five days prior to departure only half of the seats have been sold and it does not look as if demand is going to rise in the time leading up to the flight departing. If the firm calculates that the cost of taking an extra passenger is €5 (the additional cost of fuel, food and processing) then it makes sense for the firm to accept any price above €5 in the time leading up to departure.

If the standard ticket was priced at €300 but demand is weak then it is clear that the airline ought to reduce price. It could conceivably keep reducing prices down to €5 in order to fill all the seats because every additional €1 above this amount would contribute to the fixed costs and thus make it worthwhile for the airline.

Pitfall Prevention We have covered a range of pricing strategies in this section. However, it is important to remember that firms do not make pricing decisions in isolation. If a firm decides to adopt a price skimming strategy, for example, it will not do this without taking into account many other factors including what its competitors are charging, what type of product they are selling and so on, all of which may be factors that are characteristic of decision making in other pricing strategies.

IN THE NEWS

How Smart is Sony?

You might think that a firm which invents products that revolutionizes the markets it serves would be In a good position to achieve long-term success. Not so in the case of Sony, which is a good example of how strategic choices rely ultimately on human judgement which can often be found to be wanting.

Sony used to have a great brand reputation in leading electronic products reflected in the success of its Sony Walkman and Play-Station products. Its TVs were also popular and at the top of the range. Sony was the market leader for quality cathode ray tube TVs. It was far ahead of its competitors and dominated the market. As technology has developed, Sony has fallen away as indicated by the sales figures for flat screen TVs where competitors have been far more successful than Sony. In 1998, for example, Sony considered buying Samsung when that firm was struggling. Now Samsung is the king.

It seems that Sony underestimated the significance of the flat screen market. It was a latecomer to this new development. It didn't have the required production capacity and therefore had to buy components from other manufacturers. It focused on image quality rather than price but high prices seemed to turn off customers. In terms of the global flat screen market in 2013 Samsung had 21.1 percent of the share, LG 13 percent, TCL (a fast growing Chinese producer) 7 per cent with Sony only capturing 6.2 per cent.

Repeated annual losses before 2013 indicated that the business strategy and pricing had to change, but having six different people in charge of the TV division in a period of 10 years resulted in frequent changes of policy direction.

In 2012 the strategy was directed to producing larger high quality screens, although it has not ignored smaller screen sales using its brand name and has contracted out manufacturing for small screens geared at emerging markets. Part of the strategy has involved Sony TV becoming a subsidiary run entirely separately from its other business divisions.

In the market for high value-added Smart TVs, Sony's market share is higher, suggesting that this focus is working but the market leader is still Samsung having over a quarter of sales in 2013 and growing from 2012. Sony trails far behind with 14.3 per cent and LG recently overtook Sony on the sales leadership board. The trends are not looking too good as Sony's competitors are producing new products at prices people prefer. Sony's market share for Smart TVs had dropped by 1.4 per cent in 2013 compared to 2012 figures.

Questions

1. **Use the Boston Consulting Group Matrix to analyse the position of Sony's TV products in the 1990s, 2000s and in 2013. Explain your reasoning.**
2. **One of the reasons why Sony has struggled is because it could not compete on price and efficiency with its rivals. What factors might have contributed to this situation?**
3. **Discuss whether or not Sony is now aiming at a niche strategy.**
4. **Evaluate the decision of the Sony senior team to refocus its strategy in the way outlined in the article.**
5. **Discuss the factors which may have convinced the senior managers of Sony in failing to exploit its dominance in the TV market.**

References: http://ajw.asahi.com/article/business/AJ201411010008

http://www.broadbandtvnews.com/2014/02/18/samsung-global-smart-tv-market-share-reaches-26/

www.forbes.com/sites/marksparrow/2014/02/09/sony-spins-off-tv-business-in-bid-to-reconquer-market/

SUMMARY

- Strategy looks at where a firm wants to be in the future.
- Strategy involves an analysis of the firm and its market, making strategic choices and then implementing those choices.
- Firms have to consider a wide range of factors prior to adopting any strategy, not least the sort of market structure they operate in; what rivals might do in response; how consumers value the product; what the cost structures are and how these compare to rivals; the extent to which brand loyalty affects demand and the price elasticity of demand.

- There is considerable debate over strategy – ultimately we might conclude that if it was easy then everyone would do it well and be successful!
- There are a range of pricing strategies (or tactics).
- Price is only one aspect of positioning a product – i.e. where the product sits in relation to the market.
- Any decision on price will be one part of the overall strategy of the firm.

QUESTIONS FOR REVIEW

1. Give a definition of the term 'strategy'.
2. Explain how the idea of 'strategic intent' helps a firm provide a framework for strategic decision making.
3. Outline two frameworks which a business might use in strategic analysis.
4. Give a bullet point list to outline the main features of the:
   a. resource-based model
   b. emergent strategy
   c. logical incrementalism.
5. How can value chain analysis help a firm establish an appropriate pricing policy?
6. Why might niche market strategies be beneficial to small and medium-sized firms?
7. Outline three challenges facing a business in implementing strategy.
8. Explain the relevance of the concept of the margin in pricing decisions.
9. Outline two advantages and two disadvantages to a firm of using cost-based pricing policies.
10. Explain the difference between market skimming and price penetration strategies.

PROBLEMS AND APPLICATIONS

1. A chemical firm believes it has a core competency in identifying and exploiting particular chemical processes in intermediate products (i.e. chemical products which will be used to help make other chemical products/drugs, etc.). How might this core competency lead to competitive advantage?

2. 'The thicker the strategic plan the less relevant it will be'. (Quote adapted from Davies, B. and Ellison, L. 1999, *Strategic Direction and Development of the School*, London: Routledge.) To what extent do you agree with this view? Explain your reasoning.

3. Consider the models of emergent strategy and logical incrementalism. To what extent would you agree with the view that they are effectively describing the reality of decision making in an uncertain environment.

4. Using an appropriate example, explain how value chain analysis can be a source of cost leadership and competitive advantage.

5. Choose a product with which you are familiar. Explain how the firm producing that product tries to differentiate it from rivals.

6. A firm producing fancy dress costumes estimates the fixed costs per costume at €20 and the variable costs at €5.
   a. Using this information, calculate the price if:
      * The desired profit margin is 75 per cent.
      * The desired mark-up is 45 per cent.
   b. The firm knows that its rivals charge €50 per costume and it wants to undercut its rivals by 10 per cent.
      * Calculate the price, the profit margin and the mark-up.

7. Two firms operate in different markets and introduce a new product into their respective markets. One uses a price penetration strategy and the other a market skimming strategy. At the end of the first year they both make the same amount of profit. Explain how this situation could arise.

8. Explain why predatory pricing is illegal in many countries. Do you agree that it should be illegal or is this pricing strategy just an inevitable consequence of competition? Explain your reasoning.

9. The tactic of using loss leaders is sometimes referred to as the 'razor strategy' because firms who sell wet razors do so below cost but then charge high prices for replacement blades. What sort of razors do you think this sort of tactic would work with? (Hint: think of the difference between a product such as the Gillette Fusion and disposable razors such as those produced by Bic.) How does a firm prevent consumers treating the razors used as loss-leaders as disposable?

10. What factors does a firm have to have in place in order to adopt a premium pricing strategy?

PART 5

MICROECONOMICS – FACTOR MARKETS

14 LABOUR MARKETS

LEARNING OUTCOMES

After reading this chapter you should be able to:

- Explain why the labour demand curve is the value of the marginal product curve for labour.
- Explain why the labour supply curve is usually upward sloping.
- Explain why a competitive firm maximizes profit when it hires labour to the point where the wage equals the value of the marginal product of labour.
- Demonstrate the similarity between the labour market and the market for other factors of production.
- Explain why the change in the supply of one factor alters the value of the marginal product of the other factors.

THE MARKETS FOR THE FACTORS OF PRODUCTION

The factors of production of land, labour and capital have to be paid for. For many businesses one of the most significant costs they face is paying for labour. They also have to pay interest on loans and pay rent for the factor land.

The payments for factors of production provide one way of measuring the economic performance of an economy. Factor incomes are earned in various ways. Workers supply their labour in return for wages and salaries; the payment to land-owners is called rent and the owners of capital – the economy's stock of equipment and structures – receive interest. Rent, wages and interest are the prices paid for the supply of factors of production. The actual prices businesses pay for labour, capital and land is determined in part by the supply and demand of factors of production. This chapter provides the basic theory for the analysis of factor markets. When a computer firm, for example, produces a new software program, it uses programmers' time (labour), the physical space on which its offices sit (land), and an office building and computer equipment (capital). Similarly, when a petrol station sells petrol, it uses attendants' time (labour), the physical space (land), and the petrol tanks and pumps (capital).

Although in many ways factor markets resemble the goods markets we have analysed in previous chapters, they are different in one important way: the demand for a factor of production is a **derived demand**. That is, a firm's demand for a factor of production is derived (determined) from its decision to supply a good in another market. The demand for computer programmers is inextricably tied to the supply of computer software, and the demand for petrol station attendants is inextricably tied to the supply of petrol.

Our initial analysis will be based on the labour market and that firms operate in a competitive market – both for products and labour. More will be said on this later but it is worth remembering that the analysis assumes that labour is free to enter and exit the market and firms are equally free to employ and shed labour at will – in other words people can move into and out of work easily and employers can 'hire and fire' workers when they need to. In reality, of course, there are a number of imperfections in the labour market but our initial analysis serves to act as a benchmark for looking at how labour markets work in reality.

> **derived demand** when demand for a factor of production is derived (determined) from its decision to supply a good in another market

> **?** **what if . . .** labour markets were perfect markets – would there ever be any unemployment and would firms ever have problems accessing the labour market skills they need?

THE DEMAND FOR LABOUR

Labour markets, like other markets in the economy, are governed by the forces of supply and demand. This is illustrated in Figure 14.1. In panel (a) the supply and demand for apples determines the price of apples. In panel (b) the supply and demand for apple pickers determine the price, or wage, of apple pickers.

As we have already noted, the demand for labour is a derived demand. Most labour services are inputs into the production of other goods. To understand labour demand, we need to focus on the firms that hire the labour and use it to produce goods for sale. By examining the link between the production of goods and the demand for labour, we gain insight into the determination of equilibrium wages.

The Versatility of Supply and Demand

The basic tools of supply and demand apply to goods and to labour services. Panel (a) shows how the supply and demand for apples determine the price of apples. Panel (b) shows how the supply and demand for apple pickers determine the wage of apple pickers.

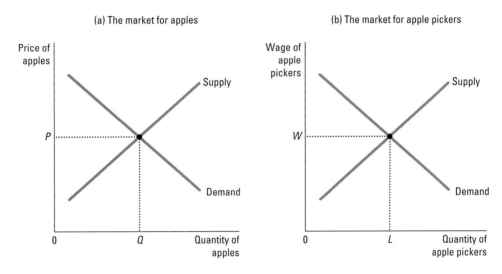

Pitfall Prevention Remember that the demand for factors of production, because of their very nature, are inextricably linked with the demand for the goods and services which they are associated with in production. This is one of the reasons why the workings of the economy as a whole is so interdependent.

The Competitive Profit-Maximizing Firm

Let's look at how a typical firm, such as an apple producer, decides the quantity of labour to demand. The firm owns an apple orchard and must decide how many apple pickers to hire to harvest its crop. After the firm makes its hiring decision, the workers pick as many apples as they can. The firm then sells the apples, pays the workers, and keeps what is left as profit.

We assume that our firm is *competitive* both in the market for apples (where the firm is a seller) and in the market for apple pickers (where the firm is a buyer). Because there are many other firms selling apples and hiring apple pickers, a single firm has little influence over the price it gets for apples or the wage it pays apple pickers. The firm takes the price and the wage as given by market conditions. It only has to decide how many workers to hire and how many apples to sell.

Second, we assume that the firm is *profit-maximizing*. Thus, the firm does not directly care about the number of workers it has or the number of apples it produces. It cares only about profit, which equals the total revenue from the sale of apples minus the total cost of producing them. The firm's supply of apples and its demand for workers are derived from its primary goal of maximizing profit.

The Production Function and the Marginal Product of Labour

To make its hiring decision, the firm must consider how the number of apple pickers affects the quantity of apples it can harvest and sell. Table 14.1 gives a numerical example. In the first column is the number of workers. In the second column is the quantity of apples the workers harvest each week.

These two columns of numbers describe the firm's ability to produce. Recall that economists use the term production function to describe the relationship between the quantity of inputs used in production and the quantity of output from production. Here the 'input' is the apple pickers and the 'output' is the apples. The other inputs – the trees themselves, the land, the firm's trucks and tractors, and so on – are held fixed for now. This firm's production function shows that if the firm hires 1 worker, that worker will pick 1000 kilos of apples per week. If the firm hires 2 workers, the two workers together will pick 1800 kilos per week and so on.

Figure 14.2 graphs the data on labour and output presented in Table 14.1. The number of workers is on the horizontal axis, and the amount of output is on the vertical axis. This figure illustrates the production function for apple pickers.

Thinking at the margin is key to understanding how firms decide what quantity of labour to hire. To take a step towards this decision, the third column in Table 14.1 gives the marginal product of labour, the increase in the amount of output from an additional unit of labour. When the firm increases the number of workers from 1 to 2, for example, the amount of apples produced rises from 1000 to 1800 kilos. Therefore, the marginal product of the second worker is 800 kilos. As we saw in Chapter 9, when a firm adds additional units of a fixed factor, in this case, labour, to a quantity of fixed factors in the short run, it will begin to experience diminishing marginal product. At first, when only a few workers are hired, they pick apples from the best trees in the orchard. As the number of workers increases, additional workers have to pick from the trees with fewer apples. Hence, as more and more workers are hired, each additional worker contributes less to the production of apples. For this reason, the production function in Figure 14.2 becomes flatter as the number of workers rises.

TABLE 14.1

How the Competitive Firm Decides How Much Labour to Hire

Labour	Output	Marginal product of labour	Value of the marginal product of labour	Wage	Marginal profit
L (number of workers)	Q (kilos per week)	$MPL = \Delta Q / \Delta L$ (kilos per week)	$VMPL = P \times MPL$ (€)	W (€)	$\Delta Profit = VMPL - W$ (€)
0	0				
		1000	1000	500	500
1	1000				
		800	800	500	300
2	1800				
		600	600	500	100
3	2400				
		400	400	500	−100
4	2800				
		200	200	500	−300
5	3000				

FIGURE 14.2

The Production Function for Apple Pickers

The production function is the relationship between the inputs into production (apple pickers) and the output from production (apples). As the quantity of the input increases, the production function gets flatter, reflecting the property of diminishing marginal product.

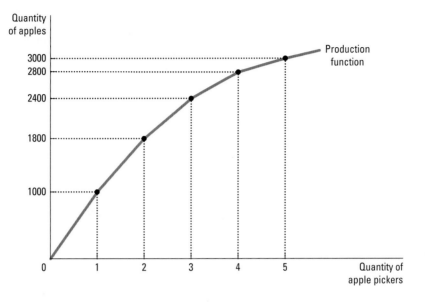

> **Pitfall Prevention** Calculating marginal product is not always easy especially when looking at service industries. Firms in these industries will have to think of how they can measure the productivity of their workers.

The Value of the Marginal Product and the Demand for Labour

Our profit-maximizing firm is concerned more with money than with apples. As a result, when deciding how many workers to hire, the firm considers how much profit each worker will bring in. Because profit is total revenue minus total cost, the profit from an additional worker is the worker's contribution to revenue minus the worker's wage.

To find the worker's contribution to revenue, we must convert the marginal product of labour (which is measured in kilos of apples) into the *value* of the marginal product (which is measured in euros). We do this using the price of apples. To continue our example, if a kilo of apples sells for €1 and if an additional worker produces 800 kilos of apples, then the worker produces €800 of revenue for the firm.

The **value of the marginal product** of any input is the marginal product of that input multiplied by the market price of the output. The fourth column in Table 14.1 shows the value of the marginal product of labour in our example, assuming the price of apples is €1 per kilo. Because the market price is constant for a competitive firm, the value of the marginal product (like the marginal product itself) diminishes as the number of workers rises. Economists sometimes call

value of marginal product
the marginal product of an input times the price of the output

this column of numbers the firm's *marginal revenue product*: it is the extra revenue the firm gets from hiring an additional unit of a factor of production.

Now consider how many workers the firm will hire. Suppose that the market wage for apple pickers is €500 per week. In this case, as you see in Table 14.1, the first worker that the firm hires is profitable: the first worker yields €1000 in revenue, or €500 in profit. Similarly, the second worker yields €800 in additional revenue, or €300 in profit. The third worker produces €600 in additional revenue, or €100 in profit. After the third worker, however, hiring workers is unprofitable. The fourth worker would yield only €400 of additional revenue. Because the worker's wage is €500, hiring the fourth worker would mean a €100 reduction in profit. Thus, the firm hires only three workers.

It is instructive to consider the firm's decision graphically. Figure 14.3 graphs the value of the marginal product. This curve slopes downward because the marginal product of labour diminishes as the number of workers rises. The figure also includes a horizontal line at the market wage. To maximize profit, the firm hires workers up to the point where these two curves cross. Below this level of employment, the value of the marginal product exceeds the wage, so hiring another worker would increase profit. Above this level of employment, the value of the marginal product is less than the wage, so the marginal worker is unprofitable. Thus, a competitive, profit-maximizing firm hires workers up to the point where the value of the marginal product of labour equals the wage.

Having explained the profit-maximizing hiring strategy for a competitive firm, we can now offer a theory of labour demand. Recall that a firm's labour demand curve tells us the quantity of labour that a firm demands at any given wage. We have just seen in Figure 14.3 that the firm makes the decision by choosing the quantity of labour at which the value of the marginal product equals the wage. As a result, the value of marginal product curve is the labour demand curve for a competitive, profit-maximizing firm.

FIGURE 14.3

The Value of the Marginal Product of Labour

This figure shows how the value of the marginal product (the marginal product times the price of the output) depends on the number of workers. The curve slopes downward because of diminishing marginal product. For a competitive, profit-maximizing firm, this value of marginal product curve is also the firm's labour demand curve.

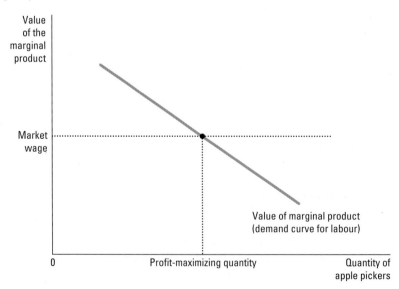

What Causes the Labour Demand Curve to Shift?

The labour demand curve reflects the value of the marginal product of labour. With this insight in mind, let's consider a few of the things that might cause the labour demand curve to shift.

The Output Price The value of the marginal product is marginal product times the price of the firm's output. Thus, when the output price changes, the value of the marginal product changes, and the labour demand curve shifts. An increase in the price of apples, for instance, raises the value of the marginal product of each worker who picks apples and, therefore, increases labour demand from the firms that supply apples. Conversely, a decrease in the price of apples reduces the value of the marginal product and decreases labour demand.

Technological Change Increases in labour productivity can be attributed in part to technological progress: scientists and engineers are constantly figuring out new and better ways of doing things. This has profound implications for the labour market. Technological advance raises the marginal product of labour, which in turn increases the demand for labour. Such technological advances allow firms to increase wages and employment but still make profits providing productivity rises faster than labour costs.

The Supply of other Factors The quantity available of one factor of production can affect the marginal product of other factors. A fall in the supply of ladders, for instance, will reduce the marginal product of apple pickers and thus the demand for apple pickers. We consider this linkage among the factors of production more fully later in the chapter.

FYI

Input Demand and Output Supply: Two Sides of the Same Coin

Remember that a competitive, profit-maximizing firm decides how much of its output to sell: it chooses the quantity of output at which the price of the good equals the marginal cost of production. We have just seen that a firm chooses the quantity of labour at which the wage equals the value of the marginal product. Because the production function links the quantity of inputs to the quantity of output, you should not be surprised to learn that the firm's decision about input demand is closely linked

to its decision about output supply. In fact, these two decisions are two sides of the same coin.

To see this relationship more fully, let's consider how the marginal product of labour (MPL) and marginal cost (MC) are related. Suppose an additional worker costs €500 and has a marginal product of 50 kilos of apples. In this case, producing 50 more kilos costs €500; the marginal cost of a kilo is €500/50, or €10. More generally, if W is the wage, and an extra unit of labour produces MPL

units of output, then the marginal cost of a unit of output is given by:

$$MC = W/MPL$$

This analysis shows that diminishing marginal product is closely related to increasing marginal cost. When our apple orchard grows crowded with workers, each additional worker adds less to the production of apples (MPL falls). Similarly, when the apple firm is producing a large quantity of apples, the orchard is already
(Continued)

crowded with workers, so it is more costly to produce an additional kilo of apples (*MC* rises).

Now consider our criterion for profit maximization. We determined earlier that a profit-maximizing firm chooses the quantity of labour so that the value of the marginal product (*P* × *MPL*) equals the wage (*W*). We can write this mathematically as:

$$P \times MPL = W$$

If we divide both sides of this equation by *MPL*, we obtain:

$$P = \frac{W}{MPL}$$

We just noted that $\frac{W}{MPE}$ equals marginal cost (*MC*). Therefore, we can substitute to obtain:

$$P = MC$$

This equation states that the price of the firm's output is equal to the marginal cost of producing a unit of output. **Thus, when a competitive firm hires labour up to the point at which the value of the marginal product equals the wage, it also produces up to the point at which the price equals marginal cost.** Our analysis of labour demand in this chapter is just another way of looking at the production decision we first saw in Chapter 9.

CASE STUDY

A Wages and Employment Conundrum

Our standard of living depends, in part, on our ability to produce goods and services. If productivity growth is weak then businesses can't increase real wages (taking into account the rate of inflation) unless they are prepared to cut their margins. If productivity is strong then wages can rise without affecting business margins. Put simply, highly productive workers are highly paid, and less productive workers are less highly paid. Therefore, as a nation becomes more productive so do the wages of its workers and consequently there is a rise in living standards. It explains why workers today are better off than workers from previous generations.

Long-run average productivity growth in the UK is around 2 to 2.5 per cent a year. However, productivity varies over time. The last few years provide an example of very low productivity changes since the 2008 crash. If trends had continued since 2007, productivity would be 15 per cent higher than before the economic downturn. In fact the UK economy's lack of productivity growth in the 7 years is unprecedented in the period since 1945. In 2014 as a whole, labour productivity saw little change from 2013, and was slightly lower than in 2007. Productivity growth is related to wage growth, so without productivity gains wages have stagnated. Unit labour costs have increased by less than 1 per cent per year on average over the last 5 years. Businesses have kept down wages and workers have prioritized getting or staying in employment above wage increases. As a consequence, unemployment rates did not rise significantly and indeed the number of people employed in the UK has risen.

The increase in the number of people working has not been matched by the hourly output of goods and services they have produced, nor have wages risen. One explanation is that those who were recently unemployed and have now gained work were prepared to accept employment for low wages. For example, there has been a reduction in UK youth unemployment and they are less skilled and less experienced, so earn lower wages. The effect has been to change the composition of the UK workforce.

Although there seems to be a close correlation between productivity and real wages in the long term, there is also a sluggishness for wages to grow despite the economic upturn in 2014. Increasing the minimum wage towards the living wage may help low earners, but will do little for others.

So the big question is how does the UK increase its productivity rates and how will this impact on real wages?

References: **http://www.bbc.co.uk/news/business-32074752**

http://**hereisthecity.com/en-gb/2015/04/02/uk-productivity-growth-is-weakest-since -second-world-war-says-on/**

http://**www.prw.com/subscriber/headlines2.html?cat=1&id=6757**

THE SUPPLY OF LABOUR

Having analysed labour demand let's turn to the other side of the market and consider labour supply. Here we discuss briefly and informally the decisions that lie behind the labour supply curve.

The Trade-Off Between Work and Leisure

One of the more obvious or more important trade-offs in any individual's life is the trade-off between work and leisure. The more hours individuals spend working, the fewer hours are available to watch TV, socialize with friends or pursue hobbies. Firms are increasingly aware of the effect on productivity of the work-life balance and how employees view this trade-off. The development in technology has meant that many workers are in touch with their work more than ever before and the temptation to put in ever more hours is considerable. This is not always a good thing for productivity. The trade-off between work and leisure lies behind the labour supply curve.

What has to be given up to get an hour of leisure? An hour of work, which in turn means an hour of wages. Thus, if an individual's wage is €15 per hour, the opportunity cost of an hour of leisure is €15. If pay rises to €20 per hour, the opportunity cost of enjoying leisure increases.

The labour supply curve reflects how workers' decisions about the work–leisure trade-off respond to a change in opportunity cost. An upward sloping labour supply curve means that an increase in the wage induces workers to increase the quantity of labour hours they supply. Because time is limited, more hours of work means that workers are enjoying less leisure. That is, workers respond to the increase in the opportunity cost of leisure by taking less of it.

It is worth noting that the labour supply curve need not be upward sloping. If pay increases from €15 to €20 per hour, the opportunity cost of leisure is now greater, but the individual is also richer than before. They might decide that with the rise they can now afford to enjoy more leisure. That is, at the higher wage, the individual chooses to work fewer hours. If so, the labour supply curve would slope backwards.

What Causes the Labour Supply Curve to Shift?

The labour supply curve shifts whenever people change the amount they want to work at a given wage. Let's now consider some of the events that might cause such a shift.

Changes in Tastes The proportion of women in the workforce in many countries is growing and has been since the 1960s. There are many explanations for this development, but one of them is changing tastes or attitudes toward work. A generation or two ago, it was the norm for women to stay at home while raising children. Today, family sizes are smaller and more mothers choose to work. The result is an increase in the supply of labour. In a number of countries governments are looking to provide incentives to get people back to work; this, along with the difficult economic conditions which many countries have faced since the financial crisis in 2007–2009, has also led to more people coming into the workforce who were previously economically inactive – in other words, they are of working age but for some reason have chosen not to be either in work or actively seeking employment.

Changes in Alternative Opportunities The supply of labour in any one labour market depends on the opportunities available in other labour markets. If the wage earned by pear pickers suddenly rises, some apple pickers may choose to switch occupations. The supply of labour in the market for apple pickers falls.

Immigration Movement of workers from region to region, or country to country, is an obvious and often important source of shifts in labour supply. When immigrants move from one European country to another – from Poland to the UK, for instance – the supply of labour in the UK increases and the supply of labour in Poland contracts. In fact, much of the policy debate about immigration centres on its effect on labour supply and, thereby, equilibrium in the labour market.

Quick Quiz Who has a greater opportunity cost of enjoying leisure – a petrol station attendant or a brain surgeon? Explain. Can this help explain why doctors work such long hours?

JEOPARDY PROBLEM

A manufacturing firm wants to increase productivity and thinks that increasing wages is the way to achieve this. It has a working system where workers have a basic working week of 35 hours and any additional hours are paid as overtime. The vast majority of its workers take advantage of the overtime opportunities whenever possible, especially when there are periods of high demand for the product. Overtime pay, especially at weekends and during periods classed as 'unsociable hours', attracts a higher rate than the normal basic pay and the firm has noticed that productivity during these periods of overtime is higher than that recorded during the normal working week. The firm announces that all workers will receive a basic 20 per cent increase in pay for the normal working week but that overtime pay will remain at previous rates. It hopes this increase in pay will boost productivity during the week. Six months after the increase an internal review shows that productivity during the week has not changed but that the amount of overtime workers are prepared to do has gone down. What could the explanation be for this situation?

Equilibrium in the Labour Market

So far we have established two facts about how wages are determined in competitive labour markets:

- The wage adjusts to balance the supply and demand for labour.
- The wage equals the value of the marginal product of labour.

At first, it might seem surprising that the wage can do both these things at once. In fact, there is no real puzzle here, but understanding why there is no puzzle is an important step to understanding wage determination.

Figure 14.4 shows the labour market in equilibrium. The wage and the quantity of labour have adjusted to balance supply and demand. When the market is in this equilibrium, each firm has bought as much labour as it finds profitable at the equilibrium wage. That is, each firm has followed the rule for profit maximization: it has hired workers until the value of the marginal product equals the wage. Hence, the wage must equal the value of the marginal product of labour once it has brought supply and demand into equilibrium.

This brings us to an important lesson: any event that changes the supply or demand for labour must change the equilibrium wage and the value of the marginal product by the same amount, because these must always be equal. This can affect the costs of firms and influence their labour structures. To see how this works, let's consider some events that shift these curves.

Shifts in Labour Supply

Suppose that immigration increases the number of workers willing to pick apples. As Figure 14.5 shows, the supply of labour shifts to the right from S_1 to S_2. At the initial wage W_1, the quantity of labour supplied now exceeds the quantity demanded. This surplus of labour puts downward pressure on the wage of apple pickers, and the fall in the wage from W_1 to W_2 in turn makes it profitable for firms to hire more workers. As the number of workers employed in each apple orchard rises, the marginal product of a worker falls, and so does the value of the marginal product. In the new equilibrium, both the wage and the value of the marginal product of labour are lower than they were before the influx of new workers.

FIGURE 14.4

Equilibrium in a Labour Market

Like all prices, the price of labour (the wage) depends on supply and demand. Because the demand curve reflects the value of the marginal product of labour, in equilibrium workers receive the value of their marginal contribution to the production of goods and services.

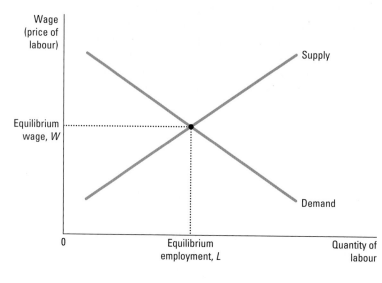

FIGURE 14.5

A Shift in Labour Supply

When labour supply increases from S_1 to S_2, perhaps because of immigration of new workers, the equilibrium wage falls from W_1 to W_2. At this lower wage, firms hire more labour, so employment rises from L_1 to L_2. The change in the wage reflects a change in the value of the marginal product of labour: with more workers, the added output from an extra worker is smaller.

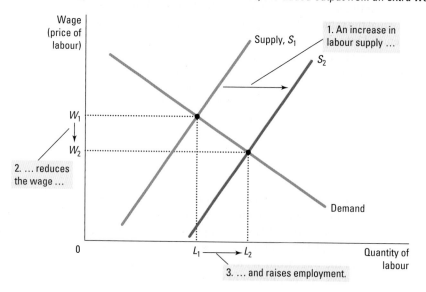

Shifts in Labour Demand

Now suppose that an increase in the popularity of apples causes their price to rise. This price increase does not change the marginal product of labour for any given number of workers, but it does raise the *value* of the marginal product. With a higher price of apples, hiring more apple pickers is now profitable. As Figure 14.6 shows, when the demand for labour shifts to the right from D_1 to D_2, the equilibrium wage rises from W_1 to W_2, and equilibrium employment rises from L_1 to L_2. Once again, the wage and the value of the marginal product of labour move together.

This analysis shows that prosperity for firms in an industry is often linked to prosperity for workers in that industry. When the price of apples rises, apple producers make greater profit and apple pickers earn higher wages. When the price of apples falls, apple producers earn smaller profit and apple pickers earn lower wages. This lesson is well known to workers in industries with highly volatile prices. Workers in oil fields, for instance, know from experience that their earnings are closely linked to the world price of crude oil.

In competitive labour markets, therefore, labour supply and labour demand together determine the equilibrium wage, and shifts in the supply or demand curve for labour cause the equilibrium wage to change. At the same time, profit maximization by the firms that demand labour ensures that the equilibrium wage always equals the value of the marginal product of labour.

FIGURE 14.6

A Shift in Labour Demand

When labour demand increases from D_1 to D_2, perhaps because of an increase in the price of the firm's output, the equilibrium wage rises from W_1 to W_2, and employment rises from L_1 to L_2. Again, the change in the wage reflects a change in the value of the marginal product of labour: with a higher output price, the added output from an extra worker is more valuable.

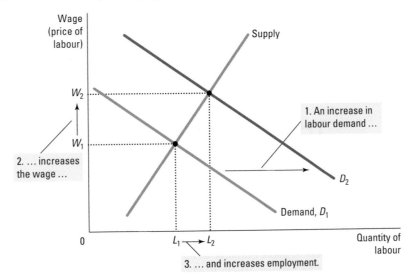

FYI

Monopsony

We have built our analysis of the labour market with the tools of supply and demand. In doing so, we assumed that the labour market was competitive. That is, we assumed that there were many buyers of labour and many sellers of labour, so each buyer or seller had a negligible effect on the wage.

Yet imagine the labour market in a small town dominated by a single large employer. That employer can exert a large influence on the going wage, and it may well use that market power to alter the outcome. Such a market in which there is a single buyer is called a *monopsony*.

A monopsony (a market with one buyer) is in many ways similar to a monopoly (a market with one seller). A monopsony firm in a labour market hires fewer workers than would a competitive firm: by reducing the number of jobs available, the monopsony firm moves along the labour supply curve, reducing the wage it pays and raising its profits. Thus, both monopolists and monopsonists reduce economic activity in a market below the socially optimal level. In both cases, the existence of market power distorts the outcome and causes deadweight losses.

In the real world, monopsonies are rare although, on a small scale, a number of towns in parts of Europe may be highly dependent on a major employer – a motor vehicle manufacturer, a steel works or chocolate manufacturer, for example. Other examples have been cited in relation to the plans by multinationals to expand into emerging markets. There have been concerns expressed in the Indian press, for example, about US grocery firm Wal-Mart's plans to further expand its operations on the Asian subcontinent. Wal-Mart faces critics in the USA who claim that it applies monopsony practices by squeezing suppliers and also using predatory pricing tactics to force out smaller competitors. If Wal-Mart does expand further then what protection can small firms and local markets expect, if any? In such situations, the analysis may have to be amended to take into consideration the effect that monopoly power of the employer has on the local labour market. In most labour markets, however, workers have many possible employers, and firms compete with one another to attract workers. In this case, the model of supply and demand is the best one to use.

Quick Quiz How does immigration of workers affect labour supply, labour demand, the marginal product of labour and the equilibrium wage?

THE OTHER FACTORS OF PRODUCTION: LAND AND CAPITAL

We have seen how firms decide how much labour to hire and how these decisions determine workers' wages. At the same time that firms are hiring workers, they are also deciding about other inputs to production. For example, our apple-producing firm might have to choose the size of its apple orchard (land), the number of ladders to make available to its apple pickers, the baskets that are used to collect the picked apples, trucks used to transport the apples and the buildings used to store the apples (capital).

Equilibrium in the Markets for Land and Capital

What determines how much the owners of land and capital earn for their contribution to the production process? Before answering this question, we need to distinguish between two prices: the purchase price and the rental price. The *purchase price* of land or capital is the price a person pays to own that factor of production indefinitely. The *rental price* is the price a person pays to use that factor for a limited period of time. It is important to keep this distinction in mind because, as we will see, these prices are determined by somewhat different economic forces.

Having defined these terms, we can now apply the theory of factor demand that we developed for the labour market to the markets for land and capital. The wage is, after all, simply the rental price of labour. Therefore, much of what we have learned about wage determination applies also to the rental prices of land and capital. As Figure 14.7 illustrates, the rental price of land, shown in panel (a), and the rental price of capital, shown in panel (b), are determined by supply and demand. Moreover, the demand for land and capital is determined just like the demand for labour. That is, when our apple-producing firm is deciding how much land and how many ladders to rent, it follows the same logic as when deciding how many workers to hire. For both land and capital, the firm increases the quantity hired until the value of the factor's marginal product equals the factor's price. Thus, the demand curve for each factor reflects the marginal productivity of that factor.

We can now explain how much income goes to labour, how much goes to landowners and how much goes to the owners of capital. As long as the firms using the factors of production are competitive and profit-maximizing, each factor's rental price must equal the value of the marginal product for that factor: labour, land and capital each earn the value of their marginal contribution to the production process.

FIGURE 14.7

The Markets for Land and Capital

Supply and demand determine the compensation paid to the owners of land, as shown in panel (a), and the compensation paid to the owners of capital, as shown in panel (b). The demand for each factor, in turn, depends on the value of the marginal product of that factor.

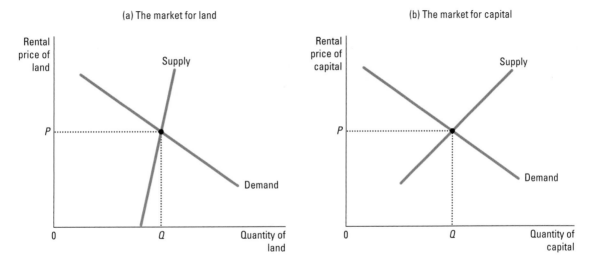

Now consider the purchase price of land and capital. The rental price and the purchase price are obviously related: buyers are willing to pay more for a piece of land or capital if it produces a valuable stream of rental income. And, as we have just seen, the equilibrium rental income at any point in time equals the value of that factor's marginal product. Therefore, the equilibrium purchase price of a piece of land or capital depends on both the current value of the marginal product and the value of the marginal product expected to prevail in the future.

Linkages Among the Factors of Production

The price paid for any factor of production – labour, land or capital – equals the value of the marginal product of that factor. The marginal product of any factor depends on the quantity of that factor that is available. Because of diminishing marginal product, a factor in abundant supply has a low marginal product and thus a low price, and a factor in scarce supply has a high marginal product and a high price. As a result, when the supply of a factor falls, its equilibrium factor price rises and so firm's costs rise.

When the supply of any factor changes, however, the effects are not limited to the market for that factor. In most situations, factors of production are used together in a way that makes the productivity of each factor dependent on the quantities of the other factors available to be used in the production process. As a result, a change in the supply of any one factor alters the earnings of all the factors.

For example, suppose one night lightning strikes the storehouse in which are kept the ladders that the apple pickers use to pick apples from the orchards, and many of the ladders are destroyed in the ensuing fire. What happens to the earnings of the various factors of production? Most obviously, the supply of ladders falls and, therefore, the equilibrium rental price of ladders rises. Those owners who were lucky enough to avoid damage to their ladders now earn a higher return when they rent out their ladders to the firms that produce apples.

Yet the effects of this event do not stop at the ladder market. Because there are fewer ladders with which to work, the workers who pick apples have a smaller marginal product. Thus, the reduction in the supply of ladders reduces the demand for the labour of apple pickers, and this causes the equilibrium wage to fall.

This story shows a general lesson: an event that changes the supply of any factor of production can alter the earnings of all the factors. The change in earnings of any factor can be found by analysing the impact of the event on the value of the marginal product of that factor.

FYI

What is Capital Income?

Labour income is an easy concept to understand: it is the wages and salaries that workers get from their employers. The income earned by capital, however, is less obvious.

In our analysis, we have been implicitly assuming that households own the economy's stock of capital – equipment, machinery, computers, warehouses and so

forth – and rent it to the firms that use it. Capital income, in this case, is the rent that households receive for the use of their capital. This assumption simplified our analysis of how capital owners are compensated, but it is not entirely realistic. In fact, firms usually own the capital they use and, therefore, they receive the earnings from this capital.

These earnings from capital, however, eventually get paid to households. Some of the earnings are paid in the form of interest to those households who have lent money to firms (anyone who has savings in a financial institution, who pays into a pension fund or an insurance policy is indirectly actually lending money to businesses). Bondholders and bank depositors are two examples of recipients of interest. Thus, when an individual receives interest on their bank account, that income is part of the economy's capital income.

In addition, some of the earnings from capital are paid to households in the form of dividends. Dividends are payments by a firm to its shareholders. A shareholder is a person who has bought a share in the ownership of the firm and, therefore, is entitled to share in the firm's profits. (This is usually called an equity or, quite simply, a share.)

A firm does not have to pay out all of its earnings to households in the form of interest and dividends. Instead, it can retain some earnings within the firm and use these earnings to buy additional capital. Although these retained earnings do not get paid to the firm's shareholders, the shareholders benefit from them nonetheless. Because retained earnings increase the amount of capital the firm owns, they tend to increase future earnings and, thereby, the value of the firm's equities.

These institutional details are interesting and important, but they do not alter our conclusion about the income earned by the owners of capital. Capital is paid according to the value of its marginal product, regardless of whether this income gets transmitted to households in the form of interest or dividends or whether it is kept within firms as retained earnings.

EARNINGS AND DISCRIMINATION

Our analysis of the labour market so far has largely been based on an assumption of a competitive market. Imperfections in the market will lead to anomalies in the way in which workers are paid and firms have to face the issues and consequences that arise as a result of these imperfections. Governments pass laws and regulations aiming to reduce the effects of imperfections in the market and firms are often the ones which pick up the bill in terms of the additional costs that have to be paid to meet legislation and regulation. In this section we consider how the characteristics of workers and jobs affect labour supply, labour demand and equilibrium wages.

Compensating Differentials

The sort of jobs firms offer varies. The wage is only one of many job attributes that have to be taken into account. Some jobs require few skills, and are 'easy' and safe; others might require considerable skill and experience; some may be very dull whilst others can be very dangerous. The 'better' the job as gauged by these non-monetary characteristics, the more people there are who are willing (and able) to do the job at any given wage. In other words, the supply of labour for jobs requiring few skills or no experience is greater than the supply of labour for highly skilled and dangerous jobs. As a result, 'good' jobs will tend to have lower equilibrium wages than 'bad' jobs. Economists use the term **compensating differential** to refer to a difference in wages that arises from non-monetary characteristics of different jobs.

compensating differential a difference in wages that arises to offset the non-monetary characteristics of different jobs

Human Capital

Human capital is the accumulation of investments in people. The most important type of human capital is education. Like all forms of capital, education represents

human capital the accumulation of investments in people, such as education and on-the-job training

an expenditure of resources at one point in time to raise productivity in the future. But, unlike an investment in other forms of capital, an investment in education is tied to a specific person, and this linkage is what makes it human capital.

Not surprisingly, workers with more human capital on average earn more than those with less human capital. University graduates in Europe and North America, for example, earn almost twice as much as those workers who end their education after secondary school. This large difference tends to be even larger in less developed countries, where educated workers are in scarce supply.

It is easy to see why education raises wages from the perspective of supply and demand. Firms – the demanders of labour – are willing to pay more for the highly educated because highly educated workers have higher marginal products. Workers – the suppliers of labour – are willing to pay the cost of becoming educated only if there is a reward for doing so. In essence, the difference in wages between highly educated workers and less educated workers may be considered a compensating differential for the cost of becoming educated.

Ability, Effort and Chance

Natural ability is important for workers in all occupations. Because of heredity and upbringing, people differ in their physical and mental attributes. Some people have physical and mental strength whereas others have less of both. Some people are able to solve complex problems, others less so. Some people are outgoing, others awkward in social situations. These and many other personal characteristics determine how productive workers are and, therefore, play a role in determining the wages they earn.

Closely related to ability is effort. Some people are prepared to put long hours and considerable effort into their work whereas others are content to do what they are required to do and no more. We should not be surprised to find that those who put in more effort may be more productive and earn higher wages. To some extent, firms reward workers directly by paying people on the basis of what they produce. Sales people, for instance, are often paid based on a percentage of the sales they make. At other times, greater effort is rewarded less directly in the form of a higher annual salary or a bonus.

Chance also plays a role in determining wages. If a person attended college to learn how to repair televisions with vacuum tubes and then found this skill made obsolete by the invention of solid-state electronics, he or she would end up earning a low wage compared to others with similar years of training. The low wage of this worker is due to chance – a phenomenon that economists recognize but do not shed much light on.

How important are ability, effort and chance in determining wages? It is hard to say, because ability, effort and chance are hard to measure. But indirect evidence suggests that they are very important. When labour economists study wages, they relate a worker's wage to those variables that can be measured – years of schooling, years of experience, age and job characteristics. Although all of these measured variables affect a worker's wage as theory predicts, they account for less than half of the variation in wages in our economy. Because so much of the variation in wages is left unexplained, omitted variables, including ability, effort and chance, must play an important role.

An Alternative View of Education: Signalling

Earlier we discussed the human capital view of education, according to which schooling raises workers' wages because it makes them more productive. Although this view is widely accepted, some economists have proposed an alternative theory which emphasizes that firms use educational attainment as a way of sorting between high-ability and low-ability workers. According to this alternative view, when people earn a university degree, for instance, they do not become more productive (indeed there are often complaints that graduates leave university without the skills that business needs), but they do *signal* their high ability to prospective employers. Because it is easier for high-ability people to earn a university degree than it is for low-ability people, more high-ability people get university degrees. As a result, it is rational for firms to interpret a university degree as a signal of ability.

The signalling theory of education is similar to the signalling theory of advertising discussed in Chapter 7. In the signalling theory of education, schooling has no real productivity benefit, but the worker signals their innate productivity to employers by their willingness to spend years at school. In both cases, an action is being taken not for its intrinsic benefit but because the willingness to take that action conveys private information to someone observing it.

According to the human capital view, increasing educational levels for all workers would raise all workers' productivity and thereby their wages. According to the signalling view, education does not enhance productivity, so raising all workers' educational levels would not affect wages. Most likely, the truth lies somewhere between these two extremes. The benefits to education are probably a combination of the productivity enhancing effects of human capital and the productivity revealing effects of signalling. The open question is the relative size of these two effects.

Above-Equilibrium Wages: Minimum Wage Laws, Unions and Efficiency Wages

For some workers, wages are set above the level that brings supply and demand into equilibrium. Let's consider three reasons why this might be so.

The Minimum Wage Market wage rates are not always at a level which are deemed appropriate. A number of countries have adopted laws to set a minimum wage including the USA and around 22 of the 28 European Union states. A statutory minimum wage dictates the lowest price for labour that any employer may pay. To examine the effects of a minimum wage, we must consider the market for labour. Panel (a) of Figure 14.8 shows the labour market subject to the forces of supply and demand. Workers determine the supply of labour, and firms determine the demand. If the government doesn't intervene, the wage normally adjusts to balance labour supply and labour demand.

Panel (b) of Figure 14.8 shows the labour market with a minimum wage. The reason for setting a minimum wage is because there may be a perception that market wage rates for some workers are too low and so the minimum wage is set above the equilibrium level. In panel (b), the minimum wage results in the quantity of labour supplied exceeding the quantity demanded. The result is unemployment. The minimum wage raises the incomes of those workers who have jobs, but the number of people who have work is less than the equilibrium wage shown in panel (a).

To fully understand the minimum wage, keep in mind that the economy contains not a single labour market, but many labour markets for different types of workers. The impact of the minimum wage depends on the skill and experience of the worker. Workers with high skills and much experience are not affected because their equilibrium wages are well above the minimum. For these workers, the minimum wage is not binding. One would therefore expect a diagram such as that in panel (b) of Figure 14.8, where the minimum wage is above the equilibrium wage and unemployment results, to apply primarily to the market for low-skilled and teenage labour. Note, however, that the *extent* of the unemployment that results depends upon the elasticities of the supply and demand for labour. In panel (c) of Figure 14.8 we have redrawn the diagram with a more elastic demand curve for labour and we can see that this results in a higher level of unemployment. It is often argued that the demand for unskilled labour is in fact likely to be highly elastic with respect to the price of labour because employers of unskilled labour, such as fast food restaurants, usually face highly price elastic demand curves for their own product and so cannot easily pass on wage rises in the form of higher prices without seeing their revenue fall.

FIGURE 14.8

How the Minimum Wage Affects the Labour Market

Panel (a) shows a labour market in which the wage adjusts to balance labour supply and demand. Panel (b) shows the impact of a binding minimum wage. Because the minimum wage is a price floor, it causes a surplus: the quantity of labour supplied exceeds the quantity demanded. The result is unemployment. Panel (c) shows that the more elastic labour demand is, the higher will be ensuing unemployment. In panel (d), because the minimum wage is binding across the whole industry, firms are able to pass a higher proportion of the wage costs onto higher prices without a drastic fall in demand for output, and so the labour demand curve for an individual firm actually shifts to the right at or above the minimum wage, so that the impact on employment is much less.

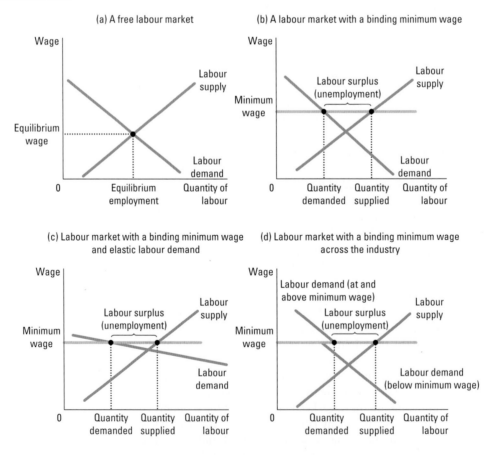

This is only true, however, if one firm raises its price while others do not. If all fast food companies are forced to raise prices slightly in order to pay the minimum wage to their staff, this may result in a much smaller fall in the demand for the output (e.g. burgers) of any one firm. If this is the case, then the imposition of a statutory minimum wage may actually lead to a rightward shift in the segment of the labour demand curve at or above the statutory minimum wage: a firm is able to pay the higher wage without drastically reducing its labour demand because it can pass on the higher wage costs by charging a higher price for its product, safe in the knowledge that other firms in the industry will have to do the same and hence that it will not suffer a dramatic fall in demand for its output. In this case – as in panel (d) of Figure 14.8 – although there is an increase in unemployment relative to the case with no minimum wage, this is mainly because the supply of labour is higher with the minimum wage imposed. This is because some workers will be attracted by the higher wage to enter the labour market – second earners, for example, or young people who otherwise would have stayed in full-time education. Businesses do face an increase in costs when having to pay the minimum wage if the minimum is higher than the market wage for those workers. Small businesses, in particular, may find the additional costs a burden and may have to defer hiring staff, let some go or, in some cases, they may find that the additional costs are too much and they have to close.

Advocates of minimum wage laws view the policy as one way to raise the income of the working poor. They correctly point out that workers who earn the minimum wage can afford only a meagre standard of living. They admit that it may have some adverse effects, including a possible rise in unemployment, but they believe that these effects are small and that, all things considered, a higher minimum wage makes the poor better off. In other words they argue that the value of the benefits of a minimum wage are greater than the value of the costs and so such a policy is worth putting into practice.

Opponents of the minimum wage contend that it is not the best way to combat poverty since it affects only the income of those in employment and may raise unemployment. In addition, they point out that not all minimum wage workers are heads of households trying to help their families escape poverty; some may be second or even third earners in relatively well-off households. To decide whether this argument is more powerful than the arguments of the advocates, economists will try and find ways to measure the size of the contrasting effects so that an informed decision can be made with regard to the value of the benefits and the costs. This is often harder than it may at first appear but is a crucial part of an economist's work.

Labour Unions   A second reason that wages might rise above their equilibrium level is the market power of labour unions. A **union** is a worker association that bargains with employers over wages and working conditions. Unions often raise wages above the level that would prevail without a union, perhaps because they can threaten to withhold labour from the firm by calling a **strike**. Studies suggest that union workers earn about 10 to 20 per cent more than similar non-union workers.

union a worker association that bargains with employers over wages and working conditions

strike the organized withdrawal of labour from a firm by a union

Efficiency Wages   A third reason for above-equilibrium wages is suggested by the theory of **efficiency wage**. This theory holds that a firm can find it profitable to pay high wages because doing so increases the productivity of its workers. In particular, high wages may reduce worker turnover (hiring and training new workers is an expensive business), increase worker effort, and raise the quality of workers who apply for jobs at the firm. In addition, a firm may feel it has to offer high wages in order to attract and keep the best people. If this theory is correct, then some firms may choose to pay their workers more than they would normally earn.

efficiency wages above-equilibrium wages paid by firms in order to increase worker productivity

Above-equilibrium wages, whether caused by minimum wage laws, unions or efficiency wages, have similar effects on the labour market. In particular, pushing a wage above the equilibrium level raises the quantity of labour supplied and reduces the quantity of labour demanded. The result is a surplus of labour, or unemployment. The study of unemployment and the public policies aimed at dealing with it is usually considered a topic within macroeconomics, so it goes beyond the scope of this chapter. But it would be a mistake to ignore these issues completely when analysing earnings. Although most wage differences can be understood while maintaining the assumption of equilibrium in the labour market, above-equilibrium wages play a role in some cases.

> **Quick Quiz** Define *compensating differential* and give an example. Give two reasons why more educated workers earn more than less educated workers.

THE ECONOMICS OF DISCRIMINATION

discrimination the offering of different opportunities to similar individuals who differ only by race, ethnic group, sex, age or other personal characteristics

Another source of differences in wages is discrimination. **Discrimination** occurs when the marketplace offers different opportunities to similar individuals who differ only by race, ethnic group, sex, age or other personal characteristics. Discrimination reflects some people's prejudice against certain groups in society. Although discrimination is an emotionally charged topic that often generates heated debate, economists try to study the topic objectively in order to separate myth from reality.

Measuring Labour Market Discrimination

How much does discrimination in labour markets affect the earnings of different groups of workers? This question is important, but answering it is not easy.

There is no doubt that different groups of workers earn substantially different wages. Different reports show that inequalities in incomes and earnings persist in many industrialized countries. Women, for example, are often reported to earn less in terms of median hourly pay for all employees and less than men for those working full time. Reports also note that people from different ethnic backgrounds are paid at different rates.

Taken at face value, such differentials appear to be evidence that there is widespread discrimination in countries against those from ethnic minorities and women. Yet there is a potential problem with this inference. Even in a labour market free of discrimination, different people have different wages. People differ in the amount of human capital they have and in the kinds of work they are able and willing to do. The wage differences we observe in the economy are, to some extent, attributable to the determinants of equilibrium wages we discussed in the preceding section. Simply observing differences in wages among broad groups – whites and blacks, men and women – does not prove that employers discriminate.

Consider, for example, the role of human capital. Whether an individual has a university degree can account for some of these differences and, in addition, the type of degree can also have an impact, for example, a first class degree in economics or maths might have more 'value' in the labour market than a degree in media arts or theatre. Some of the difference between wages can be traced to differences in educational attainment. Moreover, human capital may be more important in explaining wage differentials than measures of years of schooling suggest. In many countries measures of the quality of education across regions in terms of expenditure, class size and so on, vary considerably.

If we could measure the quality as well as the quantity of education, the differences in human capital among these groups would seem even larger. The Federal Bureau of Statistics in Germany points out that gender pay differences in Germany may be due to a number of factors including differences in educational attainment, a high proportion of women working in part-time occupations, and the type of employment they go into; many of the jobs women enter tend to be low-skilled, low-paid jobs.

Human capital acquired in the form of job experience can also help explain wage differences. In particular, women tend to have less job experience on average than men. One reason is that female labour force participation has increased in industrialized economies over the past several decades. Because of this historic change, in both Europe and North America, the average female worker today is younger than the average male worker. In addition, women are more likely to interrupt their careers to raise children. For both reasons, the experience of the average female worker is less than the experience of the average male worker.

Yet another source of wage differences is compensating differentials. Men and women do not always choose the same type of work, and this fact may help explain some of the earnings differential between men and women. For example, women are more likely to be personal assistants or receptionists and men are more likely to be lorry drivers. (Some people would argue that women get 'ushered' into these types of jobs because of stereotypes.) The relative wages of personal assistants, receptionists and lorry drivers depend in part on the working conditions of each job. Because these non-monetary aspects are hard to measure, it is difficult to gauge the practical importance of compensating differentials in explaining the wage differences that we observe.

In the end, the study of wage differences among groups does not establish any clear conclusion about the prevalence of discrimination in labour markets. Most economists believe that some of the observed wage differentials are attributable to discrimination, but there is no consensus about how much. The only conclusion about which economists are in consensus is a negative one: because the differences in average wages among groups in part reflect differences in human capital and job characteristics, they do not by themselves say anything about how much discrimination there is in the labour market.

Of course, differences in human capital among groups of workers may themselves reflect discrimination. The less rigorous curriculums historically offered to female students, for instance, can be considered a discriminatory practice. Similarly, schools which suffer from low quality may be traced to other underlying social problems. In this case, the disease is social and political, even if the symptom is economic.

? **what if . . .** a government decided to pass a law stating that every firm employing over 100 people had to have a proportion of male and female workers, able bodied and disabled workers and ethnic minorities which closely reflected the proportions found in society as a whole. Would this help reduce discrimination?

Becker's 'Employer Taste' Model

One important piece of research into the economics of discrimination is from Nobel Prize winner Gary Becker from the University of Chicago, who in 1971 revised his earlier 1957 work on the economics of discrimination. The basis of the employer taste model is that (for whatever reason) some employees will resist working with other employees, possibly because of gender or race. People may, therefore, have a 'taste' for only working with certain groups of people. Those outside this accepted group may end up being disadvantaged as a result.

Assume that a UK firm, which grows asparagus, hires workers to cut the spears. It has a choice of employing locals or migrant workers. Local people have a prejudice against migrant workers for some reason. Our analysis of a competitive firm assumes that workers will be employed up to the point at which the wage equals the marginal revenue product of labour. Assume that both local and migrant workers have the same level of productivity. If the firm has to employ workers at a going wage (which is above the minimum wage) then it may choose not to employ workers from the disadvantaged group because of the preferences of its core work-force. If, however, the firm is able to pay workers from the disadvantaged group lower wages then it faces a trade-off. There is an incentive for it to increase profits by employing these 'disadvantaged' workers – the migrant workers from Europe. If migrant workers were prepared to work for the minimum wage then the firm could lower its costs and increase profit as a result.

A discriminatory firm might employ some migrant workers but would pay these workers a lower wage to avoid upsetting their local workers. This is the 'employer taste' model – discrimination will exist because employers do not employ labour from certain genders, race, etc. unless the workers are prepared to accept lower wages. This discrimination may continue whilst there is some limit to the competition in the labour market – in this case it might be that all firms are prepared to act in the same way.

However, if there were other asparagus farmers in the area who were not discriminatory then they might choose to hire all workers at the minimum wage which would increase their overall profits. Such firms would also employ more workers (remember that the lower the wage rate the more workers a firm is willing to employ). There could be an influx of migrant workers to the area who are willing to take advantage of the jobs available. These non-discriminatory firms could not only produce more output but at a lower wage cost per unit and so make more profit, possibly driving out the discriminatory firm from the industry.

In the UK, such a situation has manifested itself in recent years. The extension of membership of the EU in 2004 led to an increase in the number of migrant workers from countries such as Poland, Lithuania and the Czech Republic coming to Britain to find work. Many of these workers appeared willing to take on jobs that paid relatively low wages, such as cutting asparagus spears. In Cambridgeshire in the south-east of England, a large number found work on farms in the region picking and packing fruit and vegetables. In the town of Wisbech, for example, there are over 2000 'local' people who are unemployed but there have been around 9000 migrant workers who have secured jobs in the area – mostly in jobs where the wages are traditionally low.

The sensitivity of the situation in Wisbech, with some of the local unemployed blaming migrant workers for their lack of work, is difficult. Some employers have been accused of exploiting migrant labour by paying them low wages but some counter that they are paying at least the minimum wage and that they find migrant workers not only willing to work for lower pay but also that their productivity levels are relatively high compared with some 'local' labour. In this case not only are migrant workers prepared to work for lower wages but their marginal product is higher at each price (wage). Some farmers claim that 'local' workers are not prepared to do the sort of work that is available and believe that it is too low paid. It seems that regardless of discrimination, employers are more concerned with getting value for money from their employees and are prepared to put profit before discrimination.

CONCLUSION

The theory developed in this chapter is called the *neoclassical theory of distribution*. According to the neoclassical theory, the amount paid to each factor of production depends on the supply and demand for that factor. The demand, in turn, depends on that particular factor's marginal productivity. In equilibrium, each factor of production earns the value of its marginal contribution to the production of goods and services.

At this point you can use the theory to answer the question that began this chapter: why are computer programmers paid more than petrol station attendants? It is because programmers can produce a good of greater market value than can a petrol station attendant. People are willing to pay relatively high prices for a good computer game, but they are willing to pay little to have their petrol pumped and their windscreen washed. The wages of these workers reflect the market prices of the goods they produce. If people suddenly got tired of using computers and decided to spend more time driving, the prices of these goods would change, and, eventually, so would the equilibrium wages of these two groups of workers.

In competitive markets, workers earn a wage equal to the value of their marginal contribution to the production of goods and services. There are, however, many things that affect the value of the marginal product. Firms pay more for workers who are more talented, more diligent, more experienced and more educated because these workers are more productive. Firms pay less to those workers against whom customers discriminate because these workers contribute less to revenue.

IN THE NEWS

China, a Rich Country with Poor Workers

Minimum wage laws exist in many countries, including China, where it is seen as a tool to reduce inequality and to ensure people have enough to live on, but raising minimum wages can have consequences on employment and competetiveness.

There is a CNN online global wage calculator tool that allows you to compare your wages with the average for the country you reside in and then compare it with selected other countries and a world average. Inputting the average wage for the UK indicates that it is over twice the world average, over three times that of China, and over 12 times that earned in India. In fact the average UK wage is 16 times the level of a teacher in Ethiopia and four times the rate earned by a health professional in Greece, as expressed in purchasing power parity (the buying power of what you earn).

(Continued)

China is the second biggest world economy, but workers using the calculator are unhappy when comparing their modest wages with that earned elsewhere. While China is rich, its workers are relatively poor. One reason, perhaps, why China has raised minimum wages. Raising the price floor of the minimum wage in China, an emerging market economy, has, however, led to lower employment. Research by the International Monetary Fund (IMF) suggests that a 10 per cent rise in the minimum wage is offset by a 1 per cent fall in employment and that the figures are far worse for the lowest income groups where the drop in employment is 1.7 per cent compared to 0.6 per cent for the highest. The minimum wage in Shanghai is equivalent to around €270 a month and has nearly doubled since 2009.

The research was based on comparing data from areas where minimum wages were increased to others where the minimum wage remained unchanged. The results of this research presents a dilemma for the Chinese government since it wants to use minimum wage increases to increase domestic consumption and reduce inequality. The policy that ensures people in employment have enough to live on will exclude some low-wage workers from jobs as firms employ fewer people.

Overall, wages in China are rising, eroding China's cost advantage for manufacturing. When China joined the World Trade Organization in 2001, wages in China averaged just €0.51 an hour; in 2015 the figure is more like €5.30 an hour.

At the same time US firms are now much leaner and less labour intensive. The average US worker is 3.4 times as productive as the Chinese counterpart and quality control is easier. Twenty years ago many US manufacturers moved to China to cut costs, but now some, with relatively low labour requirements and high transport costs, such as machinery and fabricated metals, are coming back to the US.

The minimum wage in Shanghai is equivalent to around €270 a month and has nearly doubled since 2009.

Questions

1. **Why might Chinese workers feel they have been exploited?**
2. **Why is it a Chinese policy to raise minimum wages?**
3. **In what way might an increase of 100 per cent in the minimum wage of workers in Shanghai over recent years have affected the labour market in China? Show this graphically.**
4. **Why is it complicated to assess the impact of minimum wages on overall employment levels?**
5. **Why are US workers more productive than those in China and what implication does this have for both the US and China?**

References: http://www.csmonitor.com/Business/new-economy/2012/0510/As-Chinese-wages-rise-US-manufacturers-head-back-home

http://edition.cnn.com/SPECIALS/2014/davos/global-wage-calculator/

http://qz.com/170363/the-average-chinese-private-sector-worker-earns-about-the-same-as-a-cleaner-in-thailand/

http://qz.com/288178/china-continues-to-raise-its-minimum-wage-but-employment-could-be-suffering/

SUMMARY

- The economy's income is distributed in the markets for the factors of production. The three most important factors of production are labour, land and capital.

- The demand for factors, such as labour, is a derived demand that comes from firms that use the factors to produce goods and services. Competitive, profit-maximizing firms hire each factor up to the point at which the value of the marginal product of the factor equals its price.

- The supply of labour arises from individuals' trade-off between work and leisure. An upward sloping labour supply curve means that people respond to an increase in the wage by enjoying less leisure and working more hours.

- The price paid to each factor adjusts to balance the supply and demand for that factor. Because factor demand reflects the value of the marginal product of that factor, in equilibrium each factor is compensated according to its marginal contribution to the production of goods and services.

- Because factors of production are used together, the marginal product of any one factor depends on the quantities of all factors that are available. As a result, a change in the supply of one factor alters the equilibrium earnings of all the factors.

- Workers earn different wages for many reasons. To some extent, wage differentials compensate workers for job attributes. Other things being equal, workers in hard, unpleasant jobs get paid more than workers in easy, pleasant jobs.

- Workers with more human capital get paid more than workers with less human capital. The return to accumulating human capital is high and has increased over the past two decades.

- Although years of education, experience and job characteristics affect earnings as theory predicts, there is much variation in earnings that cannot be explained by things that economists can measure. The unexplained variation in earnings is largely attributable to natural ability, effort and chance.

- Some economists have suggested that more educated workers earn higher wages not because education raises productivity but because workers with high natural ability use education as a way to signal their high ability to employers. If this signalling theory is correct, then increasing the educational attainment of all workers would not raise the overall level of wages.

- Wages are sometimes pushed above the level that brings supply and demand into balance. Three reasons for above-equilibrium wages are minimum wage laws, unions and efficiency wages.

- Some differences in earnings are attributable to discrimination on the basis of race, sex or other factors. Measuring the amount of discrimination is difficult, however, because one must correct for differences in human capital and job characteristics.

- Competitive markets tend to limit the impact of discrimination on wages. If the wages of a group of workers are lower than those of another group for reasons not related to marginal productivity, then non-discriminatory firms will be more profitable than discriminatory firms. Profit-maximizing behaviour, therefore, can reduce discriminatory wage differentials. Discrimination persists in competitive markets, however, if customers are willing to pay more to discriminatory firms or if the government passes laws requiring firms to discriminate.

QUESTIONS FOR REVIEW

1. Explain how a firm's production function is related to its marginal product of labour, how a firm's marginal product of labour is related to the value of its marginal product, and how a firm's value of marginal product is related to its demand for labour.

2. Give two examples of events that could shift the demand for labour.

3. Give two examples of events that could shift the supply of labour.

4. Explain how the wage can adjust to balance the supply and demand for labour while simultaneously equalling the value of the marginal product of labour.

5. If the population of Norway suddenly grew because of a large immigration, what would you expect to happen

to wages? What would happen to the rents earned by the owners of land and capital?

6. Why do divers employed by oil firms to survey, inspect and maintain oil rigs get paid more than other workers with similar amounts of education?

7. How might education raise a worker's wage without raising the worker's productivity?

8. Give three reasons why a worker's wage might be above the level that balances supply and demand.

9. What difficulties arise in deciding whether a group of workers has a lower wage because of discrimination?

10. Give an example of how discrimination might persist in a competitive market.

PROBLEMS AND APPLICATIONS

1. Suppose that the government proposes a new law aimed at reducing heath care costs: all citizens are required to eat one apple daily.
   a. How would this apple-a-day law affect the demand and equilibrium price of apples?
   b. How would the law affect the marginal product and the value of the marginal product of apple pickers?
   c. How would the law affect the demand and equilibrium wage for apple pickers?

2. Show the effect of each of the following events on the market for labour in the computer tablet manufacturing industry.
   a. The government buys tablets for all university students.
   b. More university students graduate in engineering and computer science.
   c. Tablet computer firms build new manufacturing factories.

3. Your enterprising uncle opens a sandwich shop that employs 7 people. The employees are paid €6 per hour and a sandwich sells for €13. If your uncle is maximizing his profit, what is the value of the marginal product of the last worker he hired? What is that worker's marginal product?

4. Suppose a harsh winter in Normandy destroys part of the French apple crop.
   a. Explain what happens to the price of apples and the marginal product of apple pickers as a result of the freeze. Can you say what happens to the demand for apple pickers? Why or why not?
   b. Suppose the price of apples doubles and the marginal product falls by 30 per cent. What happens to the equilibrium wage of apple pickers?
   c. Suppose the price of apples rises by 30 per cent and the marginal product falls by 50 per cent. What happens to the equilibrium wage of apple pickers?

5. In recent years, the UK has experienced a significant inflow of capital in the form of direct investment, especially from the Far East. For example, both Honda and Nissan have built car plants in the UK.
   a. Using a diagram of the UK capital market, show the effect of this inflow on the rental price of capital in the UK and on the quantity of capital in use.
   b. Using a diagram of the UK labour market, show the effect of the capital inflow on the average wage paid to UK workers.

6. Suppose that labour is the only input used by a perfectly competitive firm that can hire workers for €150 per day. The firm's production function is as follows:

Days of labour	Units of output
0	0
1	7
2	13
3	19
4	25
5	28
6	29

Each unit of output sells for €110. Plot the firm's demand for labour. How many days of labour should the firm hire? Show this point on your graph.

7. Assume that the supply of labour in a particular industry is determined by a union of workers.
   a. Explain why the situation faced by a labour union may resemble the situation faced by a monopoly firm.
   b. The goal of a monopoly firm is to maximize profits. Is there an analogous goal for labour unions?
   c. Now extend the analogy between monopoly firms and unions. How do you suppose that the wage set by a union compares to the wage in a competitive market? How do you suppose employment differs in the two cases?
   d. What other goals might unions have that make them different from monopoly firms?

8. A minimum wage law distorts the market for low-wage labour. To reduce this distortion, some economists advocate a two-tiered minimum wage system, with a regular minimum wage for adult workers and a lower, 'sub-minimum' wage for teenage workers. Give two reasons why a single minimum wage might distort the labour market for teenage workers more than it would the market for adult workers.

9. Hannah works for Joachim, whom she hates because of his snobbish attitude. Yet when she looks for other jobs, the best she can do is find a job paying €15 000 less than her current salary. Should she take the job? Analyse Hannah's situation from an economic point of view.

10. Imagine that someone were to offer you a choice: you could spend 4 years studying at the world's best university, but you would have to keep your attendance there a secret. Or you could be awarded an official degree from the world's best university, but you couldn't actually attend (although no one need ever know this). Which choice do you think would enhance your future earnings more? What does your answer say about the debate over signalling versus human capital in the role of education?

15 FINANCIAL MARKETS

LEARNING OUTCOMES

After reading this chapter you should be able to:

- Choose between receiving €100 now or €120 2 years from now, given an interest rate of 8 per cent.

- List and describe four important types of financial institutions.

- Describe the relationship between saving, government deficits and investment.

- Explain the slope of the supply and demand for loanable funds.

- Shift supply and demand curves in a model of the loanable funds market in response to a change in taxes on interest or investment.

- Shift supply and demand curves in a model of the loanable funds market in response to a change in the government's budget deficit.

INTRODUCTION

Businesses, whether small or large, new or existing, require funds to invest in the purchase of factor inputs. An individual entrepreneur setting up a hairdressing salon will need to fund premises, chairs, wash basins, a till, mirrors, chemicals and equipment such as scissors, trolleys and razors among other inputs. A large business manufacturing chemicals will have to purchase plant and equipment, computer systems, buildings, chemical ingredients, vessels and containers, office space, transport equipment and testing laboratories.

The funds needed to purchase these inputs have to come from somewhere. Individuals running small businesses might use savings or borrow money from a bank or from a friend or relative. Many businesses, both small and large, will raise the funds they need by convincing someone to provide the money needed for the business in exchange for a share of future profits. In either case, the investment in inputs is being financed by someone else's saving. In many economies, there are people who do not spend all their income and set aside the remainder as savings. At the same time there will be people who want to borrow in order to finance investments in new and growing businesses. The aims of each of these two groups are different. Savers may want to defer current spending to provide income in the future and look for a return on their savings which will provide them with a future stream of income. Borrowers need funds immediately to finance investment in inputs. These two groups are brought together by financial markets. **Financial markets** consist of those institutions in the economy that help to match one person's saving with another person's investment.

This chapter examines how financial markets work and how firms can access funds for investment.

financial markets financial institutions through which savers can directly provide funds to borrowers

FINANCIAL INSTITUTIONS IN THE ECONOMY

At the broadest level, the financial system moves the economy's scarce resources from savers, who could include individuals and businesses, to borrowers (people who spend more than they earn). Firms represent a significant group of these borrowers. In capitalist economic systems, savers supply their money to the financial system with the expectation that they will get it back with interest at a later date. Firms demand money from the financial system with the knowledge that they will be required to pay it back with interest at a later date. We will be exploring the workings of financial markets in a capitalist system. Not all firms will access funds through a capitalist market system. There is an increase in the role of Islamic finance where the concept of interest is not part of the interaction between savers and borrowers. We will provide a brief outline of Islamic finance but our main focus will be on capitalist financial markets.

Financial Markets

The institutions which make up financial markets are the means through which a person who wants to save can directly supply funds to a person who wants to borrow. Two of the most important financial markets in capitalist economies are the bond market and the stock market.

The Bond Market   When large corporations or the national government, or even local governments, need to borrow in order to finance the purchase of a new factory, a new jet fighter or a new school, they often do so by issuing bonds. When BP, the oil company for example, wants to borrow to finance a major new oil exploration project, it can borrow directly from the public. It can do this by selling bonds. A **bond** is a certificate of indebtedness that specifies the obligations of the borrower to the holder of the bond. The buyer of a bond gives his or her money to BP in exchange for a promise of interest and eventual repayment of the amount borrowed (called the *principal*). The buyer can hold the bond until maturity or can sell the bond at an earlier date to someone else. Put simply, a bond is an IOU. It identifies the time at which the loan will be repaid, called the *date of maturity*, and the rate of interest that will be paid periodically (called the *coupon*) until the loan matures.

bond a certificate of indebtedness

Two characteristics of bonds are most important.

The first is a bond's *term* – the length of time until the bond matures. Some bonds have short terms, such as a few months, while others have terms as long as 30 years. (The British government has even issued a bond that never matures, called a *perpetuity*. This bond pays interest forever, but the principal is never repaid.) The interest rate on a bond depends, in part, on its term. Long-term bonds are riskier than short-term bonds because holders of long-term bonds have to wait longer for repayment of principal. If a holder of a long-term bond needs their money earlier than the distant date of maturity, they have no choice but to sell the bond to someone else, perhaps at a reduced price. To compensate for this risk, long-term bonds usually (but not always) pay higher interest rates than short-term bonds.

The second important characteristic of a bond is its *credit risk* – the probability that the borrower will fail to pay some of the interest or principal. Such a failure to pay is called a *default*. Borrowers can (and sometimes do) default on their loans. When bond buyers perceive that the probability of default is high, they demand a higher interest rate to compensate them for this risk. Some government bonds are considered a safe credit risk, such as those from Germany, for example, and tend to pay low interest rates. Others are much more risky and the interest rate attached to these bonds is high, for example, the government bonds issued by Greece, Portugal, Italy and Spain in 2011–2013. Financially shaky corporations raise money by issuing *junk bonds,* which pay very high interest rates; in recent years some countries' debt has been graded as 'junk'. Buyers of bonds can judge credit risk by checking with various private agencies, such as Standard & Poor's, which rate the credit risk of different bonds. Sometimes, these bonds are referred to euphemistically but less graphically as *below investment grade bonds.*

The bond market brings together buyers and sellers of bonds. Bond buyers may be purchasing bonds as a means of saving for the future. Assume that an individual buys a bond with a €1000 principal with a term of 10 years and a coupon of 3.5 per cent. The individual can keep the bond for the full term and take the interest of €35 each year and when the bond matures receive the principal of €1000 from the borrower. Buyers of bonds do not always want to hold their bonds until maturity and may wish to sell before maturity. The bond market exists to bring buyers and sellers of bonds together. If our individual decided they wanted to sell their bond, the price they would get for it would be dependent on the demand and supply of that particular bond in the market. Demand for bonds will be determined by the returns that the bond will provide in relation to returns that could be provided by placing those funds elsewhere. The price of a bond in the market could be higher or lower than the principal. The yield of a bond (in simple terms) is given by the coupon divided by the price multiplied by 100. The price is quoted as a percentage of the principal.

$$\text{Yield} = \frac{\text{Coupon}}{\text{Price}} \times 100$$

Assume that our bond holder needs to access some cash quickly and decides to sell their bond. They sell the bond for €995. The yield on this bond is $(0.035/0.995) \times 100 = 3.52\%$. If the bond holder was able to sell the bond for €1050, then the yield would be $(0.035/1.05) \times 100 = 3.3\%$. Notice that when the price of a second hand bond rises, the yield falls. There is an inverse relationship between the price of a bond and its yield. Bond prices and yields are affected by the demand and supply of existing bonds in the market, the issue of new bonds, the likelihood of the bond issuer defaulting and the interest rates on other securities. A new bond issue will also be affected by these factors. If current interest rates are relatively high, new bond issues will require a coupon which will be competitive.

The Stock Market   Another way for BP to raise funds for its oil exploration project is to sell stock in the company. **Shares** represents ownership in a firm and are, therefore, a claim on the future profits the firm makes. For example, if BP sells a total of 1 000 000 shares, each share represents ownership of 1/1 000 000 of the business. A share is also commonly referred to as a *stock* or as an *equity*, which can be used with the term 'share' more or less interchangeably.

share (or stock or equity) a claim to partial ownership in a firm

The sale of shares to raise money is called *equity finance*, whereas the sale of bonds is called *debt finance*. Although businesses use both equity and debt finance to raise money for new investments, shares and bonds are very different. The owner of BP shares is a part owner of BP; the owner of a BP bond is a creditor of the corporation. If BP is very profitable, the shareholders enjoy the benefits of these profits, whereas the bondholders get only the interest on their bonds. And if BP runs into financial difficulty, the bondholders are paid what they are due before shareholders receive anything at all. Compared to bonds, shares offer the holder both higher risk and potentially higher return.

After a business issues shares to the public, these shares trade among shareholders on organized stock exchanges. In these transactions, the business itself receives no money when its shares change hands. Most of the world's countries have their own stock exchanges on which the shares of national companies trade.

Organized financial markets trade in a wide variety of financial and commodity products bringing together buyers and sellers from across the globe.

The prices at which shares trade on stock exchanges are determined by the supply and demand for the shares in these companies. Because shares represent ownership in a business, the demand for a share (and thus its price) reflects investor's perceptions of the business's future profitability. When investors become optimistic about a company's future, they raise their demand for its shares and thereby bid up the price. Conversely, when investors come to expect a company to have little profit or even losses, the price of a share tends to fall.

Various stock indices are available to monitor the overall level of stock prices for any particular stock market. A *stock index* is computed as an average of a group of share prices. The Dow Jones Industrial Average has been computed regularly for the New York Stock Exchange since 1896. It is now based on the prices of the shares of 30 major US companies. The Financial Times Stock Exchange (FTSE) 100 Index is based on the top 100 companies (according to the total value of their shares) listed on the London Stock Exchange (LSE), while the FTSE All-Share Index is based on all companies listed on the LSE. Indices of prices on the Frankfurt stock market, based on 30 and 100 companies respectively, are the DAX 30 and DAX 100. The NIKKEI 225 (or just plain NIKKEI Index) is based on the largest 225 companies, in terms of market value of shares, traded on the Tokyo Stock Exchange.

Because share prices reflect expected profitability, stock indices are watched closely as possible indicators of future economic conditions.

financial intermediaries financial institutions through which savers can indirectly provide funds to borrowers

Financial Intermediaries

Financial intermediaries are financial institutions through which savers can indirectly provide funds to borrowers. The term *intermediary* reflects the role of these institutions in standing between savers and borrowers. Here we consider two of the most important financial intermediaries – banks and investment funds.

Banks If the owners of a small restaurant wants to finance an expansion of their business, they probably take a strategy quite different from BP. Unlike BP, a small business person would find it difficult to raise funds in the bond and stock markets. Most buyers of shares and bonds prefer to buy those issued by larger, more familiar companies. The small business person, therefore, most likely finances their business expansion with a loan from a bank.

Banks are the financial intermediaries with which people are most familiar. A primary function of banks is to take in deposits from people who want to save and use these deposits to make loans to people who want to borrow. Banks pay depositors interest on their deposits and charge borrowers slightly higher interest on their loans. The difference between these rates of interest covers the banks' costs and returns some profit to the owners of the banks.

Besides being financial intermediaries, banks play a second important role in the economy: they facilitate purchases of goods and services by allowing people to transfer money from their account to the account of the person or corporation they are buying something from. In other words, banks help create a special asset that people can use as a *medium of exchange.* A medium of exchange is an item that people can easily use to engage in transactions. A bank's role in providing a medium of exchange distinguishes it from many other financial institutions. Shares and bonds, like bank deposits, are a possible *store of value* for the wealth that people have accumulated in past saving.

Investment Funds An **investment fund** is an institution that sells shares to the public and uses the proceeds to buy a selection, or *portfolio,* of various types of shares, bonds, or both shares and bonds. The shareholder of the investment fund accepts all the risk and return associated with the portfolio. If the value of the portfolio rises, the shareholder benefits; if the value of the portfolio falls, the shareholder suffers the loss. These intermediaries are important in providing the lifeblood of finance to businesses.

> **investment fund** an institution that sells shares to the public and uses the proceeds to buy a portfolio of stocks and bonds

We know that firms will raise finance in different ways and through different intermediaries. The decision about what to borrow, how much to borrow, from whom, for how long and at what price are key decisions that businesses need to take at some point in their existence if not at the very outset. Invariably, a business will borrow money to finance activity which will only begin to yield streams of income at some point in the future. For example, an oil company may raise finance to invest in exploration which may result in a successful discovery and supplies of oil flowing 10 years after the initial discovery. Those oil flows may then continue for the next 30 years generating income streams. A pharmaceutical company may spend many years researching and developing a new drug which may bring returns for a limited period of time depending on whether it is able to take out a patent to protect its discovery.

Businesses take decisions on such investments on the basis of whether the expected returns over a period of time are greater than the cost of the investment and, in many cases, on the size of the difference between the expected return and the cost. For example, if an investment only brought a return of 2 per cent over a 10-year period then a firm may decide that is not enough but would go ahead with the investment if the expected return was 8 per cent over the same period.

One important factor here is time – sums of money are not worth the same at different time periods and so a firm not only has to make a decision based on borrowing money at a rate of interest today to gain returns over a period of time in the future, but what the risk involved in making that decision might be. Such decisions might have a significant impact on the value of a company. We are now going to turn to these three topics. First, we discuss how to compare sums of money at different points in time. Second, we discuss how to manage risk. Third, we build on our analysis of time and risk to examine what determines the value of an asset, such as a share of stock.

> **Quick Quiz**   What factors might determine the source of funds for investment in inputs for a business?

CASE STUDY

Financial Crises

In 2008 and 2009, the US economy and many other major economies around the world experienced a financial crisis, which in turn led to a deep downturn in global economic activity. Here we outline the key elements of financial crises.

The first element of a financial crisis is a large decline in some asset prices. In 2008 and 2009, that asset was real estate. The price of housing, after experiencing a boom earlier in the decade, fell by about 30 per cent over just a few years. Such a large decline in real estate prices had not been seen in the United States since the 1930s.

The second element of a financial crisis is insolvencies at financial institutions. In 2008 and 2009, many banks and other financial firms had in effect placed bets on real estate prices by holding mortgages backed by that real estate. As interest rates rose and mortgage holders began defaulting on their payments, some financial institutions faced insolvency.

The third element of a financial crisis is a decline in confidence in financial institutions. While some deposits in banks are insured by government policies, not all are. As insolvencies mounted, every financial institution became a possible candidate for the next failure. Individuals and firms with uninsured deposits in those institutions pulled out their money. Facing a rash of withdrawals, banks started selling off assets (sometimes at reduced 'fire-sale' prices), and they cut back on new lending.

The fourth element of a financial crisis is a credit crunch. With many financial institutions facing difficulties, would-be borrowers had trouble getting loans, even if they had profitable investment projects. In essence, the financial system had trouble performing its normal function of directing the resources of savers into the hands of borrowers with the best investment opportunities.

The fifth element of a financial crisis is an economic downturn. With people unable to obtain financing for new investment projects, the overall demand for goods and services declined. As a result, national income fell and unemployment rose.

The sixth and final element of a financial crisis is a vicious circle. The economic downturn reduced the profitability of many companies and the value of many assets. Thus, we return to step one, and the problems in the financial system and the economic downturn reinforce each other.

Financial crises, such as that of 2008 and 2009, can have severe consequences. Fortunately, they do end. Financial institutions eventually get back on their feet, perhaps with some help from government, and they return to their normal function of financial intermediation but this can take many years.

MEASURING THE TIME VALUE OF MONEY

Imagine that someone offered to give you €100 today or €100 in 10 years. Which would you choose? Getting €100 today is better, because you can always deposit the money in a bank, still have it in 10 years, and earn interest on the €100 along the way. The lesson: money today is more valuable than the same amount of money in the future.

Now consider a harder question: imagine that someone offered you €100 today or €200 in 10 years. Which would you choose? To answer this question, you need some way to compare sums of money from different points in time. Economists do this with a concept called **present value**. The present value of any future sum of money is the amount today that would be needed, at current interest rates, to produce that future sum.

present value the amount of money today that would be needed to produce, using prevailing interest rates, a given future amount of money

To learn how to use the concept of present value, let's work through a couple of examples.

Question: If a business put €100 in a bank account today, how much will it be worth in N years? That is, what will be the **future value** of this €100?

Answer: Let's use r to denote the interest rate expressed in decimal form (so an interest rate of 5 per cent means $r = 0.05$). Suppose that interest is paid annually and that the interest paid remains in the bank account to earn more interest – a process called **compounding**. Then the €100 will become:

future value the amount of money in the future that an amount of money today will yield, given prevailing interest rates

$(1 + r)\, €100$	after one year
$(1 + r)\,(1 + r)\, €100$	after two years
$(1 + r)\,(1 + r)\,(1 + r)\, €100$	after three years
$(1 + r)^N\, €100$	after N years

For example, if we are investing at an interest rate of 5 per cent for 10 years, then the future value of the €100 will be $(1.05)^{10} \times €100$, which is €163.

compounding the accumulation of a sum of money in, say, a bank account where the interest earned remains in the account to earn additional interest in the future

Question: Now suppose the business was going to earn €200 in N years. What is the *present value* of this future payment? That is, how much would the business have to deposit in a bank right now to yield €200 in N years?

Answer: To answer this question, just turn the previous answer on its head. In the first question, we computed a future value from a present value by *multiplying* by the factor $(1 + r)^N$. To compute a present value from a future value, we *divide* by the factor $(1 + r)^N$. Thus, the present value of €200 in N years is $€200/(1 + r)^N$. For example, if the interest rate is 5 per cent, the present value of €200 in 10 years is $€200/1.05^{10} = €123$. €123 would have to be deposited into a bank at an interest rate of 5 per cent to generate a return of €200 in 10 years' time.

This illustrates the general formula: if r is the interest rate, then an amount X to be received in N years has present value of $X/(1 + r)^N$.

Let's now return to our earlier question: should a business choose €100 today or €200 in 10 years? We can infer from our calculation of present value that if the interest rate is 5 per cent, the business should prefer the €200 in 10 years. The future €200 has a present value of €123, which is greater than €100. You are better off waiting for the future sum.

Notice that the answer to our question depends on the interest rate. If the interest rate were 8 per cent, then the €200 in 10 years would have a present value of €200/1.08^{10}, which is only €93. In this case, the business should take the €100 today. Why should the interest rate matter? The answer is that the higher the interest rate, the more you can earn by depositing your money at the bank, so the more attractive getting €100 today becomes.

The concept of present value is useful in assessing the decisions that businesses face when evaluating investment projects. For instance, imagine that Citroën is thinking about building a new car factory. Suppose that the factory will cost €100 million today and will yield the company €200 million in 10 years. Should Citroën undertake the project? You can see that this decision is exactly like the one we have been studying. To make its decision, the company will compare the present value of the €200 million return to the €100 million cost.

The company's decision, therefore, will depend on the interest rate. If the interest rate is 5 per cent, then the present value of the €200 million return from the factory is €123 million, and the company will choose to pay the €100 million cost. By contrast, if the interest rate is 8 per cent, then the present value of the return is only €93 million, and the company will decide to forgo the project. Thus, the concept of present value helps explain why investment declines when the interest rate rises.

Here is another application of present value: suppose a small business is the subject of a takeover. The business owners are given an option about the way the takeover will work. They could either remain as part of the business and take a guaranteed sum of money over a specified period or take an upfront payment and leave the company. Imagine the owner is given the choice between €20 000 a year for 50 years (totalling €1 000 000) or an immediate payment of €400 000. Which should the owner choose? To make the right choice, they need to calculate the present value of the stream of payments. After performing 50 calculations similar to those above (one calculation for each payment) and adding up the results, they would learn that the present value of this stream of income totalling €1 million at a 7 per cent interest rate is only €276 000. The owner would be better off picking the immediate payment of €400 000. The million euros may seem like more money, but the future cash flows, once discounted to the present, are worth far less.

Quick Quiz The interest rate is 7 per cent. What is the present value of €150 to be received in 10 years?

MANAGING RISK

Life is full of gambles. If you go skiing, you risk breaking your leg in a fall. If you cycle to work or university, you risk being knocked off your bike by a car. When a business makes an investment decision, it risks the decision failing and the value of the business falling as a result. The rational response to this risk is not necessarily to avoid it at any cost, but to take it into account in your decision making. Let's consider how a business might do that.

Risk Aversion

Many businesses are **risk averse**. This means more than businesses simply dislike bad things happening to them. It means that they dislike bad things more than they like comparable good things. (This is also reflected in *loss aversion* – research suggests that losing something makes people twice as miserable as gaining something makes them happy!)

risk averse   exhibiting a dislike of uncertainty

For example, suppose a business colleague offers you the following opportunity. They flip a coin. If it comes up heads, they will pay you €1000. But if it comes up tails, you will have to pay them €1000. Would you accept the offer? You wouldn't if you were risk averse, even though the probability of winning is the same as the probability of losing. For a risk-averse person, the pain from losing the €1000 would exceed the gain from winning €1000.

Economists have developed models of risk aversion using the concept of *utility*, the subjective measure of a person's well-being or satisfaction. Every level of wealth provides a certain amount of utility, as shown by the utility function in Figure 15.1. But the function exhibits the property of diminishing marginal utility: the more wealth a person has, the less utility they get from an additional euro. Thus, in the figure, the utility function gets flatter as wealth increases. Because of diminishing marginal utility, the utility lost from losing the €1000 bet is more than the utility gained from winning it. Diminishing marginal utility is one reason why businesses can be risk averse.

Risk aversion provides the starting point for explaining various things we observe in relation to how businesses operate in the economy.

FIGURE 15.1

The Utility Function

This utility function shows how utility, a subjective measure of satisfaction, depends on wealth. As wealth rises, the utility function becomes flatter, reflecting the property of diminishing marginal utility. Because of diminishing marginal utility, a €1000 loss decreases utility by more than a €1000 gain increases it.

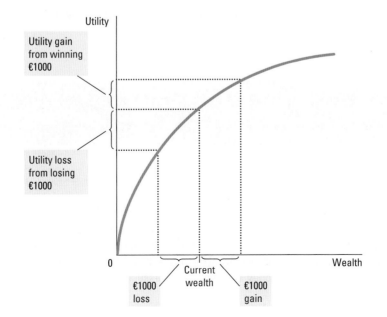

The Markets for Insurance

One way for a business to deal with risk is to buy insurance. The general feature of insurance contracts is that a business facing a risk pays a fee to an insurance company, which in return agrees to accept all or part of the risk. Firms have to take out different types of insurance. They can insure against the risk of their buildings catching fire, theft of goods and loss of revenue in certain circumstances. Businesses are also required to take out insurance to cover the risk of a customer or employees having an accident whilst on the premises and cover for damage or loss to capital equipment.

In a sense, every insurance contract is a gamble. It is possible that none of the risks insured will happen. In most years, businesses pay the insurance company the premium and get nothing in return except peace of mind. Indeed, the insurance company is counting on the fact that most businesses will not make claims on their policies; otherwise, it couldn't pay out the large claims to those few who are unlucky and still stay in business.

From the standpoint of the economy as a whole, the role of insurance is not to eliminate the risks inherent in life but to spread them around more efficiently. Consider fire insurance on a business, for instance. Owning fire insurance does not reduce the risk of losing a business in a fire. But if that unlucky event occurs, the insurance company compensates the business owners. The risk, rather than being borne by that business alone, is shared among the thousands of insurance company shareholders. Because people are risk averse, it is easier for 10 000 businesses to bear 1/10 000 of the risk than for one business to bear the entire risk itself.

The markets for insurance suffer from two types of problems that impede their ability to spread risk. One problem is *adverse selection*: a high-risk business is more likely to apply for insurance than a low-risk business. A second problem is *moral hazard*: after businesses buy insurance, they have less incentive to be careful about their risky behaviour. Insurance companies are aware of these problems, and the price of insurance reflects the actual risks that the insurance company will face after the insurance is bought. The high price of insurance is why some businesses, especially those who know themselves to be low risk, decide against buying insurance if it is not a legal requirement and, instead, endure some of life's uncertainty on their own.

Quick Quiz Describe three ways by which a risk-averse business might reduce the risk they face.

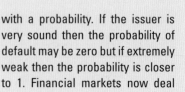

FYI

Pricing Risk

We have seen how bond issues are a means by which firms can borrow money. The bond purchaser has to have confidence that they will get their money back and also receive an appropriate reward for lending the money in the first place. There is a risk involved that the issuer will not be able to pay back the money and that risk is associated with a probability. If the issuer is very sound then the probability of default may be zero but if extremely weak then the probability is closer to 1. Financial markets now deal in pools of debt (collections of different types of loans sold to an investor). As debt is pooled the outcomes become more varied. In any given pool of business debt, for example, there will be some firms who will default and not be able to pay off their loans. Other firms may look to pay off their loans early or will increase monthly payments or pay lump sums to help reduce the repayment period of their loan and so on. Assessing probabilities with such a wide range of outcomes becomes difficult.

The risk involved with such debt is difficult to assess with any certainty. However, investors, including businesses, want to price risk as part of their decision making so that they can judge the value of an asset. If an asset is very risky then the returns expected will be higher and vice versa. In order to have an efficient market in debt, risk has to be priced and the information on which the risk is based must be reliable, accurate – and understood.

Let's consider an example. In your class there may be a number of students that you associate with every day. Take any one individual and we can identify a number of 'risks' for that person and an associated probability of the risk or outcome occurring. For example, there is a 'risk' that the individual:

- fails their exams and has to leave the course
- will be involved in a car crash
- may get mugged
- may contract a communicable disease.

What are the chances of these events happening? The analysis of such outcomes is what actuaries in the insurance industry have to do. An estimate of the probability of such events happening can be derived from analysis of data, specifically historical data. It is possible, therefore, to gather data on the average 19-year-old student coming from a particular area and with a particular background and use this data to arrive at the probability of the event occurring. Historical data tell us, for example, that young people aged between 18 and 24 are more likely to be mugged than the elderly, despite popular perception. The probability of events occurring in business can also be identified and in doing so enable the probabilities to be priced. Securities can be issued based on the probabilities of outcomes occurring – the more likely the event to occur (assuming the effects are negative), the higher the price and vice versa.

While it may be possible to identify probabilities for individual occurrences it may be more problematic when looking at relationships between occurrences. In our example, if one student in your class fails their exams what is the probability that you will also fail your exams? If one individual is involved in a car crash, what are the chances that you will also be involved in such an accident? In both cases the probability might depend on your relationship with that person. If you spend a lot of time with that person then it may be that you share similar distractions – going out every night

instead of studying, skipping lectures to play pool and so on. If this were the case then the probability of you also failing your exams and being involved in a car crash might be high but if you have no relationship at all then the chances of these events occurring are lower.

Looking at relationships between events involves the concept of correlation. If person X is involved in a car crash (and you were not in the car with them) what is the chance of you also being involved in a car crash? The chances are the correlation is very low; the probability of you both getting mugged is higher regardless of the relationship between you, and so there will be a stronger correlation in this instance. The correlation is likely to become more and more unstable the more variables are introduced (number of students in this example). In the case of pools of debt, the same problems arise and the efficiency of the information on which investors are basing their decision becomes ever more complex; probabilities become very difficult to assess and therefore to price.

Actuaries have been studying these types of correlations for some years. The job of the actuary is to provide information to the insurer on the chances of an outcome occurring under different situations. Where information becomes available indicating changes in risk factors, actuaries have to incorporate these into models to help insurers price the risk adequately (i.e. set the premiums for the policy), which in turn influence the costs that firms have to pay to get insurance.

ASSET VALUATION

Now that we have developed a basic understanding of the two building blocks of finance – time and risk – let's apply this knowledge. An **asset** is any tangible or intangible item controlled by an individual or business which has economic value,

asset a tangible or intangible item controlled by a business that has economic value that is, it can be converted into cash. Business assets can include tangible items like plant and equipment, or intangible items such as a brand or the goodwill associated with a particular business, or the value of the skills inherent in the businesses employees. Valuing assets is an important part of any business activity. For large businesses, asset valuation can make a big difference to the financial accounts of the business which it reports to its shareholders. This section considers a simple question which applies to a range of assets. What determines the price of an asset? Like most prices, the answer is supply and demand.

> **Pitfall Prevention** Always take into consideration the type of asset being analysed and note its different characteristics – shares in a business, for example, may have to be treated slightly differently, even if the same principles are applied, to a decision to launch a takeover bid for a rival firm (the asset in this case) or investing in new plant.

Fundamental Analysis

Let's imagine that a business has some cash reserves which it wants to put to use to earn a return. It is deciding how to allocate these cash reserves in different assets. These assets might include acquisition of another firm and investing in new plant and equipment to improve efficiency. When buying any asset, it is natural to consider two things: the value of the asset and the price at which the asset is being sold. If the price is less than the value, the asset is said to be *undervalued*. If the price is more than the value, the asset is said to be *overvalued*. If the price and the value are equal, the asset is said to be *fairly valued*. When buying assets, the business should prefer undervalued assets; in such cases, the business would benefit by paying less than the asset is worth.

fundamental analysis the study of an asset to determine its value

This is easier said than done. Learning the price is easy but determining the value of the asset is the hard part. The term **fundamental analysis** refers to the detailed analysis of an asset to determine its value. Many firms, especially those in the financial sector, hire analysts to conduct such fundamental analysis and offer advice about which assets to buy.

The value of an asset to a business is what they get out of owning it, which includes the present value of the stream of income and the possible final sale price or scrap value. The stream of income an asset can generate depends on a large number of factors: the demand for the product that the asset helps produce; how quickly technology renders the asset obsolete; how flexible the asset is and how easily it can be used for other purposes; and so on. The job of fundamental analysts is to take all these factors into account to determine how much an asset is worth.

JEOPARDY PROBLEM

A business does detailed analysis of a rival firm which it is thinking of taking over. It arrives at a value for the company based on fundamentals such as the current share price, profitability, earnings, the volume of shares traded in recent months, the ratio of its share price to its earnings and dividend payments. Having undertaken this analysis, the firm believes the takeover target is underpriced and that it would be beneficial to launch the takeover bid. When it announces its plans to do so, its own share price falls. What might be the reason, given the amount of analysis the firm has carried out?

SAVINGS AND INVESTMENTS IN THE NATIONAL INCOME ACCOUNTS

Access to funds for business development and growth is closely related to the rate of interest that firms have to pay to borrow money. Whether there are funds available for firms to borrow is dependent on the number of people who are willing to save money. There is a market in loanable funds and the financial institutions we looked at earlier in the chapter play a big part in this market.

The Market for Loanable Funds

We are going to build a model of financial markets. Our purpose in building this model is to explain how financial markets coordinate the economy's saving and investment and thus help channel finance to businesses that need it. The model also gives us a tool with which we can analyse various government policies that influence saving and investment which in turn can affect the amount of funds available to businesses. The supply and demand of loanable funds determines the price of loanable funds – the interest rate.

To keep things simple, we assume that the economy has only one financial market, called the **market for loanable funds**. All savers go to this market to deposit their savings, and all borrowers go to this market to get their loans. Thus, the term *loanable funds* refers to all income that people have chosen to save and lend out, rather than use for their own consumption. In the market for loanable funds, we assume there is one interest rate, which is both the return to saving and the cost of borrowing.

We can identify two types of saving in the economy, **private saving** and **public saving**. Private saving is the amount of income that households have left after paying their taxes and for their consumption. In particular, because households receive income, which we denote as Y, pay taxes of T, and spend C on consumption, private saving is $Y - T - C$. Public saving is the amount of tax revenue that the government has left after paying for its spending. The government receives T in tax revenue and spends G on goods and services. If T exceeds G, the government runs a budget surplus because it receives more money than it spends. This surplus of $T - G$ represents public saving. If the government spends more than it receives in tax revenue, then G is larger than T. In this case, the government runs a budget deficit, and public saving $T - G$ is a negative number.

market for loanable funds the market in which those who want to save, supply funds and those who want to borrow to invest, demand funds

private saving the income that households have left after paying for taxes and consumption

public saving the tax revenue that the government has left after paying for its spending

Supply and Demand for Loanable Funds

The supply of loanable funds comes from those people who have some extra income they want to save and lend out. This lending can occur directly, such as when a household buys a bond from a firm, or it can occur indirectly, such as when a household makes a deposit in a bank, which in turn uses the funds to make loans. In both cases, saving is the source of the supply of loanable funds.

The demand for loanable funds comes from households and firms who wish to borrow to make investments. This demand includes families taking out mortgages to buy homes. It also includes firms borrowing to buy new equipment or build factories. In both cases, investment is the source of the demand for loanable funds.

The interest rate is the price of a loan. It represents the amount that borrowers pay for loans and the amount that lenders receive on their saving. Because a high interest rate makes borrowing more expensive, the quantity of loanable funds demanded falls as the interest rate rises. Similarly, because a high interest rate makes saving more attractive, the quantity of loanable funds supplied rises as the interest rate rises. In other words, the demand curve for loanable funds slopes downward, and the supply curve for loanable funds slopes upward.

Figure 15.2 shows the interest rate that balances the supply and demand for loanable funds. In the equilibrium shown, the interest rate is 5 per cent, and the quantity of loanable funds demanded and the quantity of loanable funds supplied both equal €500 billion.

FIGURE 15.2

The Market for Loanable Funds

The interest rate in the economy adjusts to balance the supply and demand for loanable funds. The supply of loanable funds comes from national saving, including both private saving and public saving. The demand for loanable funds comes from firms and households that want to borrow for purposes of investment. Here the equilibrium interest rate is 5 per cent, and €500 billion of loanable funds are supplied and demanded.

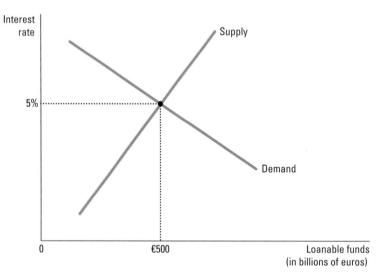

The adjustment of the interest rate to the equilibrium level occurs for the usual reasons. If the interest rate was lower than the equilibrium level, the quantity of loanable funds supplied would be less than the quantity of loanable funds demanded. The resulting shortage of loanable funds would encourage lenders to raise the interest rate they charge. A higher interest rate would encourage saving (thereby increasing the quantity of loanable funds supplied) and discourage borrowing for investment (thereby decreasing the quantity of loanable funds demanded). Conversely, if the interest rate was higher than the equilibrium level, the quantity of loanable funds supplied would exceed the quantity of loanable funds demanded. As lenders competed for the scarce borrowers, interest rates would be driven down. In this way, the interest rate approaches the equilibrium level at which the supply and demand for loanable funds exactly balance.

Economists distinguish between the real interest rate and the nominal interest rate. The nominal interest rate is the interest rate as usually reported – the monetary return to saving and cost of borrowing. The real interest rate is the nominal interest rate corrected for inflation; it equals the nominal interest rate minus the inflation rate. Because inflation erodes the value of money over time, the real interest rate more accurately reflects the real return to saving and cost of borrowing. Therefore, the supply and demand for loanable funds depend on the real (rather than nominal) interest rate, and the equilibrium in Figure 15.2 should be interpreted as determining the real interest rate in the economy.

This model of the supply and demand for loanable funds shows that financial markets work much like other markets in the economy. When the interest rate adjusts to balance supply and demand in the market for loanable funds, it coordinates the behaviour of people who want to save (the suppliers of loanable funds) and the behaviour of people who want to invest (the demanders of loanable funds). When the interest rate changes it affects the risk involved in investment for a business and affects the value of the returns. We are likely to see firms reducing their investment plans when the interest rate rises but increasing them when the interest rate falls.

We can now use this analysis of the market for loanable funds to examine various government policies that affect the economy's saving and investment and in particular the ability of firms to borrow.

Policy 1: Saving Incentives If a country can raise its saving rate, the interest rate (other things being equal) will fall and firms can invest more. This in turn leads to the growth rate of the economy to increase and, over time, the citizens of that country should enjoy a higher standard of living. The savings rate may be influenced by incentives – both positive and negative.

Savings rates in some countries can be depressed because of tax laws that discourage saving. In response to this problem, some economists and politicians have advocated replacing income taxes with a consumption tax. Under a consumption tax, income that is saved would not be taxed until the saving is later spent. A consumption tax could be a direct tax levied on an individual by calculating how much consumer expenditure they carried out over the year and taxing them on that, perhaps at higher and higher rates as the level of consumer expenditure rises.

What is more typical are incentives for people to save which shelter some of their saving from taxation. Let's consider the effect of such a saving incentive on the market for loanable funds, as illustrated in Figure 15.3.

FIGURE 15.3

An Increase in the Supply of Loanable Funds

A change in the tax laws to encourage more saving would shift the supply of loanable funds to the right from S_1 to S_2. As a result, the equilibrium interest rate would fall, and the lower interest rate would stimulate investment. Here the equilibrium interest rate falls from 5 per cent to 4 per cent, and the equilibrium quantity of loanable funds saved and invested rises from €500 billion to €600 billion.

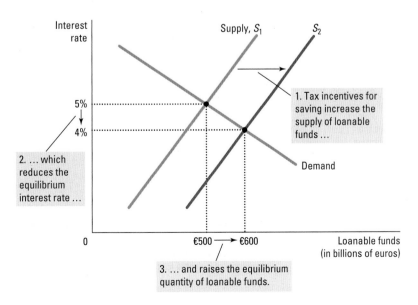

The tax change alters the incentive for households to save *at any given interest rate*, it affects the quantity of loanable funds supplied at each interest rate. Because saving would be taxed less heavily, households would increase their saving by consuming a smaller fraction of their income. Households would use this additional saving to increase their deposits in banks or to buy more bonds. The supply of loanable funds would increase, and the supply curve would shift to the right from S_1 to S_2, as shown in Figure 15.3. The demand for loanable funds would remain the same, because the tax change would not directly affect the amount that borrowers want to borrow at any given interest rate.

The increased supply of loanable funds reduces the interest rate from 5 per cent to 4 per cent. The lower interest rate raises the quantity of loanable funds demanded from €500 billion to €600 billion. That is, the shift in the supply curve moves the market equilibrium along the demand curve. With a lower cost of borrowing, households and firms are motivated to borrow more to finance greater investment. Thus, if a reform of the tax laws encouraged greater saving, the result would be lower interest rates and greater investment.

Policy 2: Investment Incentives   Suppose that the government passed a tax reform aimed at making investment more attractive. In essence, this is what the government does when it institutes an *investment allowance*, which some governments put in place. An investment allowance gives a tax advantage to any firm building a new factory or buying a new piece of equipment. Let's consider the effect of such a tax reform on the market for loanable funds, as illustrated in Figure 15.4.

FIGURE 15.4

An Increase in the Demand for Loanable Funds

If the passage of an investment allowance encouraged firms to invest more, the demand for loanable funds would increase. As a result, the equilibrium interest rate would rise, and the higher interest rate would stimulate saving. Here, when the demand curve shifts from D_1 to D_2, the equilibrium interest rate rises from 5 per cent to 6 per cent, and the equilibrium quantity of loanable funds saved and invested rises from €500 billion to €600 billion.

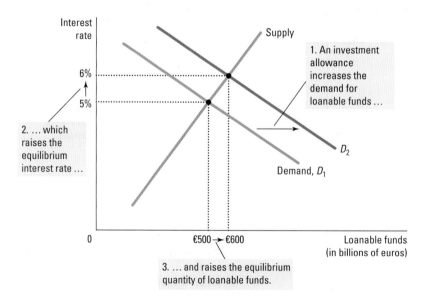

The investment allowance rewards firms that borrow and invest in new capital; it would alter investment at any given interest rate and, thereby, change the demand for loanable funds. Because firms would have an incentive to increase investment at any interest rate, the quantity of loanable funds demanded would be higher at any given interest rate. Thus, the demand curve for loanable funds would move to the right, as shown by the shift from D_1 to D_2 in the figure. By contrast, because the investment allowance would not affect the amount that households save at any given interest rate, it would not affect the supply of loanable funds.

In Figure 15.4, the increased demand for loanable funds raises the interest rate from 5 per cent to 6 per cent, and the higher interest rate in turn increases the quantity of loanable funds supplied from €500 billion to €600 billion, as households respond by increasing the amount they save.

This change in household behaviour is represented here as a movement along the supply curve. Thus, if a reform of the tax system encouraged greater investment, the result would be higher interest rates and greater saving.

Policy 3: Government Budget Deficits and Surpluses A *budget deficit* is an excess of government spending over tax revenue. Governments finance budget deficits by borrowing in the bond market, and the accumulation of past government borrowing is called the *government debt*. A *budget surplus*, an excess of tax revenue over government spending, can be used to repay some of the government debt. If government spending exactly equals tax revenue, the government is said to have a *balanced budget*.

Imagine that the government starts with a balanced budget and then, because of a tax cut or a spending increase, starts running a budget deficit. We can analyse the effects of the budget deficit as illustrated in Figure 15.5.

FIGURE 15.5

The Effect of a Government Budget Deficit

When the government spends more than it receives in tax revenue, the resulting budget deficit lowers national saving. The supply of loanable funds decreases, and the equilibrium interest rate rises. Thus, when the government borrows to finance its budget deficit, it crowds out households and firms who otherwise would borrow to finance investment. Here, when the supply shifts from S_1 to S_2, the equilibrium interest rate rises from 5 per cent to 6 per cent, and the equilibrium quantity of loanable funds saved and invested falls from €500 billion to €300 billion.

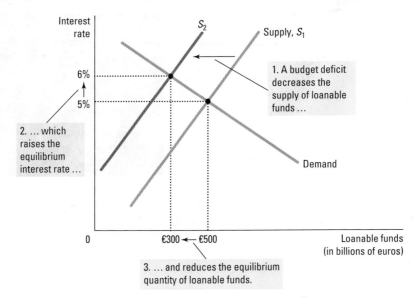

Recall that national saving – the source of the supply of loanable funds – is composed of private saving and public saving. A change in the government budget balance represents a change in public saving and, thereby, in the supply of loanable funds. When the government runs a budget deficit, public saving is negative, and this reduces national saving. In other words, when the government borrows to finance its budget deficit, it reduces the supply of loanable funds available to finance investment by households and firms. Thus, a budget deficit shifts the supply curve for loanable funds to the left from S_1 to S_2, as shown in Figure 15.5. Because the budget deficit does not influence the amount that households and firms want to borrow to finance investment at any given interest rate, it does not alter the demand for loanable funds.

When the budget deficit reduces the supply of loanable funds, the interest rate rises from 5 per cent to 6 per cent. This higher interest rate then alters the behaviour of the households and firms that participate in the loan market. In particular, many demanders of loanable funds are discouraged by the higher interest rate. Fewer families buy new homes and fewer firms choose to build new factories. The fall in investment because of government borrowing is called **crowding out** and is represented in the figure by the movement along the demand curve from a quantity of €500 billion in loanable funds to a quantity of €300 billion. That is, when the government borrows to finance its budget deficit, it crowds out private borrowers who are trying to finance investment.

crowding out a decrease in investment that results from government borrowing

Government budget surpluses work just the opposite way to budget deficits. When government collects more in tax revenue than it spends, it saves the difference by retiring some of the outstanding government debt. This budget surplus, or public saving, contributes to national saving. Thus, a budget surplus increases the supply of loanable funds, reduces the interest rate and stimulates investment. Higher investment, in turn, means greater capital accumulation and more rapid economic growth.

CASE STUDY

A Contrast of Two Countries

Yemen is a relatively poor country with over 30 million inhabitants. Yemen's external debt stood at $7.2 billion in November 2013, down $50 million from September. This sum represents the total debt owed to non-residents and payable in foreign currency.

About one half of the creditors are made up of a group of international financing organizations including the Arab Monetary Fund, International Monetary Fund (IMF) and the OPEC Fund for International Development. The rest of the money is owed to member countries of the Paris Club and also other creditor countries such as Algeria, Poland and South Korea.

Sunset over Sana, Yemen.

Yemen also owes $1.5 billion to the Saudi Development Fund, the Kuwait Fund for Arab Economic Development and the Iraqi Fund.

$7.2 billion sounds a lot of money for a desperately poor country with a large proportion of its population living in absolute poverty. The external debt represents about 20 per cent of its GDP ($35.9 billion in 2013). The percentage figure makes the debt seem quite low when compared to some other Arab nations such as the United Arab Emirates (UAE).

The Yemeni government's total debt is around 45 per cent of the GDP and it is running a budget deficit so the proportion of government debt to GDP is likely to grow. The government debt is worsening because oil revenues have declined severely and will continue to do so. Yemen needs to diversify but the government doesn't have the money to support this. Crowding out is a real potential issue. Overall investment stands at 18 per cent of GDP but needs to be higher.

Contrasting Yemen with the UAE is interesting. The UAE has a much higher per capita income and a trade surplus. In 2012, the UAE had a budget surplus of 4.5 per cent of GDP compared to the 45 per cent debt in Yemen. The UAE had begun to use oil revenues to diversify its economy some years ago by developing trade and tourism. However, the financial crisis hit the Emirates badly, especially Dubai which was heavily exposed to depressed real estate assets. The UAE external debt was just $5.9 billion in 2005 but reached $158.7 billion in 2012. Since the GDP was valued at $359 billion in 2012 the proportion of external debt to GDP reached 44 per cent and was therefore much higher than compared to Yemen. Within the UAE, Dubai has the highest debt ratio at around 130 per cent of its GDP. However, what makes it different to Yemen is that it has a government budget surplus and can continue to finance its external debt and invest in its infrastructure. Investment in fixed capital was estimated to be 29 per cent of GDP in 2012; this compares favourably to that in Yemen.

References: Al Arabiya News Monday, 6 January 2014 and the Index Mundi.

AN OVERVIEW OF ISLAMIC FINANCE

Our analysis in this chapter has been based on financial markets working in a capitalist system. There is a growing interest in other types of financial market and the globalization of business now means that access to funds for investment can be explored through these other markets. Islamic finance is a financial system governed by Islamic Shariah (an Arabic term often translated to Islamic law), comprising the principles and rules derived from Islam as a religion. Its primary sources are the holy Quran (also known as the holy book) and the Sunna, the Prophet's religious instructions and traditions. In Islamic finance all financial contracts should be consistent with Islamic Shariah principles.

The primary doctrines of Islamic finance are the avoidance of Riba (fixed interest), Gharar (uncertainty and ambiguity), and Haram (anything religiously prohibited). Therefore, any interest-based transaction is prohibited in Islamic finance. Further Islamic financial principles entail all parties sharing profits as well as the risk and that people cannot sell any asset (real or financial) that they do not own.

Shariah-compliant institutions play an intermediary role by offering the same banking services as conventional institutions. There are, however, many differences. All Shariah-compliant institutions should have a Shariah supervisory board separate from its board of directors. The main task of the Shariah board is to review, approve or disapprove financial contracts and activities. A number of European countries are reforming their financial and tax laws to become compliant with Islamic finance products and instruments.

Principles of Islamic Finance

For a financial transaction or contract to be valid from an Islamic Shariah standpoint, it should satisfy a number of conditions.

To Be Halal (Permitted)   In Shariah, Halal means permitted or legal. All financial transactions are allowed in Islamic Shariah as long as they do not include Riba and Gharar. In other words, permission is the default status in any transaction and forbidden is the exception. Practically, the Shariah supervisory board takes the responsibility for checking contracts and transactions against Islamic Shariah principles.

Avoidance of Riba   *Riba* means 'growth' or 'increase' and denotes the payment or receipt of interest for the use of money. By default, Islamic finance business and activities must be free from any interest element. Lending money for more money is forbidden because money is not a commodity in itself and cannot be rented out for a fee. It is seen as unfair that a borrower pays a fixed return (interest) regardless of the outcome of their investments or how such funds may have been used. Many Islamic practitioners believe that Riba is exploitative and unproductive as it brings a gain to the lender, who has an excess of funds, and it passes all the risk onto the borrower, who is initially short of funds.

Avoidance of Gharar   Gharar is interpreted as excessive uncertainty. Examples of Gharar are selling fish in the sea, birds in the sky and gambling, all of which cause excessive uncertainty. Fish are common resources that cannot be owned by any one person; gambling can be seen as a zero-sum game in which one party benefits at the expense of another. Because Gharar might lead to disputes caused by an unjustified term in the contract arising from fraud or misrepresentation, the contract should be clear with a full description of the subject matter and the seller should own the assets that they intended to sell.

Islamic Versus Conventional Banks

There are many similarities between Islamic and conventional banks. An Islamic bank is expected to perform the same activities as a conventional bank and carries out the role of a financial intermediary. Unlike conventional banks, Islamic banks are not allowed to borrow and lend funds based on interest. The assets of an Islamic bank include funds on a profit and loss sharing (PLS) basis usually deriving from equity financing, asset financing, and lease financing. On the liabilities side, Islamic banks mobilize agency contract funds; they can accept current, saving, and investment deposits which are treated again on the basis of PLS.

Islamic Banking Sources and Uses

With a growing international profile, Islamic finance is evolving toward a fully-fledged financial system offering a broad range of Shariah-compliant products and services to satisfy the needs of individuals as well as businesses. As with any bank, Islamic banks aim to maximize shareholders' wealth and provide adequate return to the depositors who invest their savings in the bank. Islamic banks are required to pursue those objectives with a clear understanding of their role toward the development of society as a whole. Financially, Islamic banks will achieve these objectives by operating as an intermediary between depositors, who have excess funds, and fund seekers, who have a shortage of funds.

The Main Sources of Funds

Islamic banks' depositors are seeking safe custody for their money and/or looking to earn adequate returns on their deposits. As deposit-taking institutions, which do not pay interest, the main sources of funds for Islamic banks are described below.

Shareholder Investments   Islamic banks raise their initial capital by offering equity participation in which the shareholders are owners and partners in the bank's business. The shareholders expect a return in the form of a share of the bank's profit (if any).

Current Accounts   The current account is a deposit account that entitles the account holder to receive funds on demand. The depositor can also issue cheques on the account to transfer legal ownership of funds to others. In this type of account there is no guaranteed return but sometimes the bank rewards current account clients by Hiba, or gift, which is at the bank's sole discretion. There is no limit for withdrawals from a current account.

Savings Accounts (Wadiah)   When depositors put money into a bank they expect it to be kept safely. Banks can use these savings accounts (also called Wadiah) provided the bank seeks the depositor's permission. Assuming this permission is granted the bank can employ the funds, although it guarantees the deposit principal against any damage or loss. As with the current account, the bank may pay Hiba on these accounts at its discretion and without a predetermined agreement.

Investment Accounts   Investment accounts are profit-sharing accounts, also known as Mudarabah, where banks accept deposits for a specific period. Mudarabah contracts are used as sources of funds for a bank as well as being used to finance other activities. In practice the bank pools the deposits with other funds while keeping a record of each individual account. The bank invests these funds in a Shariah-compliant investment with the aim of maximizing the return. Any return on those funds will be shared with depositors according to a predetermined profit-sharing ratio. Although these accounts are known as profit and loss sharing accounts, the depositors bear all the losses, except when the loss results from the bank's misconduct or negligence.

CONCLUSION

This chapter has developed some of the basic tools that businesses use as they make financial decisions and provides a brief outline of an alternative form of financial market.

The concept of present value reminds us that a sum of money in the future is less valuable than a sum of money today, and it gives us a way to compare sums of money at different points in time. The theory of risk management reminds us that the future is uncertain and that risk-averse businesses can take precautions to guard against this uncertainty. The study of asset valuation tells us that the value of an asset should reflect its expected future profitability.

In most economies, people borrow and lend often, and usually for good reason. You may borrow one day to start your own business or to buy a home. And people may lend to you in the hope that the interest you pay will allow them to enjoy a more prosperous retirement. The financial system has the job of coordinating all this borrowing and lending activity.

In many ways, financial markets are like other markets in the economy. The price of loanable funds – the interest rate – is governed by the forces of supply and demand, just as other prices in the economy are. In one way, however, financial markets are special. Financial markets, unlike most other markets, serve the important role of linking the present and the future. Those who supply loanable funds – savers – do so because they want to convert some of their current income into future purchasing power. Those who demand loanable funds – borrowers – do so because they want to invest today in order to have additional capital in the future to produce goods and services. Thus, well-functioning financial markets are important not only for current generations but also for future generations who will inherit many of the resulting benefits.

IN THE NEWS

India Attempts to Address Productivity Concerns

This article looks at how some government spending can encourage investment, but such spending needs to be disciplined, as the new government in India is attempting to do with some initial success.

Governments need to spend money for all sorts of reasons. They need to provide public goods and services such as defence and policing;

Nilgiri Mountain Railway, Ooty

they often spend on providing merit goods and services such as health and education. A better educated workforce should increase future productivity. They will spend on welfare to support the most needy citizens or risk unrest. Finally, they may have capital expenditures such as improving infrastructure as a strategy to encourage future economic growth. However, all these expenditures need financing. For some countries it

may be difficult to find the funds especially if there is a large informal economy where it is difficult to collect taxes or if the economy is performing poorly. A solution is to run a budget deficit and increase the national debt with the hope of paying back in better times.

India, according to the World Economic Outlook (WEO), has a real issue over its productivity. India must do something about it otherwise it will lose out to other economies. Its GDP growth rates have been falling. It was 6.8 per cent in 2011 and fell to 3.2 per cent in 2013, before recovering, mainly due to lower oil

prices which have partly masked the underlying productivity concerns. The WEO report recommends that India should do three things. First, it should increase its infrastructure spending in order to remove supply bottlenecks; second, it needs to undergo further structural reforms so that it is easier to conduct business; and, third, it needs to improve the quality of human capital and that means better training and education.

These reforms and actions don't come without a cost and involve increasing the budget deficit in the short run which stands at around 4 per cent of GDP in 2015. Public debt as a percentage of GDP rose from 50.5 per cent in 2011 to 51.8 per cent in 2013. So, will following the WEO advice lead to crowding out of private investment? Not necessarily, if the expenditure is targeted at capital projects and not at increasing welfare payments.

In fact India has already started on a plan to improve its infrastructure, by investing heavily in its famously overcrowded and archaic railway network. The hope is that this will give a boost to demand in the short term and supply in the medium term. It is also changing labour legislation. Such policy reforms, according to the WEO, have already resulted in increased investment activity.

In April 2015, Moody's changed its ratings on India to BAA3 believing its outlook has moved from stable to positive. This is an indication that the policies are beginning to address concerns, but any future upgrade will depend on the extent and outcome of the growth and institutional reforms.

The new government's fiscal consolidation map aims to reduce the fiscal deficit to 3.9 per cent in 2015–16 and finally to 3 per cent in 2017–2018. It represents an overall delay in the programme by a year in order to have funds available for its capital investment programme. The Indian Finance Minister, Arun Jaitley, predicts a rise in economic growth to 8 per cent in the financial year 2016.

Questions

1. Explain why governments are tempted to run up budget deficits.

2. Using appropriate diagrams, explain the possible effects of an increase in a government budget deficit on the supply of loanable funds and the levels of investment.

3. Using examples from the article, explain why some increases in government spending might lead to 'crowding in'.

4. Why has India decided to increase capital spending when it has a fiscal deficit?

5. Explain why a country like India and potential investors are interested in how the IMF or credit rating agencies like Moody's rates a country and forecasts trends in that country.

References: **http://www.dnaindia.com /money/report-moody-s-says-india -positive-under-modi-but-still-below -investment-grade-2075979**

http://www.imf.org/external/pubs/ft /weo/2015/update/01/pdf/0115.pdf

http://www.livemint.com/Opinion /txei05CA47qJTe9R19s4KJ/Indian -economy-Raise-productivity-to-stay -ahead.htmlhttp://mecometer.com/whats /india/government-expenditure -percentage-of-gdp/

SUMMARY

- The financial system of an advanced economy is made up of many types of financial institutions, such as the bond market, the stock market, banks and investment funds. All of these institutions act to direct the resources of households who want to save some of their income into the hands of households and firms who want to borrow.

- Because savings can earn interest, a sum of money today is more valuable than the same sum of money in the future. A person can compare sums from different times using the concept of present value. The present value of any future sum is the amount that would be needed today, given prevailing interest rates, to produce that future sum.

- Because of diminishing marginal utility, most people are risk averse. Risk-averse people can reduce risk using insurance.

- The value of an asset equals the present value of the income streams the owner of the asset will receive and the final sale price if appropriate.

- The interest rate is determined by the supply and demand for loanable funds. The supply of loanable funds comes from households who want to save some of their income and lend it out. The demand for loanable funds comes from households and firms who want to borrow for investment. To analyse how any policy or event affects the interest rate, one must consider how it affects the supply and demand for loanable funds.

- National saving equals private saving plus public saving. A government budget deficit represents negative public saving and, therefore, reduces national saving and the supply of loanable funds available to finance investment. When a government budget deficit crowds out investment, it reduces the growth of productivity and GDP.

- Islamic finance, which is based on profit and loss sharing rather than on interest, is a growing option for financing for some businesses and is growing in sophistication not only in Muslim countries but in many non-Muslim countries.

QUESTIONS FOR REVIEW

1. What is the role of the financial system? Name and describe two markets that are part of the financial system in an economy. Name and describe two financial intermediaries.

2. The interest rate is 7 per cent. Use the concept of present value to compare €200 to be received in 10 years and €300 to be received in 20 years.

3. What might be some of the advantages and disadvantages to a firm of issuing bonds or issuing shares as a source of finance?

4. A chemical processing manufacturer is considering investing in a new process to produce a constituent ingredient for an agricultural fertilizer. It expects the return on the investment to last for at least 10 years. How might it decide whether to proceed with the investment?

5. What is private saving? What is public saving? How are these two variables related?

6. What is investment? How is it related to national saving?

7. What factors should an analyst think about in determining the value of an asset?

8. Describe a change in the tax system that might increase private saving. If this policy were implemented, how would it affect the market for loanable funds?

9. What is a government budget deficit? How does it affect interest rates, investment and economic growth?

10. What is the logic behind the prohibition of interest in Islamic finance?

PROBLEMS AND APPLICATIONS

1. A company has an investment project that would cost €10 million today and yield a pay-off of €15 million in 4 years.
   a. Should the firm undertake the project if the interest rate is 11 per cent? 10 per cent? 9 per cent? 8 per cent?
   b. Can you figure out the exact cut-off for the interest rate between profitability and non-profitability?

2. For each of the following pairs, which bond would you expect to pay a higher interest rate? Explain.
   - A bond of the UK government or a bond of an East European government.
   - A bond that repays the principal in year 2017 or a bond that repays the principal in year 2035.
   - A bond from BP or a bond from a start-up software company.
   - A bond issued by the national government or a bond issued by a local authority.

3. For which kind of asset would you expect to pay the higher average return: shares in an industry that is very sensitive to economic conditions (such as a car manufacturer) or shares in an industry that is relatively insensitive to economic conditions (such as a water company). Why?

4. When the Greek government announced that it could default on its debt to foreigners in the latter part of 2011, interest rates rose on bonds issued by many other European countries but fell on German debt. Why do you suppose this happened?

5. Suppose that BP is considering exploring a new oil field.
   a. Assuming that BP needs to borrow money in the bond market to finance the purchase of new oil rigs and drilling machinery, why would an increase in interest rates affect BP's decision about whether to carry out the exploration?
   b. If BP has enough of its own funds to finance the development of the new oil field without borrowing, would an increase in interest rates still affect BP's decision about whether to undertake the new project? Explain.

6. Suppose the government borrows €5 billion more next year than this year.
   a. Use a supply-and-demand diagram to analyse this policy. Does the interest rate rise or fall?
   b. What happens to investment? To private saving? To public saving? Compare the size of the changes to the €5 billion of extra government borrowing.

c. How does the elasticity of supply of loanable funds affect the size of these changes?

d. How does the elasticity of demand for loanable funds affect the size of these changes?

e. Suppose households believe that greater government borrowing today implies higher taxes to pay off the government debt in the future. What does this belief do to private saving and the supply of loanable funds today? Does it increase or decrease the effects you discussed in parts (a) and (b)?

7. Over the past 20 years, new computer technology has enabled firms to substantially reduce the amount of inventories they hold for each unit of sales. Illustrate the effect of this change on the market for loanable funds. (Hint: expenditure on inventories is a type of investment.) What do you think has been the effect on investment in factories and equipment?

8. This chapter explains that investment can be increased both by reducing taxes on private saving and by reducing the government budget deficit.

a. Why is it difficult to implement both of these policies at the same time?

b. What would you need to know about private saving in order to judge which of these two policies would be a more effective way to raise investment?

9. Is it ever possible for fundamental analysis to tell an investor everything they need to know about the value of an asset? Explain your answer.

10. The financial crisis of 2007–2009 had a significant effect on many banks in financial markets in capitalist systems. In contrast, many Islamic financial institutions proved to be more resilient during this period. What do think might be some of the reasons for this contrast?

PART 6

INTRODUCTION TO MACROECONOMICS

16 THE MACROECONOMIC ENVIRONMENT

LEARNING OUTCOMES

After reading this chapter you should be able to:

- Demonstrate why income equals expenditure equals output.

- Explain the key words and phrases in the definition of GDP.

- Define consumption, investment, government purchases and net exports.

- Calculate real and nominal GDP using base year and current year prices.

- List the five steps necessary to calculate the inflation rate.

- Discuss three reasons why the CPI may be biased.

- Describe two differences between the CPI and GDP deflator.

- Explain the relationship between the real interest rate, the nominal interest rate, and the inflation rate.

- Show how comparative advantage explains the gains from trade.

- Describe how saving, domestic investment, and net capital outflow are related.

- Explain why net exports must always equal net capital outflow.

- Distinguish between the nominal exchange rate and the real exchange rate.

- Explain purchasing power parity as a theory of how exchange rates are determined.

- Use data on the number of employed, unemployed, and not in the labour force to calculate the unemployment rate and the labour force participation rate.

INTRODUCTION

All businesses have to operate within an external economic environment which is largely out of an individual firm's control. In some years, firms throughout the economy are expanding their production of goods and services. This helps create more business activity for other firms who act as suppliers, distributors, provide financial services or advice, and act as wholesalers. In other years, firms cut back on production; as employment declines household spending gets cut back and firms throughout the economy find that business activity has slowed and operating becomes increasingly challenging.

Because the condition of the overall economy profoundly affects businesses, changes in economic conditions are widely reported by the media. These reports include changes in the total income of everyone in the economy (gross domestic product (GDP)), the rate at which average prices are rising (inflation), the percentage of the labour force that is out of work (unemployment), total spending in shops (retail sales) and the imbalance of trade between the domestic economy and the rest of the world (the trade balance). All these statistics are *macroeconomic*. Rather than telling us about a particular household or firm, they tell us something about the entire economy.

Central to the study of macroeconomics is data. Firms pay close attention to macroeconomic data because it gives clues about the direction in which the economy, not only in the domestic country but around the world, is heading. This information can be factored into decision making so that the firm can try and anticipate events and be better prepared to be able to manage the changing macroeconomic environment as a result. For example, if data suggests the economy is slowing down, firms may put plans in place to cut back production and sell off inventory (stock). If the economy looks to be picking up firms may invest to ensure they have the capacity to meet anticipated demand.

In this chapter we will look at some key macroeconomic variables: GDP, inflation, unemployment, savings and investment and exchange rates.

THE ECONOMY'S INCOME AND EXPENDITURE

Recall that the economy is all the transactions that take place over a period of time. When judging the performance of the economy, we look at how total transactions change over time. The measure typically used is **gross domestic product** (**GDP**). GDP measures the market value of all final goods and services produced within a country in a given period of time. There are three ways to measure this market value. First, we can add up all the incomes received in the economy as a result of transactions. These incomes will have been received by firms and households and represent expenditure by other firms and households, so expenditure on the economy's output of goods and services is the second way we can measure GDP. An economy's income is the same as its expenditure because every transaction has two parties: a buyer and a seller. Every euro of spending by some buyer is a euro of income for some seller. Finally, the goods and services transacted have a value – the value of the output is the third way GDP can be measured. We will focus on the income and expenditure methods of measuring GDP.

Suppose, for instance, that John Watson, a local builder, is constructing an extension for a client and purchases €1000-worth of bricks, cement and timber

gross domestic product (GDP) the market value of all final goods and services produced within a country in a given period of time

from a local builder's merchant. The builder's merchant earns €1000 and John spends €1000. Thus, the transaction contributes equally to the economy's income and to its expenditure. GDP, whether measured as total income or total expenditure, rises by €1000.

The equality of income and expenditure can be represented as a diagram called the circular-flow as in Figure 16.1. This is a model which describes all the transactions between households and firms in a simple economy. In this economy, households buy goods and services from firms; these expenditures flow through the markets for goods and services. The firms in turn use the money they receive from sales to pay workers' wages, landowners' rent and firm owners' profit; this income flows through the markets for the factors of production. In this economy, money flows from households to firms and then back to households.

The actual economy is, of course, more complicated than the one illustrated in Figure 16.1. In particular, households do not spend all of their income. They pay

FIGURE 16.1

The Circular-Flow Diagram

Households buy goods and services from firms, and firms use their revenue from sales to pay wages to workers, rent to landowners and profit to firm owners. GDP equals the total amount spent by households in the market for goods and services. It also equals the total wages, rent and profit paid by firms in the markets for the factors of production.

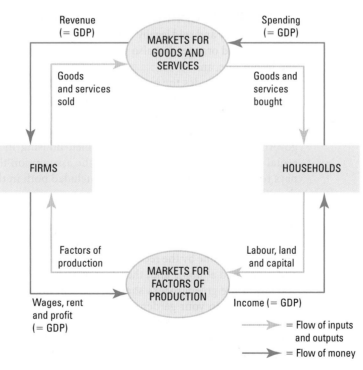

some of it to the government in taxes, and they save some for use in the future. In addition, households do not buy all goods and services produced within the economy. Some goods and services are bought by governments through taxes paid by households which represent government spending, and some are bought by firms that plan to use them in the future to produce their own output which represents investment. Some goods are bought from sellers in foreign countries (imports) and some domestic products are sold abroad (exports). Yet, regardless of whether a household, government or firm buys a good or service, the transaction has a buyer and seller. Thus, for the economy as a whole, expenditure and income are always the same.

> **Quick Quiz** In theory, income and expenditure are mirror images of a transaction. Why might the authorities find that in measuring income and expenditure in the economy they get different results for each?

The Measurement of Gross Domestic Product

The following is a more detailed breakdown of how GDP is measured:

'GDP is the Market Value ...'   GDP adds together many different kinds of products into a single measure of the value of economic activity. To do this, it uses market prices. Because market prices measure the amount people are willing to pay for different goods, they reflect the value of those goods. If the price of an apple is twice the price of an orange, then an apple contributes twice as much to GDP as does an orange.

'... Of All ...'   GDP tries to be comprehensive. It includes all items produced in the economy and sold legally in markets. GDP measures the market value of not just apples and oranges, but also pears and grapefruit, books and movies, haircuts and health care, and so on.

GDP also includes the market value of the housing services provided by the economy's stock of housing. For rental housing, this value is easy to calculate – the rent equals both the tenant's expenditure and the landlord's income. Yet many people own the place where they live and, therefore, do not pay rent. The government includes this owner-occupied housing in GDP by estimating its rental value. That is, GDP is based on the assumption that the owner, in effect, pays rent to themselves, so the rent is included both in their expenditure and in their income.

There are some products, however, that GDP excludes because measuring them is so difficult. GDP excludes items which are not transacted through official channels such as when work is done on a cash-in-hand basis and is not declared as income by the receiver. It also excludes most items that are produced and consumed at home and, therefore, never enter the marketplace. Vegetables you buy at the greengrocer's shop or the supermarket are part of GDP; vegetables you grow in your garden are not. In the UK, until 2014, other types of illegal transactions such as those involving drugs and prostitution were excluded from GDP figures. However, From September 2014, the UK's national statistical service, the Office for National Statistics (ONS) included estimates of the level of activity in illegal drugs and prostitution in order to bring the figures for the UK National Accounts in line with methods used across other European Union (EU) countries. (The ONS estimated that the average impact on the UK economy by including illegal drugs and prostitution amounts to around £11 billion per year).

'... Final ...'   When a paper company sells paper to a greetings card company, the paper is called an *intermediate good,* and the card is called a *final good.* GDP includes only the value of final goods. The reason is that the value of intermediate goods is already included in the prices of the final goods. Adding the market value of the paper to the market value of the card would be double counting. That is, it would (incorrectly) count the paper twice.

An important exception to this principle arises when an intermediate good is produced and, rather than being used, is added to a firm's inventory of goods to be used or sold at a later date. In this case, the intermediate good is taken to be 'final' at the time of the accounting, and its value as inventory investment is added to GDP. When the inventory of the intermediate good is later used or sold, the firm's inventory investment is negative, and GDP for the later period is reduced accordingly.

'... Goods and Services ...'

GDP includes both tangible goods (food, clothing, cars) and intangible services (haircuts, house cleaning, doctor visits). When you (legally) download an album by your favourite band, you are buying a good, and the purchase price is part of GDP. When you pay to hear a concert by the same band, you are buying a service, and the ticket price is also part of GDP.

'... Produced ...'

GDP includes goods and services currently produced. It does not include transactions involving items produced in the past. When Aston Martin produces and sells a new car, the value of the car is included in the GDP of the country in which Aston Martin operates. When one person sells a used car to another person, the value of the used car is not included in GDP.

'... Within a Country ...'

GDP measures the value of production within the geographic confines of a country. When an Australian citizen works temporarily in South Africa, their production is part of South African GDP. When a UK citizen owns a factory in Bulgaria, the production at their factory is not part of UK GDP (it is part of Bulgaria's GDP). Thus, items are included in a nation's GDP if they are produced domestically, regardless of the nationality of the producer.

'... in a Given Period of Time'

GDP measures the value of production that takes place within a specific interval of time. Usually that interval is a year or a quarter (three months). GDP measures the economy's flow of income and expenditure during that interval.

When GDP is reported for a quarter, it usually presents GDP 'at an annual rate'. This means that the figure is the amount of income and expenditure during the quarter multiplied by 4. This convention is used so that quarterly and annual figures on GDP can be compared more easily.

In addition, when quarterly GDP is reported, it presents data after being modified by a statistical procedure called *seasonal adjustment*. The unadjusted data show clearly that the economy produces more goods and services during some times of the year than during others. (As you might guess, December's holiday shopping season is a high point in many countries whilst the period before Ramadan is a high point for many Muslim countries.) When monitoring the condition of the economy, economists and policy makers often want to look beyond these regular seasonal changes. Therefore, national statisticians adjust the quarterly data to take out the seasonal cycle. The GDP data reported in the news are always seasonally adjusted.

FYI

Other Measures of Income

When the ONS or Eurostat computes the GDP every three months for the UK and the EU respectively, they also compute various other measures of income to arrive at a more complete picture of what's happening in the economy. These other measures differ from GDP by excluding or including certain categories of income. What follows is a brief description of five of these income measures.

- *Gross national product* (GNP) is the total income earned by a nation's permanent residents (called nationals). It differs from GDP by including income that citizens earn abroad and excluding income that foreigners earn. For most countries domestic residents are responsible for most domestic production, so GDP and GNP are quite close.
- *Net national product* (NNP) is the total income of a nation's residents (GNP) minus losses from depreciation. *Depreciation* is the wear and tear on the

economy's stock of equipment and structures, such as lorries rusting and computers becoming obsolete.

- *National income* is the total income earned by a nation's residents in the production of goods and services. It differs from net national product by excluding indirect business taxes (such as sales taxes) and including business subsidies. NNP and national income also differ because of a 'statistical discrepancy' that arises from problems in data collection.
- *Personal income* is the income that households and non-corporate businesses receive. Unlike national income, it excludes *retained earnings*, which is income that corporations have earned but have not paid out to their owners. It also subtracts corporate income taxes and contributions for social insurance. In addition, personal income includes the

interest income that households receive from their holdings of government debt and the income that households receive from government transfer programmes, such as welfare and social security payments.

- *Disposable personal income* is the income that households and non-corporate businesses have left after satisfying all their obligations to the government. It equals personal income minus personal taxes and certain non-tax payments (such as parking tickets).

Although the various measures of income differ in detail, they almost always tell the same story about economic conditions. When GDP is growing rapidly, these other measures of income are usually growing rapidly. And when GDP is falling, these other measures are usually falling as well. For monitoring fluctuations in the overall economy, it does not matter much which measure of income we use.

? **what if . . .** a business receives a cash payment for a job – does the value of the work carried out contribute to GDP? What might your answer depend upon?

THE COMPONENTS OF GDP

Spending in the economy takes many forms. At any moment, the Müller family may be having lunch in a Munich restaurant; Honda may be building a car factory on the banks of the Rhine; the German army may be procuring weapons from German arms manufacturers; and a New York investment company may be buying bonds from a German bank. German GDP includes all of these various forms of spending on domestically produced goods and services. Similarly, each country in Europe will monitor the forms of spending and income to arrive at the GDP for that country.

To understand how the economy is using its scarce resources and how this use affects business activity and planning, economists are often interested in studying the composition of GDP among various types of spending. To do this, GDP (which we denote as Y) is divided into four components: consumption (C), investment (I), government purchases (G) and net exports (NX):

$$Y \equiv C + I + G + NX$$

This equation is an *identity* – an equation that must be true by the way the variables in the equation are defined. (That's why we used the three-bar, 'identically equals' symbol, '$\equiv$', although for the most part we'll follow normal practice in dealing with identities and use the usual equals sign, '$=$'). In this case, because each pound, dirham, rand or euro of expenditure included in GDP is placed into one of the four components of GDP, the total of the four components must be equal to GDP. Let's look at each of these four components more closely.

Consumption

Consumption is spending by households on goods and services. 'Goods' include household spending on durable goods, such as cars and appliances like washing machines and fridges, and non-durable goods, such as food and clothing. 'Services' include intangible items such as haircuts and insurance. Household spending on education is also included in consumption of services (although one might argue that it would fit better in the next component).

consumption spending by households on goods and services, with the exception of purchases of new housing

Investment

Investment is the purchase of goods that will be used in the future to produce more goods and services. It is the sum of purchases of capital equipment, inventories and structures. Investment in structures include expenditure on new housing. By convention, the purchase of a new house is the one form of household spending categorized as investment rather than consumption.

It is worth remembering the way in which goods produced but not sold and added to inventories are treated on the national accounts. Inventories are treated this way because one aim of GDP is to measure the value of the economy's production, and goods added to inventory are part of that period's production.

Government Purchases

Government purchases include spending on goods and services by local and national governments. It includes the salaries of government workers and spending on public works.

government purchases spending on goods and services by local, state and national governments

The meaning of 'government purchases' requires a little clarification. When the government pays the salary of an army general, that salary is part of government purchases. But what happens when the government pays a social security benefit to one of the elderly? Such government spending is called a **transfer payment** because it is not made in exchange for a currently produced good or service. Transfer payments alter household income, but they do not reflect the economy's production. (From a macroeconomic standpoint, transfer payments are like negative taxes.) Because GDP is intended to measure income from, and expenditure on, the production of goods and services, transfer payments are not counted as part of government purchases.

transfer payment a payment for which no good or service is exchanged

Net Exports

net exports spending on domestically produced goods by foreigners (exports) minus spending on foreign goods by domestic residents (imports)

Net exports equal the purchases of domestically produced goods by foreigners (exports) minus the domestic purchases of foreign goods (imports). A domestic firm's sale to a buyer in another country, such as the sale of textbooks produced in the UK to customers in South Africa, increases UK net exports.

The 'net' in 'net exports' refers to the fact that the value of imports is subtracted from the value of exports. This subtraction is made because imports of goods and services are included in other components of GDP. For example, suppose that a UK household buys a £30 000 car from Volvo, the Swedish car maker. That transaction increases consumption in the UK by £30 000 because car purchases are part of consumer spending in the UK. It also reduces net exports by £30 000 because the car is an import (note it represents an export for Sweden). In other words, net exports include goods and services produced abroad (with a minus sign) because these goods and services are included in consumption, investment and government purchases (with a plus sign). Thus, when a domestic household, firm or government buys a good or service from abroad, the purchase reduces net exports – but because it also raises consumption, investment or government purchases, it does not affect GDP. The above example shows the importance of making sure that we focus on a particular country when discussing imports and exports because of the potential for confusion to arise.

REAL VERSUS NOMINAL GDP

As we have seen, GDP measures the total spending on goods and services in all markets in the economy. If total spending rises from one year to the next, one of two things (or a combination of the two) must be true: (1) the economy is producing a larger output of goods and services, or (2) goods and services are being sold at higher prices. When studying changes in the economy over time, economists want to separate these two effects and businesses need to be able to have an accurate and stable picture of what is happening on which to base decision making. In particular, they want a measure of the total quantity of goods and services the economy is producing that is not affected by changes in the prices of those goods and services.

The answer is *real GDP*. Real GDP presents the value of goods and services and accounts for changes in prices. It does this by valuing goods and services at prices that prevailed in some specific year in the past. By evaluating current production using prices that are fixed at past levels, real GDP shows how the economy's overall production of goods and services changes over time.

To see more precisely how real GDP is constructed, let's consider an example. Table 16.1 shows some data for an economy that produces only two goods – burgers and pizzas. The table shows the quantities of the two goods produced and their prices in the years 2015, 2016 and 2017.

To compute total spending in this economy, we would multiply the quantities of burgers and pizzas by their prices. In the year 2015, 100 burgers are sold at a price of €1 per burger, so expenditure on burgers equals €100. In the same year, 50 pizzas are sold for €2 per pizza, so expenditure on pizzas also equals €100. Total expenditure in the economy – the sum of expenditure on burgers and expenditure on pizzas – is €200. This amount, the production of goods and services valued at current prices, is called **nominal GDP**.

nominal GDP the production of goods and services valued at current prices

The table shows the calculation of nominal GDP for these 3 years. Total spending rises from €200 in 2015 to €600 in 2016 and then to €1200 in 2017. Part of this rise is attributable to the increase in the quantities of burgers and pizzas, and part is attributable to the increase in the prices of burgers and pizzas.

TABLE 16.1

Real and Nominal GDP

This table shows how to calculate nominal GDP, real GDP and the GDP deflator for a hypothetical economy that produces only burgers and pizzas.

		Prices and quantities		
Year	Price of burgers €	Quantity of burgers	Price of pizzas €	Quantity of pizzas
2015	1	100	2	50
2016	2	150	3	100
2017	3	200	4	150
Year	Calculating nominal GDP (base year 2015)			
2015	(€1 per burger × 100 pizzas) + (€2 per pizza × 50 pizzas) = €200			
2016	(€2 per burger × 150 pizzas) + (€3 per pizza × 100 pizzas) = €600			
2017	(€3 per burger × 200 pizzas) + (€4 per pizza × 150 pizzas) = €1200			
Year	Calculating real GDP (base year 2015)			
2015	(€1 per burger × 100 pizzas) + (€2 per pizza × 50 pizzas) = €200			
2016	(€1 per burger × 150 pizzas) + (€2 per pizza × 100 pizzas) = €350			
2017	(€1 per burger × 200 pizzas) + (€2 per pizza × 150 pizzas) = €500			
Year	Calculating the GDP deflator			
2015	(€200/€200) × 100 = 100			
2016	(€600/€350) × 100 = 171			
2017	(€1200/€500) × 100 = 240			

To obtain a measure of the amount produced that is not affected by changes in prices, we use **real GDP**, which is the production of goods and services valued at constant prices. We calculate real GDP by first choosing one year as a *base year*. We then use the prices of burgers and pizzas in the base year to compute the value of goods and services in all of the years. In other words, the prices in the base year provide the basis for comparing quantities in different years.

Suppose that we choose 2015 to be the base year in our example. We can then use the prices of burgers and pizzas in 2015 to compute the value of goods and services produced in 2015, 2016 and 2017. Table 16.1 shows these calculations. To compute real GDP for 2015 we use the prices of burgers and pizzas in 2015 (the base year) and the quantities of burgers and pizzas produced in 2015. (Thus, for the base year, real GDP always equals nominal GDP.) To compute real GDP for 2016, we use the prices of burgers and pizzas in 2015 (the base year) and the quantities of burgers and pizzas produced in 2016. Similarly, to compute real GDP for 2017, we use the prices in 2015 and the quantities in 2017. When we find that real GDP has risen from €200 in 2015 to €350 in 2016 and then to €500 in 2017, we know that the increase is attributable to an increase in the quantities produced, because the prices are being held fixed at base-year levels.

To sum up: nominal GDP uses current prices to place a value on the economy's production of goods and services, while real GDP uses constant base-year prices to place a value on the economy's production of goods and services. Because real

real GDP a measure of the amount produced that is not affected by changes in prices

GDP is not affected by changes in prices, changes in real GDP reflect only changes in the amounts being produced. Thus, real GDP is a measure of the economy's production of goods and services.

Our goal in computing GDP is to gauge how well the overall economy is performing. Because real GDP measures the economy's production of goods and services, it reflects the economy's ability to satisfy people's needs and desires. Thus, real GDP is a better gauge of economic well-being than is nominal GDP. When economists talk about the economy's GDP, they usually mean real GDP rather than nominal GDP. And when they talk about growth in the economy, they measure that growth as the percentage change in real GDP from one period to another.

The GDP Deflator

Nominal GDP reflects both the prices of goods and services and the quantities of goods and services the economy is producing. In contrast, by holding prices constant at base-year levels, real GDP reflects only the quantities produced. From these two statistics we can compute a third, called the GDP deflator, which reflects the prices of goods and services but not the quantities produced.

GDP deflator a measure of the price level calculated as the ratio of nominal GDP to real GDP times 100

The **GDP deflator** is calculated as follows:

$$\text{GDP Deflator} = \left(\frac{\text{Nominal GDP}}{\text{Real GDP}} \right) \times 100$$

Because nominal GDP and real GDP must be the same in the base year, the GDP deflator for the base year always equals 100. The GDP deflator for subsequent years measures the change in nominal GDP from the base year that cannot be attributable to a change in real GDP.

The GDP deflator measures the current level of prices relative to the level of prices in the base year. To see why this is true, consider a couple of simple examples. First, imagine that the quantities produced in the economy rise over time but prices remain the same. In this case, both nominal and real GDP rise together, so the GDP deflator is constant. Now suppose, instead, that prices rise over time but the quantities produced stay the same. In this second case, nominal GDP rises but real GDP remains the same, so the GDP deflator rises as well. Notice that, in both cases, the GDP deflator reflects what's happening to prices, not quantities.

Let's now return to our numerical example in Table 16.1. The GDP deflator is computed at the bottom of the table. For year 2015, nominal GDP is €200, and real GDP is €200, so the GDP deflator is 100. For the year 2016, nominal GDP is €600, and real GDP is €350, so the GDP deflator is 171. Because the GDP deflator rose in year 2016 from 100 to 171, we can say that the price level increased by 71 per cent.

> **Quick Quiz** Define real and nominal GDP. Which is a better measure of economic well-being? Why?

MEASURING THE COST OF LIVING

Distinguishing between real and nominal GDP is important but this leads us to another question – how do we measure changes in prices over time and the change in prices of all goods and services produced in the economy as opposed to the bundle of goods bought by the average household? If firms face increases in the price of component parts, raw materials and other supplies then they will have to consider whether to increase prices of finished goods to the consumer or maintain their selling price and accept lower profit margins. If they do pass on these price increases to consumers, what will rivals do and how will consumers respond?

To measure these changes in prices we use a statistic called the *consumer prices index*. The consumer prices index is used to monitor changes in the cost of living over time. Economists use the term *inflation* to describe a situation in which the economy's overall price level is rising. The *inflation rate* is the percentage change in the price level from the previous period.

The **consumer prices index (CPI)** is a measure of the overall prices of the goods and services bought by a typical consumer. It is a standard method of measuring changes in prices adopted in many countries.

consumer prices index (CPI) a measure of the overall prices of the goods and services bought by a typical consumer

CASE STUDY

Recent Macroeconomic Performance in Lebanon

Governments regularly collect macroeconomic data. It helps them understand the nature of their economy in the past, present and what is likely to happen in the future. They can then decide what actions they may need to undertake to move their economy in the desired direction. Investors and businesses also look at the published data to assist their decisions.

The macroeconomic data collected by governments need to be accurate, relevant and form the basis for comparison over time and between nations. Many countries adopt internationally accepted standards.

The Lebanese Republic Central Administration of Statistics online shows the main components that make up the consumer prices index for Lebanon.

The index shows that prices actually fell on average in 2014 but what is surprising is the further monthly drop of 2.18 per cent during January 2015. This was caused by significant falls in clothing and footwear and energy and fuel prices, the latter impacting on the costs of running housing and of transportation.

By looking at headline figures of key macroeconomics variables for Lebanon and past trends it is possible to paint a picture of the current state of the economy, something firms considering investing in the country would want to know and analyse. The past data show some interesting trends:

- GDP has risen every year from 2008 when it was US$24.58 billion to US$44.35 billion in 2013, although the rate of growth has slowed.
- Unemployment has remained steady at or around 8.8 per cent since 2008.
- Since 2008 the balance of payments has been negative and worsened until 2014 when the negative balance was reduced, but it is still above 2008 levels.
- Interest rates have remained at 10 per cent since 2010.
- The external debt was low in 2008 through to the beginning of 2012 when it rose until May 2013 before levelling off.
- The government ran a budget surplus of over 6 per cent in 2014 which followed on from 2 years of deficit budgets.
- Lebanese government debt represents 146 per cent GDP. Since 2008 this figure has varied from a low of 134 per cent to its current high.

References: **http://www.cas.gov.lb/index.php/economic-statistics-en/cpi-en#cpiresults http://www.tradingeconomics.com/lebanon/indicators**

How the Consumer Prices Index Is Calculated

To calculate the CPI and the inflation rate, national statistics offices use data on the prices of thousands of goods and services. To see exactly how these statistics are constructed, let's revisit our simple economy in which consumers buy only two goods – burgers and pizzas. Table 16.2 shows the five steps that national statistics offices follow.

- *Fix the basket.* The first step in computing the CPI is to determine which prices are most important to the typical consumer. If the typical consumer buys more burgers than pizzas, then the price of burgers is more important than the price of pizzas and, therefore, should be given greater weight in measuring the cost of living. The statistics office sets these weights by surveying consumers and finding the basket of goods and services that the typical consumer buys. In the example in the table, the typical consumer buys a basket of 4 burgers and 2 pizzas.
- *Find the prices.* The second step in computing the CPI is to find the prices of each of the goods and services in the basket for each point in time. The table shows the prices of burgers and pizzas for three different years.

TABLE 16.2

Calculating the Consumer Prices Index and the Inflation Rate: An Example

This table shows how to calculate the consumer prices index and the inflation rate for a hypothetical economy in which consumers buy only burgers and pizzas.

Step 1: Survey consumers to determine a fixed basket of goods

4 burgers, 2 pizzas

Step 2: Find the price of each good in each year

Year	Price of burgers €	Price of pizzas €
2015	1	2
2016	2	3
2017	3	4

Step 3: Compute the cost of the basket of goods in each year

2015	(€1 per burger× 4 burgers) + (€2 per pizza × 2 pizzas) = €8
2016	(€2 per burger × 4 burgers) + (€3 per pizza × 2 pizzas) = €14
2017	(€3 per burger × 4 burgers) + (€4 per pizza × 2 pizzas) = €20

Step 4: Choose one year as a base year (2015) and compute the consumer prices index in each year

2015	(€8/€8) × 100 = 100
2016	(€14/€8) × 100 = 175
2017	(€20/€8) × 100 = 250

Step 5: Use the consumer prices index to compute the inflation rate from previous year

2016	(175 − 100)/100 × 100 = 75%
2017	(250 − 175)/175 × 100 = 43%

- *Compute the basket's cost.* The third step is to use the data on prices to calculate the cost of the basket of goods and services at different times. The table shows this calculation for each of the 3 years. Notice that only the prices in this calculation change. By keeping the basket of goods the same (4 burgers and 2 pizzas), we are isolating the effects of price changes from the effect of any quantity changes that might be occurring at the same time.
- *Choose a base year and compute the index.* The fourth step is to designate 1 year as the base year, which is the benchmark against which other years are compared. To calculate the index, the price of the basket of goods and services in each year is divided by the price of the basket in the base year, and this ratio is then multiplied by 100. The resulting number is the CPI.

In the example in the table, the year 2015 is the base year. In this year, the basket of burgers and pizzas costs €8. Therefore, the price of the basket in all years is divided by €8 and multiplied by 100. The CPI is 100 in 2015. (The index is always 100 in the base year.) The CPI is 175 in 2016. This means that the price of the basket in 2016 is 175 per cent of its price in the base year. Put differently, a basket of goods that costs €100 in the base year costs €175 in 2016. Similarly, the CPI is 250 in 2017, indicating that the price level in 2017 is 250 per cent of the price level in the base year.

- *Compute the inflation rate.* The fifth and final step is to use the CPI to calculate the **inflation rate**, which is the percentage change in the price index from the preceding period. That is, the inflation rate between two consecutive years is computed as follows:

> **inflation rate** the percentage change in the price index from the preceding period

$$\text{Inflation rate in year 2} = 100 \times \frac{(\text{CPI in year 2} - \text{CPI in year 1})}{\text{CPI in year 1}}$$

In our example, the inflation rate is 75 per cent in 2016 and 43 per cent in 2017.

Although this example simplifies the real world by including only two goods, it shows how statistics offices compute the CPI and the inflation rate. Statistics offices collect and process data on the prices of thousands of goods and services every month and, by following the five foregoing steps, determine how quickly the cost of living for the typical consumer is rising.

In addition to the CPI for the overall economy, statistics offices may calculate price indices for the sub-categories of 'goods' and of 'services' separately, as well as the **producer prices index**, which measures the change in prices of a basket of goods and services bought by firms rather than consumers. Because firms eventually pass on their costs to consumers in the form of higher consumer prices, changes in the producer prices index are often thought to be useful in predicting changes in the CPI.

> **producer prices index** a measure of the change in prices of a basket of goods and services bought by firms

Problems in Measuring the Cost of Living

The goal of the CPI is to measure changes in the cost of living. In other words, the CPI tries to gauge how much incomes must rise in order to maintain a constant standard of living. The CPI, however, is not a perfect measure of the cost of living. Three problems with the index are widely acknowledged but difficult to solve.

Substitution Bias   The first problem is called *substitution bias*. When prices change from one year to the next, they do not all change proportionally: some prices rise more than others and some prices fall. Consumers respond to these differing price changes by buying less of the goods whose prices have risen and by buying more of the goods whose prices have risen less or perhaps even have fallen. That is, consumers substitute towards goods that have become relatively less expensive. For businesses, this information is important to know as part of their overall planning. If a prices index is computed assuming a fixed basket of goods, it ignores the possibility of consumer substitution and, therefore, overstates the increase in the cost of living from one year to the next.

Let's consider a simple example. Imagine that in the base year apples are cheaper than pears, and so consumers buy more apples than pears. When the statistics office constructs the basket of goods, it will include more apples than pears. Suppose that next year pears are cheaper than apples. Consumers will respond to the price changes by buying more pears and fewer apples. Yet, when computing the CPI, the statistics office uses a fixed basket, which in essence assumes that consumers continue buying the now expensive apples in the same quantities as before. For this reason, the index will measure a much larger increase in the cost of living than consumers actually experience.

Introduction of New Goods
When a new good is introduced, consumers have more variety from which to choose. Greater variety, in turn, makes each unit of currency more valuable, so consumers need fewer units to maintain any given standard of living. Yet because the CPI is based on a fixed basket of goods and services, it does not reflect this change in the purchasing power of the currency.

Unmeasured Quality Change
If the quality of a good deteriorates from one year to the next, the effective value of a unit of currency falls, even if the price of the good stays the same. Similarly, if the quality rises from one year to the next, the effective value of a unit of currency rises. National statistics offices do try to account for quality change. When the quality of a good in the basket changes – for example, when a car model has more horsepower or gets better fuel consumption from one year to the next – the statistics office adjusts the price of the good to account for the quality change. It is, in essence, trying to compute the price of a basket of goods of constant quality.

Because many businesses strive to improve quality of products as part of their drive to be competitive, this also has to be taken into consideration. For example, digital cameras were introduced into some national statistics services baskets of goods around 2004 but these products are subject to very rapid technological progress. The average price of a digital camera might remain the same over a period, and in some cases might even fall, but over that same period the average quality may have risen substantially. Statistics offices attempt to correct for this by a method known as *hedonic quality adjustment*. This involves working out the average characteristics (e.g. LCD screen size, number of megapixels, zoom features, etc.) of the average digital camera and adjusting the price when one of these average characteristics increases.

Despite these efforts, changes in quality remain a problem, because quality is so hard to measure.

Relevance
A final problem with the index is that people may not see the reported CPI measure of inflation as relevant to their particular situation. This is because their spending patterns are individual and might not be typical of the representative pattern on which the official figures are based. For example, if an individual spent a high proportion of their income on fuel and their mortgage, the effect of price rises in gas, electricity, petrol and a rise in mortgage rates would have a disproportionate effect on their own experience of inflation.

The GDP Deflator versus the Consumer Prices Index

Economists and policy makers monitor both the GDP deflator and the CPI to gauge how quickly prices are rising. Usually, these two statistics tell a similar story. Yet there are two important differences that can cause them to diverge.

The first difference is that the GDP deflator reflects the prices of all goods and services *produced domestically*, whereas the CPI reflects the prices of all goods and services *bought by consumers*. For example, suppose that the price of an aeroplane produced by Dassault, a French aerospace firm and sold to the French Air Force, rises. Even though the aeroplane is part of GDP in France, it is not part of the basket of goods and services bought by a typical consumer. Thus, the price increase shows up in the GDP deflator for France but not in the CPI.

This first difference between the CPI and the GDP deflator is particularly important when the price of oil changes. Although the UK does produce some oil, as with all of Europe and also North America, much of the oil used in the UK is imported from the Middle East. As a result, oil and oil products such as petrol and heating oil comprise a much larger share of consumer spending than they do of GDP. When the price of oil rises, the CPI rises by much more than does the GDP deflator.

The second and subtler difference between the GDP deflator and the CPI concerns how various prices are weighted to yield a single number for the overall level of prices. The CPI compares the price of a *fixed* basket of goods and services with the price of the basket in the base year. Whilst, as we have seen, statistics offices revise the basket of goods on a regular basis, in contrast, the GDP deflator compares the price of *currently produced* goods and services with the price of the same goods and services in the base year. Thus, the group of goods and services used to compute the GDP deflator changes automatically over time. This difference is not important when all prices are changing proportionately. But if the prices of different goods and services are changing by varying amounts, the way we weight the various prices matters for the overall inflation rate.

Comparing Inflation Over Time

The purpose of measuring the overall level of prices in the economy is to permit comparisons of monetary figures from different points in time. A business might want to compare what it is paying for raw materials in 2016 compared to 2000, for example. Now that we know how price indices are calculated, let's see how we might use such an index to compare a certain figure from the past to a figure in the present.

To do this we need to know the level of prices in 2000 and the level of prices in 2016. To compare prices we need to inflate the 2000 prices to turn the 2000 unit of currency (euro in this example) into today's unit of currency. A prices index determines the size of this inflation correction.

The formula for turning currency figures from *year T* into today's currency is:

$$\text{Amount in today's currency} = \text{amount in year } T \text{ currency} \times \frac{\text{Price level today}}{\text{Price level in year } T}$$

A prices index such as the CPI measures the price level and determines the size of the inflation correction.

Real and Nominal Interest Rates

Correcting economic variables for the effects of inflation is particularly important, and somewhat tricky, when we look at data on interest rates. Firms have cash deposits in bank accounts which may earn interest. Conversely, when firms borrow from a bank to buy capital equipment, they will pay interest on the loan. Interest represents a payment in the future for a transfer of money in the past. As a result, interest rates always involve comparing amounts of money at different points in time. To fully understand interest rates, we need to know how to correct for the effects of inflation.

Let's consider an example. Suppose that a firm has cash deposits of €10 000 in a bank account that pays an annual interest rate of 2 per cent. After a year passes, the firm has accumulated €200 in interest. The firm then withdraws the €10 200. Is the firm €200 richer than a year earlier?

The answer depends on what we mean by 'richer'. The firm does have €200 more than before. In other words, the number of euros has risen by 2 per cent. But if prices have risen at the same time, each euro now buys less than it did a year ago. Thus, the firm's purchasing power has not risen by 2 per cent. If the inflation rate was 1 per cent, then the amount of resources the firm can buy has increased by only 1 per cent. And if the inflation rate was 5 per cent, then the price of goods has increased proportionately more than the number of euros in the account. In that case, the firm's purchasing power has actually fallen by 3 per cent.

nominal interest rate the interest rate as usually reported without a correction for the effects of inflation

The interest rate that the bank pays is called the **nominal interest rate,** and the interest rate corrected for inflation is called the real interest rate. We can write the relationship between the nominal interest rate, the real interest rate and inflation as follows:

$$\text{Real interest rate} = \text{Nominal interest rate} - \text{Inflation rate}$$

real interest rate the interest rate corrected for the effects of inflation

The **real interest rate** is the difference between the nominal interest rate and the rate of inflation. The nominal interest rate tells you how fast the number of units of currency in your bank account rises over time. The real interest rate tells you how fast the purchasing power of your bank account rises over time.

PRODUCTION AND GROWTH

When you travel around the world, you see tremendous variation in the standard of living. The average person in many countries of Western Europe has an income more than ten times as high as the average person in countries such as India, Indonesia or Nigeria. These large differences in income are reflected in large differences in the quality of life. Richer countries have more cars, more telephones, more televisions, better nutrition, safer housing, better health care, wider access to education and longer life expectancy.

Growth rates vary substantially from country to country. In some East Asian countries, such as Singapore, South Korea and Taiwan, average income has risen about 7 per cent per year in recent decades. At this rate, average income doubles about every 10 years. These countries have, in the length of one generation, gone from being among the poorest in the world to being among the richest. In contrast, in some African countries, such as Chad, Ethiopia and Nigeria, average income has been stagnant for many years.

Productivity

Productivity is a key determinant of living standards and growth in productivity is the key determinant of growth in living standards. For businesses, productivity is an important factor in efficiency and the control of costs. The more products are produced per time period given a fixed amount of factors, the lower a business's unit costs. Higher productivity also means more products are available for consumption which improves living standards.

A nation can enjoy a high standard of living only if it can produce a large quantity of goods and services. Western Europeans live better than Nigerians because Western European workers are more productive than Nigerian workers. The Japanese have enjoyed more rapid growth in living standards than Argentineans because Japanese workers have experienced more rapidly growing productivity.

ECONOMIC GROWTH, BUSINESS AND PUBLIC POLICY

Most governments want to pursue policies that help raise productivity and living standards. These policies also have significant direct and indirect effects on businesses.

The Importance of Saving and Investment

Because capital is a produced factor of production, a society can change the amount of capital it has. If today the economy produces a large quantity of new capital goods, then tomorrow it will have a larger stock of capital and be able to produce more of all types of goods and services. Thus, one way to raise future productivity is to invest more current resources in the production of capital.

There is an important trade-off when considering the accumulation of capital. Because resources are scarce, devoting more resources to producing capital requires devoting fewer resources to producing goods and services for current consumption. That is, for society to invest more in capital, it must consume less and save more of its current income. The growth that arises from capital accumulation is not a free lunch: it requires that society sacrifice consumption of goods and services in the present in order to enjoy higher consumption in the future. Policies aimed at improving future productive capacity may mean investment in infrastructure such as transport networks, ports, bridges, technology such as super-fast internet access and so on. Firms which provide these products will benefit from policy decisions to invest in infrastructure and many other smaller firms who act as suppliers and service providers for construction and technology firms can benefit from this investment.

Investment From Abroad

Investment from abroad takes several forms. BMW might build a car factory in Portugal. A capital investment that is owned and operated by a foreign entity is called *foreign direct investment*. Alternatively, a German might buy equity in a Portuguese corporation (that is, buy a share in the ownership of the corporation); the Portuguese corporation can use the proceeds from the equity sale to build a new factory. An investment that is financed with foreign money but operated by domestic residents is called *foreign portfolio investment*. In both cases, Germans provide the resources necessary to increase the stock of capital in Portugal. That is, German saving is being used to finance Portuguese investment.

When foreigners invest in a country, they do so because they expect to earn a return on their investment. BMW's car factory increases the Portuguese capital stock and, therefore, increases Portuguese productivity and Portuguese GDP. Yet BMW takes some of this additional income back to Germany in the form of profit. Similarly, when a German investor buys Portuguese equity, the investor has a right to a portion of the profit that the Portuguese corporation earns.

Investment from abroad, therefore, does not have the same effect on all measures of economic prosperity. Recall that gross domestic product (GDP) is the income earned within a country by both residents and non-residents, whereas gross national product (GNP) is the income earned by residents of a country both at home and abroad. When BMW opens its car factory in Portugal, some of the income the factory generates accrues to people who do not live in Portugal. As a result, foreign investment in Portugal raises the income of the Portuguese (measured by GNP) by less than it raises the production in Portugal (measured by GDP).

Nevertheless, investment from abroad is one way for a country to grow. Even though some of the benefits from this investment flow back to the foreign owners, this investment does increase the economy's stock of capital, leading to higher productivity and higher wages. Moreover, investment from abroad is one way for poorer countries to learn the state-of-the-art technologies developed and used in richer countries. For these reasons, many economists who advise governments in less developed economies advocate policies that encourage investment from abroad. Often this means removing restrictions that governments have imposed on foreign ownership of domestic capital.

Businesses can both benefit and lose from investment from abroad. If a Japanese car manufacturer expands the production facilities at one of its UK plants, many smaller business may benefit from increased orders for supplies and construction firms will benefit from the contracts to build the new facilities. In some cases, however, foreign investment can provide competition for domestic businesses and if the foreign firms are large and very efficient and can benefit from economies of scale, domestic firms can be forced out of business.

Education

Education – investment in human capital – is at least as important as investment in physical capital for a country's long-run economic success. In the developed economies of Western Europe and North America, each extra year of schooling raises a worker's income by about 10 per cent on average. In less-developed countries, where human capital is especially scarce, the gap between the wages of educated and uneducated workers is even larger. Thus, one way in which government policy can enhance the standard of living is to provide good schools and to encourage the population to take advantage of them. Investment in high quality education can also mean that firms can recruit employees who have the capacity to be more productive, efficient, innovative and flexible.

Health and Nutrition

The term *human capital* usually refers to education, but it can also be used to describe another type of investment in people: expenditures that lead to a healthier population. Other things equal, healthier workers are more productive. The right investments in the health of the population provide one way for a nation to increase productivity and raise living standards and reduce business costs through days lost at work through illness.

Poverty invariably means poor living conditions, inadequate nourishment, health problems and lower productivity as a result.

Property Rights, Political Stability and Good Governance

An important prerequisite for the price system in a capitalist system to work is an economy-wide respect for *property rights.* A mining company will not make the effort to mine iron ore if it expects the ore to be stolen. The company mines the ore only if it is confident that it will benefit from the ore's subsequent sale. For this reason, courts serve an important role in a market economy: they enforce physical and intellectual property rights. Through the criminal justice system, the courts discourage direct theft. In addition, through the civil justice system, the courts ensure that buyers and sellers live up to their contracts.

Although those of us in developed countries tend to take property rights for granted, those living in less developed countries understand that lack of property rights can be a major problem. In many countries, the system of justice does not work well. Contracts are hard to enforce, and fraud often goes unpunished. In more extreme cases, the government not only fails to enforce property rights but actually infringes upon them. To do business in some countries, firms are expected to bribe powerful government officials. Such corruption impedes the coordinating power of markets. It also discourages domestic saving and investment from abroad.

One threat to property rights is political instability. When revolutions and coups are common, there is doubt about whether property rights will be respected in the future. If a revolutionary government might confiscate the capital of some businesses, domestic residents have less incentive to save, invest and start new businesses. At the same time, businesses, both domestic and foreign, have less incentive to invest in the country. One of the most important requirements for business is a degree of stability and if businesses cannot have the security of knowing that their assets, physical and human, are not protected and relatively safe, they may decide to withdraw their activities or defer future investment. This does not help to improve a nation's standard of living.

Free Trade

Trade is, in some ways, a type of technology. When businesses in a country export wheat and other businesses import steel, the country as a whole benefits in the same way as if it had invented a technology for turning wheat into steel. A country that eliminates trade restrictions will, therefore, experience the same kind of economic growth that would occur after a major technological advance.

However, some of the world's poorest countries have tried to achieve more rapid economic growth by pursuing *inward-oriented policies.* These policies are aimed at raising productivity and living standards within the country by avoiding interaction with the rest of the world. This approach gets support from some domestic firms, which claim that they need protection from foreign competition in order to compete and grow. This infant-industry argument, together with a general distrust of foreigners, has at times led policy makers in less developed countries to impose tariffs and other trade restrictions.

Research and Development

The primary reason that living standards are higher today than they were a century ago is that technological knowledge has advanced.

Although most technological advance comes from private research by firms and individual inventors, there is also a public interest in promoting these efforts. To a large extent, knowledge is a *public good*: once one person discovers an idea, the idea enters society's pool of knowledge and other people and businesses can freely use it (subject to any legal restrictions such as those imposed by intellectual property rights). Just as government has a role in providing a public good such as national defence, it also has a role in encouraging the research and development of new technologies. The governments in most advanced countries do this in a number of ways, for example through science research laboratories owned and funded by the government, or through a system of research grants offered to promising researchers. It may also offer tax breaks and concessions for firms engaging in research and development.

Yet another way in which government policy encourages research is through the patent system. When a person or firm invents a new product, such as a new drug, the inventor can apply for a patent. If the product is deemed truly original, the government awards the patent, which gives the inventor the exclusive right to make the product for a specified number of years. In essence, the patent gives the inventor a property right over their invention, turning their new idea from a public good into a private good. By allowing inventors to profit from their inventions – even if only temporarily – the patent system enhances the incentive for individuals and firms to engage in research.

Population Growth

Economists and other social scientists have long debated how population growth affects a society. The most direct effect is on the size of the labour force: a large population means more workers to produce goods and services. At the same time, it means more people to consume those goods and services and it is also likely that a larger population will be more likely to have individuals who will be enterprising, and will come up with new ideas that lead to technological progress which benefits everyone.

UNEMPLOYMENT

What Is Unemployment?

The answer to this question may seem obvious: an unemployed person is someone who does not have a job. But if you are in full-time education, for example, you do not have a full-time job in the usual sense of the word, i.e. you are not in full-time paid employment and not available for work. If you were suffering from some long-term illness that meant that you were unfit for work, although you would not have a job, we would not say that you were unemployed because you would not be available for work. From these two examples, it seems clear that we need to qualify our original definition of an unemployed person as 'someone who does not have a job' to 'someone who does not have a job and who is available for work'.

But we still need to be clear as to what we mean by 'available for work'. Suppose you were not in full-time employment and were offered a job as a research assistant for €1 a day. Would you take it? At this wage rate, probably not. At another extreme, suppose you won so much money on the Euro Millions Lottery that you decided you would leave university and live off your winnings for the rest of your life. Would you be unemployed? No, because you would still be unavailable for work, no matter what wage rate you were offered. Thus, being unemployed also depends upon whether you are willing to work (whether you are 'available for work') at going wage rates.

We are now in a position to give a more precise definition of what it means to be **unemployed**: the number unemployed in an economy is the number of people of working age who are able and available for work at current wage rates and who do not have a job.

> **unemployed** the number unemployed in an economy is the number of people of working age who are able and available for work at current wage rates and who do not have a job

Normally, economists find it more convenient to speak of the *unemployment rate*. This expresses the number unemployed as a percentage of the *labour force*, which in turn can be defined as the total number of people who could possibly be employed in the economy at any given point in time. If you think about it, this must be equal to the total number of people who are employed plus the total number of people who are unemployed.

How Is Unemployment Measured?

There are two basic ways that government agencies go about measuring the unemployment rate in the economy:

The Claimant Count   One simple way is to count the number of people who, on any given day, are claiming unemployment benefit payments from the government – the so-called *claimant count*. Since a government agency is paying out the benefits, it will be easy to gather data on the number of claimants. The government also has a good idea of the total labour force in employment, since it is receiving income tax payments from them. Adding to this the number of unemployment benefit claimants is a measure of the total labour force, and expressing the claimant count as a proportion of the labour force, is a measure of the unemployment rate.

Labour Force Surveys   The second, and probably more reliable method of measuring unemployment is through the use of surveys – in other words, going out and asking people questions – based on an accepted definition of unemployment. In many countries, the government carries out Labour Force Surveys based on the standardized definition of unemployment from the International Labour Office, or ILO. The ILO definition of an unemployed person is someone who is without a job and who is willing to start work within the next two weeks and either has been looking for work within the past four weeks or was waiting to start a job. The Labour Force Survey is carried out quarterly throughout Europe. The surveys are published in different languages but scrutinized by statisticians to ensure comparability between the surveys carried out in each member state.

Once the government has placed all the individuals covered by the survey in a category, it computes various statistics to summarize the state of the labour market. The **labour force** is defined as the sum of the employed and the unemployed:

labour force the total number of workers, including both the employed and the unemployed

Labour force = Number of people employed + number of people unemployed

Then the **unemployment rate** can be measured as the percentage of the labour force that is unemployed:

unemployment rate the percentage of the labour force that is unemployed

$$\text{Unemployment rate} = \left(\frac{\text{Number of unemployed}}{\text{Labour force}} \right) \times 100$$

The government computes unemployment rates for the entire adult population and for more narrowly defined groups – men, women, youths and so on.

The same survey results are used to produce data on labour force participation. The **labour force participation rate** measures the percentage of the total adult population of the country that is in the labour force:

labour force participation rate the percentage of the adult population that is in the labour force

$$\text{Labour force participation rate} = \left(\frac{\text{Labour force}}{\text{Adult population}} \right) \times 100$$

This statistic tells us the fraction of the population that has chosen to participate in the labour market. The labour force participation rate, like the unemployment rate, is computed both for the entire adult population and for more specific groups.

Data on the labour market also allow economists and policy makers to monitor changes in the economy over time. The normal rate of unemployment, around which the unemployment rate fluctuates, is called the **natural rate of unemployment** and the deviation of unemployment from its natural rate is called **cyclical unemployment**.

natural rate of unemployment the normal rate of unemployment around which the unemployment rate fluctuates

Unemployment figures represent an important statistic for businesses because they give an indication of the performance of the economy as a whole and thus help put together parts of the jigsaw so that businesses can make more informed decisions about the state of the economy, whether to make investments, what the labour market is like and how this might impact on wage rates and costs, and how they might fill skill shortages.

cyclical unemployment the deviation of unemployment from its natural rate

Quick Quiz How is the unemployment rate measured? How might the unemployment rate overstate the amount of joblessness? How might it understate it?

CASE STUDY

Doing Business in Africa

The World Bank publishes a *Doing Business* report annually looking at how easy it is to do business around the world. Businesses considering expansion in certain countries will want to take a close look at the report as an aid to their strategic decision-making process. The report uses over 10 000 experts to collate data that will affect business operations in 189 countries in order to make a judgement on the ease of doing business and the barriers that face domestically owned SMEs (small and medium-sized enterprises). The report also looks at regional trends to see if things are better or worse.

The top three countries in Africa are Mauritius with a global ranking of 28, South Africa, globally ranked 43 and Rwanda at number 46. Africa also hosts the bottom three countries in the world for the ease of doing business: the Central African Republic, Libya and Eritrea. Africa on the whole performs worse than other continents in terms of the ease of doing business. Afri-

A lot of businesses are based in Cape Town, South Africa

can countries making significant improvements include Benin, the Democratic Republic of Congo and the Ivory Coast. Things these countries have improved on include reducing bureaucracy such as simplifying tax returns, greater transparency and disclosure requirements, digitizing land registry and tax returns, and reducing the capital requirement to start a business.

South Africa, ranked 43 in the world, has seen a drop in ranking over 2014 of six places when it stood at 37. This is largely down to the greater difficulty in businesses getting credit. The supply of electricity remains a significant barrier to the country and it takes on average 226 days from submitting an application to being connected. This figure compares with the Organization for Economic Cooperation and Development (OECD) average of around 77 days. The cost of getting electricity represents about 730 per cent of the income per capita which is relatively expensive compared to the UK figure of 90 per cent. South Africa also has significant barriers in trading across borders in terms of time and cost. It takes on average 16 days to export and 21 days to import compared with 8 and 6 days for the UK.

References: **http://www.doingbusiness.org/data/exploreeconomies/south-africa/** **http://www.klgates.com/world-bank-publishes-new-findings-on-doing-business-in -africa-11-10-2014/**

SPECIALIZATION AND TRADE

Consider your typical day. You wake up in the morning and you make yourself some coffee from beans grown by farmers in Brazil, processed by businesses from the USA, or tea from leaves grown in Sri Lanka processed and turned into tea bags made in Europe. Over breakfast, you might listen to a radio programme on a radio set made by businesses in Japan. You get dressed in clothes manufactured in Thailand and sold by retail outlets. You might drive to the university or take public transport in a vehicle made of parts manufactured in more than a dozen countries around the world. Then you open up your business economics textbook written by three authors of whom one lives in the USA and the other two live in England, published by a company located in Hampshire and printed on paper made from trees grown in Finland.

Every day you rely on many businesses from around the world, most of whom you have never heard of, to provide you with the goods and services that you enjoy. Such interdependence is possible because people and businesses trade with one another. These people and businesses who provide you with goods and services are not totally acting out of generosity or concern for your welfare. Businesses provide you and other consumers with the goods and services they produce because they get something in return.

The principle that trade can make everyone better off explains why businesses trade with each other both within an economy and internationally. In this section we examine this principle more closely.

The Principle of Comparative Advantage

Access to resources can mean that some businesses are better at producing some goods and services than others. For example, in Spain the climate means that the production of soft fruit is much less costly in terms of resource use than would be the case in Sweden. The City of London houses a large number of banks and financial institutions and London is well known for its expertise in financial products. In the Cape, conditions allow for the growth and processing of grapes for wine and in Germany, manufacturing firms are widely recognized for their high levels of productivity and quality. We call this *specialization*. If businesses specialize and trade then everyone can be made better off.

Some countries house businesses where the cost of production is always lower, for example, a farmer in one country might be better at both rearing cattle and growing potatoes. Does that mean that a farmer in another country who also grows potatoes and rears cattle cannot gain from trade? The principle of comparative advantage suggests that specialization can still occur and benefits can be gained from trading.

absolute advantage the comparison among producers of a good according to their productivity

A key to this principle is the relative costs of production. Economists use the term **absolute advantage** when comparing the productivity of one business to that of another. The producer that requires a smaller quantity of inputs to produce a good is said to have an absolute advantage in producing that good.

A farmer can have an absolute advantage both in producing meat and in producing potatoes if they require less time than the other farmer requires to produce a unit of either good. If Farmer A needs to input only 2 hours in order to produce a kilogram of meat and 1 hour to produce a kilogram of potatoes, whereas Farmer B needs 6 hours to produce a kilogram of meat and 1.5 hours for a kilogram of potatoes, then based on this information, we can conclude that Farmer A has the lower cost of producing potatoes, if we measure cost in terms of the quantity of inputs.

Opportunity Cost and Comparative Advantage

There is another way to look at the cost of producing potatoes. Rather than comparing inputs required, we can compare the opportunity costs. Let us assume that both farmers each spend 48 hours a week working. Time spent producing potatoes, therefore, takes away from time available for producing meat. As both farmers reallocate time between producing the two goods, they give up units of one good to produce units of the other. The opportunity cost measures the trade-off between the two goods that each producer faces.

comparative advantage the comparison among producers of a good according to their opportunity cost

Economists use the term **comparative advantage** when describing the opportunity cost of two producers. The producer who gives up less of other goods to produce good X has the smaller opportunity cost of producing good X and is said to have a comparative advantage in producing it. Although it is possible for one person to have an absolute advantage in both goods (as the farmer does in our example), it is impossible for one business to have a comparative advantage in both goods. Because the opportunity cost of one good is the inverse of the opportunity cost of the other, if a business's opportunity cost of one good is relatively high, the opportunity cost of the other good must be relatively low. Comparative advantage reflects the relative opportunity cost. Unless two businesses have exactly the same opportunity cost, one business will have a comparative advantage in one good, and the other business will have a comparative advantage in the other good. If each business specializes in the product in which they have a comparative advantage and then engage in trade, both can be better off as a result and total world output can increase.

OPEN-ECONOMY MACROECONOMICS: BASIC CONCEPTS

When you next buy some fruit in the supermarket, the chances are that you will have a choice between a domestically produced fruit – perhaps apples – and fruit produced abroad, such as mangoes or bananas. When you take your next holiday, you may consider spending it in one of the cultural capitals of Europe or taking a trip to Dubai or Egypt. When you start saving for your retirement, you may choose between a unit trust that buys mainly shares in domestic companies or one that buys shares of US or Japanese companies instead.

International trade allows businesses to produce what they produce best and for households to consume the great variety of goods and services produced around the world. International trade can raise living standards in all countries by allowing each country to specialize in producing those goods and services in which it has a comparative advantage.

The International Flows of Goods and Capital

Businesses in an economy buy and sell goods and services in world product markets and they buy and sell capital assets such as stocks and bonds in world financial markets. Here we discuss these two activities and the close relationship between them.

The Flow of Goods and Services: Exports, Imports and Net Exports   **Exports** are domestically produced goods and services that are sold abroad, and **imports** are foreign-produced goods and services that are sold domestically. When Lloyd's of London insures a building in New York, it is paid an insurance premium for this service by the owner of the building. The sale of the insurance service provided by Lloyd's is an export for the United Kingdom and an import for the USA. When Volvo, the Swedish car manufacturer, makes a car and sells it to a Swiss resident, the sale is an import for Switzerland and an export for Sweden.

exports goods produced domestically and sold abroad

imports goods produced abroad and purchased for use in the domestic economy

Pitfall Prevention It can be easy to get confused about imports and exports and focus on the physical movement of the good rather than the direction of payment. For example, if a Dutch family decides to take a holiday in Dubai all members of the family physically travel to Dubai. However, what they are actually doing is buying a service – tourism in this case – from Dubai and so their visit represents an import to the Netherlands and an export to Dubai.

trade balance the value of a nation's exports minus the value of its imports; also called net exports

trade surplus an excess of exports over imports

trade deficit an excess of imports over exports

balanced trade a situation in which exports equal imports

The net exports of any country are the value of its exports minus the value of its imports. The sale of insurance services abroad by Lloyd's raises UK net exports, and the Volvo sale reduces Swiss net exports. Because net exports tell us whether a country is, in total, a seller or a buyer in world markets for goods and services, net exports are also called the **trade balance**. If net exports are positive, exports are greater than imports, indicating that the country sells more goods and services abroad than it buys from other countries. In this case, the country is said to run a **trade surplus**. If net exports are negative, exports are less than imports, indicating that the country sells fewer goods and services abroad than it buys from other countries. In this case, the country is said to run a **trade deficit**. If net exports are zero, its exports and imports are exactly equal, and the country is said to have **balanced trade**.

Some of the factors that might influence a country's exports, imports and net exports include the following:

- The tastes of consumers for domestic and foreign goods.
- The prices of goods at home and abroad.
- The exchange rates at which people can use domestic currency to buy foreign currencies.
- The incomes of consumers at home and abroad.
- The cost of transporting goods from country to country.
- The policies of the government towards international trade.

As these variables change over time, so does the amount of international trade.

The Flow of Financial Resources: Net Capital Outflow Residents of an open economy participate in world financial markets. A UK resident with £20 000 could use that money to buy a car from BMW, but they could instead use that money to buy stock in the German BMW corporation. The first transaction would represent a flow of goods, whereas the second would represent a flow of capital.

net capital outflow the purchase of foreign assets by domestic residents minus the purchase of domestic assets by foreigners

The term **net capital outflow** refers to the purchase of foreign assets by domestic residents minus the purchase of domestic assets by foreigners. (It is sometimes called *net foreign investment*.) When a UK resident buys shares in BMW, the purchase raises UK net capital outflow. When a Japanese resident buys a bond issued by the UK government, the purchase reduces UK net capital outflow.

Recall that the flow of capital abroad takes two forms. If the French car manufacturer Renault opens up a factory in Romania, that is an example of foreign *direct investment*. Alternatively, if a French citizen buys shares in a Romanian company, that is an example of *foreign portfolio investment*. In the first case, the French owner is actively managing the investment, whereas in the second case the French owner has a more passive role. In both cases, French residents are buying assets located in another country, so both purchases increase French net capital outflow.

Let's consider briefly some of the more important variables that influence net capital outflow:

- The real interest rates being paid on foreign assets.
- The real interest rates being paid on domestic assets.
- The perceived economic and political risks of holding assets abroad.
- The government policies that affect foreign ownership of domestic assets.

For example, consider German investors deciding whether to buy Mexican government bonds or German government bonds. To make this decision, German investors compare the real interest rates offered on the two bonds. The higher a bond's real interest rate, the more attractive it is. While making this comparison, however, German investors must also take into account the risk that one of these governments might *default* on its debt (that is, not pay interest or principal when it is due), as well as any restrictions that the Mexican government has imposed, or might impose in the future, on foreign investors in Mexico.

The Equality of Net Exports and Net Capital Outflow

Net exports and net capital outflow each measure a type of imbalance in these markets. Net exports measure an imbalance between a country's exports and its imports. Net capital outflow measures an imbalance between the amount of foreign assets bought by domestic residents and the amount of domestic assets bought by foreigners.

An important but subtle fact of accounting states that, for an economy as a whole, these two imbalances must offset each other. That is, net capital outflow (*NCO*) always equals net exports (*NX*):

$$NCO = NX$$

This equation holds because every transaction that affects one side of this equation must also affect the other side by exactly the same amount. This equation is an *identity* – an equation that must hold because of the way the variables in the equation are defined and measured.

To see why this accounting identity is true, consider an example. Suppose that BP sells some aircraft fuel to a Japanese airline. In this sale, a UK company (BP) gives aircraft fuel to a Japanese company, and a Japanese company gives yen to a UK company. Notice that two things have occurred simultaneously. The UK has sold to a foreigner some of its output (the fuel), and this sale increases UK net exports. In addition, the UK has acquired some foreign assets (the yen), and this acquisition increases UK net capital outflow.

Although BP most probably will not hold on to the yen it has acquired in this sale, any subsequent transaction will preserve the equality of net exports and net capital outflow. For example, BP may exchange its yen for pounds with a UK investment fund that wants the yen to buy shares in Sony Corporation, the Japanese maker of consumer electronics. In this case, BP's net export of aircraft fuel equals the investment fund's net capital outflow in Sony shares. Hence, *NX* and *NCO* rise by an equal amount.

Alternatively, BP may exchange its yen for pounds with another UK company that wants to buy computers from Toshiba, the Japanese computer maker. In this case, UK imports (of computers) exactly offset UK exports (of aircraft fuel). The sales by BP and Toshiba together affect neither UK net exports nor UK net capital outflow. That is, *NX* and *NCO* are the same as they were before these transactions took place.

The equality of net exports and net capital outflow follows from the fact that every international transaction is an exchange. When a seller country transfers a good or service to a buyer country, the buyer country gives up some asset to pay for this good or service. The value of that asset equals the value of the good or service sold. When we add everything up, the net value of goods and services sold by a country (*NX*) must equal the net value of assets acquired (*NCO*). The international flow of goods and services and the international flow of capital are two sides of the same coin.

Saving and Investment, and Their Relationship to the International Flows

A nation's saving and investment is crucial to its long-run economic growth. Let's consider how these variables are related to the international flows of goods and capital as measured by net exports and net capital outflow. We can do this most easily with the help of some simple mathematics.

Recall that the total expenditure on the economy's output of goods and services is the sum of expenditure on consumption, investment, government purchases and net exports ($Y = C + I + G + NX$). Also recall that national saving is the income of the nation that is left after paying for current consumption and government purchases. National saving (S) equals $Y - C - G$. If we rearrange the above equation to reflect this fact, we obtain:

$$Y - C - G = I + NX$$
$$S = I + NX$$

Because net exports (NX) also equal net capital outflow (NCO), we can write this equation as:

$$S = I + NCO$$
$$Saving = Domestic\ investment + Net\ capital\ outflow$$

This equation shows that a nation's saving must equal its domestic investment plus its net capital outflow. In other words, when Dutch citizens save a euro of their income for the future, that euro can be used to finance accumulation of domestic capital or it can be used to finance the purchase of capital abroad.

In a closed economy (with no external trade), net capital outflow is zero ($NCO = 0$), so saving equals investment ($S = I$). In an open economy with trade there are two uses for its saving: domestic investment and net capital outflow.

We can view the financial system as standing between the two sides of this identity. For example, suppose the Smith family decides to save some of its income for retirement. This decision contributes to national saving, the left-hand side of our equation. If the Smiths deposit their saving in an investment fund, the fund may use some of the deposit to buy shares issued by BP, which uses the proceeds to build an oil refinery in Aberdeen. In addition, the investment fund may use some of the Smiths' deposit to buy shares issued by Toyota, which uses the proceeds to build a factory in Osaka. These transactions show up on the right-hand side of the equation. From the standpoint of UK accounting, the BP expenditure on a new oil refinery is domestic investment, and the purchase of Toyota stock by a UK resident is net capital outflow. Thus, all saving in the UK economy shows up as investment in the UK economy or as UK net capital outflow.

Quick Quiz Define net exports and net capital outflow. Explain how they are related.

THE PRICES FOR INTERNATIONAL TRANSACTIONS: REAL AND NOMINAL EXCHANGE RATES

Just as the price in any market serves the important role of coordinating buyers and sellers in that market, international prices help coordinate the decisions of consumers and producers as they interact in world markets.

Nominal Exchange Rates

The **nominal exchange rate** is the rate at which a person can trade the currency of one country for the currency of another. For example, a business in Belgium trading with one in Japan might be quoted an exchange rate of 125 yen per euro. If the business gives up one euro, they would get 125 Japanese yen in return.

An exchange rate can always be expressed in two ways. If the exchange rate is 125 yen per euro, it is also 1/125 (= 0.008) euro per yen. If a euro is worth £0.88, a pound is worth 1/0.88 (= 1.136) euros. This can be a source of confusion, and there is no real hard and fast convention that people use. For example, it is customary to quote the US dollar–pound exchange rate as dollars per pound, e.g. $1.50 if £1 exchanges for $1.50. On the other hand, the pound–euro exchange rate can be quoted either way, as pounds per euro or euros per pound. In this book we shall for the most part think of the exchange rate as being the quantity of foreign currency that exchanges for one unit of domestic currency, or the foreign price of a unit of domestic currency. For example, if we are thinking of the UK as the domestic economy and the USA as the foreign economy, then the exchange rate is expressed as $1.58 per pound. If we are thinking of, say, Germany as the domestic economy, then we could express the exchange rate as dollars per euro, e.g. $1.33 dollars per euro.

Given that the exchange rate is the price of acquiring a currency, it might not be surprising to learn that the exchange of any particular currency is determined by the supply and demand of that currency on foreign exchange markets. When the exchange rate changes so that a euro buys more of another currency, this is referred to as an **appreciation** of the euro. When the exchange rate changes so that a euro buys less of another currency, this is referred to as a **depreciation** of the euro. For example, when the exchange rate rises from 125 to 127 yen per euro, the euro is said to appreciate. At the same time, because a Japanese yen now buys less of the European currency, the yen is said to depreciate. When the exchange rate falls from 125 to 123 yen per euro, the euro is said to depreciate, and the yen to appreciate. (It is sometimes helpful to think how much of the domestic currency an individual has to give up to get the required amount of the foreign currency and vice versa.)

At times you may have heard the media report that the pound or the euro is either 'strong' or 'weak'. These descriptions usually refer to recent changes in the nominal exchange rate. When a currency appreciates, it is said to *strengthen* because it can then buy more foreign currency. Similarly, when a currency depreciates, it is said to *weaken*. If the individual gets more of the foreign currency in exchange for the same amount of the domestic currency, the domestic currency is stronger. If the individual has to give up more of the domestic currency to get the same amount of the foreign currency then the domestic currency is weaker.

For any currency, there are many nominal exchange rates. The euro can be used to buy US dollars, UAE dirham, South African rand, British pounds, Mexican pesos and so on. When economists study changes in the exchange rate, they often use indices that average these many exchange rates. Just as the CPI turns the many prices in the economy into a single measure of the price level, an exchange rate index turns these many exchange rates into a single measure of the international value of the currency. So when economists talk about the euro or the pound appreciating or depreciating, they often are referring to an exchange rate index that takes into account many individual exchange rates.

nominal exchange rate the rate at which a person can trade the currency of one country for the currency of another

appreciation an increase in the value of a currency as measured by the amount of foreign currency it can buy

depreciation a decrease in the value of a currency as measured by the amount of foreign currency it can buy

Real Exchange Rates

real exchange rate the rate at which a person can trade the goods and services of one country for the goods and services of another

The **real exchange rate** is the rate at which a person can trade the goods and services of one country for the goods and services of another. For example, suppose that you go shopping and find that a kilo of Swiss cheese is twice as expensive as a kilo of English Cheddar cheese. We would then say that the real exchange rate is a ½ kilo of Swiss cheese per kilo of English cheese. Notice that, like the nominal exchange rate, we express the real exchange rate as units of the foreign item per unit of the domestic item. But in this instance the item is a good rather than a currency.

Real and nominal exchange rates are closely related. To see how, consider an example. Suppose that a kilo of British wheat sells for £1, and a kilo of European wheat sells for €3. What is the real exchange rate between British and European wheat? To answer this question, we must first use the nominal exchange rate to convert the prices into a common currency. If the nominal exchange rate is €2 per pound, then a price for British wheat of £1 per kilo is equivalent to €2 per kilo. European wheat, however, sells for €3 a kilo, so British wheat is only ⅔ as expensive as European wheat. The real exchange rate is ⅔ of a kilo of European wheat per kilo of British wheat.

We can summarize this calculation for the real exchange rate with the following formula, where we are measuring the exchange rate as the amount of foreign currency needed to buy 1 unit of domestic currency:

$$\text{Real exchange rate} = \frac{(\text{Nominal exchange rate} \times \text{Domestic price})}{(\text{Foreign price})}$$

Using the numbers in our example, the formula applies as follows:

$$\text{Real exchange rate} = \frac{(\text{€2 per pound}) \times (\text{£1 per kilo of UK wheat})}{(\text{€3 per kilo of European wheat})}$$

$$= \text{⅔ kilo of European wheat per kilo of UK wheat}$$

Thus, the real exchange rate depends on the nominal exchange rate and on the prices of goods in the two countries measured in the local currencies.

The real exchange rate is a key determinant of how much a country exports and imports. For example, when a British bread company is deciding whether to buy British or European wheat to make into flour and use in making its bread, it will ask which wheat is cheaper. The real exchange rate gives the answer.

When studying an economy as a whole, macroeconomists focus on overall prices rather than the prices of individual items. That is, to measure the real exchange rate, they use price indices, such as the CPI, which measure the prices of a basket of goods and services. By using a prices index for a UK or European basket (P), a prices index for a foreign basket (P^*) and the nominal exchange rate between the UK pound or euro and foreign currencies (e = foreign currency per pound), we can compute the overall real exchange rate between the United Kingdom or Europe and other countries as follows:

$$\text{Real exchange rate} = \frac{(e \times P)}{P^*}$$

This real exchange rate measures the price of a basket of goods and services available domestically relative to a basket of goods and services available abroad.

A country's real exchange rate is a key determinant of its net exports of goods and services. A depreciation (fall) in the real exchange rate of the euro means that EU goods have become cheaper relative to foreign goods. This change encourages consumers both at home and abroad to buy more EU goods and fewer goods from other countries. Businesses in the EU selling goods to South Africa, for example, will benefit from the depreciation whereas those buying goods and services from South Africa will find the depreciation has increased their costs. As a result, EU exports rise and EU imports fall, and both of these changes raise EU net exports. Conversely, an appreciation (rise) in the euro real exchange rate means that EU goods have become more expensive compared to foreign goods, so EU net exports fall.

It is important to remember that whilst we are talking about the prices of exports and imports changing, the domestic price for these goods and services may not change. For example, a French wine producer may have wine for sale priced at €10 per bottle. If the exchange rate between the euro and the South African rand is €1 = R9.9 then a South African buyer of wine will have to give up R69 to buy a bottle of wine. If the euro exchange rate appreciates to €1 = 10.5 then the South African buyer now has to give up R105 to buy the bottle of wine. The euro price of the wine has not changed but to the South African buyer the price has risen. Equally, if the euro exchange rate depreciated from €1 = R9.9 to €1 = R9.00 then the South African buyer would now have to give up R90 to buy the wine. Again, the euro price of the wine has not changed but the price to the South African buyer has fallen because the exchange rate between the pound and the euro has changed.

Quick Quiz Define nominal exchange rate and real exchange rate, and explain how they are related. If the nominal exchange rate changes from 100 to 120 yen per euro, has the euro appreciated or depreciated? Explain.

JEOPARDY PROBLEM

A firm based in the Netherlands buys raw materials from firms in South Africa and Saudi Arabia and sells its output to firms elsewhere in the EU and to the USA. The exchange rate between the euro and those other currencies in which it trades depreciates significantly over a period of a year. The Dutch firm finds that far from benefiting from the depreciation its profits are falling. Why might this happen?

A MODEL OF EXCHANGE RATE DETERMINATION: PURCHASING POWER PARITY

Exchange rates vary substantially over time. Economists have developed many models to explain how exchange rates are determined, each emphasizing just some of the many forces at work. Here we develop the simplest theory of exchange rates, called purchasing power parity. This theory states that a unit of any given currency should be able to buy the same quantity of goods in all countries. Many economists believe

purchasing power parity a theory of exchange rates whereby a unit of any given currency should be able to buy the same quantity of goods in all countries

that **purchasing power parity** describes the forces that determine exchange rates in the long run. We now consider the logic on which this long-run theory of exchange rates is based, as well as the theory's implications and limitations.

The Basic Logic of Purchasing Power Parity

The theory of purchasing power parity is based on a principle called the *law of one price*. This law asserts that a good must sell for the same price in all locations. Otherwise, there would be opportunities for profit left unexploited. For example, suppose that coffee beans sold for less in Munich than in Frankfurt. A person could buy coffee in Munich for, say, €4 a kilo and then sell it in Frankfurt for €5 a kilo, making a profit of €1 per kilo from the difference in price. The process of taking advantage of differences in prices in different markets is called *arbitrage*. In our example, as people took advantage of this arbitrage opportunity, they would increase the demand for coffee in Munich and increase the supply in Frankfurt. The price of coffee would rise in Munich (in response to greater demand) and fall in Frankfurt (in response to greater supply). This process would continue until, eventually, the prices were the same in the two markets.

Now consider how the law of one price applies to the international market-place. If a euro (or any other currency) could buy more coffee in Germany than in Japan, international traders could profit by buying coffee in Germany and selling it in Japan. This export of coffee from Germany to Japan would drive up the German price of coffee and drive down the Japanese price. Conversely, if a euro could buy more coffee in Japan than in Germany, traders could buy coffee in Japan and sell it in Germany. This import of coffee into Germany from Japan would drive down the German price of coffee and drive up the Japanese price. In the end, the law of one price tells us that a euro must buy the same amount of coffee in all countries.

This logic leads us to the theory of purchasing power parity. According to this theory, a currency must have the same purchasing power in all countries. That is, a euro must buy the same quantity of goods in Germany and Japan, and a Japanese yen must buy the same quantity of goods in Japan as in Germany. Indeed, the name of this theory describes it well. *Parity* means equality, and *purchasing power* refers to the value of money. *Purchasing power parity* states that a unit of all currencies must have the same real value in every country.

Implications of Purchasing Power Parity

What does the theory of purchasing power parity say about exchange rates? It tells us that the nominal exchange rate between the currencies of two countries depends on the price levels in those countries. If a euro buys the same quantity of goods in Germany (where prices are measured in euros) as in Japan (where prices are measured in yen), then the number of yen per euro must reflect the prices of goods in Germany and Japan. For example, if a kilo of coffee is priced at 500 yen in Japan and €5 in Germany, then the nominal exchange rate must be 100 yen per euro (500 yen/€5 = 100 yen per euro). Otherwise, the purchasing power of the euro would not be the same in the two countries.

To see more fully how this works, it is helpful to use just a little mathematics. Think of Germany as the home or domestic economy. Suppose that P is the price of a basket of goods in Germany (measured in euros), P^* is the price of a basket of goods in Japan (measured in yen), and e is the nominal exchange rate (the number of yen needed to buy one euro). Now consider the quantity of goods a euro can buy at home (in Germany) and abroad. At home, the price level is P, so the purchasing power of €1 at home is $1/P$. Abroad, a euro can be exchanged into e units of foreign currency, which in turn have purchasing power e/P^*. For the purchasing power of a euro to be the same in the two countries, it must be the case that:

$$\frac{1}{P} = \frac{e}{P^*}$$

With rearrangement, this equation becomes:

$$1 = \frac{eP}{P^*}$$

Notice that the left-hand side of this equation is a constant, and the right-hand side is the real exchange rate. Thus, if the purchasing power of the euro is always the same at home and abroad, then the real exchange rate – the relative price of domestic and foreign goods – cannot change.

To see the implication of this analysis for the nominal exchange rate, we can rearrange the last equation to solve for the nominal exchange rate:

$$e = \frac{P^*}{P}$$

That is, the nominal exchange rate equals the ratio of the foreign price level (measured in units of the foreign currency) to the domestic price level (measured in units of the domestic currency). According to the theory of purchasing power parity, the nominal exchange rate between the currencies of two countries must reflect the different price levels in those countries.

Limitations of Purchasing Power Parity

The theory of purchasing power parity is not completely accurate. That is, exchange rates do not always move to ensure that a euro has the same real value in all countries all the time. There are two reasons why the theory of purchasing power parity does not always hold in practice.

The first reason is that many goods are not easily traded. Imagine, for instance, that haircuts are more expensive in Paris than in New York. International travellers might avoid getting their haircuts in Paris, and some haircutters might move from New York to Paris. Yet such arbitrage would probably be too limited to eliminate the differences in prices. Thus, the deviation from purchasing power parity might persist, and a euro (or dollar) would continue to buy less of a haircut in Paris than in New York.

The second reason that purchasing power parity does not always hold is that even tradable goods are not always perfect substitutes when they are produced in different countries. For example, some consumers prefer German cars, and others prefer Japanese cars. Moreover, consumer tastes can change over time. If German cars suddenly become more popular, the increase in demand will drive up the price of German cars compared to Japanese cars. But despite this difference in prices in the two markets, there might be no opportunity for profitable arbitrage because consumers do not view the two cars as equivalent.

Thus, both because some goods are not tradable and because some tradable goods are not perfect substitutes with their foreign counterparts, purchasing power parity is not a perfect theory of exchange rate determination. For these reasons, real exchange rates fluctuate over time. Nonetheless, the theory of purchasing power parity does provide a useful first step in understanding exchange rates. The basic logic is persuasive: as the real exchange rate drifts from the level predicted by purchasing power parity, people have greater incentive to move goods across national borders. Even if the forces of purchasing power parity do not completely fix the real exchange rate, they provide a reason to expect that changes in the real exchange rate are most often small or temporary. As a result, large and persistent movements in nominal exchange rates typically reflect changes in price levels at home and abroad.

CONCLUSION

The purpose of this chapter has been to develop some basic concepts in macro-economics that businesses need to be aware of and indeed monitor. GDP gives an indication of how the economy is performing and inflation and unemployment are closely linked to this. If economic activity is growing then businesses might be tempted to expand output and invest but how easily they can do this might depend on the level of savings in the economy which might in turn be dependent on the level of interest rates and inflation. During periods of a slowdown in economic activity, firms may choose to cut production and lay off workers thus raising unemployment, but if the economy is growing then unemployment may be falling and firms might find it more difficult to attract new workers with the skills they need and may also find that they have to pay higher wages to attract these workers.

Many businesses will engage in some form of trade with the rest of the world. If they are buying goods and services from abroad, or selling goods and services abroad, then the rate of exchange will have an effect on relative prices and sales. Understanding the determinants of the exchange rate better, as well as how exchange rates might vary with the performance of the economy, might be important in making business decisions. The macroeconomic variables defined here offer a starting point for analysing an economy's interactions with the rest of the world and how they have an effect on businesses.

IN THE NEWS

The Effects of Exchange Rates on Businesses

This article looks at how exchange rate movements can have effects on business performance by changing the costs and revenues that the business pays and receives.

The Swiss government want important businesses operating in Switzerland to be successful. They provide employment, tax and are often a source of export revenues. Swatch is one example of a big business located in Switzerland. Swatch is a Swiss watch-making firm that exports nearly all of its products around the world. In 2014 Swatch had a turnover of over CHF 9 billion (€8.7 billion). It has

Nick Hayek Jr, CEO of Swatch

production in Switzerland but has marketing and distribution networks in 50 countries throughout the world. Swatch, along with companies involved in the Swiss tourist industry, takes a keen interest in currency fluctuations.

Currency charts are live and plot the changes in the exchange rate between any two currencies. At the close of day on 13 April 2015, one Swiss franc (CHF) could be exchanged for €0.968, but the rate varies all the time. Earlier in the day at around 7.30am one CHF was worth €0.962 and three months ago it was worth over €1.

Big businesses trading overseas often hedge their bets to negate the effect of exchange rate movements by using forward markets. Forward markets are designed to even out the exchange rate fluctuations businesses buying and selling across countries might otherwise experience. It would have been a very good idea for Swiss companies trading abroad to have hedged their bets earlier this year.

Early on Thursday morning of the 15 January 2015 one CHF would buy €0.83 but within a few minutes that morning it had risen in value by 30 per cent to command €1.15 after the announcement by the Swiss central bank that it was ending the Swiss franc-euro cap. The cap was originally introduced in September 2011 to protect Swiss businesses like Swatch and those involved in the tourist industry. Any jump over 2 per cent is considered big in the foreign exchange market, so this event was huge. Later in the day the exchange rate settled down at one CHF to €0.98.

The effect was devastating to some currency traders caught out by the unexpected announcement, but the rapid rise in the value of the Swiss franc also had a significant impact on Swiss tourism, which was felt immediately in ski resorts and for Swiss manufacturers like Swatch. Nick Hayet, the chief executive of Swatch, described the move by the central bank as a tsunami for the export industry.

Questions

1. Assume Swatch sells watches in the eurozone countries that are priced at CHF100. If the exchange rate between the Swiss franc and the euro is CHF1 = €0.83, what is the price of the transaction in euros?
2. Assume now that the exchange rate changes to CHF1 = €0.98, what is the new euro price of the product? What effect would you expect this change to have on Swatch's business in the eurozone countries?
3. A Swiss company imports materials for its manufacturing from the USA. The company buys a quantity of materials each month priced at $15 000. The exchange rate between the Swiss franc and the US dollar at the beginning of the year is CHF1 = $0.98. Several months later the value of the Swiss franc against the dollar changes to CHF1 = $1.03. What effect does this have on the Swiss importer?
4. Swatch sells some of its products to customers in Europe and some to Japan. Assume the Swiss franc depreciates against the euro but appreciates against the yen. What would determine the overall outcome for Swatch of these different movements in the exchange rate?
5. How might Swatch protect itself from exchange rate movements by using forward exchange rate markets?

References: http://www.ozforex.com.au/currency-converter/chf/eur/1000000/false http://www.theguardian.com/business/2015/jan/15/currency-markets-switzerland-franc

SUMMARY

- Economic prosperity, as measured by GDP per person, varies substantially around the world.

- Because every transaction has a buyer and a seller, the total expenditure in the economy must equal the total income in the economy.

- Gross domestic product (GDP) measures an economy's total expenditure on newly produced goods and services and the total income earned from the production of these goods and services. More precisely, GDP is the market value of all final goods and services produced within a country in a given period of time.

- The standard of living in an economy depends on the economy's ability to produce goods and services.

- Government policies can try to influence the economy's growth rate by encouraging saving and investment, encouraging investment from abroad, fostering education, maintaining property rights and political stability, allowing free trade, promoting the research and development of new technologies, and controlling population growth.

- Nominal GDP uses current prices to value the economy's production of goods and services. Real GDP uses constant base-year prices to value the economy's production of goods and services. The GDP deflator – calculated from the ratio of nominal to real GDP – measures the level of prices in the economy.

- The CPI shows the changes in the prices of a basket of goods and services relative to the prices of the same basket in the base year. The index is used to measure the overall level of prices in the economy. The percentage change in the consumer prices index measures the inflation rate.

- The CPI is an imperfect measure of the cost of living for three reasons. First, it does not take into account consumers' ability to substitute towards goods that become relatively cheaper over time. Second, it does not take into account increases in the purchasing power of money due to the introduction of new goods. Third, it is distorted by unmeasured changes in the quality of goods and services. Because of these measurement problems, the CPI overstates true inflation.

- The nominal interest rate is the interest rate usually reported; it is the rate at which the amount of money in a savings account increases over time. In contrast, the real interest rate takes into account changes in the value of money over time. The real interest rate equals the nominal interest rate minus the rate of inflation.

- An economy's saving can be used either to finance investment at home or to buy assets abroad. Thus, national saving equals domestic investment plus net capital outflow.

- The unemployment rate is the percentage of those who would like to work who do not have jobs. The government calculates this statistic monthly based on a survey of thousands of households.

- The unemployment rate is an imperfect measure of joblessness. Some people who call themselves unemployed may actually not want to work, and some people who would like to work have left the labour force after an unsuccessful search.

- Net exports are the value of domestic goods and services sold abroad minus the value of foreign goods and services sold domestically. Net capital outflow is the acquisition of foreign assets by domestic residents minus the acquisition of domestic assets by foreigners. Because every international transaction involves an exchange of an asset for a good or service, an economy's net capital outflow always equals its net exports.

- The nominal exchange rate is the relative price of the currency of two countries, and the real exchange rate is the relative price of the goods and services of two countries. When the nominal exchange rate changes so that each unit of domestic currency buys more foreign currency, the domestic currency is said to *appreciate* or *strengthen*. When the nominal exchange rate changes so that each unit of domestic currency buys less foreign currency, the domestic currency is said to *depreciate* or *weaken*.

- According to the theory of purchasing power parity, a unit of currency should be able to buy the same quantity of goods in all countries. This theory implies that the nominal exchange rate between the currencies of two countries should reflect the price levels in those countries. As a result, countries with relatively high inflation should have depreciating currencies, and countries with relatively low inflation should have appreciating currencies.

QUESTIONS FOR REVIEW

1. Explain why an economy's income must equal its expenditure.

2. What does the level of a nation's GDP measure? What does the growth rate of GDP measure? Would you rather live in a nation with a high level of GDP and a low growth rate, or in a nation with a low level of GDP and a high growth rate?

3. A farmer sells wheat to a baker for €2. The baker uses the wheat to make bread, which is sold for €3. What is the total contribution of these transactions to GDP?

4. Which do you think has a greater effect on the consumer prices index: a 10 per cent increase in the price of chicken or a 10 per cent increase in the price of caviar? Why?

5. Over a long period of time, the price of a chocolate bar rose from €0.10 to €0.60. Over the same period, the consumer prices index rose from 150 to 300. Adjusted for overall inflation, how much did the price of the chocolate bar change?

6. Why do economists use real GDP rather than nominal GDP to gauge economic well-being?

7. What is the GDP deflator and how does it differ to the consumer prices index?

8. Define net exports and net capital outflow. Explain how and why they are related.

9. If a Japanese car is priced at 500 000 yen, a similar German car is priced at €10 000, and a euro can buy 100 yen, what are the nominal and real exchange rates?

10. Describe the economic logic behind the theory of purchasing power parity.

PROBLEMS AND APPLICATIONS

1. Below are some data from the land of milk and honey.
   a. Compute nominal GDP, real GDP and the GDP deflator for each year, using 2016 as the base year.
   b. Compute the percentage change in nominal GDP, real GDP and the GDP deflator in 2017 and 2018 from the preceding year. For each year, identify the variable that does not change. Explain in words why your answer makes sense.
   c. Did economic well-being rise more in 2017 or 2018? Explain.

Year	Price of milk €	Quantity of milk (litres)	Price of honey €	Quantity of honey (litres)
2016	1	100	2	50
2017	1	200	2	100
2018	2	200	4	100

2. One day Boris the Barber, collects €400 for haircuts. Over this day, his equipment depreciates in value by €50. Of the remaining €350, Boris sends €30 to the government in sales taxes, takes home €220 in wages, and retains €100 in his business to add new equipment in the future. From the €220 that Boris takes home, he pays €70 in income taxes. Based on this information, compute Boris' contribution to the following measures of income:
   a. gross domestic product
   b. net national product
   c. national income
   d. personal income,
   e. disposable personal income.

3. Suppose that a borrower and a lender agree on the nominal interest rate to be paid on a loan. Then inflation turns out to be higher than they both expected:
   a. Is the real interest rate on this loan higher or lower than expected?
   b. Does the lender gain or lose from this unexpectedly high inflation? Does the borrower gain or lose?

4. Do you think that firms in small towns or in cities have more market power in hiring? Do you think that firms generally have more market power in hiring today than 50 years ago, or less? Explain.

5. How would the following transactions affect UK net capital outflow? Also, state whether each involves direct investment or portfolio investment.
   a. A British mobile telephone company establishes an office in the Czech Republic.
   b. A US company's pension fund buys shares in BP.
   c. Toyota expands its factory in Derby, England.
   d. A London-based investment trust sells its Volkswagen shares to a French investor.

6. How would the following transactions affect UK exports, imports and net exports?
   a. A British art lecturer spends the summer touring museums in Italy.
   b. Students in Paris flock to see the Royal Shakespeare Company perform *King Lear* on tour.
   c. The British art lecturer buys a new Volvo.
   d. A student in Munich buys a Manchester United official team shirt (in Munich).
   e. A British citizen goes to Calais for the day to stock up on French wine.

7. International trade in each of the following products has increased over time. Suggest some reasons why this might be so.
   a. Wheat.
   b. Banking services.
   c. Computer software.
   d. Automobiles.

8. Would each of the following groups be happy or unhappy if the euro appreciated against all currencies? Explain.
   a. US pension funds holding French government bonds.
   b. German manufacturing industries.
   c. Australian tourists planning a trip to Europe.
   d. A British firm trying to purchase property overseas.

9. Suppose that a car company owned entirely by South Korean citizens opens a new factory in the north of England.
   a. What sort of foreign investment would this represent?
   b. What would be the effect of this investment on UK GDP?
   c. Would the effect on UK GNP be larger or smaller?

10. What is happening to the Swiss real exchange rate in each of the following situations? Explain.
    a. The Swiss nominal exchange rate is unchanged, but prices rise faster in Switzerland than abroad.
    b. The Swiss nominal exchange rate is unchanged, but prices rise faster abroad than in Switzerland.
    c. The Swiss nominal exchange rate declines, and prices are unchanged in Switzerland and abroad.
    d. The Swiss nominal exchange rate declines, and prices rise faster abroad than in Switzerland.

17 AGGREGATE DEMAND AND AGGREGATE SUPPLY

LEARNING OUTCOMES

After reading this chapter you should be able to:

- Outline three key facts about economic fluctuations.
- Explain the difference between the short run and the long run.

- Analyse at least three reasons why the aggregate demand and aggregate supply curve can shift.
- Assess the effect of a shift in either the aggregate demand curve or the aggregate supply curve.

INTRODUCTION

economic activity the amount of buying and selling (transactions) that take place in an economy over a period of time

Economic activity fluctuates from year to year. In most years, the production of goods and services rises. Because of increases in the labour force, increases in the capital stock and advances in technological knowledge, the economy can produce more and more over time.

In some years, however, this normal growth does not occur. Firms find themselves unable to sell all of the goods and services they have to offer, so they cut back on production. Workers are laid off, unemployment rises and firms have excess capacity. With the economy producing fewer goods and services, real GDP and other measures of income fall. Such a period of falling incomes and rising unemployment is called a **recession** if it is relatively mild and a **depression** if it is more severe.

recession a period of declining real incomes and rising unemployment. The technical definition gives recession occurring after two successive quarters of negative economic growth

What causes short-run fluctuations in economic activity? How are businesses affected by these fluctuations and how do they react? What, if anything, can public policy do to moderate swings in economic activity? These are the questions that we take up now.

depression a severe recession

The variables that we study in relation to these questions include GDP, unemployment and the price level. The main policy instruments include government spending, taxes, and the money supply and interest rates. Many of these policies are designed to influence how the economy works in the short run. Although there remains some debate among economists about how to analyse short-run fluctuations, at an introductory level it is appropriate to use the *model of aggregate demand and aggregate supply*. This chapter introduces the model's two key elements – the aggregate demand curve and the aggregate supply curve.

THREE KEY FACTS ABOUT ECONOMIC FLUCTUATIONS

Short-run fluctuations in economic activity occur in all countries and in all times throughout history. As a starting point for understanding these year-to-year fluctuations, let's discuss some of their most important properties.

Fact 1: Economic Fluctuations Are Irregular and Unpredictable

Fluctuations in the economy are often called the *business cycle*. As this term suggests, economic fluctuations correspond to changes in business conditions. When real GDP grows rapidly, firms find that customers are plentiful and that profits are growing. On the other hand, during periods of economic contraction, many firms experience declining sales and dwindling profits.

The term *business cycle* is somewhat misleading, however, because it seems to suggest that economic fluctuations follow a regular, predictable pattern. In fact, economic fluctuations are not at all regular, and they are almost impossible to predict with much accuracy. Over a period of time, the general trend in real GDP is to rise steadily in many countries but the path of GDP is not always smooth. We can define a recession as occurring when real GDP falls for two successive quarters. From this definition we can identify recessions in almost every decade since the 1960s in Europe and across other parts of the world. The most recent global recession which began around 2008 has caused major uncertainty and many firms have either gone out of business or found carrying out business extremely difficult.

Fact 2: Most Macroeconomic Quantities Fluctuate Together

Real GDP is the variable that is most commonly used to monitor short-run changes in the economy because it is the most comprehensive measure of economic activity. Real GDP measures the total income (adjusted for inflation) of everyone in the economy.

In monitoring short-run fluctuations it does not really matter which measure of economic activity one looks at. Most macroeconomic variables that measure some type of income, spending or production fluctuate closely together. When real GDP falls in a recession, so do personal income, corporate profits, consumer spending, investment spending, industrial production, retail sales, home sales, auto sales and so on. Because recessions are economy-wide phenomena, they show up in many sources of macroeconomic data.

Although many macroeconomic variables fluctuate together, they fluctuate by different amounts. In particular, investment spending by businesses varies greatly over the business cycle. When economic conditions deteriorate, much of the decline is attributable to reductions in spending on new factories, housing and inventories.

Fact 3: As Output Falls, Unemployment Rises

Changes in the economy's output of goods and services are strongly correlated with changes in the economy's utilization of its labour force so when real GDP declines unemployment rises. When firms choose to produce a smaller quantity of goods and services, they lay off workers, expanding the pool of unemployed. However, there is generally a time-lag between any downturn in economic activity and a rise in unemployment and vice versa. Even when positive growth resumes, therefore, unemployment is likely to continue to rise for some time afterwards. For this reason, unemployment is referred to as a 'lagged indicator'.

> **Quick Quiz** If economic activity falls, what would you expect to happen to the overall level of consumption, investment, government spending and net exports? What would you expect to happen to the price level?

EXPLAINING SHORT-RUN ECONOMIC FLUCTUATIONS

Describing the patterns that economies experience as they fluctuate over time is easy. Explaining what causes these fluctuations is more difficult. The theory of economic fluctuations remains controversial.

How the Short Run Differs From the Long Run

There are a number of theories to explain what determines most important macroeconomic variables in the long run. Much of this analysis is based on two

real variables variables measured in physical units

nominal variables variables measured in monetary units

related ideas – the classical dichotomy and monetary neutrality. The classical dichotomy is the separation of variables into **real variables** (those that measure physical units, quantities or relative prices) and **nominal variables** (those measured in terms of money). Monetary neutrality refers to the assumption that changes in the money supply affect nominal variables but not real variables.

The Classical Dichotomy and Monetary Neutrality

The political philosopher David Hume (1711–1776) suggested that all economic variables should be divided into nominal variables and real variables. For example, the income of dairy farmers is a nominal variable because it is measured in euros, whereas the quantity of milk they produce is a real variable because it is measured in litres. Similarly, nominal GDP is a nominal variable because it measures the euro value of the economy's output of goods and services; real GDP is a real variable because it measures the total quantity of goods and services produced and is not influenced by the current prices of those goods and services. This separation of variables into these groups is now called the **classical dichotomy**. (A *dichotomy* is a division into two groups, and *classical* refers to the earlier economic thinkers or classical economists.)

classical dichotomy the theoretical separation of nominal and real variables

Application of the classical dichotomy is somewhat tricky when we turn to prices. Prices in the economy are normally quoted in terms of money and, therefore, are nominal variables. For instance, when we say that the price of corn is €2 a kilo or that the price of wheat is €1 a kilo, both prices are nominal variables. But what about a **relative price** – the price of one thing compared to another? In our example, we could say that the price of a kilo of corn is two kilos of wheat. Notice that this relative price is no longer measured in terms of money. When comparing the prices of any two goods, the euro signs cancel, and the resulting number is measured in physical units. The lesson is that money prices (e.g. in pounds, euros or dollars) are nominal variables, whereas relative prices are real variables.

relative price the ratio of the price of one good to the price of another

This lesson has several important applications. For instance, the real wage (the money wage adjusted for inflation) is a real variable because it measures the rate at which the economy exchanges goods and services for each unit of labour. Similarly, the real interest rate (the nominal interest rate adjusted for inflation) is a real variable because it measures the rate at which the economy exchanges goods and services produced today for goods and services produced in the future.

Why bother separating variables into these two groups? Hume suggested that the classical dichotomy is useful in analysing the economy because different forces influence real and nominal variables. In particular, he argued, nominal variables are heavily influenced by developments in the economy's monetary system, whereas the monetary system is largely irrelevant for understanding the determinants of important real variables.

Hume's idea is implicit in discussions of the real economy in the long run. Real GDP, saving, investment, real interest rates and unemployment are determined without any mention of the existence of money. The economy's production of goods and services depends on productivity and factor supplies, the real interest rate adjusts to balance the supply and demand for loanable funds, the real wage adjusts to balance the supply and demand for labour, and unemployment results when the real wage is for some reason kept above its equilibrium level. These important conclusions have nothing to do with the quantity of money supplied.

Changes in the supply of money, according to Hume, affect nominal variables but not real variables. When the central bank doubles the money supply, the price level doubles, the euro wage doubles, and all other euro values double. Real variables, such as production, employment, real wages and real interest rates, are unchanged. This irrelevance of monetary changes for real variables is called **monetary neutrality**.

An analogy sheds light on the meaning of monetary neutrality. As the unit of account, money is the yardstick we use to measure economic transactions. When a central bank doubles the money supply, all prices double, and the value of the unit of account falls by half. A similar change would occur if a European Union directive reduced the definition of the metre from 100 to 50 centimetres: as a result of the new unit of measurement, all *measured* distances (nominal variables) would double, but the *actual* distances (real variables) would remain the same. The euro, like the metre, is merely a unit of measurement, so a change in its value should not have important real effects.

Is this conclusion of monetary neutrality a realistic description of the world in which we live? The answer is, not completely. A change in the length of the metre from 100 to 50 centimetres would not matter much in the long run, but in the short run it would certainly lead to confusion and various mistakes. Similarly, most economists today believe that over short periods of time – within the span of a year or two – there is reason to think that monetary changes do have important effects on real variables. Hume himself also doubted that monetary neutrality would apply in the short run. Most economists today accept Hume's conclusion as a description of the economy in the long run. Over the course of a decade, for instance, monetary changes have important effects on nominal variables (such as the price level) but only negligible effects on real variables (such as real GDP). When studying long-run changes in the economy, the neutrality of money offers a good description of how the world works.

Beyond a period of several years, changes in the money supply affect prices and other nominal variables but do not affect real GDP, unemployment or other real variables. When studying year-to-year changes in the economy, however, the assumption of monetary neutrality is no longer appropriate. Most economists believe that, in the short run, real and nominal variables are highly intertwined. In particular, changes in the money supply can temporarily push output away from its long-run trend.

To understand the economy in the short run, therefore, we need a different model. To build this new model, we rely on many of the tools we have developed in previous chapters, but we have to abandon the classical dichotomy and the neutrality of money.

The Basic Model of Economic Fluctuations

Our model of short-run economic fluctuations focuses on the behaviour of two variables. The first variable is the economy's output of goods and services, as measured by real GDP. The second variable is the overall price level, as measured by the CPI or the GDP deflator. Notice that output is a real variable, whereas the price level is a nominal variable. Hence, by focusing on the relationship between these two variables, we are highlighting the breakdown of the classical dichotomy.

We analyse fluctuations in the economy as a whole with the **model of aggregate demand and aggregate supply**, which is illustrated in Figure 17.1. On the vertical axis is the overall price level in the economy. On the horizontal axis is the overall quantity of goods and services. The **aggregate demand curve** shows the quantity of goods and services that households, firms and the government want to buy at each price level. The **aggregate supply curve** shows the quantity of goods and services that firms produce and sell at each price level. According to this model, the price level and the quantity of output adjust to bring aggregate demand and aggregate supply into balance.

It may be tempting to view the model of aggregate demand and aggregate supply as nothing more than a macro version of the model of market demand and

monetary neutrality the proposition that changes in the money supply do not affect real variables

model of aggregate demand and aggregate supply the model that many economists use to explain short-run fluctuations in economic activity around its long-run trend

aggregate demand curve a curve that shows the quantity of goods and services that households, firms and the government want to buy at each price level

aggregate supply curve a curve that shows the quantity of goods and services that firms choose to produce and sell at each price level

market supply. Yet in fact this model is quite different. When we consider demand and supply in a particular market – wheat, for instance – the behaviour of buyers and sellers depends on the ability of resources to move from one market to another. When the price of wheat rises, the quantity demanded falls because buyers will use their incomes to buy products other than wheat. Similarly, a higher price of wheat raises the quantity supplied because firms that produce wheat can increase production by hiring workers away from other parts of the economy. This *microeconomic* substitution from one market to another is impossible when we are analysing the economy as a whole. After all, the quantity that our model is trying to explain – real GDP – measures the total quantity produced in all of the economy's markets. To understand why the aggregate demand curve is downwards sloping and why the aggregate supply curve is upwards sloping, we need a *macroeconomic* theory. Developing such a theory is our next task.

FIGURE 17.1

Aggregate Demand and Aggregate Supply

Economists use the model of aggregate demand and aggregate supply to analyse economic fluctuations. On the vertical axis is the overall level of prices. On the horizontal axis is the economy's total output of goods and services. Output and the price level adjust to the point at which the aggregate supply and aggregate demand curves intersect.

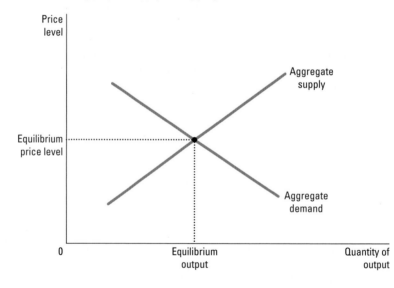

Quick Quiz How does the economy's behaviour in the short run differ from its behaviour in the long run? Draw the model of aggregate demand and aggregate supply. What variables are on the two axes?

THE AGGREGATE DEMAND CURVE

The aggregate demand curve tells us the quantity of all goods and services demanded in the economy at any given price level. As Figure 17.2 illustrates, the aggregate demand curve is downwards sloping. This means that, other things equal, a fall in the economy's overall level of prices (from, say, P_1 to P_2) tends to raise the quantity of goods and services demanded (from Y_1 to Y_2).

FIGURE 17.2

The Aggregate Demand Curve

A decrease in the price level from P₁ to P₂ increases the quantity of goods and services demanded from Y₁ to Y₂. There are three reasons for this negative relationship. As the price level falls, real wealth rises, interest rates fall and the exchange rate depreciates. These effects stimulate spending on consumption, investment and net exports. Increased spending on these components of output means a larger quantity of goods and services demanded.

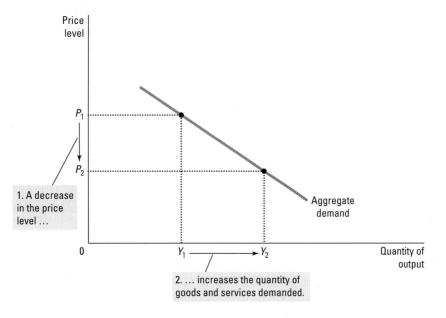

Why the Aggregate Demand Curve Slopes Downwards

Why does a fall in the price level raise the quantity of goods and services demanded? To answer this question, it is useful to recall that $GDP = C + I + G + NX$. Let us assume that government spending is fixed by policy. The other three components of spending – consumption, investment and net exports – depend on economic conditions and, in particular, on the price level. To understand the downwards slope of the aggregate demand curve we must examine how the price level affects the quantity of goods and services demanded for consumption, investment and net exports.

The Price Level and Consumption: The Wealth Effect Consider the money that you hold in your pocket and your bank account. The nominal value of this money is fixed, but its real value is not. When prices fall, this money is more valuable because then it can be used to buy more goods and services. Thus, a decrease in the price level makes consumers wealthier, which in turn encourages them to spend more. The increase in consumer spending means a larger quantity of goods and services demanded.

The Price Level and Investment: The Interest Rate Effect The price level is one determinant of the quantity of money demanded. The lower the price level, the less money households need to hold to buy the goods and services they want. When the price level falls, therefore, households try to reduce their holdings of money by lending some of it out. For instance, a household might use its excess money to buy interest-bearing bonds. Or it might deposit its excess money in an interest-bearing savings account, and the bank would use these funds to make more loans. In either case, as households try to convert some of their money into interest-bearing assets, they drive down interest rates. Lower interest rates, in turn, encourage borrowing by firms that want to invest in new factories and equipment and by households who want to invest in new housing. Thus, a lower price level reduces the interest rate, encourages greater spending on investment goods, and thereby increases the quantity of goods and services demanded.

The Price Level and Net Exports: The Exchange Rate Effect   As we have just discussed, a lower price level lowers the interest rate. In response, some investors will seek higher returns by investing abroad. For instance, as the interest rate on European government bonds falls, an investment fund might sell European government bonds in order to buy US government bonds. As the investment fund tries to convert its euros into dollars in order to buy the US bonds, it increases the supply of euros in the market for foreign currency exchange. The increased supply of euros causes the euro to depreciate relative to other currencies. Because each euro buys fewer units of foreign currencies, non-European goods (i.e. imports) become more expensive to European residents but exporters find that foreign buyers get more euros for each unit of their currency. This change in the real exchange rate (the relative price of domestic and foreign goods) increases European exports of goods and services and decreases European imports of goods and services. Net exports, which equal exports minus imports, also increase. Thus, when a fall in the European price level causes European interest rates to fall, the real value of the euro falls, and this depreciation stimulates European net exports and thereby increases the quantity of goods and services demanded in the European economy.

It is important to keep in mind that the aggregate demand curve (like all demand curves) is drawn holding 'other things equal'. In particular, our three explanations of the downwards sloping aggregate demand curve assume that the money supply is fixed. That is, we have been considering how a change in the price level affects the demand for goods and services, holding the amount of money in the economy constant. As we will see, a change in the quantity of money shifts the aggregate demand curve. At this point, just keep in mind that the aggregate demand curve is drawn for a given quantity of money.

Why the Aggregate Demand Curve Might Shift

The downwards slope of the aggregate demand curve shows that a fall in the price level raises the overall quantity of goods and services demanded. Many other factors, however, affect the quantity of goods and services demanded at a given price level. When one of these other factors changes, the aggregate demand curve shifts.

Let's consider some examples of events that shift aggregate demand. We can categorize them according to which component of spending is most directly affected.

Shifts Arising From Consumption   Suppose people suddenly become more concerned about saving for retirement and, as a result, reduce their current consumption. Because the quantity of goods and services demanded at any price level is lower, the aggregate demand curve shifts to the left. Conversely, imagine that a stock market boom makes people wealthier and less concerned about saving. The resulting increase in consumer spending means a greater quantity of goods and services demanded at any given price level, so the aggregate demand curve shifts to the right.

Thus, any event that changes how much people want to consume at a given price level shifts the aggregate demand curve. One policy variable that has this effect is the level of taxation. When the government cuts taxes, it encourages people and businesses to spend more, so the aggregate demand curve shifts to the right. When the government raises taxes, people and businesses cut back on their spending and the aggregate demand curve shifts to the left.

Shifts Arising From Investment Any event that changes how much firms want to invest at a given price level also shifts the aggregate demand curve. For instance, imagine that the telecommunications industry introduces faster broadband access, and many firms decide to invest in this new access. Because the quantity of goods and services demanded at any price level is higher, the aggregate demand curve shifts to the right. Conversely, if firms become pessimistic about future business conditions, they may cut back on investment spending, shifting the aggregate demand curve to the left.

Tax policy can also influence aggregate demand through investment. An investment allowance (a tax rebate tied to a firm's investment spending) increases the quantity of investment goods that firms demand at any given interest rate. It therefore shifts the aggregate demand curve to the right. The repeal of an investment allowance reduces investment and shifts the aggregate demand curve to the left.

Another policy variable that can influence investment and aggregate demand is the money supply. An increase in the money supply lowers the interest rate in the short run. This makes borrowing less costly, which stimulates investment spending and thereby shifts the aggregate demand curve to the right. Conversely, a decrease in the money supply raises the interest rate, discourages investment spending, and thereby shifts the aggregate demand curve to the left. Many economists believe that changes in monetary policy have been an important source of shifts in aggregate demand in most developed economies at some points in their history.

CASE STUDY

Investment or Consumption? Which Has Led to Economic Growth?

According to the Office for National Statistics (ONS) the UK economy grew by 0.6 per cent in the fourth quarter of 2014 which equates to an overall growth rate of 2.8 per cent for the year. The growth was driven by an increase in household consumption rather than by business investment which fell by 0.9 per cent in the final quarter of 2014. Record low inflation, caused partly by significant falls in oil prices to below $60 a barrel, resulted in workers experiencing real wage increases for the first time since 2007. This feel-good factor may well diminish as the oil price reductions feed through the system and if inflation once again rises to normal levels from the March 2015 rate of 0 per cent.

Wages, which rose by 1.6 per cent in 2014, would need to rise by a much faster rate in 2015 to match the potential rise in inflation and for economic growth to be sustainable. To make economic growth sustainable requires business investment, but here is the catch. Wage increases result from investment and consequent increases in productivity but 2015 investment forecasts from the British Chambers of Commerce (BCC) have been reduced from 7.5 per cent to just 3.5 per cent representing a big drop from the 2014 figure of 6.8 per cent. Uncertainty is a key factor deriving from both external and internal factors. Businesses are worried about EU stagnation, global tensions and the planned UK referendum on its position in the EU in 2017. The Chief Economist of the BCC, David Kern, notes that 'greater efforts are needed to rebalance our economy, away from growth that is dependent on consumer spending towards long-term growth that is based on business investment and exports'. The current consumer spending boom in the UK may be a temporary thing and when added to weaker consumer spending in the export market of the EU, makes investment decisions more risky. In such circumstance some of any increased investment may lead to a rise in capacity and the potential for unsold stock to build up, adding to business costs and reducing profitability. As a result, the temptation for many businesses is to sit on the cash and wait, especially since only time will tell if the recent growth is sustainable. A survey of 500 firms by ICAEW, which represents the accountancy and finance profession, found that two-thirds of firms have more cash than a year ago holding reserves upwards of £550 billion.

References: **http://www.ft.com/cms/s/0/12dc0348-d780-11e4-94b1-0144feab7de.html #axzz3XNPKMZ66**
http://uk.blastingnews.com/economics/2015/03/is-britain-s-recent-economic -growth-sustainable-00328081.html
http://video.cnbc.com/gallery/?video=3000369639

Shifts Arising From Government Purchases The most direct way that policy makers shift the aggregate demand curve is through government purchases. For example, suppose the government decides to reduce purchases of new weapons systems. Because the quantity of goods and services demanded at any price level is lower, the aggregate demand curve shifts to the left. Conversely, if the government starts building more motorways, the result is a greater quantity of goods and services demanded at any price level, so the aggregate demand curve shifts to the right.

Shifts Arising From Net Exports   Any event that changes net exports for a given price level also shifts aggregate demand. For instance, when the USA experiences a recession, it buys fewer goods from Europe. This reduces European net exports and shifts the aggregate demand curve for the European economy to the left. When the USA recovers from its recession, it starts buying European goods again, shifting the aggregate demand curve to the right.

Net exports sometimes change because of movements in the exchange rate. Suppose, for instance, that international speculators bid up the value of the euro in the market for foreign currency exchange. This appreciation of the euro would make goods produced in the eurozone more expensive compared to foreign goods, which would depress net exports and shift the aggregate demand curve to the left. Conversely, a depreciation of the euro stimulates net exports and shifts the eurozone aggregate demand curve to the right.

Table 17.1 summarizes what we have learned so far.

TABLE 17.1

The Aggregate Demand Curve: Summary

Why does the aggregate demand curve slope downwards?
- *The wealth effect:* A lower price level increases real wealth, which encourages spending on consumption.
- *The interest-rate effect:* A lower price level reduces the interest rate, which encourages spending on investment.
- *The exchange-rate effect:* A lower price level causes the real exchange rate to depreciate, which encourages spending on net exports.

Why might the aggregate demand curve shift?
- *Shifts arising from consumption:* An event that makes consumers spend more at a given price level (a tax cut, a stock market boom) shifts the aggregate demand curve to the right. An event that makes consumers spend less at a given price level (a tax increase, a stock market decline) shifts the aggregate demand curve to the left.
- *Shifts arising from investment:* An event that makes firms invest more at a given price level (optimism about the future, a fall in interest rates due to an increase in the money supply) shifts the aggregate demand curve to the right. An event that makes firms invest less at a given price level (pessimism about the future, a rise in interest rates due to a decrease in the money supply) shifts the aggregate demand curve to the left.
- *Shifts arising from government purchases:* An increase in government purchases of goods and services (greater spending on defence or motorway construction) shifts the aggregate demand curve to the right. A decrease in government purchases on goods and services (a cutback in infrastructure spending, a reduction in spending on welfare benefits) shifts the aggregate demand curve to the left.
- *Shifts arising from net exports:* An event that raises spending on net exports at a given price level (a boom overseas, an exchange rate depreciation) shifts the aggregate demand curve to the right. An event that reduces spending on net exports at a given price level (a recession overseas, an exchange rate appreciation) shifts the aggregate demand curve to the left.

Quick Quiz   Explain the three reasons why the aggregate demand curve slopes downwards. Give an example of an event that would shift the aggregate demand curve. Which way would this event shift the curve?

THE AGGREGATE SUPPLY CURVE

The aggregate supply curve tells us the total quantity of goods and services that firms produce and sell at any given price level. Unlike the aggregate demand curve, which is always downwards sloping, the aggregate supply curve shows a relationship that depends crucially on the time horizon being examined. In the long run, the aggregate supply curve is vertical, whereas in the short run, the aggregate supply curve is upwards sloping. To understand short-run economic fluctuations, and how the short-run behaviour of the economy deviates from its long-run behaviour, we need to examine both the long-run aggregate supply curve and the short-run aggregate supply curve.

Why the Aggregate Supply Curve Is Vertical in the Long Run

In the long run, an economy's production of goods and services (its real GDP) depends on its supplies of labour, capital and natural resources, and on the available technology used to turn these factors of production into goods and services. In the long run these resources are fixed and so there is a finite amount that can be produced with these given resources. Because the price level does not affect these long-run determinants of real GDP, the long-run aggregate supply curve is vertical, as in Figure 17.3.

The vertical long-run aggregate supply curve is, in essence, just an application of the classical dichotomy and monetary neutrality. As we have already discussed, classical macroeconomic theory is based on the assumption that real variables do not depend on nominal variables. The long-run aggregate supply curve is consistent with this idea because it implies that the quantity of output (a real variable) does not depend on the level of prices (a nominal variable). As noted earlier, most economists believe that this principle works well when studying the economy over a period of many years, but not when studying year-to-year changes. Thus, the aggregate supply curve is vertical only in the long run.

FIGURE 17.3

The Long-Run Aggregate Supply Curve

In the long run, the quantity of output supplied depends on the economy's quantities of labour, capital and natural resources and on the technology for turning these inputs into outputs. The quantity supplied does not depend on the overall price level. As a result, the long-run aggregate supply curve is vertical at the natural rate of output.

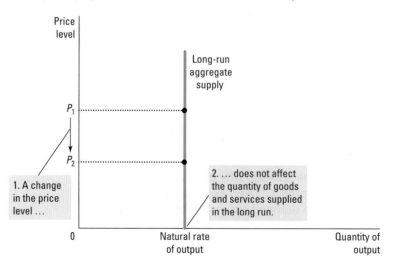

One might wonder why supply curves for specific goods and services can be upwards sloping if the long-run aggregate supply curve is vertical. The reason is that the supply of specific goods and services depends on *relative prices* – the prices of those goods and services compared to other prices in the economy. For example, when the price of ice cream rises, holding other prices in the economy constant, there is an incentive for suppliers of ice cream to increase their production by taking labour, milk, chocolate and other inputs away from the production of other goods, such as frozen yoghurt. By contrast, the economy's overall production of goods and services is limited by its labour, capital, natural resources and technology. Thus, when all prices in the economy rise together, there is no change in the overall quantity of goods and services supplied because relative prices and thus incentives have not changed.

Why the Long-Run Aggregate Supply Curve Might Shift

The position of the long-run aggregate supply curve shows the quantity of goods and services predicted by classical macroeconomic theory. This level of production is sometimes called *potential output* or *full-employment output*. To be more accurate, we call it the **natural rate of output** because it shows what the economy produces when unemployment is at its natural, or normal, rate. The natural rate of output is the level of production towards which the economy gravitates in the long run.

Any change in the economy that alters the natural rate of output shifts the long-run aggregate supply curve. Because output in the classical model depends on labour, capital, natural resources and technological knowledge, we can categorize shifts in the long-run aggregate supply curve as arising from these sources.

natural rate of output the output level in an economy when all existing factors of production (land, labour, capital and technology resources) are fully utilized and where unemployment is at its natural rate

Shifts Arising From Labour Imagine that an economy experiences an increase in immigration from abroad. Because there would be a greater number of workers, the quantity of goods and services supplied would increase. As a result, the long-run aggregate supply curve would shift to the right. Conversely, if many workers left the economy to go abroad, the long-run aggregate supply curve would shift to the left.

The position of the long-run aggregate supply curve also depends on the natural rate of unemployment, so any change in the natural rate of unemployment shifts the long-run aggregate supply curve. For example, if the government were to raise the minimum wage substantially, the natural rate of unemployment would rise, and the economy would produce a smaller quantity of goods and services. As a result, the long-run aggregate supply curve would shift to the left. Conversely, if a reform of the unemployment insurance system were to encourage unemployed workers to search harder for new jobs, the natural rate of unemployment would fall, and the long-run aggregate supply curve would shift to the right.

? **what if ...** a country experiences a high level of immigration with people of poor education but sees high levels of emigration of some of its most talented workers? What effect would you expect to see on the long run aggregate supply curve?

Shifts Arising From Capital An increase in the economy's capital stock increases productivity and, thereby, the quantity of goods and services supplied. As a result, the long-run aggregate supply curve shifts to the right. Conversely, a decrease in the economy's capital stock decreases productivity and the quantity of goods and services supplied, shifting the long-run aggregate supply curve to the left. Notice that the same logic applies regardless of whether we are discussing physical capital or human capital. An increase either in the number of machines or in the number of university degrees will raise the economy's ability to produce goods and services. Thus, either would shift the long-run aggregate supply curve to the right.

This highlights the trade-off which many nations face in investment in infrastructure projects which boost future productive capacity and shift the long run aggregate supply curve to the right but which take resources away from current consumption.

Shifts Arising From Natural Resources   An economy's production depends on its natural resources, including its land, minerals and climate. A discovery of a new mineral deposit shifts the long-run aggregate supply curve to the right. A change in weather patterns that makes farming more difficult shifts the long-run aggregate supply curve to the left.

In many countries, important natural resources are imported from abroad. A change in the availability of these resources can also shift the aggregate supply curve.

Shifts Arising From Technological Knowledge   Perhaps the most important reason that the economy today produces more than it did a generation ago is that our technological knowledge has advanced. The invention of the computer, for instance, has allowed us to produce more goods and services from any given amounts of labour, capital and natural resources. As a result, it has shifted the long-run aggregate supply curve to the right.

Although not literally technological, there are many other events that act like changes in technology. Opening up international trade has effects similar to inventing new production processes, so it also shifts the long-run aggregate supply curve to the right. Conversely, if the government passed new regulations preventing firms from using some production methods, perhaps because they were too dangerous for workers, the result would be a leftward shift in the long-run aggregate supply curve.

A Way to Depict Long-Run Growth and Inflation

Having introduced the economy's aggregate demand curve and the long-run aggregate supply curve, we now have a way to describe the economy's long-run trends. Figure 17.4 illustrates the changes that occur in the economy from decade to decade. Notice that both curves are shifting. Although there are many forces that govern the economy in the long run and can in principle cause such shifts, the two most important in practice are technology and monetary policy. Technological progress enhances the economy's ability to produce goods and services, and this continually shifts the long-run aggregate supply curve to the right. At the same time, because the central bank increases the money supply over time, the aggregate demand curve also shifts to the right. As the figure illustrates, the result is trend growth in output (as shown by increasing Y) and continuing inflation (as shown by increasing P).

The purpose of developing the model of aggregate demand and aggregate supply is to provide a framework for short-run analysis. As we develop the short-run model, we keep the analysis simple by not showing the continuing growth and inflation depicted in Figure 17.4. But always remember that long-run trends provide the background for short-run fluctuations. Short-run fluctuations in output and the **price level** should be viewed as deviations from the continuing long-run trends.

price level the price of a basket of goods and services measured as the weighted arithmetic average of current prices

FIGURE 17.4

Long-Run Growth and Inflation in the Model of Aggregate Demand and Aggregate Supply

As the economy becomes better able to produce goods and services over time, primarily because of technological progress, the long-run aggregate supply curve shifts to the right. At the same time, as the central bank increases the money supply, the aggregate demand curve also shifts to the right. In this figure, output grows from Y$_{1995}$ to Y$_{2005}$ and then to Y$_{2015}$, and the price level rises from P$_{1995}$ to P$_{2005}$ and then to P$_{2015}$. Thus, the model of aggregate demand and aggregate supply offers a way to describe the classical analysis of growth and inflation.

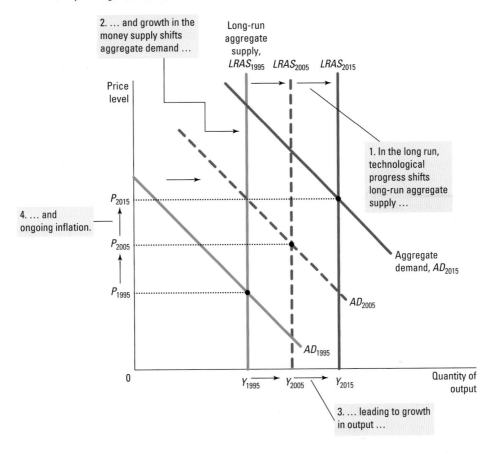

Why the Aggregate Supply Curve Slopes Upwards in the Short Run

As we have already discussed, the long-run aggregate supply curve is vertical. By contrast, in the short run, the aggregate supply curve is upwards sloping, as shown in Figure 17.5. That is, over a period of a year or two, an increase in the overall level of prices in the economy tends to raise the quantity of goods and services supplied, and a decrease in the level of prices tends to reduce the quantity of goods and services supplied.

What causes this positive relationship between the price level and output? Macro-economists have proposed three theories for the upwards slope of the short-run aggregate supply curve. In each theory, a specific market imperfection causes the supply side of the economy to behave differently in the short run than it does in the long run. Although each of the following theories will differ in detail, they share a common theme: the quantity of output supplied deviates from its long-run, or 'natural' level when the price level deviates from that people expected to prevail. When the price level rises above the expected level, output rises above its natural rate, and when the price level falls below the expected level, output falls below its natural rate.

FIGURE 17.5

The Short-Run Aggregate Supply Curve

In the short run, a fall in the price level from P₁ to P₂ reduces the quantity of output supplied from Y₁ to Y₂. This positive relationship could be due to sticky wages, sticky prices or misperceptions. Over time, wages, prices and perceptions adjust, so this positive relationship is only temporary.

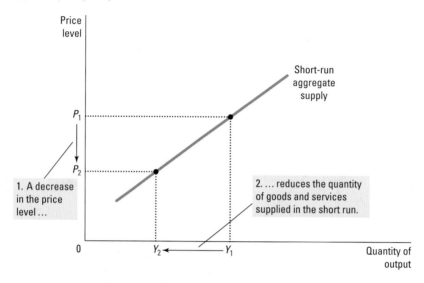

The Sticky Wage Theory   The first and simplest explanation of the upwards slope of the short-run aggregate supply curve is the sticky wage theory. According to this theory, the short-run aggregate supply curve slopes upwards because nominal wages are slow to adjust, or are 'sticky', in the short run. To some extent, the slow adjustment of nominal wages is attributable to long-term contracts between workers and firms that fix nominal wages, sometimes for as long as 3 years. In addition, this slow adjustment may be attributable to social norms and notions of fairness that influence wage setting and that change only slowly over time.

To see what sticky nominal wages mean for aggregate supply, imagine that a firm has agreed in advance to pay its workers a certain nominal wage based on what it expected the price level to be. The wage that a firm pays to a worker is closely related to the amount of output produced. Productivity measures the amount produced per time period per factor of production. Imagine that a picker in an online retail distribution centre processes 50 parcels per hour. Each parcel has a retail price of €25. The value of the output of the worker to the firm is 50 × €25 = €1250. If the worker gets paid €20 per hour then every €1 the firm pays the worker results in €62.50 worth of output to the firm. If the price of the goods fall from €25 to €22 but the wage and productivity stays the same at €20 per hour and 50 parcels, then each €1 the firm pays to the worker now only generates €50 worth of output. The cost of production to the firm has effectively increased.

If the price level *P* falls below the level that was expected and the nominal wage remains stuck at *W*, then the real wage rises above the level the firm planned to pay. The firm responds to these higher costs by hiring less labour and producing a smaller quantity of goods and services. In other words, because wages do not adjust immediately to the price level, a lower price level makes employment and production less profitable, so firms reduce the quantity of goods and services they supply.

FYI

Calculating Real Wages

Over time wages increase but so does the price level. If wages increased at the same rate as prices, the amount of goods each euro buys would stay the same. When prices rise at different rates to wages, purchasing power, or the real wage, will either rise or fall. In simple terms, if wages over a period rise by 2 per cent but prices rise over the same period by 4 per cent, people are worse off because their income cannot buy the same amount of goods at the end of the period as it did at the start.

The real wage is a measure of the wage measured in the currency of another year.

$$\text{Real wage rate} = \frac{\text{Nominal wage rate}}{\left(\dfrac{\text{Base CPI}}{\text{Current CPI}}\right)}$$

Imagine that in June 2006 you earned €6.66 an hour. How much would you have to earn in 2016 to buy the same amount of goods as €6.66 an hour would have bought in 2006? Assume that the CPI for June 2016 was 180 and that the CPI in June 2006 was 100 (the base year). The real wage would be calculated as follows:

$$\text{Real wage rate} = \frac{6.66}{\left(\dfrac{100}{180}\right)} \quad \text{Real wage rate} = \text{€12.00 (rounded up)}$$

This tells us that you would have to earn €12.00 per hour in 2016 to buy the same amount of goods that €6.66 would have bought in 2006. If your nominal wage is higher than €12.00 an hour in 2016 then you would be better off compared to 2006 as your wage will buy you more goods but if your wage is less than €12.00 you would be worse off. You would be able to buy fewer goods compared to 2006.

We can also look at comparisons of yearly earnings over time. For example, assume that you currently earn €35 000 in 2016 but in 1996 you were on a salary of €12 000. Are you better off now than you were in 1996? To calculate this you need to know the CPI in 1996. Assume that it was 65.

The formula used is:

$$\text{Real wage in 1996 currency} = \frac{\text{Current nominal wage}}{\left(\dfrac{\text{Current CPI}}{\text{Base (1996) CPI}}\right)}$$

Substituting the figures into the formula we get:

$$\text{Real wage in 1996 currency} = \frac{35\,000}{\left(\dfrac{180}{65}\right)}$$

$$\text{Real wage in 1996 currency} = \frac{35\,000}{2.77}$$

$$\text{Real wage in 1996 currency} = \text{€12 635.38}$$

The result tells you that you were better off in 1996. Your annual wage in that year would have bought you more goods than your current salary does. The rate of growth of prices between 1996 and 2016 has risen by more than the rate of your wage growth over the time period.

The Sticky Price Theory   Some economists have advocated another approach to the short-run aggregate supply curve, called the sticky price theory. As we just discussed, the sticky wage theory emphasizes that nominal wages adjust slowly over time. The sticky price theory emphasizes that the prices of some goods and services also adjust sluggishly in response to changing economic conditions. This slow adjustment of prices occurs in part because there are costs to adjusting prices, called *menu costs*. These menu costs include the cost of printing and distributing price lists or mail-order catalogues, changes to prices in back-office systems which feed through to various accounting and supply chain systems, down to the physical time required to change price tags. As a result of these costs, prices as well as wages may be sticky in the short run.

To see the implications of sticky prices for aggregate supply, suppose that each firm in the economy announces its prices in advance based on the economic conditions it expects to prevail. Then, after prices are announced, the economy experiences an unexpected contraction in the money supply, which will reduce the overall price level in the long run. Although some firms reduce their prices immediately in response to changing economic conditions, other firms may not want to incur additional menu costs and, therefore, may temporarily lag behind. Because these lagging firms have prices that are too high, their sales decline. Declining sales, in turn, cause these firms to cut back on production and employment. In other words, because not all prices adjust instantly to changing conditions, an unexpected fall in the price level leaves some firms with higher-than-desired prices, and these higher-than-desired prices depress sales and induce firms to reduce the quantity of goods and services they produce.

The Misperceptions Theory   A third approach to the short-run aggregate supply curve is the misperceptions theory. According to this theory, changes in the overall price level can temporarily mislead suppliers about what is happening in the individual markets in which they sell their output. As a result of these short-run misperceptions, suppliers respond to changes in the level of prices, and this response leads to an upwards sloping aggregate supply curve.

To see how this might work, suppose the overall price level falls below the level that people expected. When suppliers see the prices of their products fall, they may mistakenly believe that their *relative* prices have fallen. For example, wheat farmers may notice a fall in the price of wheat before they notice a fall in the prices of the many items they buy as consumers. They may infer from this observation that the reward to producing wheat is temporarily low, and they may respond by reducing the quantity of wheat they supply. Similarly, workers may notice a fall in their nominal wages before they notice a fall in the prices of the goods they buy. They may infer that the reward to working is temporarily low and respond by reducing the quantity of labour they supply. In both cases, a lower price level causes misperceptions about relative prices, and these misperceptions induce suppliers to respond to the lower price level by decreasing the quantity of goods and services supplied.

Pitfall Prevention   Misperception on changes in prices is not only a mistake that businesses and consumers make but also economics students. There is a difference between changes in the overall price level and particular prices of goods and services and there is always the danger of generalizing one from the other too easily.

Summary

There are three alternative explanations for the upwards slope of the short-run aggregate supply curve: (1) sticky wages, (2) sticky prices and (3) misperceptions. Economists debate which of these theories is correct, and it is very possible each contains an element of truth. For our purposes in this book, the similarities of the theories are more important than the differences. All three theories suggest that output deviates from its natural rate when the price level deviates from the price level that people expected. We can express this mathematically as follows:

$$
\begin{pmatrix} \text{Quantity} \\ \text{of output} \\ \text{supplied} \end{pmatrix} = \begin{pmatrix} \text{Natural} \\ \text{rate of} \\ \text{output} \end{pmatrix} + a \begin{pmatrix} \text{Actual} \\ \text{price} \\ \text{level} \end{pmatrix} - \begin{pmatrix} \text{Expected} \\ \text{price} \\ \text{level} \end{pmatrix}
$$

where *a* is a number that determines how much output responds to unexpected changes in the price level.

Notice that each of the three theories of short-run aggregate supply emphasizes a problem that is likely to be only temporary. Whether the upwards slope of the aggregate supply curve is attributable to sticky wages, sticky prices or misperceptions, these conditions will not persist forever. Eventually, as people adjust their expectations, nominal wages adjust, prices become unstuck and misperceptions are corrected. In other words, the expected and actual price levels are equal in the long run, and the aggregate supply curve is vertical rather than upwards sloping.

Why the Short-Run Aggregate Supply Curve Might Shift

When thinking about what shifts the short-run aggregate supply curve, we have to consider all those variables that shift the long-run aggregate supply curve plus a new variable – the expected price level – that influences sticky wages, sticky prices and misperceptions.

Let's start with what we know about the long-run aggregate supply curve. As we discussed earlier, shifts in the long-run aggregate supply curve normally arise from changes in labour, capital, natural resources or technological knowledge. These same variables shift the short-run aggregate supply curve. For example, when an increase in the economy's capital stock increases productivity, both the long-run and short-run aggregate supply curves shift to the right. If an increase in the minimum wage raises the natural rate of unemployment, both the long-run and short-run aggregate supply curves shift to the left.

The important new variable that affects the position of the short-run aggregate supply curve is people's expectation of the price level. As we have discussed, the quantity of goods and services supplied depends, in the short run, on sticky wages, sticky prices and misperceptions. Yet wages, prices and perceptions are set on the basis of expectations of the price level. So when expectations change, the short-run aggregate supply curve shifts.

To make this idea more concrete, let's consider a specific theory of aggregate supply – the sticky wage theory. According to this theory, when workers and firms expect the price level to be high, they are more likely to negotiate high nominal wages. High wages raise firms' costs and, for any given actual price level, reduce the quantity of goods and services that firms supply. When the expected price level rises, wages are higher, costs increase, and firms supply a smaller quantity of goods and services at any given actual price level. Thus, the short-run aggregate supply curve shifts to the left. Conversely, when the expected price level falls, wages are lower, costs decline, firms increase production at any given price level, and the short-run aggregate supply curve shifts to the right.

A similar logic applies in each theory of aggregate supply. The general lesson is the following: an increase in the expected price level reduces the quantity of goods and services supplied and shifts the short-run aggregate supply curve to the left. A decrease in the expected price level raises the quantity of goods and services supplied and shifts the short-run aggregate supply curve to the right. As we will see in the next section, this influence of expectations on the position of the short-run aggregate supply curve plays a key role in reconciling the economy's behaviour in the short run with its behaviour in the long run. In the short run, expectations are fixed, and the economy finds itself at the intersection of the aggregate demand curve and the short-run aggregate supply curve. In the long run, expectations adjust, and the short-run aggregate supply curve shifts. This shift ensures that the economy eventually finds itself at the intersection of the aggregate demand curve and the long-run aggregate supply curve.

You should now have some understanding about why the short-run aggregate supply curve slopes upwards and what events and policies can cause this curve to shift. Table 17.2 summarizes our discussion.

TABLE 17.2

The Short-Run Aggregate Supply Curve: Summary

Why does the short-run aggregate supply curve slope upwards?

- *The sticky wage theory:* An unexpectedly low price level raises the real wage, which causes firms to hire fewer workers and produce a smaller quantity of goods and services.
- *The sticky price theory:* An unexpectedly low price level leaves some firms with higher-than-desired prices, which depresses their sales and leads them to cut back production.
- *The misperceptions theory:* An unexpectedly low price level leads some suppliers to think their relative prices have fallen, which induces a fall in production.

Why might the short-run aggregate supply curve shift?

- *Shifts arising from labour:* An increase in the quantity of labour available (perhaps due to a fall in the natural rate of unemployment) shifts the aggregate supply curve to the right. A decrease in the quantity of labour available (perhaps due to a rise in the natural rate of unemployment) shifts the aggregate supply curve to the left.
- *Shifts arising from capital:* An increase in physical or human capital shifts the aggregate supply curve to the right. A decrease in physical or human capital shifts the aggregate supply curve to the left.
- *Shifts arising from natural resources:* An increase in the availability of natural resources shifts the aggregate supply curve to the right. A decrease in the availability of natural resources shifts the aggregate supply curve to the left.
- *Shifts arising from technology:* An advance in technological knowledge shifts the aggregate supply curve to the right. A decrease in the available technology (perhaps due to government regulation) shifts the aggregate supply curve to the left.
- *Shifts arising from the expected price level:* A decrease in the expected price level shifts the short-run aggregate supply curve to the right. An increase in the expected price level shifts the short-run aggregate supply curve to the left.

TWO CAUSES OF ECONOMIC FLUCTUATIONS

Now that we have introduced the model of aggregate demand and aggregate supply, we have the basic tools we need to analyse fluctuations in economic activity. In particular, we can use what we have learned about aggregate demand and aggregate supply to examine the two basic causes of short-run fluctuations.

To keep things simple, we assume the economy begins in long-run equilibrium, as shown in Figure 17.6. Equilibrium output and the price level are determined by the intersection of the aggregate demand curve and the long-run aggregate supply curve, shown as point A in the figure. At this point, output is at its natural rate. The short-run aggregate supply curve passes through this point as well, indicating that wages, prices and perceptions have fully adjusted to this long-run equilibrium. That is, when an economy is in its long-run equilibrium, wages, prices and perceptions must have adjusted so that the intersection of aggregate demand with short-run aggregate supply is the same as the intersection of aggregate demand with long-run aggregate supply.

FIGURE 17.6

The Long-Run Equilibrium

The long-run equilibrium of the economy is found where the aggregate demand curve crosses the long-run aggregate supply curve (point A). When the economy reaches this long-run equilibrium, wages, prices and perceptions will have adjusted so that the short-run aggregate supply curve crosses this point as well.

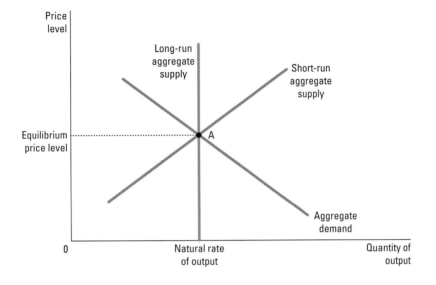

The Effects of a Shift in Aggregate Demand

Suppose that for some reason a wave of pessimism suddenly overtakes the economy. The cause might be a government scandal, a banking crisis, a crash in the stock market or uncertainty caused by increases in acts of terrorism across the world. Because of this event, many people lose confidence in the future and alter their plans. Households cut back on their spending and delay major purchases, and firms put off buying new equipment.

What is the impact of such a wave of pessimism on the economy? Such an event reduces the aggregate demand for goods and services. That is, for any given price level, households and firms now want to buy a smaller quantity of goods and services. As Figure 17.7 shows, the aggregate demand curve shifts to the left from AD_1 to AD_2.

In this figure we can examine the effects of the fall in aggregate demand. In the short run, the economy moves along the initial short-run aggregate supply curve AS_1, going from point A to point B. As the economy moves from point A to point B, output falls from Y_1 to Y_2, and the price level falls from P_1 to P_2. The falling level of output indicates that the economy is in a recession. Although not shown in the figure, firms respond to lower sales and production by reducing employment. Thus, the pessimism that caused the shift in aggregate demand is, to some extent, self-fulfilling: pessimism about the future leads to falling incomes and rising unemployment.

What should policy makers do when faced with such a recession? One possibility is to take action to increase aggregate demand. As we noted earlier, an increase in government spending or an increase in the money supply would increase the quantity of goods and services demanded at any price and, therefore, would shift the aggregate demand curve to the right. If policy makers can act with sufficient speed and precision, they can offset the initial shift in aggregate demand, return the aggregate demand curve back to AD_1, and bring the economy back to point A.

FIGURE 17.7

A Contraction in Aggregate Demand

A fall in aggregate demand, which might be due to a wave of pessimism in the economy, is represented with a leftward shift in the aggregate demand curve from AD_1 to AD_2. The economy moves from point A to point B. Output falls from Y_1 to Y_2, and the price level falls from P_1 to P_2. Over time, as wages, prices and perceptions adjust, the short-run aggregate supply curve shifts to the right from AS_1 to AS_2, and the economy reaches point C, where the new aggregate demand curve crosses the long-run aggregate supply curve. The price level falls to P_3, and output returns to its natural rate, Y_1.

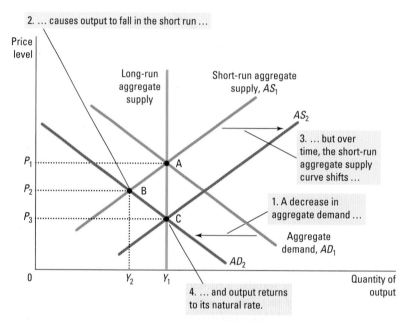

Even without action by policy makers, the recession will remedy itself over a period of time. Because of the reduction in aggregate demand, the price level falls. Eventually, expectations catch up with this new reality, and the expected price level falls as well. Because the fall in the expected price level alters wages, prices and perceptions, it shifts the short-run aggregate supply curve to the right from AS_1 to AS_2 in Figure 17.7. This adjustment of expectations allows the economy over time to approach point C, where the new aggregate demand curve (AD_2) crosses the long-run aggregate supply curve.

In the new long-run equilibrium, point C, output is back to its natural rate. Even though the wave of pessimism has reduced aggregate demand, the price level has fallen sufficiently (to P_3) to offset the shift in the aggregate demand curve. Thus, in the long run, the shift in aggregate demand is reflected fully in the price level and not at all in the level of output. In other words, the long-run effect of a shift in aggregate demand is a nominal change (the price level is lower) but not a real change (output is the same).

To sum up, this story about shifts in aggregate demand has two important lessons:

- In the short run, shifts in aggregate demand cause fluctuations in the economy's output of goods and services.
- In the long run, shifts in aggregate demand affect the overall price level but do not affect output.

The Effects of a Shift in Aggregate Supply

Imagine once again an economy in its long-run equilibrium. Now suppose that suddenly some firms experience an increase in their costs of production. For example, bad weather might destroy some agricultural crops, driving up the cost of producing food products. Or a dispute in the Middle East might interrupt the shipping of crude oil, driving up the cost of producing oil products. What is the macroeconomic impact of such an increase in production costs? For any given price level, firms now want to supply a smaller quantity of goods and services. Thus, as Figure 17.8 shows, the short-run aggregate supply curve shifts to the left from AS_1 to AS_2. (Depending on the event, the long-run aggregate supply curve might also shift. To keep things simple, however, we will assume that it does not).

In this figure we can trace the effects of the leftward shift in aggregate supply. In the short run, the economy moves along the existing aggregate demand curve, going from point A to point B. The output of the economy falls from Y_1 to Y_2, and the price level rises from P_1 to P_2. Because the economy is experiencing both *stagnation* (falling output) and *inflation* (rising prices), such an event is sometimes called **stagflation**.

stagflation a period of falling output and rising prices

FIGURE 17.8

An Adverse Shift in Aggregate Supply

When some event increases firms' costs, the short-run aggregate supply curve shifts to the left from AS_1 to AS_2. The economy moves from point A to point B. The result is stagflation: output falls from Y_1 to Y_2, and the price level rises from P_1 to P_2.

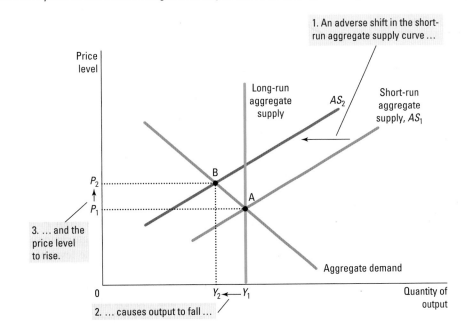

What should policy makers do when faced with stagflation? There are no easy choices. One possibility is to do nothing. In this case, the output of goods and services remains depressed at Y_2 for a while. Eventually, however, the recession will remedy itself as wages, prices and perceptions adjust. A period of low output and high unemployment, for instance, puts downwards pressure on workers' wages. Lower wages, in turn, increase the quantity of output supplied. Over time, as the short-run aggregate supply curve shifts back toward AS_1, the price level falls, and the quantity of output approaches its natural rate. In the long run, the economy returns to point A, where the aggregate demand curve crosses the long-run aggregate supply curve. This is the view that believers of free markets might adopt.

Alternatively, policy makers who control monetary and fiscal policy might attempt to offset some of the effects of the shift in the short-run aggregate supply curve by shifting the aggregate demand curve. This possibility is shown in Figure 17.9.

FIGURE 17.9

Accommodating an Adverse Shift in Aggregate Supply

Faced with an adverse shift in aggregate supply from AS$_1$ to AS$_2$, policy makers who can influence aggregate demand might try to shift the aggregate demand curve to the right from AD$_1$ to AD$_2$. The economy would move from point A to point C. This policy would prevent the supply shift from reducing output in the short run, but the price level would permanently rise from P$_1$ to P$_3$.

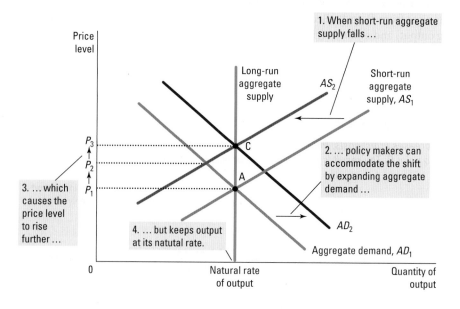

In this case, changes in policy shift the aggregate demand curve to the right from AD_1 to AD_2 – exactly enough to prevent the shift in aggregate supply from affecting output. The economy moves directly from point A to point C. Output remains at its natural rate, and the price level rises from P_1 to P_3. In this case, policy makers are said to *accommodate* the shift in aggregate supply because they allow the increase in costs to permanently affect the level of prices. This intervention by policy makers would be seen as being desirable by supporters of John Maynard Keynes. In 1936, Keynes published an influential book entitled *The General Theory of Employment Interest and Money*, which attempted to explain short run fluctuations in economic activity. The fundamental idea Keynes put forward was that downturns in economic activity could occur because of a lack of aggregate demand. Policy makers, he argued, could manipulate fiscal policy to influence aggregate demand. Following the Second World War, a number of countries adopted demand management policies which reflected the ideas Keynes put forward. By the end of the 1970s, these policies seemed to be failing and attention turned to monetary and supply-side policies. The recession which followed the financial crisis of 2007–2009 led to a revival of interest in the use of Keynesian

demand management. These different views on policy action form a key aspect of the debate between economists about action in the face of short-run fluctuations in economic activity.

To sum up, this story about shifts in aggregate supply has two important lessons:

- Adverse shifts in aggregate supply can cause stagflation – a combination of recession (falling output) and inflation (rising prices).
- Policy makers who can influence aggregate demand cannot offset both of these adverse effects simultaneously.

Quick Quiz Suppose that the election of a popular prime minister suddenly increases people's confidence in the future. Use the model of aggregate demand and aggregate supply to analyse the effect on the economy.

JEOPARDY PROBLEM

Over a period of 20 years an economy has found that despite periods of growth it has ended up with higher inflation rates and a level of unemployment no different to that it started with at the beginning of the time period. Explain, using aggregate demand and supply diagrams, why this may have occurred.

IN THE NEWS

Economic Growth in BRIC Countries

There has been much talk in recent years about the emerging economies such as the so-called BRIC countries of Brazil, Russia, India and China. Much hope has been pinned on these countries providing investment opportunities and driving global growth. As this article shows, these countries face very different problems and their future strong performance is not guaranteed.

In 2001 Jim O'Neill coined the acronym BRIC to describe four emerging and fast growing economies, Brazil, Russia, India and China, that had the potential to reshape the world economy.

The current performances of the BRIC countries are mixed, which shouldn't be too surprising. What they shared in the past was strong economic growth, but their economies were, and still are, all very different.

Brazil's economic growth can be linked to the exports of iron ore and agricultural commodities including soya, sugar and coffee. Economic growth averaged close to 4 per cent from 2001 to the end of the decade, but from 2010 to 2014 growth slowed to less than 2 per cent. Having a dependency on a few key commodities is fine when world demand and prices are high, but this can mask

weaknesses in the wider economy. It is a country that needs to diversify its risk and make itself more attractive to inward investment. That includes improving labour competitiveness.

Russia's economic growth in the decade from 2001 has averaged nearly 5 per cent a year. Its success was through exporting resources such as oil and gas. Things have changed in the past few years and the average growth rate from 2010 to 2014 had slowed by over half. By the end of 2014 the economy had stagnated and fell into recession as oil and gas prices fell worldwide. Matters have not been helped by

sanctions from the EU over the conflict in Ukraine. All these factors have contributed to an economic downturn, made worse by investors, concerned at the future, who have been far more reluctant to risk their money in new projects. A UN report on global investment trends identified that foreign direct investment (FDI) in Russia had fallen by 70 per cent and this is despite a drop in the value of the rouble which makes potential investments cheaper. Russia is seen as a geopolitical risk.

India's economic growth rate from 2001 to 2011 averaged close to 8 per cent before falling back to below 6 per cent in 2012 and 2013, but has recently picked up again and the economy is now growing faster than that of China. Recent economic reforms focussed on easing the ability to do to business are making India more competitive and have acted as a strong signal for foreign investors who are now keen to buy Indian assets. The falls in commodity prices, which have hurt commodity exporters like Brazil and Russia, have benefited India which imports four-fifths of all the oil it consumes. As well as improving its balance of trade, the fall in commodity prices has reduced inflation, allowed for interest rates to be cut and raised disposable income. However, a key to the future lies in the ability of the government to carry out its proposed reforms. It is spending more on infrastructure, improving education and training, and making it easier to do business and such measures are intended to attract more foreign investment.

China's phenomenal growth rates averaging 10 per cent a year would be hard to keep up for ever, especially since it is largely based on very high rates of investment, somewhat close to half the GDP. This makes the economy highly dependent on export growth. This growth has been affected by the world financial crisis with growth rates in China falling to around 8 per cent on average between 2010 and 2014. The growth rate in 2015 is expected to be 7 per cent. China wants to rebalance its economy so that it is driven by domestic consumption, so it sees lower growth rates as the norm, however that is not an easy strategy to deliver.

Questions

1. Why is it important for Brazil to consider diversifying its economy and improving its labour competitiveness?

2. Using an aggregate demand and supply diagram, explain how a decline in FDI in Russia might impact on the future economy of Russia.

3. Explain how a cut in interest rates in India combined with a fall in inflation might be expected to give a boost to India's economy.

4. What measure might a country like India take to improve FDI?

5. Why does the Chinese government want to rebalance its economy and why might this be a difficult challenge?

References: http://in.rbth.com/economics /2015/03/12/economic_slowdown_a_test _for_india-russia_business_ties_41953. html

http://www.bbc.co.uk/news/business -29960335

http://www.economist.com/news /business-and-finance/21642656-indias -economy-grew-faster-chinas-end -2014-catching-dragon

CONCLUSION

In this chapter we have discussed some of the important facts about short-run fluctuations in economic activity. We have introduced the model of aggregate demand and aggregate supply to explain these fluctuations. We will use this model in later chapters in order to understand more fully what causes fluctuations in the economy and how policy makers might respond to these fluctuations.

SUMMARY

- All societies experience short-run economic fluctuations around long-run trends. These fluctuations are irregular and largely unpredictable. When recessions do occur, real GDP and other measures of income, spending and production fall, and unemployment rises.

- Economists analyse short-run economic fluctuations using the model of aggregate demand and aggregate supply. According to this model, the output of goods and services and the overall level of prices adjust to balance aggregate demand and aggregate supply.

- The aggregate demand curve slopes downwards for three reasons. First, a lower price level raises the real value of households' money holdings, which stimulates consumer spending. Second, a lower price level reduces the quantity of money households' demand; as households try to convert money into interest-bearing assets, interest rates fall, which stimulates investment spending. Third, as a lower price level reduces interest rates, the local currency depreciates in the market for foreign currency exchange, which stimulates net exports.

- Any event or policy that raises consumption, investment, government purchases or net exports at a given price level increases aggregate demand. Any event or policy that reduces consumption, investment, government purchases or net exports at a given price level decreases aggregate demand.

- The long-run aggregate supply curve is vertical. In the long run, the quantity of goods and services supplied depends on the economy's labour, capital, natural resources and technology, but not on the overall level of prices.

- Three theories have been proposed to explain the upwards slope of the short-run aggregate supply curve.

According to the sticky wage theory, an unexpected fall in the price level temporarily raises real wages, which induces firms to reduce employment and production. According to the sticky price theory, an unexpected fall in the price level leaves some firms with prices that are temporarily too high, which reduces their sales and causes them to cut back production. According to the misperceptions theory, an unexpected fall in the price level leads suppliers to mistakenly believe that relative prices have fallen, which induces them to reduce production. All three theories imply that output deviates from its natural rate when the price level deviates from the price level that people expected.

- Events that alter the economy's ability to produce output, such as changes in labour, capital, natural resources or technology, shift the short-run aggregate supply curve (and may shift the long-run aggregate supply curve as well). In addition, the position of the short-run aggregate supply curve depends on the expected price level.

- One possible cause of economic fluctuations is a shift in aggregate demand. When the aggregate demand curve shifts to the left, for instance, output and prices fall in the short run. Over time, as a change in the expected price level causes wages, prices and perceptions to adjust, the short-run aggregate supply curve shifts to the right, and the economy returns to its natural rate of output at a new, lower price level.

- A second possible cause of economic fluctuations is a shift in aggregate supply. When the aggregate supply curve shifts to the left, the short-run effect is falling output and rising prices – a combination called stagflation. Over time, as wages, prices and perceptions adjust, the price level falls back to its original level, and output recovers.

QUESTIONS FOR REVIEW

1. Name two macroeconomic variables that decline when the economy goes into a recession. Name one macroeconomic variable that rises during a recession.

2. Draw a diagram with aggregate demand, short-run aggregate supply and long-run aggregate supply. Be careful to label the axes correctly.

3. List and explain the three reasons why the aggregate demand curve is downwards sloping.

4. Explain why the long-run aggregate supply curve is vertical.

5. List and explain the three theories for why the short-run aggregate supply curve is upwards sloping.

6. What might shift the aggregate demand curve to the left? Use the model of aggregate demand and aggregate supply to trace through the effects of such a shift.

7. What might shift the aggregate supply curve to the left? Use the model of aggregate demand and aggregate supply to trace through the effects of such a shift.

8. Use an aggregate supply and aggregate demand diagram to show how an economy can experience rising prices and falling growth (stagflation) at the same time.

9. Why do recessions ultimately come to an end?

10. What sort of policy do you think would be the most appropriate to bring about a reduction in a country's natural rate of unemployment?

PROBLEMS AND APPLICATIONS

1. Why do you think that investment is more variable over the business cycle than consumer spending? Which category of consumer spending do you think would be most volatile: durable goods (such as furniture and car purchases), non-durable goods (such as food and clothing) or services (such as haircuts and social care)? Why?

2. Suppose that the economy is in a long-run equilibrium:
   a. Use a diagram to illustrate the state of the economy. Be sure to show aggregate demand, short-run aggregate supply and long-run aggregate supply.
   b. Now suppose that a financial crisis causes aggregate demand to fall. Use your diagram to show what happens to output and the price level in the short run. What happens to the unemployment rate?
   c. Use the sticky wage theory of aggregate supply to explain what will happen to output and the price level in the long run (assuming there is no change in policy). What role does the expected price level play in this adjustment? Be sure to illustrate your analysis with a graph.

3. Explain whether each of the following events will increase, decrease or have no effect on long-run aggregate supply:
   a. The country experiences a wave of immigration.
   b. The government raises the minimum wage above the national average wage level.
   c. A war leads to the destruction of a large number of factories.

4. In Figure 17.7, how does the unemployment rate at points B and C compare to the unemployment rate at point A? Under the sticky wage explanation of the short-run aggregate supply curve, how does the real wage at points B and C compare to the real wage at point A?

5. Explain why the following statements are false:
   a. 'The aggregate demand curve slopes downwards because it is the horizontal sum of the demand curves for individual goods.'
   b. 'The long-run aggregate supply curve is vertical because economic forces do not affect long-run aggregate supply.'

   c. 'If firms adjusted their prices every day, then the short-run aggregate supply curve would be horizontal.'
   d. 'Whenever the economy enters a recession, its long-run aggregate supply curve shifts to the left.'

6. For each of the three theories for the upwards slope of the short-run aggregate supply curve, explain:
   a. How the economy recovers from a recession and returns to its long-run equilibrium without any policy intervention.
   b. What determines the speed of the recovery?

7. Suppose the central bank expands the money supply, but because the public expects this action, it simultaneously raises its expectation of the price level. What will happen to output and the price level in the short run? Compare this result to the outcome if the central bank expanded the money supply but the public didn't change its expectation of the price level.

8. Suppose that the economy is currently in a recession. If policy makers take no action, how will the economy evolve over time? Explain in words and using an aggregate demand/aggregate supply diagram.

9. Suppose workers and firms suddenly believe that inflation will be quite high over the coming year. Suppose also that the economy begins in long-run equilibrium, and the aggregate demand curve does not shift.
   a. What happens to nominal wages? What happens to real wages?
   b. Using an aggregate demand/aggregate supply diagram, show the effect of the change in expectations on both the short-run and long-run levels of prices and output.
   c. Were the expectations of high inflation accurate? Explain.

10. Explain whether each of the following events shifts the short-run aggregate supply curve, the aggregate demand curve, both, or neither. For each event that does shift a curve, use a diagram to illustrate the effect on the economy.
    a. Households decide to save a larger share of their income.
    b. Cattle farmers suffer a prolonged period of foot-and-mouth disease which cuts average cattle herd sizes by 80 per cent.
    c. Increased job opportunities overseas cause many people to leave the country.

18 MACROECONOMICS – EMPLOYMENT AND UNEMPLOYMENT

LEARNING OUTCOMES

After reading this chapter you should be able to:

- Explain why some unemployment is inevitable.
- Illustrate in a diagram the impact of the minimum wage on high wage and low wage sectors.

- List the reasons why unions cause unemployment and, alternatively, why unions might increase efficiency in some cases.
- Describe the four reasons why firms may choose to pay wages in excess of the competitive wage.

INTRODUCTION

Businesses rely on workers who provide labour services in return for payment. This payment allows the individual to provide for themselves and their families. For the business, the payment represents an investment in terms of the returns that the individual can help generate for the business. We have seen in Chapter 14 how marginal revenue product (MRP) for labour is related to the wage rate. For firms, when the MRP falls below the wage rate for whatever reason, there is a risk that the worker will have to be released.

Losing a job can be the most distressing economic event in a person's life. Most people rely on their labour earnings to maintain their standard of living, and many people get from their work not only income but also a sense of personal accomplishment. A job loss means a lower living standard in the present, anxiety about the future and reduced self-esteem. It is not surprising, therefore, that politicians campaigning for office often speak about how their proposed policies will help create jobs.

Businesses have a considerable impact on the number of people employed in a society and to a certain extent the number of people who are out of work. The level of unemployment provides an indicator to the state of the labour market. If the demand for labour is higher than the available supply we say the labour market is 'tight'. If labour supply exceeds labour demand then there is likely to be a high level of unemployment and the labour market could be described as being 'loose'.

In previous chapters we have seen some of the forces that determine the level and growth of a country's standard of living. A country that saves and invests a high fraction of its income, for instance, enjoys more rapid growth in its capital stock and GDP than a similar country that saves and invests less. An even more obvious determinant of a country's standard of living is the amount of unemployment it typically experiences. People who would like to work but cannot find a job are not contributing to the economy's production of goods and services. Although some degree of unemployment is inevitable in a complex economy with thousands of firms and millions of workers, the amount of unemployment varies substantially over time and across countries. When a country keeps its workers as fully employed as possible, it achieves a higher level of GDP than it would if it left many of its workers standing idle.

The problem of unemployment is usefully divided into two categories – the long-run problem and the short-run problem. The economy's *natural rate of unemployment* refers to the amount of unemployment that the economy normally experiences. *Cyclical unemployment* refers to the year-to-year fluctuations in unemployment around its natural rate, and it is closely associated with the short-run ups and downs of economic activity. In this chapter we discuss the determinants of an economy's natural rate of unemployment. As we will see, the designation *natural* does not imply that this rate of unemployment is desirable. Nor does it imply that it is constant over time or impervious to economic policy. It merely means that this unemployment does not go away on its own, even in the long run.

IDENTIFYING UNEMPLOYMENT

Recall that the labour force is defined as the sum of the employed and the unemployed; that the unemployment rate is measured as the percentage of the labour force that is unemployed and the labour force participation rate measures the percentage of the total adult population of the country that is in the labour force.

To see how these data are computed, consider the figures for Germany in February 2015. According to data from the Federal Statistical Office, 42.512 million people were employed and 2.21 million people were unemployed.

The labour force was:

$$42.512 + 2.21 = 44.772 \text{ million}$$

The unemployment rate was:

$$(2.21/42.512) \times 100 = 5.2\%$$

Because the adult population (the number of people aged between 16 and 65) was around 53.4 million, the labour force participation rate was:

$$(42.512/53.4) = 79.6\%.$$

We know that any economy will always have some unemployment. In this chapter we examine why there is always some unemployment in market economies.

> **?** **what if ...** the population of a country is stable but is experiencing an ageing population. What will happen to the labour force?

CASE STUDY

Identifying Unemployment Across OECD Countries

The Organization for Economic Cooperation and Development (OECD) represents over 30 countries which are committed to both democracy and the free market. Events such as the financial crisis and differing government policies can influence the numbers unem-

The World Bank Office Building in Washington DC.

ployed in any country. Therefore, although unemployment across the OECD countries averaged 7.1 per cent in February 2015, the rate has changed over recent years and also masks differences between OECD countries.

Some 43 million people were unemployed within the OECD countries in February 2015, around 8.6 million more than at the start of the financial crisis in 2008, but 6.7 million less than at the peak of the recession in the spring of 2010.

Spain's unemployment remains stubbornly high at just under 25 per cent, but Spain has a large informal economy, which like Greece (with unemployment above 27 per cent) accounts for close to one-quarter of the GDP. Their unemployment figures compare unfavourably with the 5 per cent jobless rate in Germany. These large difference exist despite all being members of the EU and sharing a common currency. The countries where it is easiest to gain employment are Korea and Japan, where unemployment was below 4 per cent in 2014.

Young people face particular challenges in seeking employment. Lacking the required skills and experience means that young people on average may find it both more difficult to get a job and to keep it. Youth unemployment across the OECD countries averaged just under 15 per cent in 2014, having dropped from a peak in 2009. Some Euro countries have an exceptionally high youth unemployment figure, headed by Greece and Spain with over 50 per cent of young people being without work and Italy with a rate of over 40 per cent. The UK comes in around the average of all OECD countries.

The unemployment rates between females and males across the OECD countries is about the same, although in Ireland and the UK, for example, the chances of being employed are better for females than males but in Turkey males have the advantage.

Demographics have a part to play in the longer-term trends in age related unemployment. In most OECD countries, active workers make up more than half of the total population. According to the World Bank, those under 15 years old make up 18 per cent of the UK's population. Comparison between OECD countries and Arab countries shows potential problems ahead in Arab countries where those under 15 represent around one-third of the total population. In the future more of the population in Arab nations will be seeking jobs placing even more pressure on the levels of youth unemployment.

References: **http://data.worldbank.org/indicator/SP.POP.0014.TO.ZS**
http://www.oecd.org/std/labour-stats/HUR-Feb15.pdf

How Long Are the Unemployed Without Work?

In judging how serious the problem of unemployment is, one question to consider is whether unemployment is typically a short-term or long-term condition. If unemployment is short term, one might conclude that it is not a big problem. Workers may require a few weeks between jobs to find the openings that best suit their tastes and skills. Yet if unemployment is long term, one might conclude that it is a serious problem. Workers unemployed for many months are more likely to suffer economic and psychological hardship.

Because the duration of unemployment can affect our view about how big a problem it is, economists have identified that most spells of unemployment are short, and most unemployment observed at any given time is long term.

To see how this statement can be true, consider an example. Suppose that you visited the government's unemployment office every week for a year to survey the unemployed. Each week you find that there are four unemployed workers. Three of these workers are the same individuals for the whole year, while the fourth person changes every week. Based on this experience, would you say that unemployment is typically short term or long term?

Some simple calculations help answer this question. In this example, you meet a total of 55 unemployed people; 52 of them are unemployed for 1 week, and 3 are unemployed for the full year. This means that 52/55, or 95 per cent, of unemployment spells end in 1 week. Thus, most spells of unemployment are short. Yet consider the total amount of unemployment. The 3 people unemployed for 1 year (52 weeks) make up a total of 156 weeks of unemployment. Together with the 52 people unemployed for 1 week, this makes 208 weeks of unemployment. In this example, 156/208, or 75 per cent, of unemployment is attributable to those individuals who are unemployed for a full year. Thus, most unemployment observed at any given time is long term.

This subtle conclusion implies that economists and policy makers must be careful when interpreting data on unemployment and when designing policies to help the unemployed. Most people who become unemployed will soon find jobs. Yet most of the economy's unemployment problem is attributable to the relatively few workers who are jobless for long periods of time.

Why Are There Always Some People Unemployed?

In an ideal labour market, wages would adjust to balance the quantity of labour supplied and the quantity of labour demanded. This adjustment of wages would ensure that all workers are always fully employed. Of course, reality does not resemble this ideal. There are always some workers without jobs, even when the overall economy is doing well. In other words, the unemployment rate never falls to zero; instead, it fluctuates around the natural rate of unemployment. To understand this natural rate, the remaining sections in the chapter examine the reasons why actual labour markets depart from the ideal of full employment.

To preview our conclusions, we will find that there are four ways to explain unemployment in the long run. The first explanation is that it takes time for workers to search for the jobs that are best suited for them. The unemployment that results from the process of matching workers and jobs is sometimes called **frictional unemployment**, and it is often thought to explain relatively short spells of unemployment.

The next three explanations for unemployment suggest that the number of jobs available in some labour markets may be insufficient to give a job to everyone who wants one. This occurs when the quantity of labour supplied exceeds the quantity demanded. Unemployment of this sort is sometimes called **structural unemployment**, and it is often thought to explain longer spells of unemployment. As we will see, this kind of unemployment results when wages are, for some reason, set above the level that brings supply and demand into equilibrium. We will later examine three possible reasons for an above-equilibrium wage: minimum wage laws, unions and efficiency wages.

frictional unemployment unemployment that results because it takes time for workers to search for the jobs that best suit their tastes and skills

structural unemployment unemployment that results because the number of jobs available in some labour markets is insufficient to provide a job for everyone who wants one

Quick Quiz How is the unemployment rate measured? How might the unemployment rate overstate the amount of joblessness? How might it understate it?

Since the 1930s there has been an ongoing debate in economics about the principal causes of unemployment and the extent to which these causes stem from the supply side of the economy or the demand side. Policies designed to improve the workings of the supply side of the economy which includes cutting taxes, investing in training and education, changing the benefits system and improving incentives to get work, have to be viewed alongside those which affect the level of aggregate demand in the economy. In essence, the debate centres on the extent to which unemployment is cyclical or structural – the latter accounting for the level of unemployment not due to changes in the economic cycle. As we build the theoretical building blocks of macroeconomics it must be remembered that policies to cut unemployment still deeply divide opinion in the economics profession.

JOB SEARCH

One reason why economies always experience some unemployment is job search. **Job search** is the process of matching workers with appropriate jobs. If all workers and all jobs were the same, so that all workers were equally well suited for all jobs, job search would not be a problem. Laid-off workers would quickly find new jobs that were well suited for them. But workers differ in their tastes and skills, jobs differ in their attributes, and information about job candidates and job vacancies is disseminated slowly among the many firms and households in the economy.

job search the process by which workers find appropriate jobs given their tastes and skills

Why Some Frictional Unemployment Is Inevitable

Frictional unemployment is often the result of changes in the demand for labour among different firms. When consumers decide that they prefer Brand X to Brand Y, the company producing Brand X increases employment, and the other firm lays off workers. The former Brand Y workers must now search for new jobs, and the Brand X producer must decide which new workers to hire for the various jobs that have opened up. The result of this transition is a period of unemployment.

Similarly, because different regions of the country produce different goods, employment can rise in one region while it falls in another. Consider, for instance, what happens when the world price of oil falls. Firms extracting oil from the fields below the North Sea off the coast of Scotland respond to the lower price by cutting back on production and employment. At the same time, cheaper petrol stimulates car sales, so car manufacturing firms in northern and central England raise production and employment. Changes in the composition of demand among industries or regions are called *sectoral shifts*. Because it takes time for workers to search for jobs in the new sectors, sectoral shifts temporarily cause unemployment.

Frictional unemployment is inevitable simply because the economy is always changing. Fifty years ago, manufacturing played a much larger role in the UK economy than it does today. The number of people employed in manufacturing was much higher as a result. On the other hand, business services and finance contributed only about 3 per cent of UK GDP in the mid-1950s but contribute more than a quarter today. Similar structural changes have taken place across other European countries. As these transitions take place, jobs are created in some firms and destroyed in others. The end result of this process has been higher productivity and higher living standards. But, along the way, workers in declining industries find themselves out of work and searching for new jobs. The skill sets they have may not match to the jobs that are being created by the development of new firms and industries.

In addition to the effects of sectoral shifts on unemployment, workers will leave their jobs sometimes because they realize that the jobs are not a good match for their tastes and skills and they wish to look for a better job. Many of these workers, especially younger ones, find new jobs at higher wages, although given the vast improvements in information technology in recent years (especially the Internet) it is likely that many people search for new jobs without actually quitting their current job. Nevertheless, this churning of the labour force is normal in a well-functioning and dynamic market economy, and the result is some amount of frictional unemployment.

Public Policy and Job Search

Even if some frictional unemployment is inevitable, the precise amount is not. The faster information spreads about job openings and worker availability, the more rapidly the economy can match workers and firms. Public policy may play a role in reducing the time it takes unemployed workers to find new jobs and in doing so, it can reduce the economy's natural rate of unemployment.

Government policies try to facilitate job search in various ways. One is through government-run employment agencies or job centres, which give out information about job vacancies. Another is through public training schemes, which aim to ease the transition of workers from declining to growing industries and to help disadvantaged groups escape poverty. Advocates of these policies believe that they make the economy operate more efficiently by keeping the labour force more fully employed, and that they reduce the inequities inherent in a constantly changing market economy.

Critics of these policies question whether the government should get involved with the process of job search. They argue that it is better to let the private market match workers and jobs. In fact, most job search in the economy takes place without intervention by the government. Newspaper advertisements, internet job sites, headhunters and word of mouth all help spread information about job openings and job candidates. Similarly, much worker education is done privately, either through schools or through on-the-job training. These critics contend that the government is no better – and most likely worse – at disseminating the right information to the right workers and deciding what kinds of worker training would be most valuable. They claim that these decisions are best made privately by workers and employers.

Unemployment Insurance

One government policy that increases the amount of frictional unemployment, without intending to do so, is **unemployment insurance** (or, as it is called in the UK, national insurance). This policy is designed to offer workers partial protection against job loss. The unemployed who quit their jobs, were fired for just cause or who have just entered the labour force are not eligible. Benefits are paid only to the unemployed who are laid off because their previous employers no longer needed their skills.

unemployment insurance
a government programme that partially protects workers' incomes when they become unemployed

While unemployment insurance reduces the hardship of unemployment, it is argued that it can also increase the amount of unemployment. Because unemployment benefits stop when a worker takes a new job, the unemployed it is argued, devote less effort to job search and are more likely to turn down unattractive job offers. In addition, because unemployment insurance makes unemployment less onerous, workers are less likely to seek guarantees of job security when they negotiate with employers over the terms of employment. However, research on unemployment insurance in Europe gives a different perspective. In a paper by Konstantinos Tatsiramos, the benefits to workers searching for jobs and receiving unemployment insurance is greater than the costs:

> *This paper provides evidence on the effect of unemployment benefits on unemployment and employment duration in Europe, using individual data from the European Community Household Panel for eight countries. Even if receiving benefits has a direct negative effect, increasing the duration of unemployment spells, there is also a positive indirect effect of benefits on subsequent employment duration. This indirect effect is pronounced in countries with relatively generous benefit systems, and for recipients who have remained unemployed for at least six months. In terms of the magnitude of the effect, recipients remain employed on average two to four months longer than nonrecipients. This represents a ten to twenty per cent increase relative to the average employment duration, compensating for the additional time spent in unemployment.*

> *Source:* Tatsiramos, K. (2006) Unemployment Insurance in Europe: Unemployment Duration and Subsequent Employment Stability. Institute for the Study of Labor Discussion Paper no. 2280.

The effect of unemployment insurance is likely to be related to the way the scheme is designed and operated. In one US study, when unemployed workers applied to collect unemployment insurance benefits, some of them were randomly selected and each offered a $500 bonus if they found new jobs within 11 weeks. This group was then compared with a control group not offered the incentive. The average spell of unemployment for the group offered the bonus was 7 per cent shorter than the average spell for the control group. This experiment suggests that the design of the unemployment insurance system influences the effort that the unemployed devote to job search.

Several other studies examined search effort by following a group of workers over time. Unemployment insurance benefits, rather than lasting forever, usually run out after six months or a year. These studies found that when the unemployed become ineligible for benefits, the probability of their finding a new job rises markedly. It is argued, therefore, that receiving unemployment insurance benefits does reduce the search effort of the unemployed.

Even if this is indeed the case, we should not necessarily conclude that the policy is a bad one. The policy can achieve its primary goal of reducing the income uncertainty that workers face. In addition, when workers turn down unattractive job offers, they have the opportunity to look for jobs that better suit their tastes and skills. Some economists have argued that unemployment insurance improves the ability of the economy to match each worker with the most appropriate job.

Quick Quiz How would an increase in the world price of oil affect the amount of frictional unemployment? Is this unemployment undesirable? What public policies might affect the amount of unemployment caused by this price change?

STRUCTURAL UNEMPLOYMENT

Having seen how frictional unemployment results from the process of matching workers and jobs, let's now examine how structural unemployment results when the number of jobs is insufficient for the number of workers.

Minimum Wage Laws

To understand structural unemployment, we begin by reviewing how unemployment arises from minimum wage laws. We introduced the idea of minimum wages in Chapter 14. Recall that a minimum wage above the equilibrium wage rate can lead to unemployment. Minimum wages have an important effect on certain groups with particularly high unemployment rates. An analysis of minimum wages is a natural place to start because it can be used to understand some of the other reasons for structural unemployment.

As noted in Chapter 14, the extent to which minimum wage laws lead to unemployment is dependent on the relative elasticity of demand for labour and the nature of the industry. Most workers in the economy, however, are likely to have wages well above the legal minimum and so it is unlikely that minimum wage laws will be a predominant reason for structural unemployment. Minimum wage laws are binding most often for the least skilled and least experienced members of the labour force, such as teenagers. It is only among these workers that minimum wage laws explain the existence of unemployment.

Our brief analysis of minimum wage laws allows us to draw a more general lesson: if the wage is kept above the equilibrium level for any reason, the result is unemployment. Minimum wage laws are just one reason why wages may be 'too high'. In the remaining two sections of this chapter, we consider two other reasons why wages may be kept above the equilibrium level – unions and efficiency wages.

At this point, however, we should stop and notice that the structural unemployment that arises from an above-equilibrium wage is, in an important sense, different from the frictional unemployment that arises from the process of job search. The need for job search is not due to the failure of wages to balance labour supply and labour demand. When job search is the explanation for unemployment, workers are *searching* for the jobs that best suit their tastes and skills. By contrast, when the wage is above the equilibrium level, the quantity of labour supplied exceeds the quantity of labour demanded, and workers are unemployed because they are *waiting* for jobs to open up.

Pitfall Prevention The logic is for the minimum wage to be set at a level above market equilibrium. Assuming this is the case then a minimum wage is an example of a price floor – a legal minimum imposed by a government which is above the market equilibrium. It should not be confused with a price ceiling which is a legal maximum price that can be charged.

Quick Quiz Draw the supply curve and the demand curve for a labour market in which the wage is fixed above the equilibrium level. Show the quantity of labour supplied, the quantity demanded and the amount of unemployment.

Unions and Collective Bargaining

A union is a worker association that bargains with employers over wages and working conditions. Union density measures the proportion of the workforce that is unionized, excluding people who cannot, for legal or other reasons, be members of a union – for example, members of the armed forces. Broadly speaking, this amounts to expressing the number of union members as a proportion of civilian employees plus the unemployed. In the UK in 2013, some 13 million employees were members of trade unions representing union density at 25.6 per cent. Density has been steadily falling since 1995 when it stood at around 32.4 per cent and an even greater marked fall from the beginning of the 1980s, when it was over 50 per cent. In other European countries there is a similar trend of falling union density. In Germany, density has fallen from 25.3 per cent in 1999 to 17.7 per cent in 2013, in Austria the fall has been from 37.4 per cent to 27.4 per cent and in the Netherlands from 24.7 per cent to 17.6 per cent in the same period. However, there are exceptions with countries like Finland, Denmark and Sweden having stable densities between 67 per cent and 70 per cent. In the United States, by comparison, density is 10.8 per cent and in Australia 17.0 per cent (figures for 2013).

The Economics of Unions

A union is a type of cartel. Like any cartel, a union is a group of sellers acting together in the hope of exerting their joint market power. Businesses have had conflict with unions for hundreds of years and relations can often be strained. The basis of union activity is that individually a worker cannot bargain for improvements in pay and conditions in the face of the might of the business but as a group they have more 'power'. Workers in a union, therefore, act as a group when discussing their wages, benefits and working conditions with their employers. The process by which unions and firms agree on the terms of employment is called **collective bargaining**.

When a union bargains with a firm, it asks for higher wages, better benefits and better working conditions than the firm would offer in the absence of a union. If

collective bargaining the process by which unions and firms agree on the terms of employment

the union and the firm do not reach agreement, the union can take various steps to put pressure on employers to come to an agreement including working to rule (doing only what is agreed in the contract of employment) and as a last resort organizing a withdrawal of labour from the firm, called a strike. Because a strike reduces production, sales and profit, a firm facing a strike threat is more likely to agree to pay higher wages than it otherwise would.

When a union raises the wage above the equilibrium level, it raises the quantity of labour supplied and reduces the quantity of labour demanded, resulting in unemployment. Those workers who remain employed are better off, but those who were previously employed and are now unemployed are worse off. Indeed, unions are often thought to cause conflict between different groups of workers – between the *insiders* who benefit from high union wages and the *outsiders* who do not get the union jobs.

The outsiders can respond to their status in one of two ways. Some of them remain unemployed and wait for the chance to become insiders and earn the high union wage. Others take jobs in firms that are not unionized. Thus, when unions raise wages in one part of the economy, the supply of labour increases in other parts of the economy. This increase in labour supply, in turn, reduces wages in industries that are not unionized. In other words, workers in unions reap the benefit of collective bargaining, while workers not in unions bear some of the cost.

The role and effectiveness of unions in securing above market wage rates in the economy depends in part on the national laws that govern union organization and collective bargaining. Normally, explicit agreements among members of a cartel are illegal. Unions are given exemption from these laws in the belief that workers need greater market power as they bargain with employers.

Legislation affecting the market power of unions is a perennial topic of political debate. In the past 30 years, legislation in the UK has tightened the rules under which unions operate and can call industrial action. Part of the reason for this legislation is the belief in some political circles that unions had too much power and that their behaviour was undemocratic and damaging to the economy as well as the interests of its members. Opponents of increased legislation argue that it has been a politically motivated movement to restrict workers' rights and that the interests of employers have been unfairly prioritized.

JEOPARDY PROBLEM

A firm had been in dispute with workers represented by a trade union for a number of months. The union was pushing for a pay rise 5 per cent above inflation and the firm was only prepared to initially offer an inflation-related rise. In the end, the dispute was resolved with workers getting a 4 per cent pay rise in return for specified productivity increases linked to the length of the working week and changes to working practices. Why might the firm have been prepared to agree fairly closely to the demands of the union?

Are Unions Good or Bad for the Economy?

Economists disagree about whether unions are good or bad for the economy as a whole. Let's consider both sides of the debate.

Critics of unions argue that unions are merely a type of cartel. When unions raise wages above the level that would prevail in competitive markets, they reduce the quantity of labour demanded, cause some workers to be unemployed and reduce the wages in the rest of the economy. The resulting allocation of labour is, critics argue, both inefficient and inequitable. It is inefficient because high union wages reduce employment in unionized firms below the efficient, competitive level. It is inequitable because some workers benefit at the expense of other workers.

Advocates of unions contend that unions are a necessary antidote to the market power of the firms that hire workers. In some regions where one particular company is the dominant employer, if workers do not accept the wages and working conditions that the firm offers, they may have little choice but to move or stop working. In the absence of a union, therefore, the firm could use its market power to pay lower wages and offer worse working conditions than would prevail if it had to compete with other firms for the same workers. In this case, a union may balance the firm's market power and protect the workers from being at the mercy of the firm owners.

Advocates of unions also claim that unions are important for helping firms respond efficiently to workers' concerns. Whenever a worker takes a job, the worker and the firm must agree on many attributes of the job in addition to the wage: hours of work, overtime, holidays, sick leave, health benefits, promotion schedules, job security and so on. By representing workers' views on these issues, unions allow firms to provide the right mix of job attributes. In many countries unions have now taken on additional roles in supporting workers with respect to offering legal support in the event of an individual dispute at work, advice on pensions, financial services such as insurance and support for those who have been injured or disabled at work and have to retire early. Even if unions have the adverse effect of pushing wages above the equilibrium level and causing unemployment, they have the benefit of helping firms keep a happy and productive workforce.

In the end, there is no consensus among economists about whether unions are good or bad for the economy. Like many institutions, their influence is probably beneficial in some circumstances and adverse in others.

The Theory of Efficiency Wages

A fourth reason why economies always experience some unemployment is suggested by the theory of efficiency wages. According to this theory, firms operate more efficiently if wages are above the equilibrium level. Therefore, it may be profitable for firms to keep wages high even in the presence of a surplus of labour.

In some ways, the unemployment that arises from efficiency wages is similar to the unemployment that arises from minimum wage laws and unions. In all three cases, unemployment is the result of wages above the level that balances the quantity of labour supplied and the quantity of labour demanded. Yet there is also an important difference. Minimum wage laws and unions prevent firms from lowering wages in the presence of a surplus of workers. Efficiency wage theory states that such a constraint on firms is unnecessary in many cases because firms may be better off keeping wages above the equilibrium level.

Why should firms want to keep wages high? This decision may seem odd at first, given that wages are a large part of firms' costs. Normally, we expect profit-maximizing firms to want to keep costs – and therefore wages – as low as possible. The novel insight of efficiency wage theory is that paying high wages might be profitable because they might raise the efficiency of a firm's workers. There are several types of efficiency wage theory. Each type suggests a different explanation for why firms may want to pay high wages. Let's now consider four of these types.

Worker Health   The first and simplest type of efficiency wage theory emphasizes the link between wages and worker health. Better paid workers eat a more nutritious diet, and workers who eat a better diet are healthier and more productive.

A firm may find it more profitable to pay high wages and have healthy, productive workers than to pay lower wages and have less healthy, less productive workers.

This type of efficiency wage theory is more relevant for firms in less developed countries where inadequate nutrition is a more common problem. Unemployment is high in the cities of many poor African countries, for example. In these countries, firms may fear that cutting wages would, in fact, adversely influence their workers' health and productivity. In other words, concern over nutrition may explain why firms do not cut wages despite a surplus of labour.

Worker Turnover A second type of efficiency wage theory emphasizes the link between wages and worker turnover. Workers quit jobs for many reasons – to take jobs in other firms, to move to other parts of the country, to leave the labour force and so on. The frequency with which they quit depends on the entire set of incentives they face, including the benefits of leaving and the benefits of staying. The more a firm pays its workers, the less often its workers will choose to leave. Thus, a firm can reduce turnover among its workers by paying them a high wage.

Firms care about turnover because it is costly for firms to hire and train new workers. Moreover, even after they are trained, newly hired workers are not as productive as experienced workers. Firms with higher turnover, therefore, will tend to have higher production costs. Firms may find it profitable to pay wages above the equilibrium level in order to reduce worker turnover.

Worker Effort A third type of efficiency wage theory emphasizes the link between wages and worker effort. In many jobs, workers have some discretion over how hard to work. As a result, firms monitor the efforts of their workers, and workers caught shirking their responsibilities can be disciplined and possibly dismissed. But not all shirkers are caught immediately because monitoring workers is costly and imperfect. A firm can respond to this problem by paying wages above the equilibrium level. High wages make workers more eager to keep their jobs and, thereby, give workers an incentive to put forward their best effort.

This particular type of efficiency wage theory is similar to the Marxist idea of the 'reserve army of the unemployed'. Marx thought that employers benefited from unemployment because the threat of unemployment helped to discipline those workers who had jobs. In the worker effort variant of efficiency wage theory, unemployment fills a similar role. If the wage were at the level that balanced supply and demand, workers would have less reason to work hard because if they were fired, they could quickly find new jobs at the same wage. Therefore, firms raise wages above the equilibrium level, causing unemployment and providing an incentive for workers not to shirk their responsibilities.

Worker Quality A fourth and final type of efficiency wage theory emphasizes the link between wages and worker quality. When a firm hires new workers, it cannot perfectly gauge the quality of the applicants. By paying a high wage, the firm attracts a better pool of workers to apply for its jobs.

To see how this might work, consider a simple example. Waterwell Company owns one well and needs one worker to pump water from the well. Two workers, Singh and Patel, are interested in the job. Singh, a proficient worker, is willing to work for €10 per hour. Below that wage, he would rather start his own car washing business. Patel, a complete incompetent, is willing to work for anything above €2 per hour. Below that wage, he would rather sit on the beach. Economists say that Singh's *reservation wage* – the lowest wage he would accept – is €10, and Patel's reservation wage is €2.

What wage should the firm set? If the firm were interested in minimizing labour costs, it would set the wage at €2 per hour. At this wage, the quantity of workers supplied (one) would balance the quantity demanded. Patel would take the job, and Singh would not apply for it. Yet suppose Waterwell knows that only one of these two applicants is competent, but it does not know whether it is Singh or Patel. If the firm hires the incompetent worker, he may damage the well, causing the firm huge losses. In this case, the firm has a better strategy than paying the equilibrium wage of €2 and hiring Patel. It can offer €10 per hour, inducing both Singh and Patel to apply for the job. By choosing randomly between these two applicants and turning the other away, the firm has a 50:50 chance of hiring the competent one. By contrast, if the firm offers any lower wage, it is sure to hire the incompetent worker.

This story illustrates a general phenomenon. When a firm faces a surplus of workers, it might seem profitable to reduce the wage it is offering. But by reducing the wage, the firm induces an adverse change in the mix of workers. In this case, at a wage of €10, Waterwell has two workers applying for one job. But if Waterwell responds to this labour surplus by reducing the wage, the competent worker (who has better alternative opportunities) will not apply. Thus, it is profitable for the firm to pay a wage above the level that balances supply and demand.

CONCLUSION

In this chapter we discussed the reasons why economies always experience some degree of unemployment. We have seen how job search, minimum wage laws, unions and efficiency wages can all help explain why some workers do not have jobs. Which of these four explanations for the natural rate of unemployment are the most important? Unfortunately, there is no easy way to tell. Economists differ in which of these explanations of unemployment they consider most important.

The analysis of this chapter yields an important lesson: although the economy will always have some unemployment, its natural rate is not immutable. Many events and policies can change the amount of unemployment the economy typically experiences. As the information revolution changes the process of job search, as government adjusts the minimum wage, as workers join or quit unions, and as firms alter their reliance on efficiency wages, the natural rate of unemployment evolves. Unemployment is not a simple problem with a simple solution. But how we choose to organize our society can profoundly influence how prevalent a problem it is.

IN THE NEWS

Is the Minimum Wage a Good Thing?

In a number of countries around the world, governments pass laws designed to achieve some specific policy objective. One legislation common to many countries has been to introduce a legal minimum wage. This article looks at the effects of such a policy.

The UK government, like many other governments across the world, has a national minimum wage. As part of its enforcement, the UK government names and shames exploitative firms and fines them. It employs compliance

Indentured servant on the streets of London

officers to detect the firms disobeying the legislation. It has identified the care sector as a particular problem and has targeted this sector.

At the time of writing, the minimum wage rates in the UK are set at £6.70 per hour for an adult, £5.30 for 18- to 20-year-olds, £3.87 for 16- to 17-year-olds and £3.30 for apprentices. It poses two questions. First, is this enough for people to live on and, second, why is it considered necessary to have different rates? If £6.70 per hour is considered a reasonable rate for a 21-year-old, how can it be justifiable to have a lower rate for 20-year-olds and other rates below this level? A further complication is the minimum wage is nationally set so an adult on the minimum wage in London receives the same rate as one working in a part of the country where living costs are lower. Many experts believe that all workers in London should receive at least

the London Living Wage (LLW), which in 2014 was set at £9.15 an hour. In 2014 nearly 20 per cent or 900 000 of London's workers earned less than the LLW. Low paid workers would also be concerned about the increase in zero hours contracts which affects some 77 000 London workers.

Some strongly believe that the UK should adopt city-level floors for wages such as has been happening in several US cities. According to Arindrajit Dube, from the University of Massachusetts, recent evidence suggests raising the minimum wage results in a modest negative employment effect but is also marked by a sizable reduction in labour turnover since more workers choose to stick with their jobs. Higher pay rates are designed to lift people out of poverty. An increase in minimum pay raises the disposable income of the lowest paid leading to greater consumption from this group of workers. The boost in demand goes some way to offset the effects of higher wages on employers.

Not everyone shares these ideas about demand offsetting higher wages. China has used minimum wage increases to increase domestic consumption and reduce inequality. For example, the minimum wage in Shanghai is equivalent to around £200 a month (€270) and has nearly doubled since 2009. The Chinese policy that ensures people in employment have enough to live on, will end up excluding some low-wage workers from jobs as firms employ fewer staff. Research by the IMF suggests that a 10 per cent rise in the minimum wage is offset by a 1 per cent fall in employment and that the figures are far worse for the

lowest income groups where the drop in employment is 1.7 per cent compared to 0.6 per cent for the highest.

The research was based on comparing data from areas where minimum wages were increased to others where the minimum wage remained unchanged.

It is difficult to assess what is the acceptable level of tradeoff between minimum pay and extra unemployment which will no doubt form the debate between all those affected by employment legislation.

Questions

1. If a government raises the minimum wage by 20 per cent, what would you expect to happen to the employment levels based on the evidence from China?

2. Why do many governments have minimum wage legislation?

3. Explain possible arguments for and against the idea of city or regional level minimum wage floors.

4. Why do you think there are different minimum wage levels according to age in the UK?

5. What is the difference between the idea of a 'living wage' and a 'minimum wage' in countries like the UK?

References: https://www.gov.uk /government/news/government-names -and-shames-largest-ever-number -of-national-minimum-wage-offenders

http://www.theguardian.com/uk-news /davehillblog/2015/mar/26/should -london-have-its-own-higher-legal -minimum-wage

http://www.newsmax.com /FastFeatures/minimum-wage -employment-levels-new-hiring /2015/04/06/id/636750/

SUMMARY

- The unemployment rate is an imperfect measure of joblessness. Some people who call themselves unemployed may actually not want to work, and some people who would like to work have left the labour force after an unsuccessful search.

- In many advanced economies, most people who become unemployed find work within a short period of time. Nevertheless, most unemployment observed at any given time is attributable to the few people who are unemployed for long periods of time.

- One reason for unemployment is the time it takes for workers to search for jobs that best suit their tastes and skills. Unemployment insurance is a government policy that, while protecting workers' incomes, increases the amount of frictional unemployment.

- A second reason why an economy may always have some unemployment is if there is a minimum wage that exceeds the wage that would balance supply and demand for the workers who are eligible for the minimum wage. By raising the wage of unskilled and inexperienced workers above the equilibrium level, minimum wage laws raise the quantity of labour supplied and reduce the quantity demanded. The resulting surplus of labour represents unemployment.

- A third reason for unemployment is the market power of unions. When unions push the wages in unionized industries above the equilibrium level, they create a surplus of labour.

- A fourth reason for unemployment is suggested by the theory of efficiency wages. According to this theory, firms find it profitable to pay wages above the equilibrium level. High wages can improve worker health, lower worker turnover, increase worker effort and raise worker quality.

QUESTIONS FOR REVIEW

1. What is the difference between the labour force and the population of working age?

2. Explain how the number of people employed and the number of people unemployed can both rise at the same time.

3. Why is there an apparent contradiction between short spells of unemployment and unemployment being long term?

4. Why is frictional unemployment inevitable? How might the government reduce the amount of frictional unemployment?

5. Explain how minimum wage laws can lead to an increase in unemployment.

6. Are minimum wage laws a better explanation for structural unemployment among teenagers or among university graduates? Why?

7. How do unions affect the natural rate of unemployment?

8. How does the existence of unions add to a firm's costs?

9. What claims do advocates of unions make to argue that unions are good for the economy?

10. Explain four ways in which a firm might increase its profits by raising the wages it pays.

PROBLEMS AND APPLICATIONS

1. If the unemployment rate is rising in a country, does this mean that firms will find it easier to be able to hire new workers? What might your answer depend on?

2. Should firms be forced to contribute to the costs of improving job search? Explain your answer.

3. Assume that there is an increase in the labour participation rate in a country with a growing number of females entering the workforce. What would you expect to happen to the average wage rate and how would firms respond to such a trend?

4. Are the following workers more likely to experience short-term or long-term unemployment? Explain.
   a. A construction worker laid off because of bad weather.
   b. A manufacturing worker who loses her job at a plant in an isolated area.

c. A bus industry worker laid off because of competition from the railway.

d. A short-order cook who loses his job when a new restaurant opens across the street.

e. An expert welder with little formal education who loses her job when the company installs automatic welding machinery.

5. Using a diagram of the labour market, show the effect of an increase in the minimum wage on the wage paid to workers, the number of workers supplied, the number of workers demanded and the amount of unemployment.

6. Consider the minimum wage law.

a. Suppose the minimum wage is above the equilibrium wage in the market for unskilled labour. Using a supply and demand diagram of the market for unskilled labour, show the market wage, the number of workers who are employed and the number of workers who are unemployed. Also show the total wage payments to unskilled workers.

b. Now suppose the minister for employment proposes an increase in the minimum wage. What effect would this increase have on employment? Does the change in employment depend on the elasticity of demand, the elasticity of supply, both elasticities, or neither?

c. What effect would this increase in the minimum wage have on unemployment? Does the change in unemployment depend on the elasticity of demand, the elasticity of supply, both elasticities, or neither?

d. If the demand for unskilled labour were inelastic, would the proposed increase in the minimum wage raise or lower total wage payments to unskilled workers? Would your answer change if the demand for unskilled labour were elastic?

7. Do you think that firms in small towns or in cities have more market power in hiring? Do you think that firms generally have more market power in hiring today than 50 years ago, or less? How do you think this change over time has affected the role of unions in the economy? Explain.

8. Consider an economy with two labour markets, neither of which is unionized. Now suppose a union is established in one market.

a. Show the effect of the union on the market in which it is formed. In what sense is the quantity of labour employed in this market an inefficient quantity?

b. Show the effect of the union on the non-unionized market. What happens to the equilibrium wage in this market?

9. Some workers in the economy are paid a flat salary and some are paid by commission.

a. Which compensation scheme would require more monitoring by supervisors?

b. In which case do firms have an incentive to pay more than the equilibrium level (as in the worker effort variant of efficiency wage theory)?

c. What factors do you think determine the type of compensation firms choose?

10. Suppose that the government passes a law requiring employers to provide employees some benefit (such as a guaranteed pension) that raises the cost of an employee by €4 per hour.

a. What effect does this new law have on the demand for labour? (In answering this and the following questions, be quantitative when you can.)

b. If employees place a value on this benefit exactly equal to its cost, what effect does the new law have on the supply of labour?

c. If the wage is free to balance supply and demand, how does this law affect the wage and the level of employment? Are employers better or worse off? Are employees better or worse off?

d. If a minimum wage law prevents the wage from balancing supply and demand, how does the new law affect the wage, the level of employment and the level of unemployment? Are employers better or worse off? Are employees better or worse off?

e. Now suppose that workers do not value the benefit arising from the new law at all. How does this alternative assumption change your answers to parts (b), (c) and (d) above?

19

MACROECONOMICS – INFLATION AND PRICE STABILITY

LEARNING OUTCOMES

After reading this chapter you should be able to:

- Explain why money has no impact on real variables in the long run.

- Explain the concept of an inflation tax.

- Explain who gains and who loses on a loan contract when inflation rises unexpectedly.

- Draw a graph of a short-run Phillips curve.

- Draw a graph of a long-run Phillips curve.

- Show the relationship between a shift in the short-run aggregate supply curve and a shift in the short-run Phillips curve.

- Explain the sacrifice ratio.

- Explain why more than rational expectations are needed to reduce inflation costlessly.

MONEY GROWTH AND INFLATION

In advanced economies, most prices tend to rise over time. This increase in the overall level of prices is called *inflation*. Although inflation has been the norm in more recent history, there has been substantial variation in the rate at which prices rise. Inflation in the UK during the late 1990s and the first half of the 2000s was low and stable at around 2 per cent or so. However, in the mid-1970s, annual UK inflation, as measured by increases in the retail prices index, exceeded 20 per cent.

International data show an even broader range of inflation experiences. In recent times there have been episodes of hyperinflation in the former Yugoslavia and in Zimbabwe. Inflation in Yugoslavia ran at 5 quadrillion per cent (5 with 15 zeros after it) between October 1993 and January 1995. In January 2009, the Zimbabwean authorities announced that inflation had reached 231 million per cent in June 2008. What that means is that a product (say a loaf of bread) priced at Z$1 in June 2007 would have a price tag of Z$2.31 million in June 2008. The Zimbabwean central bank reported that some goods on the black market had risen by 70 million per cent. Laundry soap was one of the goods that had risen by this much, but cooking oil also rose by 60 million per cent and sugar by 36 million per cent. Inflation made almost every Zimbabwean a billionaire. Unskilled workers earned around Z$200 billion a month – at the time, equivalent to about US$10. In July 2008 the government issued a Z$100 billion note. If you had one it would just about have bought you a loaf of bread. In Europe in early 2015, the price level actually fell, meaning the European economy was experiencing deflation, a phenomena which Japan has struggled with for a number of years.

This theory of inflation can explain both moderate inflations and hyperinflations, such as those outlined above.

THE CLASSICAL THEORY OF INFLATION

We begin our study of inflation by developing the quantity theory of money. This theory is often called 'classical' because it was developed by some of the earliest thinkers about economic issues back in the 18th century such as David Hume, who are often referred to as the 'classical economists'.

The Level of Prices and the Value of Money

Our first insight about inflation is that it is more about the value of money (the goods and services any given amount of money can be exchanged for) than about the value of goods. Inflation is an economy-wide phenomenon that concerns, first and foremost, the value of the economy's medium of exchange and so affects businesses and their customers.

The economy's overall price level can be viewed in two ways. We can view the price level as the price of a basket of goods and services as we saw when looking at how to measure inflation in Chapter 16. When the price level rises, businesses and people have to pay more for the goods and services they buy. Alternatively, we can view the price level as a measure of the value of money. A rise in the price level means a lower value of money because each unit of money now buys a smaller quantity of goods and services.

It may help to express these ideas mathematically. Suppose P is the price level as measured, for instance, by the consumer prices index (CPI) or the GDP deflator.

Then P measures the number of euros needed to buy a basket of goods and services. Now turn this idea around: the quantity of goods and services that can be bought with €1 equals $1/P$. In other words, if P is the price of goods and services measured in terms of money, $1/P$ is the value of money measured in terms of goods and services. Thus, when the overall price level rises, the value of money falls.

> **Pitfall Prevention** Remember to link the increase in the price level to that for incomes/wages so that the distinction can be made between nominal and real income.

Money Supply, Money Demand and Monetary Equilibrium

Supply and demand determines the value of money. First consider money supply. The central bank, together with the banking system, determines the supply of money. In this chapter, we take the quantity of money supplied as a policy variable that the central bank controls. The demand for money reflects how much wealth people want to hold in liquid form. Many factors influence the quantity of money demanded. The amount of currency that businesses and people hold at any one time depends in part on their view of the future, how much they rely on credit to make purchases and the ease with which cash can be accessed. For consumers this might depend on whether an automatic cash dispenser is easy to find. The quantity of money demanded depends on the interest rate that businesses and consumers could earn by using the money to buy an interest-bearing security rather than holding it as cash or in a low interest bank account.

Although many variables affect the demand for money, one variable stands out in importance: the average level of prices in the economy. Businesses and people hold money because it is the medium of exchange. Unlike other assets, such as bonds or stocks, money can be used to buy the raw materials, equipment, and goods and services to operate and to live. How much money they choose to hold for this purpose depends on the prices of those goods and services. The higher prices are, the more money the typical transaction requires, and the more money businesses and people will choose to hold as cash and in bank accounts. That is, a higher price level (a lower value of money) increases the quantity of money demanded.

What ensures that the quantity of money the central bank supplies balances the quantity of money people demand depends on the time horizon being considered? *In the long run, the overall level of prices adjusts to the level at which the demand for money equals the supply.* Figure 19.1 illustrates this idea. The horizontal axis of this graph shows the quantity of money. The left-hand vertical axis shows the value of money $1/P$, and the right-hand vertical axis shows the price level P. Notice that the price level axis on the right is inverted: a low price level is shown near the top of this axis, and a high price level is shown near the bottom. This inverted axis illustrates that when the value of money is high (as shown near the top of the left axis), the price level is low (as shown near the top of the right axis).

The two curves in this figure are the supply and demand curves for money. The supply curve is vertical because it is assumed that the central bank fixes the quantity of money available. The demand curve for money is downward sloping, indicating that when the value of money is low (and the price level is high), people demand a larger quantity of it to buy goods and services. At the equilibrium, shown in the figure as point A, the quantity of money demanded balances the quantity of money supplied. This equilibrium of money supply and money demand determines the value of money and the price level.

FIGURE 19.1

How the Supply and Demand for Money Determine the Equilibrium Price Level

The horizontal axis shows the quantity of money. The left vertical axis shows the value of money, and the right vertical axis shows the price level. The supply curve for money is vertical because the quantity of money supplied is fixed by the central bank. The demand curve for money is downwards sloping because people want to hold a larger quantity of money when each euro buys less. At the equilibrium, point A, the value of money (on the left axis) and the price level (on the right axis) have adjusted to bring the quantity of money supplied and the quantity of money demanded into balance.

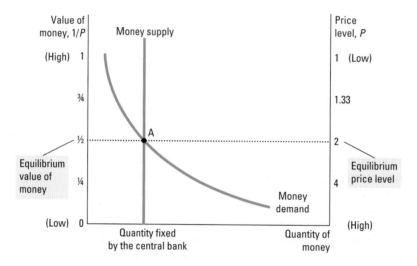

To summarize, if the price level is above the equilibrium level, businesses and people will want to hold more money than the central bank has created, so the price level must fall to balance supply and demand. If the price level is below the equilibrium level, people will want to hold less money than the central bank has created, and the price level must rise to balance supply and demand. At the equilibrium price level, the quantity of money that people want to hold exactly balances the quantity of money supplied by the central bank.

> **?**
>
> **what if ...** the assumption that the central bank can control the money supply was dropped and instead the supply of money was positively related to the interest rate. What effect would a rise in the demand for money have on interest rates in comparison to that when the supply of money is assumed to be fixed?

The Effects of a Monetary Injection

Let's now consider the effects of a change in monetary policy. Assume that the economy is in equilibrium and then, suddenly, the central bank doubles the supply of money by printing large amounts of money. This may be done through the central bank injecting money into the economy by buying some government bonds from the public in open-market operations (this is the basis of quantitative easing).

Figure 19.2 shows what happens after such a monetary injection. The monetary injection shifts the supply curve to the right from MS_1 to MS_2, and the equilibrium moves from point A to point B. As a result, the value of money (shown on the left axis) decreases from ½ to ¼, and the equilibrium price level (shown on the right axis) increases from 2 to 4. In other words, when an increase in the money supply makes euros more plentiful, the result is an increase in the price level that makes each euro less valuable.

FIGURE 19.2

An Increase in the Money Supply

When the central bank increases the supply of money, the money supply curve shifts from MS₁ to MS₂. The value of money (on the left axis) and the price level (on the right axis) adjust to bring supply and demand back into balance. The equilibrium moves from point A to point B. Thus, when an increase in the money supply makes euros more plentiful, the price level increases, making each euro less valuable.

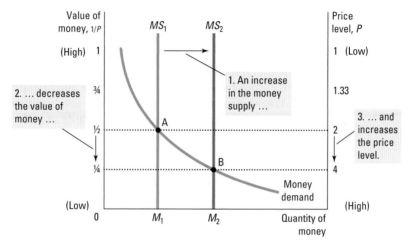

This explanation of how the price level is determined and why it might change over time is called the **quantity theory of money**. According to the quantity theory, the quantity of money available in the economy determines the value of money, and growth in the quantity of money is the primary cause of inflation.

quantity theory of money
a theory asserting that the quantity of money available determines the price level and that the growth rate in the quantity of money available determines the inflation rate

A Brief Look at the Adjustment Process

The immediate effect of a monetary injection is to create an excess supply of money. Before the injection, the economy was in equilibrium (point A in Figure 19.2). At the prevailing price level, people had exactly as much money as they wanted. But after the increase in the money supply, businesses and people hold more euros as cash than they need to buy goods and services. At the prevailing price level, the quantity of money supplied now exceeds the quantity demanded.

This excess supply of money is used in various ways. It might be used to buy more raw materials or goods and services. Or it might be used to make loans to others by buying bonds or by depositing the money in a bank savings account. These loans allow other businesses and people to buy goods and services. In either case, the injection of money increases the demand for goods and services.

The economy's ability to supply goods and services, however, has not changed. The economy's output of goods and services is determined by the available labour, physical capital, human capital, natural resources and technological knowledge. None of these is altered by the injection of money.

Thus, the greater demand for goods and services causes the prices of goods and services to increase. The increase in the price level, in turn, increases the quantity of money demanded because people are using more euros for every transaction. Eventually, the economy reaches a new equilibrium (point B in Figure 19.2) at which the quantity of money demanded again equals the quantity of money supplied. In this way, the overall price level for goods and services adjusts to bring money supply and money demand into balance.

THE COSTS OF INFLATION

Many business leaders rank inflation, at too high a level, as a serious problem that must be kept under control although many would agree that some inflation is desirable. In this next section we will look at some of the costs of inflation to businesses and people in general.

A Fall in Purchasing Power? The Inflation Fallacy

If you ask the typical business or person why inflation is bad, they will tell you that the answer is obvious: inflation robs them of the purchasing power of hard-earned money. When prices rise, each euro buys fewer goods and services. Thus, it might seem that inflation directly lowers living standards and affects the ability of businesses to buy.

Yet further thought reveals a fallacy in this answer. When prices rise, buyers of goods and services pay more for what they buy. At the same time, however, businesses get more for what they sell. Because most people earn their incomes by selling their services, such as their labour, inflation in incomes goes hand in hand with inflation in prices. *Thus, inflation does not in itself reduce peoples' real purchasing power.*

The inflation fallacy is an issue because of the principle of monetary neutrality. A worker who receives an annual rise of 10 per cent in their salary, for example, tends to view that rise as a reward for their own talent and effort. When an inflation rate of 6 per cent reduces the real value of that pay rise to only 4 per cent, the worker might feel that they have been cheated of what is rightfully their due. In fact, real incomes are determined by real variables, such as physical capital, human capital, natural resources, and the available production technology. Nominal incomes are determined by those factors and the overall price level. If the central bank were to succeed in lowering the inflation rate from 6 per cent to zero, our worker's annual rise might only be 4 per cent rather than 10 per cent. They might feel less robbed by inflation, but their real income would not rise more quickly.

If nominal incomes tend to keep pace with rising prices, why then is inflation a problem? It turns out that there is no single answer to this question. Instead, economists have identified several costs of inflation. Each of these costs shows some way in which persistent growth in the money supply does, in fact, have some effect on real variables.

Shoe Leather Costs

Inflation is like a tax on the holders of money. The tax itself is not a cost to society: it is only a transfer of resources from households to the government. Yet most taxes give people an incentive to alter their behaviour to avoid paying the tax, and this distortion of incentives causes deadweight losses for society as a whole. Like other taxes, the **inflation tax** also causes deadweight losses because businesses and people waste scarce resources trying to avoid it.

inflation tax the revenue the government raises by creating money

How can a business or person avoid paying the inflation tax? Because inflation erodes the real value of the money held, you can avoid the inflation tax by holding less money. One way to do this is to manage cash flow more carefully. For example, if a business can keep more cash in interest-bearing accounts the effect of inflation is reduced. Active management of cash flow in all businesses, but especially in large businesses where the amounts of cash reserves being held can be significant, is a vital part of overall financial management of the business.

The cost of reducing money holdings is called the **shoe leather cost** of inflation because such active cash management involves the time and convenience that must be sacrificed to keep less money on hand than you would if there were no inflation – it is in effect a *transaction cost*.

shoe leather cost the resources wasted when inflation encourages people to reduce their money holding

Menu Costs

Most firms do not change the prices of their products every day. Instead, firms often announce prices and leave them unchanged for weeks, months or even years. Firms change prices infrequently because there are costs involved in changing prices. Costs of price adjustment are called **menu costs**, a term derived from a restaurant's cost of printing a new menu. Menu costs include the cost of deciding on new prices, the cost of printing new price lists and catalogues, the cost of sending these new price lists and catalogues to dealers and customers, amending prices on websites and internal systems, the cost of advertising the new prices, and even the cost of dealing with customer annoyance over price changes.

menu costs the costs of changing prices

Inflation increases the menu costs that firms must bear. In an economy with low inflation of just a few percentage points a year, annual price adjustment is an appropriate business strategy for many firms. But when high inflation makes firms' costs rise rapidly, annual price adjustment is impractical. If inflation is rising strongly then firms may have to adjust prices more regularly and this can not only be expensive but disruptive.

Relative Price Variability and the Misallocation of Resources

Suppose that the Eatabit Eatery prints a new menu with new prices every January and then leaves its prices unchanged for the rest of the year. If there is no inflation, Eatabit's relative prices – the prices of its meals compared with other prices in the economy – would be constant over the course of the year. By contrast, if the inflation rate is 12 per cent per year, Eatabit's relative prices will automatically fall by 1 per cent each month. The restaurant's relative prices (that is, its prices compared with others in the economy) will be high in the early months of the year, just after it has printed a new menu, and low in the later months. And the higher the inflation rate, the greater is this automatic variability. Thus, because prices change only once in a while, inflation causes relative prices to vary more than they otherwise would.

This matters because market economies rely on relative prices to allocate scarce resources. Consumers decide what to buy by comparing the quality and prices of various goods and services. Through these decisions, they determine how the scarce factors of production are allocated among industries and firms. When inflation distorts relative prices, consumer decisions are distorted, and markets are less able to allocate resources to their best use.

Inflation-Induced Tax Distortions

Almost all taxes distort incentives, cause businesses and people to alter their behaviour, and lead to a less efficient allocation of the economy's resources. Many taxes, however, become even more problematic in the presence of inflation. Economists who have studied the tax system conclude that inflation tends to raise the tax burden on income earned from savings.

The taxes on nominal capital gains and on nominal interest income are two examples of how the tax system interacts with inflation. There are many others. Because of these inflation-induced tax changes, higher inflation tends to discourage people from saving. If a business has cash reserves that are attracting interest of 5 per cent, for example, and the inflation rate is 7 per cent, the cash reserves are effectively diminishing in value at a rate of 2 per cent. This provides a disincentive for holding cash reserves. Recall that the economy's saving provides the resources for investment, which in turn is a key ingredient to long-run economic growth. Thus, when inflation raises the tax burden on saving, it tends to depress the economy's long-run growth rate. There is, however, no consensus among economists about the size of this effect.

Confusion and Inconvenience

Imagine that we took a poll and asked people the following question: 'This year the metre is 100 centimetres. How long do you think it should be next year?' Assuming we could get people to take us seriously, they would tell us that the metre should stay the same length – 100 centimetres. Anything else would just complicate life needlessly.

What does this finding have to do with inflation? Money, as the economy's unit of account, is what we use to quote prices and record debts. In other words, money is the yardstick with which we measure economic transactions. The job of the central bank is to ensure the reliability of a commonly used unit of measurement. When the central bank increases the money supply and creates inflation, it erodes the real value of the unit of account.

It is difficult to judge the costs of the confusion and inconvenience that arise from inflation. Accountants can incorrectly measure firms' earnings when prices are rising over time. Because inflation causes money at different times to have different real values, computing a firm's profit – the difference between its revenue and costs – is more complicated in an economy with high inflation. Therefore, to some extent, inflation makes investors less able to sort out successful from unsuccessful firms, which in turn impedes financial markets in their role of allocating the economy's saving to alternative types of investment.

CASE STUDY

Does Deflation Matter?

It is clear that a persistent rise in the price level results in some winners and some losers. For example, those with fixed rate mortgages set when inflation was lower, will benefit from rising prices because in effect they pay back over time with a devalued currency, whereas retired people with fixed pensions lose out as over time their income has less buying power. In this way inflation is having an arbitrary effect. It is harder, however, to determine the effects of deflation on people.

In the UK in the first three months of 2015, inflation was around 0 per cent. The government sets the target rate of inflation for the Bank of England and

2 per cent is considered an acceptable rate which is sufficient to encourage growth. For some time there had been talk that the UK might experience deflation where the average price level actually falls (as opposed to price rises slowing) and this actually happened in May 2015 when the Office for National Statistics announced that the CPI for April 2015 fell by 0.1%. Falling prices might sound like good news but there are arguments put forward to suggest that it is not.

With deflation, interest rates could become negative and banks end up having to pay people to borrow money while savers, in effect 'pay interest' on their savings. With deflation, prices fall over a period of time. People lending money for a year find that when they get it back it buys more goods and services. Meanwhile the borrower has lost out as the amount repaid is worth a lot more than when it was borrowed. Obviously there is a need to factor in risk and a service charge.

Falling prices could lead people to defer spending, because goods and services will be cheaper in the future. Demand falls and businesses postpone investment. There is some evidence that this happened in Japan when it experienced deflation for many years, but there is no agreement among economists as to the strength of this effect and even whether people do make decisions on this basis. It may have an effect when deciding to buy higher priced items like white goods (fridges, washing machines and so on) but for everyday items, it seems less likely that this would be a factor in decision making.

If the UK experiences deflation which persists over time should it be a cause of concern? If it is the Bank of England would need to use monetary tools to inflate the economy. Making interest rates negative would reduce the cost of money and encourage spending, but there is a real danger that people might withdraw cash from banks. That leaves the central bank with the challenge to increase the money supply through quantitative easing.

The Bank of England does not appear to be too worried and is forecasting inflation in 2016 and beyond rather than any persistent deflation. Falling prices in the UK have owed much to the fall in world oil and commodity prices which is not likely to continue indefinitely. Lower fuel prices have benefitted firms by reducing input prices and benefitted households who have more disposable income to spend. The main losers are the North Sea oil firms.

Reference: **http://www.globalchange.com/inflation-and-deflation-winners-and-losers.htm**

A Special Cost of Unexpected Inflation: Arbitrary Redistributions of Wealth

So far, the costs of inflation we have discussed occur even if inflation is steady and predictable. Inflation has an additional cost, however, when it comes as a surprise. Unexpected inflation redistributes wealth among the population in a way that has nothing to do with either merit or need. These redistributions occur because many loans in the economy are specified in terms of the unit of account – money.

Consider an example. Suppose that a small business takes out a €20 000 loan from a bank at a 7 per cent interest rate to expand the business. In 10 years the loan will have to be repaid. After the debt has compounded for 10 years at 7 per cent, the business will owe the bank €39 343. The real value of this debt will depend on inflation over the decade. If the economy experiences high inflation, wages and prices will rise so high that it will find it easier to be able to pay the €39 343 debt. Recall that the value of money is lower in the future than it is today. In contrast, if the economy goes through a major deflation, then wages and prices will fall, and the business will find the €39 343 debt a greater burden than anticipated.

This example shows that unexpected changes in prices redistribute wealth among debtors and creditors. A higher inflation rate enriches the business (borrowers) at the expense of the bank (lenders) because it diminishes the real value of the debt; the business can repay the loan in less valuable euros than anticipated. Deflation enriches the bank at the business' expense because it increases the real value of the debt; in this case, the business has to repay the loan in more valuable euros than anticipated. If inflation were predictable, then the bank and the business could take inflation into account when setting the nominal interest rate. But if inflation is hard to predict, it imposes risk on the business and the bank that both would prefer to avoid.

This cost of unexpected inflation is important to consider together with another fact: inflation is especially volatile and uncertain when the average rate of inflation is high. This is seen most simply by examining the experience of different countries. Countries with low average inflation, such as Germany in the late 20th century, tend to have stable inflation. Countries with high average inflation, such as many countries in Latin America, tend also to have unstable inflation. There are no known examples of economies with high, stable inflation. This relationship between the level and volatility of inflation points to another cost of inflation. If a country pursues a high-inflation monetary policy, it will have to bear not only the costs of high expected inflation but also the arbitrary redistributions of wealth associated with unexpected inflation.

JEOPARDY PROBLEM

In ten successive years, the rate of inflation in a country increases, rising from 3 per cent in year one to 35 per cent in year ten. However, at the same time, incomes rise in line with inflation. A poll of workers suggests that few have a problem with the rate of inflation in the country. Explain why this might be and whether, as a result, the government should not worry about the rising inflation rate.

Deflation

In 2014, there were concerns expressed that the UK and the Eurozone might face deflation – a fall in the price level. In such a scenario, the CPI would be negative suggesting that prices, on average, had fallen. The Eurozone actually experienced deflation of 0.3 per cent in the year to January 2015 and the UK CPI was −0.1 per cent in the year to April 2015 as noted in the Case Study. It is important to note the distinction between a fall in average prices and a slowdown in the rate of growth of prices. If the CPI reports inflation at 2.5 per cent in March and then 2.0 per cent in April, the rate of growth of prices has slowed down, not fallen, but if the CPI is recorded as -0.75 per cent in May, then prices have, on average, fallen.

Deflation is a relatively rare phenomenon; most economies experience inflation at varying levels and indeed an inflation rate of around 2 per cent is seen as being beneficial to an economy as it encourages businesses to expand and helps create a more dynamic economy. Where deflation has occurred it has tended not to last for very long and indeed the German and UK authorities were predicting that the deflation experienced in early 2015 would be short-lived. When deflation persists for some time, as it has done in Japan, for example, problems can arise. Japan experienced deflation from the mid-1990s until the latter part of the first decade of the 2000s. One of the problems faced was a reluctance of consumers to spend when the expectation is that prices will be lower in the future. This argument has some logic and may apply to particular types of goods such as high-priced consumer goods – furniture, TVs and electrical goods, fridges, washing machines, dishwashers and so on. For many everyday goods like food, the likelihood of consumers deferring purchasing in the expectation that prices will be lower is less relevant. The evidence that consumers would delay purchases and thus plunge the economy into recession as consumption spending falls is not clear, especially where deflation does not persist for any length of time.

Other potential problems with deflation are related to interest rates. In the Eurozone and in the UK, interest rates are at historically low levels. Central banks would be reluctant to cut rates much further and would think carefully before having negative interest rates. Negative interest rates would be an incentive for savers to withdraw their deposits to prevent the value of them falling (a negative interest rate would in effect mean banks taking money out of savers deposits). If enough savers did this then this could put pressure on banks and reduce the amount available for lending to businesses.

A period of deflation further affects borrowers and lenders. Banks lending to business would find that the sum lent would purchase more in future when the debt is paid back if prices continued to fall, whereas firms borrowing funds would find that the burden of the debt would increase. In such a situation it might be that businesses would be more reluctant to borrow for investment resulting in a fall in aggregate demand.

One way in which businesses can reduce real wages in a period of inflation is to put a freeze on pay increases for workers. In a period of deflation a pay freeze leads to the opposite result and increases real wages which in effect increases the costs of businesses. If prices are falling, firms might press workers to accept a reduction in wages. If the reduction in wages was less than the rate at which prices are falling, workers would not be any worse off in real terms. However, it is extremely difficult for firms to put through pay cuts so at the very least, a pay freeze is the most likely option. If firms' costs rise, then it is possible that supply is cut or employees are laid off and if either of these outcomes occur throughout the economy, it can trigger a slowdown in economic activity. Given that all these effects could be experienced together, one of the fears of a period of persistent deflation is that the economy suffers from a downward spiral which is difficult to break. Given that interest rates are already likely to be low, the option of providing a stimulus through further interest rate cuts is unlikely.

INFLATION AND UNEMPLOYMENT

Having looked at unemployment in Chapter 18 and inflation in this chapter we now look at the extent to which these two key variables are related. The natural rate of unemployment depends on various features of the labour market, such as minimum wage laws, the market power of unions, the role of efficiency wages and the effectiveness of job search. The inflation rate depends primarily on growth in the money supply, which a nation's central bank controls. In the long run, therefore, inflation and unemployment are largely unrelated problems.

In the short run, just the opposite is true. If monetary and fiscal policy makers expand aggregate demand and move the economy up along the short-run aggregate supply curve, they can lower unemployment for a while, but only at the cost of higher inflation. If policy makers contract aggregate demand and move the economy down the short-run aggregate supply curve, they can lower inflation, but only at the cost of temporarily higher unemployment. The best way to understand this relationship is to see how thinking about it has evolved over time.

THE PHILLIPS CURVE

'Probably the single most important macroeconomic relationship is the Phillips curve.' These are the words of economist George Akerlof from the lecture he gave when he received the Nobel Prize for Economics in 2001. The Phillips curve is the short-run relationship between inflation and unemployment.

Origins of the Phillips Curve

In 1958, a New Zealand economist working at the London School of Economics, A.W. Phillips, published an article in the British journal *Economica* that would make him famous. The article was entitled 'The Relationship between Unemployment and the Rate of Change of Money Wages in the United Kingdom, 1861–1957'. In it, Phillips showed a negative correlation between the rate of unemployment and the rate of inflation. That is, Phillips showed that years with low unemployment tend to have high inflation, and years with high unemployment tend to have low inflation. (Phillips examined inflation in nominal wages rather than inflation in prices, but for our purposes that distinction is not important. These two measures of inflation usually move together.) Phillips concluded that two important macroeconomic variables – inflation and unemployment – were linked in a way that economists had not previously appreciated.

Although Phillips's discovery was based on data for the United Kingdom, researchers quickly extended his finding to other countries. Two years after Phillips published his article, economists Paul Samuelson and Robert Solow published an article in the *American Economic Review* called 'Analytics of Anti-inflation Policy' in which they showed a similar negative correlation between inflation and unemployment in data for the USA. They reasoned that this correlation arose because low unemployment was associated with high aggregate demand, which in turn puts upward pressure on wages and prices throughout the economy. Samuelson and Solow dubbed the negative association between inflation and unemployment the Phillips curve. Figure 19.3 shows an example of a Phillips curve like the one found by Samuelson and Solow.

As the title of their paper suggests, Samuelson and Solow were interested in the Phillips curve because they believed that it held important lessons for policy makers. In particular, they suggested that the Phillips curve offers policy makers a menu of possible economic outcomes. By altering monetary and fiscal policy to influence aggregate demand, policy makers could choose any point on this curve. Point A offers high unemployment and low inflation. Point B offers low unemployment and high inflation. Policy makers might prefer both low inflation and low unemployment, but the historical data as summarized by the Phillips curve indicate that this combination is impossible. According to Samuelson and Solow, policy makers face a trade-off between inflation and unemployment, and the Phillips curve illustrates that trade-off.

FIGURE 19.3

The Phillips Curve

The Phillips curve illustrates a negative association between the inflation rate and the unemployment rate. At point A, inflation is low and unemployment is high. At point B, inflation is high and unemployment is low.

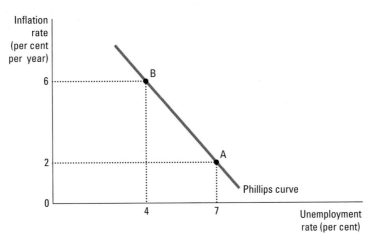

Aggregate Demand, Aggregate Supply and the Phillips Curve

The model of aggregate demand and aggregate supply provides an easy explanation for the menu of possible outcomes described by the Phillips curve. The Phillips curve simply shows the combinations of inflation and unemployment that arise in the short run as shifts in the aggregate demand curve move the economy along the short-run aggregate supply curve. As we saw in Chapter 17, an increase in the aggregate demand for goods and services leads, in the short run, to a larger output of goods and services and a higher price level. Larger output means greater employment and, thus, a lower rate of unemployment. In addition, whatever the previous year's price level happens to be, the higher the price level in the current year, the higher the rate of inflation. Thus, shifts in aggregate demand push inflation and unemployment in opposite directions in the short run – a relationship illustrated by the Phillips curve.

To see more fully how this works, let's consider an example. To keep the numbers simple, imagine that the price level (as measured, for instance, by the CPI) equals 100 in the year 2016. Figure 19.4 shows two possible outcomes that might occur in year 2017. Panel (a) shows the two outcomes using the model of aggregate demand and aggregate supply. Panel (b) illustrates the same two outcomes using the Phillips curve.

In panel (a) of the figure, we can see the implications for output and the price level in the year 2016. If the aggregate demand for goods and services is relatively low, the economy experiences outcome A. The economy produces output of 7500, and the price level is 102. By contrast, if aggregate demand is relatively high, the economy experiences outcome B. Output is 8000, and the price level is 106. Thus, higher aggregate demand moves the economy to an equilibrium with higher output and a higher price level.

FIGURE 19.4

How the Phillips Curve is Related to the Model of Aggregate Demand and Aggregate Supply

This figure assumes a price level of 100 for the year 2016 and charts possible outcomes for the year 2017. Panel (a) shows the model of aggregate demand and aggregate supply. If aggregate demand is low, the economy is at point A; output is low (7500), and the price level is low (102). If aggregate demand is high, the economy is at point B; output is high (8000), and the price level is high (106). Panel (b) shows the implications for the Phillips curve. Point A, which arises when aggregate demand is low, has high unemployment (7 per cent) and low inflation (2 per cent). Point B, which arises when aggregate demand is high, has low unemployment (4 per cent) and high inflation (6 per cent).

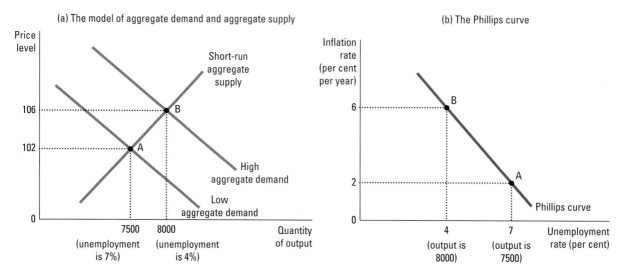

In panel (b) of the figure, we can see what these two possible outcomes mean for unemployment and inflation. Because firms need more workers when they produce a greater output of goods and services, unemployment is lower in outcome B than in outcome A. In this example, when output rises from 7500 to 8000, unemployment falls from 7 per cent to 4 per cent. Moreover, because the price level is higher at outcome B than at outcome A, the inflation rate (the percentage change in the price level from the previous year) is also higher. In particular, since the price level was 100 in year 2016, outcome A has an inflation rate of 2 per cent, and outcome B has an inflation rate of 6 per cent. Thus, we can compare the two possible outcomes for the economy either in terms of output and the price level (using the model of aggregate demand and aggregate supply), or in terms of unemployment and inflation (using the Phillips curve).

We will see in Chapter 20 how monetary and fiscal policy can shift the aggregate demand curve. Monetary and fiscal policy can move the economy along the Phillips curve. Increases in the money supply, increases in government spending, or cuts in taxes expand aggregate demand and move the economy to a point on the Phillips curve with lower unemployment and higher inflation. Decreases in the money supply, cuts in government spending, or increases in taxes contract aggregate demand and move the economy to a point on the Phillips curve with lower inflation and higher unemployment. In this sense, the Phillips curve offers policy makers a menu of combinations of inflation and unemployment.

Quick Quiz Draw the Phillips curve. Use the model of aggregate demand and aggregate supply to show how policy can move the economy from a point on this curve with high inflation to a point with low inflation.

THE ROLE OF EXPECTATIONS

The Phillips curve seems to offer policy makers a menu of possible inflation–unemployment outcomes. But does this menu remain stable over time? Is the Phillips curve a relationship on which policy makers can rely? Economists took up these questions in the late 1960s, shortly after Samuelson and Solow had introduced the Phillips curve into the macroeconomic policy debate.

The Long-Run Phillips Curve

In 1968, economist Milton Friedman published a paper in the *American Economic Review*, based on an address he had recently given as president of the American Economic Association. The paper, entitled 'The Role of Monetary Policy', contained sections on 'What Monetary Policy Can Do' and 'What Monetary Policy Cannot Do'. Friedman argued that one thing monetary policy cannot do, other than for only a short time, is pick a combination of inflation and unemployment on the Phillips curve. At about the same time, another economist, Edmund Phelps, also published a paper denying the existence of a long-run trade-off between inflation and unemployment.

Friedman and Phelps based their conclusions on classical principles of macroeconomics. Classical theory points to growth in the money supply as the primary determinant of inflation. But classical theory also states that monetary growth does not have real effects – it merely alters all prices and nominal incomes proportionately. In particular, monetary growth does not influence those factors that determine the economy's unemployment rate, such as the market power of unions, the role of efficiency wages, or the process of job search. Friedman and Phelps concluded that there is no reason to think the rate of inflation would, *in the long run*, be related to the rate of unemployment.

Here, in his own words, is Friedman's view about what the central bank can hope to accomplish in the long run:

> *The monetary authority controls nominal quantities – directly, the quantity of its own liabilities* [currency plus bank reserves]. *In principle, it can use this control to peg a nominal quantity – an exchange rate, the price level, the nominal level of national income, the quantity of money by one definition or another – or to peg the change in a nominal quantity – the rate of inflation or deflation, the rate of growth or decline in nominal national income, the rate of growth of the quantity of money. It cannot use its control over nominal quantities to peg a real quantity – the real rate of interest, the rate of unemployment, the level of real national income, the real quantity of money, the rate of growth of real national income, or the rate of growth of the real quantity of money.*

These views have important implications for the Phillips curve. In particular, they imply that monetary policy makers face a long-run Phillips curve that is vertical, as in Figure 19.5. If the central bank increases the money supply slowly, the inflation rate is low, and the economy finds itself at point A. If the central bank increases the money supply quickly, the inflation rate is high, and the economy finds itself at point B. In either case, the unemployment rate tends towards its normal level, called the *natural rate of unemployment*. The vertical long-run Phillips curve illustrates the conclusion that unemployment does not depend on money growth and inflation in the long run.

FIGURE 19.5

The Long-Run Phillips Curve

According to Friedman and Phelps, there is no trade-off between inflation and unemployment in the long run. Growth in the money supply determines the inflation rate. Regardless of the inflation rate, the unemployment rate gravitates towards its natural rate. As a result, the long-run Phillips curve is vertical.

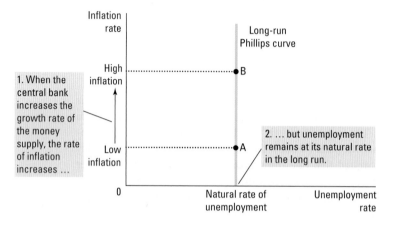

The vertical long-run Phillips curve is, in essence, one expression of the classical idea of monetary neutrality. As you may recall, we expressed this idea in Chapter 17 with a vertical long-run aggregate supply curve. Indeed, as Figure 19.6 illustrates, the vertical long-run Phillips curve and the vertical long-run aggregate supply curve are two sides of the same coin. In panel (a) of this figure, an increase in the money supply shifts the aggregate demand curve to the right from AD_1 to AD_2. As a result of this shift, the long-run equilibrium moves from point A to point B.

FIGURE 19.6

How the Long-Run Phillips Curve is Related to the Model of Aggregate Demand and Aggregate Supply

Panel (a) shows the model of aggregate demand and aggregate supply with a vertical aggregate supply curve. When expansionary monetary policy shifts the aggregate demand curve to the right from AD_1 to AD_2, the equilibrium moves from point A to point B. The price level rises from P_1 to P_2, while output remains the same. Panel (b) shows the long-run Phillips curve, which is vertical at the natural rate of unemployment. Expansionary monetary policy moves the economy from lower inflation (point A) to higher inflation (point B) without changing the rate of unemployment.

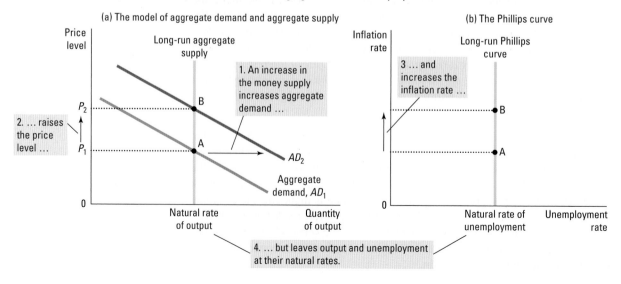

The price level rises from P_1 to P_2, but because the aggregate supply curve is vertical, output remains the same. In panel (b), more rapid growth in the money supply raises the inflation rate by moving the economy from point A to point B. But because the Phillips curve is vertical, the rate of unemployment is the same at these two points. Thus, the vertical long-run aggregate supply curve and the vertical long-run Phillips curve both imply that monetary policy influences nominal variables (the price level and the inflation rate) but not real variables (output and unemployment). Regardless of the monetary policy pursued by the central bank, output and unemployment are, in the long run, at their natural rates.

What is so 'natural' about the natural rate of unemployment? Friedman and Phelps used this adjective to describe the unemployment rate towards which the economy tends to gravitate in the long run. Yet the natural rate of unemployment is not necessarily the socially desirable rate of unemployment. Nor is the natural rate of unemployment constant over time. For example, suppose that a newly formed union uses its market power to raise the real wages of some workers above the equilibrium level. The result is an excess supply of workers and, therefore, a higher natural rate of unemployment. This unemployment is 'natural' not because it is good but because it is beyond the influence of monetary policy. More rapid money growth would not reduce the market power of the union or the level of unemployment; it would lead only to more inflation.

Although monetary policy cannot influence the natural rate of unemployment, other types of policy can. To reduce the natural rate of unemployment, policy makers should look to policies that improve the functioning of the labour market. Earlier in the book we discussed how various labour market policies, such as minimum wage laws, collective bargaining laws, unemployment insurance, and job-training schemes, affect the natural rate of unemployment. A policy change that reduced the natural rate of unemployment would shift the long-run Phillips curve to the left. In addition, because lower unemployment means more workers are producing goods and services, the quantity of goods and services supplied would be larger at any given price level, and the long-run aggregate supply curve would shift to the right. The economy could then enjoy lower unemployment and higher output for any given rate of money growth and inflation.

Reconciling Theory and Evidence

At first, the conclusion of Friedman and Phelps of a long-run trade-off between inflation and unemployment might not seem persuasive. Their argument was based on an appeal to *theory*. In contrast, the negative correlation between inflation and unemployment documented by Phillips, Samuelson and Solow was based on *data*. Why should anyone believe that policy makers faced a vertical Phillips curve when the world seemed to offer a downward sloping one? Shouldn't the findings of Phillips, Samuelson and Solow lead us to reject the classical conclusion of monetary neutrality?

Friedman and Phelps were well aware of these questions, and they offered a way to reconcile classical macroeconomic theory with the finding of a downward sloping Phillips curve in data from the UK and the USA. They claimed that a negative relationship between inflation and unemployment holds in the short run but that it cannot be used by policy makers in the long run. In other words, policy makers can pursue expansionary monetary policy to achieve lower unemployment for a while, but eventually unemployment returns to its natural rate, and more expansionary monetary policy leads only to higher inflation.

Friedman and Phelps' reasoning was based on the difference between the short-run and long-run aggregate supply curves. As you may recall, the short-run aggregate supply curve is upward sloping, indicating that an increase in the price level raises the quantity of goods and services that firms supply. In contrast, the long-run aggregate supply curve is vertical, indicating that the price level does not influence quantity supplied in the long run. Chapter 17 presented three theories to explain the upward slope of the short-run aggregate supply curve: sticky wages, sticky prices and misperceptions about relative prices. Because wages, prices and perceptions adjust to changing economic conditions over time, the positive relationship between the price level and quantity supplied applies in the short run but not in the long run. Friedman and Phelps applied this same logic to the Phillips curve. Just as the aggregate supply curve slopes upward only in the short run, the trade-off between inflation and unemployment holds only in the short run. And just as the long-run aggregate supply curve is vertical, the long-run Phillips curve is also vertical.

To help explain the short-run and long-run relationship between inflation and unemployment, Friedman and Phelps introduced a new variable into the analysis: *expected inflation*. Expected inflation measures how much people expect the overall price level to change. The expected price level affects the wages and prices that people set and the perceptions of relative prices that they form. As a result, expected inflation is one factor that determines the position of the short-run aggregate supply curve. In the short run, the central bank can take expected inflation (and thus the short-run aggregate supply curve) as already determined. When the money supply changes, the aggregate demand curve shifts, and the economy moves along a given short-run aggregate supply curve. In the short run, therefore, monetary changes lead to unexpected fluctuations in output, prices, unemployment and inflation. In this way, Friedman and Phelps explained the Phillips curve that Phillips, Samuelson and Solow had documented.

Yet the central bank's ability to create unexpected inflation by increasing the money supply exists only in the short run. In the long run, people come to expect whatever inflation rate the central bank chooses to produce. Because wages, prices and perceptions will eventually adjust to the inflation rate, the long-run aggregate supply curve is vertical. In this case, changes in aggregate demand, such as those due to changes in the money supply, do not affect the economy's output of goods and services. Thus, Friedman and Phelps concluded that unemployment returns to its natural rate in the long run.

The Short-Run Phillips Curve

The analysis of Friedman and Phelps can be summarized in the following equation:

$$\text{Unemployment rate} = \text{Natural rate of unemployment} - a\left(\text{Actual inflation} - \text{Expected inflation}\right)$$

This equation relates the unemployment rate to the natural rate of unemployment, actual inflation and expected inflation, and is reflective of a similar equation given in Chapter 17. In the short run, expected inflation is given. As a result, higher actual inflation is associated with lower unemployment. (How much unemployment responds to unexpected inflation is determined by the size of *a*, a number that in turn depends on the slope of the short-run aggregate supply curve.) In the long run, however, people come to expect whatever inflation the central bank produces. Thus, actual inflation equals expected inflation, and unemployment is at its natural rate.

This equation implies there is no stable short-run Phillips curve. Each short run Phillips curve reflects a particular expected rate of inflation. (To be precise, if you graph the equation, you'll find that the short-run Phillips curve intersects the long-run Phillips curve at the expected rate of inflation.) Whenever expected inflation changes, the short-run Phillips curve shifts.

According to Friedman and Phelps, it is dangerous to view the Phillips curve as a menu of options available to policy makers. To see why, imagine an economy at its natural rate of unemployment with low inflation and low expected inflation, shown in Figure 19.7 as point A. Now suppose that policy makers try to take advantage of the trade-off between inflation and unemployment by using monetary or fiscal policy to expand aggregate demand. In the short run when expected inflation is given, the economy goes from point A to point B. Unemployment falls below its natural rate, and inflation rises above expected inflation. Over time, people get used to this higher inflation rate, and they raise their expectations of inflation. When expected inflation rises, firms and workers start taking higher inflation into account when setting wages and prices. The short-run Phillips curve then shifts to the right, as shown in the figure. The economy ends up at point C, with higher inflation than at point A but with the same level of unemployment.

Thus, Friedman and Phelps concluded that policy makers do face a trade-off between inflation and unemployment, but only a temporary one.

FIGURE 19.7

How Expected Inflation Shifts the Short-Run Phillips Curve

The higher the expected rate of inflation, the higher the short-run trade-off between inflation and unemployment. At point A, expected inflation and actual inflation are both low, and unemployment is at its natural rate. If the central bank pursues an expansionary monetary policy, the economy moves from point A to point B in the short run. At point B, expected inflation is still low, but actual inflation is high. Unemployment is below its natural rate. In the long run, expected inflation rises, and the economy moves to point C. At point C, expected inflation and actual inflation are both high, and unemployment is back to its natural rate.

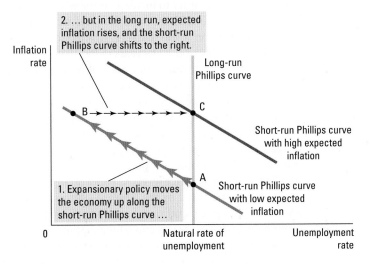

The Unemployment–Inflation Trade-Off

Friedman and Phelps had made a bold prediction in 1968: if policy makers try to take advantage of the Phillips curve by choosing higher inflation in order to reduce unemployment, they will succeed at reducing unemployment only temporarily. This view – that unemployment eventually returns to its natural rate, regardless of the rate of inflation – is called the **natural-rate hypothesis**.

natural-rate hypothesis the claim that unemployment eventually returns to its normal, or natural, rate, regardless of the rate of inflation

To some economists at the time, it seemed ridiculous to claim that the Phillips curve would break down once policy makers tried to use it. But, in fact, that is exactly what happened in both the UK and the United States. Beginning in the late 1960s, the UK government, for example, followed policies that expanded the aggregate demand for goods and services. On top of this, the UK and many other developed economies in the late 1960s and early 1970s experienced an increase in aggregate demand due to American involvement in the Vietnam War, increasing US government spending (on the military), which boosted US aggregate demand and also net exports from other countries to the USA. In addition, in 1971, as a result of the relaxation of certain controls on bank lending, the UK experienced a major expansion in the money supply. In the following year, the government announced an extraordinarily expansionary fiscal policy, in terms of extra spending and tax reduction, and the economy began seriously to overheat and inflation started to rise. But, as Friedman and Phelps had predicted, unemployment did not stay low.

THE ROLE OF SUPPLY SHOCKS

Friedman and Phelps had suggested in 1968 that changes in expected inflation shift the short-run Phillips curve, and the experience of the early 1970s convinced most economists that Friedman and Phelps were right. Within a few years, however, the economics profession would turn its attention to a different source of shifts in the short-run Phillips curve: shocks to aggregate supply.

This time, the shift in focus came not from two economics professors but from a group of Arab sheikhs. Conflict between Israel and its Arab neighbours triggered a series of oil price shocks as Arab oil producers used their market power to exert political pressure on western governments who supported Israel. In 1974, the Organization of Petroleum Exporting Countries (OPEC) also began to exert its power as a cartel in order to increase its members' profits. The countries of OPEC, such as Saudi Arabia, Kuwait and Iraq, restricted the amount of crude oil they pumped and sold on world markets. This reduction in supply caused the price of oil to almost double over a few years in the 1970s.

supply shock an event that directly alters firms' costs and prices, shifting the economy's aggregate supply curve and thus the Phillips curve

A large increase in the world price of oil is an example of a supply shock. A **supply shock** is an event that directly affects firms' costs of production and thus the prices they charge; it shifts the economy's aggregate supply curve and, as a result, the Phillips curve. Oil is a constituent part of so many production processes that increases in its price have far-reaching effects. For example, when an oil price increase raises the cost of producing petrol, heating oil, tyres, plastic products, distribution and many other products, it reduces the quantity of goods and services supplied at any given price level. As panel (a) of Figure 19.8 shows, this reduction in supply is represented by the leftward shift in the aggregate supply curve from AS_1 to AS_2. The price level rises from P_1 to P_2, and output falls from Y_1 to Y_2. The combination of rising prices and falling output is sometimes called *stagflation*.

This shift in aggregate supply is associated with a similar shift in the short-run Phillips curve, shown in panel (b). Because firms need fewer workers to produce the smaller output, employment falls and unemployment rises. Because the price level is higher, the inflation rate – the percentage change in the price level from the previous year – is also higher. Thus, the shift in aggregate supply leads to higher unemployment and higher inflation. The short-run trade-off between inflation and unemployment shifts to the right from PC_1 to PC_2.

FIGURE 19.8

An Adverse Shock to Aggregate Supply

Panel (a) shows the model of aggregate demand and aggregate supply. When the aggregate supply curve shifts to the left from AS_1 to AS_2, the equilibrium moves from point A to point B. Output falls from Y_1 to Y_2, and the price level rises from P_1 to P_2. Panel (b) shows the short-run trade-off between inflation and unemployment. The adverse shift in aggregate supply moves the economy from a point with lower unemployment and lower inflation (point A) to a point with higher unemployment and higher inflation (point B). The short-run Phillips curve shifts to the right from PC_1 to PC_2. Policy makers now face a worse trade-off between inflation and unemployment.

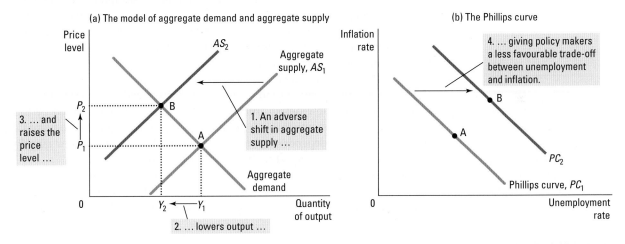

Confronted with an adverse shift in aggregate supply, policy makers face a difficult choice between fighting inflation and fighting unemployment. If they contract aggregate demand to fight inflation, they will raise unemployment further. If they expand aggregate demand to fight unemployment, they will raise inflation further. In other words, policy makers face a less favourable trade-off between inflation and unemployment than they did before the shift in aggregate supply: they have to live with a higher rate of inflation for a given rate of unemployment, a higher rate of unemployment for a given rate of inflation, or some combination of higher unemployment and higher inflation.

An important question is whether this adverse shift in the Phillips curve is temporary or permanent. The answer depends on how businesses and people adjust their expectations of inflation. If both view the rise in inflation due to the supply shock as a temporary aberration, expected inflation does not change, and the Phillips curve will soon revert to its former position. But if it is believed the shock will lead to a new era of higher inflation, then expected inflation rises, and the Phillips curve remains at its new, less desirable position.

Quick Quiz Give an example of a favourable shock to aggregate supply. Use the model of aggregate demand and aggregate supply to explain the effects of such a shock. How does it affect the Phillips curve?

THE COST OF REDUCING INFLATION

Economic theory suggests that controlling the money supply is a way of reducing inflation. But what is the short-run cost of disinflation?

The Sacrifice Ratio

To reduce the inflation rate, the central bank has to pursue contractionary monetary policy. Figure 19.9 shows some of the effects of such a decision. When the central bank slows the rate at which the money supply is growing, it contracts aggregate demand. The fall in aggregate demand, in turn, reduces the quantity of goods and services that firms produce, and this fall in production leads to a fall in employment. The economy begins at point A in the figure and moves along the short-run Phillips curve to point B, which has lower inflation and higher unemployment. Over time, as people come to understand that prices are rising more slowly, expected inflation falls, and the short-run Phillips curve shifts downward. The economy moves from point B to point C. Inflation is lower, and unemployment is back at its natural rate.

Thus, if a nation wants to reduce inflation, it must endure a period of high unemployment and low output. In Figure 19.9, this cost is represented by the movement of the economy through point B as it travels from point A to point C. The size of this cost depends on the slope of the Phillips curve and how quickly expectations of inflation adjust to the new monetary policy.

Many studies have examined the data on inflation and unemployment in order to estimate the cost of reducing inflation. The findings of these studies are often summarized in a statistic called the **sacrifice ratio**.

sacrifice ratio the number of percentage points of annual output lost in the process of reducing inflation by 1 percentage point

---

FIGURE 19.9

Disinflationary Monetary Policy in the Short Run and Long Run

When the central bank pursues contractionary monetary policy to reduce inflation, the economy moves along a short-run Phillips curve from point A to point B. Over time, expected inflation falls, and the short-run Phillips curve shifts downward. When the economy reaches point C, unemployment is back at its natural rate.

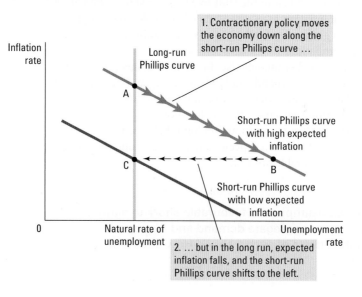

The sacrifice ratio is the number of percentage points of annual output lost in the process of reducing inflation by 1 percentage point. A typical estimate of the sacrifice ratio is around 3 to 5. That is, for each percentage point that inflation is reduced, 3 to 5 per cent of annual output must be sacrificed in the transition.

According to studies of the Phillips curve and the cost of disinflation, this sacrifice could be paid in various ways. An immediate reduction in inflation by a significant amount would depress output for a single year, but the cost in terms of lost output would be extremely harsh even for the most hardline inflation hawks. It would be better, many argued, to spread out the cost over several years. If the reduction in inflation took place over 5 years, for instance, then the cost would be lower each year. An even more gradual approach would be to reduce inflation slowly over a decade. Whatever path was chosen, however, it seemed that reducing inflation would not be easy.

Rational Expectations and the Possibility of Costless Disinflation

Just as policy makers were pondering how costly reducing inflation might be, a group of economics professors were leading an intellectual revolution that would challenge the conventional wisdom on the sacrifice ratio. This group included such prominent economists as Robert Lucas, Thomas Sargent and Robert Barro. Their revolution was based on a new approach to economic theory and policy called **rational expectations**. According to the theory of rational expectations, people optimally use all the information they have, including information about government policies, when forecasting the future.

rational expectations the theory according to which people optimally use all the information they have, including information about government policies, when forecasting the future

This new approach has had profound implications for many areas of macroeconomics, but none is more important than its application to the trade-off between inflation and unemployment. As Friedman and Phelps had first emphasized, expected inflation is an important variable that explains why there is a trade-off between inflation and unemployment in the short run but not in the long run. How quickly the short-run trade-off disappears depends on how quickly expectations adjust. Proponents of rational expectations built on the Friedman-Phelps analysis argue that when economic policies change, people adjust their expectations of inflation accordingly. Studies of inflation and unemployment that tried to estimate the sacrifice ratio had failed to take account of the direct effect of the policy regime on expectations. As a result, estimates of the sacrifice ratio were, according to the rational expectations theorists, unreliable guides for policy.

In a 1982 paper entitled 'The End of Four Big Inflations' (one of which was the UK inflation of the late 1970s and early 1980s), Thomas Sargent described this new view as follows:

> An alternative 'rational expectations' view denies that there is any inherent momentum to the present process of inflation. This view maintains that firms and workers have now come to expect high rates of inflation in the future and that they strike inflationary bargains in light of these expectations. However, it is held that people expect high rates of inflation in the future precisely because the government's current and prospective monetary and fiscal policies warrant those expectations.... An implication of this view is that inflation can be stopped much more quickly than advocates of the 'momentum' view have indicated and that their estimates of the length of time and the costs of stopping inflation in terms of forgone output are erroneous. This is not to say that it would be easy to eradicate inflation. On the contrary, it would require more than a few temporary restrictive

fiscal and monetary actions. It would require a change in the policy regime....
How costly such a move would be in terms of forgone output and how long it
would be in taking effect would depend partly on how resolute and evident the
government's commitment was.

According to Sargent, the sacrifice ratio could be much smaller than suggested
by previous estimates. Indeed, in the most extreme case, it could be zero. If the government made a credible commitment to a policy of low inflation, people would
be rational enough to lower their expectations of inflation immediately. The short-
run Phillips curve would shift downward, and the economy would reach low inflation quickly without the cost of temporarily high unemployment and low output.
The credibility of government or central bank policy is thus of prime importance.

Does this experience refute the possibility of costless disinflation as suggested
by the rational expectations theorists? Some economists have argued that the
answer to this question is a resounding 'yes'.

Yet perhaps there is good reason not to reject the conclusions of the rational
expectations theorists so quickly. Even though disinflation can impose a cost of
temporarily high unemployment, the cost may not be as large as many economists had initially predicted. Most estimates of the sacrifice ratio based on
UK disinflation policies in the 1980s are smaller than estimates that had been
obtained from previous data. One explanation is that a tough stand on inflation
does have some direct effect on expectations, as the rational expectations theorists claimed.

Quick Quiz What is the sacrifice ratio? How might the credibility
of the government's commitment to reduce inflation affect the
sacrifice ratio?

CONCLUSION

This chapter has discussed the causes and costs of inflation. The primary cause of
inflation is simply growth in the quantity of money. When the central bank creates money in large quantities, the value of money falls quickly. To maintain stable
prices, the central bank must maintain strict control over the money supply.

The costs of inflation are more subtle. They include shoe leather costs, menu
costs, increased variability of relative prices, unintended changes in tax liabilities,
confusion and inconvenience, and arbitrary redistributions of wealth. Are these
costs, in total, large or small? All economists agree that they become huge during
hyperinflation. But their size for moderate inflation – when prices rise by less than
10 per cent per year – is more open to debate.

When the central bank reduces the rate of money growth, prices rise less rapidly, as the quantity theory suggests. Yet as the economy makes the transition to
this lower inflation rate, the change in monetary policy will have disruptive effects
on production and employment. That is, even though monetary policy is neutral
in the long run, it has profound effects on real variables in the short run.

We also examined how economists' thinking about inflation and unemployment has evolved over time. We have discussed the ideas of many of the best
economists of the 20th century: from the Phillips curve of Phillips, Samuelson
and Solow, to the natural-rate hypothesis of Friedman and Phelps, to the rational
expectations theory of Lucas, Sargent and Barro.

IN THE NEWS

India's Central Bank Faces a Dilemma

India is one of the emerging economies, a country with a population of around 1.26 billion people and a GDP of over $2 trillion, making GDP per capita over $1600. Economic growth has been around 7–10 per cent in recent years with latest estimates putting 2015 growth at 7.5 per cent, a level that will surpass that of China and will be over double the rate of global growth.

Despite these impressive-sounding figures there are problems within the country. Until recently inflation in particular has proved difficult to get under control. The CPI has hovered around double digits at times since 2005 through to 2013, despite attempts by the central bank to reduce inflation below this level to targets of around 4–5 per cent.

The central bank, the Reserve Bank of India (RBI) increased base rates 13 times between 2010 and 2012 to try and curtail inflation. Part of the reason why its attempts proved difficult was because of the approach of the government at the time, which some argued was borrowing too much and not spending the money wisely on things that would help boost aggregate supply in the economy. Rather than spending money on infrastructure and helping Indian businesses to boost investment, the government borrowed heavily to fund so-called 'populist measures' which have included subsidies on food and fuel.

This borrowing to fund subsidies led to crowding out of private investment and a credit squeeze which in turn led to lower than expected growth levels, slowing below the 9 per cent predicted a few years ago. The fear was that India might face stubborn inflation and sluggish growth (in comparison to expectations).

A change of government has seen a shift in the emphasis of macroeconomic policy. The primary objective of the Reserve Bank of India's monetary policy is price stability, giving less importance to government borrowing. In February 2015, the government and the central bank agreed to set a consumer inflation target of 4 per cent, with a band of plus or minus 2 percentage points, from the financial year ending in March 2017. The interest rate was cut to 7.5 per cent in March 2015, partly because of external factors helping to reduce overall inflation rates in 2014. This was the result of a world fall in oil, commodity and food prices. India as a net importer of energy will benefit from lower fuel prices.

Lower interest rates raise disposable incomes but it is the new government's proposed reforms that will provide the key to developing a sustainable economy. It is spending money, but the spending is not so much on subsidies but on improving infrastructure, education, training and making it easier to do business. This is something of a priority since in 2015 it is ranked only 142nd in the world.

Questions

1. What is meant by the term 'crowding out' (see Chapter 15)?
2. Explain how a change in interest rates would be expected to feed through to a change in the rate of inflation.
3. Why had the previous government been spending money on subsidizing food and fuel and why was this not deemed as being a priority in 2014?
4. What is the relevance to business of the new government's priority of spending on capital projects and education?
5. Should the RBI focus its policy on controlling inflation or boosting economic growth in India? Justify your view.

References: http://statisticstimes.com/economy/gdp-capita-of-india.php

http://www.tradingeconomics.com/india/inflation-cpi

SUMMARY

- The overall level of prices in an economy adjusts to bring money supply and money demand into balance. When the central bank increases the supply of money, it causes the price level to rise. Persistent growth in the quantity of money supplied leads to continuing inflation.

- A government can pay for some of its spending simply by printing money. When countries rely heavily on this 'inflation tax', the result is hyperinflation.

- Many people think that inflation makes them poorer because it raises the cost of what they buy. This view is a fallacy, however, because inflation also raises nominal incomes.

- Economists have identified six costs of inflation: shoe leather costs associated with reduced money holdings; menu costs associated with more frequent adjustment of prices; increased variability of relative prices; unintended changes in tax liabilities due to non-indexation of the tax system; confusion and inconvenience resulting from a changing unit of account; and arbitrary redistributions of wealth between debtors and creditors. Many of these costs are large during hyperinflation, but the size of these costs for moderate inflation is less clear.

- The Phillips curve describes a negative relationship between inflation and unemployment. By expanding aggregate demand, policy makers can choose a point

on the Phillips curve with higher inflation and lower unemployment. By contracting aggregate demand, policy makers can choose a point on the Phillips curve with lower inflation and higher unemployment.

- The trade-off between inflation and unemployment described by the Phillips curve holds only in the short run. In the long run, expected inflation adjusts to changes in actual inflation, and the short-run Phillips curve shifts. As a result, the long-run Phillips curve is vertical at the natural rate of unemployment.

- The short-run Phillips curve also shifts because of shocks to aggregate supply. An adverse supply shock, such as the increase in world oil prices during the 1970s, gives policy makers a less favourable trade-off between inflation and unemployment. That is, after an adverse supply shock, policy makers have to accept a higher rate of inflation for any given rate of unemployment, or a higher rate of unemployment for any given rate of inflation.

- When the central bank contracts growth in the money supply to reduce inflation, it moves the economy along the short-run Phillips curve, which results in temporarily high unemployment. The cost of disinflation depends on how quickly expectations of inflation fall. Some economists argue that a credible commitment to low inflation can reduce the cost of disinflation by inducing a quick adjustment of expectations.

QUESTIONS FOR REVIEW

1. Explain how an increase in the price level affects the real value of money.

2. In what sense is inflation like a tax? How does thinking about inflation as a tax help explain hyperinflation?

3. What are the costs of inflation? Which of these costs do you think are most important for the economy of the country in which you live?

4. If inflation is less than expected, who benefits – debtors or creditors? Explain.

5. Explain how business planning can be affected by inflation rising at rates deemed to be 'too fast'.

6. Draw the short-run trade-off between inflation and unemployment. How might the central bank move the economy from one point on this curve to another?

7. Draw the long-run trade-off between inflation and unemployment. Explain how the short-run and long-run trade-offs are related.

8. What's so natural about the natural rate of unemployment? Why might the natural rate of unemployment differ across countries?

9. Suppose a drought destroys farm crops and drives up the price of food. What is the effect on the short-run trade-off between inflation and unemployment?

10. The central bank decides to reduce inflation. Use the Phillips curve to show the short-run and long-run effects of this policy. How might the short-run costs be reduced?

PROBLEMS AND APPLICATIONS

1. Suppose that changes in bank regulations expand the availability of credit cards, so that people need to hold less cash.
   a. How does this event affect the demand for money?
   b. If the central bank does not respond to this event, what will happen to the price level?
   c. If the central bank wants to keep the price level stable, what should it do?

2. The economist John Maynard Keynes wrote: 'Lenin is said to have declared that the best way to destroy the capitalist system was to debauch the currency. By a continuing process of inflation, governments can confiscate, secretly and unobserved, an important part of the wealth of their citizens.' Justify Lenin's assertion.

3. Suppose that a country's inflation rate increases sharply. What happens to the inflation tax on the holders of money? Why is wealth that is held in savings accounts not subject to a change in the inflation tax? Can you think of any way in which holders of savings accounts are hurt by the increase in the inflation rate?

4. What are your shoe leather costs of going to the bank? How might you measure these costs in euros? How do you think the shoe leather costs of the head of your university or college differ from your own?

5. Explain whether the following statements are true, false or uncertain.
   a. 'Inflation hurts borrowers and helps lenders, because borrowers must pay a higher rate of interest.'
   b. 'If prices change in a way that leaves the overall price level unchanged, then no one is made better or worse off.'
   c. 'Inflation does not reduce the purchasing power of most workers.'

6. Suppose the natural rate of unemployment is 6 per cent. On one graph, draw two Phillips curves that can be used to describe the four situations listed here. Label the point that shows the position of the economy in each case.

   a. Actual inflation is 5 per cent and expected inflation is 3 per cent.
   b. Actual inflation is 3 per cent and expected inflation is 5 per cent.
   c. Actual inflation is 5 per cent and expected inflation is 5 per cent.
   d. Actual inflation is 3 per cent and expected inflation is 3 per cent.

7. Illustrate the effects of the following developments on both the short-run and long-run Phillips curves. Give the economic reasoning underlying your answers.
   a. A rise in the natural rate of unemployment.
   b. A decline in the price of imported oil.
   c. A rise in government spending.
   d. A decline in expected inflation.

8. Suppose that a fall in consumer spending causes a recession.
   a. Illustrate the changes in the economy using both an aggregate supply/aggregate demand diagram and a Phillips curve diagram. What happens to inflation and unemployment in the short run?
   b. Now suppose that over time expected inflation changes in the same direction that actual inflation changes. What happens to the position of the short-run Phillips curve? After the recession is over, does the economy face a better or worse set of inflation–unemployment combinations?

9. Suppose the central bank announced that it would pursue contractionary monetary policy in order to reduce the inflation rate. Would the following conditions make the ensuing recession more or less severe? Explain.
   a. Wage contracts have short durations.
   b. There is little confidence in the central bank's determination to reduce inflation.
   c. Expectations of inflation adjust quickly to actual inflation.

10. Imagine an economy in which all wages are set in 3-year contracts. In this world, the central bank announces a disinflationary change in monetary policy to begin immediately. Everyone in the economy believes the central bank's announcement. Would this disinflation be costless? Why or why not? What might the central bank do to reduce the cost of disinflation?

20

MACROECONOMICS – FISCAL, MONETARY AND SUPPLY-SIDE POLICY

LEARNING OUTCOMES

After reading this chapter you should be able to:

- Give a clear definition to outline the differences between monetary, fiscal and supply-side policies.

- Explain the difference between planned and actual spending, saving and investment.

- Draw a diagram of the Keynesian cross and use it to show both an inflationary and deflationary gap.

- Be able to calculate the value of the multiplier given data on the marginal propensities to withdraw.

- Draw a diagram to explain the relevance of the slope of the expenditure line in relation to changes in autonomous expenditure.

- Show what an increase in the money supply does to the interest rate in the short run.

- Illustrate what an increase in the money supply does to aggregate demand.

- Analyse how fiscal policy affects interest rates and aggregate demand.

- Discuss the debate over whether policy makers should try to stabilize the economy.

- Describe how a change in the money supply (both increase and decrease) feeds through to the interest rate in the short run.

- Explain crowding out.

MONETARY POLICY, FISCAL POLICY AND SUPPLY-SIDE POLICY

In this chapter we are going to examine three main policies used to control the economy. These policies are *monetary policy, fiscal policy* and *supply-side policy*. In each case policy is designed to influence economic activity but in different ways. The effects on business and consumer behaviour in each case can be very different and the consequences for the economy will also vary. A change in monetary and fiscal policy can lead to short-run fluctuations in output and prices; the effects of changes to supply-side policy tend to be longer term. Fiscal and monetary policies tend to have an impact on aggregate demand whereas supply-side policies are focused on the aggregate supply curve.

Many factors influence aggregate demand besides monetary and fiscal policy. In particular, desired spending by households and firms determines the overall demand for goods and services. When desired spending changes, aggregate demand shifts. If policy makers do not respond, such shifts in aggregate demand cause short-run fluctuations in output and employment. As a result, monetary and fiscal policy makers sometimes use the policy levers at their disposal to try to offset these shifts in aggregate demand and thereby stabilize the economy. Here we discuss the theory behind these policy actions and some of the difficulties that arise in using this theory in practice.

MONETARY POLICY

Monetary policy refers to attempts to influence the level of economic activity (the amount of buying and selling in the economy) through changes to the amount of money in circulation and the price of money – short-term interest rates. The basis of the relationship between the money supply and inflation is set out in the classical quantity theory of money encapsulated in the formula:

$$MV = PY$$

where M = the money stock, V = velocity of circulation, P = price level and Y = level of national income. This can be stated more formally as:

$$M_d = kPY$$

where P is the price level, Y is the level of real national income, M_d is demand for money for transactions purposes, and k = proportion of national income held as transactions balances.

In equilibrium $M_d = M_s$, so:

$$P = (1/kY \times Ms).$$

It follows that a rise in M_s will lead to a proportional rise in P.

The main weapon used to control the money supply is interest rates set by the central bank. Changes in the rate at which the central bank lends to the banking system helps determine the structure of interest rates throughout the financial system. The structure of interest rates then feeds through to different parts of the economy through the *interest rate transmission mechanism*. This transmission mechanism is summarized in Figure 20.1. In panel (a), changes in interest rates affect the amount of borrowing by businesses and individuals which in turn affect levels of consumption and investment. At the same time, businesses which have existing loans may find that the cost of servicing the loan changes if interest rates rise. Higher interest rates affects costs and margins and may cause firms to cut back production or find other ways to reduce costs such as shed employment. If workers lose their jobs and their incomes fall, this affects consumption.

monetary policy the set of actions taken by the central bank in order to affect the money supply

FIGURE 20.1

The Interest Rate Transmission Mechanism

The three panels (a), (b) and (c) show the effect of changes in interest rates on different parts of the economy. In panel (a), the effect is traced through changes to borrowing by individuals and firms on consumption and investment. In panel (b) the effect is traced through mortgage holders and savers and in panel (c) the effect on exchange rates, import and export prices and the subsequent demand for imports and exports is shown, which together have an impact on net exports.

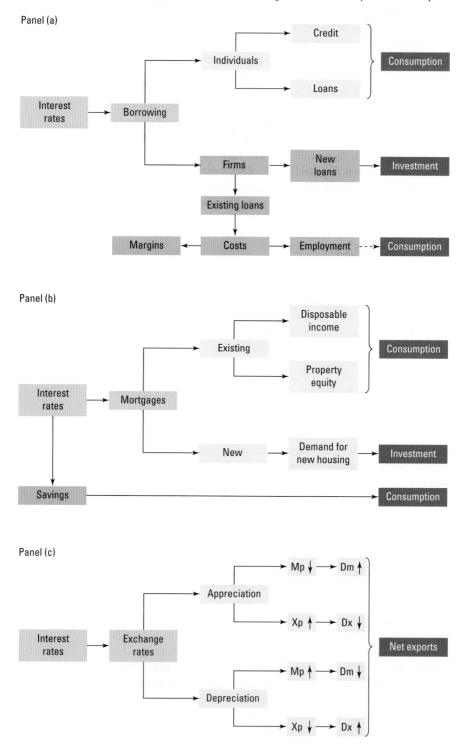

In panel (b), the effect occurs through mortgages and savings. Changes to interest rates affect those with mortgages and can impact on disposable income thus affecting consumption. It will also affect the demand for new mortgages and can feed through to investment in housing stock. There might also be changes to property prices which can affect homeowners' equity. For example, if interest rates rise significantly the demand for mortgages might fall, which in turn slows down the housing market causing a fall in house prices. The fall in house prices can leave some homeowners in a position where the value of their mortgage is greater than the value of the property. If they have to sell they end up saddled with debt and this may lead to them cutting their consumption. There will also be effects from changes in interest rates on savings. Between 2009 and 2015, interest rates across the developed world have remained very low and savers have found that returns have been weak as a result. This affects their consumption. Low interest rates also tend to discourage saving and this can not only lead to increased consumption (remember, $Y = C + S$) but also have an effect on funds available for investment through the financial system.

Panel (c) shows how changes in interest rates feed through to exchange rates. If the central bank changes interest rates and other countries interest rates remain constant, then the difference in relative interest rates affects the demand and supply of currencies as traders look to move funds to higher interest rate countries to improve returns. This affects the demand and supply of currencies causing an appreciation or depreciation which in turn affects import and export prices (denoted by M_p and X_p respectively), and the demand for imports and exports. There will be a resulting effect on net exports.

The Central Bank's Tools of Monetary Control

The central bank is responsible for controlling the supply of money in the economy. When the central bank decides to change the money supply, it must consider how its actions will work through the banking system.

In general, a central bank has three main tools in its monetary toolbox: open-market operations, the refinancing rate and reserve requirements.

Open-Market Operations   If the central bank wants to increase the money supply, it can create currency and use it to buy bonds from the public in the bond market. After the purchase, the extra currency is in the hands of the public. Thus, an open-market purchase of bonds by the central bank increases the money supply. If, on the other hand, the central bank wants to decrease the money supply, it can sell bonds from its portfolio to the public. After the sale, the currency it receives for the bonds is out of the hands of the public. Thus an open-market sale of bonds by the central bank decreases the money supply. To be precise, the open-market operations discussed in these simple examples are called outright open-market operations, because they each involve an outright sale or purchase of non-monetary assets to or from the banking sector without a corresponding agreement to reverse the transaction at a later date.

The Refinancing Rate   The central bank of an economy will set an interest rate at which it is willing to lend to commercial banks on a short-term basis.

The way in which the central bank lends to the banking sector is through a special form of open-market operations. In the previous paragraph we discussed the use of outright open-market operations. Although outright open-market operations have traditionally been used by central banks to regulate the money supply, central banks nowadays more often use a slightly more sophisticated form of open-market operations that involves buying bonds or other assets from banks and at the same time agreeing to sell them back later. When it does this, the central bank has effectively made a loan and taken the bonds or other assets as collateral or security on the loan. The central bank will have a list of eligible assets that it will accept as collateral – 'safe' assets such as government bonds or assets issued by large corporations, on which the risk of default by the issuer is negligible. The interest rate that the central bank charges on the loan is the refinancing rate. Because the central bank has bought the assets but the seller has agreed to buy them back later at an agreed price, this kind of open-market operation is often called a repurchase agreement or 'repo' for short. To see how central bank's use repos as a means of controlling the money supply and how this is affected by the refinancing rate, we need to look a little more closely at the way commercial banks lend money to one another and borrow from the central bank.

Banks need to carry enough reserves to cover their lending and will generally aim for a certain ratio of reserves to deposits, known as the reserve ratio. The minimum reserve ratio may be set by the central bank, but even if it isn't, banks will still have a reserve ratio that they consider prudent. Now, because deposits and withdrawals at banks can fluctuate randomly, some banks may find that they have an excess of reserves one day (i.e. their reserve ratio is above the level the bank considers prudent or above the minimum reserve ratio, or both), while other banks may find that they are short of reserves and their reserve ratio is too low. Therefore, the commercial banks in an economy will generally lend money to one another on a short-term basis – overnight to a couple of weeks – so that banks with excess reserves can lend them to banks who have inadequate reserves to cover their lending. This market for short-term reserves is called the money market. If there is a general shortage of liquidity in the money market (because the banks together have done a lot of lending), then the short-term interest rate at which they lend to one another will begin to rise, while it will begin to fall if there is excess liquidity among banks. The central bank closely monitors the money market and may intervene in it in order to affect the supply of liquidity to banks, which in turn affects their lending and hence affects the money supply.

Suppose, for example, that there is a shortage of liquidity in the market because the banks have been increasing their lending and they need to increase their reserves. A commercial bank may then attempt to obtain liquidity from the central bank by selling assets to the central bank and at the same time agreeing to purchase them back a short time later. As we said before, in this type of open-market operation the central bank effectively lends money to the bank and takes the assets as collateral on the loan. Because the commercial bank is legally bound to repurchase the assets at a set price, this is called a 'repurchase agreement' and the difference between the price the bank sells the assets to the central bank and the price at which it agrees to buy them back, expressed as an annualized percentage of the selling price, is called the repurchase or repo rate by the Bank of England and the refinancing rate by the European Central Bank. The ECB's refinancing rate is thus the rate at which it will lend to the banking sector of the euro area, while the repo rate is the rate at which the Bank of England lends short term to the UK banking sector.

In the example given, the central bank added liquidity to the banking system by lending reserves to banks. This would have the effect of increasing the money supply. Because the loans made through open-market operations are typically very short term, with a maturity of at most two weeks, the banks are constantly having to repay the loans and borrow again, or 'refinance' the loans. If the central bank wants to mop up liquidity it can simply decide not to renew some of the loans. In practice, however, the central bank will set a reference rate of interest – the Bank of

England's repo rate or the ECB's refinancing rate – and will conduct open-market operations, adding to or mopping up liquidity, close to this reference rate.

In the USA the interest rate at which the Federal Reserve lends to the banking sector (corresponding to the ECB's refinancing rate or the Bank of England's repo rate) is called the discount rate.

Now we can see why the setting of the central bank's refinancing rate is the key instrument of monetary policy. If the central bank raises the refinancing rate, commercial banks will try and rein in their lending rather than borrow reserves from the central bank, and so the money supply will fall. If the central bank lowers the refinancing rate, banks will feel freer to lend, knowing that they will be able to borrow more cheaply from the central bank in order to meet their reserve requirements, and so the money supply will tend to rise.

Reserve Requirements   The central bank may also influence the money supply with reserve requirements, which are regulations on the minimum amount of reserves that banks must hold against deposits. Reserve requirements influence how much money the banking system can create with each euro of reserves.

The amount of money the banking system generates with each euro of reserves is called the **money multiplier**. It is important to remember that when banks make loans no new 'cash' (actual notes and coins) is created. Most transactions in modern economies are simply 'book entries'; when you get a bank statement telling you that there is a balance of €1500 in your current account there is not a box with this sum of money stored somewhere in the bank's vault. The banking system is such that we have trust that if we did wish to withdraw all that money in cash the bank would have sufficient funds to be able to meet our demand. The size of the money multiplier is the reciprocal of the reserve ratio. If R is the reserve ratio for all banks in the economy, then each euro of reserves generates euros of money. If the reserve ratio is set at $R = \frac{1}{10}$, the money multiplier is 10.

> **money multiplier** the amount of money the banking system generates with each unit of reserves

This reciprocal formula for the money multiplier makes sense. If a bank holds €1000 in deposits, then a reserve ratio of $\frac{1}{10}$ (10 per cent) means that the bank must hold €100 in reserves. The money multiplier just turns this idea around: if the banking system as a whole holds a total of €100 in reserves, it can have only €1000 in deposits. In other words, if R is the ratio of reserves to deposits at each bank (that is, the reserve ratio), then the ratio of deposits to reserves in the banking system (that is, the money multiplier) must be $\frac{1}{r}$.

If the reserve ratio is changed by the central bank then the money multiplier changes. If the reserve ratio were $\frac{1}{20}$ (5 per cent), then the banking system would have 20 times as much in deposits as in reserves, implying a money multiplier of 20. Each euro of reserves would generate €20 of money. Similarly, if the reserve ratio were $\frac{1}{5}$ (20 per cent), deposits would be 5 times reserves, the money multiplier would be 5, and each euro of reserves would generate €5 of money. Thus, the higher the reserve ratio, the less of each deposit banks lend out and the smaller the money multiplier.

Central banks have traditionally tended to use changes in reserve requirements only rarely because frequent changes would disrupt the business of banking. When the central bank increases reserve requirements, for instance, some banks find themselves short of reserves, even though they have seen no change in deposits. As a result, they have to curtail lending until they build their level of reserves to the new required level.

Following the financial crisis, negotiations have taken place on improving banks' reserves to avoid the problems faced during the crisis. The so-called Basel III negotiations between 27 countries set new reserve requirements in September 2010. The new rules came into force in 2013 and will be phased in over a period of 6 years. The regulations mean that banks will have to have higher reserves to support lending; for every €50 of lending banks will have to have €3.50 of reserves compared to €1 prior to the Basel III agreement. This obviously more than triples the amount of reserves that banks will have to keep. If banks do not adhere to the new regulations then they risk seeing the authorities placing restrictions on their activities, including paying out dividends to shareholders and bonuses to staff.

Problems in Controlling the Money Supply

Through the setting of its refinancing rate and the associated open-market operations, the central bank can exert an important degree of control over the money supply. Yet the central bank's control of the money supply is not precise. The central bank must wrestle with two problems, each of which arises because much of the money supply is created by the system of fractional-reserve banking.

The first problem is that the central bank does not control the amount of money that households choose to hold as deposits in banks. The more money that households deposit, the more reserves banks have, and the more money the banking system can create. The less money households deposit, the less reserves banks have, and the less money the banking system can create. To see why this is a problem, suppose that one day people begin to lose confidence in the banking system and, therefore, decide to withdraw deposits and hold more cash. When this happens, the banking system loses reserves and creates less money. The money supply falls, even without any central bank action.

The second problem of monetary control is that the central bank does not control the amount that bankers choose to lend. When money is deposited in a bank, it creates more money only when the bank lends it out. Because banks can choose to hold excess reserves instead, the central bank cannot be sure how much money the banking system will create. For instance, suppose that one day bankers become more cautious about economic conditions and decide to make fewer loans and hold greater reserves. In this case, the banking system creates less money than it otherwise would. This is a situation which has arisen following the financial crisis and the consequences are that many businesses have found it harder to secure vital loans for managing their business or for expansion or that the price of securing a loan is prohibitively high. Because of the bankers' decision, the money supply falls.

> **Quick Quiz** If the ECB wanted to use all three of its policy tools to decrease the money supply, what would it do?

FISCAL POLICY

fiscal policy influencing the level of economic activity through manipulation of government income and expenditure

Fiscal policy involves influencing the level of economic activity though manipulation of government income and expenditure. It works through affecting key variables in aggregate demand, consumption, investment and government spending. In most developed countries, government spending accounts for around 40 per cent of total spending. This fact alone suggests that governments can have a significant effect on economic activity.

In 1936, economist John Maynard Keynes published a book entitled *The General Theory of Employment, Interest and Money*, which attempted to explain short-run economic fluctuations in general and the Great Depression in particular. Keynes' primary message was that recessions and depressions can occur because of inadequate aggregate demand for goods and services. Keynes had long been a critic of classical economic theory because it could explain only the long-run effects of policies.

When he published *The General Theory*, the world's economies were suffering very high levels of unemployment. Keynes advocated policies to increase aggregate demand through the government manipulating its own income and expenditure through changing taxes and government spending on public works. Keynes argued that short-run interventions in the economy could lead to improvements in the economy that would be beneficial rather than waiting for the long-run equilibrium to establish itself.

The Keynesian Cross

Classical economics placed a fundamental reliance on the efficiency of markets and the assumption that they clear. At a macro level, this meant that if the economy was in disequilibrium and unemployment existed, wages and prices would adjust to bring the economy back into equilibrium at full employment. **Full employment** is defined as a point where those people who want to work at the going market wage level are able to find a job. Any unemployment that did exist would be classed as voluntary unemployment. The experience of the Great Depression of the 1930s brought the classical assumptions under closer scrutiny; the many millions suffering from unemployment could not all be volunteering to not take jobs at the going wage rates so some must, therefore, have been involuntarily unemployed.

Fundamental to Keynesian analysis is the distinction between planned and actual decisions by households and firms. **Planned spending, saving or investment** refers to the desired or intended actions of firms and households. A publisher may plan to sell 1000 copies of a textbook in the first three months of the year, an individual may plan to go on holiday to Turkey in the summer and to save up to finance the trip, a person may intend to save €1000 over the year to pay for a wedding in the following year.

Actual spending, saving or investment refers to the realized, ex post (after the event) outcome. The publisher may only sell 800 copies in the first three months and so has a build-up of stock of 200 more than planned; the holidaymaker may fall ill and so is unable to go on holiday and so actual consumption is lower than planned (whereas actual saving is more than planned) and the plans for saving for the wedding may be compromised by the need to spend the money on repairing a house damaged by a flood.

Planned and actual outcomes might be very different as briefly outlined above. As a result Keynes argued that there was no reason why equilibrium national income would coincide with full employment output. Wages and prices might not adjust in the short run (so-called sticky wages and prices) and so the economy could be at a position where the level of demand in the economy was insufficient to bring about full employment. It is useful at this point to refer back to the circular flow of income described in Chapter 16. Households and firms interact in the market for goods and services and in the factor market. Recall also the identity given in Chapter 16 which described how a country's gross domestic product (national income, Y) is divided among four components, i.e. consumption spending, investment spending, spending by government and net exports. Figure 20.2 summarizes this analysis.

In panels (a) and (b), the 45° line connects all points where consumption spending would be equal to national income. This line can be thought of as the equivalent of the capacity of the economy – the aggregate supply (*AS*) curve. The economy is in equilibrium where the $C + I + G + NX$ line cuts the 45° line at Y_1. In panel (a) the equilibrium is less than that required to give full employment output (Y_f). At this equilibrium there is spare capacity in the economy and unemployment will rise. The difference between full employment output and the expenditure required

full employment a point where those people who want to work at the going market wage level are able to find a job

planned spending, saving or investment the desired or intended actions of households and firms

actual spending, saving or investment the realized or ex post outcome resulting from actions of households and firms

deflationary/inflationary gap the difference between full employment output and the expenditure required to meet it

to meet it is termed the **deflationary gap**. In panel (b) equilibrium is above full employment output and in this case the economy does not have the capacity to meet the demand. This will trigger inflationary pressures in the economy. The difference between full employment output and the expenditure line here is called the **inflationary gap**. To eradicate these gaps governments can influence the components of aggregate demand through both fiscal and monetary policy to bring about an equilibrium that is closer to the desired full employment output.

FIGURE 20.2

Deflationary and Inflationary Gaps

The 45° line shows all the points where consumption spending equals income. The vertical intercept of the expenditure line shows autonomous expenditure. The economy is in equilibrium where the expenditure line, $C + I + G + NX$, cuts the 45° line. In panel (a) this equilibrium is lower than full employment output Y_f; at Y_1 there is insufficient demand to maintain full employment output. The government would need to shift the expenditure line up to $C + I + G + NX_1$ to eliminate the deflationary gap as shown. In panel (b) the equilibrium is higher than full employment output – the economy does not have the capacity to meet demand. In this case the government needs to shift the $C + I + G + NX$ line down to $C + I + G + NX_2$ to eliminate the inflationary gap.

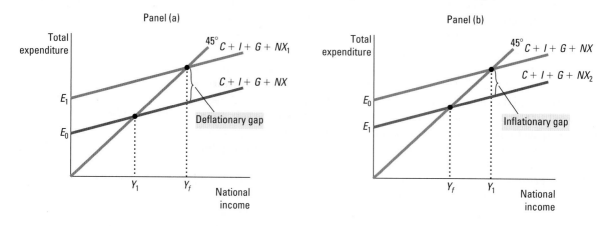

The Multiplier Effect

When a government makes a purchase, say a contract for €10 billion to build a new nuclear power generating station, that purchase has repercussions. The immediate impact of the higher demand from the government is to raise employment and profits at the construction company (which we shall call Nucelec). Nucelec, in turn, has to buy resources from other contractors to carry out the job and so these suppliers also experience an increase in orders. Then, as the workers see higher earnings and the firm owners see higher profits, they respond to this increase in income by raising their own spending on consumer goods. As a result, the government purchase from Nucelec raises the demand for the products of many other firms and consumers in the economy. Because each euro spent by the government can raise the aggregate demand for goods and services by more than a euro, government purchases are said to have a **multiplier effect** on aggregate demand.

multiplier effect the additional shifts in aggregate demand that result when expansionary fiscal policy increases income and thereby increases consumer spending

This multiplier effect continues even after this first round. When consumer spending rises, the firms that produce these consumer goods hire more people and experience higher profits. Higher earnings and profits stimulate consumer spending once again and so on. Thus, there is positive feedback as higher demand leads to higher income, which in turn leads to even higher demand. Once all these effects are added together, the total impact on the quantity of goods and services demanded can be much larger than the initial impulse from higher government spending.

This multiplier effect arising from the response of consumer spending can be strengthened by the response of investment to higher levels of demand. For instance, Nucelec might respond to the higher demand for building services by buying more cranes and other mechanized building equipment. In this case, higher government demand spurs higher demand for investment goods. This positive feedback from demand to investment is sometimes called the investment accelerator.

A Formula for the Spending Multiplier

A little algebra permits us to derive a formula for the size of the multiplier effect that arises from consumer spending. An important number in this formula is the **marginal propensity to consume** (*MPC*) – the fraction of extra income that a household spends rather than saves. For example, suppose that the marginal propensity to consume is ¾. This means that for every extra pound or euro that a household earns, the household spends 75p or 75c of it and saves 25p or 25c. The **marginal propensity to save** is the fraction of extra income that a household saves rather than consumes. With an *MPC* of ¾, when the workers and owners of Nucelec earn €10 billion from the government contract, they increase their consumer spending by ¾ × €10 billion, or €7.5 billion.

> **marginal propensity to consume** the fraction of extra income that a household spends rather than saves

> **marginal propensity to save** the fraction of extra income that a household saves rather than consumes

To gauge the impact on aggregate demand of a change in government purchases, we follow the effects step-by-step. The process begins when the government spends €10 billion, which implies that national income (earnings and profits) also rises by this amount. This increase in income in turn raises consumer spending by *MPC* × €10 billion, which in turn raises the income for the workers and owners of the firms that produce the consumption goods. This second increase in income again raises consumer spending, this time by *MPC* × (*MPC* × €10 billion). These feedback effects go on and on.

To find the total impact on the demand for goods and services, we add up all these effects:

Change in government purchases	= €10 billion
First change in consumption	= *MPC* × €10 billion
Second change in consumption	= MPC^2 × €10 billion
Third change in consumption	= MPC^3 × €10 billion
Total change in demand	= $(1 + MPC + MPC^2 + MPC^3 = ...)$ × €10 billion

Here, '...' represents an infinite number of similar terms. Thus, we can write the multiplier as follows:

$$\text{Multiplier} = 1 + MPC + MPC^2 + MPC^3 + \cdots$$

This multiplier tells us the demand for goods and services that each euro of government purchases generates.

To simplify this equation for the multiplier, recall from your school algebra that this expression is an infinite geometric series. For *x* between −1 and 1:

$$1 + x + x^2 + x^3 + \cdots = \frac{1}{(1 - x)}$$

The sum of this series, as the number of terms tends to infinity, is given by the expression:

$$\frac{1}{1 - x}$$

In our case, *x* = *MPC*. Thus:

$$\text{Multiplier} = \frac{1}{(1 - MPC)}$$

Note, the $MPC + MPS = 1$ so the multiplier can also be expressed as:

$$\text{Multiplier} = \frac{1}{MPS}$$

For example, if MPC is ¾, the multiplier is $1/(1-¾)$, which is 4. In this case, the €10 billion of government spending generates €40 billion of demand for goods and services.

This formula for the multiplier shows an important conclusion: the size of the multiplier depends on the marginal propensity to consume. While an MPC of ¾ leads to a multiplier of 4, an MPC of ½ leads to a multiplier of only 2. Thus, a larger MPC means a larger multiplier. To see why this is true, remember that the multiplier arises because higher income induces greater spending on consumption. The larger the MPC is, the greater is this induced effect on consumption, and the larger is the multiplier.

? **what if** ...the government did some research and found that the MPC for the wealthiest 20 per cent of the population was 0.3 but that the MPC for the poorest 20 per cent was 0.95. What might the explanation for this difference be and how might this affect policy decisions on tax changes to boost the economy?

Other Applications of the Multiplier Effect

Because of the multiplier effect, a euro of government purchases can generate more than a euro of aggregate demand. The logic of the multiplier effect, however, is not restricted to changes in government purchases. Instead, it applies to any event that alters spending on any component of GDP – consumption, investment, government purchases or net exports.

For example, suppose that a recession overseas reduces the demand for German net exports by €1 billion. This reduced spending on German goods and services depresses German national income, which reduces spending by German consumers. If the MPC is ¾ and the multiplier is 4, then the €1 billion fall in net exports means a €4 billion contraction in aggregate demand.

As another example, suppose that a stock market boom increases households' wealth and stimulates their spending on goods and services by €2 billion. This extra consumer spending increases national income, which in turn generates even more consumer spending. If the MPC is ¾ and the multiplier is 4, then the initial impulse of €2 billion in consumer spending translates into an €8 billion increase in aggregate demand.

The multiplier is an important concept in macroeconomics because it shows how the economy can amplify the impact of changes in spending. A small initial change in consumption, investment, government purchases or net exports can end up having a large effect on aggregate demand and, therefore, on the economy's production of goods and services.

autonomous expenditure spending which is not dependent on income

Another important concept in this analysis is that of **autonomous expenditure** – spending which does not depend on income – government spending being a key element of this expenditure. The amount spent in each successive 'round' of spending is termed induced expenditure. The multiplier showed how the eventual change in income would be determined by the size of the MPC and the MPS – the proportion of an extra €1 spent or saved by consumers. The higher the MPC the greater the multiplier effect.

In an open economy with government, any extra €1 is not simply either spent or saved, some of the extra income may be spent on imported goods and services or go to the government in taxation. These are all classed as withdrawals from the circular flow of income. Withdrawals (W) from the circular flow are classed as endogenous as they are directly related to changes in income. There are also injections to the circular flow of income. Governments receive tax revenue but use it to spend on the goods and services they provide for citizens, firms earn revenue from selling goods abroad (exports) and firms, as we have seen, use savings as a source of funds to borrow for investment. Injections into the circular flow are exogenous – they are not related to the level of output or income – and are investment (I), government spending (G) and export earnings (X).

The slope of the expenditure line, therefore, will be dependent on how much of each extra €1 is withdrawn. There will be a marginal propensity to taxation (MPT), a marginal propensity to import (MPM) in addition to the MPS. Collectively these are referred to as the marginal propensity to withdraw (MPW). The multiplier (k) would be expressed as:

$$k = \frac{1}{MPS + MPT + MPM}$$

or:

$$k = \frac{1}{MPW}$$

A higher MPW will reduce the value of the multiplier and thus the impact on national income. In equilibrium, planned withdrawals would equal planned injections:

$$\text{Planned } S + T + M = \text{Planned } I + G + X$$

At this point all the output being produced by the economy would be 'bought' by households and firms. However, if actual withdrawals are greater than planned injections then the economy would be experiencing a deficiency in demand. For example, assume that equilibrium output is €100 billion. Planned withdrawals amount to €60 billion. If this planned withdrawal level is not 'bought' by governments, firms and foreigners (i.e. planned injections) then firms will build up stocks and plan to cut back on output in the next period. This leads to a fall in income and as withdrawals are endogenous, planned withdrawals for the next period will fall. The process will continue until planned withdrawals equal planned injections once again, and the economy is in equilibrium.

In situations where the economy is experiencing such demand deficiency, the government can budget for a deficit (i.e. spend more than it receives in tax revenue by borrowing or cutting taxes) to boost spending in the economy. It could also influence monetary policy to cut the cost of borrowing and so boost investment; there may also have been an incentive to find ways of boosting exports or cutting imports through imposing various trade barriers and offering export subsidies. However, if the emphasis is primarily on fiscal policy, the direct influence the government can have over tax and spending can mean that the effect is more immediate. The multiplier process means that the increase in government spending does not need to be as high as the size of the inflationary or deflationary gap. The steeper the slope of the expenditure line the greater the size of the multiplier, as shown in Figure 20.3.

The Keynesian cross, as it is known, gives us a picture of the economy in short-run equilibrium. (Note, if you access a copy of Keynes' *General Theory* you might be surprised to see a complete absence of Keynesian cross diagrams. The use of these diagrams to explain Keynesian ideas was developed by later economists to help portray Keynes' ideas.) In equilibrium, planned expenditure (E), ($C + I + G + \text{NX}$)

real money balances what money can actually buy given the ratio of the money supply to the price level	equals actual income (GDP or national income (Y)), (E = Y). This equilibrium is referred to as equilibrium in the goods market. Equilibrium in the money market is given by the intersection of the demand for money and the supply of **real money balances**. The goods market and the money market are both inter-related with the linking factor being the interest rate.

FIGURE 20.3

The Slope of the Expenditure Line and Changes in Autonomous Expenditure

Panel (a) shows a relatively shallow expenditure line which would mean that the marginal propensity to withdraw would be high and the value of the multiplier relatively low. The impact on national income (ΔY) of a change in government spending (ΔG) would be more limited in comparison to the effect as shown in panel (b) where the expenditure line is much steeper, reflecting a higher value of the multiplier where the MPW was relatively low. In this case it takes a smaller rise in government spending to achieve the same increase in national income.

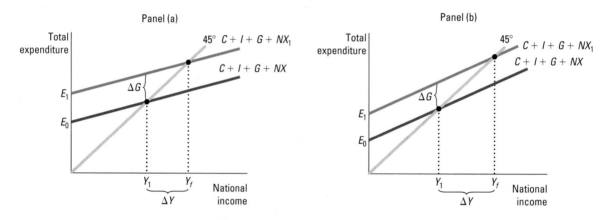

JEOPARDY PROBLEM

Over a 30-year period a government adopts demand management policies as its primary weapon in managing its economy. After 20 years, politicians are congratulating themselves on maintaining low levels of inflation, consistent growth of around 2 per cent a year and unemployment below 5 per cent. However, in the next few years things seem to go wrong. Unemployment starts to rise and inflation accelerates to over 9 per cent. What might have gone wrong?

CASE STUDY

Job Generation in Clusters

Governments are keen to point out the magic of the multiplier effect when making additional domestic purchases, encouraging inward investment or indeed when consumer spending increases, is influenced by whatever macroeconomic policy is in force. The point being that the positive effect on employment and income is a multiple of the initial cause of change.

However, the geographical impact of the multiplier is not evenly felt. One argument put forward is that certain cities or regions gain whilst others are left behind. The regional imbalance in house price changes in a country might provide some evidence to support this view.

The Millennium Bridge in Newcastle.

Research by Enrico Moretti in the US points to a divergence between go-getting cities like Austin in Texas, Boston in Massachusetts, and Seattle in Washington State, which are becoming engines of prosperity, and other cities and regions of the country. He points out that workers in these growing cities are producing two to three times the levels identical workers are making in cities that are losing ground.

He points out that job generation happens in clusters, because these growing cities have the 'right' industries and a solid base of human capital. They, in turn, attract growing companies. These, often, high-tech companies can generate five times as many indirect jobs as direct ones. What's more, these indirect jobs include skilled work such as lawyers and teachers, as well as unskilled work such as restaurant service staff.

Moretti suggests that the innovation sector's multiplier effect is three times larger than for manufacturing. It implies that the best way to increase low skilled job opportunities in a city is to attract high-tech companies. However, can government really influence where these industries locate and create job hubs? Moretti doesn't think so. He has proposed that a government should encourage those out of work in areas of high unemployment to move to areas of stronger economic activity.

What would this mean for the UK? Since 2010 there has been a notable shift in jobs from the public sector to the private sector. Areas such as Wales and North-East England, where dependency on public sector employment was higher than average, have suffered most. Wales and North-East England had the poorest gross value added (GVA) per head figures in 2013. Between 2010 and 2013 London's performance outshone those of other cities. The next best city was Birmingham. Liverpool and Bristol showed a decline in GVA per head over the period. What is more, unemployment rates are highest in several of the older northern industrial cities including those in North-East England. It implies a problem and according to Moretti, unemployed in these areas should be encouraged to move to where the growth is such as London, but house prices in the capital are already well beyond the reach of many. Sorting out regional inequality is an enormous challenge.

Another option would be to shift capital spending north from London. The Conservative government elected in May 2015 has committed to a £15bn infrastructure investment plan for five northern cities to make them better connected and create a so-called 'northern powerhouse'. But looking at the spend per resident on publicly funded infrastructure shows that far more is spent in London per person than anywhere else. The figure is £5 426 per head compared to £1 248 for the north-west and as low as £223 for the north-east according to a report by the Institute for Public Policy and Research (IPPR).

References: **http://sloanreview.mit.edu/article/the-multiplier-effect-of-innovation-jobs/**

https://www.gov.uk/government/uploads/system/uploads/attachment_data/file/396740/bis-15-4-growth-dashboard.pdf

http://www.publicfinance.co.uk/news/2014/08/ippr-north-seeks-infrastructure-ideas/

SUPPLY-SIDE POLICIES

supply-side policy policy aimed at influencing the level of aggregate supply in the economy

Supply-side policy is a macroeconomic policy that seeks to improve the efficiency of the operation of markets to increase the capacity of the economy. The aim of such a policy is to shift the aggregate supply curve to the right and in so doing generate economic growth (and thus reduce unemployment) but without creating inflationary pressures.

This is illustrated in Figure 20.4. The aggregate supply curve is shown as a curve which gets steeper as it approaches full employment output Y_f, where the long-run aggregate supply would be vertical. Assume equilibrium output is initially at a price level of 2.3 per cent and an output level of Y_0 where the *AD* curve cuts the *AS* curve.

If the capacity of the economy was increased by policies which shift the *AS* curve to the right to AS_1, then the economy could not only support a higher level of output (and hence reduce unemployment) but also reduce the price level to 2.0 per cent.

FIGURE 20.4

Shifting Aggregate Supply

Successful supply-side policies could increase the capacity of the economy by shifting the AS curve to the right to AS₁. Given aggregate demand (AD), the economy could now support an increased level of capacity from Y_f to Y_{f2} and lower inflation from 2.3 per cent to 2.0 per cent.

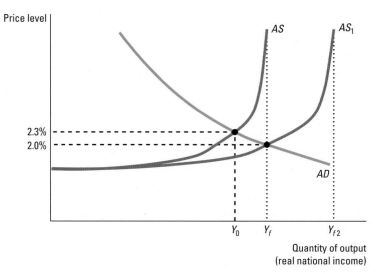

Supply-side policies are characterized by a number of features detailed in the following subsections.

Deregulation

deregulation the removal of controls, laws or rules governing a particular market aimed at improving the economic efficiency of that market and therefore the performance of the economy at the microeconomic level

Deregulation refers to the removal of controls, laws or rules governing a particular market aimed at improving the economic efficiency of that market and therefore the performance of the economy at the microeconomic level. An example would be the abandonment of a licensing system for taxis or reducing the processes, procedures and paperwork that entrepreneurs need to go through in order to set up a new business. **Deregulation** aims to help promote enterprise, risk and incentives and create a climate where private businesses can go about their activities unencumbered by bureaucracy and distractions.

Tax Laws

Reducing the tax burden on individuals and companies is seen as a key part of supply-side policy with the aim of promoting incentives which may include incentives to work rather than claim benefits, to be entrepreneurial, to invest and to expand. Part of such tax changes might include reductions in business taxes on profits and payroll and reductions in income taxes. The emphasis may instead be switched from direct to indirect taxes so that people have choices as to whether they spend money on items that attract indirect taxes such as value added tax (VAT) but do not have such choices with regard to their income. Part of the basis for reducing income taxes is linked to the Laffer curve. So the story goes, in 1974, the American economist Arthur Laffer sat in a Washington restaurant with some prominent journalists and politicians. He took out a napkin and drew a figure on it to show how tax rates affect tax revenue. It looked much like Figure 20.5. Laffer then suggested that the USA was on the downward sloping side of this curve. Tax rates were so high, he argued, that reducing them would actually raise tax revenue. Economists have, however, found it hard to trace any strong incentive effects of tax cuts leading to increases in total tax revenue, as the Laffer curve would suggest. A study by the UK Institute for Fiscal Studies (IFS), for example, concluded that at most about 3 per cent of the increase in tax revenue between 1980 and 1986 in the UK could be attributed to income tax cuts in 1980. Evidence from the US was less convincing.

Laffer's argument is not completely without merit, however. Although an overall cut in tax rates normally reduces revenue, some taxpayers at some times may be on the wrong side of the Laffer curve. The idea that cutting taxes can raise revenue may be correct if applied to those taxpayers facing the highest tax rates, but most people face lower marginal rates. Where the typical worker is on the top end of the Laffer curve, it may be more appropriate. In Sweden in the early 1980s, for instance, the typical worker faced a marginal tax rate of about 80 per cent. Such a high tax rate provides a substantial disincentive to work. Studies have suggested that Sweden would indeed have raised more tax revenue if it had lowered its tax rates.

Part of the disagreement over the Laffer curve is about the size of the relevant elasticities. The more elastic supply and demand are in any market, the more taxes distort behaviour, and the more likely it is that a tax cut will raise tax revenue. There is no debate, however, about the general lesson: how much revenue the government gains or loses from a tax change cannot be computed just by looking at tax rates. It also depends on how the tax change affects people's behaviour.

FIGURE 20.5

The Laffer Curve

The Laffer curve is the name given to the relationship between tax and revenue which shows that tax revenue rises at first but then falls.

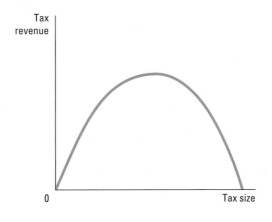

CASE STUDY

Why Would We Lower the Tax Rates of the Biggest Earners?

The concept behind the Laffer curve is not actually a recent one. It dates right back to the 14th century and the ideas of Ibn Khaldun of Tunis. He made many significant contributions to the field of economics, but of relevance for this chapter are his views on tax and the role of government.

According to Ibn Khaldun, at the beginning of a ruling dynasty, taxation yields large revenues from small assessments. Tax revenues of the ruling dynasty increase because of business prosperity, which flourishes with easy, not excessive taxes. The idea is that charging small rates of tax will bring in lots of tax revenue. 'When tax assessments and imposts upon the subjects are low, the latter have the energy and desire to do things. Cultural enterprises grow and increase, because the low taxes bring satisfaction. … When cultural enterprises grow, the number of individual imposts and assessments mount. In consequence, the tax revenue, which is the sum total of the individual assessments, increases.' However, at the end of the dynasty after increases in tax levels, taxation yields small revenue from large assessments, because of the loss of incentives.

He was therefore the first in history to lay the foundation of a theory for the optimum rate of taxation, a theory that was adopted by Arthur Laffer among others. The Laffer curve is merely a graphical presentation of the ideas of Ibn Khaldun.

Reference: An article by Ibrahim M. Oweiss **http://www9.georgetown.edu/faculty/imo3 /ibn.htm**

Welfare Reform The welfare policies adopted by countries are designed to help support those in society who are most vulnerable. Welfare benefits may include some sort of health insurance, unemployment insurance, disability and housing benefits and so on. However, whilst the system is designed to support the most vulnerable, it is invariably also open to abuse and accusations that some individuals in society come to rely on state benefits rather than helping themselves. When this happens, long-term unemployment becomes more likely and not only is the opportunity cost of lost output a factor in reducing the efficiency of the economy, but government spending increases.

Adjustments to welfare policy, therefore, aim to reverse these incentives and to encourage those out of work to try to find employment rather than rely on the state. This might include amendments to the tax and benefits system that make the hoops people have to go through to claim benefit harder, as well as making the financial incentive of getting work more significant. Such a policy is fraught with problems because every individual who feels they have a need which society should help them with, might expect some support, but the definition of what those needs are and what level of support is required, vary tremendously. There is also the problem of the poverty trap, the problems people face when moving from state support to work whereby tax systems may mean an individual can be worse off by having a job because they become liable for paying tax. Every government is very aware of the potential for damaging news headlines about how policies have left families 'in need' hungry, destitute and worse off as a result.

Flexible Labour Markets Flexible labour markets focus on the ease with which the demand and supply of labour responds to changing wage conditions. This determines the extent to which unemployment or underemployment will exist in the economy. **Underemployment** is a situation where a worker has a job but may not be working to full capacity or does not have all their skills utilized or is working for a lower income than their qualifications, training or experience might suggest.

Elements of reforming the labour market to make it more flexible might include new employment regulations or legislation relating to the hiring, firing and dealing with employees. A firm with a very seasonal operation, for example, may need large numbers of workers at certain times of the year but very few at others. If the market mechanism is working effectively then, in theory, the firm will be able to do this but if there are restrictions to the working of the labour market then this may not be possible and as such, workers may be left without jobs that technically are available; or where a firm has labour which is underutilized because they have to be retained and paid even if there is insufficient work for them.

The more flexibility firms have to match the workforce to their output needs, the more efficient they can be but this can mean that workers' rights can be compromised. Measures may be taken to help improve job search as mentioned in Chapter 19, through helping both **geographical mobility**, the ease with which people can move to different parts of the country where jobs may be available, and **occupational mobility**, the ease with which people are able to move from occupation to occupation including the degree to which skills and qualifications are transferable between occupations.

Education and Training
Investment in human capital to help improve productivity, innovation and creativity are factors we have mentioned earlier in the book. However, important questions emerge about whom should pay for training – the state or the employer – and what type of qualifications structure should a country put in place? Should science and engineering courses be prioritized at the expense of arts and humanities courses? Should education and training be aimed at preparing people for work or is education more than that? Should students in higher education pay for their studies or should the state subsidize it?

Whatever the answers to these questions, the importance of having a well-educated workforce is crucial to the economic well-being of a country and it is generally agreed that the link between high standards and levels of education in a country and productive capacity (aggregate supply in other words) is clear.

Infrastructure
Investment in infrastructure can take on many forms but ultimately the aim is to help the economy operate more efficiently. Whether this be through improved transport links which help speed up delivery and distribution, reducing congestion, providing better schools and medical facilities (including keeping the population healthy and thus reducing days missed at work through ill-health), promoting entrepreneurship, reliable energy supplies, or technology solutions and communications. The latter is particularly important in an economy that is based around knowledge and information exchange, which many service industry economies are. Having fast broadband access, good telephone links, widespread and strong mobile and cell phone signals is essential for knowledge-based economies and service industries.

Investment in new technologies for information exchange, for example, can also help job search by providing help to both employers and employees seeking information about vacancies and skills available as well as helping improve geographical mobility.

Trade Unions
We saw in Chapter 14 how trade union activity can distort the working of the labour market. Partly because of the belief by some politicians that trade unions had become too powerful and that the distorting effects too significant, and partly because of changed working practices, the role of trade unions in many countries has changed in the last 20 years. The number of days lost to

underemployment a situation where a worker has a job but may not be working to full capacity or does not have all their skills utilized or is working for a lower income than their qualifications, training or experience might suggest

geographical mobility the ease with which people can move to different parts of the country where jobs may be available

occupational mobility the ease with which people are able to move from occupation to occupation including the degree to which skills and qualifications are transferable between occupations

industrial action has fallen and unions now tend to take on roles that help support workers in legal disputes, with certain types of welfare and financial advice as well as representing the views of workers in national policy debates.

Summary

The three main policies outlined above are not used independently of each other nor exclusively. The extent to which a country has control over fiscal and monetary policy does depend on particular circumstances. In Europe, for example, governments in the eurozone have surrendered control of monetary policy to the European Central Bank and discussions are ongoing regarding greater fiscal unity within the eurozone. In the UK, South Africa and parts of the Middle East, governments have control over fiscal policy but have handed over control of monetary policy to the country's central bank.

Where countries do have some control over fiscal policy, decisions made are not simply designed to influence macroeconomic variables like growth, unemployment or inflation but also to focus on specific microeconomic goals which may be associated with a broader supply-side policy. Examples include increasing funds available for research into science and technology or improving transport and communication networks which are publicly funded.

> **Pitfall Prevention** Remember that monetary, fiscal and supply-side policies tend to be used together in order to target not only macroeconomic objectives but also microeconomic objectives which may help boost the overall efficiency of the economy. Given the prevailing economic orthodoxy of the day, one policy might take more prominence than another but the reality is that the three have to work in harmony.

HOW MONETARY POLICY INFLUENCES AGGREGATE DEMAND

In this next section we are going to look at how monetary and fiscal policy affect aggregate demand. To understand how policy influences aggregate demand, we need to examine the interest rate effect in more detail. Here we develop a theory of how the interest rate is determined, called the **theory of liquidity preference**, which was originally developed by John Maynard Keynes in the 1930s.

The Theory of Liquidity Preference

theory of liquidity preference Keynes' theory that the interest rate adjusts to bring money supply and money demand into balance

The theory is, in essence, just an application of supply and demand. According to Keynes, the interest rate adjusts to balance the supply and demand for money. In the analysis that follows, we hold constant the expected rate of inflation. (This assumption is reasonable for studying the economy in the short run.) Thus, when the nominal interest rate rises or falls, the real interest rate that people expect to earn rises or falls as well. For the rest of this chapter, when we refer to changes in the interest rate, you should envision the real and nominal interest rates moving in the same direction.

Money Supply The first element of the theory of liquidity preference is the supply of money. The money supply is assumed to be controlled by the central bank which can alter the money supply by changing the quantity of reserves in the banking system through the purchase and sale of government bonds in outright open-market operations. In addition to these open-market operations, the central bank can alter the money supply by changing reserve requirements (the amount of reserves banks must hold against deposits) or the refinancing rate (the interest rate at which banks can borrow reserves from the central bank). For the purpose of our analysis we are going to assume that the quantity of money supplied in the economy is fixed at whatever level the central bank decides to set it.

Because the quantity of money supplied is fixed by central bank policy, it does not depend on other economic variables. In particular, it does not depend on the interest rate. Once the central bank has made its policy decision, the quantity of money supplied is the same, regardless of the prevailing interest rate. We represent a fixed money supply with a vertical supply curve in Figure 20.6.

FIGURE 20.6

Equilibrium in the Money Market

According to the theory of liquidity preference, the interest rate adjusts to bring the quantity of money supplied and the quantity of money demanded into balance. If the interest rate is above the equilibrium level (such as at r_1), the quantity of money people want to hold (M_1^d) is less than the quantity the central bank has created, and this surplus of money puts downward pressure on the interest rate. Conversely, if the interest rate is below the equilibrium level (such as at r_2), the quantity of money people want to hold (M_2^d) is greater than the quantity the central bank has created, and this shortage of money puts upward pressure on the interest rate. Thus, the forces of supply and demand in the market for money push the interest rate towards the equilibrium interest rate, at which people are content holding the quantity of money the central bank has created.

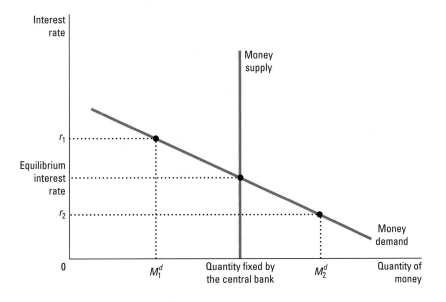

Money Demand   The second element of the theory of liquidity preference is the demand for money. Any asset's *liquidity* refers to the ease with which that asset is converted into the economy's medium of exchange. Money is the economy's medium of exchange, so it is by definition the most liquid asset available. The liquidity of money explains the demand for it: businesses and people choose to hold money instead of other assets that offer higher rates of return because money can be used to buy raw materials, equipment and goods and services.

Although many factors determine the quantity of money demanded, the one emphasized by the theory of liquidity preference is the interest rate. The reason is that the interest rate is the opportunity cost of holding money. That is, when wealth is held as cash, instead of as an interest-bearing bond or bank account, the benefits of the interest which could have been earned (the opportunity cost) are foregone. An increase in the interest rate raises the opportunity cost of holding money. Figure 20.6 shows the money demand curve sloping downward. At higher interest rates the opportunity cost in terms of foregone interest is higher and so demand for money as cash is lower than at lower interest rates.

Equilibrium in the Money Market   According to the theory of liquidity preference, the interest rate adjusts to balance the supply and demand for money. There is one interest rate, called the *equilibrium interest rate*, at which the quantity of money demanded exactly balances the quantity of money supplied. If the interest rate is at any other level, businesses and people will try to adjust their portfolios of assets and, as a result, drive the interest rate toward the equilibrium.

For example, suppose that the interest rate is above the equilibrium level, such as r_1 in Figure 20.6. In this case, the quantity of money that businesses and people want to hold, M_1^d, is less than the quantity of money that the central bank has supplied. Those who are holding the surplus of money will try to get rid of it by buying interest-bearing bonds or by depositing it in an interest-bearing bank account. Because bond issuers and banks prefer to pay lower interest rates, they respond to this surplus of money by lowering the interest rates they offer. As the interest rate falls, people become more willing to hold money until, at the equilibrium interest rate, businesses and people are happy to hold exactly the amount of money the central bank has supplied.

Conversely, at interest rates below the equilibrium level, such as r_2 in Figure 20.6, the quantity of money that people want to hold, M_2^d, is greater than the quantity of money that the central bank has supplied. As a result, businesses and people try to increase holdings of money by reducing their holdings of bonds and other interest-bearing assets. As holdings of bonds are reduced, bond issuers find that they have to offer higher interest rates to attract buyers. Thus, the interest rate rises and approaches the equilibrium level.

The Downward Slope of the Aggregate Demand Curve   Suppose that the overall level of prices in the economy rises. What happens to the interest rate that balances the supply and demand for money, and how does that change affect the quantity of goods and services demanded?

The price level is one determinant of the quantity of money demanded. At higher prices, more money is exchanged every time a good or service is sold. As a result, businesses and people will choose to hold a larger quantity of money. That is, a higher price level increases the quantity of money demanded for any given interest rate. Thus, an increase in the price level from P_1 to P_2 shifts the money demand curve to the right from MD_1 to MD_2, as shown in panel (a) of Figure 20.7.

Notice how this shift in money demand affects the equilibrium in the money market. For a fixed money supply, the interest rate must rise to balance money supply and money demand. The higher price level has increased the amount of money businesses and people want to hold, and has shifted the money demand curve to the right. Yet the quantity of money supplied is unchanged, so the interest rate must rise from r_1 to r_2 to discourage the additional demand.

This increase in the interest rate has ramifications not only for the money market but also for the quantity of goods and services demanded, as shown in panel (b). At a higher interest rate, the cost of borrowing and the return to saving are greater. Fewer households choose to borrow to buy a new house, and those who do buy smaller houses, so the demand for residential investment falls. Fewer firms choose to borrow to build new factories and buy new equipment, so business investment falls. Thus, when the price level rises from P_1 to P_2, increasing money demand from MD_1 to MD_2 and raising the interest rate from r_1 to r_2, the quantity of goods and services demanded falls from Y_1 to Y_2.

FIGURE 20.7

The Money Market and the Slope of the Aggregate Demand Curve

An increase in the price level from P₁ to P₂ shifts the money demand curve to the right, as in panel (a). This increase in money demand causes the interest rate to rise from r₁ to r₂. Because the interest rate is the cost of borrowing, the increase in the interest rate reduces the quantity of goods and services demanded from Y₁ to Y₂. This negative relationship between the price level and quantity demanded is represented with a downward sloping aggregate demand curve, as in panel (b).

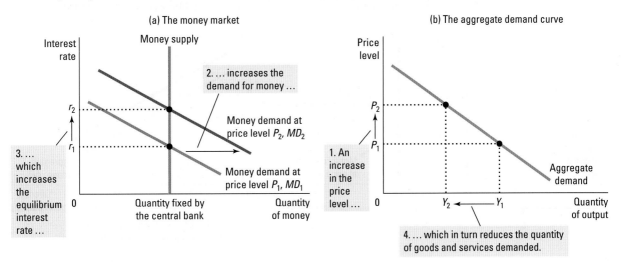

Of course, the same logic works in reverse as well: a lower price level reduces money demand, which leads to a lower interest rate, and this in turn increases the quantity of goods and services demanded. The end result of this analysis is a negative relationship between the price level and the quantity of goods and services demanded, which is illustrated with a downward sloping aggregate demand curve.

Changes in the Money Supply

Whenever the quantity of goods and services demanded changes *for a given price level*, the aggregate demand curve shifts. Suppose that the central bank increases the money supply by buying government bonds in open-market operations. As panel (a) of Figure 20.8 shows, an increase in the money supply shifts the money supply curve to the right from MS_1 to MS_2. Because the money demand curve has not changed, the interest rate falls from r_1 to r_2 to balance money supply and money demand. That is, the interest rate must fall to induce people to hold the additional money that the central bank has created.

Once again, the interest rate influences the quantity of goods and services demanded, as shown in panel (b) of Figure 20.8. The lower interest rate reduces the cost of borrowing and the return to saving. Households buy more and larger houses, stimulating the demand for residential investment. Firms spend more on new factories and new equipment, stimulating business investment. As a result, the quantity of goods and services demanded at a given price level $\bar{P}$, rises from Y_1 to Y_2. Of course, there is nothing special about $\bar{P}$: the monetary injection raises the quantity of goods and services demanded at every price level. Thus, the entire aggregate demand curve shifts to the right. Conversely, when the central bank contracts the money supply, the interest rate rises to bring the money market into equilibrium and reduces the quantity of goods and services demanded for any given price level, shifting the aggregate demand curve to the left.

FIGURE 20.8

A Monetary Injection

In panel (a), an increase in the money supply from MS$_1$ to MS$_2$ reduces the equilibrium interest rate from r$_1$ to r$_2$. Because the interest rate is the cost of borrowing, the fall in the interest rate raises the quantity of goods and services demanded at a given price level from Y$_1$ to Y$_2$. Thus, in panel (b), the aggregate demand curve shifts to the right from AD$_1$ to AD$_2$.

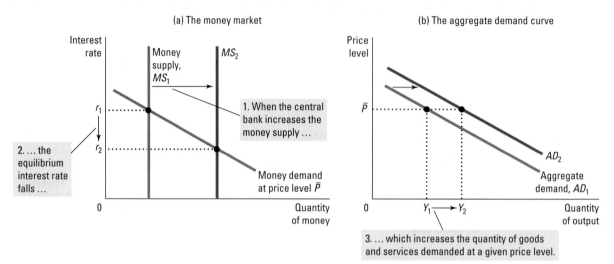

(a) The money market

(b) The aggregate demand curve

1. When the central bank increases the money supply ...

2. ... the equilibrium interest rate falls ...

3. ... which increases the quantity of goods and services demanded at a given price level.

The Role of Interest Rates

Our discussion so far in this chapter has treated the money supply as the central bank's policy instrument. When the central bank buys government bonds in open-market operations, it increases the money supply and expands aggregate demand. When the central bank sells government bonds in open-market operations, it decreases the money supply and contracts aggregate demand.

Often, however, discussions of central bank policy treat the interest rate, rather than the money supply, as the central bank's policy instrument. Some central banks conduct policy by setting the interest rate at which they will lend to the banking sector – the refinancing rate for the European Central Bank, the repurchase or 'repo' rate for the Bank of England, and the discount rate for the Federal Reserve.

The central bank's decision to set interest rates rather than target a certain level (or rate of growth) of the money supply does not fundamentally alter our analysis of monetary policy. The theory of liquidity preference illustrates an important principle: monetary policy can be described either in terms of the money supply or in terms of the interest rate. When the central bank sets a target for the refinancing rate of, say, x per cent, the central bank's bond traders are told: 'Conduct whatever open-market operations are necessary to ensure that the equilibrium interest rate equals x per cent.' In other words, when the central bank sets a target for the interest rate, it commits itself to adjusting the money supply in order to make the equilibrium in the money market hit that target.

As a result, changes in monetary policy can be viewed either in terms of a changing target for the interest rate or in terms of a change in the money supply.

Quick Quiz Use the theory of liquidity preference to explain how a decrease in the money supply affects the equilibrium interest rate. How does this change in monetary policy affect the demand curve?

HOW FISCAL POLICY INFLUENCES AGGREGATE DEMAND

In the short run, the primary effect of fiscal policy is on the aggregate demand for goods and services.

Changes in Government Purchases

We have seen that changes in autonomous spending can have an effect on the level of spending in the economy which is greater than the initial injection. The multiplier effect means that aggregate demand will shift by a larger amount than the increase in government spending. However, the **crowding-out effect** suggests that the shift in aggregate demand could be *smaller* than the initial injection.

crowding-out effect the offset in aggregate demand that results when expansionary fiscal policy raises the interest rate and thereby reduces investment spending

The Crowding-Out Effect

To see why crowding out occurs, let's consider what happens in the money market when the government invests in a nuclear power station from Nucelec. As we have discussed, this increase in demand raises the incomes of the workers and owners of this firm (and, because of the multiplier effect, of other firms as well). As incomes rise, households plan to buy more goods and services and, as a result, choose to hold more of their wealth in liquid form. That is, the increase in income caused by the fiscal expansion raises the demand for money.

The effect of the increase in money demand is shown in panel (a) of Figure 20.9.

FIGURE 20.9

The Crowding-Out Effect

Panel (a) shows the money market. When the government increases its purchases of goods and services, the resulting increase in income raises the demand for money from MD_1 to MD_2, and this causes the equilibrium interest rate to rise from r_1 to r_2. Panel (b) shows the effects on aggregate demand. The initial impact of the increase in government purchases shifts the aggregate demand curve from AD_1 to AD_2. Yet, because the interest rate is the cost of borrowing, the increase in the interest rate tends to reduce the quantity of goods and services demanded, particularly for investment goods. This crowding out of investment partially offsets the impact of the fiscal expansion on aggregate demand. In the end, the aggregate demand curve shifts only to AD_3.

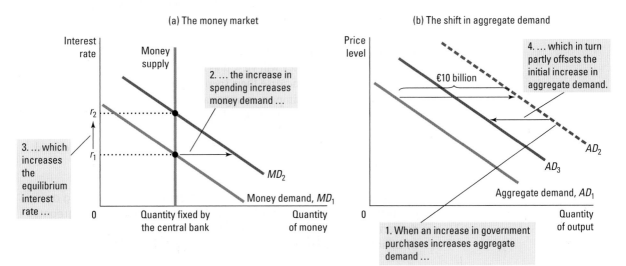

Because the central bank has not changed the money supply, the vertical supply curve remains the same. When the higher level of income shifts the money demand curve to the right from MD_1 to MD_2, the interest rate must rise from r_1 to r_2 to keep supply and demand in balance.

The increase in the interest rate, in turn, reduces the quantity of goods and services demanded. In particular, because borrowing is more expensive, the demand for residential and business investment goods declines. That is, as the increase in government purchases increases the demand for goods and services, it may also crowd out investment. This crowding-out effect partially offsets the impact of government purchases on aggregate demand, as illustrated in panel (b) of Figure 20.9. The initial impact of the increase in government purchases is to shift the aggregate demand curve from AD_1 to AD_2, but once crowding out takes place, the aggregate demand curve drops back to AD_3.

To sum up: when the government increases its purchases by €10 billion, the aggregate demand for goods and services could rise by more or less than €10 billion, depending on whether the multiplier effect or the crowding-out effect is larger.

Changes in Taxes

The other important instrument of fiscal policy, besides the level of government purchases, is the level of taxation. When the government cuts personal income taxes, for instance, it increases households' take-home pay. Households will save some of this additional income, but they will also spend some of it on consumer goods. Because it increases consumer spending, the tax cut shifts the aggregate demand curve to the right. Similarly, a tax increase depresses consumer spending and shifts the aggregate demand curve to the left.

The size of the shift in aggregate demand resulting from a tax change is also affected by the multiplier and crowding-out effects. When the government cuts taxes and stimulates consumer spending, earnings and profits rise, which further stimulates consumer spending. This is the multiplier effect. At the same time, higher income leads to higher money demand, which tends to raise interest rates. Higher interest rates make borrowing more costly, which reduces investment spending. This is the crowding-out effect. Depending on the size of the multiplier and crowding-out effects, the shift in aggregate demand could be larger or smaller than the tax change that causes it.

In addition to the multiplier and crowding-out effects, there is another important determinant of the size of the shift in aggregate demand that results from a tax change: households' perceptions about whether the tax change is permanent or temporary. For example, suppose that the government announces a tax cut of €1000 per household. In deciding how much of this €1000 to spend, households must ask themselves how long this extra income will last. If households expect the tax cut to be permanent, they will view it as adding substantially to their financial resources and, therefore, increase their spending by a large amount. In this case, the tax cut will have a large impact on aggregate demand. By contrast, if households expect the tax change to be temporary, they will view it as adding only slightly to their financial resources and, therefore, will increase their spending by only a small amount. In this case, the tax cut will have a small impact on aggregate demand.

Quick Quiz Suppose that the government reduces spending on motorway construction by €1 billion. Which way does the aggregate demand curve shift? Explain why the shift might be larger than €1 billion. Explain why the shift might be smaller than €1 billion.

CONCLUSION

Before policy makers make any change in policy, they need to consider all the effects of their decisions. In this chapter we looked at three main policies that can be adopted to influence the economy. We then examined the short-run effects of monetary and fiscal policy. We saw how these policy instruments can change the aggregate demand for goods and services and, thereby, alter the economy's production and employment in the short run. When the government reduces spending in order to balance the budget, it needs to consider both the long-run effects on saving and growth and the short-run effects on aggregate demand and employment. When the central bank reduces the growth rate of the money supply, it must take into account the long-run effect on inflation as well as the short-run effect on production.

CASE STUDY

The Accelerator Principle

The accelerator principle relates the rate of change of aggregate demand to the rate of change in investment. To produce goods, a firm needs equipment. Imagine that a machine is capable of producing 1000 DVDs per week. Demand for DVDs is currently 800. A rise in demand for DVDs of up to 200 is capable of being met without any further investment in new machinery. However, if the rate of growth of demand continues to rise, it may be necessary to invest in a new machine.

Imagine that in year 1, demand for DVDs rises by 10 per cent to 880. The business can meet this demand through existing equipment. In year 2, demand increases by 20 per cent and is now 1056. The existing capacity of the machine means that this demand cannot be met but the shortage is only 56 units so the firm decides that it might increase price rather than invest in a new machine. In year 3, demand rises by a further 25 per cent. Demand is now 1320 but the machine is only capable of producing a maximum of 1000 DVDs. The firm decides to invest in a new machine. The manufacturers of the new machine will therefore see a rise in their order books as a result of the increase in demand. An increase in demand of 25 per cent has led to an 'accelerated' rise in investment of 100 per cent. Investment is a component of aggregate demand and so economists are interested in the way investment adjusts to changes in demand in the economy. As this brief example shows, the relationship between an increase in demand and an increase in investment is not a simple one.

IN THE NEWS

Ending Deflation Can be a Difficult Challenge

This article looks at the various policies on offer for the Japanese government in attempting to end deflation.

Between 1983 and 1991 the Japanese economy grew by an average of 4.7 per cent per year making it the envy of many developed economies. However, since 1991 growth rates have been less than 1 per cent yearly. Japan entered a phase of chronic deflation where people cut back on spending as prices fell.

The Japanese government has undertaken a series of measures in an attempt to end deflation and promote economic growth. The net effect of these measures has been to raise the national debt fourfold from 64 per cent of GDP in 1991 to 240 per cent in 2013, but it did not result in the desired rapid growth.

In 2013 the Japanese government adopted a three-pronged approach to the problem which was dubbed 'Abenomics' after the Prime Minister, Shinzo Abe. The measures were designed to promote economic growth, raise inflation to 2 per cent and make the country more competitive.

First, the government introduced a series of fiscal stimulus initiatives. For example, in 2013 the government spent an extra $110 billion, so that public spending rose to 43 per cent of GDP and increased the budget deficit. Second, in 2013 it used quantitative

easing to supply the banks with excess reserves leading to a further devaluation of the yen. The weaker yen has increased the production cost of industry since oils and metals are priced in dollars. Third, Japan introduced over 200 reforms to regulations to liberalize the labour market and cut corporation tax.

According to Alan Reynolds from an article in the *Investor's Business Daily*, what the country really needs is a more pro-growth strategy of supply-side tax cuts. He believes that Japan needs a tax system that helps improve incentives to work and invest and to encourage innovation. He commented way back in 1998 that the dramatic deterioration in economic growth could be traced back to a number of tax increases between 1989 and 1992. He demonstrated that as a share of GDP, tax revenues in 1995 were no higher than they had been in 1980. It was a system of high income tax levels and low income tax revenues.

Reynolds claims that Japan should follow the example of dynamic Asian economies that have cut top individual income tax rates significantly. India, for example, cut the top rate of tax to 30 per cent in 1999 (it was 60 per cent in 1986). It has seen an average

economic growth rate of 7 per cent a year which doubles real GDP in a decade. Reynolds believes the way forward is to reduce the top rate of tax, cut public spending and cut subsidies.

Questions

1. Explain the effect of introducing a range of various tax increases had on the Japanese economy between 1989 and 1992.
2. What fiscal policies did Japan use to attempt to inflate the economy and how might the impact of these policies be affected by crowding out?
3. Use diagrams to show how quantitative easing might work in Japan.
4. What is meant by the statement 'high income tax levels lead to low income tax revenues'?
5. Do you think the principle of the Laffer curve is relevant to Japan's policy makers? Justify your view.

References: http://www.cato.org /publications/commentary/stagnant -for-decades-japan-needs-supply-side -tax-cuts

http://www.cfr.org/japan/abenomics -japanese-economy/p30383

SUMMARY

- The three main policies used to affect economic activity are monetary policy, fiscal policy and supply-side policy.

- Keynes developed the general theory as a response to the mass unemployment which existed in the 1930s. He advocated governments intervene to boost demand through influencing aggregate demand.

- The Keynesian cross diagram shows how the economy can be in equilibrium when $E = Y$.

- This equilibrium may not be sufficient to deliver full employment output and so the government can attempt to boost demand to help achieve full employment.

- Supply-side policies aim to improve the efficiency of the economy and increase the capacity of the economy by shifting the aggregate supply curve to the right.

- Key elements of a supply-side policy include tax and welfare reforms, improving the flexibility of labour markets including trade union reform, education and training, and investing in improved infrastructure.

- In developing a theory of short-run economic fluctuations, Keynes proposed the theory of liquidity preference to explain the determinants of the interest rate. According to this theory, the interest rate adjusts to balance the supply and demand for money.

- An increase in the price level raises money demand and increases the interest rate that brings the money market into equilibrium. Because the interest rate represents the cost of borrowing, a higher interest rate reduces investment and, thereby, the quantity of goods and services demanded. The downward sloping aggregate demand curve expresses this negative relationship between the price level and the quantity demanded.

- Policy makers can influence aggregate demand with monetary policy. An increase in the money supply reduces the equilibrium interest rate for any given price level. Because a lower interest rate stimulates investment spending, the aggregate demand curve shifts to the right. Conversely, a decrease in the money supply raises the equilibrium interest rate for any given price level and shifts the aggregate demand curve to the left.

- Policy makers can also influence aggregate demand with fiscal policy. An increase in government purchases or a cut in taxes shifts the aggregate demand curve to the right. A decrease in government purchases or an increase in taxes shifts the aggregate demand curve to the left.

- When the government alters spending or taxes, the resulting shift in aggregate demand can be larger or smaller than the fiscal change. The multiplier effect tends to amplify the effects of fiscal policy on aggregate demand. The crowding-out effect tends to dampen the effects of fiscal policy on aggregate demand.

QUESTIONS FOR REVIEW

1. Define monetary policy, fiscal policy and supply-side policy.

2. Explain how the interest rate transmission mechanism works to bring about changes in the components of aggregate demand and helps to boost growth.

3. Distinguish between planned expenditure and actual expenditure.

4. Draw a Keynesian cross diagram to show the effects of a rise in autonomous expenditure on an economy operating below full employment output.

5. Explain how the marginal propensity to withdraw affects the outcome of a rise in autonomous expenditure.

6. How can supply-side policies help an economy to produce greater output, reduce unemployment but reduce the price level at the same time?

7. Why are flexible labour markets such an important element in supply-side policies.

8. What is the theory of liquidity preference? How does it help explain the downward slope of the aggregate demand curve?

9. Use the theory of liquidity preference to explain how a decrease in the money supply affects the aggregate demand curve.

10. The government spends €50 million to buy a new fleet of police cars. Explain why aggregate demand might increase by more than €50 million. Explain why aggregate demand might increase by less than €50 million.

PROBLEMS AND APPLICATIONS

1. Prior to national elections, the existing government says that if elected again it wants to focus on delivering the following:
   a. a reduction in child poverty
   b. improvements in productivity in manufacturing industries
   c. increases in investment by businesses
   d. a reduction in the rate of inflation
   What policy options would you suggest the government use to deliver these objectives?

2. Explain, using an appropriate diagram, how a deflationary gap can occur and how this gap can be eliminated.

3. Suppose economists observe that an increase in government spending of €10 billion raises the total demand for goods and services by €30 billion.
   a. If these economists ignore the possibility of crowding out, what would they estimate the marginal propensity to consume (MPC) to be?
   b. Now suppose the economists allow for crowding out. Would their new estimate of the MPC be larger or smaller than their initial one? Explain your answer.

4. Suppose the government reduces taxes by €2 billion, that there is no crowding out, and that the marginal propensity to consume is 0.75:
   a. What is the initial effect of the tax reduction on aggregate demand?
   b. What additional effects follow this initial effect? What is the total effect of the tax cut on aggregate demand?
   c. How does the total effect of this €2 billion tax cut compare to the total effect of a €2 billion increase in government purchases? Why?

5. Explain how each of the following developments would affect the supply of money, the demand for money and the interest rate. Illustrate your answers with diagrams.
   a. The central bank's bond traders buy bonds in open-market operations.
   b. An increase in credit card availability reduces the cash people hold.
   c. The central bank reduces banks' reserve requirements.
   d. Households decide to hold more money to use for holiday shopping.
   e. A wave of optimism boosts business investment and expands aggregate demand.
   f. An increase in oil prices shifts the short-run aggregate supply curve to the left.

6. Suppose banks install automatic teller machines on every street corner and, by making cash readily available, reduce the amount of money people want to hold.
   a. Assume the central bank does not change the money supply. According to the theory of liquidity preference, what happens to the interest rate? What happens to aggregate demand?
   b. If the central bank wants to stabilize aggregate demand, how should it respond?

7. Consider two policies – a tax cut that will last for only 1 year, and a tax cut that is expected to be permanent. Which policy will stimulate greater spending by consumers? Which policy will have the greater impact on aggregate demand? Explain.

8. The economy is in a recession with high unemployment and low output.
   a. Use a graph of aggregate demand and aggregate supply to illustrate the current situation. Be sure to include the aggregate demand curve, the short-run aggregate supply curve and the long-run aggregate supply curve.
   b. Identify an open-market operation that would restore the economy to its natural rate.
   c. Use a graph of the money market to illustrate the effect of this open-market operation. Show the resulting change in the interest rate.
   d. Use a graph similar to the one in part (a) to show the effect of the open-market operation on output and the price level. Explain in words why the policy has the effect that you have shown in the graph.

9. In which of the following circumstances is expansionary fiscal policy more likely to lead to a short-run increase in investment? Explain.
   a. When the effect on investment is large, or when it is small?
   b. When the interest sensitivity of investment is large, or when it is small?

10. Assume the economy is in a recession. Explain how each of the following policies would affect consumption and investment. In each case, indicate any direct effects, any effects resulting from changes in total output, any effects resulting from changes in the interest rate and the overall effect. If there are conflicting effects making the answer ambiguous, say so.
    a. An increase in government spending.
    b. A reduction in taxes.
    c. An expansion of the money supply.

PART 7

GLOBAL BUSINESS
AND ECONOMICS

21 THE GLOBAL ECONOMY

LEARNING OUTCOMES

After reading this chapter you should be able to:

- Explain the key features of a currency area and a single market.

- Explain and illustrate with diagrams the macroeconomic effects of asymmetric shocks in a common currency area, wherein exchange rate adjustment is not possible.

- Explain and illustrate with diagrams how fiscal policy could be used for macroeconomic stabilization in the absence of exchange rate adjustment and independent monetary policy.

- Explain the advantages and disadvantages of globalization.

- Outline key issues facing businesses in a global environment.

- Give a definition of an emerging market.

- Outline at least three key characteristics of an emerging market.

- Be able to present an argument outlining the costs and benefits of doing business in an emerging market.

- Present an argument on the costs and benefits of outsourcing.

THE SINGLE EUROPEAN MARKET AND THE EURO

Following the devastation of two world wars in the first half of the 20th century, each of which had initially centred on European conflicts, some of the major European countries (in particular France and Germany) expressed a desire to make further wars impossible between them through a process of strong economic integration that, it was hoped, would lead to greater social and political harmony. This led to the development of the European Economic Community (EEC) – now referred to as the European Union, or EU. The official website of the European Union defines the EU as 'a family of democratic European countries, committed to working together for peace and prosperity'.

Initially the EU consisted of just six countries: Belgium, Germany, France, Italy, Luxembourg and the Netherlands. In 1973, Denmark, Ireland and the United Kingdom joined. Greece joined in 1981, Spain and Portugal in 1986, and Austria, Finland and Sweden in 1995. In 2004 the biggest ever enlargement took place with 10 new countries joining. Croatia became a member in 2013 and at the time of writing there are seven 'candidate countries' on the road to membership. These countries are Albania, Iceland, Montenegro, Serbia, the former Yugoslav Republic of Macedonia and Turkey. Bosnia and Herzegovina, and Kosovo are both classed as 'potential candidates'.

The EU has certainly been successful in its original central aim of ensuring European peace: countries such as France, England, Germany, Italy and Spain who have been at war with each other on and off for centuries, now work together for mutual benefit. This has led to greater emphasis being given to the EU's second objective – namely prosperity – and, to this end, a desire to create a **single European market** (SEM), throughout which labour, capital, goods and services can move freely. As member states got rid of obstacles to trade between themselves, it was argued, companies would start to enjoy economies of scale as they expanded their market across Europe. At the same time, inefficient firms would be exposed to more cross-border competition, either forcing them out of business or forcing them to improve their efficiency. The aim was to provide businesses with an environment of fair competition in which economies of scale could be reaped and a strong consumer base developed from which they could expand into global markets. Households, on the other hand, would benefit from lower prices, greater choice of goods and services, and work opportunities across a wide area, while the economy in general would benefit from the enhanced economic growth that would result.

Early steps towards the creation of the SEM included the abolition of internal EU tariff and quota barriers in 1968 and a movement towards greater harmonization in areas such as indirect taxation, industrial regulation and, in common EU-wide policies, towards agriculture and fisheries.

Nevertheless, it proved difficult to make progress on the more intangible barriers to free movement of goods, services, capital and labour. For example, even though internal tariffs and quotas had been abolished in the EU, local tax systems and technical regulations on goods and services still differed from country to country so that it was, in practice, often difficult to export from one country to another. A car produced in the UK might have to satisfy different emission and safety requirements in different European countries. A qualified engineer might find that their qualifications, obtained in Italy, were not recognized in Germany. The result was that during the 1970s and early 1980s, growth in the EU member

single European market a (still not complete) EU-wide market, throughout which labour, capital, goods and services can move freely

states began to lag seriously behind that of international competitors – especially the USA and Japan. Therefore, in 1985 a discussion document (in the jargon, a 'White Paper') was produced by the European Commission that subsequently led to a European Act of Parliament – the 1986 Single European Act. This identified some 300 measures that would have to be addressed in order to complete the Single European Market and set 31 December 1992 as the deadline for completion. The creation of the SEM was to be brought about by EU Directives telling the governments of member states what changes needed to be put into effect in order to achieve four goals:

- The free movement of goods, services, labour and capital between EU member states.
- The approximation of relevant laws, regulations and administrative provisions between member states.
- A common, EU-wide competition policy, administered by the European Commission.
- A system of common external tariffs implemented against countries who are not members of the EU.

Over 20 years on from the Single European Act, the SEM is still far from complete. In particular, there still exist strong differences in national fiscal systems which have come sharply into focus during the debt crisis, while academic and professional qualifications are not easily transferable and labour mobility across EU countries is generally low. Some of the reasons for this are hard to overcome: language barriers and relative levels of economic development hamper the movement of factors and member states continue to compete with one another economically, at times seeking their own national interest rather than the greater good of the EU.

Nevertheless, the years between 1985 and 1992 did see some important steps in the development of the SEM and the resulting achievements of the SEM project were not negligible: the European Commission estimates that the SEM helped create 2.5 million new jobs and generated €800 billion in additional wealth in the ten years or so following 1993.

In the context of the Single European Market project, the creation of a single European currency was seen as a final step towards 'completing the market', by which was meant two things: (a) getting rid of the transaction costs from intra-EU trade that result from different national currencies (and which act much as a tariff); and (b) removing the uncertainty and swings in national competitiveness among members that result from exchange rate movements. Before European Economic and Monetary Union (EMU), most EU countries participated in the Exchange Rate Mechanism (ERM), a system designed to limit the variability of exchange rates between members' currencies. However, the ERM turned out not to be a viable way of reducing volatility in exchange rates and, in any case, had no effect on the transaction costs arising from bank charges associated with changing currencies when engaging in intra-EU trade.

The benefits of adopting a single currency across a geographical area can be analysed more generally using macroeconomic theory. Moreover, these benefits must be weighed against the costs of joining a common currency area.

COMMON CURRENCY AREAS AND EUROPEAN MONETARY UNION

During the 1990s, a number of European nations decided to give up their national currencies and use a new, common currency called the *euro*.

common currency area (or currency union or monetary union) a geographical area throughout which a single currency circulates as the medium of exchange

A **common currency area** is a geographical area throughout which a single currency circulates as the medium of exchange. Another term for a common currency area is a *currency union*, and a closely related phenomenon is a *monetary union*: a monetary union is, strictly speaking, a group of countries that have adopted permanently and irrevocably fixed exchange rates among their various currencies. Nevertheless, the terms common currency area, currency union and monetary union are often used more or less interchangeably, and in this chapter we'll follow this practice.

Usually we speak of common currency areas when the people of a number of economies, generally corresponding to different nation states, have taken a decision to adopt a common currency as their medium of exchange, as was the case with the euro.

The Euro

European Economic and Monetary Union (EMU) the European currency union that has adopted the euro as its common currency

By 2015 19 countries had joined **European Economic and Monetary Union (EMU).** (Note that 'EMU' stands for 'Economic and Monetary Union', not European Monetary Union, as is often supposed.) The countries that form the Euro Area are Austria, Belgium, Cyprus, Estonia, Finland, France, Germany, Greece, Ireland, Italy, Latvia, Lithuania, Luxembourg, Malta, the Netherlands, Portugal, Slovenia, Slovakia and Spain. The move towards a single European currency has a very long history but we can set out the main landmarks in its formation, starting in 1992 with the Maastricht Treaty (formally known as the Treaty on European Union), which laid down, among other things, various criteria for being eligible to join the proposed currency union. In order to participate in the new currency, member states had to meet strict criteria such as a government budget deficit of less than 3 per cent of GDP, a government debt-to-GDP ratio of less than 60 per cent, combined with low inflation and interest rates close to the EU average. The Maastricht Treaty also laid down a timetable for the introduction of the new single currency and rules concerning the setting up of a European Central Bank (ECB). The ECB actually came into existence in June 1998 and forms, together with the national central banks of the countries making up the common currency area, the European System of Central Banks (ESCB), which is given responsibility for ensuring price stability and implementing the single European monetary policy.

The single European currency – the euro – officially came into existence on 1 January 1999 when 12 countries adopted it (although Greece did not join EMU until 1 January 2001). On this date, exchange rates between the old national currencies of Euro Area countries were irrevocably locked and a few days later the financial markets began to trade the euro against other currencies such as the US dollar, as well as to trade securities denominated in euros.

The period from the beginning of 1999 until the beginning of 2002 was a transitional phase, with national currencies still circulating within the Euro Area countries and prices in shops displayed in both euros and local currency. On 1 January 2002 the first euro notes and coins came into circulation and, within a few months, the switch to the euro as the single medium of exchange was complete throughout the Euro Area. The launch of the euro also saw monetary policy become the responsibility of the independent European Central Bank (ECB) and the currency is now used by some 338 million inhabitants of the 19 countries which make up the Euro Area.

> **?** ■ **what if** . . . a country joins a single currency but is at a different stage in the business cycle to other countries in the single currency area. Is it still possible for the country to successfully embrace the single currency?

Benefits of a Single Currency

Elimination of Transaction Costs

One obvious and direct benefit of a common currency is that it makes trade easier between members and, in particular, there is a reduction in the transaction costs involved in trade between members of the common currency area. When a German company imports French wine, it no longer has to pay a charge to a bank for converting German marks into French francs with which to pay the wine producer, it can just pay in euros. Of course, the banking sector loses out on the commission it used to charge for converting currencies, but this does not affect the fact that the reduction in transaction costs is a net gain. This is because paying a cost to convert currencies is in fact a deadweight loss in the sense that companies pay the transaction cost but get nothing tangible in return.

Reduction in Price Discrimination

It is sometimes argued that a second, albeit indirect gain, to the members of a common currency area results from the reduction in price discrimination that should ensue when there is a single currency. If goods are priced in a single currency it should be much harder to disguise price differences across countries. This argument assumes that the transparency in prices that results from a common currency will lead to arbitrage in goods across the common currency area: people will buy goods where they are cheaper (tending to raise their price in that location) and reduce their demand for goods where they are more expensive (tending to reduce the price in that location).

Overall, however, EMU seems unlikely to bring an end to price discrimination across Euro Area countries. For items like groceries, having a single currency is unlikely to be much of an impetus to price convergence across the common currency area because of the large transaction costs (mainly related to travelling) involved in arbitraging, relative to the prices of the goods themselves.

Reduction in Foreign Exchange Rate Variability

A third argument relates to the reduction in exchange rate variability and the consequent reduction in uncertainty that results from having a single currency. Exchange rates can fluctuate substantially on a day-to-day basis. Before EMU, when a German supermarket imported wine from France to be delivered, say, 3 months later, it had to worry about how much a French franc would be worth in terms of German marks in three months' time and therefore what the total cost of the wine would be in marks. This uncertainty might deter the supermarket company from importing wine at all, and instead lead them to concentrate on selling German wines, thereby foregoing gains from trade and reducing economic welfare. The supermarket could have eliminated the uncertainty by getting a bank to agree to sell the francs at an agreed rate against marks to be delivered three months later (an example of a forward foreign exchange contract). But the bank would charge for this service, and this charge would be equivalent to a tariff on the imported wine and so would represent a deadweight loss to society.

The reduction in uncertainty arising from the removal of exchange rate fluctuations may also affect investment in the economy. This would clearly be the case for companies that export a large amount of their output to other Euro Area countries, since less uncertainty concerning the receipts from their exports means that they are able to plan for the future with less risk, so that investment projects such as building new factories appear less risky. An increase in investment will benefit the whole economy because it is likely to lead to higher economic growth.

Costs of a Single Currency

The major cost to an economy in joining a common currency area relates to the fact that it gives up its national currency and thereby gives up its freedom to set its own monetary policy and the possibility of macroeconomic adjustment coming about through movements in the external value of its currency. Clearly, if the nations of the Euro Area have only one money, they can have only one monetary policy, which is set and implemented by the ECB. This must be the case because, since there is only one currency, it's not possible to have a different set of interest rates in different countries. Why is this a potential problem?

Suppose, for example, that there is a shift in consumer preferences across the common currency area away from goods and services produced in one country (Germany, say) and towards goods and services produced in another country (France, say). This situation is depicted in Figure 21.1, which shows a leftward shift in the German short-run aggregate demand curve and a rightward shift in the French short-run aggregate demand curve. What should policy makers in France and Germany do about this? One answer to this is, nothing: in the long run, each economy will return to its natural rate of output. In Germany, this will occur as the price level falls and wages, prices and perceptions adjust. In particular, as unemployment rises in Germany, wages eventually begin to fall. Lower wages reduce firms' costs and so, for any given price level, the amount supplied will be higher. In other words, the German short-run aggregate supply curve will shift to the right, until eventually it intersects with the new short-run aggregate demand curve at the natural rate of output. The opposite happens in France, with the short-run aggregate supply curve shifting to the left. The adjustment to the new equilibrium levels of output are also shown in Figure 21.1.

Note that, if Germany and France had maintained their own currencies and a flexible foreign exchange rate, then the short-term fluctuations in aggregate demand would be alleviated by a movement in the exchange rate: as the demand for French goods rises and falls for German goods, this would increase the demand for French francs and depress the demand for German marks, making the value of francs rise in terms of marks in the foreign currency exchange market. This would make French goods more expensive to German residents since they now have to pay more marks for a given number of French francs. Similarly, German goods become less expensive to French residents. Therefore, French net exports would fall, leading to a fall in aggregate demand. This is shown in Figure 21.2, where the French aggregate demand schedule shifts back to the left until equilibrium is again established at the natural rate of output. Conversely – and also shown in Figure 21.2 – German net exports rise and the German aggregate demand schedule shifts to the right until equilibrium is again achieved in Germany.

FIGURE 21.1

A Shift in Consumer Preferences Away from German Goods Towards French Goods

The German fall in aggregate demand leads to a fall in output from Y_1^G to Y_2^G, and a fall in the price level from P_1^G to P_2^G. The increase in French aggregate demand raises output from Y_1^F to Y_2^F. Over time, however, wages and prices will adjust, so that German and French output return to their natural levels, Y_1^G and Y_1^F, with lower prices in Germany, at P_3^G, and higher prices in France, at P_3^F.

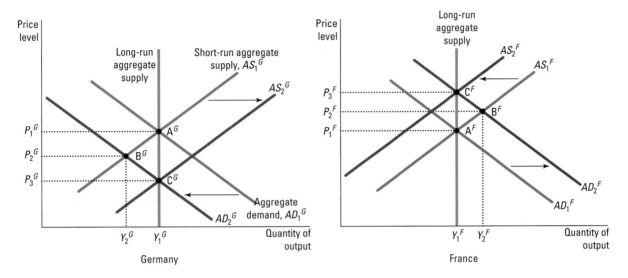

Germany   France

FIGURE 21.2

A Shift in Consumer Preferences with Flexible Exchange Rates

The fall in German aggregate demand leads, before prices have had time to adjust, to a fall in output from Y_1^G to Y_3^G. However, because this is due to a fall in net foreign demand, the value of the German currency falls, making German goods cheaper abroad. This raises net exports and restores aggregate demand. The converse happens in France: the increase in net foreign demand raises the external value of the French currency, making French goods more expensive abroad and choking off aggregate demand to its former level.

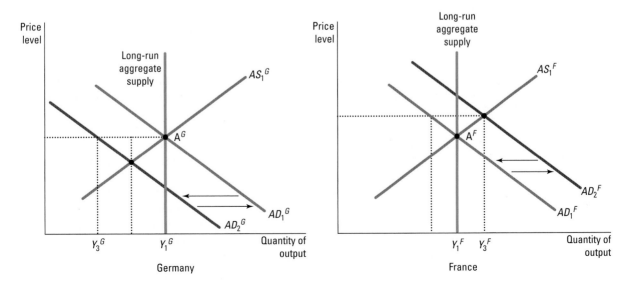

Germany   France

In a currency union, however, this automatic adjustment mechanism is not available, since, of course, France and Germany have the same currency (the euro). The best that can be done is to wait for wages and prices to adjust in France and Germany so that the aggregate supply shifts in each country, as in Figure 21.1. The resulting fluctuations in output and unemployment in each country will tend to create tensions within the monetary union, as unemployment rises in Germany and inflation rises in France. German policy makers, dismayed at the rise in unemployment, will favour a cut in interest rates in order to boost aggregate demand in their country, while their French counterparts, worried about rising inflation, will be calling for an increase in interest rates in order to curtail French aggregate demand. The ECB will not be able to keep both countries happy. Most likely, it will set interest rates higher than the German desired level and lower than the French desired level. The ECB pursues an inflation targeting strategy, and the inflation rate it targets is based upon a consumer prices index constructed as an average across the Euro Area. If a country's inflation rate (or expected inflation rate) is below the Euro Area average, the ECB's monetary policy will be too tight for that country; if it is above the average, the ECB's monetary policy will be too loose for it. All that is possible is a 'one size fits all' monetary policy. It is for this reason that entry to the eurozone is restricted to those countries that can meet the criteria outlined above where inflation and interest rates are close to the EU average.

> **Quick Quiz** A business based in Spain generates a high proportion of its revenues from selling goods to buyers in the USA. In response to weak economic growth in the Euro Area, the ECB cuts interest rates to 0.05 per cent. Over the next 9 months, the euro–dollar exchange rate changes from €1 = \$1.4 to €1 = \$1.1. What effect might this change in the exchange rate have on the Spanish firm?

Characteristics That Increase the Benefits of a Single Currency

High Degree of Trade Integration The greater the amount of trade that takes place between a group of countries – i.e. the greater the degree of trade integration – the more they will benefit from adopting a common currency. One of the principal benefits of a currency union, and the most direct benefit, is the reduction in transaction costs that are incurred in trade transactions between the various countries when there is a constant need to switch one national currency into another on the foreign currency exchange market. Clearly, therefore, the greater the amount of international trade and resulting foreign currency transactions that are carried out between member countries, the greater the reduction in transaction costs that having a common currency entails.

Currency unions can also help reduce exchange rate volatility and this reduction will also be larger the greater is the degree of intra-union trade, since more firms will benefit from knowing with certainty exactly the revenue generated from their sales to other currency union members, rather than having to bear the uncertainty associated with exchange rate fluctuations.

FISCAL POLICY AND COMMON CURRENCY AREAS

While adopting a common currency does mean that countries will have to give up autonomy in monetary policy, there is nothing in the adoption of a common currency that implies that members of the currency union should not still retain independence in fiscal policy. For instance, in our example of an asymmetric demand shock that expands demand in France and contracts aggregate demand in Germany, the French government could reduce government spending in order to offset the demand shock, while the German government could expand government spending. In fact, even if France and Germany did not make up an optimal currency because wages were sticky and labour mobility was low between the countries, national fiscal policy could, in principle, still be used to ameliorate the loss of monetary policy autonomy.

Fiscal Federalism

Suppose that a currency union had a common fiscal policy in the sense of having a single, common fiscal budget covering tax and spending decisions across the common currency area. This means that fiscal policy in the currency union would work much as fiscal policy in a single national economy works, with a surplus of government tax revenue over government spending in one region used to pay for a budget deficit in another region. Return again to our example of an asymmetric demand shock that expands aggregate demand in France and contracts aggregate demand in Germany, as in Figure 21.1. Since almost all taxes are closely related to the level of economic activity in the economy, tax revenue will automatically decline in Germany as a result of the aggregate demand shock that shifts it into recession. At the same time, transfer payments in the form of unemployment benefit and other social security benefits will also rise in Germany. These effects are referred to as automatic stabilizers built into the fiscal policy of an economy that automatically stimulate aggregate demand when the economy goes into recession without policy makers having to take any deliberate action. The opposite will be true in France, where the automatic stabilizers will be operating in reverse as transfer payments fall and tax receipts rise with the level of economic activity. These changes will tend to expand aggregate demand in Germany and contract it in France, to some extent offsetting the asymmetric demand shock.

Now, if the governments of France and Germany have a common budget, then the increased net government revenue in France can be used to offset the reduction in net government revenue in Germany. If the resulting movements in aggregate are not enough to offset the demand shock, then the French and German governments may even go further and decide to increase government expenditure further in Germany and pay for it by reducing spending and perhaps raising taxes in France.

This kind of arrangement – a fiscal system for a group of countries involving a common fiscal budget and a system of taxes and fiscal transfers across countries – is known as **fiscal federalism**. The problem with it is that the taxpayers of one country (here France) may not be happy in paying for government spending and transfer payments in another country (in this example, Germany).

fiscal federalism a fiscal system for a group of countries involving a common fiscal budget and a system of taxes and fiscal transfers across countries

Pitfall Prevention Being a member of a single currency does not mean that control over fiscal policy has to be surrendered. In a country like the USA, for example, although all states use the dollar, each has control over its own fiscal policy. The drive to a greater degree of fiscal coordination in Europe in some critics' eyes, is an attempt to move to a European super-state and is primarily political rather than economic.

National Fiscal Policies in a Currency Union: The Free-Rider Problem

During 2010 and 2011, difficulties in Greece, Ireland, Portugal, Spain and Italy led to EU leaders having to negotiate successive bailouts because of problems arising from the sovereign debt crisis. The Greek government borrowed heavily during the first decade of the 20th century but the financial crisis and subsequent recession hit the country hard. The government did not have sufficient funds to pay off loans as they became due. The government accepted a deal to help provide it with financial support from the EU in return for cuts in public spending and increases in taxes in order to impose financial discipline. The so-called 'austerity measures' have had wide-ranging effects on the Greek population with unemployment rising and standards of living for many falling significantly. The difficulties experienced by the population led to the election of an anti-bailout party called Syriza in elections in early 2015. Syriza has been in negotiations with the EU and the ECB to restructure the bail-out and at the time of writing further support for Greece has been agreed but the situation is far from stable with Greece still facing many challenges.

Similar problems have been experienced by Portugal, Italy, Ireland and Spain. The European Central Bank can control short-term interest rates but not those on long-term 10–20-year bonds. As the stresses inside the Euro Area build, interest rates on debt finance are pushed up and at a time of fragile economic activity this is not good news for longer-term economic recovery. If the economy stalls then tax revenues go down, government spending on benefits increases and the debt problem intensifies.

One explanation for the debt problem in countries like Greece is the *free-rider problem*. Given that there is a single currency in the EU but there is no fiscal federalism, there is the possibility of individual members of the currency union using fiscal policy to offset asymmetric macroeconomic shocks that cannot be dealt with by the common monetary policy. For example, Spain might choose to run a big government budget deficit in order to counteract a fall in aggregate demand and borrowing heavily in order to finance its deficit. The effects of Spain's decision impact on other members of the currency union.

Whenever a government raises its debt to very high levels, there is an increased risk of default. In general, this can be done in one of two ways. Where a country is not a member of a currency union and controls its own monetary policy, it can engineer inflation by increasing the money supply, so that the real value of the debt shrinks. When there is a sharp rise in the price level, this will usually be accompanied by a sharp fall in the foreign currency value of the domestic currency. This means that, valued in foreign currency, the stock of government debt will now be worth far less. Thus, the government has in effect defaulted on a large portion of its debt by reducing its value both internally and externally.

If the markets believe in this possibility then the debt will not be seen as risky as it otherwise would be and so the interest rates charged to the debtor country on its debt will not be as high as they otherwise might be. The net effect is for that government to pay interest rates on its large stock of debt that are lower. This is because of the implicit belief that it will be bailed out if it has problems servicing the debt. All other members of the currency union pay higher interest rates on their debt because the financial markets become flooded with euro-denominated government bonds. This is the free-rider problem; a government is enjoying the benefits of a fiscal expansion without paying the full costs.

In addition, if that government is using the proceeds of its borrowing to fund a strong fiscal expansion, this may undo or work against the anti-inflationary monetary policy of the ECB by stoking up aggregate demand throughout the whole of the Euro Area.

In order to circumvent some of these problems, the currency union members can enter into a 'no bailout' agreement which states that member countries cannot expect other members to come to their rescue if their debt levels become unsustainable as an attempt to convince the markets to charge profligate spend-and-borrow countries higher interest rates on their debt. In fact, exactly such a no bailout agreement exists among members of EMU. Unfortunately, however, it seems clear that the no bailout clause is not credible.

At the outset of EMU, a set of fiscal rules was drawn up and agreed to by EMU members. This set of rules was known as the **Stability and Growth Pact** (SGP). The Stability and Growth Pact was a set of formal rules by which members of EMU were supposed to be bound in their conduct of national fiscal policy. Its main components were as follows:

Stability and Growth Pact a set of formal rules by which members of EMU were supposed to be bound in their conduct of national fiscal policy

- Members should aim to achieve balanced budgets.
- Members with a budget deficit of more than 3 per cent of GDP will be subject to fines that may reach as high as 0.5 per cent of GDP unless the country experiences exceptional circumstances (such as a natural disaster) or a very sharp recession in which GDP declines by 2 per cent or more in a single year.

If EMU members adhered to the SGP, it would rule out any free-rider problems associated with excessive spending and borrowing in any one member country by forcing members to put a limit on the national government budget. The choice of a maximum budget deficit of no more than 3 per cent of GDP was related to a clause in the 1992 Maastricht Treaty which suggested that a 'prudent' debt-to-GDP ratio should be no more than 60 per cent. This itself was perhaps somewhat arbitrary – although it was very close to the actual debt-to-GDP ratio of Germany in 1992. To see how a 60 per cent ratio of debt to GDP could entail 'prudent' budget deficits of no more than 3 per cent a year, let's do some simple budgetary arithmetic.

Suppose a country is enjoying real GDP growth of 3 per cent a year and inflation of 2 per cent a year, so that nominal GDP is growing at the rate of 5 per cent a year. This means that the nominal value of its government debt can grow at a rate of 5 per cent a year and still be sustainable. But if the debt-to-GDP ratio is 60 per cent, this means that debt can increase by 5 per cent of 60 per cent, or 3 per cent of GDP a year while keeping the debt-to-GDP ratio constant. In other words, it can run a budget deficit of 3 per cent of GDP a year.

While there was some logic in setting a maximum budget deficit of 3 per cent a year (given a maximum prudent debt-to-GDP ratio of 60 per cent), it is not clear why the SGP suggested that members should aim for a balanced budget. From the budgetary arithmetic just discussed, it is not imprudent for countries to run small budget deficits so long as they are enjoying sustained long-term growth in GDP. The effective straitjacketing of national fiscal policy that the SGP implied, may have reflected a desire among the architects of EMU for the ECB to maintain an effective monopoly on demand management, so that its policies could not be countered by national fiscal policies.

The crucial question for the SGP, however, was whether or not the maximum allowable budget deficit would be enough for a country to let its automatic fiscal stabilizers come into play when it goes into recession. This is crucial in a monetary union because member countries will have already given up their right to pursue an independent monetary policy and they cannot use the exchange rate as an instrument of policy.

In practice, the SGP proved to be something of a toothless watchdog. As the Euro Area experienced sluggish growth in the early years of EMU, several member countries – and in particular France and Germany, two of the largest member countries – found themselves in breach of the SGP excessive deficit criteria. However, both France and Germany managed to persuade other EMU members not to impose fines and, in 2004, the European Commission drew up guidelines for softening the SGP. These guidelines included considering more widely the sustainability of countries' public finances on an individual basis, paying more attention to overall debt burdens and to long-term liabilities such as pensions, rather than to a single year's deficit.

The Sovereign Debt Crisis

The SGP was effectively rendered redundant by the sovereign debt crisis. The debt crisis developed because countries like Portugal, Greece and Ireland were able to access funds at low interest rates. Greece, for example, borrowed extensively to finance the 2004 Olympic Games and the expansion of public debt built to around 115 per cent of GDP and its deficit stood at 14 per cent of GDP. Recall that the recommended maximum was 3 per cent of GDP.

The financial crisis of 2007–2008, which led to the credit crunch, resulted in access to funds for countries like Greece drying up. The cost of acquiring new debt rose and banks, investors and financial institutions across Europe and elsewhere faced massive losses if Greece and the others were allowed to default. This would almost certainly have plunged the world into another deep and damaging recession.

Moves to find a way of preventing sovereign debt default led to the establishment of the European Financial Stability Fund (EFSF) to provide support for countries that faced default. €750 billion was initially set aside along with help from the International Monetary Fund. The initial bailout of Greece accounted for €110 billion of these funds; Ireland's €85 billion and Portugal around €80 billion. The establishment of the EFSF may have resolved some of the more immediate problems that existed in 2010 but merely led to the markets turning their attention to other states deemed to be in danger of default, notably Spain and Italy. The latter was of significance because it accounted for a much larger proportion of total EU GDP than Greece. If Italy were to default the consequences for the Euro Area then the global economy would be dire.

The bailout terms include implementation of significant measures to reduce public spending. It has been argued that the austerity measures have exacerbated the slowdown in economic activity and as a result, the chances of generating tax revenue to pay off debt and invest in improving the economy have been limited.

By March 2012, negotiations led to an agreement to set aside €529 billion for long-term refinancing operations (LTRO) which meant that the total funds allocated to the bailouts broke the €1 trillion level. In addition, the negotiations led to the setting up of what has been termed the Fiscal Compact. The Treaty came into force on 1 January 2013 and is designed to place a greater degree of fiscal discipline on EU members. Strict rules on government spending and borrowing will be imposed, designed to ensure that government budgets are either balanced or in surplus. To see the relevance of this we need to identify two types of deficit. A **cyclical deficit** occurs when government spending and income is disrupted by the 'normal' economic cycle. In times of strong economic growth government revenue from taxes will rise and spending on welfare and benefits will fall and so public finances will move into surplus (or the deficit shrinks appreciably). In times of economic slowdown the opposite occurs and the size of the budget deficit will rise (or the surplus shrinks). A **structural deficit** refers to a situation where the deficit is not dependent on movements in the economic cycle but where a government is 'living beyond its means' – spending what it has not got. The Fiscal Compact states that structural deficits must not exceed 0.5 per cent of GDP at market prices although this can rise to 1 per cent provided government debt as a whole is 'significantly' less than 60 per cent of GDP at market prices. If countries breach this limit fines will be imposed of up to 0.1 per cent of GDP and 'a correction mechanism' designed to correct any imbalance will be automatically triggered. The Treaty also requires countries to report in advance plans for major bond sales and economic reforms to EU institutions and for Euro Area summits to be held at least twice a year.

cyclical deficit a situation when government spending and income is disrupted by the 'normal' economic cycle

structural deficit a situation where the deficit is not dependent on movements in the economic cycle

JEOPARDY PROBLEM

A country with very high levels of sovereign debt announces that it is aiming to raise funds by borrowing on the bond market. It needs to raise €7 billion. As the time nears for the auction, the price of its existing debt starts to fall and yields rise. At the same time, the price of sovereign debt bonds of a country with a low level of debt starts to rise and yields fall.

Why might this be happening?

GLOBAL BUSINESS, CULTURE AND ETHICS

The term **globalization** refers to the growth of interdependence amongst world economies usually seen as resulting from the removal of many international regulations affecting financial flows. In one respect this means that it is becoming easier for firms to conduct business across national boundaries and to engage in trade around the world. This clearly opens up major opportunities but also presents difficulties and challenges that have to be recognized and managed, not least the ethical and cultural issues of carrying out business in a global market.

Doing business globally means that a firm can get its product and brand positioned anywhere in the world. It is highly likely that regardless of where you are in the world, for example, you will be able to find a store that sells Coca-Cola. Many businesses have expanded their reach by setting up operations in different countries but are headquartered in their country of origin. These types of organizations are referred to as **multinationals** or multinational corporations (MNCs). These firms have developed, and seek to exploit, a global brand presence. It is not only firms in product markets who have such a global presence, other markets, such as commodity and financial markets, could be argued to be even more global.

globalization the growth of interdependence amongst world economies usually seen as resulting from the removal of many international regulations affecting financial flows

multinationals organizations characterized by having operations in a number of countries although their main headquarters will be in one country – normally the country in which the firm originally developed

CASE STUDY

The Global Market for Higher Education

The UK government offers advice to businesses on how to expand into new markets abroad. It makes good sense for the government and also for businesses. For the latter it provides a chance to develop new markets away from saturated domestic markets and can offer a chance to reduce costs if production moved abroad or was outsourced to a foreign-based company.

Research shows that business organizations become more innovative and productive by expanding into foreign markets but there are certainly obstacles to overcome. These obstacles include potential currency risks, dealing with different labour and tax regulations, cultural differences and the risk of non-payment. Distance is now not a barrier. Technology has improved communications and logistics to help the world become more interdependent.

Using the case of Higher Education can help us understand the processes and options. There is a growing demand for Higher Education globally and universities want to exploit this. One option is for universities to market their Degree offers heavily abroad to encourage foreign students to come to study. London universities are making the most of this strategy as they have a good reputation and London is a desirable place to live. For example, Imperial College is spending £3bn in developing a new campus in West London and University College London is spending £350 million on a new campus on the Olympic site in East London. In fact UCL describes itself as 'London's global university'. Both of these developments are the result of attempting to attract more foreign students. But it doesn't end there. Some universities are establishing branch campuses abroad often as joint ventures with existing universities in target countries. The US leads the way with over 82 campuses in 37 countries with the UK following with 22 campuses and Australia with 15. The key destinations are the UAE with 35 foreign-based universities and China with 15. Such an expansion means the universities can generate additional revenues and develop their global brand. For example three UK universities, Nottingham, Newcastle and Southampton have branch campuses in Malaysia.

References: **http://www.ft.com/cms/s/0/11fcec5e-e4e5-11e4-8b61-00144feab7de.html#axzz 3Y7pTMBkX**

https://www.gov.uk/government/uploads/system/uploads/attachment_data /file/371945/From_local_to_global_-_how_to_expand_your_business_overseas.pdf

http://www.usatoday.com/story/news/nation/2013/11/14/colleges-go-abroad-with -branch-campuses/3189495/

International students in Paris

The Reasons for Globalization

One of the main reasons for the development of global markets has been technological change, particularly the Internet, but also transport and other forms of communication. Firms have been able to exploit the developments in these technologies to increase efficiency, gain scale economies, and produce and communicate 365 days of the year. The main reasons for globalization can be summarized as follows:

Transport and Logistics   Investing in production facilities in different countries can present challenges but the developments in low-cost transport systems and improvements in infrastructure in many countries around the world mean that component parts can travel across the globe many times as part of a production process before being assembled into a final product. Crucially, the cost of producing in this way has not increased at the same rate as the productivity benefits and as a result unit costs are kept low which means that firms are still able to offer consumers high quality products at relatively low and competitive prices.

Developments in transport infrastructures mean that firms can analyse and devise logistics to increase productivity. In particular, the advancements in containerization as a means of transporting goods enables firms to move far more goods per hour and with much lower levels of labour than was the case 50 years ago. Containers come in standardized sizes and can be loaded in very large quantities onto ships and then at the port onto freight trains and lorries to be delivered to factories, warehouses and distribution hubs.

A paper published in 2013 by Bernhofen, El-Sahli and Kneller on 'Estimating the effects of the container revolution in international trade' (**http://www.uv.es /inteco/jornadas/jornadas10/BEK_Nov25.pdf**) suggested that containerization increased bilateral trade (the trade of goods between two countries) between developed countries in the northern hemisphere by some 700 per cent in the period between 1966 and 1990. For developments in technologies like containerization to be commercially viable, there has to be appropriate infrastructure available. Investment in port facilities to handle the size of ships that carry containers is essential and once containers arrive in port, there needs to be road and rail systems available for the onward journey of cargo to distribution hubs, warehouses and finally retail outlets. The importance of having this infrastructure is highlighted by the fact that countries which have developed ports to cope with the demands of containerization are most likely to see the economic benefits of increased trade. For poorer countries, the inability to invest in this sort of infrastructure holds them back in their development.

Capital Mobility

Trade requires a medium of exchange. Countries will have different regulations and laws associated with their currencies and if these make it harder to engage in international trade then the benefits are going to be less. Over the past 50 years, many countries have relaxed currency laws and regulation which has meant that capital is able to flow more freely between countries. This has increased the ability of firms to invest in developing operations in other countries and to move funds around to maximize returns. In so doing, the benefits of international trade are shared across more countries.

The Expansion of Global Credit Markets

The complexity of financial markets has increased and part of the reason is the development of new products designed to boost access to credit for businesses across the globe. Firms looking to borrow funds for investment and expansion can increasingly look at global financial markets and access cheaper credit. Products developed to help firms insure their debt more effectively have also improved the credit worthiness of global businesses and as a result they can benefit from financial economies of scale.

The Collapse of the Soviet Bloc and Emerging Markets

A significant proportion of the world's countries operated under a different economic system until the early part of the 1990s. Social, political and economic change in Eastern Europe has led to countries gaining independence, embracing the market economy and opening up their borders to trade. It is not only the former Soviet Bloc countries which have increased trade with the rest of the world, many countries in South America, Africa and Asia, some of which are classed as emerging economies, have seen their share of trade as a percentage of national income increase. The ratio of exports plus imports to national income is called **trade openness**. The extent to which trade openness leads to wider economic benefits for the countries involved is debated but there has been empirical research which suggests a causal link between increased trade openness and improved economic growth. Of course, the extent to which all citizens share in the improved economic growth has to be investigated if broader conclusions on the benefits are to be drawn.

trade openness the ratio of exports plus imports to gross domestic product

The Growth of Multinational Companies   Sometimes, statistics can tell a story with far more clarity than words. The World Trade Organization (WTO), has noted that the top 500 multinational corporations account for almost 70 per cent of global trade. If the turnovers of MNCs were compared to the GDP of countries, then 51 of the 100 largest economies of the world are corporations (source: **http://www.gatt.org/trastat_e.html**). These statistics highlight the importance of MNCs in global trade and the way in which they have contributed to the growth in trade across borders in the last 50 years.

THE COSTS AND BENEFITS OF GLOBALIZATION

Economic theory predicts that trade can benefit everyone and few economists would disagree with that bald statement. However, as with many things in economics, it is highly dependent on a number of assumptions. Globalization has brought benefits to billions of people but the extent to which everyone can share these benefits is still open to question.

The Benefits of Globalization

Choice and Price   The opportunity to expand sales globally means that many businesses can invest in production systems that result in economies of scale. The lower unit costs can be passed on to consumers in the form of lower prices. In addition, consumers have access to a much wider choice of goods and services and assuming the principle of 'more is preferred to less' this improves standards of living.

Shareholder Value   Businesses can exploit global markets to source cheaper factor inputs which not only lowers unit cost but improves the flexibility of firms to improve their competitiveness around the world. The wider access to markets means firms can increase revenues and with lower unit costs, can improve profitability.

Inward Investment   As businesses expand in different countries, investment can create a multiplier effect which not only improves the living standards of local people but also generates opportunities for local businesses to expand as suppliers and in turn increase employment. Inward investment also means that technologies and knowledge is more widely shared and this is also likely to have economic benefits.

The Costs of Globalization

The links between globalization and the benefits outlined above have been the subject of research and it is not clear just how far these benefits extend. The WTO has noted that despite trade liberalization, the number of people living on less than $2 per day has risen to represent almost half of the world's population since 1980. In addition it notes that the poorest 49 per cent of countries account for only 0.4 per cent of world trade but represent 10 per cent of the world's population. Given these figures, we have to be mindful of the costs of globalization.

The Power of Multinationals   The statistic noting that 51 of the top 100 'economies' is a corporation is an indicator as to the size and global reach of MNCs. Whilst their size can bring the benefits outlined above, the power that these corporations can wield has been highlighted as a cause for concern. This power might manifest itself in pressure on governments to make decisions on investment and planning which may not be in the best interests of the majority of citizens. The desire to secure inward investment might be transitory with MNCs capable of switching investments from country to country seeking out the most favourable returns. Knowledge of this may lead to some governments relaxing the regulatory environment which may not always improve the welfare of the population as a whole. MNCs are also criticized for driving down wages and for using suppliers who may seek to exploit workers in order to maintain lucrative contracts. The pay and conditions of workers in factories in developing and emerging countries is often publicized although most MNCs claim that they have rigorous and robust codes of practice in place which seek to minimize such exploitation. Consumers also have a role to play here. Many consumers are willing to buy goods at low prices which can be seen to be considered as being disposable without necessarily considering the pay and conditions of the workers who make these products.

There are arguments which suggest that inward investment by MNCs can help to create employment and increase standards of living. The size of such an effect will depend on the nature of the business and the number and type of people employed. If the MNC is capital intensive then the effect on job creation might be relatively small. It might also depend on the number of local people employed and how many high skilled workers the MNC brings in from its own ranks. If MNCs are producing goods which are also produced in the domestic economy, the competition they bring in might be too great for local firms, leading to them closing down and putting domestic labour out of work. The dynamics of inward investment by MNCs is complex and the relative costs and benefits have to be considered on a case-by case basis.

Standardization   One feature of global business is the increase in standardization; wherever you go in the world, the customer experience of many products are very similar. Whether it be a Mcdonald's burger, Windows operating system, Apple's iPad, Coca-Cola, Head and Shoulders shampoo, Colgate toothpaste or BMW cars, regardless of where you are in the world these are highly standardized products. In one respect it might be argued that this is a good thing in that quality can be assured and all customers get the same experience, but standardization also results in a lack of product diversity and sets up barriers to entry for domestic businesses to compete effectively.

Climate Change   Proponents of the view that man-made increases in carbon dioxide emissions is resulting in changes in the climate which could bring devastating effects on some countries (and potential benefits to others it must be noted) argue that globalization is contributing to the problem. Attempts at agreement between global leaders to reduce carbon emissions have been extremely difficult to secure, partly because developing countries that are seeking to improve living standards for their populations through economic growth are being asked by the richer nations to cut their carbon emissions and thus compromising their attempts at growth. Many developing nations take the view that the extent of the problem has been caused by the richer nations' profligacy in the past 100 years. Developing nations want to see the developed world take far more responsibility for their actions and have much greater involvement in solving the problem.

Interdependence   The global financial crisis highlighted the extent to which financial institutions around the world are highly interdependent. The expansion of global credit and the reduction in the barriers to flows of capital across borders mean that more than ever before, shocks which occur in one country can very quickly affect businesses across the globe and exacerbate the effects of the shock. In product markets there are similar problems. Many businesses rely on complex logistics and supply chains for their production processes and if problems arise in one country this can affect global production. An earthquake in Japan, for example, could have a significant effect on car manufacturers and component suppliers in European countries.

Inequality and Equity   Most economics textbooks would point to the benefits that international trade can bring to individuals and communities. The benefits of trade, however, are not shared equally between all citizens in a country and even between countries. Trade between countries in the northern hemisphere and many countries in the southern hemisphere will tend to favour the richer northern countries whilst it may be that within countries a relatively small number of people will become richer and richer whilst the majority remain in relative poverty. When the gap between rich and poor increases and where poverty persists, there is unrest and the potential for civil and political turmoil and terrorism. Impoverished people may see that they are not sharing in wealth creation and in some cases see no other option but to resort to violence to advance their cause or simply to survive. The problems of piracy off the coast of Somalia and the continued supply of heroin from Afghanistan exist in part because those involved have few alternatives to make a living. Despite the risks involved, the alternative is not sufficiently rewarding to encourage them to do anything else.

The Wider Implications of Globalization

There are wider social and environmental implications of globalization in addition to those outlined above, not least the potential damage to eco-systems, the increasing use of non-renewable resources and damage to indigenous cultures. Firms are increasingly aware of these potential difficulties and make considerable attempts to demonstrate transparency in their actions and accountability. Many large firms produce social and environmental accountability reports which aim to highlight how they are managing their operations to limit the negative effects of their activities on stakeholders.

Cultural and Religious Sensitivities

Cultural and religious differences present challenges to businesses trading abroad. There are many examples of different cultural sensitivities which need to be taken into account such as how to greet people, how the use of colour can have different meanings in different parts of the world, and how certain gestures and body language can be interpreted very differently throughout the world. For example, showing the soles of the feet is considered highly offensive in many Muslim countries. Touching has different interpretations in different parts of the world. Touching the head in parts of Asia is not polite because the head houses the soul; in Islamic and Hindu cultures the use of the left hand for social interaction is considered insulting. Having hands in pockets or sitting cross-legged is considered disrespectful in Turkey, while making eye contact is expected in the West and in some Arabic cultures but not in Japan, parts of Africa, the Caribbean and parts of Latin America. For firms seeking to do business in different parts of the world and where individuals travel to conduct business on behalf of firms, it is imperative that an understanding, appreciation and respect of local cultures and sensitivities is recognized and followed if firms are to trade successfully.

BUSINESS IN EMERGING MARKETS

The economies of the developed world tend to dominate textbooks and the global news media. However, in the last 20 years political and economic changes have meant that increasing focus is now centred on economies in other countries termed 'emerging economies' or 'emerging markets'. An **emerging market economy** is one where the per capita income of the population is in the middle to low range compared to other global economies. The United Nations puts the number of emerging economies at 120 out of the 160 it recognizes.

emerging market economy
a country where the per capita income of the population is in the middle to low range compared to other global economies

Each country differs in its state of development but major attention has been focused in recent years on the so-called BRIC countries, Brazil, Russia, India and China. These are countries with huge productive potential due in part to their respective size, population and resource endowment. However, there are a growing number of countries which deserve to be classed in a similar category to these countries in terms of their increasing GDP per capita. These countries include Turkey, South Africa, Mexico, Malaysia, Taiwan, Hungary, Poland, Czech Republic, Chile, Indonesia, Philippines, Thailand, the United Arab Emirates, Saudi Arabia, Egypt, Colombia, Peru and Morocco.

Characteristics of Emerging Markets

One of the reasons why these countries are categorized in the terms outlined above is because of their state of economic development. It is not just size that matters but the internal economic structures that are important. Countries like China, Russia, Saudi Arabia and Poland, for example, have been under different types of political regime which have shaped their economic development over the last 100 years. Russia and Poland were former states within the Union of Soviet Socialist Republics (USSR) where a planned market economy was the economic system which determined resource allocation. China was similarly governed by a communist regime although would claim to be following a different brand of communism. In a planned economy, state planning authorities sought to answer the three basic questions of any economic system: what is to be produced, how is it going to be produced and who gets what is produced?

In the former USSR, the state central planning authority was called Gosplan. Its function was to identify what goods and services were needed by the people, how these goods and services would be produced and how the state output would be distributed. Agencies were given the resources that the planners had worked out would be necessary for producing that output. Most factories and farms were given output targets to reach; once produced, it might be the job of another body to ensure that goods were distributed. In return for the labour expended in producing this output, a wage was given. This wage, however, bore no relation to the value of the output being produced. The wage was planned to allow workers to be able to buy the things the planners had worked out they needed to live on. To enable this to happen, prices were also set by the planning authorities.

In theory, everyone had enough to live on. Wage differentials were minimal – whether you were a highly qualified university professor or a street cleaner, wages only varied by a relatively small amount. Most people had a job if they wanted one, regardless of the type of job; unemployment was therefore zero. Inflation did not exist as we know it because of the system of price fixing and there were very few homeless people – the state provided housing.

State planning, however, was not without its problems. The assumption that people would work hard for the common good was not always realized. Factories found that if they met their targets or even exceeded them, they were given higher targets next year but not necessarily the resources to achieve them, nor any extra wages – so what was the point? Targets soon appeared to become subject to what has been called 'Goodhart's law', where targets used to manage something become corrupted to the extent that they cease to be able to be used to measure what you want them to measure.

The communication between the different sectors of the economy was not always good. It was estimated that something of the order of 40 per cent of all agricultural produce rotted before it could be processed or reach its intended markets. Price-fixing meant that shortages and surpluses developed and often persisted. Product quality fell, negative externalities like pollution increased and inefficiency was endemic.

In Saudi Arabia the situation was somewhat different given the key resource endowment of oil. The country has been able to generate massive wealth as a result of its reserves of oil but its political system is dominated by the Al Saud family. The King fulfils the role of commander-in-chief of the military, prime minister, head of government and chief of state. Saudi Arabia is an Islamic state and justice is governed by Islamic law. There are no political parties in Saudi.

All the countries mentioned above are changing and making economic reforms; the establishment of institutions and bodies which reflect broader international standards and regulations are being developed. Many of the emerging economies are embracing market reforms, engaging in trade, establishing private property and opening up their economies to outside investment. In order for these countries to take a growing part in the global economy it is essential that they have institutions and governance which reflect those of the developed world – why would a business risk investing in setting up operations in these countries if it believed there was not the same or at least similar rules of governance that existed in their home country? It is accepted that there are still, in some cases, major obstacles to the integration of many emerging countries into the global economic system. Not least problems with corruption, questions over human rights and issues over corporate governance and the rule of law, particularly in relation to intellectual property. However, it is also recognized that no country can move from being an essentially closed economy to a fully integrated market economy overnight. This is part of the reason why these economies are referred to as emerging.

Many emerging economies will also have specific advantages which their respective governments are recognizing have some economic value. It might be something to do with resource endowment such as the reserves of oil and gas that exist in Russia, discoveries of oil off the Brazilian coast, copper in Zambia and minerals in other parts of Africa. Or it might be something to do with the huge human resources at the disposal of many emerging economies: China and India both have populations in excess of one billion and this provides huge reserves of relatively cheap labour.

Some of the changes which have brought emerging economies into the global business environment have included a greater degree of political stability. Western governments may disagree fundamentally with the political systems in China and Saudi Arabia, for example, but these countries are stable and this provides an incentive for investment by businesses. The development of banking and financial sectors, systems and institutions to settle commercial disputes, having more harmonized business law as well as stock markets, have further helped accelerate investment into emerging economies.

Why are Emerging Markets So Important?

There is a simple answer to this question – opportunity. Businesses in the developed world are finding that many of the 'traditional' markets they are operating in are mature. The opportunities for growth in these markets are limited; growth is likely to occur in some but only at low rates. Take mobile or cell phones, for example. In the UK, USA, Canada and countries of northern Europe and Scandinavia, penetration into the market is almost total. Virtually every person who wants a cell phone has now got (at least) one device and this limits the potential for growth. Opportunities exist if new more sophisticated models are brought out, but unless they do something very different the incentive for an individual to give up their existing phone and buy a new one is limited.

However, in a country like Vietnam, for example, cell phone ownership has been growing at a rapid rate. Its 86 million people, therefore, represent a huge market for mobile phone manufacturers and service operators. This is a crucial reason for businesses seeking to do business in emerging markets – there are billions of potential customers. Equally important, many of these people are becoming wealthier and entering the middle classes where spending on the sort of consumer goods which could be classed as luxuries is likely to rise dramatically in the next 50 years.

The links between the increasing development of these economies and the rise in wages of workers in the countries has not been lost on businesses in the developed world. As they continue to industrialize and expand, workers will add more value, get paid more and will have more disposable income. The process may not be rapid but businesses have to look ahead to the next 10 to 20 years for sustained revenue and sales growth rather than the next 5 years.

It is not only businesses selling consumer goods that see the opportunities for securing new markets and growth in sales. Business-to-business (B2B) operations are also recognizing that part of the continued development of emerging economies rests on improved infrastructure. We saw in Chapter 20 how investment in infrastructure was an important feature in improving efficiency and the supply-side of the economy. Investment in energy supplies, telecommunications, internet supplies, construction plant, distribution networks, road and transport networks, and water and sewerage systems are all vital to the continued growth of emerging economies, and firms in the developed world have looked to invest heavily in such opportunities.

Firms that see and seize first mover opportunities may find that there are numerous problems in setting up and doing business in emerging economies but despite these challenges, if they are in a position to become established, the medium and longer-term benefits in terms of growth opportunities can be extensive. Mistakes will be made but the experience they gain and the scale opportunities that exist mean most want to be involved sooner rather than later for fear of missing the chances that exist.

Problems Facing Business in Emerging Markets

The opportunities for future growth may be large but there are many challenges. One of the biggest is the fact that businesses need to understand the markets they are getting into. Typical of the early forays into emerging markets have been attempts to replicate successful business models in Western developed market economies. Many businesses have found that this replication model has not worked and that major changes to the way in which the business operates in these countries is required. Part of the reason may be the different political, cultural and religious systems and norms in place in some emerging economies. Another reason may be that assumptions about the markets and consumers within that market are flawed. Selling hi-tech gadgets in a country where there are very few people who own these may present a huge potential opportunity. This opportunity may only exist if there are enough people who are (a) wealthy enough to have the disposable income to be able to afford (and want) these gadgets; (b) that there are not other products which are deemed more important or valuable to these consumers; and (c) that the way consumers in developed economies see the products may not be the same as those in emerging economies.

The needs of customers in these markets may not be the same as those in developed economies and so the business may find that its model is fundamentally flawed. This sort of problem was noted by C.K. Prahalad, the noted management thinker who died in April 2010. In his book, *The Fortune at the Bottom of the Pyramid: Eradicating Poverty Through Profits (2004)*, Prahalad sought to show how poverty could be tackled by focusing products on the world's poorest people – around 5 billion of them. Not only could firms make a real difference to the world's poor but they could also secure new profits and growth in the process. The key questions businesses need to ask in this regard are whether a market exists and if it does what sort of scale exists? Does the market and the scale enable profits to be made? If the answers to these questions are 'yes' then there are opportunities to be exploited. This means that firms can look at generating revenue from people who may only be earning very small incomes. One example is the market for shampoo. Do consumers in emerging markets want to buy shampoo in the same way as those in the Netherlands, for example? Prahalad suggested that these consumers may have a lot in common, not least their desire to purchase well-respected branded items such as Pantene shampoo produced by Procter & Gamble. However, whilst consumers in the Netherlands may want to purchase their shampoo in 500ml bottles for around €5, for consumers in India this may represent a week's wages. The solution might be to supply the same product in single-serve sachets so that the shampoo market in India (which in terms of size is potentially as large as in the USA) can be served.

Business Strategies in Emerging Markets

There are a number of different but often complementary strategies that have been identified for conducting business in emerging markets.

Hit and Run Strategies   Firms might enter a market with the intention of 'creaming off' the value in the market and then getting out. They sell their products to those that can afford them, take the profits and then leave the market. The advantage is a boost to short-term profits but the disadvantage is that long-term growth prospects and business relationships are sacrificed and these relationships may be more profitable in the long run.

Enclave Strategies   This is often associated with firms doing business in emerging economies exploiting natural resources. The intention is to set up operations which do not depend on local supply networks and where local businesses and people have minimal involvement in the operation. This may be because the firm believes the local business environment is less efficient and reliable but might also be because of concerns over security. Firms may engage with the local military to help provide that security. One of the problems of this is that such involvement can raise ethical questions about how the firm operates and the extent to which the payment to the local military is transparent. In addition it can also attract attention to the business, especially in more politically volatile areas where local conflicts and terrorism might be problematic. It also alienates the firm from the local stakeholders.

Learn to Earn   Committing to investing in emerging markets for the long term may involve the firm having to accept that in the short run profits will be slim if non-existent. By being involved in the economy, however, the firm will learn and as it does it develops longer term relationships and a better understanding of the market. In the long term it is hoped that this improved understanding and experience will lead to higher and more consistent profits.

Summary

There are many emerging markets – some more advanced than others, but the opportunities for business facing limited growth in domestic, mature markets are significant. However, firms have to be prepared to be flexible in their approach to doing business in emerging markets and be prepared to make mistakes, learn from experience and invest in time and new business models to succeed. Building relationships with governments, local suppliers, regional government and understanding cultural, political and religious differences are part of the process of developing sustainable platforms for future growth.

OUTSOURCING

The existence of emerging economies with large labour resources which often have high literacy levels but low wage costs, has encouraged a number of companies to look to move parts of their operations to these countries. The contracting out of a part of the business' operations to another organization is referred to as **outsourcing**. While the focus has been on outsourcing labour operations to low-wage economies, outsourcing also refers to any operation. This might include accountancy activities, IT, various human resources activities such as payroll management, and recruitment and training. Outsourcing does not have to mean the operation goes abroad – many businesses will outsource operations to other organizations within the domestic country.

outsourcing contracting out of a part of the business' operations to another organization

The main reason for outsourcing is to reduce costs and to improve efficiency. Taking advantage of the expertise of other organizations that may specialize in particular operations is a major factor in decision making. By outsourcing production and obtaining supplies from low-cost manufacturers, companies are able to focus their attention on their core competencies – the key strengths that they have. This leads to a more efficient operation whilst allowing the business concerned to benefit from economies of scale.

The benefit to the consumer is that they get good quality products – and more of them – at lower prices. The clothing industry is an excellent example of where these changes have been happening. Primark is one business that has adopted this business model. Owned by Associated British Foods, Primark has placed itself as a 'value retailer' offering low-priced but good quality clothing, and along with other value retailers like Matalan now account for around a quarter of total fashion spending in the UK.

The benefits of outsourcing have to be weighed against the possible disadvantages. There are costs associated with outsourcing, not least of which involve the setting up of the agreement with the contractor, but also the cost of closing down operations which the outsourced activity is replacing. Outsourcing call centre operations has been a high profile news story in the UK with sometimes thousands of domestic workers losing their jobs to outsourced operations in countries like India, where labour costs are significantly lower. The ethics of the decision of firms to outsource have been questioned and the firm has to consider the effect on its reputation.

In addition to this, some firms have found that the expected benefits have not been as large as they anticipated; there are complex issues that have arisen which may not have been foreseen. Customers, for example, have complained about the service they are receiving from outsourced services. Outsourced workers may not have the 'local' knowledge and understanding necessary to meet customer needs. Training of outsourced workers has also been a problem for some firms which has led companies like Newcastle Building Society and Lloyds TSB to move some operations back to the UK. In other cases, firms in financial services have found that security is an issue. Handling and protecting customer data is an important part of the business of financial services and something which is highly regulated. The UK insurance and financial services firm Aviva has encountered such problems of maintaining security, which have cost it an estimated £10 million in efforts to ensure that its outsourced operations meet regulatory requirements.

There are also problems associated with how some outsourced operations do business. The development of social networking sites and the ease with which individuals can post information and videos onto the Internet have meant that firms are acutely aware of the damage to their reputation from stories about abuse of workers in outsourced operations. A number of firms have attempted to counter stories that workers in plants in China are working long hours for low wages. A series of apparent suicides in a factory in Shenzhen in China which make products for Apple, Nokia, Dell, Sony and Nintendo, were linked to the stresses imposed as a result of the conditions that workers have to operate in. For these types of companies which have a main demographic of young, socially aware individuals, when reports such as these filter through, a balance has to be drawn between the benefits of the low cost of using outsourced manufacture, and the potential for the image of the company to be damaged. Similar reports have been released about worker abuse in clothing factories supplying big-name Western retailers which can be equally as damaging and the speed with which many of these firms react to the claims is perhaps testament to the potential for damage to the firm.

FOREIGN DIRECT INVESTMENT

Globalization has led to an increase in the investments firms make abroad. These investments might include the construction of new plant and equipment abroad, the development of new or expanded production facilities and the acquisition of businesses. This investment leads to funds flowing into the host country and is termed **foreign direct investment** (FDI). The World Bank defines FDI as: 'Net inflows of investment to acquire a lasting management interest (defined as 10 per cent or more of voting stock) in an enterprise operating in an economy other than that of the investor.' FDI has been made easier because of the opening up of trade borders by countries, the growth in the internet and communications technologies which makes it easier for different regional operations to keep in touch, and by the deregulation of capital markets.

foreign direct investment inflows of investment into a host country from external businesses

The sums of money involved in FDI are difficult to comprehend. The OECD notes that the level of FDI in 2007 was around $2170 billion ($2.1 trillion) but fell back following the financial crisis and amounted to around $1600 billion ($1.6 trillion) in 2011. The United Nations Conference on Trade and Development (UNCTAD) estimated that global FDI would reach $1800 billion ($1.8 trillion) in 2015. UNCTAD also reported that developing economies accounted for 52 per cent of global FDI in 2012.

Features of FDI

The growth in FDI is closely linked to the growth in MNCs and many of the costs and benefits of FDI also mirror the costs and benefits of MNCs outlined above. For the investing firms, there are the potential benefits of new markets, new distribution channels, access to new technology, skills and finance, and the potential for lower unit costs. In addition, FDI can help a firm avoid trade barriers especially given the growth in free trade agreements, or trading blocs, between countries. There may also be tax benefits or access to grants and allowances to firms investing in foreign countries. For the host countries, the investments can lead to higher living standards for its citizens, access to new technologies, capital, processes, products and skills, the potential for an expansion in employment and the development of infrastructure to further boost economic growth.

One feature of FDI has been the investment in new technology start-ups. These are often small firms which have grown in a country, in some cases having arisen out of the research and development which takes place at universities. The spin-offs from this research and development can take the form of small businesses set up by the researchers, and firms from abroad then acquire these start-ups or engage in licensing and technology transfer arrangement which allows the start-ups to expand. For larger firms, the risk associated with research and development is reduced as this risk is assumed by these start-ups. The large firm comes in when a lot of the development work has taken place and its resources can be used to build commercially viable production. In some cases, large firms may collaborate with researchers on projects. Changes to rules on intellectual property ownership have meant that researchers in universities who develop new products or processes are allowed to issue licence agreements to commercial businesses to further develop the ideas, with some of the funding feeding back into the university. In some countries, the close links between business and higher education institutions are fostered by the development of science and innovation parks constructed in and around university towns and cities. In Cambridge, in the UK, the high quality research carried out by academics at the University of Cambridge is particularly attractive and the Cambridge Science Park located on the outskirts of the city is an example of this sort of relationship.

In some cases, two firms in a similar industry may enter into an agreement to use their distribution networks and logistics systems to distribute each other's products. For example, two brewery businesses in different countries may agree to a regional distribution agreement whereby their respective beers are made available in pubs and clubs in each country. This saves both firms the costs of investment in new distribution networks in the foreign country and utilizes local knowledge, expertise and market access of the host firm. In each case, the firms get access to new markets but at lower unit costs and also reduce the competition they face.

Joint ventures involve partnerships between firms with different opportunities, markets or skills, allowing the partners to develop new products or exploit new markets. Such ventures are justified by the opportunities to exploit synergies and economies of scale reducing average costs and also reducing some of the need to spend large sums on research and development. Despite these potential benefits, the success of joint ventures is not strong with relatively high failure rates recorded.

CONCLUSION

This chapter has examined business in the wider context of trading across the world. Emerging markets provide the potential for existing companies to be able to exploit growth opportunities that increasingly do exist in the developed world. We also developed some of the main issues around common currency areas, focusing in particular on European Monetary Union. Where there is a high degree of trade among a group of countries, there are benefits to be had from forming a currency union, largely arising from the reduction of transaction costs in international trade and reductions in exchange rate uncertainty. However, there are also costs associated with joining a monetary union, mainly associated with the loss of monetary autonomy (member countries are no longer free to set their own interest rates), and the loss of exchange rate movements as a means of achieving macroeconomic adjustment. Any decision to form a currency union must weigh these costs and benefits against one another to see if there is an overall net benefit. Although, in the long run, the loss of exchange rate adjustment and monetary autonomy may have little effect on the equilibrium levels of output and unemployment in the economies involved, there may be substantial short-term economic fluctuations in these macroeconomic variables as a result of joining the currency union. This is particularly the case if there are asymmetric demand shocks impacting on the currency union so that it is impossible to design a 'one-size-fits-all' monetary policy to suit every country. Short-run adjustment will also be long and painful when wages do not adjust very quickly, although this problem may be overcome by labour mobility across the member countries. The sovereign debt crisis in Europe has brought the whole single currency project into question and there are considerable challenges that still exist across many European countries.

Firms doing business abroad and using outsourced operations have to weigh up the costs and benefits of doing so. Some of the costs, including being alert to cultural, religious and social sensitivities, along with the effects on the environment and the potential for such operations to be questioned on ethical grounds, can mean that decisions to carry out business abroad in some form can be challenging.

IN THE NEWS

Trading Blocs and Bilateral Agreements

The ultimate aim of multinational institutions such as the IMF and WTO is to have global free trade. At present trade is dominated by the existence of a number of geographical trading blocs, but even these are changing, creating both winners and losers.

Trading blocs have been set up across the world to foster more free trade for goods and services, develop mutual interdependence and bring greater prosperity to members working together under common regulations and agreements. They are geo-political in nature. For example, the Pacific Alliance is made up of Mexico, Peru, Columbia, Chile and Costa Rica. The Pacific Alliance nations are expected to grow much faster than their big neighbour, Brazil. Their current GDP of $2.2 trillion is similar in size to the GDP of the Eurasian Economic Union (EEU), formed in 2015 comprising of Russia, Belarus, Kazakhstan and Armenia. The EEU has around $900 billion worth of trade.

Many regional trading blocs have a dominant country. For example, Russia dominates the EEU and the US dominates NAFTA - the North American Free Trade Association. They have tended to be geo-political regional power blocs as dominant countries are able to make their neighbours more economically reliant on them. For example, Russia wanted to bring the Ukraine into the EEU, but Ukraine feared its freedom would be compromised and resisted.

Trading blocs have their own common rules and regulations and external tariffs. They exist uncomfortably alongside multinational institutions such as the IMF and

WTO targeting free trade for all and also the large global multinational companies which operate within different trading blocs living by each bloc's different legislation.

It is difficult to predict future trends, but some nations are beginning to reject the shared belief of prosperity within trading blocs while others think things do not go far enough. For example, the Transatlantic Trade and Investment Partnership (TTIP) is currently being negotiated at the time of writing. It is trying to formalize a bilateral agreement between the EU and the USA by streamlining standards and reducing barriers to trade on products including manufacturing, services and agriculture. It is something that big business is eager to see, especially considering that the EU is the world's largest economy followed by the USA, a combination creating a market for over 800 million of the world's richest consumers. The advantage is that costs for some businesses might fall, benefitting producers and consumers, and that corporations will be more willing to invest. However, it is not without resistance.

Opponents believe that the agreement removes regulations that currently protect health and workers' rights, public services and the environment, including having an impact on climate change. When agreement has been reached companies will have the right to sue governments if they make public policy decisions which could harm their future profits.

Another problem is that although it is a bilateral agreement other close trading partners would need to comply but would not have been party to the negotiations.

The USA is also negotiating a bilateral agreement with Japan. If such bilateral agreements become more common, the role and impact of multinational organizations is reduced. Finally, give a thought for the economically weaker countries. What should they do or what can they do?

Questions

1. What is the purpose of a trading bloc?
2. How does a trading bloc work in favour of its members?
3. Why might global institutions like the IMF and WTO have less impact on trade than in the past?
4. Who are the potential winners and losers from a Transatlantic Trade and Investment Partnership?
5. Discuss your views on whether large trading blocs or large multinationals have more power on modern global markets.

References: http://action.globaljustice.org
.uk/ea-campaign/action.retrievestaticpage
.do?ea_static_page_id=3521&gclid=CN
_ovY6vjMUCFfOZtAodr0IAIg
http://www.ft.com/cms/s/0/11fcec5e
-e4e5-11e4-8b61-00144feab7de
.html#axzz3Y7pTMBkX
http://yaleglobal.yale.edu/content
/will-ttip-harm-global-trading-system

SUMMARY

- A common currency area (currency union or monetary union) is a geographical area through which one currency circulates and is accepted as the medium of exchange.

- The formation of a common currency area can bring significant benefits to the members of the currency union, particularly if there is already a high degree of international trade among them (i.e. a high level of trade integration). This is primarily because of the reductions in transaction costs in trade and the reduction in exchange rate uncertainty.

- There are, however, costs of joining a currency union, namely the loss of independent monetary policy and also of the exchange rate as a means of macroeconomic adjustment. Given a long-run vertical supply curve, the loss of monetary policy and the lack of exchange rate adjustment affect mainly short-run macroeconomic adjustment.

- These adjustment costs will be lower the greater is the degree of real wage flexibility, labour mobility and capital market integration across the currency union, and also the less the members of the currency union suffer from asymmetric demand shocks.

- The problems of adjustment within a currency union may be alleviated by fiscal federalism – a common fiscal budget and a system of taxes and fiscal transfers across member countries. In practice, however, fiscal federalism may be difficult to implement for political reasons.

- The national fiscal policies of the countries making up a currency union may be subject to a free-rider problem, whereby one country issues a large amount of government debt and pays a lower interest rate on it than it might otherwise have paid, but also leads to other member countries having to pay higher interest rates. It is for this reason that a currency union may wish to impose rules on the national fiscal policies of its members.

- Globalization has led to the rise of very large firms which account for a significant proportion of total world sales.

- There are costs and benefits of globalization – not only to society as a whole but to firms, which have to be taken into account.

- Emerging markets refer to countries which are between developed and developing status and have low to medium GDP per capita.

- Limited growth opportunities in developed countries mean that more businesses are turning to investing in emerging economies as the source of future growth.

- Existing business models often cannot be replicated in emerging markets and as a result more creative and innovative ways of doing business may have to be thought of which meet the needs of populations with limited incomes.

- Businesses have used outsourcing as a means of cutting costs and increasing efficiency but there can be problems which have to be taken into consideration in making any decision to outsource.

- There are cultural, religious and social issues that are involved in carrying out business abroad. The reduction in global boundaries means that more and more businesses operate in a global business environment and so these factors have to be taken into consideration.

QUESTIONS FOR REVIEW

1. What are the main advantages of forming a currency union? What are the main disadvantages?

2. Are the advantages and disadvantages you have listed in answer to Question 1 long run or short run in nature?

3. What is fiscal federalism? How might the problems of macroeconomic adjustment in a currency union be alleviated by fiscal federalism?

4. Why might the members of a currency union wish to impose rules on the conduct of national fiscal policies?

5. Define the terms 'globalization', 'emerging economies' and 'foreign direct investment'.

6. Outline three costs and three benefits of globalization.

7. Why do an increasing number of firms believe that investment in emerging economies represents their future?

8. What are the main costs and benefits of doing business in emerging economies?

9. What is 'outsourcing' and what are the main costs and benefits to a firm of outsourcing?

10. What are the main challenges to firms doing business in a global environment?

PROBLEMS AND APPLICATIONS

1. Consider two countries that trade heavily with one another – Cornsylvania and Techoland. The national currency of Cornsylvania is the cob, while the Techoland national currency is the byte. The output of Cornsylvania is mainly agricultural, while the output of Techoland is mainly high-technology electronic goods. Suppose that each economy is in a long-run macroeconomic equilibrium.
   a. Use diagrams to illustrate the state of each economy. Be sure to show aggregate demand, short-run aggregate supply and long-run aggregate supply.
   b. Now suppose that there is an increase in demand for electronic goods in both countries, and a simultaneous decline in demand for agricultural goods. Use your diagrams to show what happens to output and the price level in the short run in each country. What happens to the unemployment rate in each country?
   c. Show, using your diagrams, how each country could use monetary policy to reduce the short-run fluctuation in output.
   d. Show, using your diagrams, how movements in the cob–byte exchange rate could reduce short-run fluctuations in output in each country.

2. Suppose Techoland and Cornsylvania form a currency union and adopt the electrocarrot as their common currency. Now suppose again that there is an increase in demand for electronic goods in both countries, and a simultaneous decline in demand for agricultural goods. As president of the central bank for the currency union, would you raise or lower the electrocarrot interest rate, or keep it the same? Explain. (Hint: you are charged with maintaining low and stable inflation across the electrocarrot area.)

3. Suppose that Techoland and Cornsylvania decide to engage in fiscal federalism and adopt a common fiscal budget.
   a. Show, again using aggregate demand/aggregate supply diagrams, how fiscal policy can be used to alleviate the short-run fluctuations generated by the asymmetric demand shock.
   b. Given the typical lags in the implementation of fiscal policy, would you advise the use of federal fiscal policy to alleviate short-run macroeconomic fluctuations?

4. The USA can be thought of as a non-trivial currency union since, although it is a single country, it encompasses many states that have economies comparable in size to those of some European countries. Given that the USA has had a single currency for 200 years, it may be thought of as a successful currency union. Yet many of the American states produce very different products and services, so that they are likely to be impacted by different kinds of macroeconomic shocks (expansionary and recessionary) over time. For example, Texas produces oil, while Kansas produces agricultural goods. How do you explain the long-term success of the US currency union given this diversity? Are there any lessons or predictions for Europe that can be drawn from the US experience?

5. Explain, giving reasons, whether the following statements are true or false.
   a. 'A high degree of trade among a group of countries implies that there would be benefits from them adopting a common currency and forming a currency union.'
   b. 'A high degree of trade among a group of countries implies that they should definitely adopt a common currency and form a currency union.'

6. Do you think that the free-rider problem associated with national fiscal polices in a currency union, as we discussed in the text, is likely to be a problem in actual practice? Justify your answer.

7. A firm is planning to invest in setting up a new manufacturing facility in an emerging economy. It aims to use some of its existing highly skilled workforce to help in the setting up of the new facility. Examine some of the challenges that the firm might typically face in executing its plans.

8. In order to be able to get permission to obtain a licence to do business in an emerging economy, senior managers have been left in no doubt that a private payment to local administrative officials will be necessary. The opportunity to do business in this country is seen as being essential to the survival of the business in the medium term and to the security of 2 000 jobs in the home country. How should the senior managers handle this situation? Explain your answer.

9. A firm closes its call centre operations in Belgium with the loss of 3000 jobs which has a significant impact on the local economy where the call centre was located. It outsources the operation to Malaysia and its press release says that it will reduce costs as a result by €1 million a year. After the first six months the firm begins to receive complaints from customers that they are not happy with the level of service which they receive from the new call centre operation. What should the firm do in this situation? (Hint – you might want to consider as part of your answer why customers use the call centre in the first place.)

10. To what extent would you agree with the view that globalization brings more benefits than costs to the world economy?

GLOSSARY

abnormal profit the profit over and above normal profit

absolute advantage the comparison among producers of a good according to their productivity

accounting profit total revenue minus total explicit cost

actual spending, saving or investment the realized or ex post outcome resulting from actions of households and firms

added value the difference between the cost of factor inputs into production and the amount consumers are prepared to pay (the value placed on the product by consumers)

adverse selection the tendency for the mix of unobserved attributes to become undesirable from the standpoint of an uninformed party

agency theory where managers act as the agents of shareholders and as a result there may be a divorce between ownership and control such that managers pursue their own self-interests rather than the interests of shareholders

agent a person who is performing an act for another person, called the principal

aggregate demand curve a curve that shows the quantity of goods and services that households, firms and the government want to buy at each price level

aggregate supply curve a curve that shows the quantity of goods and services that firms choose to produce and sell at each price level

aims the long-term goals of a business

appreciation an increase in the value of a currency as measured by the amount of foreign currency it can buy

asset a tangible or intangible item controlled by a business that has economic value

autonomous expenditure spending which is not dependent on income

average fixed cost fixed costs divided by the quantity of output

average revenue total revenue divided by the quantity sold

average total cost total cost divided by the quantity of output

B2B business business activity where the business sells goods and services to another business

balanced trade a situation in which exports equal imports

bond a certificate of indebtedness

bounded rationality the idea that humans make decisions under the constraints of limited, and sometimes unreliable, information that they are unable to fully process

branding the means by which a business creates an identity for itself and highlights the way in which it differs from its rivals

budget constraint the limit on the consumption bundles that a consumer can afford

business cycle fluctuations in economic activity, such as employment and production

C2C business business activity where consumers exchange goods and services often facilitated by a third party such as an online auction site

capital any item used in production which is not used for its own sake but for what it contributes to production

capitalist economies systems where resource inputs are largely owned by private individuals and where the motive for exchange takes place primarily for profit

cartel a group of firms acting in unison

classical dichotomy the theoretical separation of nominal and real variables

collective bargaining the process by which unions and firms agree on the terms of employment

collusion an agreement among firms in a market about quantities to produce or prices to charge

common currency area (or currency union or monetary union) a geographical area throughout which a single currency circulates as the medium of exchange

common resources goods that are rival but not excludable

communist economies systems where resource inputs are largely owned by the state and exchange and trade is based on social, political and economic motives which may be primarily based on a belief of greater equality

comparative advantage the comparison among producers of a good according to their opportunity cost

compensating differential a difference in wages that arises to offset the non-monetary characteristics of different jobs

competition a market situation when two or more firms are rivals for customers

complements two goods for which an increase in the price of one leads to a decrease in the demand for the other (and vice versa)

compounding the accumulation of a sum of money in, say, a bank account where the interest earned remains in the account to earn additional interest in the future

concentration ratio the proportion of total sales in an industry accounted for by a given number of firms

constant returns to scale the property whereby long-run average total cost stays the same as the quantity of output changes

consumer prices index (CPI) a measure of the overall prices of the goods and services bought by a typical consumer

consumer surplus the amount a buyer is willing to pay for a good minus the amount the buyer actually pays for it

consumption spending by households on goods and services, with the exception of purchases of new housing

contribution the difference between the selling price and the variable cost per unit

core competencies the things a business does which are the source of competitive advantage over its rivals

cost the payment to factor inputs in production

cost leadership a strategy to gain competitive advantage through reducing costs below competitors

cross-price elasticity of demand a measure of how much the quantity demanded of one good responds to a change in the price of another good, computed as the percentage change in quantity demanded of the first good divided by the percentage change in the price of the second good

crowding out a decrease in investment that results from government borrowing

crowding-out effect the offset in aggregate demand that results when expansionary fiscal policy raises the interest rate and thereby reduces investment spending

cyclical deficit a situation when government spending and income is disrupted by the 'normal' economic cycle

cyclical unemployment the deviation of unemployment from its natural rate

deadweight loss the fall in total surplus that results from a market distortion, such as a tax

deflationary/inflationary gap the difference between full employment output and the expenditure required to meet it

demand curve a graph of the relationship between the price of a good and the quantity demanded

demand schedule a table that shows the relationship between the price of a good and the quantity demanded

depreciation a decrease in the value of a currency as measured by the amount of foreign currency it can buy

depression a severe recession

deregulation the removal of controls, laws or rules governing a particular market aimed at improving the economic efficiency of that market and therefore the performance of the economy at the microeconomic level

derived demand when demand for a factor of production is derived (determined) from its decision to supply a good in another market

differentiation the way in which a firm seeks to portray or present itself as being different or unique in some way

diminishing marginal product the property whereby the marginal product of an input declines as the quantity of the input increases

diminishing marginal utility a 'law' that states that marginal utility will fall as consumption increases

discrimination the offering of different opportunities to similar individuals who differ only by race, ethnic group, sex, age or other personal characteristics

diseconomies of scale the property whereby long-run average total cost rises as the quantity of output increases

dominant strategy a strategy that is best for a player in a game regardless of the strategies chosen by the other players

economic activity the amount of buying and selling (transactions) that take place in an economy over a period of time

economic growth the increase in the amount of goods and services in an economy over a period of time

economic profit total revenue minus total cost, including both explicit and implicit costs

economics the study of how society makes decisions in managing scarce resources

economies of scale the property whereby long-run average total cost falls as the quantity of output increases

efficient scale the quantity of output that minimizes average total cost

elasticity a measure of the responsiveness of quantity demanded or quantity supplied to one of its determinants

emerging market economy a country where the per capita income of the population is in the middle to low range compared to other global economies

enterprise the act of taking risks in the organization of factors of production to generate business activity

equilibrium or clearing price the price that balances quantity supplied and quantity demanded

equilibrium quantity the quantity supplied and the quantity demanded at the equilibrium price

ethical responsibility the moral basis for business activity and whether what the business does 'is right' and is underpinned by some moral purpose – doing what is 'right'

European Economic and Monetary Union (EMU) the European currency union that has adopted the euro as its common currency

excludable the property of a good whereby a person can be prevented from using it when they do not pay for it

expected utility theory the idea that buyers can rank preferences from best to worst (or vice versa)

explicit costs input costs that require an outlay of money by the firm

exports goods produced domestically and sold abroad

externality the uncompensated impact of one person's actions on the well-being of a bystander or third party

factors of production a classification of inputs used in business activity which includes land, labour, capital and enterprise

financial intermediaries financial institutions through which savers can indirectly provide funds to borrowers

financial markets financial institutions through which savers can directly provide funds to borrowers

fiscal federalism a fiscal system for a group of countries involving a common fiscal budget and a system of taxes and fiscal transfers across countries

fiscal policy influencing the level of economic activity through manipulation of government income and expenditure

fixed costs costs that are not determined by the quantity of output produced

foreign direct investment inflows of investment into a host country from external businesses

free cash flow the cash generated from the firm's operations minus that spent on capital assets

frictional unemployment unemployment that results because it takes time for workers to search for the jobs that best suit their tastes and skills

full employment a point where those people who want to work at the going market wage level are able to find a job

fundamental analysis the study of an asset to determine its value

future value the amount of money in the future that an amount of money today will yield, given prevailing interest rates

game theory the study of how people behave in strategic situations

GDP deflator a measure of the price level calculated as the ratio of nominal GDP to real GDP times 100

geographical mobility the ease with which people can move to different parts of the country where jobs may be available

globalization the growth of interdependence amongst world economies usually seen as resulting from the removal of many international regulations affecting financial flows

government purchases spending on goods and services by local, state and national governments

gross domestic product (GDP) the market value of all final goods and services produced within a country in a given period of time

gross domestic product (GDP) per head the market value of all final goods and services produced within a country in a given period of time divided by the population of a country to give a per capita figure

heuristics rules of thumb or shortcuts used in decision making

human capital the accumulation of investments in people, such as education and on-the-job training

implicit costs input costs that do not require an outlay of money by the firm

imports goods produced abroad and purchased for use in the domestic economy

income effect the change in consumption that results when a price change moves the consumer to a higher or lower indifference curve

income elasticity of demand a measure of how much the quantity demanded of a good responds to a change in consumers' income, computed as the percentage change in quantity demanded divided by the percentage change in income

indifference curve a curve that shows consumption bundles that give the consumer the same level of satisfaction

inferior good a good for which, other things being equal, an increase in income leads to a decrease in demand (and vice versa)

inflation an increase in the overall level of prices in the economy

inflation rate the percentage change in the price index from the preceding period

inflation tax the revenue the government raises by creating money

internalizing an externality altering incentives so that people take account of the external effects of their actions

investment making money available to develop a project which will generate future returns including increasing future productive capacity

isocost line the different combination of factor inputs which can be purchased with a given budget

job search the process by which workers find appropriate jobs given their tastes and skills

labour all the human effort, mental and physical, which is used in production

labour force the total number of workers, including both the employed and the unemployed

labour force participation rate the percentage of the adult population that is in the labour force

land all the natural resources of the Earth which can be used in production

law of demand the claim that, other things being equal, the quantity demanded of a good falls when the price of the good rises

law of supply the claim that, other things being equal, the quantity supplied of a good rises when its price rises

law of supply and demand the claim that the price of any good adjusts to bring the quantity supplied and the quantity demanded for that good into balance

long run the period of time in which all factors of production can be altered

macroeconomic environment the national or global economy within which the business operates

margin the amount of profit a firm makes on each sale

margin of safety the distance between the break-even output and current production where total revenue is greater than total cost

marginal changes small incremental adjustments to a plan of action

marginal cost the increase in total cost that arises from an extra unit of production

marginal product the increase in output that arises from an additional unit of input

marginal propensity to consume the fraction of extra income that a household spends rather than saves

marginal propensity to save the fraction of extra income that a household saves rather than consumes

marginal rate of technical substitution the rate at which one factor input can be substituted for another at a given level of output

marginal revenue the change in total revenue from an additional unit sold

marginal utility the addition to total utility as a result of one extra unit of consumption

market a group of buyers and sellers of a particular good or service who come together to agree a price for exchange

market economy an economy that allocates resources through the decentralized decisions of many firms and households as they interact in markets for goods and services

market equilibrium a situation in which the price has reached the level where quantity supplied equals quantity demanded

market failure a situation in which a market left on its own fails to allocate resources efficiently

market for loanable funds the market in which those who want to save, supply funds and those who want to borrow to invest demand funds

market niche a small segment of an existing market with specific wants and needs which are not currently being met by the market

market power the ability of a single economic agent (or small group of agents) to have a substantial influence on market prices

market share the proportion of total sales accounted for by a product/business in a market

menu costs the costs of changing prices

merit good a good which could be provided by the private sector but which may also be offered by the public sector because it is believed that a less than optimal amount would be available to the public if resource allocation was left entirely to the private sector

microeconomic environment factors and issues that affect an individual firm operating in a particular market or industry

mixed economies economic systems that include elements of both private and public ownership of resources to answer the fundamental questions

model of aggregate demand and aggregate supply the model that many economists use to explain short-run fluctuations in economic activity around its long-run trend

monetary neutrality the proposition that changes in the money supply do not affect real variables

monetary policy the set of actions taken by the central bank in order to affect the money supply

money multiplier the amount of money the banking system generates with each unit of reserves

monopolistic competition a market structure in which many firms sell products that are similar but not identical

monopoly a firm that is the sole seller of a product without close substitutes

moral hazard the tendency of a person who is imperfectly monitored to engage in dishonest or otherwise undesirable behaviour

multinationals organizations characterized by having operations in a number of countries although their main headquarters will be in one country – normally the country in which the firm originally developed

multiplier effect the additional shifts in aggregate demand that result when expansionary fiscal policy increases income and thereby increases consumer spending

Nash equilibrium a situation in which economic actors interacting with one another each choose their best strategy given the strategies that all the other actors have chosen

natural monopoly a monopoly that arises because a single firm can supply a good or service to an entire market at a smaller cost than could two or more firms

natural rate of output the output level in an economy when all existing factors of production (land, labour, capital and technology resources) are fully utilized and where unemployment is at its natural rate

natural rate of unemployment the normal rate of unemployment around which the unemployment rate fluctuates

natural-rate hypothesis the claim that unemployment eventually returns to its normal, or natural, rate, regardless of the rate of inflation

net capital outflow the purchase of foreign assets by domestic residents minus the purchase of domestic assets by foreigners

net exports spending on domestically produced goods by foreigners (exports) minus spending on foreign goods by domestic residents (imports)

nominal exchange rate the rate at which a person can trade the currency of one country for the currency of another

nominal GDP the production of goods and services valued at current prices

nominal interest rate the interest rate as usually reported without a correction for the effects of inflation

nominal variables variables measured in monetary units

normal good a good for which, other things being equal, an increase in income leads to an increase in demand (and vice versa)

normal profit the minimum amount required to keep factors of production in their current use

objectives the means by which a business will be able to achieve its aims

occupational mobility the ease with which people are able to move from occupation to occupation including the degree to which skills and qualifications are transferable between occupations

oligopoly competition amongst the few – a market structure in which only a few sellers offer similar or identical products and dominate the market

opportunity cost the cost expressed in terms of the benefits sacrificed of the next best alternative

outsourcing contracting out of a part of the business' operations to another organization

Phillips curve a curve that shows the short-run trade-off between inflation and unemployment

Pigovian tax a tax enacted to correct the effects of a negative externality

planned spending, saving or investment the desired or intended actions of households and firms

present value the amount of money today that would be needed to produce, using prevailing interest rates, a given future amount of money

price discrimination the business practice of selling the same good at different prices to different customers

price elasticity of demand a measure of how much the quantity demanded of a good responds to a change in the price of that good, computed as the percentage change in quantity demanded divided by the percentage change in price

price elasticity of supply a measure of how much the quantity supplied of a good responds to a change in the price of that good, computed as the percentage change in quantity supplied divided by the percentage change in price

price the amount of money a buyer (a business or a consumer) has to give up in order to acquire something

price level the price of a basket of goods and services measured as the weighted arithmetic average of current prices

principal a person for whom another person, called the agent, is performing some act

prisoners' dilemma a particular 'game' between two captured prisoners that illustrates why cooperation is difficult to maintain even when it is mutually beneficial

private goods goods that are both excludable and rival

private saving the income that households have left after paying for taxes and consumption

private sector business activity which is owned, financed and organized by private individuals

producer prices index a measure of the change in prices of a basket of goods and services bought by firms

producer surplus the amount a seller is paid minus the cost of production

product life cycle a diagram representing the life cycle of a product from launch through to growth, maturity and decline

production function the relationship between the quantities of inputs used to make a good and the quantity of output of that good

production isoquant a function which represents all the possible combinations of factor inputs that can be used to produce a given level of output

productivity the quantity of goods and services produced from each hour of a worker's time

profit the reward for taking risk in carrying out business activity

property rights the exclusive right of an individual, group or organization to determine how a resource is used

public goods goods that are neither excludable nor rival

public saving the tax revenue that the government has left after paying for its spending

public sector business activity owned, financed and organized by the state on behalf of the population as a whole

purchasing power parity a theory of exchange rates whereby a unit of any given currency should be able to buy the same quantity of goods in all countries

quantity supplied the amount of a good that sellers are willing and able to sell

quantity theory of money a theory asserting that the quantity of money available determines the price level and that the growth rate in the quantity of money available determines the inflation rate

rational expectations the theory according to which people optimally use all the information they have, including information about government policies, when forecasting the future

real exchange rate the rate at which a person can trade the goods and services of one country for the goods and services of another

real GDP a measure of the amount produced that is not affected by changes in prices

real interest rate the interest rate adjusted to take account of the effect of inflation calculated as the nominal interest rate minus the inflation rate

real money balances what money can actually buy given the ratio of the money supply to the price level

real variables variables measured in physical units

recession a period of declining real incomes and rising unemployment. The technical definition gives recession occurring after two successive quarters of negative economic growth

relative prices the ratio of the price of one good to the price of another

risk the extent to which a decision leading to a course of action will result in some loss, damage, adverse effect or otherwise undesirable outcome to the decision maker

risk averse exhibiting a dislike of uncertainty

rival the property of a good whereby one person's use diminishes other people's use

sacrifice ratio the number of percentage points of annual output lost in the process of reducing inflation by one percentage point

scarcity the limited nature of society's resources in relation to wants and needs

screening an action taken by an uninformed party to induce an informed party to reveal information

share (or stock or equity) a claim to partial ownership in a firm

shareholder value the overall value delivered to the owners of business in the form of cash generated and the reputation and potential of the business to continue growing over time

shoe leather costs the resources wasted when inflation encourages people to reduce their money holding

short run the period of time in which some factors of production cannot be changed

shortage a situation in which quantity demanded is greater than quantity supplied

signalling an action taken by an informed party to reveal private information to an uninformed party

single European market a (still not complete) EU-wide market throughout which labour, capital, goods and services can move freely

social responsibility the responsibility a firm has for the impact of their product and activities on society

Stability and Growth Pact a set of formal rules by which members of EMU were supposed to be bound in their conduct of national fiscal policy

stagflation a period of falling output and rising prices

stakeholders groups or individuals with an interest in a business, such as workers, managers, suppliers, the local community, customers and owners.

standard of living a measure of welfare based on the amount of goods and services a person's income can buy

strategic intent a framework for establishing and sharing a vision of where a business wants to be at some point in the future and encouraging all those involved in the business to understand and work towards achieving this vision

strategy a series of actions, decisions and obligations that lead to the firm gaining a competitive advantage and exploiting the firm's core competencies

strike the organized withdrawal of labour from a firm by a union

structural deficit a situation where the deficit is not dependent on movements in the economic cycle

structural unemployment unemployment that results because the number of jobs available in some labour markets is insufficient to provide a job for everyone who wants one

subsidy a payment to buyers and sellers to supplement income or lower costs and which thus encourages consumption or provides an advantage to the recipient

substitutes two goods for which an increase in the price of one leads to an

increase in the demand for the other (and vice versa)

substitution effect the change in consumption that results when a price change moves the consumer along a given indifference curve to a point with a new marginal rate of substitution

sunk cost a cost that has already been committed and cannot be recovered

supply chain the various processes, activities, organizations and resources used in moving a product from business to business or business to consumer

supply curve a graph of the relationship between the price of a good and the quantity supplied

supply schedule a table that shows the relationship between the price of a good and the quantity supplied

supply shock an event that directly alters firms' costs and prices, shifting the economy's aggregate supply curve and thus the Phillips curve

supply-side policy policy aimed at influencing the level of aggregate supply in the economy

surplus a situation in which quantity supplied is greater than quantity demanded

SWOT analysis an analysis of the firm's strengths, weaknesses, opportunities and threats

synergy a situation where the combination of two or more businesses or business operations brings total benefits which are greater than those which would arise from the separate business entities

tactic short-term framework for decision making

tax incidence the manner in which the burden of a tax is shared among participants in a market

technology the application or use of knowledge in some way which enables individuals or businesses to have greater control over their environment

the economy the collective interaction between individuals in the process of production and exchange in a defined area

theory of liquidity preference Keynes' theory that the interest rate adjusts to bring money supply and money demand into balance

third sector business activity owned, financed and organized by private individuals but with the primary aim of providing needs and not making profit

total cost the market value of the inputs a firm uses in production

total expenditure the amount paid by buyers, computed as the price of the good times the quantity purchased

total revenue the amount received by sellers of a good, computed as the price of the good times the quantity sold

trade balance the value of a nation's exports minus the value of its imports; also called net exports

trade deficit an excess of imports over exports

trade openness the ratio of exports plus imports to gross domestic product

trade surplus an excess of exports over imports

transfer payment a payment for which no good or service is exchanged

transformation process the process in which businesses take factor inputs and process them to produce outputs which are then sold

underemployment a situation where a worker has a job but may not be working to full capacity or does not have all their skills utilized or is working for a lower income than their qualifications, training or experience might suggest

unemployed the number unemployed in an economy is the number of people of working age who are able and available for work at current wage rates and who do not have a job

unemployment insurance a government programme that partially protects workers' incomes when they become unemployed

unemployment rate the percentage of the labour force that is unemployed

unintended consequences the outcomes of decision making or policy changes which are not anticipated and are unforeseen

union a worker association that bargains with employers over wages and working conditions

utility the satisfaction derived from consumption

value chain the activities and operations which a firm carries out and how value is added at each of these stages

value for money a situation (mostly subjective) where the satisfaction gained from purchasing and consuming a product is greater than the amount of money the individual had to hand over to acquire it (the price)

value the worth to an individual of owning an item represented by the satisfaction derived from its consumption

value of marginal product the marginal product of an input times the price of the output

variable costs costs that are dependent on the quantity of output produced

willingness to pay a measure of how much a buyer values a good by the amount they are prepared to pay to acquire the good

abnormal profit 247, 557
absolute advantage 410, 557
absorption cost pricing 322
accelerator principle 521
accounting profit 209–10, 557
actual spending, saving or investment 503, 557
added value 36–8, 557
adverse selection 169, 557
advertising 164
  critique 165–6
  debate concerning 164–6
  defence of 166
  as prisoner's dilemma 301–2
  as signal of quality 166–7
agency theory 199, 557
agent 169, 557
aggregate demand
  changes in money supply 517–18
  contraction 446
  influence of fiscal policy 519–20
  influence of monetary policy 514–18
  and Phillips curve 481–2
  role of interest rates 518
  shifts 445–6
  theory of liquidity preference 514–17
aggregate demand curve 429, 430–1, 557
  consumption shift 432–3
  downward slope 431–2, 516–17
  government purchases shift 434
  investment shift 433
  net exports shifts 435
  summary 435
aggregate supply
  adverse shock 488–9
  and Phillips curve 481–2
  shifts 447–9
aggregate supply curve 429, 436, 557
  capital shifts 437–8
  labour shifts 437
  long-run growth/inflation 438–9
  natural resources shifts 438
  reasons for short-run shift 443
  summary 442–3
  technological knowledge shifts 438
  upward slope in short run 439–42
  vertical in long run 436–7
agricultural technologies 110–11
aims 180–1, 557
Akerlof, George 169
aluminium 131
appreciation 415, 557
asset 369, 557
  valuation 369–70
asymmetric information 168–9
  hidden actions 169–70
  screening to induce information revelation 171
  signalling to convey private information 170
auctions 125–6
autonomous expenditure 508, 557
average cost 10, 215–16
average cost curve 217
average fixed cost 215, 557
average revenue 186, 261, 557
average total cost 215, 557
  profit as area between price/average total cost 244
  relationship with marginal cost 218
  short-run/long-run relationship 220–1
  U-shaped 218
average variable cost 215

B2B business 34, 557
B2C business 34
balanced trade 412, 557
banks 363
  India's central bank 493
  Islamic sources/uses 378–9
  Islamic vs conventional 378
  see also central bank
Becker, Gary 354–5
behavioural economics 161–4
below investment grade bonds 361
bilateral agreements 553
bond 360–2, 557
  below investment grade 361
  coupon 361
  credit risk 361
  date of maturity 361
  default 361
  junk 361
  long-term 361
  perpetuity 361
  principal 361
  term 361
Boston Consulting Group matrix 314–15
bounded rationality 161, 557
brand names 167–8
brand recognition 201–2
branding 167, 557
break-even analysis 190–1
  cost minimization 196–8
  effect of break-even output of changes in price 192
  limitations 191–2
  revenue maximization 192–6
  shareholder value 198–9
BRIC countries (Brazil, Russia, India, China) 449–50
budget
  constraint 153, 557
  deficits/surpluses 375–6
business activity 4–6
business cycle 17, 426, 557
business decision making *see* decision making
business economics *see* economics
business environment 47–8
  PESTLE framework 39–46
  shareholder value/stakeholders 46–7
  transformation process 34–8
business policy 403–4
business strategy *see* strategy
buyers
  clearly defined 55
  many 54

C2C business 34, 557
capital 34–5, 344, 557
  aggregate supply curve 437–8
  equilibrium in markets 345–6
  mobility 541
capital intensive 210
capitalist economies 5, 557
car emissions 124
cartel 293–4, 557
case studies
  accelerator principle 521
  added value through use of technology 37
  advertising 164–5
  Apple gaining market share 24–5
  aviation in the long run 221–2
  cheap milk 40
  complex transformation process 38–9
  contrasting Yemen/UAE 376–7
  deflation 476–7
  diamond monopoly 58
  doing business in Africa 408–9
  financial crises 364–5
  global market for higher education 540
  homogeneity of tobacco products 55
  importance of customer retention 29
  industry quotas in Nigeria 11
  investment/consumption 433–4
  job generation in clusters 508–9
  local authorities 184–5
  measuring business in Wales 6
  OPEC/world oil market 294–5
  price of tickets 320–1
  production decisions 241–2
  short-term monopoly drugs 269–70
  tax rates 512
  travel/fuel prices 94–5
  unemployment in OECD countries 455–6
  wages/employment conundrum 338–9
central bank 499
  open-market operations 499
  refinancing rate 499–501
  reserve requirements 501–2
  see also banks

CEO *see* chief executive officer
Chartered Institute of Marketing 28
chief executive officer (CEO) 34
China 145–6, 355–6
circular-flow diagram 389–90
claimant count 407
classical dichotomy 428, 557
classical theory 428–9, 483
classical theory of inflation 470–4
clearing price (or equilibrium) 70
climate change 543–4
collective bargaining 461–2, 557
collusion 557
command-and-control policies 135
common currency area 530, 557
    fiscal policy 535–8
common resources 180, 302, 557
    game 303
communist economies 5, 7, 557
comparative advantage 410–11, 557
compensating differential 347, 557
competition 57, 236–7, 293–4, 557
    with differentiated products 285
    law 304–5
    monopoly vs 260–1
    perfect/imperfect 57
    policy controversies 305–7
    pricing 325
competitive firm
    long run supply curve 243
    measuring profit 243–4
    staying in business with zero profit 247
competitive markets 236–7
    supply curve in 244–50
competitive profit-maximizing firm
    333–4
complements 68, 557
compounding 365, 557
concentration ratio 292, 557
constant returns to scale 222, 557
consumer prices index (CPI) 397, 557–8
    calculation of 398–9
    choose base year/compute index 399
    compare basket's cost 399
    compute inflation rate 399
    find the prices 398
    fix the basket 398
    vs GDP deflator 401
Consumer Reports 161
consumer surplus 125, 125–6, 558
    measuring using demand curve 127–8
consumers
    changes in income affect choice 156–7
    changes in prices affect choice 157–9
    goods/services bought by 401
    optimization 155–6
    preferences 154–5, 533
    what they can afford 152–3
consumption 393, 558
    aggregate demand curve shifts 432–3
contestable markets 291
contribution 191, 558
contribution cost pricing 322
core competencies 315, 558
cost of capital 209
cost curves 217

marginal cost/average total cost rela-
    tionship 218
    rising marginal cost 217
    typical 218–20
    U-shaped average total cost 218
cost leadership 317–18, 558
cost of living 396–7
    consumer prices index 398–9
    introduction of new goods 400
    problems of measuring 399–400
    relevance 400
    substitution bias 399–400
    unmeasured quality change 400
cost minimization 196–7
    productivity 197
    supply chain 198
cost-benefit 123
    of globalization 542–4
cost-plus pricing 321–2
costs 54, 558
    average/marginal 215–17
    economic vs accounting profit 209–10
    explicit 208
    fixed/variable 215
    implicit 208
    isoquants/isocosts 224–9
    measures of 213–20
    opportunity 208–9
    production and 210–13
    shoe leather 475
    short-run/long-run 220–3
    single currency 532, 534
    total 207–8
coupon 361
CPI *see* consumer prices index
credit markets, global 541
credit risk 361
cross-price elasticity of demand 103–4, 558
crowding out 376, 558
crowding-out effect 519–20, 558
cultural sensitivities 544–5
currency union 530, 557
    national fiscal policies 536–8
currently produced goods 401
customers, acquiring/keeping 28, 29
cyclical deficit 539, 558
cyclical unemployment 408, 454, 558

date of maturity 361
David Lloyd Leisure 184–5
deadweight loss 129–30, 266–8, 558
debt finance 362
decision making 25
    acquiring/keeping customers 28
    business 25–8
    costs/benefits 123
    effects of 23
    external effects 124–5
    growth/expansion 27–8
    human 161–4
    investment 26–7
    long run to exit/enter a market 242–3
    supply 237–9
    trade-offs 8
default 361
deflation 478–9

deflationary gap 504, 558
demand
    change in 75–6
    excess 71
    increase/decrease 65, 67, 69
    market vs individual 64–5
    money 471–2, 515–16
    price/quantity relationship 64
    shift in short run/long run 247–9
demand curve 64, 558
    measuring consumer surplus 127–8
    shifts vs movements 65–9
    variety of 98
demand for labour
    causes of shift in demand curve 337
    competitive profit-maximizing firm
        333–4
    production function/marginal product
        of 334–5
    shifts in 343
    value of marginal product/demand for
        labour 335–6
demand schedule 64, 558
demand-supply 70
    analysing changes in equilibrium 75–80
    equilibrium 70–2
depreciation 415, 558
depression 426, 558
deregulation 510, 558
derived demand 332, 558
destroyer pricing 324
dichotomy 428
differentiation 318, 558
diminishing marginal product 213
diminishing marginal utility 152, 558
discrimination 352, 558
    Becker's 'employer taste' model 354–5
    measuring labour market 352–3
diseconomies of scale 222, 558
disinflation
    costless 491–2
    monetary policy 490
disposable personal income 392
dominant strategy 299–300, 558
duopoly 292–3

earnings 347
    ability, effort, chance 348
    above-equilibrium wages 349–52
    compensating differentials 347
    education 348–9
    human capital 347–8
economic activity 426, 558
economic fluctuation 444
    basic model 429–30
    effects of shift in aggregate demand 445–6
    effects of shift in aggregate supply 447–9
    irregular/unpredictable 426
    macroeconomic quantities 427
    as out falls, unemployment rises 427
    short run vs long run 427–8
economic growth 14, 403–6, 433–4, 558
economic profit 209–10, 558
economics 4, 7, 22, 30, 41–2, 558
    business decision making 25–8
    science/art of decision making 22–4

economies of scale 222–3, 558
implications 223
the economy 8, 562
education 134, 404, 513, 540
signalling 348–9
efficiency 122
allocative 122
productive 122
social 122
technical 122
efficiency wages 351, 463
worker effort 464
worker health 463–4
worker quality 464–5
worker turnover 464
efficient level of output 266
efficient scale 218, 558
EFSF *see* European Financial Stability
Fund
elasticity 87, 558
mathematics of 104–9
and tax incidence 139–40
electronic news 203
emergent strategy 316
emerging market economy 545, 558
emerging markets 541–2
business strategies in 548–9
characteristics 545–7
importance of 547–8
problems facing business in 548
employees, effect on business 43
employer taste model (Becker's) 354–5
employment 338–9
full 503
hidden actions 169–70
EMU *see* European Economic and Monetary Union
enclave strategies 549
enterprise 35, 558
entrepreneur 35–6
entry/exit 55, 242–3, 245–7
environment 45–6
carbon emissions/climate change 46
recycling 45–6
regulation 135
environmental objectives 200–1
equality of net exports 414
equilibrium
analysing changes in 75–80
labour market 341
market for land/capital 346
money 471–2
for oligopoly 295–8
price level 472
quantity 70, 558
shifts in aggregate demand 445–6
equilibrium (or clearing price) 70, 558
equity 544
equity finance 362–3
ERM *see* Exchange Rate Mechanism
ethical objectives 200–1
ethical responsibility 144–5, 558
EU *see* European Union
EU Competition Commission 304–5
Euro 530–1
European Central Bank (ECB) 536, 537

European Economic and Monetary Union
(EMU) 529, 530–1, 537, 558
European Financial Stability Fund
(EFSF) 538
European System of Central Banks
(ESCB) 530
European Union (EU) 7, 528–9
excess capacity 288–9
exchange rate
effect 432
effect on businesses 420–1
nominal 415
real 416–17
shift in consumer preferences 433
Exchange Rate Mechanism (ERM) 529
excludable 180, 558
expectations 63, 69
expected utility theory 155, 163–4, 558
explicit costs 208, 558
exports 411, 558
net 394, 413, 414, 435, 560
external growth 259
externalities 14, 123, 558
elasticity/tax incidence 139–40
formal analysis of taxes/subsidies 138
government command-and-control
policies 135
market outcomes 124
market-based policies 135–6
negative 123, 131–3
objections to economic analysis of pollution 143–4
positive 123, 133–4
property rights 142–3
social/ethical responsibility 144–5
subsidies affect market outcomes 141–2
taxes on sellers affect market outcomes
138–9
tradable pollution permits 136–8
variety of 124–5
welfare economics 125

factors of production 34–6, 558
capital 34–5
labour 34
land 34
markets for 332
mobility of 88–9
fair trade 305–6
FDI *see* foreign direct investment
final good 390–1
finance, Islamic *see* Islamic finance
financial crisis (2007–2009) 42
financial intermediaries 362–3, 558
banks 363
investment funds 363–4
financial markets 360, 558
bond market 360–2
stock market 362
financial objectives 185
identifying point of profit maximization
187–9
profit maximization 185–7
financial resources 412–13
Financial Times Stock Exchange (FTSE) 362
firm cooperation 302–4

firm size 88
fiscal federation 535, 558
fiscal policy 502–3, 559
common currency areas 535–8
Keynesian cross 503–4
multiplier effect 504–8
Five Forces model (Porter's) 315
fixed basket of goods 401
fixed costs 215, 559
flexible labour markets 512–13
foreign direct investment (FDI) 403–4,
551, 559
features 551–2
foreign exchange rate 531–2
foreign investment 30–1
foreign portfolio investment 412
framing effects 163–4
Frankfurt stock market 362
free cash flow 199, 559
free trade 405–6
free-rider problem 536–8
frictional unemployment 457, 559
as inevitable 458
Friedman, Milton 483–8
full employment 503, 559
fundamental analysis 370, 559
future value 365, 559

game theory 298–9, 559
GDP *see* gross domestic product
GDP deflator 396, 559
vs consumer prices index 401
geographical mobility 513, 559
global business, culture, ethics 539, 540–2
global credit markets 541
globalization 539, 559
benefits 542
capital mobility 541
choice/price 542
climate change 543–4
collapse of Soviet bloc/emerging
markets 541–2
costs 543–4
cultural/religious sensitivities 544–5
expansion of global credit markets 541
growth of multinational companies 542
inequality/equity 544
interdependence 544
inward investment 542
power of multinations 543
reasons for 540–2
shareholder value 542
standardization 543
transport/logistics 540–1
wider implications of 544
GNP *see* gross national product
goals 180
aims/objectives 180–1
public/private sectors 182–4
strategies/tactics 181–2
goods 123, 391, 393
bought by consumers 401
currently produced 401
domestically produced 401
fixed basket 401
introduction of new 400

goods (*Continued*)
  private 180
  public 180
  unmeasured quality change 400
Google 279–80
government
  aggregate demand curve shift 434
  budget deficits/surpluses 375–6
  changes in pruchases 519
  command-and-control policies 135
  good governance 405
  intervention 13–14
  market-based policies 135–6
  monopoly creation 258
  printing money 16–17
  public policy toward oligopolies 304–7
  public policy towards monopolies 275–8
  purchases 393, 559
gross domestic product (GDP) 15–16,
    388–90, 404, 559
  components 392–4
  comprehensive 390
  final good 390–1
  in a given period of time 391
  goods/services 391
  market value 390
  measurement of 390–1
  produced 391
  real vs nominal 394–6
  within a country 391
gross national product (GNP) 392, 404
growth
  economic 403–6
  population 406
  rates 402

health 405
heuristics 162, 559
  anchoring 162
  availability 162–3
  persuasion 163
  representativeness 163
  simulation 163
hidden action 169
hidden characteristic 169
hit and run strategies 549
homoeconomicus 161
homogenous goods 54, 55
human capital 347–8, 352–3, 559
human mistakes
  confirmation of existing view/
    hypothesis 162
  expected utility theory/framing effects
    163–4
  overconfidence 161
  reluctance to change mind 162
  rules of thumb/heuristics 162–3
  weight given to observations 161–2
Hume, David 428, 470

identity 393
IFS *see* Institute for Fiscal Studies
image 202
immigration 340
immunization programmes 124–5
imperfect competition 256–7, 285

implicit costs 208, 559
imports 559
incentives 10–11
  investment 374–5
  saving 373–4
income 67
  changes affect consumer choice 156–7
  disposable personal 392
  measurement 392
  national 392
  personal 392
  proportion devoted to product 96–7
income effect 67, 159–60, 559
income elasticity of demand 103, 559
India 380–1, 493
indifference curve 154, 559
industry size 88
inequality 123, 544
inferior good 67, 158, 559
inflation 16–17, 447, 559
  classical theory 470–4
  comparison over time 401
  confusion/inconvenience 476
  cost of reducing 490–2
  costs of 474–9
  fallacy 474
  long-run 438–9
  rate 399, 599
  special cost of unexpected inflation 477–9
  tax 474–5, 559
  and unemployment 479–80
  unemployment-inflation trade-off 488
inflation-induced tax distortions 476
inflationary gap 504, 558
information
  asymmetry 168–71
  for life insurance 172–3
  perfect 55
  private 170
  revelation 171
infrastructure 513
input demand 337–8
input prices 62
Institute for Fiscal Studies (IFS) 511
insurance 368
  unemployment 459–60
interdependence 544
interest rate
  effect 431–2
  role 518
  transmission mechanism 498
intermediary 362–3
intermediate good 390
internalizing an externality 133, 559
International Monetary Fund (IMF) 41
international transactions 414–15
  equality of net exports 414
  net capital outflow 414
  nominal exchange rates 415
  real exchange rates 416–17
inventory, ease of storing 90
investment 26–7, 48, 393, 559
  actual 503
  aggregate demand curve shifts 433
  foreign portfolio 412
  from abroad 403–4

fund 363
  importance of 403
  incentives 374–5
  inward 542
  Islamic accounts 379
  planned 503
  relationship to international flows 414
inward investment 542
inward-oriented policies 405–6
Islamic finance 377–8
  avoidance of Gharar 378
  avoidance of Riba 378
  banking sources/users 378–9
  current accounts 379
  investment accounts 379
  Islamic vs conventional banks 378
  principles 378
  savings accounts (Wadiah) 379
  shareholder investments 379
  sources 379
  to be Halal (permitted) 378
isocost line 225–8, 559
isoquants 224–5

jeopardy problems 17, 27
job search 457, 559
  public policy 458–9
junk bonds 361

Keynes, John Maynard 448, 502–3

labour 34, 559
  aggregate supply curve 437
  demand for 332–8
  supply of 339–43
labour demand curve 337
labour force 408, 559
  participation rate 408, 599
Labour Force Surveys 407
labour market
  earnings/discrimination 347–52
  economics of discrimination 352–5
  flexible 512–13
  measuring discrimination 352–3
Laffer, Arthur 511
Laffer curve 511
lagged indicator 427
land 34, 344, 559
  equilibrium in market 345–6
law of demand 64, 559
law of supply 59, 559
law of supply and demand 559
laws/regulation 44–5
learn to earn strategy 549
least-cost input combination 228–9
linear demand curve 101–3
loanable funds
  market for 371
  supply/demand for 371–6
logical incrementalism 316
logistics 540–1
London Stock Exchange (LSE) 362
long run 211, 559
  aggregate supply curve 436–9
  decision to exit/enter a market 242–3
  disinflationary monetary policy 490

market supply with entry/exit 245–7
Phillips curve 483–5
shift in demand 247–9
supply curve sloping upwards 249–50
long run average total cost 220–1
long run equilibrium 287–8
long-term bond 361
long-term refinancing operation (LTRO)
    538–9
LTRO *see* long-term refinancing operation
luxuries 96

M&A *see* merger and acquisition
macroeconomic environment 42, 559
macroeconomic variables 427
macroeconomics 388
    open-economy 411-14
    imports 411
margin 320, 559
margin of safety 191, 559
marginal changes 10, 559
marginal cost 10, 215–16, 559
    mark-up over 289–90
    relationship with average total cost 218
    rising 217
marginal cost curve 217
    firm's supply decision 237–9
marginal product 212–13, 559
    demand for labour 335–6
    of labour 334–5
marginal propensity to consume 505, 559
marginal propensity to save 505, 559
marginal rate of substitution (MRS) 152,
    154, 156
marginal rate of technical substitution
    (MRTS) 224, 559
marginal revenue 186, 559
marginal revenue product (MRP) 454
marginal utility 151–2, 560
marginal-cost pricing 325–6
margins, mathematics of 216
mark-up over marginal cost 289–90
market 56, 560
    definition 96
    economy 12–13, 560
    equilibrium 70, 560
    exit/entry 242–3
    inefficiencies 131
    niche 318–19, 560
    power 14, 123, 199–200, 236, 560
    share 200, 560
    skimming 323–4
    types 56–7
market failure 14
    sources 122–3
market for loanable funds 371
market outcomes 13–14
    size of oligopoly 297–8
    and subsidies 141–2
    tax on sellers 138–9
market supply
    long run 245–7
    short run 245
market-based policies 135–6
market-based strategy 316–17
    differentiation 318

niche strategies 318–19
    value chain analysis 317–18
medium of exchange 363
menu costs 475, 560
merger and acquisition (M&A) 27
merit good 183, 560
microeconomic environment 42, 560
microeconomic substitution 430
minimum wage laws 460–1
minimum wages 349–50, 465–6
misperception theory 442
mixed economies 7
model of aggregate demand and aggregate
    supply 429, 560
monetary multiplier 560
monetary neutrality 429, 560
monetary policy 497–9, 560
    central banks' tools 499–502
    disinflationary 490
    problems controlling money supply 502
monetary union 530, 557
money
    adjustment process 473–4
    controlling supply 502
    demand 471–2
    effects of monetary injection 472–3
    equilibrium 471–2, 516
    growth 470
    multiplier 501–2
    quantity theory of 473
    real balances 508
    time value 365–6
    value of 470–1
money supply 471–2
    changes in 517–18
monopolistic competition 285, 560
    long run equilibrium 287–8
    short run 285–7
    vs perfect competition 288–90
monopoly 57, 255, 257, 293–4
    deadweight loss 266–8
    external growth 259
    government-increased 258
    inefficiency 267
    natural 258–9
    prevalence of 278–9
    profit 264
    profit maximization 262–4
    profit as social cost 268
    public ownership 277
    public policy towards 275–8
    regulation 276–7
    resources 257–8
    revenue 261–2
    supply curve 265
    vs competition 260–1
    welfare cost 266–8
monopsony 344
moral hazard 169, 560
MRP *see* marginal revenue product
MRS *see* marginal rate of substitution
MRTS *see* marginal rate of technical
    substitution
multinational companies 539, 542, 543
multiplier effect 504–5, 560
    applications 506–8

multiplier, formula for spending 505–6

naive empiricism 162
Nash equilibrium 296–7, 560
national income 392
national income accounts 371
    market for loanable funds 371
    supply/demand for loanable funds
        371–6
natural factors 63
natural monopoly 258–9, 560
natural rate of output 437, 560
natural rate of unemployment 408, 454,
    483, 485
natural resources 438
natural-rate hypothesis 488, 560
necessities 96
negative externality 123, 131–3
net capital outflow 412–13, 414, 560
net exports 394, 413, 414, 435, 560
net national product (NNP) 392
niche strategies 318–19
NIKKEI Index 362
NNP *see* net national product
nominal exchange rate 415, 560
nominal GDP 394–5, 560
nominal interest rate 402, 560
nominal variables 428, 560
non-financial objectives 199
    brand recognition 201–2
    market power 199–200
    reputation/image 202
    satisficing 199
    social enterprise 202
    social, ethical, environmental objectives
        200–1
normal good 67, 560
normal profit 247, 560
not-for-profit 202
nutrition 405

objectives 180–1, 560
occupational mobility 513, 560
oil prices 81
oligopoly 57, 291–2, 560
    competition, monopolies, cartels 293–4
    duopoly example 292–3
    equilibrium for 295–7
    Ishaq & Coralie game 303
    markets with few dominant sellers 292
    as prisoner's dilemma 300–1
    size affects market outcome 297–8
online shopping 125–6
open skies international policy 308
open-economy macroeconomics 411
    equality of net exports 413
    international flows of goods/capital
        411–13
    net capital outflow 413
    saving/investment & international flows
        414
open-market operations 499
opportunity cost 9, 208–9, 560
    and comparative advantage 410–11
    cost of capital 209
optimum 155–6

output
    efficient level of 266
    price 337
    supply 337–8
    and unemployment 427
outsourcing 549–50, 560

penetration pricing 323
People and Places 184
perfect competition 288–90
perfect price discrimination 272–3
perpetuity of bond 361
personal income 392
PESTLE framework 39, 47
    economic 41–2
    environment 45–6
    legal 44–5
    political 41
    social 43
    technological 44
Phelps, Edmund 483–8
Phillips, A.W. 480
Phillips curve 17, 480, 560
    aggregate demand/supply 481–2
    long-run 483–5
    origins 480–1
    reconciling theory/evidence 485–6
    short-run 486–7
Pigou, Arthur 135
Pigovian taxes 135–6, 561
    equivalence with pollution
        permits 137
planned spending, saving or investment
    503, 561
political stability 405
politics 41
pollution
    carbon emissions 45–6
    government regulation 135
    objections to economic analysis 143–4
    pricing 145–6
    and social optimum 132
    tradable permits 136–8
population
    ageing 43
    growth 406
    size/structure 69
positive externality 123, 133–4
POST (purpose, objectives, strategies,
    tactics) 314
predatory pricing 306, 324
premium pricing 324–5
present value 365, 366, 561
price discrimination 270, 561
    airline prices 274
    analytics 272–3
    cinema tickets 274
    discount coupons 274
    examples 274
    parable about pricing 270–2
    quantity discounts 274
    reduction in 531
    welfare and 273
price elasticity of demand 94, 561
    applications 110–13
    availability of close substitutes 96

changing along demand curve/marginal
    revenue 194
    computing 97
    definition of market 96
    determinants 96–7
    elasticity/total expenditure along linear
        demand curve 101–3
    necessities vs luxuries 96
    proportion of income devoted to prod-
        uct 96–7
    time horizon 97
    total expenditure 98–101
    total revenue 98–101
    using midpoint method 98
    variety of demand curves 98
price elasticity of supply 87–8, 561
    applications 110–13
    computing 89
    ease of stock/inventory 89
    midpoint method of calculating per-
        centage changes/
        elasticities 89–90
    mobility of factors of production 88–9
    productive capacity 88
    size of firm/industry 88
    time period 88
    total revenue and 93–4
price leadership 325
price level 438, 470–1, 561
price/s 54, 561
    affect on consumer surplus 127
    allocation of resources 83
    benefits of globalization 542
    changes affect consumer choice 157–9
    computing CPI 398
    and consumption 431
    input 62
    international transactions 414–17
    and investment 431–2
    and net exports 432
    output 337
    profit as area between price/average
        total cost 244
    of related goods 68
    relative 153
    as signals 82
    sticky price theory 441–2
pricing
    parable 270–2
    pollution 145–6
    predatory 306, 324
    premium 324–5
    psychological 323
    risk 368–9
pricing strategies 320
    competition 325
    contribution/absorption cost pricing
        322
    cost-plus 321–2
    destroyer/predatory 324
    loss-leader 324
    marginal-cost 325–6
    market skimming 323–4
    penetration 323
    predatory 306
    premium/value 324–5

    price leadership 325
    psychological 323
principal 169, 561
principles
    decision making involves trade-offs 8
    governments can improve market out-
        comes 13–14
    inflation/unemployment trade-off 17
    markets as way to organized economic
        activity 12–13
    opportunity cost 9
    prices rise when government prints too
        much
        money 16–17
    responding to incentives 10–11
    standard of living 15–16
    thinking at the margin 9–10
    trade can make everyone better off
        11–12
print news 203
prisoners' dilemma 299–300, 561
    advertising 301–2
    common resources 302
    oligopolies as 300–1
private costs 123–5
private goods 180, 561
private information 170
private saving 371, 561
private sector 4–5, 182–4, 561
producer prices index 399, 561
producer surplus 128, 561
    cost/willingness to sell 128
    market inefficiencies 131
    measuring using supply curve 129–30
    negative externalities 131–3
    positive externalities 133–4
product life cycle 561
product/s
    differentiation 285
    life cycle 196
    proportion of income devoted to 96–7
    success/failure 36–8
production 402
    costs 207
    function 210–11, 212, 334–5, 561
    isoquant 224, 225, 226, 561
productive capacity 88
productivity 16, 197, 403, 561
profit 4, 207–8, 561
    abnormal 247
    as area between price/average total cost
        244
    measuring 243–4
    monopoly 264, 268
    normal 247
    zero 247, 289
profit maximization 185–7, 195, 262–4,
    333–4
    identifying point of 187–9
    mathematics of 189
property rights 13–14, 55, 142–3, 405, 561
psychological pricing 323
public goods 180, 561
public policy 403–4
    controversies over competition policy
        305–7

doing nothing 278
job search 458–9
public ownership 277
regulation 276–7
restraint of trade/competition law 304–5
toward monopolies 275–8
toward oligopolies 304–7
public saving 371, 561
public sector 5, 182–4, 561
ownership of monopolies 277
purchasing power 474
purchasing power parity 417–18, 561
basic logic of 418
implications of 418–19
limitations of 419–20
pure market economy 12–13

quantity demand 64, 69
quantity supplied 58–9, 561
quantity theory of money 473, 561

R&D *see* research and development
RAS *see* reticular activation system
rational behaviour 9–10, 22–3, 56
rational expectations 491–2, 561
real exchange rate 416–17, 561
real GDP 395–6, 427, 561
real interest rate 402, 561
real money balances 508, 561
real variables 428, 561
real wages 441
recession 426, 561
redistribution of wealth 477–8
refinancing rate 499–501
relative price 428, 561
relative price of goods 153
relative price variability 475
religious sensitivities 544–5
rental price 345
reputation 202
resale price maintenance 305–6
research and development (R&D) 124, 406
reserve requirements 501–2
resource immobility 123
resource-based model 315–16
resources
common 180
misallocation of 475
price allocation 83
scarce 22–3
retained earnings 392
reticular activation system (RAS) 162
revenue maximization 192–5
risk 27, 561
risk averse 367, 561
risk management 366
markets for insurance 368
risk aversion 367
rival 180, 561

sacrifice ratio 490–1, 561
sales revenue maximization 192–3
graphical representation 193–5
Samuelson, Paul 480
Sargent, Thomas 491–2
satisficing 199

saving
actual 503
importance of 403
incentives 373–4
planned 503
relationship to international flows 414
scarce resources 22–3
scarcity 7, 561
screening 171, 561
seasonal adjustment 391
sellers
clearly defined 55
number of 54, 63
variables that influence 63
SEM *see* single European market
services 391
bought by consumers 401
domestically produced 401
SGP *see* Stability and Growth Pact
shareholder value 46–7, 198–9, 561
benefits of globalization 542
shares 362
shoe leather cost 475, 561
short run 211, 561
aggregate supply curve 439–40, 443, 444
decision to shut down 239–41
disinflationary monetary policy 490
economic fluctuations 427–8
market supply with fixed number of firms 245
monopolistically competitive firm 285–7
Phillips curve 486–7
shift in demand 247–9
short run average total cost 220–1
short run supply curve 241
shortage 71, 562
shutdown 239
signalling 170, 348–9, 562
Simon, Herbert 199
single currency
benefits 531–2, 534
costs 532, 534
elimination of transaction costs 531
high degree of trade integration 534
reduction in foreign exchange rate variability 531–2
reduction in price discrimination 531
single European market (SEM) 528–9, 562
ski holidays 111–13
Smith, Adam 13
smoking 113–14
social
change 43
enterprise 184, 202
factors 63
networking 43
objectives 200–1
optimism 134
responsibility 144–5, 562
social costs 123–5
monopoly profit 268
society 6–7
Solow, Robert 480
Sony 326–7
South Africa 7, 30–1

sovereign debt crisis 538–9
Soviet bloc 541–2
specialization 409–11
Spence, Michael 169
Stability and Growth Pact (SGP) 537–8, 562
stagflation 447, 562
stagnation 447
stakeholders 26, 46–7, 562
standard economic model 150
standard of living 16, 562
standardization 543
sticky price theory 441–2
sticky wage theory 440
Stiglitz, Joseph 169
stock
ease of storing 89
index 362
market 362
store of value 363
strategic intent 313, 562
strategy 181–2, 313, 562
definition 313
emergent strategy 316
enclave 549
hit and run 549
learn to earn 549
logic incrementalism 316
market-based strategy 316–19
resource-based model 315–16
strategic hierarchy 313
strategic implementation 319
strategic planning 314–15
strike 351, 562
structural deficit 539, 562
structural unemployment 457, 562
economics of unions 461–2
efficiency wages 463–5
minimum wage laws 460–1
unions as good/bad for economy 462–3
unions/collective bargaining 461
subsidy 141, 562
affect on market outcomes 141–2
on rail transport 141
substitutes 68, 96, 562
substitution bias 399–400
substitution effect 67, 159–60, 562
sunk cost 239, 240, 562
SuperJam 229–30
supply 58
change in 77
excess 71
market vs individual 60
money 471–2, 473, 514–15
price/quantity relationship 58–9
see also demand-supply
supply chain 198, 562
supply curve 58–9, 562
in competitive market 244–50
long run sloping upwards 249–50
marginal cost 238, 239
measuring producer surplus 129–30
monopoly 265
shifts vs movements 60–3
short run 241
variety of 90–2

supply and demand 54
  assumptions 54–6
  buyers/sellers clearly defined 55
  freedom of entry/exit 55
  homogenous goods 54
  labour 332–43
  law of 559
  many buyers/sellers 54
  perfect information 55
  property rights clearly defined 55
  rational behaviour 56
  versatility of 333
  zero transaction costs 56
supply of labour 339
  causes of labour supply curve shift 340
  changes in alternative opportunities 340
  changes in tastes 340
  equilibrium in market 341
  immigration 340
  shifts in 341–2
  trade-off between work/leisure 339–40
supply schedule 59, 562
supply shock 488–9, 562
supply-side policies 510, 562
  deregulation 510
  education/training 513
  flexible labour markets 512–13
  infrastructure 513
  tax laws 510–11
  trade unions 513–14
  welfare reform 512
surplus 71, 562
SWOT analysis 314, 562
synergy 27, 562

Tablet market 250–1
tactic 181–2, 562
tastes/fashion 68
tax
  affect on welfare 130
  burden of tax as dividend 140
  changes in 520
  inflation-induced distortions 476
  laws 510–11
  levied on sellers 138–9
  policy 433
tax incidence 138, 562
  elasticity and 13–40
TDR 184–5
technological change 337
technological knowledge 438
technology 44, 62–3, 562
term 361
Tesco 48–9

theory of liquidity preference 514, 518, 562
  downward slope of aggregate demand
    curve 516–17
  equilibrium in money market 516
  money demand 515–16
  money supply 514–15
third sector 5, 202, 562
time period 88
time value of money 365–6
Tokyo Stock Exchange 362
total cost 207–8, 562
total cost curve 214
total expenditure 98–101, 562
total revenue 93–4, 98–101, 207–8, 261,
  562
total revenue curve 194
total utility 151–2
trade
  balance 412, 562
  deficit 412, 562
  openness 542, 562
  restraint 304–5
  specialization and 409–11
  surplus 412, 562
trade unions *see* unions
trade-offs 8
  short-run 17
  unemployment-inflation 488
  work/leisure 339–40
trading blocs 553
training 513
transaction costs
  elimination of 531
  zero 56
transfer payment 393, 562
transformation process 34, 562
  adding value 36–8
  factors of production 34–6
transport 124, 141, 540–1
tying 306–7

U-shaped average total cost 218
UNCTAD *see* United Nations Conference
  on Trade and Development
underemployment 513, 562
unemployed 407, 562
unemployment 427
  cyclical 408, 454
  definition 406–7
  frictional 457, 458
  identifying 454–5
  and inflation 479–80
  insurance 459–60, 562
  job search 457, 458–9

  length of time 456
  measuring 407–8
  natural rate of 408, 454, 483, 485
  rate 408, 562
  structural 457, 460–5
unemployment-inflation trade-off 488
unintended consequences 10–11, 562
unions 351, 513–14, 562
  collective bargaining 461
  economics of 461–2
  as good/bad for economy 462–3
United Kingdom 7
United Nations Conference on Trade and
  Development (UNCTAD) 551
university education 18
utility 151, 367, 563
utility function 367

value 150–1, 563
value chain 317, 563
value of the marginal product 335–6, 562
value for money 24, 563
value pricing 324–5
variable costs 215, 563

wages 338–9
  above-equilibrium 349–52
  calculating real wages 441
  efficiency 351–2, 463–5
  labour unions 351
  minimum 349–51, 465–6
  sticky wage theory 440
wants/needs 22–3
wealth
  arbitrary redistributions 477–8
  effect 431
welfare
  cost of monopoly 266–8
  tax affects 130
  with/without price discrimination 273
welfare economics 125
welfare reform 512
willingness to pay 125, 562
women in workforce 340
work/leisure trade-off 339–40
worker
  effort 464
  health 463–4
  quality 464–5
  turnover 464
World Trade Organization (WTO) 542
WTO *see* World Trade Organization

zero-profit 247, 289

FORMULAS

1. **Average Revenue:**

$$AR = \frac{\text{Total revenue } (TR)}{\text{Output } (Q)}$$

2. **Average Total Cost:**

$$\text{Average total cost} = \text{Total cost/Quantity}$$
$$ATC = \frac{TC}{Q}$$

3. **Break-Even Output:**

$$\text{Break-even} = \frac{\text{Fixed costs}}{\text{Contribution per unit}}$$

4. **Calculating the Inflation Rate between Consecutive Years:**

$$\text{Inflation rate in year 2} = 100 \times \frac{(\text{CPI in year 2} - \text{CPI in year 1})}{\text{CPI in year 1}}$$

5. **Classical Quantity Theory of Money:**

$$MV = PY$$
$$M_d = kPY$$

6. **Comparing Inflation Over Time:**

$$\text{Amount in today's currency} = \text{Amount in year } T \text{ currency} \times \frac{\text{Price level today}}{\text{Price level in year } T}$$

7. **Consumer Optimum in the Standard Economic Model:**

$$\frac{MU_x}{P_x} = \frac{MU_y}{P_y}$$

8. **Cross Price Elasticity of Demand:**

$$\text{Cross price elasticity of demand} = \frac{\text{Percentage change in quantity demanded of good 1}}{\text{Percentage change in the price of good 2}}$$

9. **Desired Margin Level:**

$$\text{Selling price} = \frac{\text{Total cost per unit}}{(1 - \text{Margin})}$$

10. **Entry Point:**

$$\text{Enter if } P > ATC$$

11. **Exit Point:**

$$\text{Exit if } P < ATC$$

12. **Gross Domestic Product (Expenditure Method):**

$$GDP\,(Y) = C + I + G + NX$$

13. GDP Deflator:

$$\text{GDP deflator} = \left(\frac{\text{Nomimal GDP}}{\text{Real GDP}} \right) \times 100$$

14. Income Elasticity of Demand:

$$\text{Income elasticity of demand} = \frac{\text{Percentage change in quantity demanded}}{\text{Percentage change in income}}$$

15. Labour Force Participation Rate:

$$\text{Labour force participation rate} = \left(\frac{\text{Labour force}}{\text{Adult population}} \right) \times 100$$

16. Marginal Cost:

$$\text{Marginal cost} = \text{Change in total cost / Change in quantity}$$

$$MC = \frac{\Delta TC}{\Delta Q}$$

17. Marginal Revenue:

$$MR = \frac{\Delta TR}{\Delta Q}$$

18. Marginal Propensity to Consume:

$$MPC = \frac{\Delta C}{\Delta Y}$$

19. Marginal Propensity to Save:

$$MPS = \frac{\Delta S}{\Delta Y}$$

20. Mark-Up:

$$\text{Mark-up (per cent)} = \left(\frac{\text{Selling price} - \text{Total cost per unit}}{\text{Total cost}} \right) \times 100$$

21. Market Equilibrium:

$$\text{Market equilibrium occurs where } Qd = Qs$$

22. Multiplier (k):

$$\text{Multiplier} = \frac{1}{(1 - MPC)}$$

$$\text{Multiplier} = \frac{1}{MPS}$$

$$k = \frac{1}{MPS + MPT + MPM}$$

$$k = \frac{1}{MPW}$$

23. Opportunity Cost:

$$\text{Opportunity cost} = \frac{\text{Sacrifice}}{\text{Gain}}$$

24. Price Elasticity of Demand:

$$\text{Price elasticity of demand} = \frac{\text{Percentage change in quantity demanded}}{\text{Percentage change in price}}$$

25. Price Elasticity of Supply:

$$\text{Price elasticity of supply} = \frac{\text{Percentage change in quantity supplied}}{\text{Percentage change in price}}$$

26. Production Function (Assuming Two Factor Inputs, Land and Capital):

$$Q = f(L_1, K_1)$$

27. Productivity:

$$\text{Productivity} = \frac{\text{Total output}}{\text{Units of the factor}}$$

28. Profit:

$$\text{Profit} = \text{Total revenue} - \text{Total cost} \ (\pi = TR - TC)$$

29. Profit Maximizing Output:

$$\text{where } MC = MR$$

30. Real Exchange Rate:

$$\text{Real exchange rate} = \frac{(\text{Nominal exchange rate} \times \text{Domestic price})}{(\text{Foreign price})}$$

$$\text{Real exchange rate} = \left(\frac{e \times P}{P*} \right)$$

31. Real Interest Rate:

$$\text{Real interest rate} = \text{Nominal interest rate} - \text{Inflation rate}$$

32. Real Money Balances:

$$\frac{M}{P}$$

33. Saving:

$$S \quad = \quad\quad\quad I \quad\quad + \quad\quad NCO$$

$$\text{Saving} = \text{Domestic investment} + \text{Net capital outflow}$$

34. Shut-Down Point:

$$\text{Shut down if } P < AVC$$

35. The Demand Function:

$$D = f(P_n, P_n \dots P_{n-1}, Y, T, P, A, E)$$

Where:

- P_n = Price
- $P_n \dots P_{n-1}$ = Prices of other goods (substitutes and complements)
- Y = Incomes (the level and distribution of income)
- T = Tastes and fashions
- P = The level and structure of the population
- A = Advertising
- E = Expectations of consumers

36. The Equilibrium of the Economy:

$$\text{Planned } S + T + M = \text{Planned } I + G + X$$

37. The Supply Function:

$$S = f(P_n, P_n \ldots P_{n-1}, H, N, F_1 \ldots F_m, E, S_f)$$

Where:
- P_n = Price
- $P_n \ldots P_{n-1}$ = Profitability of other goods in production and prices of goods in joint supply
- H = Technology
- N = Natural shocks
- $F_1 \ldots F_m$ = Costs of production
- E = Expectations of producers
- S_f = Social factors

38. The Least-Cost-Input Combination:

$$\frac{MP_K}{P_K} = \frac{MP_L}{P_L}$$

39. The Marginal Rate of Substitution:

$$MRS = \frac{\Delta P_x}{\Delta P_y}$$

40. The Mid-point Method of Calculating Price Elasticity of Supply:

$$\text{Price elasticity of supply} = \frac{(Q_2 - Q_1)/([Q_2 + Q_1]/2)}{(P_2 - P_1)/([P_2 + P_1]/2)}$$

41. The Mid-point Method of Calculating Price Elasticity of Demand:

$$\text{Price elasticity of demand} = \frac{(Q_2 - Q_1)/([Q_2 + Q_1]/2)}{(P_2 - P_1)/([P_2 + P_1]/2)}$$

42. Total Cost:

$$\text{Total cost} = \text{Fixed costs} + \text{Variable cost } (TC = FC + VC)$$

43. Total Revenue:

$$TR = P \times Q$$

44. Unemployment Rate:

$$\text{Unemployment rate} = \left(\frac{\text{Number of unemployed}}{\text{Labour force}} \right) \times 100$$